D1285065

FATHER ED DOWLING

FATHER ED DOWLING

Bill Wilson's Sponsor

GLENN F. CHESNUT

iUniverse

FATHER ED DOWLING
BILL WILSON'S SPONSOR

Copyright © 2015 Glenn F. Chesnut.

All rights reserved. No part of this book may be used or reproduced by any means, graphic, electronic, or mechanical, including photocopying, recording, taping or by any information storage retrieval system without the written permission of the publisher except in the case of brief quotations embodied in critical articles and reviews.

Scriptures are taken from Douay —Rheims 1899 edition of the John Murphy Company, Baltimore, Maryland

iUniverse books may be ordered through booksellers or by contacting:

iUniverse
1663 Liberty Drive
Bloomington, IN 47403
www.iuniverse.com
1-800-Authors (1-800-288-4677)

Because of the dynamic nature of the Internet, any web addresses or links contained in this book may have changed since publication and may no longer be valid. The views expressed in this work are solely those of the author and do not necessarily reflect the views of the publisher, and the publisher hereby disclaims any responsibility for them.

Any people depicted in stock imagery provided by Thinkstock are models, and such images are being used for illustrative purposes only. Certain stock imagery © Thinkstock.

ISBN: 978-1-4917-7085-6 (sc)
ISBN: 978-1-4917-7087-0 (e)

Print information available on the last page.

iUniverse rev. date: 07/15/2015

QUOTES

"The two greatest obstacles to democracy in the United States are, first, the widespread delusion among the poor that we have a democracy, and second, the chronic terror among the rich, lest we get it." Edward Dowling, *Chicago Daily News*, July 28, 1941.

Father Ed rejoiced that in "moving therapy from the expensive clinical couch to the low-cost coffee bar, from the inexperienced professional to the informed amateur, AA has democratized sanity."[1]

"At one Cana Conference he commented, 'No man thinks he's ugly. If he's fat, he thinks he looks like Taft. If he's lanky, he thinks he looks like Lincoln.'"[2]

Edward Dowling, S.J., of the *Queen's Work* staff, says, "Alcoholics Anonymous is natural; it is natural at the point where nature comes closest to the supernatural, namely in humiliations and in consequent humility. There is something spiritual about an art museum or a symphony, and the Catholic Church approves of our use of them. There is something spiritual about A.A. too, and Catholic participation in it almost invariably results in poor Catholics becoming better Catholics." Added as an appendix to the Big Book in 1955.[3]

"'God resists the proud, assists the humble. The shortest cut to humility is humiliations, which AA has in abundance. The achievements of AA, which grew out of this book, are profoundly significant. Non-alcoholics should read the last nine words of 12th Step, page 72.' — Edward Dowling, S.J., The Solidarity of Our Lady, St. Louis, Mo." A quote from Fr. Dowling on the book jacket for *Alcoholics Anonymous*, beginning with the ninth printing of the first edition in January 1946.[4]

Bill W., A.A. *Grapevine* (Spring 1960), "Father Ed, an early and wonderful friend of AA, died as this last message went to press. He was the greatest and most gentle soul to walk this planet. I was closer to him than to any other human being on earth."

TABLE OF CONTENTS

Father Dowling's Later Life: 1940–1960

Father Dowling's Early Life

Chapter 1

The Route to Becoming a Priest: 1898-1931

Father Edward Patrick Dowling, nicknamed "Puggy" as a schoolboy, was born on September 1, 1898 in St. Louis, Missouri. [5] Many Jesuits were moved around to varying locations over the course of their years in the order, but Fr. Dowling spent nearly his entire life in or near the great riverboat city. St. Louis was at that time the fourth largest city in the United States, an energetic, ambitious, bustling town which in 1904 (the year young Ed turned six) hosted both the World's Fair and the Olympic Games. His grandfather had come to America shortly before the American Civil War, forced by the great potato famine to leave his Irish homeland (the Dowlings came from Ballagh, Kilroosky in County Roscommon[6]), but the family prospered after settling in St. Louis. His grandfather started a railroad construction company, which was later managed by Ed's father Edward P. Dowling (1871-1956). Ed's mother, Annie Cullinane Dowling (1866-1934), belonged to an Irish family which owned a livery stable and an undertakers establishment. [7]

Childhood and youth: Ed's family lived on 8224 Church Road, just two city blocks west of the Mississippi River, in the tiny suburb of Baden on the north side of St. Louis.[8] The first church to be established in Baden had been Holy Cross Roman Catholic Church, which was just one block south of where he lived: dominated by German immigrants, the church's parochial school even had its classes in German.

The Irish had felt very uncomfortable even attending mass there, and eventually split off in 1873 to form their own parish, Our Lady of Mount Carmel (located three blocks north of where the Dowling family lived), with their own parochial school added the next year.[9] Ed was baptized at Our Lady of Mount Carmel.

But from the résumé which Father Dowling put together later on, it appears that his parents did not wish to send their son, while he was very young, to either of the nearby parochial schools, the German or the Irish, and instead sent him at first to the Baden public school.[10] And yet they were an extremely religious family: Ed's mother went to 8 a.m. mass every morning.

There were five children in all: Father Ed (Sept. 1, 1898 – Mar. 30, 1960) was the oldest. His sister Anna (Nov. 21, 1899 - March, 1980), the second oldest, never married and took care of Father Ed at the end of his life when he was left blind and severely crippled from arthritis; she acted as his reader and his secretary, and traveled with him. The next child James was born in 1903 and died in October 1918 at the young age of fifteen while he was a student at St. Mary's College in Kansas, a victim of the great Influenza Pandemic of 1918-1919. The next-to-youngest child, Paul Vincent Dowling (May 12, 1905 – Nov. 10, 1955), tried the Jesuit novitiate but decided not to stay, and became a newspaper reporter. In 1939 he married Beatrice F. (1909-2003), they had two children (Paul and Mary), and then he died at the young age of fifty while his children were still not out of their teens. Beatrice however survived down to almost her ninety-fourth birthday. The youngest child Mary (Feb. 17, 1907 - Dec. 16, 1976), became a Religious of the Sacred Heart and librarian at Maryville College. This institution was originally located in south St. Louis, but in 1961 moved to a new campus over on the far west side of St. Louis, and is now called Maryville University. Mary and Anna established the Dowling Archives at the new campus, a collection of material which is important for Father Dowling studies: nearly all of the surviving letters between him and Bill Wilson are preserved there.[11]

As a child, Fr. Dowling came under the influence of Jesuit ideals at a very early age. Although he went to public school when he was very small, as soon as he was old enough to take the streetcar by himself, he was sent to Holy Name Parochial School in the College Hill neighborhood (on the north side of town, like Baden, but over where the St. Louis University College Farm was located). This parochial school was run by the Sisters of St. Joseph, a women's order founded by the Jesuit priest Jean Paul Médaille. Young Ed Dowling then continued

4

his education with three years at the St. Louis Academy (now called the St. Louis University High School), which is located on the campus of the Jesuit's St. Louis University (an excellent academic institution, the oldest American university west of the Mississippi river).[12]

It was a quite academically oriented educational track which the young Ed Dowling was taking, but in later years, he nevertheless made a point of mentioning in his résumé that he had also spent the summers during his high school years (1913-16) doing factory labor. At all points during his adult life, Fr. Dowling identified with the problems of ordinary working people, and he wanted everyone to know that he had first hand experience of factories and manual labor.[13]

He traveled around during the summer of 1916 playing as a semi-pro catcher in exhibition baseball games, and tried out unsuccessfully for two major league teams (the Boston Red Sox and the St. Louis Browns), before giving up on his dream of becoming a professional baseball player.[14]

He did two years of undergraduate work— presumably for the 1916-17 and 1917-18 academic years—at St. Mary's College, the school where both his father and grandfather had gone. Located in St. Mary's, Kansas, twenty-five miles west of Topeka, the college was operated as a Jesuit institution from its beginnings as a mission to the Potawatomi Indians until it was closed in 1968.[15]

Newspaper reporter and brief military service: Direct United States involvement in the First World War began on April 6, 1917, when the U.S. declared war on Germany, and continued down to the Armistice on November 11, 1918. It is not clear how this affected young Ed Dowling's plans. But instead of finishing his degree at St. Mary's, he went back to St. Louis in 1918 and got a brief job as a reporter for the *St. Louis Globe-Democrat* (working for ten dollars a week). The other reporters called him "Eddie."[16] But then he went into the Army as a private on October 28, 1918, just two weeks before the war ended. It appears as though he served six months however, in a student army training program at St. Louis University. He then went back to the reporter's job at the *Globe-Democrat*, but again for only a short time.[17]

For most of its history, the *Globe-Democrat* was St. Louis' conservative newspaper. The liberal voice for that part of the Midwest was provided by Joseph Pulitzer's *St. Louis Post-Dispatch*. One cannot help but wonder if young Ed Dowling would have simply stayed in the newspaper business if he had gotten his first job on the Pulitzer paper, whose editorial philosophy matched so much more closely with his own spirit. Joseph Pulitzer, in his retirement speech on April 10, 1907, had said that he wanted the newspaper to continue to adhere to the platform he had tried to live by all his life: [18]

> I know that my retirement will make no difference in its cardinal principles, that it will always fight for progress and reform, never tolerate injustice or corruption, always fight demagogues of all parties, never belong to any party, always oppose privileged classes and public plunderers, never lack sympathy with the poor, always remain devoted to the public welfare, never be satisfied with merely printing news, always be drastically independent, never be afraid to attack wrong, whether by predatory plutocracy or predatory poverty.

Entered the Jesuit order in 1919: his seminary years. At any rate, whether it was in part because of the *St. Louis Globe-Democrat*'s conservative philosophy, or for other reasons, Dowling recognized fairly quickly that working for this newspaper was not where God wanted him to devote the rest of his life, and made the decision to enter the priesthood. We can note a whole host of other things which could also have been involved—his World War I experiences may have played some role, or perhaps the death of his fifteen-year-old brother James in October 1918—but in 1919 (the year young Ed Dowling turned twenty-one) he decided to join the Jesuit order. He entered St. Stanislaus Seminary, which was located in Florissant, a small town of 680 people, historically mostly French-speaking, located just north of St. Louis.[19] One of the other people at the newspaper later told how his friends got the news:

> It was in an all-night cafe frequented by *Globe-Democrat* reporters that he announced he would enter the seminary at Florissant the next morning. An astounded fellow staff member who had an automobile volunteered to drive the

young newsman to the seminary. The friend reported that Dowling wore his favorite candy-striped silk shirt for the occasion, and his only luggage was a pair of canvas duck trousers he carried under his arm. En route, the friend unsuccessfully tried to persuade the young man to turn back. Fr. Dowling said that he was startled a few days later when he saw the seminary floors being swabbed with rags including his silk shirt.[20]

The Florissant seminary's central structure was the Rock Building with its three-foot-thick walls, built in 1840 and still standing today, constructed of limestone quarried from the banks of the Missouri river and walnut logged by the Jesuits on the property. The seminary was originally completely self-sufficient, like a medieval European Benedictine monastery, surrounded by almost a thousand acres where they raised cattle and chickens, and maintained large wheat fields and an orchard. They had a bakery, a creamery, and a butchery for preparing the food.[21] Back in those days the meals were hearty; as one older Jesuit remembered it: "Three times a week, we had corn bread and stew for breakfast. The number of square feet of corn bread and the number of barrels of stew consumed over the course of a year would probably astonish even" the editors of Ripley's *Believe It or Not*. The cornbread was either mashed up into the stew, or eaten on the side, slathered with syrup.[22]

And of course, soon after he entered the seminary, young Ed was led for the first time through the *Spiritual Exercises* of St. Ignatius Loyola,[23] the great spiritual masterpiece which lay at the heart of the Jesuit understanding of the spiritual life. The author of the book, Ignatius Loyola (1491-1556), had been a Spanish soldier, a knight from an aristocratic Basque family, whose military career was brought to an end after a serious wound from a cannon ball at the Battle of Pamplona in 1521 left him crippled (like Father Ed Dowling) in his legs. But the next year, Loyola had a vision of the Virgin Mary at the shrine at Montserrat and God gave him a new career: he went live in a cave close to the nearby town of Manresa, where he began praying for many hours a day while putting together the fundamental principles of his *Spiritual Exercises*, and eventually formed the Society of Jesus, the Catholic religious order which devoted itself for centuries to going into places too dangerous for any other priests to venture.

The *Exercises*, among other things, made heavy use of a method of prayer called contemplation. We were asked to spend hours visualizing a scene such as the crucifixion of Jesus, filling in all the physical details in our minds to as great a degree as possible, and also imagining inside our minds the inner emotions and feelings of all the participants. What would we have done in that situation? Would we have eagerly hammered the nails into his hands and feet? Would we have stood on the side, jeering and making fun of him? Or would we have at least tried to help him carry the cross? Would we have at least attempted to wipe the sweat and blood off his face with a clean cloth? Or if forced to stand helpless in mute horror, would we have at least helped lift his body down from the cross afterwards, and participated in giving his body a decent burial? What were all these people actually feeling, and what was our own emotional reaction?

Real life is made up of continual choices, and one of the central goals of Ignatian spirituality was to help us practice *discernment* about the true nature of these choices. When all was said and done, did I want to be one of the people who laughed and jeered and went for what was popular and easy and made them lots of money, and involved no pain or suffering on their part? Or did I want to be one of the people who did what was right, no matter how they appeared in the eyes of the world? Who were my real heroes? In the New Testament—and in fact in the entire Bible, and throughout the history of the Christian Church—the real heroes were the ones who carried out God's work regardless of how much pain and suffering it brought them. But when, on the other hand, we refused to serve God and rebelled against him and cursed him because we could not tolerate a world in which real pain and suffering occurred, it turned us into despicable human beings.

The idea that God would reward those who faithfully served him by continually giving them lives of ease and prosperity, where neither they nor their parents or children or other loved ones ever fell ill or died or was the victim of gross cruelty and injustice, was a purely pagan fantasy that had nothing to do with the Bible or the faith of the Catholic

Church or even elementary common sense and simple observation of real life.

But we need to study more than just the *Spiritual Exercises* in order to fully understand the Jesuit way of life: we also need to listen to the stories they told within the order. For example, the seminary at Florissant was named for the patron saint of Jesuit novices, St. Stanislaus Kostka, a Polish lad who, at the age of fifteen, had a vision of Mary visiting him and placing the baby Jesus in his arms, which he regarded as a divine call to enter the Society of Jesus. The older members of the order would tell his story to the new people who were just joining. Young Stanislaus trudged 450 miles on foot, penniless, to apply to the order. After additional struggle, suffering and self-sacrifice, but still humbly and obediently following the divine vision which had assigned him to his task, he was finally accepted into the Jesuit novitiate at Rome on his seventeenth birthday. Even though he died only ten months later, he was "obedient unto death" (as it says in the great Christ Hymn in Philippians, the foundational statement of so much traditional Catholic spirituality) to the divine vision he had been granted.[24]

As we think of the way in which this story would have been embedded in the young Fr. Dowling's mind at a formative level, we can see what lay behind some of the impact on him later on, when he first encountered Bill Wilson's story of visions and penniless struggle. It also helps us to better understand the kind of pastoral advice which he gave to Bill, when the A.A. leader was feeling especially beset by his struggles: embracing any necessary suffering was a necessary part of true obedience to God and "pain was the touchstone of all spiritual progress."[25] Whether Bill succeeded or failed, he was not going to be released by God from the task of attempting to help the alcoholics of the world. It was not just the *Spiritual Exercises*, but the entire Jesuit ethos and understanding of the spiritual life which enabled Fr. Dowling to identify with Bill Wilson's life mission, and which in addition allowed him to give such good spiritual advice to Bill.

Beginning of Father Ed's health problems: crippling arthritis develops c. 1920-1928. It was also during this same general period, while young Ed was at the Jesuit seminary at Florissant, when the great physical burden of his life first appeared. He was walking along the Missouri River when he started feeling pain in one of his legs. When he went for a medical check, it was discovered that he had incurable arthritis, which was actually centered in his back, although one of his greatest pains came from walking. When he reached thirty, his spine would "turn to stone," as he put it. It was not rheumatoid arthritis, but some other form of severely crippling arthritis.[26] It should be remembered that in spite of this, all the way to the end of his life, he remained busy traveling around the country, hobbling along on a cane, in spite of the enormous pain that he must have experienced doing things like climbing up the metal stairs into a train carriage, or walking the length of a railroad station. And there were very few elevators in the United States in those days.

When Fr. Dowling came to visit Bill Wilson for the first time, it caused him enormous pain to climb the stairs to the second floor room where Bill was staying: nevertheless, he walked up to meet the A.A. leader, one laborious step at a time, instead of asking him to come downstairs. But this was part of the message of St. Ignatius Loyola and the Jesuits which Fr. Dowling had come to deliver to Bill. If it was God's mission which we were carrying out, then it was our duty to do our best, regardless of any personal suffering or agony that might be involved. God gives us real tasks, requiring real heroism.

Crisis of faith c. 1920: Young Ed Dowling had to learn suffering himself at first hand, and not only through the constant pain from his arthritis. In the second year of his novitiate he underwent a major crisis of faith which took him two years to work himself out of. As he later described it, in his own words:

> But here tonight, I am discussing a problem to which I am not entirely alien. Up to the age of 21 my spirituality, my religion, my faith was a comfortable, unchallenged nursery habit. Then over a course of some months, the most important months of my life saw that faith, that religion, drift away. It began to make demands. And as it ceased to be comfortable and comforting to big and important I, when it ceased to "yes" my body and soul, I found that I moved away from it. I am not utterly unacquainted with atheism. I know and respect agnosticism and I have been a bed-fellow

with spiritual confusion, not merely the honest and sincere kind, but the self-kidding kind.[27]

Earning his degrees at St. Louis University (1921-1925): But to go on with the story of Fr. Dowling's early life, men who entered the Jesuit order were ordinarily expected to do a certain amount of graduate study in both philosophy and theology, and those who had no completed college degree were required to finish a bachelor's degree first, usually in philosophy. So after finishing his two-year-long novitiate (1919-1921), young Ed Dowling spent three years (1921-1924) taking the coursework for a major in philosophy at the Jesuit's St. Louis University. He was awarded his A.B. degree in 1924, and then spent an additional year at the university earning a master's degree, which he was awarded in 1925.[28]

Regency teaching at Loyola Academy (1926-1929), involvement in Catholic Action and Christian Family movements. After the period of their Novitiate and First Studies, the young men who were preparing to be Jesuits then went through a three-year period called their Regency, when they were most usually (in those days) assigned to teaching at a secondary school. In Fr. Dowling's case, he taught from 1926 to 1929 at Loyola Academy, which in those days was located in Rogers Park on the far North Side of Chicago, on the Loyola University campus. The academy was a typical exclusive prep school, where students were required to wear coat and tie at all times. They were also forbidden to talk when walking about the campus, and had to attend the academy's weekly mass.[29]

In spite of the formal atmosphere, however, Fr. Dowling began what were to be lifelong friendships with his students there. One of these was a young man named Pat Crowley, who eventually married a woman named Patty. In later years, Pat and Patty Crowley (along with Burnie Bauer and his wife Helene in South Bend, Indiana) founded the Christian Family Movement.[30]

> Loyola in those days was a small, intimate school whose students came from prosperous Catholic families all over the city .... The Jesuits ran a tight ship, but there were men

like Father Brooks and Father Ed Dowling, for whom the students had great admiration. Father Dowling, in particular, had enormous influence on Pat's circle of friends—and on all the students at Loyola .... Even after he moved to St. Louis, Dowling kept alive a network of graduates whom he visited and counseled whenever he could. His meetings with the Loyola graduates who remained in Chicago led eventually to his association with the Cana Conference, a movement for married Catholics that blossomed in the late 1940s.[31]

Burnie Bauer, when he was a student at the University of Notre Dame, had been a member of the first Catholic Action group started by Father Louis Putz, C.S.C. All of them—Pat and Patty, Burnie and Helene—had been involved in both formal and informal lay Catholic groups which used what was called the Jocist method. They were linked, in other words, to that side of early twentieth century Catholicism which believed in social involvement and strong social activism. "Jocism" referred to a Belgian priest named Joseph Cardijn, who started a group called Young Trade Unionists in 1919. In 1924, the name of his group was changed to Jeunesse Ouvrière Chrétienne ("young Christian workers") or JOC for short, which was why the movement came to be referred to as "Jocism." Dorothy Day described her Catholic Worker Movement as an only slightly more radical version of Father Cardijn's Jocist movement. It was with this kind of background that Pat and Patty Crowley met Helene and Burnie Bauer at the Cana Convention in August 1948, and laid the foundations of the Christian Family Movement.[32]

Pat and Patty Crowley spent the 1950's and 60's traveling about preaching a new kind of message about the Christian family. A good Catholic marriage ought to be a special gift of God's grace, they proclaimed, to both the church and the world. The Christian Family Movement made major breaks with a number of traditional ways of doing things: it was the first major Catholic movement in the United States, for example, to be started by laypeople. The group was made up of men and women working together, at a time when Catholic organizations tended to be same sex. Because of their prominence in this movement, the Crowley's were invited to Rome in 1966 to serve on Pope Paul VI's Birth Control Commission. Patty later on stated her position in the *Chicago Tribune* (in 1994): "I think women should have the choice to use contraception. They want to have children, but they want to have them responsibly." She presented the members of the Commission with a large collection of correspondence from Catholics begging the church to stop forbidding artificial birth control. The Commission's majority report ended up agreeing with her, but the small number of members who remained unconvinced went separately to the pope, and persuaded him to continue the ban on artificial contraception.[33]

The well-known Catholic novelist Fr. Andrew Greeley, who was also a longtime friend of the Crowleys, made the bold assertion that "In terms of lay activism, Patty was the most important woman of her time, and CFM [the Christian Family Movement] was the most important movement of the pre-conciliar church."[34] Those who know Greeley's novels are well aware of the way that they continually emphasize the positive role of romantic love and sexual passion in a good Catholic marriage.

Monsignor John Joseph Egan, who eventually ended up heading the Cana Conference program in the Chicago archdiocese from 1946 to 1959, described Dowling as "a man of great generosity who would take the train from St. Louis to Chicago, sit with a couple in difficulty, and get on the midnight train back to St. Louis for work the next morning." Msgr. Egan, it should be said, was one of the great Catholic social activists of that period, a good priest who cared about the poor and the helpless, and believed that taking the gospel seriously required us to make radical changes in the structure of human society. He served as chaplain not only to the Christian Family Movement (from 1947 to 1953) but also the Young Christian Workers (from 1943 to 1955).[35] It is important to note that these are the sort of people whom we encounter over and over again when writing about Fr. Dowling's life: people like Pat and Patty Crowley and Msgr. Jack Egan and Fr. Andrew Greeley, who cared deeply about their fellow human beings.

When Father Ed first encountered the new Alcoholics Anonymous movement in 1940, alcoholics bore a terrible stigma. They were considered the lowest of the low, people who refused to take even the most basic moral responsibility for themselves, people who deserved only to be punished, lectured at, fired from their jobs, and thrown in prisons or insane asylums. But Dowling believed in a Lord who had also been despised by the proud and arrogant, as the *Spiritual Exercises* emphasized, and this was a Lord who commanded that we help the poor and despised segments of society instead of condemning them and discriminating against them (cf. James 2:1-7, 2:15-17, and 5:1-6).

And then by the autumn of 1940, Father Ed seems to have come to the conclusion that something even more amazing was going on. These poor drunks, whom everyone derided and scorned, had been given a special spiritual key to the godly life which they would cheerfully share with everyone around them. As it said in Isaiah 53:2-5,

> He had no form or comeliness that we should look at him, and no beauty that we should desire him. He was despised and rejected by men; a man of sorrows, and acquainted with grief; and as one from whom men hide their faces, he was despised and we esteemed him not. Surely he has borne our griefs and carried our sorrows; yet we esteemed him stricken, smitten by God, and afflicted. But he was wounded for our transgressions, he was bruised for our iniquities; upon him was the chastisement that made us whole, and with his stripes we are healed.

When Alcoholics Anonymous first came to public attention, it took someone like Father Ed, a courageous Jesuit who was not afraid of ideas and movements simply because they were new and different and unconventional—or even perhaps looked dangerous to some people—if it looked like they might help any of God's people, no matter how humble or disregarded and ignored.

Theology at St. Mary's College in Kansas in 1929: Dowling is failed out of the academic track in philosophical theology. After finishing his Regency, which (as we have seen) he spent teaching high school at Loyola Academy in Chicago, Fr. Dowling was sent to spend four years studying theology at St. Mary's College in Kansas.[36] This was in 1929, the year he turned 31. It was a two-tiered system: those who were considered the academically brighter students were enrolled in the "long course," and if they did well, had a chance at earning a Ph.D. somewhere and then coming back to a prestigious teaching position in a Jesuit university. Those they regarded as the less able students were enrolled instead in the "short course."

Father Dowling did not arrive at St. Mary's with completely glowing recommendations from his three-year Regency period. His superior at Loyola, a man named Father Moran, sent an evaluation letter saying rather cautiously:

> He is ambitious, wants to get ahead, and possesses a good deal of shrewdness in getting what he wants from people and from circumstances .... He is eccentric and has a very distinctive and original personality. He is careless about small things, and is very absent-minded. He is self-conscious at times and somewhat sensitive.[37]

Nevertheless, they enrolled him in the upper level theology course work at St. Mary's College, which in those days meant the study of Thomistic philosophy and theology, studied in the context of general medieval scholastic thought. Young Fr. Dowling lasted until the second year, when he failed the Latin oral exam thesis on the question of whether angels have bodies.[38] Now the question itself was a simple one, which anyone who had been paying attention in class should have been able to answer easily. An angel according to Thomistic doctrine is composed of pure form (it is a completely ideal being), and has no material body. This means that the answer, for example, to the famous question about "how many angels can dance on the head of a pin," is that this question is meaningless, because beings which have no matter cannot have a spatial location. Any moderately intelligent student should have been able to answer that question.

It was not a completely trivial question, incidentally, because it was closely tied to the question of whether the human soul could enjoy any kind of individual immortality after death. Aristotle had said that the soul was only the form of the body, so that when the material body died and decomposed, there was no longer anything for the soul to be "the form of." Some of the medieval Muslim philosophers used this argument to deny the immortality of the human soul, while others allowed only for the survival of the part of the human intellect which knew universal intellectual truths (such as that two plus two equals four, the Pythagorean theorem in mathematics, and so on). St. Thomas Aquinas tried to work out a way that he could accept at least a modified Aristotelian doctrine of the soul without automatically denying the possibility of any kind of life after death, and his theories about angels' bodies were linked to the doctrine of the immortality of the human soul.

So it was a question which a good seminary student should have been able to answer at either a simple level or a more complicated one, but apparently whatever the young Fr. Dowling did, his examiners were not pleased, and not only removed him from the advanced academic track, but reprimanded him for spending too much time on what they regarded as triviality—working to keep other priests-in-training aware of important events going on the world around them.

> Both the rector and the provincial reprimanded him for spending too much time on a bulletin board with news items and not enough time on his theology. He wrote to both that he had learned much from this exchange, listed how much time he spent on theology, and added frankly that the thesis was a footnote and not really covered in class. The bulletin board took little time; he merely put up news items others had received in their mail.[39]

As a result of Dowling's being flunked out of the advanced theological curriculum, some of his fellow Jesuits, who admired the skilled scholastic theologians among their order, tended to write him off as "a disorganized, intellectual lightweight."[40] But one of his friends, Father Ben Fulkerson, who was much more perceptive, remarked that:

> Dowling was a kind of knave in the king's court. He would grunt. But he was smarter than all the king's councilors. His manners and ways of expressing himself went against him. He seemed disorganized, a bit slap-happy, a roughneck.[41]

And there was something even more important going on here. By this point in the 1930's, the younger Roman Catholic theologians were beginning to become more and more dissatisfied with the straightjacket of medieval Thomist orthodoxy. Some of Father Ed's contemporaries began quietly becoming involved in patristics studies instead (like Jean Daniélou, S.J. 1905-1974) or in New Testament studies. Others became directly involved in social activism (joining people like Dorothy Day, 1897-1980, in working for a better society). At the Second Vatican Council (1962-1965), which began only two years after Fr. Dowling's death, the overwhelming majority of the citations listed in the conciliar decrees were from Biblical and patristic sources, not medieval scholastic sources. After Vatican II was over, to give just one typical example of the effect of the council on Catholic education, no member of the Theology Department at Notre Dame University in South Bend, Indiana—one of the top ranking American Catholic universities at that time—taught any course on Thomistic theology at all for many years.[42]

Young Fr. Dowling refused to take medieval Thomistic theology seriously—even if it meant being bumped off the track to a university professorship—because he believed it was no longer relevant to the twentieth century church. He threw himself instead into supporting the Catholic social activists, making sure the new Alcoholics Anonymous movement was a safe place for Catholics, and other missions of that sort.

Ordination as a priest in 1931, early stages of the black civil rights movement, Dred Scott's grave. On June 25, 1931, at the age of 32, Dowling was ordained in St. Louis by Archbishop John Joseph Glennon.[43] This prelate was an Irishman, born in Kinnegad, County Meath, who served as Archbishop of St. Louis from 1903 until his death in 1946. He became involved in major public furor when he began trying to block certain members of the Jesuit order who were attempting to bring racial integration to the Catholic schools of the city. In spite of the Archbishop's opposition, the racial barrier was finally broken in the summer of 1944 when St. Louis University admitted its first African American students.[44]

There were some members of the Catholic clergy who were strong defenders of black Americans. Monsignor John Joseph Egan, for example (whom we mentioned before) was one of the clergymen who marched with Rev. Martin Luther King, Jr. in the 1965 protest march from Selma to Montgomery, Alabama.[45] The desegregation of St. Louis University in 1944 came ten years before the Supreme Court's Brown v. Board of Education decision in 1954 outlawed segregated public schools.

In 1956 Fr. Dowling stood up as one of the Catholic clergy who were working to bring honor and dignity to the black community. 1957 would mark the one hundredth anniversary of the Supreme Court's Dred Scott decision.[46] Scott was an African-American slave who, while living in St. Louis, had sued to obtain freedom for himself and his wife and two daughters on the grounds that they had lived for a while in areas where slavery was illegal. When the legal battle eventually rose to the level of the U.S. Supreme Court, the justices rendered the decision that since slaves were private property, the federal government could not declare slaves freed simply on the basis of their having lived at some point in a free state or territory (Illinois and the Wisconsin Territory in this case), and that furthermore, any person descended from Africans, whether slave or free, was not a citizen of the United States, so that Scott had no right to sue in federal court. This decision, issued by the Supreme Court on March 6, 1857 helped catalyze public outrage over the institution of slavery during the four years which followed, culminating in the outbreak of the great Civil War in 1861.

Dred Scott had died in St. Louis in 1858, and was buried in an unmarked grave. Fr. Dowling used his skills as a genealogist to locate the gravesite in Calvary Cemetery, whose trees and green lawns, dotted with tombstones, began just three streets south of his childhood home. There is a wonderful photograph of him standing with Scott's great-grandson John A. Madison on March 6, 1957, with Dowling pointing with his cane to the section of grass where the former slave was buried and announcing their plans: "We have in mind putting up only a simple monument. Then if someone some day wants to put up a better monument it will at least be known where Dred Scott lies." A descendant of the white family which had originally owned Scott carried out Fr. Dowling's wishes and paid for a gravestone. For a long time afterward, people who visited the gravesite would leave Lincoln head pennies on top of the stone, to honor both Scott and Lincoln.[47]

CHAPTER 2

The Queen's Work and the Cana Conference movement

The Queen's Work: In 1932, the year Fr. Dowling turned 34, he was assigned to the Central Office of the Jesuit-sponsored Sodalities of Our Lady, to help in the editorial work for their magazine, *The Queen's Work* — the job where the Jesuits kept him all the way down to his death in 1960.[48] Dowling had apparently caught the eye of Fr. Daniel A. Lord, S.J. who had in 1925, only two years after his own ordination, been appointed director of the sodality.

The Sodality of the Blessed Virgin Mary was considered a dying organization when Fr. Lord took over. It was made up of a scattered network of Catholic student groups at Jesuit schools, devoted to prayer and charitable work. Fr. Lord used a revitalized version of the sodality magazine, *The Queen's Work*, to quickly raise the membership to two million members. It affected nearly every Catholic school in the United States. The magazine gave instruction in Catholic doctrine and pushed for the evangelization of non-Catholics. Fr. Lord wrote songs and poems and put on plays and musical pageants in addition to publishing a long series of educational pamphlets, with titles like "The Call to Catholic Action" and "When Sorrow Comes—Reflections on the Problem of Pain and the Mystery of Suffering and Sorrow" in 1935, "Atheism doesn't make sense" and "They're Married! AKA Christian Marriage AKA Catholic Marriage" in 1936, and later (in 1938) "Prayers Are Always Answered."[49] One can see instantly both how this fit in with the developing interests of young Fr. Dowling, and also how fascinated he would become when he read the A.A. Big Book shortly after its publication and noticed how it was focusing on so many of the same kinds of topics.

God's reporter: Although Fr. Ed had only been a reporter for the *St. Louis Globe Democrat* for a year or so at most, nevertheless, given his role as one of the principal editors on *The Queen's Work*—in 1957, "Edward Dowling" was listed at the beginning of the list of fourteen names on the official letterhead of the magazine—he continued to regard himself as basically a newspaperman, even if of a different kind. He continued to be a member of the National Press Club, and was a delegate from the St. Louis local of the American Newspaper Guild to both their Toronto and their San Francisco conventions.[50] An editorial in the *St. Louis Post-Dispatch*, written right after Fr. Dowling's death, expressed the love which his fellow St. Louis newspapermen had for him:

> The Rev. Edward Dowling, S.J., was a kindly man who never allowed kindliness to keep him from speaking his mind. He made friends wherever he went, especially among newspaper people. He left the city room for the Jesuit Seminary, but he was like the old firehorse. Crippling arthritis restricted his activities but a cane always got him to a Newspaper Guild meeting, to a party for a Pulitzer Prize winner, or any journalistic bull session which promised to bring out the "inside story" of what made the wheels turn. Eddie Dowling did not vaunt his kindliness; he used it quietly to help those who needed help. They will remember him as long as those who only learned from him that the world is never too gloomy for cheerfulness ....[51]

His desire to continue to play an ongoing role in the newspaper world gives an interesting insight into what he believed himself to be doing at *The Queen's Work*. The word prophet in the original ancient Greek (*prophêtês*) meant someone who "spoke for" God (*phêmi* = speak + *pro* = for, in behalf of). Dowling gave that idea an interesting twist by at least subconsciously regarding his vocation as a Jesuit as one of serving as something like "God's reporter"—or perhaps even "God's press secretary." His job (as he understood it) was not to be a great formative theologian or a great philosophical thinker. His role was to represent God to the public in the same quiet way that the American president's press secretary explained and spoke in behalf of the president. His task was to explain in clear and simple language what God was currently doing and whom God had chosen to carry out his work. Or as his reporter friend Sam Lambert put it, Father Ed's job as one of the editors of *The Queen's Work* was "a cover-up for his real job, being 'God's ambassador to humanity.'"[52] That was why he threw himself into backing Bill Wilson in every possible way, and worked so hard to try to make it clear to the world that one of God's great works was underway, with the twelve step program at its spear point. Dowling regarded that as part of his own special God-given mission.

A colorful character: Father Ed was a colorful character across the board. Every weekday morning he would leave his lodgings at St. Louis University and walk out and stand in the middle of Grand Boulevard, which ran through the center of campus. *The Queen's Work* was located two miles south, at the corner of Tower Grove Park, at 3115 S. Grand Boulevard. Father Ed would blow a whistle, and then hitch a ride with any vehicle that stopped for him. He was seen arriving at *The Queen's Work* one day riding in a limousine driven by the Mayor's chauffeur, and not long afterward sitting in the cab of a garbage truck, and having a wonderful time on both trips. Taxicab drivers cruising for fares near the Melbourne Hotel (now Jesuit Hall, the faculty residence at St. Louis University) would rush to pick him up when they heard his whistle. Father Ed would insist that the driver also pick up anyone else they saw looking for a cab along the two-mile journey, so he could chat with them too.[53]

Father Larry Chumminatto said he was visiting Father Ed in his office one day, when the priest opened the middle drawer of his desk and drew out a children's toy cap pistol. He fired two loud bangs, and a young woman suddenly appeared at his door. He asked her to bring him several items, and then explained to Father Chuminatto that this was their temporary device until they got the office buzzer system fixed.[54]

As was noted earlier, Father Ed had tried out for a couple of major league baseball teams in 1916, when he was seventeen,[55] and he continued to enjoy watching baseball games in his later years. In the

Spring of 1950, after going to a game at Cardinal Park with a newspaper sportswriter, he commented the next day:

> Baseball wastes more time than any other sport. Last night I took a stop watch out and timed the minutes they wasted winding up, fouling off pitches, etc. I am going to write some new rules and … see if they will work. Then I am going to send the results to the commissioner.

Instead of the old traditional American rule of three strikes and four balls, Fr. Ed wanted to speed up the change of batters by reducing the count to two strikes and three balls. For the sake of television coverage, he also proposed taking the regulation baseball diamond and "squeezing it in from the sides," so the speak, so that the distance across the diamond transversely from third base to first base would be much shorter than the vertical distance from home plate to second base. In that way, a single television camera placed behind home plate would be able to show all the action going on at all of the bases simultaneously without having to pan back and forth. Such was the power of his persuasive tongue, that he actually talked some amateur players into playing a game that way, and then sent his proposals to the U.S. baseball commissioner, who was not however so easily persuaded to change the old rules![56]

Father Ed's love affair with the cross: humility as the willingness to be crucified if necessary in the battle against evil. He loved people, and he loved being with people. Yet he did also have his quiet times. He began every morning by celebrating the eucharist at the St. Louis College Church, and then would sit afterwards in the sacristy and silently contemplate the crucifix on the wall. Only after this quiet time would he go to the telephone and start arranging his day's business.[57]

At the beginning of his career as a Jesuit, when he had finished his two-year novitiate, and had taken his permanent vows of poverty, chastity, and obedience, he had taken the name Dismas as his vow name.[58] This was, according to later Catholic tradition, the name of one of the two thieves who were crucified on either side of Jesus: the good thief, who prayed to Jesus and was rewarded with Jesus' eternal blessing. See Luke 23:39-43 (in the old Roman Catholic Douay-Rheims translation):

And one of those robbers who were hanged, blasphemed him, saying: If thou be Christ, save thyself and us. But the other answering, rebuked him, saying: Neither dost thou fear God, seeing thou art condemned under the same condemnation? And we indeed justly, for we receive the due reward of our deeds; but this man hath done no evil. And he said to Jesus: Lord, remember me when thou shalt come into thy kingdom. And Jesus said to him: Amen I say to thee, this day thou shalt be with me in paradise.

Many years later Father Dowling wrote a famous article on "Catholic Asceticism and the Twelve Steps," in which he referred to "Christ's love affair with the cross." In that piece, as I interpret it, Father Dowling was saying that Jesus had to do more than merely passively acquiesce in his death on the cross. He had to actively desire his crucifixion—his battle to the death with the forces of evil—as a fight that had to be fought in order for him to save the human race. In that article, Father Ed went on to say that likewise people in A.A. had to carry out what they called their Sixth Step, in which they became "entirely ready to have God remove all [their] defects of character." They had to want the agony they would suffer, as the grasping, clutching, deeply embedded claws of these defects were wrenched loose from their hearts, because it was a necessary part of a battle where they knew they were going to have to triumph, in order to save their own souls.[59]

This vision of what was truly meant by the virtue of humility was one that Dowling successfully imparted to Bill Wilson during the 1940's and early 1950's. We can see it coming out powerfully in 1953 in Wilson's chapter on Step Seven in *Twelve Steps and Twelve Traditions*, where the whole chapter turns into a description of the virtue of humility as the tool which we can use to remove all our other shortcomings.

His problems with smoking and overeating: Father Ed had more than one path of suffering which he was going to have to walk. In addition to his crippling arthritis, he smoked so heavily that even the St. Louis A.A. members, in a period of history when so many A.A. men and women were heavy smokers themselves, saw the way it was endangering his health and begged him to stop. So in 1944 (the year he turned forty-six), he used the twelve steps on his smoking, but like many people who stop, he then began compulsively overeating instead.[60]

His weight rose to 242 pounds (110 kg). He would sometimes gorge himself in grotesque food binges: doing things, for example, like eating a quarter pound of butter and an entire box of saltine crackers at one sitting. Once he started on one of these binges, he was unable to make himself stop. One night, to give another example, he came into the kitchen and ended up eating all the strawberries that had been prepared for the entire Jesuit community. He became so deathly ill he had to be given the last rites.[61]

Trying to go on diets did not work. The other Jesuits joked about it, because he would carefully eat the items on his restricted diet, but then end up consuming as much in "extra helpings" afterwards as he had eaten before he tried going on the diet.[62] Or it would take place in the reverse order: first the almost oblivious, blind bingeing, and then sitting down and eating the carefully limited diet meal. Mary Wehner, who was on the staff at *The Queen's Work,* told of an incident she observed at one of their staff buffet dinners.

> I happened to be standing next to him (Father Ed) at the buffet table watching a group square dancing. As we stood there completely absorbed, Father Ed would take a piece of bread, slap a piece of ham on it, fold it over and gulp it down. This happened several times, maybe five or six.
>
> I said, knowing he was notorious for being oblivious to what he ate, Oh, Father, why don't you let me get you some decent food?"
>
> "No thanks, dear, I'm on a strict diet."[63]

All of this had a terrible effect on his heart and arteries. In 1952 he had a retinal stroke that left him unable to read, and by 1958 (the year he turned sixty) he had had one or two more strokes and finally, at roughly the beginning of August in that year, a heart attack, which required him to carry a portable oxygen tank with him wherever he went. He finally got his weight down to 167 pounds by November 1958, but it was too late to do much good. A year and a half later, in Memphis, Tennessee, he had another heart attack and died.[64]

The conversion of Heywood Broun: One well known newspaperman of that period was Heywood Broun, who was famous for his defense of the underdog and the liberal positions he took on the social issues of the day. He believed that journalists had a duty to campaign against societal injustice, especially when it was the government itself which was supporting the evil doers. In 1933 he helped found the American Newspaper Guild, a labor union for journalists (it is still in existence, and currently has 32,000 members all over North America). The Guild still sponsors a Heywood Broun Award to be given annually to the journalist who does the most to help right a public wrong.

He was a member of the famous lunch group called the Algonquin Round Table in New York City, along with famous literary figures Dorothy Parker, Alexander Woollcott, and Robert Benchley, and was also close friends with the Marx Brothers (the famous comedy team from early twentieth-century vaudeville and movies).

Broun had published numerous attacks on conservative Christian political and ecclesiastical figures who, he believed, were denying people's civil liberties in their attempt to prevent the publishing of certain kinds of things: this included anything on topics they regarded as obscene, anything on the use of birth control devices, or anything defending the drinking of alcoholic beverages. As a 1939 *Time* magazine article put it, "To many a U. S. churchman, Heywood Broun was a Red, certainly a freethinker, probably an atheist." But then he began talking to Fr. Dowling, and as Broun put it in a column he wrote in March 1939,

> Quite recently I talked to a newspaper friend of mine who is now a priest. I said to him that I wanted to know if there was anything in Catholicism which stood in the way of any person who believed in political and economic progressivism. And my friend smiled and answered: "Don't you realize that you're a little naïve, Heywood? You like to call yourself a radical, but the doctrines of the Church to which I belong imply so many deep changes in human relationship that when they are accomplished—and they will be—your own notions will be nothing more than an outmoded pink liberalism." Whenever the Church militant begins to march there is no force in the armaments of dictators which can stay its progress.[65]

Broun was received into the Roman Catholic Church at the end of May 1939. Father Dowling had successfully made his convert,[66] by making it clear to him that he did not need to sacrifice his dedication to righting social wrongs in order to be a good Catholic.

Democracy: the poor vs. the rich. Fr. Dowling was in fact even more dedicated than Heywood Broun to defending the poor and downtrodden against the wealthy and powerful. The most famous statement attributed to Dowling on this topic was one that has been quoted almost three million times on the internet according to one standard search engine. It is sometimes identified as having first appeared in the *Chicago Daily News* on 28 July 1941:

> The two greatest obstacles to democracy in the United States are, first, the widespread delusion among the poor that we have a democracy, and second, the chronic terror among the rich, lest we get it.

His basic attitude towards power came out especially clearly in a letter he wrote to Bill Wilson in 1947: "Christ has always been associated with the weak, the poor and the human," he said. Christ's followers, as Father Ed and the members of so many of the major Catholic religious orders knew, were commanded to go out to the thirsty, those who had no food, immigrants looking for work, those without adequate clothing, the sick, and the people locked up in the jails and prisons (Matthew 25:31-46). And Christ's association with the helpless, the downtrodden, and the weak and easily tempted ran through the whole course of his life, Father Ed said, "from his nine months stay in the womb of his mother, to his years with his bungling, ostentatious, little college of twelve cardinals."[67] There was an important warning in that final little turn of phrase: the cardinals who ran the modern Roman Catholic Church from their palaces in Rome were no different from the twelve apostles from whom they were descended. They were inalterably human, which meant that they could sometimes be catastrophically weak.

Any kind of organization which Bill W. devised for Alcoholics Anonymous would be subject to the same human limitations, which was why Father Ed warned him, "Leadership should be on tap, not on top."[68] Guards against tyranny needed to be built into the A.A. structure at every possible point, because just as was the case in all other human institutions, those in A.A. who were given power would sometimes fall prey to the temptation to run roughshod over everyone else.

The radically democratic nature of A.A.'s organizational structure and its Twelve Traditions has long been noted. Some have pointed to the influence on Bill W. and Dr. Bob of their childhood memories of the New England town meeting. But certainly of even greater importance was the fact that the majority of the Protestants in early A.A. came from denominations (Congregationalists, Baptists, and so on) which practiced a pure congregationalist church polity (a method of church government in which each local church congregation is independent and autonomous from all the others, making its own decisions about the way in which matters of faith and practice are to be interpreted within its own congregation), or (in many other cases) they came from denominations such as the Presbyterians which were governed by a hierarchy of committees in which no single person was given any great amount of power for more than a limited and non-repeatable term of office.

But in addition to all this, we must not ignore what must have been the powerful influence of Fr. Dowling's spirit on the way Bill W. organized A.A. The movement's radical protection of the rights of minority groups went far beyond anything seen in New England town meetings or Protestant church organizations. It was the protection of small minority groups (black people and so on) and powerless groups (like factory workers or married women who had to stay home and care for numerous small children) which was at the focus of all Fr. Dowling's political involvement, and something which would automatically have come up every time he and Bill Wilson got together.

1942: the Cana Conference movement. An unfortunate number of American Catholic priests of Father Dowling's generation were of an authoritarian mindset, and viewed it as their mission to draw up hundreds of rules and then enforce them on their parishioners, who were regarded as helpless and foolish, and unable to make their own moral decisions. This kind of authoritarian pastor believed that only the priest had St. Peter's keys to the kingdom of heaven, and could serve as an effective conduit of divine grace. Father Ed on the contrary spent his whole life trying to devise and foster various kinds of self-help groups, both within the Church and outside the Church, where laypeople would minister to one another and serve as agents of healing grace, with such powerful success that no sensible observer could deny that God himself was working through these good laypeople.

One of the most famous self-help groups which he devised was directed toward married couples. In American Catholicism in the 1940's there often tended to be a rather Jansenistic attitude toward marriage: strait-laced, ridden with rigid rules, and filled with enormous fears about experiencing physical pleasure. In 1947, the German psychiatrist Karl Stern, who had immigrated to Canada and converted to Catholicism, was invited to speak to a Christian Family Movement convention, where he spoke quite strongly on this issue: "A great number of Catholics," he said, "have toward sexuality a strange, puritanical attitude; a Manichean attitude of fear as though the flesh in itself was something evil or dirty." (Manicheism, we remember, was an ancient non-Christian religious movement which proclaimed that the only way the human spirit could be saved was through an extraordinary denial of the human body and its needs and desires, including the practice of complete sexual abstinence.) Even though official Church doctrine condemned that kind of false teaching, "it is very prevalent. The strange thing is that the child in contact with a mother who has this kind of inner attitude towards sexual morality, even long before a conscious awareness of sex, is imbued with (the same attitude)."[69]

Fr. Dowling decided to become involved in a counter-campaign, one designed to bring more love and less fear into Catholic marriages, by founding the Cana Conference marriage enrichment program. He set up the first gathering in St. Louis in or before 1942, and devised the name for the program. The word "Cana" of course referred to the story of Jesus turning water into wine at the wedding feast described in John 2:1-11, but Dowling turned the word into an acronym which stressed the idea of a fellowship of mutual support involving devoted Catholic men and women: C-A-N-A = Couples Are Not Alone. He talked about all this in a letter which he wrote to Bill Wilson in 1942, explaining how "he had started a national movement for married couples to help each other through the twelve steps." He used the twelve steps to help them with their theological, intellectual and psychological problems, as well as scruples and sexual compulsions.[70] The basic format was to bring these married couples together for a one day conference involving three talks and a group discussion based on inquiries drawn from a question box, followed by a ceremony in which the couple renewed their wedding vows.[71]

When Cardinal Samuel Strich (the Archbishop of Chicago) appointed Father (later Msgr.) John Egan to head the Cana program in Chicago—a position he held from 1947 to 1948—Egan became a major leader in the movement. Because of his personality, drive, and public prominence, he came to be better known than Fr. Dowling in many parts of the United States.[72]

But Fr. Dowling never ceased his work for the movement, using the twelve steps to give Cana conferences for families at least once a month from 1942 until his death in 1960 (in fact, it has been calculated that he put on more than 300 conferences during that period). Sometimes he doubled up on Cana and Alcoholics Anonymous, such as on April 29, 1947, when he was the principal speaker in the morning (at the Hotel Tallcorn) for the third anniversary celebration of the A.A. group in Marshalltown, Iowa, and then led a Cana Conference meeting for Catholic couples that afternoon.[73]

And in fact when he died, we remember, it was the morning after meeting with one of the Cana groups he had established, a group of devoted Catholic couples in Memphis, Tennessee. Right after his death, Monsignor DeBlanc, who was the director of the Family Life Bureau of NCWC (the National Catholic Welfare Council, today the United States Conference of Catholic Bishops), sent a wire saying simply but eloquently: "Fr. Dowling's death an irreparable personal loss." Monsignor Egan, the aforementioned director of Chicago Cana, telegraphed a similar message: "Our debt to him for what he was and what he did will never be repaid."[74]

In Bill W.'s letter to Fr. Ed of May 20, 1946, he talked about how impressed he was with the way the Cana marriage conferences worked within the context of the Catholic Church. Although A.A. had had informal family groups meeting in some cities since 1941, one still cannot help but wonder if the example of the Cana Conference movement might not have helped inspire Lois Wilson when she joined with Anne B. in setting up a more formal Al-Anon Family Groups organization in 1951.[75]

The Queen's Work and its Summer School of Catholic Action: Fr. Dowling was a well-known member of the faculty of the Summer School of Catholic Action for over twenty-five years, traveling to around twenty-five cities in the United States and Canada, and speaking to large audiences. This was one of the most influential nationwide endeavors carried out by the famous Jesuit leader Fr. Daniel A. Lord, who had revitalized The Sodality of the Blessed Virgin Mary and its magazine *The Queen's Work* when he was appointed director in 1925.[76]

> In these stops across the country at big city hotels, *The Queen's Work* staff offered young people talks, discussions, and liturgies. Father Dan Lord directed their singing and dancing in his large musicals. Dowling himself gave talks on social justice, marriage, the family, proportional representation, suffering, A.A.—whatever his current interest.[77]

Fr. Ed especially liked to show how the *Spiritual Exercises* of St. Ignatius could be applied to dealing with the everyday stresses of family life.[78] But as one of the other staff remembered, he did it with a light-handed style, reminiscent of the way a good newspaper columnist would talk: "He would speak from current newspaper 'clippings,' which he would have in his hands in seeming disorder, and all of this 'stuff' was spontaneous and bristled with one liners."[79]

Large numbers of young American Catholics—the best and brightest of their generation—had their earliest exposure to good Catholic thought at these summer schools, and were inspired to dedicate their lives to serving the Church as clergy, religious, or enthusiastic lay people.

CHAPTER 3

Cognitive Behavioral Psychology and Small Group Therapy

What kind of psychological system to employ? The use of Neo-Freudian psychiatry among A.A.'s of Protestant background. A book called *The Psychology of Alcoholism*, written by A.A. author William E. Swegan, was the most detailed statement from the important wing of early A.A. which stressed the psychological interpretation of the steps and largely or wholly ignored their spiritual side. Swegan was an atheist or near-atheist from a Protestant background (during his childhood his parents had listened on Sundays to the weekly "hot gospel" program broadcast by a Protestant fundamentalist radio evangelist named E. Howard Cadle, but the child found it grotesque and unbelievable even at that young age).[80] Swegan was very typical of many early A.A.'s from Protestant backgrounds: he preferred to combine the twelve steps with some form of Neo-Freudian psychiatry which stressed the importance of issues which arose during childhood and adolescence as the major source of later adult psychological problems. This approach rejected Freud's almost exclusive focus on the problems of early infancy. The psychiatrists Alfred Adler (1870-1937), Karen Horney (1885-1952), and Erik Erikson (1902-1994) were typical of this type of Neo-Freudian approach.

The Neo-Freudians then further modified orthodox Freudian doctrine by talking about the importance of issues such as social factors, interpersonal relations, and cultural influences in personality development and in the development of psychological illnesses and disorders. They believed that social relationships were fundamental to the formation and development of personality. So in other words, they tended to reject Freud's emphasis on sexual problems as the cause of neurosis, and were more apt to regard fundamental human psychological problems as psychosocial rather than psychosexual.

Bill Wilson's name was linked to that of three of the Neo-Freudians: Adler, Horney, and Jung. His mother, Dr. Emily Griffith Wilson, had studied with Adler in Vienna, and after taking up residence in San Diego, California, lectured on Adlerian psychiatry and maintained a practice as an Adlerian psychoanalyst. In a 1956 letter, Bill W. gave special praise to the writings of another famous Neo-Freudian, Karen Horney. It should further be noted that from 1945 to 1949, Bill was working continuously on his depression with a psychiatrist named Dr. Frances Weeks who was a Jungian, and that the psychiatrist Carl Jung was also usually regarded as one of the Neo-Freudians, even if of a different sort.[81]

The kind of A.A. which Jack Alexander was exposed to when he was carrying out his research in the Fall of 1940 for the *Saturday Evening Post* article that appeared in March of 1941, used this kind of Neo-Freudian approach. Alexander picked up on these ideas and summarized them in his article, which (as we remember) immediately produced an outflowing of eager interest in A.A. all over the United States:

> Only one note is found to be common to all alcoholics— emotional immaturity. Closely related to this is an observation that an unusually large number of alcoholics start out in life as an only child, as a younger child, as the only boy in a family of girls or the only girl in a family of boys. Many have records of childhood precocity and were what are known as spoiled children.
>
> Frequently, the situation is complicated by an off-center home atmosphere in which one parent is unduly cruel, the other overindulgent. Any combination of these factors, plus a divorce or two, tends to produce neurotic children who are poorly equipped emotionally to face the ordinary realities of adult life. In seeking escapes, one may immerse himself in his business, working twelve to fifteen hours a day, or in what he thinks is a pleasant escape in drink. It bolsters his opinion

of himself and temporarily wipes away any feeling of social inferiority, which he may have. Light drinking leads to heavy drinking. Friend and family are alienated and employers become disgusted. The drinker smolders with resentment and wallows in self-pity. He indulges in childish rationalizations to justify his drinking: He has been working hard and he deserves to relax; his throat hurts from an old tonsillectomy and a drink would ease the pain; he has a headache; his wife does not understand him; his nerves are jumpy; everybody is against him; and on and on. He unconsciously becomes a chronic excuse-maker for himself.[82]

What is especially important is to see how Neo-Freudian ideas affected the way A.A. figures carried out their fourth steps. Bill Swegan, for example, the author of *The Psychology of Alcoholism* mentioned above, explains in his book how he underwent a great trauma after his mother died when he was a small child. This operated on the little boy's mind at an unconscious level, in such a way that it caused him to attack other children because he was jealous of the love and attention they were receiving from their mothers. Bill's family was also very poor, so that he had to go to school wearing old and worn-out clothes, which caused him to withdraw socially and skip out on solitary fishing expeditions instead of learning how to interrelate with other children. Again, this was an unconscious connection, in that young Bill was aware that he felt unbearably self-conscious about his clothes, but was not really fully consciously aware of the fact that this was the real reason why he so often said, "I'd rather go fishing," and was certainly not consciously aware of the fact that the lack of adequate social training which this produced, was one of the chief reasons for the disasters that occurred when he attempted to date and court young women during his later adolescence.[83]

Nick Kowalski was a member of one of the two most famous early A.A. prison groups (his story is told in the book *The Factory Owner & the Convict*). Although brought up Roman Catholic, he was originally taught a Protestant style of A.A. with its heavy emphasis upon human powerlessness and the saving power of free unmerited grace. Like Bill Swegan, Nick was shaped at a profound level by the death of his mother when he was a little boy. In Nick's case however, an extra dimension was added when one of the people at the orphanage commented right after he arrived on the first day, "Why he's such a brave little boy, he doesn't even cry." The small boy was in fact totally shell-shocked and unable to even begin to comprehend what was happening to him as his father abandoned him and drove away. But little Nick decided, on the basis of the woman's offhand remark, that praiseworthy behavior meant closing off all your emotions and driving off anyone who ever tried to get close to you, so you could stand there stiffly and pretend to feel nothing. And the diet at the orphanage was so poor, that he developed rickets, and his ribcage was partially sunken in. One of the other children at the orphanage told him (cruelly and ignorantly) that his sunken ribcage was because he was a "queer," that is, a homosexual, which resulted in little Nick spending years trying never to let any of the other children see him with his shirt off. What developed was social isolationism, just as in Bill Swegan's case, and a failure to learn how to function in normal society, but with Nick there was also the development of more and more dangerous attempts to "prove his manhood" and show he was a "tough guy" by falling into increasing criminality and violence. Nick ended up getting drunk out of his mind one night, and shooting and killing a stranger in a house of prostitution, for which he received a life sentence at the Indiana state penitentiary.[84]

Recovering alcoholics are often able to pinpoint the exact year in their childhoods during which some kind of trauma blocked much of their further emotional growth. We could look for example at the life of Nancy Olson, a recovered alcoholic who became Senator Harold Hughes' chief aide in charge of alcoholism legislation while the Hughes Act was being passed in 1970. A glance at a photograph taken when Nancy was nine years old, right after her mother and father had separated, shows a little girl with a thousand-yard stare of uncomprehending horror and grief, and a sticker pasted on the photo saying "Tomorrow Will You Know My Name?" Even as a highly competent adult, many years later, when Nancy was placed under certain kinds of stress, she reverted emotionally to behaving like that scared and angry little girl.[85]

Submarine Bill C., when he was twelve years old, almost died as the result of a ruptured spleen received in a fall off a high cliff. As the youngest in a large family, he was already something of a spoiled child, but was now simply given everything he wanted, with never a hint of having to take any other person's feelings and wishes into account, and grew into an adult who would explode (or seethe) in anger if he did not receive instant perfect gratification. Compounding the problem, when he was sixteen he contracted rheumatic fever and had to spend a year in bed. After being totally bedridden for so long, he was left quite physically weakened at first, and had a classical Adlerian response of an inferiority complex followed by over-compensation. He won a football scholarship to college, went out for Golden Gloves boxing, shot the prize deer in the Pennsylvania woods, and eventually became involved in sordid bar room fights, flirting with the ladies, and other activities of that sort: "playing the tough guy" and continually "trying to prove his manhood."[86]

If I may give my own interpretation of how I have seen this theory applied in practice, the people in the A.A. group who have already been sober for a long period of time "re-parent" the new arrivals. They serve as good fathers and good mothers, good older brothers and good older sisters, good uncles and aunts, and good grandparents, patiently showing the troubled alcoholic how to behave like an adult. Little children throw childish, out-of-control temper tantrums, while adults know how to express anger and disagreement in ways that make their disputes easier to resolve. Little children demand instant gratification, while adults learn to show patience and look toward delayed gratification. Little children can see only one moral issue at a time, while adults learn how to analyze situations in which several different competing moral claims may be placed on them simultaneously. 1 Corinthians 13 was cited again and again in early A.A. because it stated this so clearly. 1 Cor. 13:4-7 explains what adult love is, as opposed to childish love. For children to act like children is not evil, but after I reach my adult years, continuing to act in a childish and infantile manner is something that needs correcting: "When I was a child, I spoke like a child, I thought like a child, I reasoned like a child; when I became an adult, I gave up childish ways" (1 Cor. 13:11).

Now although many Protestants in early A.A. found it very useful to employ this kind of analysis when working with deeply troubled alcoholics—Kenneth G. Merrill, the devout Episcopalian factory owner in the aforementioned book, *The Factory Owner & the Convict*, laid out the basic theory in especially clear fashion in an article he wrote called "Drunks Are a Mess"[87]—Roman Catholic thinkers were often made uneasy by parts of this approach.

I remember when I was serving as editor for Ernest Kurtz, the best Catholic philosopher and theologian of A.A.'s second generation—this was when he was writing the second edition[88] of his famous book on *Shame & Guilt*—that Kurtz made it clear how uncomfortable it made him to hear people in A.A. use phrases like "we're as sick as our secrets." He believed that the attempt to force people to make public their most shameful and humiliating experiences while everyone else gaped and stared, only made the trauma even more horribly unbearable. It was not psychologically healing, in Kurtz's estimation, but made the person's guilt and shame far worse and even more deeply crippling.

The Catholic choice: instead of Freudianism, the cognitive behavioral psychology of Dr. Abraham A. Low. Father Dowling and Father Ralph Pfau were likewise not only deeply opposed to classical Freudianism but were also uncomfortable with the later Neo-Freudian approaches that were attracting so many of the A.A.'s who came from Protestant backgrounds.[89]

That was one of the reasons Father Dowling was so appreciative of the twelve step program as practiced by simple laypeople in the ordinary work-a-day rooms of A.A. As he put it, in "moving therapy from the expensive clinical couch to the low-cost coffee bar, from the inexperienced professional to the informed amateur, A.A. has democratized sanity."[90] It put moral considerations back on the basis of everyday common sense, and took things out of the hands of over-intellectualized psychiatrists who were all too often deeply hostile to religion and spirituality, and attacked religious beliefs at every turn as superstitious and "neurotic."

Father Dowling and Father Pfau were not totally hostile, however, to all varieties of psychology and psychotherapy. Both of them were strong supporters of the approach taken by Chicago psychiatrist Dr. Abraham A. Low (1891-1954), the original founder of the kind of cognitive-behavioral therapy which (in the 1950's and 60's) was further developed by Albert Ellis and Aaron T. Beck. In 1937 Dr. Low started a program to teach his system, which he called Recovery Inc., which quickly spread across the United States and Canada, particularly after the *Saturday Evening Post* published an article describing their recovery groups in December 6, 1952. Low publicized his ideas in two important bodies of work, which came out in 1943 and 1950 respectively.[91] In 2007, Recovery Inc. changed its name to Recovery International, and in 2009 became Abraham Low Self-Help Systems, and is still active today, with over six hundred groups meeting in the U.S. and several other countries. The program can give enormous help to patients who are dealing with a wide range of different psychological problems, including phobias, general anxiety and panic attacks, depression, obsessive-compulsive disorder, and bi-polar disorder. It can even help in anger management and make it easier for patients to manage schizophrenic symptoms.

The question we must ask here though, is why were Dowling and Pfau so attracted to Abraham Low's method, but so deeply repelled by Freudian psychiatry of any kind? As Father Dowling saw it, *Low preserved the Catholic insistence on the vital role of human free will in human moral and spiritual development*. As he put it in a speech to the N.C.C.A. in 1953:

> Doctor Abraham A. Low, rejects psychoanalysis as philosophically false and practically ineffective. He writes: "Life is not driven by instincts but is guided by the will."[92]

Dowling recommended Recovery, Inc. in his speech to the N.C.C.A. in 1953,[93] and himself founded the first Recovery, Inc. group in St. Louis.[94] He began by traveling to Chicago to learn more at first hand about how to run their program, and then opened that society's St. Louis group in one of the offices at *The Queen's Work*, where he could directly supervise it.[95]

Fr. Ralph Pfau likewise recommended Recovery, Inc., several times in his autobiography,[96] and told how he went to their group meetings in Louisville in addition to his participation in A.A. One of the modern experts on the Recovery program is Ernest Kurtz's wife, Linda Farris Kurtz, DPA, who is now Professor Emeritus at Eastern Michigan

University's School of Social Work, and who also highly praises the group.[97]

Abraham Low's system is designed help people deal with a large number of psychological problems, including phobias, anxiety, panic attacks, depression, feelings of low self-worth, outbursts of uncontrollable anger, obsessive compulsive disorder, social anxiety, crippling shyness, psychologically induced tremors or dizziness, suicidal thoughts, and certain types of sleep problems. It can also help people manage their symptoms when they are being treated for attention deficit disorder, bipolar disorder, borderline personality disorder, schizoaffective disorder, and schizophrenia.

A triggering event will cause us to fall into either a "fearful temper" or an "angry temper." In either case, the feeling is produced by a certain kind of judgment that our minds have made about the triggering situation. A fearful temper arises from the belief that *we have done something wrong*, which gives rise to feelings of fearfulness, shame and inadequacy. An angry temper is produced by the belief that *we have been wronged*, which produces feelings such as indignation and impatience.

If we respond to this initial flash of temper by using more and more "temperamental lingo" in our internal self-dialogue, the incapacitating and/or destructive emotions will grow greater and greater. Temperamental lingo includes using overly judgmental language about right and wrong ("good people *always* do such-and-such," "I am a totally and absolutely bad person," etc.), and the use of defeatist and fatalistic language to describe our symptoms: "intolerable," "unbearable," "uncontrollable," "irresistible," and so on.

Abraham Low's Recovery, Inc. program stresses the power of human free will. It rejects the psychoanalytical idea of the subconscious, and argues that any therapeutic system which teaches that human behavior is determined by unconscious motives, instincts, and drives will of necessity be self-defeating. Human beings have the power to analyze what they are feeling and what is going on in their lives, and then working out rational ways to deal with those problems, and acting upon their carefully considered conclusions. We do not have to accept every thought that arises, nor do we have to act on every impulse that springs up. And even more important, we can use our free will to devise training programs where we replace the old destructive thoughts and feelings which used to pop up automatically in our minds with a new set of habitual responses built up out of self-affirming inner thoughts and positive external behaviors.

Group members are trained to respond to unsetting situations by going through a four-part process of analysis. (1) This begins with a brief statement of the situation: for example, the clerk at a store helped someone else before taking my order, even though I had been there first; I had to ride up ten floors in an elevator even though I suffer from extreme claustrophobia; I did not know the answer to the first question on the exam, and immediately fell into such a panic that I could not even remember the answers to problems which I would otherwise have been able to work easily.

(2) I note any feelings which I then experienced: for example, angry thoughts, fearful thoughts, a wave of pure despair, wanting to scream, wanting to cry, mental confusion, or what have you. Also physical symptoms: things like sweaty palms, trembling hands, pounding heart, a knot in my stomach, clenched teeth, feeling myself growing red in the face, or what have you. The object here is to be as objective and analytical as possible, to help defuse and lower the emotional level.

(3) *Spotting* means analyzing my thoughts and feelings so as to identify the places where I am violating the principles of the Recovery, Inc. program in ways which will increase my anger and fear. *Reframing* means changing the way I have been viewing the situation and my role in it.

(4) I then remind myself of how I would have mishandled this situation before I began working the Recovery, Inc. program, and what a catastrophe I would have made out of things, as a way of giving myself positive reinforcement for my new behavioral pattern.

This kind of extremely rationalistic approach fit much better with typical Jesuit modes of thought, than psychological approaches which talked too much about the unconscious or fell too heavily into rejecting all human self-will. St. Ignatius, for example, had taught the Jesuits how to practice discernment when they had to make difficult decisions: the Ignatian method of discernment was a systematic analysis of the person's own thoughts and feelings which had many similarities to Dr. Abraham Low's methodology.

Ever since the sixteenth century Reformation, Catholic theologians had feared that Protestant theologians had too great a tendency to let people just sit around until they spontaneously felt like they would enjoy changing. Catholic theologians believed that ordinary human beings needed direction from people who were more knowledgeable, and that sometimes they needed to be told to buck up their will power and *make* themselves do things which would help them grow spiritually, even if this meant deliberately doing things which involved pain and suffering. The idea of engaging in strenuous psychological exercises through the Recovery, Inc. program, in order to train our wills to be stronger and in better control, was something that Catholic theologians could find extremely attractive.

And in the history of Christian spirituality, we need to remember, the word asceticism originally came from the ancient desert monks, who took the pagan Greek word *askêsis* (which referred to the kind of hard, sweaty, difficult physical training which athletes underwent) and turned it into a term referring to the kind of rigorous and often painful *spiritual* training which the monks underwent as they prayed and meditated for hours without cease in the heat of the Egyptian desert.

And to make my own comment, we also need to remember that there is no reason to make an either-or issue out of the differences between cognitive behavioral therapy and the Neo-Freudian psychosocial analysis of childhood development. A.A. members who developed low self esteem and a continually self-sabotaging inferiority complex as children, can be helped enormously by simple behavioral techniques such as drawing up a list of their good attributes and reading these over every morning. Likewise, making a gratitude list and reading it every morning can help to recondition and reframe people's minds when their habitually negative self-talk drives them into chronic depression.

Even if the person's problems arose out of specific childhood traumas, many of the best old-time A.A. sponsors would tell their sponsees to "perform the right motion until you feel the right emotion," or similar advice. This was the standard behaviorist observation that when people acted in a certain way over and over, they would eventually begin to feel the emotions that went with those actions. Submarine Bill, one of the A.A. old-timers from my part of the U.S., was told by his sponsor to perform a good deed every day for one of his brothers-in-law—the person whom he hated and resented more than any other person in the world—until he learned to love that man. Bill found that after enough weeks of doing this, he could spend time with the brother-in-law without being driven into out-of-control anger and attacks. Bill at first despised and looked down upon the other A.A. members, so his sponsor made him stand by the front door and greet every person who entered, shaking that person's hand, looking the other person in the eye, and greeting the person by name. After enough weeks of that, Bill's mind had been reframed and his emotions had been reconditioned, so that he was actually feeling cheery and welcoming when he shook the person's hand, and he found himself slowly coming to genuinely like the other people at the meeting.

Given the important role that early Catholic members played in getting A.A. to employ cognitive behavioral methods as a regular part of the A.A. toolbox, they did an enormous service to the movement.

The Montserrat Circle for scrupulosity and other emotional self-help groups. Father Dowling later also formed an additional group in St. Louis, modeled on the therapeutic method used by Recovery, Inc., which he dedicated to working with Catholics who suffered from scrupulosity. He called this new group the Montserrat Circle, naming it after the place in Spain where St. Ignatius Loyola, the founder of the Jesuits, had his vision of the Virgin Mary and the infant Jesus in March 1522.[98]

Scrupulosity is a self-tormenting tendency among some religious people in which they feel pathological guilt over their own behavior in minor or trivial situations which they have convinced themselves involve serious moral issues or a blasphemous mistake in the performance of a religious ritual. St. Ignatius Loyola once spoke of accidentally stepping on two straws which had fallen to the ground in the form of a cross, and suddenly feeling that he had committed a grave sin. Martin Luther in similar fashion said that on one occasion he accidentally left out the word *enim* ("for") in one passage while saying mass, and suddenly was overwhelmed with the feeling that he had committed a sin as grave as divorcing a spouse or murdering a parent. (It is ironic that Loyola and Luther, although on opposite sides of the sixteenth-century Protestant Reformation, were two of the most famous sufferers from scrupulosity in the history of the disorder—both the *Spiritual Exercises* and the Lutheran interpretation of the gospel message in the Apostle Paul's letter to the Romans were attempts to devise methods of treating and healing scrupulosity.)

In addition to his Montserrat Circle for Catholics suffering from scrupulosity, Dowling also set up two additional self-help groups (meeting at *The Queen's Work*) for people who suffered from nervous disorders. It was a bustling place: people belonging to these two groups were continually coming and going from Fr. Ed's office, or holding long consultations with him over the telephone. Ernest Kurtz believes that this may have been an early version of what was later known as Neurotics Anonymous or Emotions Anonymous.[99]

Group therapy: God working through the group. A.A. members in particular, Dowling stated on one occasion, "know the wonders that can come from amateur group psychotherapy based on the human will aided by God's help."[100] The twelve steps, he discovered, provided one of the best disciplines ever seen for turning a small group therapy session into a context in which the grace of God and the power of the divine Spirit could operate in and through the members of the group. It was not just alcoholism that could be healed in that fashion, nor was it just addictive behaviors, but an incredibly wide range of human moral and relationship problems.

Combining A.A. with Recovery Inc., Cana, and a 1950's movement called Divorcées Anonymous. When Fr. Dowling discovered Alcoholics Anonymous at the end of 1940, he quickly became convinced of the special power of the twelve steps as a spiritual tool. In the following years he liked to incorporate insights and teaching techniques from A.A. into his work with other groups. He sometimes put together interesting combinations of group therapies, as we see in the letter he wrote Bill and Lois Wilson at Christmas time 1953:

> The Recovery Inc. people borrow strength from the 12
> Steps .... Last month we experimented with a Cana

Conference, confined to couples from A.A., Recovery Inc., Divorcees Anonymous, and Cana.

They discussed in small groups, three and four couples each and then processed to new groupings. The case presented involved money, in-laws, jealousy, sex. Then asked the question, "What could A.A. contribute to this situation?" What would Recovery? What would Cana? What would Divorcees Anonymous?[101]

Divorcées Anonymous (DA) —one of the groups he mentions here—was a new group which was trying to deal with a new problem: the increasing number of marriages in the United States that were ending in divorce. The group was started in 1949 by a Chicago attorney named Samuel M. Starr, and its philosophy was very much a product of attitudes towards women in the United States in that historical era. DA used the feminine form—*divorcée,* that is, divorced *woman*; not *divorcé,* divorced *man*—and to put it quite frankly, the group was designed to teach married women how to use their wiles and manipulative abilities to bring back straying husbands and change their husbands' behaviors when they were grumpy, angry, and so on. It assumed that if the marriage was not working, this was the wife's responsibility.[102]

Father Ed was also a man of that era, just like Samuel Starr, and some of his words about marriage counseling seem quite dated today. He argued, for example, that America needed "an 'internship in housework' for society debutantes and college girls," displaying an attitude toward male and female marital roles that would enrage one of today's feminists. But when he "urged married couples to write each other love notes to make up for the lag in conversation," although this might at first sound to some modern men and women like a piece of sentimentality from a 1950's American television show, in fact, getting family members to explicitly tell other family members that they love them, and say it — really meaning it — on a regular basis, can play a vital role in healing all sorts of dysfunctional family relationships.[103] How many men and women in twelve-step programs for example, never heard their fathers, or their mothers, telling them that they loved them, but instead received only harsh words, put-downs, and constant denigration?

Why did Divorcées Anonymous come into being at that time, in 1949? People in the United States had been alarmed by the sudden sharp peak in the divorce rate that occurred right after the Second World War, even though the divorce rate went back down quickly. There had been nothing like that before in all of U.S. history. This 1946-47 outbreak was almost as high (even though not nearly as long-lasting) as a second peak which began its rise in the later 1960s and 1970s and continued through the 1980s before it began turning back down slightly.

It is to Fr. Dowling's credit that, instead of reacting to the crisis that had broken out within the U.S. marriage system by preaching condemnatory sermons denouncing men and women who got divorced and threatening them with hellfire—and instead of trying vainly to bring down the divorce rate by conducting political campaigns against the legalization of divorce (or against birth control or against other women's rights, as some conservatives in the U.S. and Europe were doing at that time)—he devoted his energies to trying to lend his help to the best available marital therapy group which a Catholic priest of that period could endorse.

CHAPTER 4

Father Ed Receives a Gift of Grace: 1940

When Father Dowling discovered the Alcoholics Anonymous movement in the Fall of 1940, then began experimenting with setting up twelve step groups himself, and finally got to meet Bill Wilson himself in December of that year, it was one of the most momentous few months of his life. As Father Robert Fitzgerald, S.J. noted in his article in *The Catholic Digest*,[104]

> Father Ed counted many gifts from Bill. He had told his sister, Anna, that the graces he received from their meeting were equivalent to those received at his own ordination. And he thanked Bill for letting him "hitchhike" on the twelve steps.

That is an extraordinary statement to make: *a gift of divine grace as great as the one conveyed by the Holy Spirit at his ordination as a Catholic priest.*

But Father Ed meant it. He was able to apply what he learned from his study of the twelve steps to all the small group programs and religious activities he was involved in all over the United States: Recovery Inc., the Montserrat Circle, Divorcées Anonymous, the Catholic Action summer school programs, the Christian Family movement, his writing for *The Queen's Work*, and so on.

But meeting Bill Wilson seems to have also given him a personal boost that filled him with a new life and creativity and dedication to serving God by helping his fellow human beings.

Father Ed and Bill Wilson: Two Spiritual Masters

CHAPTER 5

Discovering A.A. and Meeting Bill W: 1940

Fr. Dowling founds the first A.A. meeting in St. Louis on October 30, 1940: In April 1939, the new Alcoholics Anonymous movement published 4,730 copies of its Big Book, which set out its famous twelve steps and explained in careful detail how the program worked. The Big Book said they had one hundred members, who were centered mainly in Akron, New York City, and Cleveland.

By the Fall of 1940 (when Father Dowling first became involved with the Alcoholics Anonymous program), there were A.A. groups holding regular weekly meetings in twenty-two American cities, still concentrated mostly on the East Coast and in the upper Midwest (although there were now A.A. groups in Little Rock, Arkansas; Houston, Texas; and in San Francisco and Los Angeles, California). The total membership however was still small—1,400 men and women, according to A.A.'s New York office—and not very many copies of the first printing of the Big Book had sold.[105]

We are told that Father Ed Dowling first became involved in A.A. during the Fall of 1940 when he "was contacted by F., who said his son-in-law had a drinking problem. Of course, it was F. himself who had the drinking problem and was seeking help." Father Ed took F. up to Chicago with him, along with four other problem drinkers whom he had recruited there in St. Louis, to see how a well-run A.A. group actually functioned.[106]

How did Father Ed know about Chicago A.A.? He had important Catholic connections in that city, dating back to when he had been a young Jesuit doing his Regency teaching at Loyola Academy in

1926-1929. But several of the Chicago A.A. members were newspaper people, and he continued to keep in contact with the newspaper world for his whole life, so he may also have known about A.A. through those friendships.[107]

Mrs. Marty Mann commented on this later on, in an article with an interesting topic: "The Pastor's Resources in Dealing with Alcoholics: Alcoholics Are Consumed with Guilt; They Do Not Need to Be Reminded of Their Sins."[108] Father Dowling, Marty said, was a superb example of the good pastor: instead of condemning and scolding alcoholics from the pulpit and increasing their sense of being stigmatized, he climbed down out of the pulpit, took these alcoholics by the hand, and climbed on a railroad train with them and went *with them* to visit the Chicago A.A. group. This good priest, Marty said, who was both extraordinarily brave and totally humble, was one of the stories from early A.A. that showed us how to do it right:

> Ten years ago when there were not many groups, a Catholic priest in St. Louis shepherded several alcoholics whom he was trying to interest in A.A. up to Chicago where they could see it for themselves. The St. Louis group was started.[109]

It is also important, on a pastoral note, to pay special attention to one line from the obituary which Bill W. wrote for Fr. Dowling after his death in 1960: "St. Louis old-timers recalled how he helped start their group; it had turned out to be largely Protestant, but this fazed him not a bit."[110] The truly good people who were associated with the new A.A. movement—the ones who had really worked the twelve steps or their equivalent in their own spiritual system—acted out of pure love toward all. Catholics like Fr. Dowling and Fr. Pfau helped Protestants in the same way that they helped Catholics, with never a thought as to which was which, and the Protestants responded with undying gratitude.

Chicago A.A. 1937-1940: The central figure in early Chicago A.A. was an alcoholic named Earl Treat, who originally came from the Akron area. His story, "He Sold Himself Short," is in the 2nd, 3rd and 4th eds. of the Big Book. In 1937, Earl's father brought him back to Akron to visit the newly formed A.A. group there. He sobered up with the help of Dr. Bob and the early Akron group, and returned to Chicago, where he had one brief slip in July 1937, but then sobered up again.[111] As Earl explained it, he was at first totally on his own, but "I would go to Akron every two months for a meeting in order to maintain my sobriety and work with others." "It took a year before I could find anyone to work with [in Chicago], and two years without the book before we had six people."[112]

Sylvia Kauffmann (whose story, "The Keys to the Kingdom," is in the 2nd, 3rd, and 4th eds. of the Big Book) was another important member of the early Chicago A.A. group. Earl Treat sent her to Akron, and after spending time there and in Cleveland, she came back to Chicago where she eventually got sober on September 13, 1939.[113]

On September 20, 1939, Chicago had its first official group meeting in Earl Treat's apartment in the Chicago suburb of Evanston. There were only eight present: Earl, Earl's wife Katie, Sylvia Kauffmann, Dick R., Ken A., Sadie I., George M., and a nonalcoholic, Grace Cultice (Sylvia Kauffmann's personal secretary), who became the group's secretary. But the group grew with amazing speed over the next few months, and in January 1940, when Bill Wilson came to visit, there were thirty people present at Sylvia's apartment for the dinner and meeting.[114] And by the end of that year, when Jack Alexander visited, he reported in the *Saturday Evening Post* article which he wrote immediately afterward, that "in Chicago, twenty-five doctors work hand in hand with Alcoholics Anonymous, contributing their services and referring their own alcoholic patients to the group, which now numbers around 200." One of the things that most impressed Jack (as a newspaperman) was that in Chicago, "on one of the most influential newspapers in the country, I found that the city editor, the assistant city editor, and a nationally known reporter were A.A.s, and strong in the confidence of their publisher.[115] That would have similarly impressed Father Ed, an old newspaperman himself.

So Father Dowling and his little group from St. Louis were able to see a large and vigorous A.A. community at work when they visited Chicago in the Fall of 1940.

The St. Louis A.A. group: 1940-45. As soon as they got back from Chicago, Father Ed and the five alcoholics used what they had learned to set up the first St. Louis A.A. group:

> [They] held the first A.A. meeting in St. Louis ... on October 30, 1940, at the Gibson Hotel, 5883 Enright Avenue. The first newcomer got sober December 11 and the second on January 8, 1941. And on December 26, 1940, the *St. Louis Star-Times* ran a favorable article under the headline, "Alcoholics Anonymous, Fraternity that Streamlined the Waterwagon, Has Formed a Group in St. Louis."[116]

The St. Louis group was not only going to grow and prosper, it was almost immediately going to play a decisive role in a major event in A.A. history. While the group was still in its initial organizational period—the winter of 1940-41— the publisher of the *Saturday Evening Post* magazine assigned one of its reporters, Jack Alexander, to investigate the new Alcoholics Anonymous movement.[117] Jack had been born in St. Louis,[118] and had worked for the *St. Louis Star* and then the *St. Louis Post-Dispatch* (one of the largest and most influential Midwestern newspapers, founded by Joseph Pulitzer) before leaving St. Louis and moving to the East Coast in 1930. He spent the remainder of his career in New York City, working for the *Daily News* (a New York newspaper owned by the publishers of the *Chicago Tribune*), the *New Yorker* magazine, and finally the *Saturday Evening Post* magazine.[119]

In an article he wrote for the A.A. *Grapevine* later on, Jack Alexander described how his attitude toward the Alcoholics Anonymous movement changed as he continued his research. He began his research, he said, by spending a week talking with Bill Wilson and the New York A.A. group. At the end of the week, he told Bill that he frankly did not believe all the marvelous things he was being told. The A.A.'s sounded to him like actors playing a role on stage, and his ear did not seem to be hearing the ring of truth. So Bill took Jack to Philadelphia to spend all day Sunday, December 15, 1940, and then took him that Sunday night to see the people in Akron. While they were there, Dr. Bob drove

Jack and Bill to visit the A.A. group in Cleveland, so he could see yet a further group in action.[120]

Jack Alexander said that he began to lose a little of his skepticism by the time they had finished talking to the people in Cleveland, as he began to note that, although the alcoholics in all the different cities came from widely different backgrounds—factory workers, lawyers, accountants, professional men (whom Jack characterized as being kind of "oily"), along with people in hospitals and psychopathic wards who had recently been undergoing the blind staggers—they nevertheless told the same stories and displayed the same patterns.[121]

But the grand tour of early A.A. did not stop there. They continued on, to Chicago and finally to Father Dowling's town, St. Louis. As Jack Alexander described it:

> The pattern was repeated also in Chicago, the only variation there being the presence at the meetings of a number of newspapermen. I had spent most of my working life on newspapers and I could really talk to these men. The real clincher, though, came in St. Louis, which is my hometown. Here I met a number of my own friends who were A.A.s, and the last remnants of skepticism vanished. Once rollicking rumpots, they were now sober. It didn't seem possible, but there it was.[122]

Jack Alexander must have arrived in St. Louis around the end of the third week in December, and Bill Wilson said that Jack was planning to write his article there, so he seems to have been combining his research with a visit back home for Christmas.[123] The article Jack authored, which appeared in the *Saturday Evening Post* for March 1, 1941, gained A.A. its first major national recognition. At the beginning of that year, A.A. had had a total membership of only 2,000 or so. After the article came out, alcoholics from all over the United States (and their relatives) began contacting the New York A.A. office, and within less than a year, their membership tripled.

The important thing to note for our story here, is that the little A.A. group in St. Louis which had been created by a St. Louis journalist who became a priest—created to help some of his hard-drinking buddies from the newspaper world—was the force that made Jack Alexander a believer. What an extraordinary thing Father Dowling accomplished for alcoholics all over the world, by struggling through the pain of his arthritis to climb on a train to Chicago, and setting up meetings in St. Louis hotel rooms instead of staying at home in the evenings and giving his legs and back a rest, and putting his personal time and energy into trying to help a little group of people who were despised by almost everyone else, simply because he was a good man and a courageous priest.

St. Louis forms the first black A.A. group: The Jesuits in St. Louis had consistently been one of the groups in the forefront of the black civil rights movement in that city. In the summer of 1944 they got the first African American students admitted to St. Louis University (a great Jesuit educational institution and their pride and joy, the oldest U.S. university west of the Mississippi river). This was a decade before the Supreme Court outlawed segregation in the public schools and Martin Luther King, Jr., started the Montgomery, Alabama, bus boycott in 1954-55.

It is perhaps not surprising then that the first black A.A. group in the United States was formed in St. Louis. They held their first meeting on January 24, 1945, with five members present, and designated Torrence S. as their secretary. Proud of their accomplishment, they called themselves the "AA-1 Group." Eight months later, in September, another member of the group, Howard W., wrote Bobbie Burger at the Alcoholic Foundation (the central A.A. office in New York City) asking the New York office and the A.A. *Grapevine* to "withhold publicity about our group that may occasion controversial discussions of racial problems within A.A." That is, the existence of the black A.A. group was kept almost totally secret, at their request, for fear that white racists would try to raise a public controversy about it. But at the beginning of 1946, still going strong, they celebrated with their First Annual Dinner Meeting with "two Negro doctors, the secretary of the YMCA, and a representative of the Urban League" as honored guests.[124]

Because of the St. Louis black A.A. group's desire to stay out of the public limelight, even the people in New York forgot about their existence, and very quickly. By 1955, the official New York A.A.

position, which subsequently was simply repeated over and over for the next half century, was that the first black group was formed in Washington D.C. in March 1945. But in fact the order in which the first three black A.A. groups were started was St. Louis on January 24, 1945, Chicago in March 1945, and Washington D.C. in April 1945.[125]

Father Ed meets Bill W.—early December 1940—at the A.A. clubhouse on West 24th Street. In September 1936, when Lois' father died, the bank foreclosed on the mortgage on the house he owned at 182 Clinton St. in Brooklyn. But the bank told Lois and Bill Wilson that they could continue living there for twenty dollars a month until the house was sold.[126] In April 1939, that day finally came. The very week the Big Book was published, the bank told Bill and Lois that they had found a buyer for the house, and that they had to leave now.[127] They moved all their belongings out of 182 Clinton St. on April 26, 1939, and for almost two years, they had to move continually from place to place (54 different places according to Lois).[128]

In February 1940, the first ever A.A. clubhouse was set up at 334½ West 24th St. in New York City, and Bill and Lois finally decided to take advantage of that, and on November 4, 1940, moved into one of the two small upstairs bedrooms where they stayed for about a year.[129] Lois' diary entry for June 11, 1940, described the clubhouse building: "One large room, with fireplace and paneled in knotty pine, and kitchen are downstairs. Upstairs there is a large room with skylights and two small bedrooms and two toilets." The bedroom was barely big enough for a double bed, but she tore out some of the shelving to give a bit more room. Then she painted the walls white and the trim red, and sewed curtains to put over the window and to cover the fronts of the orange crates which she had converted into dressers.[130]

There was almost no real privacy. The other upstairs bedroom was used by old Tom Mulhall, a former New York fireman living on his fireman's pension, who had been rescued from the Rockland Asylum to make coffee for the A.A.'s, work in the kitchen, put coal in the furnace, and help lead drunks outside if they got too unruly.

This was where Father Dowling met Bill Wilson for the first time. It is important to note that Dowling had not only read the Big Book *before* he traveled to New York, but had also visited the highly successful

Chicago A.A. group, and begun working with alcoholics himself in St. Louis (where his little A.A. group had already held its first meeting on October 30, 1940).[131]

The date was sometime at the end of 1940. Bill and Lois did not actually move into the A.A. clubhouse until November 4, so the visit had to have taken place after that point. In the earliest account of Dowling's visit,[132] it was described as a "wild" and "wintry" night where "hail and sleet beat on the tin roof," and Father Ed's black hat was described as "plastered with sleet." It could have been the end of November, but was more likely early December. Father Ed's visit had to have taken place before December 15, because that was when Bill Wilson went out of town with Jack Alexander to visit the A.A. group in Philadelphia.

Bill W. had been walking the path of disappointment and suffering: It is necessary to remember how rough the preceding year and a half had been for Bill Wilson. When they finally got the Big Book published in April 1939, they had started to settle back into warm fantasies about being able to take it easy now. The book would instantly be a huge publishing success, and they would start raking in unbelievably large sums of money. Everyone knew—or thought they knew—how much money successful popular authors made! Alcoholics Anonymous would rapidly gain tens of thousands of members, they fantasized, and would set up alcoholism treatment centers and clubhouses all over the country. But the reality, sadly, was one disappointment after another.

> April 1939 — 4,730 copies of the Big Book were printed— many in early Alcoholics Anonymous thought the book would be an instant success and Bill Wilson and Hank Parkhurst thought it was going to earn them a million dollars.[133] But hardly any copies sold.
>
> An editor at the *Reader's Digest* had promised them a story about A.A. as soon as the book was published, but he now denied any such agreement.
>
> April 26, 1939 — Bill and Lois had to move out of their home at 182 Clinton Street in Brooklyn and were homeless for the next two years.

April 29, 1939 — Morgan Ryan (one of the first two Roman Catholics in A.A.) appeared on Gabriel Heatter's radio program. The A.A. group mailed out 20,000 post cards, addressed to all of the physicians in the U.S. east of the Mississippi, expecting thousands of orders for the book. But they only got twelve replies, only two of which were serious orders for the new book.

September 30, 1939 — Fulton Oursler, the editor of *Liberty* magazine, published an article called "Alcoholics and God," which brought in around 800 inquiries about A.A., a number which was better than anything they had accomplished before, but was still disappointingly small by typical popular market book publishing standards.

October 14, 1939 — the review of the Big Book in the *Journal of the American Medical Association* was very unfavorable— the medical profession looked like it was going to be almost totally against them.

February 8, 1940 — John D. Rockefeller Jr. held a dinner for A.A. (Nelson Rockefeller ended up representing his father, who was ill). It raised a little money for A.A.—$2,200—and they continued to provide about $3,000 a year for several years after that. But this was still far indeed from the huge financial and organizational success which Bill Wilson had been dreaming of.

April, 1940 — Hank Parkhurst, who had been sober for four years, had been Bill Wilson's closest A.A. associate on the East Coast, in some ways closer than Dr. Bob—but now Hank started drinking again. He wanted to divorce his wife and marry Ruth Hock (Hank and Bill's secretary). She turned him down, but this made Hank's drunken rages (and dangerously violent temper) even worse. Hank also never forgave Bill W. for moving the Alcoholic Foundation's central office from New Jersey to New York City (which Bill had done in March).

May/June, 1940 — Hank Parkhurst went to Cleveland and made the totally and ludicrously false claim that Bill W. was getting rich by taking huge sums of money from Rockefeller, from Big Book sales, and from other A.A.-related sources, and was putting the money in his own pocket. Hank teamed up with Henrietta Seiberling in Akron and Clarence Snyder in Cleveland to start an anti-Bill Wilson movement. Clarence kept on attacking Bill for a long time afterward, and claiming that he (not Bill) was the real founder of A.A.

In fact, events were getting ready to change in a much more positive direction, but at the time Father Dowling made his visit to meet Bill, there was no way that Bill could have known what was in the process of taking place.

October, 1940 — Bill W. went to Philadelphia to try to get Curtis Bok, one of the owners of the *Saturday Evening Post*, to do an article on A.A. But there had already been enough disappointments in that area, from the *Reader's Digest* article that totally fell through to the *Liberty* magazine article that got published but helped much less than they had hoped.

December 1940 — *Saturday Evening Post* reporter Jack Alexander was assigned to the story, but after his initial conversations with Bill W. and the New York A.A. group, told Bill frankly that he did not believe what the group was telling him.

March 1, 1941 — but then when the Jack Alexander article was actually published in the *Saturday Evening Post* it was glowingly positive, and beautifully and compellingly written. In response, over 6,000 appeals for help were received in the A.A. postbox in New York. Over the course of that year, A.A. membership increased from 2,000 to 8,000.

April 11, 1941 — Bill and Lois Wilson were finally able to obtain their own home (Stepping Stones), a seven-room house on almost two acres of land in Bedford Hills, New York.

With hindsight, we can see that A.A. was just getting ready to burst forth as a rapidly growing national (and then international) movement, but Bill Wilson did not know any of that on this freezing winter evening in December 1940 when Father Dowling came to visit him.

Bill Wilson had been trying to fight his disappointments by working even harder at spreading the A.A. message. But as Robert Thomsen described the A.A. leader's private feelings (relying on Bill Wilson's autobiographical tape recordings):[134]

> He was beginning to sense that both his famous drive and his wildly active schedule were a release mechanism for his pent-up fury—fury at himself, at his world and at his failure to transform A.A. from a small society into the big-time operation he knew it must be.
>
> His depression, his deep dissatisfaction, was beginning to color everything; even his A.A. talks were beginning to take on a flavor of self-pity and self-dramatization. After one such talk in Baltimore, when he had moved in heavily on the horrors and the terrifying isolation of the alcoholic, a young clergyman came up to him at the close of the meeting. He thanked Bill and then went on to say that one thing he did not understand was why Bill put such emphasis on his great misfortune. It seemed to the young man that it was indeed these very experiences, terrible as they were, which in the end had humbled Bill so completely that his eyes and his heart had been opened, and had led directly to the wondrous experience of A.A. .... "You A.A.s," he said, "are certainly a privileged people."
>
> These remarks from a man he would never see again had a profound and frightening effect on Bill. He'd known that something was wrong, desperately wrong, but he had tried to override it ....
>
> As he battled these questions ... on many nights .... this stock-taking led to a depression which, in its prolonged intensity, was worse than any he had experienced since Towns Hospital. And with the depression there was a sense of guilt because he could feel this way, he who had been given so much, whom others looked up to. This, in time, led to a new and hideous fear. What if he should break, if he, Bill W., should crack up as he had seen other men crack ...?

Hank Parkhurst, who had been one of the key leaders of the new A.A. movement, had gone back to drinking in April, 1940. That meant that it was possible that Bill Wilson could too. How was he going to deal with all the pain and suffering he was sinking into without eventually suffering the same fate as Hank?

CHAPTER 6

Pain and Suffering: (1) Emmet Fox

Emmet Fox and New Thought: One extreme answer to the problem of pain and suffering was given in the New Thought movement, which had a great influence on many of the Protestants in early A.A. These New Thought authors taught that pain and suffering were fundamentally produced, not by external conditions, but by wrong thinking. If we changed the way we thought, the external world would change to match our new ideas. This group of American and British teachers, preachers, writers, and healers included Phineas Parkhurst Quimby (1802-1866), Emma Curtis Hopkins (1849–1925), Thomas Troward (1847-1916), James Allen (1864-1912), and Emmet Fox (1886-1951). I would also include, as part of this tradition, a number of more recent figures such as Louise Hay (b. 1926), Helen Schucman (1909-1981), and Marianne Williamson (b. 1952), although these three latter figures of course had no influence on the world of early A.A.

The New Thought movement has at this time not been studied much or usually even taken with much seriousness by academic theologians and scholarly historians of thought. Even the largest New Thought denominational organizations (Unity Church, Church of Divine Science, and Religious Science) are quite small. Yet Louise Hay's *You Can Heal Your Life* (1984) has sold 35 million copies to date (as opposed to 30 million copies for the A.A. Big Book), and even the works of some of the other New Thought authors have sometimes sold quite well. Marianne Williamson's *A Return to Love: Reflections on the Principles of A Course in Miracles* (1992) has sold 3 million copies. Helen Schucman's *A Course in Miracles* (1975) has sold 2 million copies. Emmet Fox's *Sermon on the Mount* has sold 600,000 copies and his

Power Through Constructive Thinking over 500,000, so just counting these two books alone, over a million copies of his writings have been sold. New Thought has been a big movement in the English-speaking world, and its popularity has been growing continuously over the last century. It definitely made its mark on some of the beliefs of early Alcoholics Anonymous.

Influence of Hinduism and the doctrine of karma. The New Thought movement was deeply influenced in its earliest stages by the world of Asian religions: Hindu Vedanta thought[135] and, especially in James Allen's case, Buddhism as well.[136] They believed that the phenomenal world external to our own minds was a form of what the Hindu tradition called *maya*, that is, they held that the material world around us was simply an "illusion," a screen of false and unreal things which blocked us from knowledge of the transcendent Godhead. And they taught that events within this realm of *maya* followed what Hindu and Buddhist spirituality called the law of *karma*.

New Thought spirituality taught that we captives to the world-illusion could be freed from the chains of karma by learning how to "see through" the illusion and discover its falsity. If we were feeling pain and suffering—including inner resentment, continual inner rage, fear, worry, anxiety, shame, and guilt, but also pain and suffering caused by external and material things such as physical illness, problems in our relationships with other people, money problems, lawsuits, and so on—we could heal these problems simply by learning how to think about them differently.

The ancient Greek philosopher Plato influenced the New Thought authors in many similar directions. In the Allegory of the Cave, ancient Platonic philosophy had spoken of ordinary unenlightened human beings as living like prisoners chained since birth in a dark cave where they could see only a world of black and white images, the shadows of a puppet show cast on the back wall of the cave by the light from a flickering fire behind them. The prisoners had never been allowed to turn their heads and see either the puppet masters or the puppets, so they believed that the shadows cast on the wall of the cave were the real world. In Plato's allegory, this shadow world represented the realm of *doxa*, mere "opinion" or "belief," based on things other people had told us and the indoctrination we had received as children about the way we "should" believe.

In the more extreme forms of Platonic philosophy, *doxa* meant something very close to what Hinduism called *maya*, that is, a world of pure illusion and falsehood. In Plato's metaphor, if we prisoners could become freed from our chains, we would be able to climb out of the cave and ascend up into the real world, which was the realm of the true ideas of things, lit by the light of the Good Itself. Most of the Catholic and Orthodox theologians of early Christianity were Christian Platonists, who equated Plato's supreme Good with the Christian God, and believed that it was the spiritual world (not the material world) which was eternal and far more truly real.

The way New Thought ideas helped shape early Alcoholics Anonymous teaching. New Thought teachers put this basic Vedanta Hindu and Platonic doctrine at the center of their system of thought: we human beings were all captives to illusion who could only be freed from our chains by learning how to "see through" the illusion and discover its falsity. We can immediately see the enormous impact of this idea on the A.A. movement across the board. Whenever someone in an A.A. group starts complaining about his or her life and the way other people are behaving, it does not take long for a good old timer to say words to this effect: "What saved my life was discovering that it was not other people who were the real problem in my life, it was me, and what was going on in my own head. What finally brought me peace of mind was discovering that it was not external circumstances which were destroying me, but the way I was thinking about them. The enemy is not out there; my greatest enemy is inside my own head." This absolutely central A.A. belief, and the enormous emphasis placed upon it, came from New Thought. It did not come from the Oxford Group or the Protestant fundamentalists, nor did it come from the liberal Protestants or from the huge wave of Roman Catholics who began joining A.A. in the Spring of 1939.

William James' *Varieties of Religious Experience*—a book which was read by Bill Wilson and many other early A.A. people—talked about the New Thought movement in the chapter on "The Religion of Healthy-Mindedness," where James sometimes referred to it as the "mind-cure" movement, making special reference to their frequent claims that they could teach people to cure physical ailments by learning to think positive and healthy thoughts.[137] James' main criticism of New Thought, repeated several times in that section of the book, was that their philosophy never explained where evil was coming from or how it could arise. It was all well and good to say that all human pain and suffering were the product of illusion, but in a good universe created by a good and loving God, how could such an illusion have come into being in the first place? This was an interesting question, but the lack of a good answer did not seem to have bothered early A.A. people.

The major connecting link between New Thought and Alcoholics Anonymous was Emmet Fox (1886-1951), one of the most famous New Thought speakers and authors of the 1930's and 40's. He had been chosen in 1931 to be the minister of the Church of the Healing Christ in New York City. His most famous book, *The Sermon on the Mount*, first came out in 1934. Another well known work of his, *Power Through Constructive Thinking*, was not published until 1940 (after the A.A. Big Book came out in 1939), but was constructed from pamphlets and leaflets on a variety of spiritual topics, some of them copyrighted as early as 1932.[138] So I will occasionally cite this latter book as well: the early A.A.'s were also exposed to those ideas during the years 1935 to 1939, from going to hear Fox's sermons and from picking up pamphlets and leaflets while they were there, even though this material had not yet been printed up in book form.

Fox's importance to A.A. history was pointed out at an early date by Jim Burwell, a famous early A.A. member who came into the program in New York City in 1938. At some point prior to the end of 1947, Jim wrote a little history of early A.A. entitled "Memoirs of Jimmy: The Evolution of Alcoholics Anonymous."[139] Commenting on the way Bill Wilson wrote the Big Book, he said:

> Bill probably got most of his ideas from ... James' "Varieties of Religious Experience." I have always felt this was because Bill himself had undergone such a violent spiritual experience. He also gained a fine basic insight of spirituality through Emmet Fox's "Sermon on the Mount," and a good portion of the psychological approach of A.A. from Dick Peabody's "Common Sense of Drinking."

Although one could argue that the claim that these three books supplied most of the ideas in the Big Book was an oversimplification, one should note the way in which one of the major early East Coast A.A.'s emphasized the importance of Emmet Fox for understanding many aspects of the Big Book and early A.A. thought.

A.A. historian Mel B., who had his first encounter with A.A. in the late 1940's and got permanently sober in 1950 (he now has sixty-four years of sobriety), had the blessing of having frequent contact with Bill W. during one point in his life, when Mel was living in the New York City area and was on the *Grapevine* committee at A.A. headquarters. This gave him an opportunity to ask Bill directly about the sources of many of his ideas. Mel later stated in an article he wrote on Emmet Fox that

> I have long believed that some of my best spiritual help has come from reading the books of Emmet Fox, especially *The Sermon on the Mount*. I also learned in a brief discussion with Bill W. that he and the other pioneer A.A.'s attended Emmet Fox's lectures in New York in the late 1930's and benefitted from them.[140]

And Doug B., likewise a very knowledgeable and reliable A.A. historian, also dated the New York A.A. group's devoted following of Emmet Fox back into the 1930's. In Doug's case this information came through his own family:

> My mother-in-law used to attend many of Emmet Fox's talks in New York in the 30's and 40's. She said she would see Bill W. at many of them and that Bill always had a group of men with him. When I asked her if there was anything about Bill's group that she remembered, like fidgeting, coughing, smoking, talking, etc., she replied that the only thing that stood out, besides the fact that they all stayed close together, was that they were always "very well dressed."[141]

It was not just Bill Wilson who was interested in Emmet Fox's ideas. Igor I. Sikorsky, Jr., in his book on Fox and Jung, noted that "five of the original stories in the Big Book were by early A.A. members deeply influenced by Emmet Fox."[142] In Akron, Dr. Bob would regularly give newcomers a copy of Fox's *Sermon on the Mount* to read.[143] Mel B., in his book *New Wine*, said that "Mike E., the second A.A. member from Detroit, often mentioned the inspiration he received from Fox's book when he started his recovery in 1938, even before the publication of *Alcoholics Anonymous*."[144] Later on, Glenn "Tex" Brown, who was a leader in A.A. in the Chicago area for 53 years, said that Emmet Fox's *Sermon on the Mount* was as popular as the Big Book when he first came into A.A. in the Chicago suburb of Skokie, Illinois on February 6, 1947.[145] A.A. historian Mel B., speaking of his own personal experience of early A.A., said in a message to an A.A. history group that "I am very grateful that I spent my first months in sobriety [in 1950] in Pontiac, Michigan, where the group offered Emmet Fox's *The Sermon on the Mount* and other items that have been very helpful to me over the years."[146]

In March 1944, a special kind of link was established between Emmet Fox and the A.A. movement, when the son of Fox's secretary joined A.A. This was a man named Harold A. "Al" Steckman. He became very active in A.A. He was the author of the Responsibility Pledge recited at the Toronto International in 1965 ("I am responsible. When anyone, anywhere, reaches out for help, I want the hand of A.A. always to be there. And for that I am responsible") and also wrote the Declaration of Unity used at the Miami International in 1970. In his later years, he wrote a book called *Bert D.: Hardhat, Inebriate, Scholar*. He was at various points Director of the New York Intergroup Association, a Trustee, *Grapevine* Director and *Grapevine* Editor.[147]

> When Al became the *Grapevine* Editor in 1949, the magazine wasn't too well known around the country. There were many months when he wrote the entire issue by himself, signing each article with a different set of initials and giving a different locality.[148]

As editor of the *Grapevine*, Al also changed the basic nature of the major A.A. periodical when he "shifted editorial emphasis away from drunk stories to You're Not Drinking—Now What."[149]

A profound shift in A.A. had taken place around the time the Big Book was published in 1939. At the point when the book came off the press, one important segment of the A.A. movement (the part in the Akron-Cleveland area) were still linked to the Oxford Group. But in the A.A. literature written in the decade following (that is, during the 1940's) there were no mentions of books on the Oxford Group, and no recommendations—none at all—that anyone read any of the major books written by prominent Oxford Group members. The Oxford Group connection was dead.

On the other hand, there was a significant contingent within the A.A. fellowship during the 1940's which was strongly devoted to Emmet Fox and New Thought spirituality, as we have just seen, and newcomers *were* very strongly urged to read New Thought books.

The effect of this on A.A. was extremely positive. In the first four years of A.A. history (1935-39) A.A. membership grew 20 times larger, which may seem quite impressive until we look at what happened over the next ten years (1939-49), when A.A. membership grew over 750 times larger. Breaking with the Oxford Group and shifting (in part) to a major emphasis on the writings of Emmet Fox and the New Thought movement was an intrinsic part of the era which saw the greatest growth in all of Alcoholics Anonymous history.[150]

> Time Span — Total Members
> 1935 — growth to 5 members
> 1935-1939 — growth to 100 members
> 1939-1949 — growth to 75,625 members

As an example of the way that the newer A.A. literature of the 1940's was emphasizing the importance of New Thought ideas, there was a suggested reading list at the end of the first edition of the little pamphlet called the *Akron Manual* (published c. June 1942) which was handed out to alcoholics when they entered St. Thomas Hospital in Akron for detoxing. This pamphlet, which presumably had the approval of both Dr. Bob and Sister Ignatia, strongly recommended that alcoholics who were new to the A.A. program read Emmet Fox's *Sermon on the Mount*, as well as another New Thought classic, James Allen's *As a Man Thinketh* (1902).[151]

As a second example, after the publication of the Big Book, the most commonly used beginners lessons in early A.A. were based on the four-week Beginners Lessons that began to be used in early Detroit A.A. in June 1943. The pamphlet which outlined these lessons was printed and reprinted by A.A. groups all over the U.S. in subsequent years, and referred to variously as the *Detroit Pamphlet*, the *Washington D.C. Pamphlet* (the first version printed on a printing press), the *Tablemate*, the *Table Leader's Guide*, and so on. There were also printed editions published in Seattle, Oklahoma City, Minneapolis, etc.[152]

The Detroit version had a long passage from Emmet Fox at the end, a little piece called "Staying on the Beam."[153]

> Today most commercial flying is done on a radio beam. A directional beam is produced to guide the pilot to his destination, and as long as he keeps on this beam he knows that he is safe, even if he cannot see around him for fog, or get his bearings in any other way.
>
> As soon as he gets off the beam in any direction he is in danger, and he immediately tries to get back on to the beam once more. Those who believe in the All-ness of God, have a spiritual beam upon which to navigate on the voyage of life. As long as you have peace of mind and some sense of the Presence of God you are on the beam, and you are safe, even if outer things seem to be confused or even very dark; but as soon as you get off the beam you are in danger.
>
> You are off the beam the moment you are angry or resentful or jealous or frightened or depressed; and when such a condition arises you should immediately get back on the beam by turning quietly to God in thought, claiming His Presence, claiming that His Love and Intelligence are with you, and that the promises in the Bible are true today.
>
> If you do this you are back on the beam, even if outer conditions and your own feelings do not change immediately. You are back on the beam and you will reach port in safety.
>
> Keep on the beam and nothing shall by any means hurt you.

Now Fox warns here, in the next-to-last paragraph, that you will sometimes find yourself in situations in which "outer conditions and your own feelings do not change immediately." You cannot expect all your pain and suffering to vanish instantly, he cautions, simply by turning your thoughts away from the problems and towards God.

Nevertheless, Fox promises that if we keep turning to God and reminding ourselves of the divine presence and power, every possible kind of pain and hardship will disappear fairly quickly, even if not instantly:

> Let us suppose, for the sake of example, that on a certain Monday, your affairs are in such a condition that, humanly speaking, certain consequences are sure to follow before the end of the week. These may be legal consequences, perhaps of a very unpleasant nature following upon some decision of the courts; or they may be certain physical consequences in the human body. A competent physician may decide that a perilous operation will be absolutely necessary, or he may even feel it his duty to say that there is no chance for the recovery of the patient. Now, if someone can raise his consciousness above the limitations of the physical plane in connection with the matter—and this is only a scientific description of what is commonly called prayer—then the conditions on that plane will change, and, in some utterly unforeseen and normally impossible manner, the legal tragedy will melt away, and to the advantage, be it noted, of all parties to the case; or the patient will be healed instead of having to undergo the operation, or of having to die.
>
> In other words, miracles, in the popular sense of the word, can and do happen as the result of prayer. *Prayer does change things* .... It makes no difference at all what sort of difficulty you may be in. It does not matter what the causes may have been that led up to it. Enough prayer will get you out of your difficulty if only you will be persistent enough in your appeal to God.[154]

And Fox assures us that if we only turned to God and sought God first, there would never be any need to fall into sickness or ill-health, or to fall into material poverty, or to experience family troubles and quarrels.[155]

The problem was that in December 1940, when Father Dowling visited Bill Wilson for the first time, Bill had been mired in what seemed to be continuous defeat and disappointment for so long, that the optimistic New Thought instruction to simply think about God and think positive thoughts until the problems went away, no longer seemed in the slightest bit realistic.

Emmet Fox: radical New Thought ideas against an Irish Catholic background. One of the biggest problems which most newcomers to A.A. have in dealing with the spiritual aspects of the program when they first come in, is that they are absolutely terrified of God. In fact this is the case with most people in the western world: each time they start to come into real contact with the living presence of God, their first instinctive reaction is to shut their eyes, plug their ears, and jerk back in raw fear. This is why effective spiritual teaching has to continually work at reassuring people that God loves them, and is not going to harm them but is going to befriend them and heal them. Early A.A. switched from Oxford Group literature to Emmet Fox's *Sermon on the Mount* because Fox did such a much better job of calming the newcomers' fears. And he still does: his book still works just as well today. Fox told newcomers point blank that the idea of a cruel, vindictive, punishing God which scared them so much was nothing but an imaginary bogeyman from an ancient and superstitious world:

> Men built up absurd and very horrible fables about a limited and man-like God who conducted his universe very much as a rather ignorant and barbarous prince might conduct the affairs of a small Oriental kingdom. All sorts of human weaknesses, such as vanity, fickleness, and spite, were attributed to this being. Then a farfetched and very inconsistent legend was built up concerning original sin, vicarious blood atonement, infinite punishment for finite transgressions; and, in certain cases, an unutterably horrible doctrine of predestination to eternal torment, or eternal bliss, was added. Now, no such theory as this is taught in the Bible. If it were the object of the Bible to teach it, it would be clearly

stated in a straightforward manner in some chapter or other; but it is not.[156]

The real Jesus did not go around inventing hundreds of rules and laws, Fox said, and telling us that we would suffer eternal hellfire for breaking a single one of them. In fact he discouraged "hard-and-fast rules and regulations of every kind. What he insisted upon was a certain spirit in one's conduct, and he was careful to teach principles only, knowing that when the spirit is right, details will take care of themselves." That is, Jesus certainly never denied that we had to act morally toward our fellow human beings. But it was the spirit of the law rather than the letter of the law that we needed to follow, where the spirit of the law could normally be summed up as a command to treat other human beings with love and compassion.[157]

Emmet Fox, in spite of the radical form into which his ideas eventually grew, was born in 1886 (during the middle of the notoriously straitlaced, moralistic Victorian era) into a pious Roman Catholic family in Ireland and received his early formative education at a Catholic grammar school run by Jesuits: St. Ignatius' College at Stamford Hill in north London. At a young age however, he began to fall under the influence of the New Thought movement, and eventually came over to America, where in 1931 he was ordained by the Divine Science Church, one of the three largest New Thought denominations in the United States, and appointed as pastor of the Church of the Healing Christ in New York City.

So he ended up as a *pro forma* Protestant, according to the normal definition of that term. Yet I believe that to speak of him in this way is at one level misleading. It is true that Fox's religious position was quite radical—there was no conceivable way that the Vatican or any proper believer could ever have regarded many of his teachings as anything other than a total denial of the Roman Catholic faith!—but there were still strongly Catholic elements in his thought.

So for example, Fox did not interpret the Bible literally (in the typical Protestant fashion) but in the kind of allegorical fashion which was used by the Catholic and Orthodox authors of the Early Christian period, beginning in the first century A.D. (the New Testament often read the Old Testament in allegorical fashion), and extending through the second and third century and beyond, all the way through to the end of the Middle Ages. By allegorical, I mean in the broadest sense, the kind of interpretive method used in medieval Catholic art and scriptural interpretation where various items in the biblical text were interpreted as symbols or metaphors of higher realities.

So in biblical phrases like "give us this day our daily bread," the word bread symbolizes not only physical food, Fox teaches, but also things like "spiritual perception, spiritual understanding, and preeminently spiritual realization." The word heart does not refer to the organ in my chest which pumps blood, but is a symbol for what modern psychology calls the subconscious mind. The word city in the Bible always stands allegorically for my human consciousness, Fox says, and the terms hill or mountain refer metaphorically to prayer or spiritual activity. So when the Bible speaks of the need to become like "a city set upon a hill," this means allegorically that your proper goal is to build your human consciousness upon a foundation of prayer and turn it into "the Golden City, the City of God" that shines out over all the world. Likewise when the Bible speaks of bringing offerings and placing them upon an altar, the "altar" is our own human consciousness, and the "offerings" which we bring are the prayers we speak. When we are asked in the Bible to make offerings which are described as "burnt sacrifices," what we are really being asked to do is to take all our erroneous thoughts about life and the world, and destroy or burn away these wrong thoughts upon the divine altar of our human consciousness.[158]

I have never made a systematic study, but I believe that most of Fox's allegorical interpretations were drawn by him directly from some point or other within the ancient Catholic tradition. Some of his interpretations were especially profound and led the early A.A.'s straight to the heart of a life truly dedicated to God. They were like the ecstatic cries of the greatest of the medieval Catholic saints and mystics, such as Fox's deeply moving interpretation of the phrase "poor in spirit":

> To be poor in spirit means to have emptied yourself of all desire to exercise personal self-will, and, what is just as important, to have renounced all preconceived opinions in

the wholehearted search for God. It means to be willing to set aside your present habits of thought, your present views and prejudices, your present way of life if necessary; to jettison, in fact, anything and everything that can stand in the way of your finding God.[159]

For Fox, God was conceived in fundamentally the same way as the medieval Catholic tradition had understood him, as a divine *Nous* (the Greek word for Mind) or *Intellectus* (the Latin word for Intelligence) which presided over the universe. Fox therefore characteristically described God as the "Divine Mind," the "Great Mind," or "Infinite Mind."[160]

Like a number of other modern philosophers however, Fox was deeply impressed with all the new twentieth-century scientific discoveries about universal process. He saw the need to introduce a more dynamic element into the concept of God. God could no longer believably be thought of in medieval fashion as merely the passive Unmoved Mover in a universe based on teleological causal processes. Modern science understood causation in a different way. We had to talk of God today as an *Energetikos*, a Power or Force, "a source of energy stronger than electricity, more potent than high explosive; unlimited and inexhaustible." If God was mind or intelligence, this divine reality had to be more than a realm of pure, unchanging Platonic ideas. God had to be in some way a *Creative Intelligence* (the term Bill Wilson later liked to use),[161] a Mind which "is ever seeking for more and new expression." This divine drive for continual creativity and novelty underlies all human life at a profound level: an individual human being is in fact God's-creativity-in-action, "the dynamic Thinking of that Mind," an opening through which Infinite Energy is seeking a creative outlet."[162]

Emmet Fox states that God comes to consciousness within us, in such a way that God sees the universe through our eyes, as we begin to become conscious of God in ourselves. This sounds radical indeed, and yet it is especially here that we hear echoes of a number of Catholic and Orthodox authors from the early Christian and medieval periods — John Scotus Eriugena (an Irishman just like Emmet Fox) and

Meister Eckhart, for example — along with the great fourth century Cappadocian theologians who spoke of each individual human spirit as an individual *hypostasis* of God, and who spoke of the created universe (taken as a totality) as a temporal *energeia* (operation, energy, or act) of God's eternal divine *ousia* (being or substance). Fox expressed his version of this idea as follows:

> Man being manifestation or expression of God has a limitless destiny before him. His work is to express, in concrete, definite form, the abstract ideas with which God furnishes him, and in order to do this, he must have creative power. If he did not have creative power, he would be merely a machine through which God worked—an automaton. But man is not an automaton; he is an individualized consciousness. God individualizes Himself in an infinite number of distinct focal points of consciousness, each one quite different; and therefore each one is a distinct way of knowing the universe, each a distinct experience .... The consciousness of each one is distinct from God and from all others, and yet none are separated. How can this be? How can two things be one, and yet not one and the same? The answer is that in matter, which is finite, they cannot; but in Spirit, which is infinite, they can. With our present limited, three-dimensional consciousness, we cannot see this; but intuitively we can understand it through prayer. If God did not individualize Himself, there would be only one experience; as it is, there are as many universes as there are individuals to form them through thinking.[163]

Fox talked about this idea in even greater detail in the chapter on "The Wonder Child" which is placed at the beginning of his book *Power Through Constructive Thinking*. The divine power which runs through each of us, Fox says, is the power of *Being Itself*:

> This extraordinary Power, mystic though I have rightly called it, is nevertheless very real, no mere imaginary abstraction, but actually the most practical thing there is. The existence of this Power is already well known to thousands of people in

the world today, and has been known to certain enlightened souls for tens of thousands of years. This Power is really no less than the primal Power of Being, and to discover that Power is the Divine birthright of all men. It is your right and your privilege to make your contact with this Power, and to allow it to work through your body, mind, and estate, so that you need no longer grovel upon the ground amid limitations and difficulties, but can soar up on wings like an eagle to the realm of dominion and joy.

But where, it will naturally be asked, is the wonderful, mystic Power to be contacted? Where may we find it? and how is it brought into action? The answer is perfectly simple— this Power is to be found within your own consciousness, the last place that most people would look for it. Right within your own mentality.[164]

Emmet Fox: God as Creative Intelligence and the power of Being Itself. Now it is important to say once again, that I am not trying to turn Fox into an orthodox Roman Catholic theologian. Not at all! He had moved far beyond anything that could have been taught in a Roman Catholic school or university, or preached from a Roman Catholic pulpit. Even if he had tried to moderate his ideas to some degree, and leave a few of his most radical notions unspoken, if Fox had tried to stay in the Catholic Church, I feel sure that he would have suffered the same fate as a contemporary of his, the Jesuit priest Father Pierre Teilhard de Chardin (1881-1955), a member of the faculty at the Institut Catholique de Paris who in the 1920's was forbidden to teach anymore by both the Vatican and his Jesuit superiors. Although he was allowed to continue his paleontological work, his books and ideas were condemned, and the Catholic Church kept him fairly much totally muzzled for the rest of his life.

And yet, St. Thomas Aquinas himself—the standard of Roman Catholic orthodox theological teaching—had said that the only literal statement we could make about who God was, was to say that he was the power of Being Itself. That was the central idea of God in traditional Catholic teaching. Aquinas taught that anything else we said about God was only symbol or metaphor or allegory, or analogy, or involved *via negativa* statements or the like. This was fairly much what Emmet Fox was saying, and using the same technical language.

And that preeminently proper Catholic author Étienne Gilson, the greatest Thomistic scholar of the early twentieth century, made statements on occasion that also sounded just like what Fox was saying. God is not forced to create the universe or anything in it by any kind of natural necessity, Gilson wrote:

> If God freely chooses to create … it can be said that creation is the proper action of God—*creatio est propria Dei actio* …. In every being, to be is the prime act … consequently, it belongs to every being, inasmuch as it is act, to desire to communicate its own perfection and to do so by causing effects similar to itself. And this is the very meaning of efficient causality. A universe of beings imitating God in that they are and are causes, such is the universe of Thomas Aquinas. In it, the actuality of being is an ontological generosity: *omne ens actu natum est agere aliquid actu existens*; that is to say: "It is natural, for all being in act, to produce some actually existing being."[165]

But that was what Fox was saying. Gilson is saying here that God is *Creative Intelligence*, who is pure act, which in Thomistic language means that God is Being-in-action, Being-that-can-do-something, Being-that-can-be-the-cause-of-something-else. All the Beings in the universe which God creates then attempt to imitate him, in so far as their nature allows them to do so. That means that they themselves then try to create other things and cause other things to happen, and continually seek out (insofar as they are able) creative and novel ways of doing this.

And as Fox points out, human beings, who have more intelligence than any other of God's created beings living here on this earth, by that ability have the greatest power to imitate God and be creative themselves. Above all, human beings have the power within their own minds, to create new ideas and new understandings of things, which is what is meant by the act of Being Itself. The technical term "act of Being Itself" refers to what takes place when we think of a new way of looking at things or a new way of doing things, or otherwise arrive at some new *creative insight* (to use the technical term employed by the great Jesuit Thomistic philosopher Bernard Lonergan[166]) which will change the whole nature of the world of separate Beings which surrounds us.

This divine creativity within the human soul, that is, this ability to have new insights, to make a creative reassessment of my life, and change my fundamental way of looking at myself and the world around me—which provides me with my ability to change the basic cognitive structures of my mind, including even my most deeply cherished concepts and all my assumptions about "what good people should always do" and "what good people ought never to do"—is what Fox calls the Wonder Child:

> This is the real meaning of such sayings in the Bible as "The Kingdom of God is within you" .... This Indwelling Power, the Inner Light, or Spiritual Idea, is spoken of in the Bible as a child, and throughout the Scriptures the child symbolically always stands for this. Bible symbolism has its own beautiful logic, and just as the soul is always spoken of as a woman, so this, the Spiritual Idea that is born to the soul, is described as a child. The conscious discovery by you that you have this Power within you, and your determination to make use of it, is the birth of the child. And it is easy to see how very apt the symbol is, for the infant that is born in consciousness is just such a weak, feeble entity as any new-born child, and it calls for the same careful nursing and guarding that any infant does in its earliest days.[167]

By nurturing this ability, we allow ourselves to be illuminated, Fox says, by the divine Light:

> Isaiah says: "The people that walked in darkness have seen a great light: they that dwell in the land of the shadow of death, upon them hath the light shined." This is a marvelous description of what happens when the Spiritual Idea, the child, is born to the soul. Walking in darkness, moral or physical, dwelling in the land of the shadow of death—the

death of joy, or hope, or even self-respect [people suddenly discover their deliverer]. "For unto us a child is born, unto us a son is given: and the government shall be upon his shoulder: and his name shall be called Wonderful, Counsellor, The Mighty God, The Everlasting Father, The Prince of Peace" .... Once you have contacted the mystic Power within, and have allowed it to take over your responsibilities for you, it will direct and govern all your affairs from the greatest to the least without effort, and without mistakes, and without trouble to you. The government shall be upon his shoulder. You are tired, and driven, and worried, and weak, and ill, and depressed, because you have been trying to carry the government upon your own shoulder; the burden is too much for you, and you have broken down under it. Now, immediately you hand over your self-government, that is, the burden of making a living, or of healing your body, or erasing your mistakes, to the Child, He, the Tireless One, the All-Powerful, the All-Wise, the All-Resourceful, assumes it with joy; and your difficulties have seen the beginning of the end.[168]

We can see a powerful influence from this kind of New Thought teaching on Bill Wilson's description of God in the Big Book. At first, Bill said, he was willing to accept the idea of a God who was "Creative Intelligence, Universal Mind or Spirit of Nature," as long as this was construed in such a way that human beings would still be allowed the freedom to think for themselves and come up with their own creative ideas. But he could never accept the idea, he said, of some kind of authoritarian, all-controlling "Czar of the Heavens," even if the theologians argued that, when God was running everything and denying us any real freedom, he was doing so out of his love for us. In fact, Bill eventually discovered that we human beings had to retain the power to ask questions and raise new issues and think for ourselves at all times, because this was a necessary part of our creativity—if we were not being creative and innovative, we were not imitating the Creator God successfully. But we also had to acknowledge that a true Higher Power existed, a cosmic power of creativity and truth, because that was where we had to go to receive real power and direction. That was the key thing he discovered he had to do in order to begin his new spiritual life, as Bill W. explained in the Second and Third Steps: he had to allow God back into his life. But "as soon as we admitted the possible existence of a Creative Intelligence, a Spirit of the Universe underlying the totality of things, we began to be possessed of a new sense of power and direction."[169]

Atheists fell into their self-defeating mindset, Bill Wilson said, because they refused to acknowledge that their freedom and creativity was supposed to be spent working out ever more creative and novel ways of advancing a divine cosmic loving-goodness and beauty, and instead began regarding their own most selfish desires as a sufficient foundation to build their lives upon: "Instead of regarding ourselves as intelligent agents, spearheads of God's ever advancing Creation, we agnostics and atheists chose to believe that our human intelligence was the last word, the alpha and the omega, the beginning and end of all."[170]

We already knew who God was, Bill Wilson said. We already knew that we had this divine power within ourselves to devise creative new ways of thinking which would be able to break through the denials and false beliefs of the past. We already knew that when we used this power to change the way we thought about the world, that the world around us would change in response, and that miraculous changes could be made in our own lives and in what was going on in the world around us. "Deep down in every man, woman, and child, is the fundamental idea of God," Bill W. said. "It may be obscured by calamity, by pomp, by worship of other things, but in some form or other it is there. For faith in a Power greater than ourselves, and miraculous demonstrations of that power in human lives, are facts as old as man himself."[171]

Now this life-changing power was only there in its fullness, when we stopped trying to deny the fact that it was God's creative energy which we were channeling when we ourselves attempted to be creative too. The faith which saved was simply the intuitive, immediate awareness of the divine cosmic energy of love, goodness, novelty, and the desire to know the truth, which kept flowing into us continually as long as we are willing to accept God as our friend instead of our foe. We could sense it in the same way that we could sense the love of a good friend who had just walked into the room at a time when we were sad or despairing. As Bill W. put it: "We finally saw that faith in some kind of God was a part of our make-up, just as much as the feeling we have for a friend. Sometimes we had to search fearlessly, but He was there. He was as much a fact as we were. We found the Great Reality deep down within us."[172]

Now one of Bill Wilson's basic convictions about God—that a person did not have to begin with a belief in any kind of completely orthodox traditional doctrine of God and Christ in order to be saved—could well have come in part from Oxford Group leader Dr. Sam Shoemaker. The latter stated in numerous ways that a person could start his spiritual journey by giving "as much of himself as he can, to as much of Christ as he understands."[173]

But the specific concept of God which Bill in fact recommended was based on Emmet Fox and New Thought, not on Oxford Group ideas.

Transmigration of souls: There were one or two quite surprising teachings in Emmet Fox's works — for example, in his book *Power Through Constructive Thinking*, there was a major section on the doctrine of reincarnation,[174] showing yet another influence of Vedic Hindu thought on his ideas. The doctrine of transmigration and reincarnation, Fox said, explained why some babies were born deformed or blind, and why some were born into successful and well-to-do families while others were born into rags, poverty, and even the chains of slavery. It explained why some people were born into families with good and loving parents while others were born into dysfunctional families where they suffered continuous physical, sexual, and psychological abuse. It explained why some babies died just a few days or weeks after they were born, and had no chance at any kind of real life. The way I think not only has powerful consequences on my present life, but as was taught in the writings of ancient India, will also affect many of the future lives that I will lead. If I am thinking in this present life about myself and the world in ways that are bringing continual pain and suffering down upon me, Fox said, and I die without ever having changed the way I think, then the next life I will be born into will obviously be filled, from the beginning, with the same kind of pain and suffering.[175]

Now Bill Wilson (and some of the other early A.A.'s and their spouses, including Bill's wife Lois and Dr. Bob and Anne Smith) believed that they had spoken with the spirits of the dead by going into trances, using ouija boards, and through other methods,[176] which means that they believed that the spirits of those who had left this life continued to exist in some other realm somewhere.

Bill never attempted (to the best of my knowledge) to use a doctrine of reincarnation to provide an explanation for any kind of pain and suffering that we were undergoing in this life. On the other hand, we know from *Pass It On* page 265 that Bill and Lois recited a prayer together every morning which said:

> Oh Lord, we thank Thee that Thou art, that we are from everlasting to everlasting .... Oh Lord ... Thou art everlasting love. Accordingly, Thou has fashioned for us a destiny passing through Thy many mansions, ever in more discovery of Thee and in no separation between ourselves.

The line that says "we are from everlasting to everlasting" seems unmistakably to be laying out a doctrine of preexistence, asserting that our souls have always existed from infinite times past, going back to long before their incarnation in this present life. But the line that talks about "passing through Thy many mansions, ever in more discovery of Thee" is a bit more ambiguous, and could be interpreted in several different ways. The prayer may have implied a belief that our spirits would be reincarnated in future lives on this planet earth. But it could also have been expressing the belief that our spirits would be reincarnated in material existences on other planets in other parallel multiverses (in some way similar perhaps to the one that C. S. Lewis described in the seven books of his Chronicles of Narnia, which were published between 1950 and 1956). And it is also possible that, in quasi-Swedenborgian fashion,[177] the prayer simply assumed that after our deaths, we would pass through a series of different heavenly realms (the "house of many mansions" in John 14:2), in each one of which we would learn additional new and different things about God. Or in other words, even if Bill and Lois's prayer was not speaking of reincarnation into additional lives on this earth (or on other planets or in parallel universes elsewhere), it was at least implying an eternal spiritual journey in the world to come, through ever new dimensions and spheres of existence.

The important thing is that Bill and Lois's prayer clearly says not only that all of our individual human spirits had always existed in some realm or other, but that they would always exist for all eternity, and would continue to have fresh experiences and adventures forever. So there were similarities at least between this prayer and Emmet Fox's teaching about transmigration of souls and reincarnation.

Now the way that Alcoholics Anonymous eventually incorporated Emmet Fox's Hindu ideas about karma into its everyday teaching, was to refuse to absolutize this concept. Or this is what I have observed in practice. When a newcomer starts complaining about how some other person did such-and-and-such a bad thing to him (or her), an A.A. oldtimer is apt to snap back instantly, "And what was your contribution?" Submarine Bill C. was sometimes a bit kinder, and would simply ask sternly, "And have you been keeping your own side of the street swept clean?" Over and over, when A.A. people are talking about themselves, one can hear them saying, "I always have to remember that the real problem is usually not in the outside world, but inside my own head."

In other words, a good deal of the time—perhaps even most of the time—A.A. people have found that the New Thought people are correct in pointing out the way my own attitudes and beliefs end up shaping what the world around me is going to be like. If I approach all human relationships with suspicion and pent up anger-waiting-to-explode, expecting the other person to attack me or cheat me, I will eventually find myself surrounded by people most of whom are looking for an opportunity to attack me or cheat me. If I fall ill and lose my will to live, and simply lie there expecting to die, the longer I lie there thinking that way, the greater the chances become that I will in fact die.

But in present day A.A. practice, in my observation, this is never absolutized in the way that Emmet Fox so often did it. People who have never done any harm to anybody sometimes become the victims of other people's wickedness: say the little children in an elementary school who are killed by a madman with a gun who storms into their school shooting at random everywhere he goes. Good hardworking and dependable people sometimes lose their jobs for reasons that are no fault of their own. People of deep faith can also get cancer and die, or be crippled by degenerative disc disease or multiple sclerosis, or find themselves sitting in A.A. meetings during their old age (like one of the greatest among my own spiritual teachers) drooling continually from Parkinson's disease—and bravely rising above their own false pride and ego, and accepting the humiliation, and continuing to go to their A.A. meetings anyway. Another A.A. oldtimer, racked with enormous pain from rheumatoid arthritis, and filled with constant sorrow about the way his wife's life was going—she was hideously depressed, and her anti-depressive medication was no longer working properly—once said to me simply, "I'm learning to live life on life's terms."

As we can see, modern day A.A. is shaped to the core by teachings drawn from Emmet Fox and the New Thought tradition, but it refuses to say that *all* human problems can be *completely cured* by simply thinking positive thoughts. It is too easy nowadays to find people who have been sober (or drug-free or attending Al-Anon meetings or whatever) for twenty or thirty years or more, so that we simply know far more than anyone did back in December 1940 about the things that can go wrong in human lives even when they are leading exemplary spiritual lives.

When Bill Wilson met Father Ed Dowling for the first time, however, it *was* December 1940 and Bill was feeling like a failure. According to Emmet Fox, any person who had suffered as much poverty and disappointment as Bill had, must have been doing something badly wrong at the spiritual level. Over a year and a half of repeated failure was too much.

CHAPTER 7

Pain and Suffering: (2) Matt Talbot

Matt Talbot and self-punishment: Within the Catholic historical tradition one sometimes saw an attitude toward pain and suffering that was the diametric opposite to the New Thought method. As a way of stopping alcoholics from drinking, we see this self-punitive approach at its most vivid in the life of Matt Talbot (1856-1925), an Irishman whose recovery from alcoholism turned him into a powerful hero to many Catholics during the years after his death.

There was no compulsory school attendance in those days, so Matt ran free until he was rounded up at the age of eleven and put in a school designed to teach the basics. But he began playing truant before he had even learned how to read and write. Around the age of twelve, he got a job as a messenger boy for E. & J. Burke Wine Merchants (who in fact bottled beer and stout), and soon discovered the pleasures of drinking the dregs from the returned bottles. Two years later, he switched to a job at the Port and Docks board which gave him access to the barrels of whiskey in their stores, and by the age of sixteen was often visibly drunk when he came home from work. He eventually got a job at Pembertons the building contractors, as a hodman, carrying bricks and mortar to the bricklayers, and then got a job as a common laborer at Martin's timber yard. He was drinking up his entire pay by the end of his drinking career, and even that was not enough to keep him as drunk as he wanted. He was being forced to do things like holding people's horses outside pubs for tips, and once stole a fiddle from a blind man to get money for the increasing amounts of alcohol he needed.[178]

Finally, one evening in 1884 (he was in his late twenties by then), he was standing around outside a pub without a penny to his name, making fruitless humiliating attempts to get one of his drinking companions to buy him a drink, when he stalked off in disgust and went to Holy Cross College, where he "took the pledge" for three months, that is, he took a solemn ritual vow to God that he would drink no alcohol for that period of time. He never had another drink after that promise. He got through those 90 days somehow, then took the pledge for six months, and finally took the pledge for life.[179]

Talbot devised a rigorous program for continuing to stay sober. He allowed himself only four or five hours sleep per night and got up at 5 a.m. every weekday to attend early Mass and take communion. He would go back home for breakfast afterwards, and then head for work at T. & C. Martin's lumberyard. Any time there was no job immediately at hand, he would go off to some quiet place and pray. He joined many religious associations, so in the evening after work he might attend one of their meetings. Or he could be found on his knees, praying before the Stations of the Cross, or reciting devotions to the Blessed Mother. He taught himself to read and write so he could read the Bible and the lives of the saints, as well as various religious books and pamphlets. He spent every evening, from 9 or 10 p.m. until 1 a.m. in the morning, on this kind of spiritual reading. On Sunday's, the only day he did not work, he went to one of the many churches in Dublin and knelt in an unnoticed corner from the first mass of the day at 6 a.m. until lunch time.[180]

In addition, he ate very little at best, fasted frequently, and performed other acts of physical mortification. After his mother died in 1915, he lived in a tiny rented flat with almost no furniture, sleeping on a plank bed and using only a piece of timber for his pillow. When he finally died in 1925 (collapsing of heart failure on his way to Sunday Mass), they found that he had a heavy chain wound around his waist, more chains wrapped around an arm and a leg, and cords wrapped around his other arm and leg. Dr. Michael Hickey, Professor of Philosophy in Clonliffe College, had given him one of the chains. Wearing one light weight chain in loose fashion was a way that some devout Catholics symbolized their slavery to Mary our Mother. Talbot characteristically went far beyond the usual practice.[181]

Talbot rapidly turned into a hero for the Irish temperance organization called the Pioneer Total Abstinence Association, and stories about him started being spread everywhere in the world that Irish immigrants had settled, including the large Irish-American communities in the United States. A movement started to have him declared a saint. His remains, which had originally been buried in what was little more than a pauper's grave, were moved to a glass-fronted tomb in Our Lady of Lourdes church in Dublin in 1972. In 1977 Pope Paul VI declared him to be the Venerable Matt Talbot, the first stage on the path of sainthood.[182]

We can see Matt Talbot's name appearing in A.A. circles almost from the beginning in Cleveland, Ohio, the birthplace of Roman Catholic A.A. We remember that on May 10-11, 1939, the Cleveland A.A. members, for the sake of the Roman Catholics among their number, repudiated the Akron A.A. group's Oxford Group connection and formed their own separate group. Clarence Snyder then wrote to Ruth Hock on December 12, 1939 (half a year later) about the creation of an A.A. spinoff or associated group in Cleveland called the "Matt Talbot Wagon Club," telling her that it now had 88 members and "is doing a wonderful job." The wagons were used to collect old furniture which they then refurbished and sold. This was to provide themselves with food and shelter. They were "transients, stumblebums, and social outcasts," Clarence said, who had no money for hospitalization, had to detox from alcohol on their own, and would have to undergo a period of recovery before they could find jobs once more. Clarence said that the Matt Talbot club had been inspired by the September 30, 1939 *Liberty* magazine article and the Elrick B. Davis articles which appeared in the Cleveland *Plain Dealer* in the latter part of October 1939. They were basing their program on A.A., Clarence told Ruth, "using our stuff and following much the same pattern in every way that it can be applied to their needs and setup."[183]

Matt Talbot was a major inspirational figure for the first Roman Catholic priest to get sober in A.A. This was Father Ralph Pfau (1904-1967), who came into the A.A. program on November 10, 1943 in Indianapolis. The A.A. Central Office in that city has in its archives one of the original souvenir booklets printed and distributed at the A.A. weekend spiritual retreat at St. Joseph College in Rensselaer, Indiana on June 6-8, 1947, containing the text of the talks that Father Ralph gave during the course of the weekend conference. The little book had a picture of Matt Talbot at the back, a short account of his life, and a prayer for Talbot's canonization as a saint. Father Pfau started receiving requests for copies of the book from all over the U.S. and Canada, and had to reprint it over and over again. This was the start of his career as one of the four most-published A.A. authors. For most years between 1947 and 1964, an additional Golden Book was published, giving the talks for that year's spiritual retreat, under Ralph's pseudonym of "Father John Doe." He created his own publishing company for publishing and distributing these pamphlets (along with his other longer books) which was called The SMT Guild, Inc., and was eventually headquartered in a three-room suite at the Good Shepherd Convent in Indianapolis. One of Pfau's nieces who had worked closely with her uncle told me that the SMT stood for Sons of Matt Talbot.[184]

There are also today what are called Matt Talbot spiritual retreats for alcoholics all over the world, which seem to be linked to A.A. to varying degrees, but which all give honor to Talbot's name.

Now Matt Talbot's devotion to prayer is a good recommendation for any alcoholic who wishes to stay sober and find a deep and satisfying spiritual life. Continuous periods of prayer throughout the day formed an intrinsic part of Catholic monastic life for centuries. That is not where the real issue arises when one uses his life as an example for Catholic alcoholics.

The problem is raised by the regimen of severe self-punishment to which Talbot subjected himself: sleep-deprivation, wearing chains, sleeping on a wooden plank with another hard piece of wood for a pillow, and so on. There is a Catholic tradition of that kind of practice as well, in forms which unfortunately sometimes became quite cruel and perverse. In the later medieval period (running from the mid-1200's till the mid-1300's) groups of flagellants marched through many parts of Europe, whipping themselves savagely until the blood flowed. The Church finally had to condemn it as a heresy, and eventually (and somewhat ironically) began burning large groups of flagellants at the stake in the early 1400's in an effort to bring the parades under control. In the seventeenth and eighteenth century, some of the Spanish and French Catholic spiritual works spoke of going to great lengths in wearing scratchy haircloth garments next to their skin, sleeping on bare stone floors, and engaging in other practices designed to inflict severe physical discomfort. At various periods of Catholic history, one can read spiritual writers bragging about the way in which certain saintly figures permanently destroyed their health by denying themselves almost all food for extended periods of time (when the human body has to go without food for too long, in an effort to supply enough energy to keep the lungs breathing and the heart beating, the body will start to digest and permanently destroy some of its own internal organs).

We can see part of the origin of this kind of practice in a Bible which Matt Talbot owned. He had marked one passage very heavily, Luke 13:3, which says in the old Douay Catholic translation, "No, I say to you: but except you do penance, you shall all likewise perish."[185] In the language of the medieval Latin Vulgate which the Roman Catholic Church was still reading from in its church services, this verse read: *Non dico vobis sed si non paenitentiam egeritis omnes similiter peribitis.* This passage warned us that we had to perform *paenitentia*, that is, do "penance," and this was what Matt was trying to do.

We see an even more famous version of this Biblical command in Matthew 4:17, which comes shortly before Jesus's Sermon on the Mount, and was intended by the author of the gospel to announce the beginning of, and also declare the central theme of, Jesus's preaching ministry. Let us give the passage in three versions. The first is the sixteenth-century Douay Catholic translation, the next is the fourth-century Latin Vulgate version associated with the name of St. Jerome (and used as the official Bible of the Roman Catholic Church down to the Second Vatican Council in 1962-65), and the last is the original Greek text of the gospel passage (put down in writing in its present form c. 80-90 A.D.).

> From that time Jesus began to preach, and to say: Do penance, for the kingdom of heaven is at hand.
>
> *Exinde coepit Iesus praedicare et dicere: paenitentiam agite, adpropinquavit enim regnum caelorum.*
>
> *Apo tote êrxato ho Iêsous kêrussein kai legein: metanoeite, êggiken gar hê basileia tôn ouranôn.*

Now *paenitentia*, the Latin word that means penance or repentance, is connected with the Latin word *poena*, which refers to money paid as an atonement or a fine, and generally means penalty or punishment, blood money, or compensation for some wrong done. So when Matt Talbot and other good Catholics read the phrase "do penance," and assumed that this meant that they had to punish themselves for their sins before they could obtain God's forgiveness, this was a reasonable response to what their Bibles seemed to be telling them over and over throughout the New Testament. When the Protestant Reformation came in the sixteenth century, this idea did not totally die, for to this day, large numbers of Protestant Christians believe that they have to do the psychological equivalent of whipping and flagellating and beating themselves up before God will forgive their sins, only they do it to themselves with cruel words spoken inside their heads instead of with whips and floggings applied to their bodies. But they believe just as strongly as poor Matt Talbot that God will never forgive me for anything I did until I can make myself suffer enough for it.

In the original Greek however, Jesus did not say "punish yourselves" or make yourselves suffer. He said *metanoeite*, which means something entirely different. Now *metanoia* (Jesus' word) can on some occasions mean "afterthought" in ancient Greek, that is, realizing after I have done something that my original idea was very badly conceived, on the basis of the catastrophic consequences which occurred. And this can sometimes be a painful realization, nevertheless the pain is not what the word *metanoia* is pointing toward, but the change in my understanding.

The Greek root *no* in itself referred neither to painful punishments nor to emotions of any kind (either painful or pleasant), but to thoughts, concepts, and ideas that we held in our minds and intellects. It referred above all to the underlying cognitive framework of our minds, the basic principles which we assumed were true, and upon which we decided all our behavior. It referred to beliefs such as "I must always tell the truth," "I must always get revenge if someone harms me," "good boys always do such-and-such," "good girls never do thus-and-so," "I am a loser who will come to a bad end," "if I don't scream and yell no one will take me seriously," "life is a jungle and if I don't attack other people first I will be destroyed," and so on.

The Greek prefix *meta* often functioned a good deal like the Latin prefix *trans* which, as we can see in English words like *trans*mit, *trans*fer, *trans*port, *trans*it, and *trans*form, refers to moving something from one place to another, or otherwise transforming or changing it. When Jesus was portrayed by the gospel of Matthew as saying "*metanoeite*, for the kingdom of heaven is at hand" prior to delivering the Sermon on the Mount, this introductory sentence was informing us that the sermon was going to be a description of a new set of principles and rules for behaviors, which we should use to replace the old principles we used to live by. A way of life based on ego, arrogance, raw selfishness, continually turning other people into nothing but sex objects, vengefulness, trying to impress other people with how religious we were, unwillingness to forgive other people, and so on, was the cause of our inner misery and unhappiness. The way of life Jesus was preaching would however give us the kingdom of God on earth, and the strength to handle anything which life threw at us.

There was nothing at all in there about punishing ourselves, or having to do anything else to "earn" God's love and forgiveness. All God asked us to do was to *change our minds*, to embrace a new and better set of inner principles. The minute we actually stopped blaming other people for everything that was going wrong with our lives, and started forgiving and accepting both them and ourselves as beloved children of God, we had done all God had ever asked us to do, and the entire heavenly realm was singing for pure joy at the sight of our return to the land of the blessed.

Fortunately for Bill Wilson, the person who appeared to preach to him on that cold and blustery evening in December 1940, was not someone who was going to tell him that God hated and despised him so much that he was going to have to start punishing himself with even more pain and suffering before God would ever forgive him. Father Dowling was not going to tell poor Bill to beat himself down even harder with self-recriminations and feelings of being a bad and evil person. He was not going to instruct Bill to lash himself even more viciously with tearful thoughts of how he had failed both God and man.

Father Dowling, as a good Jesuit, had been schooled in the *Spiritual Exercises* of St. Ignatius Loyola, with an underlying foundation in some of the best kinds of Catholic spirituality, and that was the precious gift he was going to give Bill Wilson, at the time when he needed it most.

CHAPTER 8

Pain and Suffering: (3) Ignatian Spirituality

The Two Standards (Las Dos Banderas): When Father Ed met Bill W. for the first time in December 1940 at the A.A. clubhouse on West 24th Street in New York City, one of the first things he said was that he had been fascinated by the parallels between the Twelve Steps and the *Spiritual Exercises* of St. Ignatius. When Bill said that he knew nothing whatever about St. Ignatius and had never heard of the *Spiritual Exercises*, Father Dowling, instead of looking displeased, seemed totally delighted. Because the parallels were indeed there, and over the years which followed, he was going to be able to teach Bill how to use those linking concepts to discover even more about some of the most profound teachings of Catholic spirituality, and incorporate them into A.A. belief and practice. We can especially see some of these important things that Bill learned from Father Dowling by reading certain parts of the *Twelve Steps and Twelve Traditions*, which Bill wrote twelve years after he met Father Ed.[186]

To fully understand the *Spiritual Exercises*, it is useful to know a bit about its background and authorship. The Jesuit order to which Father Dowling belonged, had been founded by a Spanish knight named Ignatius Loyola, born in 1491, the year before Columbus arrived in America. Loyola spent his younger years as a dashing aristocratic soldier, one of the last generation of medieval knights to walk the pages of European history. But then around the age of thirty he was severely injured while fighting in the Battle of Pamplona in northeastern Spain near the French border (the site in modern times of the famous Running of the Bulls). A French cannon ball passed between his legs, tearing open his left calf and breaking his right leg. The break did not heal properly, and the leg eventually had to be rebroken and reset, a protruding piece of bone sawn off, and the leg (now too short) had to be stretched out with weights. All this was done without anesthetics, and even after this, Loyola (like Father Dowling) walked with a limp.

During this painful period of surgeries and recuperation, Loyola wrote a work called the *Spiritual Exercises* which laid out a program of spiritual development which was carried out as a month-long series of meditations, and then repeated at various later points in life. Many American Catholic priests and nuns were heavily influenced in their spiritual training by the *Spiritual Exercises*, including Sister Ignatia (born Bridget Della Mary Gavin) who took St. Ignatius's name as her own after becoming a nun. When new A.A. people left her treatment center at St. Thomas Hospital in Akron, she would give each one a booklet containing excerpts from the writings of St. Ignatius Loyola (or a copy of Thomas à Kempis' *Imitation of Christ*).

One of the most famous sections of Loyola's *Spiritual Exercises* is the one on the "Two Standards" (*Las Dos Banderas*, the two battle flags), which portrays the Christian life as a war between elemental Good and Evil. This meditation comes on the fourth day of the second week, and begins with the famous words:[187]

> *Meditación de dos banderas, la una de Christo, summo capitán y Señor nuestro; la otra de Lucifer, mortal enemigo de nuestra humana natura.*

> Meditation on two battle standards, the one belonging to Christ, our high Captain and Lord; the other belonging to Lucifer, mortal enemy of our human nature.

We are typically asked in the meditations to bring all our senses into play, imagining in our minds how some vivid scene would look to our eyes were we physically there, and how everything would sound and feel. We must be creative: the more we can make the scene come alive in our minds, the more powerful the effect of this meditation will be, and the more strongly it will affect our souls all the way down into the depth of our subconscious. In this case we are asked to imagine two huge battlefields:[188]

> *... un gran campo de toda aquella región de Hierusalén, adonde el summo capitán general de los buenos es Christo nuestro Señor; otro campo en región de Babilonia, donde el caudillo de los enemigos es Lucifer.*

> ... one great field comprising all that region around Jerusalem, where the high Captain and General of the good people is Christ our Lord; the other field in the region around Babylon, where the leader of the enemies is Lucifer.

The flag of Babylon and the flag of Jerusalem: Pride vs. Humility.

Loyola then asks us to begin supplying additional detail to this imaginary scene, because part of his method involves a heavy use of what modern psychologists call guided imagery. The more vivid and realistic we can make our imaginary picture—using all five senses if we can—the more powerfully it will extend its influence down into our subconscious minds. In this scene, Satan tells his demons to tempt human beings into the deadly sins beginning with three of them first, because if they can lure them into these, the others will quickly follow: (1) greed for material things (*avaritia*), (2) vainglory (*vana gloria*), and (3) pride (*superbia*).[189]

> The first point is to imagine the leader of all the enemy as if he had seated himself in that great field of Babylon, in a great chair of fire and smoke, in shape horrible and terrifying. The second, is to think about how he calls forth innumerable demons and how he spreads them around, some to such-and-such a city and others to another, and so on throughout all the world, not leaving out any individual provinces, places, states, nor peoples anywhere. The third is to think about the sermon which he gives them, and how he tells them to cast out nets and chains; because they first have to tempt with a longing for riches—which is what he usually does with most people—so they may more easily fall into the desire for the vain honor of this world, and afterwards into mounting pride. So the first step will be riches; the second, honor; the third, pride; and from these three steps he induces them into all the other vices.

Then Loyola asks us to picture Christ standing in the beautiful fields surrounding the holy city of Jerusalem, and calling on all of us who are his true followers and friends, to go out to all the earth attempting to help all people everywhere:[190]

> ... by bringing them first to the highest spiritual poverty, and if His Divine Majesty would be served and would want to choose them, no less to actual poverty; the second is to be of scornful reproach and disparagement; because from these two things humility follows. So that there are to be three steps; the first, poverty against riches; the second, scornful reproach and disparagement against worldly honor; the third, humility against pride. And from these three steps they will induce them into all the other virtues.

The forces of evil recruit us to their cause by leading us into greater and greater degrees of destructive Pride; we allow the power of universal good to flood into our hearts and minds and rescue us *by replacing Pride with Humility.*

So we see how the Jesuit spiritual vision is one of spiritual combat, a great cosmic war between Good and Evil. The question which the exercises therefore ask us over and over again is a simple one, but one we cannot evade answering. It is the same question which was chanted over and over in the chorus to the famous song written by Florence Reece in 1931[191] when the mines in Harlan County, Kentucky, were unionizing: "Which side are you on?" It is a battle song.

Which side are you on? In St. Ignatius' version of this question, it is a truly elemental decision which I am being asked to make: if I refuse to declare myself *by my actions* as being on the side of Goodness, then I have declared my willingness to turn the world and my entire life over to the power of Evil. Because in this unrelenting cosmic war, Evil will always sweep in where Good refuses to fight for itself.

> A SIDE NOTE: If we look at the history of the way the Jesuit order first developed in the sixteenth century, the Jesuit vision of the world was not only one of a continual underlying spiritual warfare, it was also a vision in which the Jesuits

were designed to be the Special Forces, the troops who were sent as missionaries to places like the lawless tribal territories of North America or sent undercover into countries and regions where Catholic priests were executed on the spot. This included many parts of the British Colonies in North America prior to the American revolution, such as the Massachusetts Bay colony, where the Puritans passed a law in 1647 requiring the death penalty for "all and every Jesuit, seminary priest, missionary or other spiritual or ecclesiastical person … from the Pope or See of Rome." A law passed in New York in 1700 demanded life imprisonment for Jesuits caught in their colony. For most of the colonial period, Jesuits continued to maintain Catholic schools in Maryland, even though the colony had fallen back under the control of anti-Roman Catholic persecutors in 1692, but these schools frequently had to be clandestine. As a result, the history of the Roman Catholic Church in the Thirteen Colonies was almost exclusively the history of the Jesuits, since no other group of Catholic priests had the courage to begin operating on the ground until over a decade after the Revolution.[192]

St. Ignatius was a knight, a Spanish soldier, who had fought in numerous bloody battles before he was crippled. So he knew what real war was like (as opposed to most accounts of war in books, television, and Hollywood movies). In real war, people get killed and hurt. In war, innocent people sometimes suffer and die. In a war, soldiers are asked to keep on going even if they are hungry, cold, or wounded. It was Father Dowling's responsibility to keep on doing his job, no matter how much it hurt when he walked. And if good people had to suffer from material poverty and lack of public recognition or appreciation, this could paradoxically give them greater strength. Satan tries to lead human beings into destructive Pride and Egotism, which will always ultimately lead them to their doom. God armors his people against this with the virtue of Humility. Humble Jesuit missionaries had demonstrated over and over again that they could spread God's message successfully in a land even when the wealthy and powerful of that land were trying their best to thwart the Jesuit mission.

We can see how deeply Bill Wilson was affected by this teaching by looking at his *Twelve Steps and Twelve Traditions*, where the chapter on Step Seven is a long discourse on humility that in many places almost looks like it was written by a Jesuit. That is because it was written after Father Dowling had spent twelve years acting as his sponsor and spiritual director, and instructing him in Ignatian spirituality. So we see Bill explaining, how after we begin to work the steps, we begin to

> ... enjoy moments in which there is something like real peace of mind .... This newfound peace is a priceless gift .... Where humility had formerly stood for a forced feeding on humble pie, it now begins to mean the nourishing ingredient which can give us serenity. This improved perception of humility starts another revolutionary change in our outlook .... Until now, our lives have been largely devoted to running from pain and problems. We fled from them as from a plague. We never wanted to deal with the fact of suffering. Escape via the bottle was always our solution. Character-building through suffering might be all right for saints, but it certainly didn't appeal to us. Then, in A.A., we looked and listened .... We heard story after story of how humility had brought strength out of weakness. In every case, pain had been the price of admission into a new life. But this admission price had purchased .... a measure of humility, which we soon discovered to be a healer of pain. We began to fear pain less, and desire humility more than ever.[193]

The motif of the great cosmic conflict between Good and Evil went back in the Christian tradition long before Loyola's time, and stood at the heart of St. Augustine's teaching. In his great book *The City of God*, Augustine explained how all human beings throughout all the pages of history can be divided into two groups (two "cities" as he metaphorically called them): the City of God and the Earthly City. The City of God was made up of all those men and women who took God as their greatest love (or *ultimate concern* to put it into modern existentialist philosophical language). The Earthly City was made up of all those who took *something less than God* as their greatest love (the *ultimate concern* which they had chosen as the basic goal of their lives). The members of the Earthly City were dominated by *superbia*, a kind of overweening pride and egotism which turned them into would-be *super*-men and *super*-women, driven by insatiable desire for the *gloria mundi* (the fame and glory of this world) and the *libido dominandi* (the lust to control and dominate all the other human beings around us).[194]

Ernest Kurtz, the great Roman Catholic A.A. historian and essayist, called upon this classic motif in 1979 in the title of his history of how A.A. began. He called the book *Not-God*, because he believed that human beings had to make an ultimate either-or choice before they could make any progress at all in the spiritual life: they had to realize that God is God, he said, and that they are Not-God and never can be God.[195] Until they stopped pursuing their own self-centered desires and loves as their highest goal and purpose in life—that is, until they stopped treating themselves as their own gods—they would be unable to even begin working the Twelve Steps.

In Augustine's *City of God*, the Two Cities were defined by the Two Loves, and this kind of Love in turn was made up of a bundle of emotional drives: desire (*epithumia*), fear (*phobos*), joy (*hêdonê*, the feeling of pleasure), and sorrow (*lupê*). These were called the Four Passions in ancient Stoic philosophy. So when we said the members of the City of God loved God above all other things, this meant that they desired to be with him, feared displeasing him, felt their greatest joy or pleasure in his presence, and would fall into unbearable sorrow and grief if they lost his love.

To produce such truly dedicated and committed human action, it was not enough simply to convince people rationally at the intellectual level. People had to *desire* that course of action in such a way that they could feel its compelling force coming out of the deepest and most authentic levels of *their own inmost desires*. Loyola agreed completely with Augustine on this.

Loyola then developed this idea even further into a systematic method of meditation and prayer. If we wanted to change people's inmost desires, we needed some way to reach down into their minds at the subconscious level, and the best way to do this was through what a modern psychologist would call guided imagery. If we can get people to imagine a scene which will make them feel the emotions we need them to feel, and then meditate on that at the deepest level (using all of their five senses to fill in the details of the imaginary scene), we will eventually get them making everyday decisions on that new basis with enormous enthusiasm and total commitment.

So in his *Spiritual Exercises*, during the Third Week, Loyola had men and women visualize the crucifixion of Jesus, and then ask themselves over and over—because this is what effectually happens if we spend enough time meditating on these scenes—which of the figures in that scene would I rather have been if I had been present there? Would I genuinely have wanted to be one of the people who were jeering Jesus and laughing at him and making fun of him? Would I have genuinely wanted to be one of the soldiers who pounded the nail into one of his wrists? Would I really have had the arrogance to smirk and lecture the people who were weeping on the sidelines — Mary our Mother and Mary Magdalen and St. John and the rest — about how this was simply the kind of thing that had turned me into an atheist, and why didn't they act like intelligent people and become atheists too?

Or if I could have done nothing else, would I have stepped forward to try to help Simon of Cyrene carry Jesus' cross? Would I have stepped forward like St. Veronica to try to wipe his face? Or at least would I have sat on the ground like Mary our Mother and cradled my dead son's body in my arms as I wept over him afterwards?

At the A.A. International in St. Louis in 1955, Father Dowling told the crowd:

> I think the passage where a dying God rests in the lap of a human mother is as far down as divinity can come, and probably the greatest height that humanity can reach.[196]

In any story which is told with a coherent plot (whether a real story or a fictional account) there will of necessity be heroes and villains: people in the story whom we admire and others whom we end up holding in contempt. As we let ourselves be drawn into the story deeper and deeper, we will find ourselves internalizing at a deeper and deeper level what-is-so-praiseworthy-about-this-particular-kind-of-heroism and what-is-so-despicable-about-this-particular-kind-of-wickedness.

And Loyola asks me to meditate as well on how I would have felt if I had been this particular character or that. Or what I would have wanted to do if I had been present in that situation. In a situation where good people are undergoing unbearable pain and suffering, and *there is nothing I can do to relieve their suffering*, which would I rather be able to say afterwards that I had done? that I had stood around and lectured to people about how this was the kind of thing that had made me an atheist? Or would I have to admit that I just collapsed on the ground and felt sorry for myself "because there was so much pain and suffering in the world"? Or could I at least have stepped forward and wiped the dying man's face with a cold washcloth?

When a poor alcoholic named Ruby staggered into her first A.A. meeting in South Bend seventy years ago, shaking uncontrollably, they simply put their arms around her and held a cup of coffee to her shaking lips and reassured her that everyone in the meeting would help her in any way that they could.

Before you the reader start complaining that what St. Ignatius was doing was leading us into an unreal world of fantasy and imagination, let us look more carefully at what he was doing. This battle-scarred Spanish knight was looking at us with his stern eyes and saying to us, "Time for you to quit playing games and start getting real!" In the real world, people suffer and feel pain. So are you going to try to help the situation, or just stand around complaining? Are you going to refuse to help if it requires that you also get your hands dirty? Are you going to refuse to help if it means that you also will have to feel suffering and pain in your own person?

And this was the message that Father Dowling was carrying to Bill Wilson, even if a little more gently. Alcoholics Anonymous was designed to be one of the great tools that the good heavenly powers would be able to use to fight against the powers of darkness and destruction. Bill Wilson's job was to spearhead the first thrust in that campaign, and that meant that his duty was to keep on going, no matter how much it hurt.

God was not asking Bill W. to wear chains or a haircloth shirt, or sleep on a bare wooden plank, or whip himself on the back with a cat o' nine tails like Matt Talbot and the medieval flagellants had done. But on the other hand, spending all of your time attempting to think positive thoughts in order to obtain worldly goods and honor among your fellows (in the way Emmet Fox taught, if you made no modifications in his teaching) was not and had never been the way the great spiritual heroes of the human race had ever lived.

This did not mean that Father Dowling wished to condemn Bill W. to perpetual unhappiness. He was trying to teach him an even greater form of happiness than Bill had even dreamed of before. As Bill wrote in the passage we cited above from the *Twelve and Twelve*, it was true that "pain had been the price of admission into a new life. But this admission price had purchased .... a measure of humility" which ended up healing the pain and bringing a profound *serenity* which surpassed any other good one could ever wish for.

The centerpiece of traditional Catholic spirituality: Humility in the Christ Hymn in Philippians 2:3-11. Father Dowling cited two pieces of scripture during his first meeting with Bill Wilson. Robert Thomsen, who based many parts of his biography of Bill W. upon a set of autobiographical tape recordings which Bill had made before his death, said that the first words which Dowling spoke to Bill when he walked into the little room at the A.A. clubhouse on West 24th Street in New York City, was to quote this piece of scripture to him:[197] "'I thank my God upon every remembrance of you,' Philippians 1:3."

Now we must remember that Father Dowling and some of the other Jesuits in St. Louis were initially convinced, after reading the A.A. Big Book, that Bill Wilson was a highly trained theologian who had some knowledge of St. Ignatius's *Spiritual Exercises*. So his opening words to Bill consisted of a clever biblical reference which he was sure Wilson would immediately recognize, and probably respond to in kind.

The letter was written while the Apostle Paul was imprisoned, probably at the time he was under house arrest in Rome, powerless to carry on his work and very much aware that he was facing a possible death sentence when he finally appeared before the crazed and sadistic Emperor Nero. So perhaps Father Dowling meant to make a wry little reference to the fact that Bill's having to live in the bare, sparsely furnished room in the A.A. clubhouse was a kind of house arrest too, to show his sympathy for the hardship which Bill and Lois were undergoing at that time.

But there was far more than that implied by that piece of scripture, if one looked at it in context. The opening words of the letter (Philippians 1:1-6) taken as a whole made it clear that Father Dowling had already decided, instantly and on the spot, that he and Bill were going to have to be partners in spreading this message of salvation to the world, whether Bill realized that yet or not!

> Paul and Timothy, servants of Christ Jesus, To all the saints in Christ Jesus who are at Philippi, with the bishops and deacons: Grace to you and peace from God our Father and the Lord Jesus Christ. I thank my God in all my remembrance of you, always in every prayer of mine for you all making my prayer with joy, thankful for your partnership in the gospel from the first day until now. And I am sure that he who began a good work in you will bring it to completion at the day of Jesus Christ.

And there was more yet in Paul's epistle, which was drawn on repeatedly through the centuries to lay out the grand central themes of Catholic spirituality, particularly the verses found in the great Christ Hymn in Philippians 2:5-11. Now modern Protestant commentators all too often focus on this hymn solely as a theological commentary on the incarnation and the relationship between the divine and human in Christ, looking particularly at verse 7 which speaks of how the divine Christ "emptied (*ekenôsen*) himself" in order to take on the form of a frail human being.

But Catholic commentators have always seen that the opening line in Philippians 2:5-11 ("Have the mind among you which is in Christ Jesus") refers to us, not to Jesus.[198] We are the principal point of the message, not him. The Apostle Paul wrote those words, not simply to muse about some kind of speculative "Kenotic Christology," but primarily to remind us of the nature of the true spiritual life, and to admonish us to start following that path:

Have the mind among you which is in Christ Jesus,
who, though he was in the form of God,
    did not count equality with God a thing to be grasped,
but emptied himself, taking the form of a servant,
    being born in the likeness of human beings.
And being found in human form he humbled himself
    and became obedient unto death, even death on a cross.
Therefore God has highly exalted him and bestowed on him
    the name which is above every name,
that at the name of Jesus every knee should bow,
    in heaven and on earth and under the earth,
and every tongue confess that Jesus Christ is Lord,
    to the glory of God the Father.

So it could perhaps better be called, not the Christ Hymn in Philippians, but the Hymn to Humility. We especially need to note how in verse 3, which precedes and introduces this hymn, Paul commanded the people of Philippi to "Do nothing from selfishness or conceit, but in humility count others better than yourselves." It is a hymn about us, and it is the heart of Catholic spirituality.

The Apostle Paul certainly never asked anyone to punish themselves with unnecessary pain and suffering: to wear chains when you did not have to, or sleep on bare wooden planks or a stone floor when it was not necessary. On the other hand, Paul was at two separate points in his life put in chains by agents of the evil emperor Nero, and he was ultimately beheaded outside the city walls of Rome at Nero's order. In the great cosmic war between good and evil, God did not tell his troops that they would never have to suffer and die.

The kind of humility which Bill Wilson had to develop at this point, involved the realization that over the centuries greater people than him had suffered far more than him in rendering service to God. He was not too important to suffer! And no one who read the Bible seriously could possibly say that good people never suffered.

But on the other hand, embracing divine humility did not mean giving up the fight, or whimpering and backing down while saying "I'm not good enough to take on a task so great." In my interpretation of what Father Dowling was doing by quoting from this particular letter of Paul's, he had almost immediately begun to recognize, from the moment he walked into that little upstairs room, that Bill Wilson had not even begun to understand how God had chosen him to do something truly extraordinary. Bill Wilson had to be made to realize that pride and arrogance could doom him, but also that a false humility that left him refusing to carry out the task which he had been given, would be equally much an act of treason against God.

Puffing yourself up with a false self-importance was the opposite of true humility, but refusing to follow God's orders and go into battle when you were commanded was also the opposite of true humility, even if you defended your cowardice—your abject surrender to the enemy— by pleading that "I am too weak, I have so little skill or talent, I am such a failure." If God thought Bill Wilson was capable of leading the A.A. movement, then true humility meant that Bill had to quit thinking that he knew more than God about what was possible and what was not possible, and he had to quit thinking that he (rather than God) was the one who was supposed to be picking the goals for his life.

When Bill wrote the *Twelve and Twelve* in 1953, he talked about falling into the swamp of guilt, self-loathing, and despair, and made exactly that point: thoughts of this sort are simply "pride in reverse," the loss of "all genuine humility."[199]

Blessed are those who hunger and thirst for righteousness: humility instead of perfectionism. The second piece of scripture which Father Dowling quoted at Bill Wilson was the first part of Matthew 5:6, one of the Beatitudes at the beginning of Jesus's Sermon on the Mount, which in full reads: "Blessed are those who hunger and thirst for righteousness, for they will be filled."

This was after Bill had finally fully opened up to him, and come to trust Father Dowling so completely that he began carrying out his first full Fifth Step, confessing all of his wrongs and defects to another human being—Father Dowling in this case—for the first time in his life. The Oxford Group had had no true equivalent to that kind of Roman Catholic general confession. Frank Buchman would typically push a potential convert until the other person blurted out some secret sin for the first time, and then encourage the person to make restitution in some fashion if possible. But this confession usually included no more than a few things. Buchman admitted to only a single sin when he "came to Christ" in 1908 at Keswick, namely the fact that he felt a lingering resentment at the six trustees at the hostel in Philadelphia where he had finally quit in disgust. His restitution consisted of simply writing each of them a letter of apology. Dr. Bob Smith, on the day he had his last drink, was able to carry out all of his acts of restitution that very day, in a matter of just a few hours.[200] The example of a fourth and fifth step in the Big Book (see page 65) is likewise very primitive, to say the least: we are given the impression that all the person in the example had to do was to stop the affair with the mistress and quit padding his expense account (and perhaps admit that because of these two things he had left himself open to what his wife, his boss, Mr. Brown, and Mrs. Jones were saying about him and/or threatening to do to him). The Big Book seems to be saying that if the man did that, he would automatically and immediately be able to stop drinking, and would never be forced to drink again.

I believe that it was the influence of all the Roman Catholics who began joining A.A. in May 1939, first in Cleveland and then elsewhere, which caused typical A.A. practice to start to shift (among Protestants as well as Catholics) to envisaging the fourth and fifth steps as something much more like a traditional Roman Catholic general confession. A look at early twentieth century Catholic guides to confession will quickly show how detailed and thorough such confessions were expected to be, going far beyond anything I have ever read in any Oxford Group literature. Such a general confession was supposed to be a special and quite lengthy private confession where we gave an account of all the sins we had committed over our whole lives, or at least a major part of our lives. It was often recommended for Catholics who were entering an important new stage of life, such as going into the priesthood or joining a monastery or convent. People with guilty consciences might also do it before marriage or something else of that sort, where they wanted to start their lives over with a clean slate.

It should be said that during the years that followed this transition to having longer and more comprehensive fourth step inventories, the average length of sobriety in A.A. has been continuously growing longer and longer. Taking the time to do a more thorough fourth step is an important way to improve your chances of dying sober, and the best way of making sure that those years will be happy ones, both for you and for the people who have to live with you. The Catholic Church, which had centuries of practice in guiding human souls to the greatest heights of the spiritual life, had something very useful to teach A.A. in this area.

At any rate, under Father Dowling's guidance, Bill Wilson did that kind of Fifth Step for the first time. And apparently he must have appeared to be even more cast down than before into self-reproach, guilt, shame, and feelings of being worthless, because Father Dowling quoted the first part of Matthew 5:6 at him:

> "Blessed are they which do hunger and thirst." The saints, he said, were always distinguished by their yearnings, their restlessness, and their thirst. When Bill asked if there was never to be any satisfaction, the old man snapped back, "Never. Never any." There was only a kind of divine dissatisfaction that would keep him going, reaching out always.
>
> Bill had made a decision, Father Ed reminded him, to turn his life and his will over to the care of God, and having done this, he was not now to sit in judgment on how he or the world was proceeding. He had only to keep the channels open—and be grateful, of course; it was not up to him to decide how fast or how slowly A.A. developed. He had only to accept. For whether the two of them liked it or not, the world was undoubtedly proceeding as it should, in God's good time.[201]

The Roman empire in Jesus's time was like India in the early twentieth century, or parts of Africa in more recent years: in bad times human beings literally died of starvation by the thousands. Taking the wrong path in the barren deserts which stretched inland from the Mediterranean in many places could quickly bring you to a painful end as you died of unbearable thirst. So when Jesus referred in his Fourth Beatitude to people "hungering and thirsting" for righteousness, this was a very powerful metaphor. At first glance it was a terrifying image of torture, desperation, and stomach-clenching despair. Now if the Beatitudes were designed to take tormented people and show them the path to feeling better, how did they turn this from a negative message of doom into a positive message of hope? They called out to us in our brokenness and taught us to start looking at our problems from a new and different angle, and promised us that when we did so, we would receive the kingdom of heaven, we would be comforted, we would inherit the earth, we would obtain mercy, we would learn to see God, and we would end up being called the sons and daughters of God.

And in this Beatitude, Jesus promised his hearers that those who had started on the true spiritual path and "hungered and thirsted for righteousness" would find themselves *chortasthêsontai*, that is, put in a feeding lot where, like hungry cattle, they would be fattened up by being given—to translate the Greek completely literally—just as much hay and fodder as they could possibly eat. Every time the spiritual seeker eats the feed trough empty of the new and more glorious ways of righteousness which it contains, God (the good farmer) fills it back up to the top with even better things of goodness and beauty which are even more extraordinary and delicious than those we had tasted before. Bill Wilson was so used to feeling abandoned and without hope, that for years, whenever he spotted any inadequacy within himself, he regarded this as yet one more indication that he was a total failure and could never be anything else. He believed that this knowledge of his own imperfection was a sign of what an irredeemably bad person he was. Father Dowling was trying to get him to realize that the opposite was true: that his driving hunger and thirst for righteousness and yet more righteousness was instead the sign that he was one of the saints.

This was yet another of the blessings brought by true humility. The true spiritual life was like enrolling in a school or college in which each new semester's course offerings were even more fascinating and exciting than the one before. And as long as Bill kept hungering and thirsting spiritually, and staying humble, he would remain teachable, and find the school of the spirit filled with even more talented teachers, at whose feet he could sit and learn. He would never get stale or stodgy, but remain, like Father Ed, perpetually young at heart, forever eager to learn from anyone and everyone around him.

Father Dowling, Father Ralph Pfau, and in the next generation of Catholic A.A. authors, Ernest Kurtz,[202] all realized that one of the greatest dangers to the spiritual life is the myth of perfection: that is, the erroneous belief that people can become morally perfect in this world, and the conviction that we therefore need to drive people at all times with fanatical exhortations to achieve Absolute Unselfishness, Perfect Love, and a totalitarian concept of a Purity so great that not one single sinful thought ever pops up in our minds, even for the slightest instant, in any circumstance whatever. The real Catholic tradition knew better than that: as early as the fifth century A.D., St. Augustine had proclaimed that there was no sinless perfection in this world. After the Fall from Paradise, we were all sinners, down at a deep subconscious level if nowhere else, in a way that could not be completely healed in this world or in this life.

In the thirteenth century, St. Thomas Aquinas set out what was going to be the standard for Catholic teaching on that subject from that point on. To be sure that I was correct in the way I had been reading him on this topic, a number of years ago, I did a word study in which I took a concordance to Aquinas' *Summa Theologica*, and looked up every single place in which he had used the words *perfectus, perfectio,* and other words from that root.[203] I sorted them into categories, and soon discovered that there were really only three important ways in which he had used the concept:

1. To refer to those who had entered the monastic life and had taken the "three counsels of perfection," that is, had taken the vows of poverty, chastity, and obedience.
2. To describe the totally sinless perfection which is granted the saved in heaven after death.
3. To refer to those who are living in this world in a state of grace where they are involved in no mortal sins, that is, are committing no deliberate, conscious, thoughtful violations of any known law of God.

But the people in the third group, even though they commit no mortal sins and will end up going to heaven when they die, still continue to commit venial sins as long as they are in this life. So it is vital to remember that there is no sinless perfection for normal human beings anywhere on the face of this earth, not even among the greatest saints.

I should point out that even in the Baltimore Catechism (which was the standard Catholic school text in the United States from 1885 to the late 1960s, and presented an extremely strict version of Catholic moral teaching) it was stated clearly that no ordinary human beings were able to avoid committing venial sins after Adam and Eve's fall from grace. In Questions 56 and 57, for example, the Baltimore Catechism said:[204]

> Question 56. To make a sin mortal three things are necessary: a grievous matter, sufficient reflection, and full consent of the will.
>
> "Grievous matter." To steal is a sin. Now, if you steal only a pin the act of stealing in that case could not be a mortal sin, because the "matter," namely, the stealing of an ordinary pin, is not grievous. But suppose it was a diamond pin of great value, then it would surely be "grievous matter."
>
> "Sufficient reflection," that is, you must know what you are doing at the time you do it. For example, suppose while you stole the diamond pin you thought you were stealing a pin with a small piece of glass, of little value, you would not have sufficient reflection and would not commit a mortal sin till you found out that what you had stolen was a valuable diamond; if you continued to keep it after learning your mistake, you would surely commit a mortal sin.
>
> "Full consent." Suppose you were shooting at a target and accidentally killed a man: you would not have the sin of murder, because you did not will or wish to kill a man.
>
> Therefore three things are necessary that your act may be a mortal sin: (1) The act you do must be bad, and sufficiently important; (2) You must reflect that you are doing it, and know that it is wrong; (3) You must do it freely, deliberately, and willfully.
>
> Question 57. Venial sin is a slight offense against the law of God in matters of less importance, or in matters of great importance it is an offense committed without sufficient reflection or full consent of the will.

Father Dowling, as a good priest who knew the actual Catholic standards, was able to advise Bill Wilson to ignore the Oxford Group's Four Absolutes[205] and any other supposed spiritual teachings which proclaimed sinless perfection as the goal we should strive for, and instead taught him to embrace true scriptural humility. Bill had already realized that at least at the intellectual level, as we can see from the famous words on page 60 of the Big Book:

> No one among us has been able to maintain anything like perfect adherence to these principles. We are not saints. The point is, that we are willing to grow along spiritual lines. The principles we have set down are guides to progress. We claim spiritual progress rather than spiritual perfection.

But sometimes our hearts can be plagued by doubts even when our intellects know better. That was the point where Father Dowling could use his position as a priest to speak directly to Bill Wilson's heart with the authority of the apostles: Bill needed to stop beating himself up because he was not yet perfect, and needed instead to start gazing with awe and amazement at a future that shone with the bright and shining vision of all the truly incredible things yet to come, for both him and the Alcoholics Anonymous movement.

CHAPTER 9

Bill Wilson's First Great Epiphany: November 1934

The sense of the divine Presence: its centrality to Bill W.'s spiritual life. There were several very important occasions during which Bill Wilson felt himself overwhelmed or nearly overwhelmed by a powerful sense of the divine Presence. Some were mentioned in the Big Book, one was described in full detail for the first time in Bill's talk at the A.A. International Convention in St. Louis in 1955, and two others were recorded by Robert Thomsen in his biography of Bill W., and seem to have come from the autobiographical remarks Bill made on tape at the end of his life.

When he went back to his childhood memories of life in Vermont, Bill W. said,[206]

> I could almost hear the sound of the preacher's voice as I sat, on still Sundays, way over there on the hillside; there was ... my grandfather's good natured contempt of some church folk and their doings; his insistence that the spheres really had their music; but his denial of the preacher's right to tell him how he must listen; his fearlessness as he spoke of these things just before he died.

This was an auditory experience of the divine, where at one level the preacher's words were simply human words, but where young Bill was also impressed by some kind of divine Presence which was vaguely sensed or hinted at in the drone of the preacher's sermon.

But he also remembered that his grandfather had progressed much further in the spiritual life than he had at that time, and that his grandfather said that on occasion he had actually heard what was the auditory version of a supernatural vision, that is, "the music of the spheres." This was usually described as a high-pitched musical sound, like many voices singing together in some unknown language, rising and falling in pitch in a way totally different from any known human melodic form. It was traditionally said to be the singing of the angels who sang around the heavenly throne and presided over the sun and moon and planets. English choirboys singing in a cathedral, or people in a Pentecostal congregation singing in angelic tongues, would give a partial impression of how this was usually experienced. Or one might listen meditatively to the long continuous high notes, with their distinct vibrato, in the opening five minutes or so of John Tavener's *The Protecting Veil*, a 1988 piece for cello and strings by a prominent Eastern Orthodox composer, written to celebrate the Orthodox feast of the Protecting Veil of the Mother of God.

The choir in a Greek Orthodox service, as it sings the Cherubic Anthem (the most sacred part of the holy liturgy), is also attempting to give some partial impression of the song of the angels, insofar as it could be expressed in normal earthly sounds and effects. The very words to that hymn in fact explain that what is going on in the church building is a mystery rite, in which the human choir represents, on a lower ontological level, the ranks of angelic warriors who surround the divine throne up in heaven. A literal translation of the Greek words of the hymn would read:

> We who serve in this mystery rite as a Platonic image of the Cherubim sing the thrice-holy hymn to the life-giving Trinity. Let us now lay aside all earthly cares that we may receive the King of all things, invisibly escorted by the angelic armies. Alleluia, alleluia, alleluia.[207]

The next time Bill referred to this sense of Presence was when he described what he felt and experienced, as a young artillery officer, when he watched the sun rise as the troopship *Lancashire* approached the coast of England in the summer of 1918:[208]

> When finally Bill was relieved of his watch and had crawled up the hatchway and out onto deck, the sky was growing brighter in the east. A thin rim of gold had appeared on the horizon and at its center he could see, or thought he could see, a dim shadowy indication of land straight ahead.
>
> The sun came up strong and bright and he had been right, the dot ahead was land. Within minutes he was in the midst of a sparkling world of blue sea and tumbling whitecaps. Then suddenly there was another dot, higher up and moving toward them—a British blimp coming out to meet them. The sight of it drawing nearer and nearer pierced him with a thrill of delight. They had made it. The old tub had held beneath them and the speck of land ahead looked solid and hospitable. But more, much more than this, he had come through the night, faced terror and escaped humiliation .... and as he stood watching the blimp's approach he felt more complete in himself than ever before. He was in harmony with himself, with everything that was happening. And yet, it was the damnedest thing, at this moment of relief, pride and physical excitement, there was once again that sense of something more, as if he were on a borderline of understanding something just beyond what he was conscious of. He couldn't explain the feeling.

When Bill W. thought of this sense of divine Presence, there were strong links with what the English Romantic poet William Wordsworth (1770-1850) referred to in *My Heart Leaps Up* as "natural piety,"[209] that is, the feeling of awe and reverence which sometimes comes upon us when we are beholding a scene of great natural beauty and magnificence — a feeling of wonder which makes us aware that the hand of an all-powerful divine Creator lies behind the beauty that so enthralls us.

Bill W. would have been familiar with Wordsworth's poetry from his school days, and would probably also have known something about

John Muir (1838-1914), the father of the American national parks system, who led the fight which led to the creation of both the Yosemite and Sequoia National Parks in 1890. Muir spent a famous night in 1903 camping out with President Theodore Roosevelt in Yosemite Park, and was a great admirer of Ralph Waldo Emerson, the leader of the New England Transcendentalists, who offered him a professorship at Harvard (which he nevertheless turned down). John Muir fought to preserve as much as he could of the American wilderness, because he devoutly believed that the place where we could most clearly see God's presence revealed to us was in beholding such things as the wild mountain peaks, the giant sequoia trees, and the light beaming down out of the skies and illuminating the crags and rocks. In fact the whole American national parks system is a monument to not only the belief that we can sense the divine Presence in the beauty and majesty of nature, but to a conviction that the solemn beauty of the vistas at the national parks are the American equivalent to the grandeur of the great European cathedrals. The parks are places where God reveals himself to us, and where we can go and find God.

Nevertheless, even though Bill Wilson's sunrise experience off the coast of England in 1918 was impressive enough for him to remember it even years later, it was not yet the fully conscious awareness of the divine Presence. As Robert Thomsen put it, it was as if Bill "were on a borderline of understanding something just beyond what he was conscious of." But it was still only a hint, an inexplicable feeling of something more out there.

The first time this awareness of the divine Presence broke into his consciousness in a fully gripping and ecstatic manner came shortly afterwards. Bill W.'s artillery unit, after disembarking in England, was stationed outside Winchester for a while before being sent over to France. The war news was ominous: the Germans were on the offensive and the newly arrived American troops were being sent in as reinforcements in all the most dangerous spots along the line. With this surely on his mind—was he going to die in France, as so many other young men had gone to their deaths?—he decided to visit Winchester's great medieval cathedral. He opened his story in the Big Book by speaking of that visit:[210]

We landed in England. I visited Winchester Cathedral. Much moved, I wandered outside. My attention was caught by a doggerel on an old tombstone:

> "Here lies a Hampshire Grenadier
> Who caught his death
> Drinking cold small beer.
> A good soldier is ne'er forgot
> Whether he dieth by musket
>   Or by pot."

Ominous warning—which I failed to heed.

Bill W. gave almost no detail: his experience inside the cathedral was simply summed up in the two words "much moved." But it was on page one of Chapter 1 of the Big Book, and he referred back to it again on page ten to emphasize its significance.

Robert Thomsen, presumably building on the tape recordings which Bill W. made, gives far more information in his account of that experience:[211]

Bill had no idea where the coast artillery would be needed or when they'd be sent. But the moment he stepped into the cool hush of the cathedral, all such thoughts, indeed any kind of conscious thinking, seemed to be taken from him. He moved slowly up the great main aisle, then, halfway to the altar, he paused. His head went back and he stood transfixed, legs spread, gazing up at a shaft of pure light streaming in from the uppermost point of a stained-glass window, absorbing the total silence around him, which seemed part of some vast universal silence, and all his being yearned to go on to become a part of that silence. Then, hardly knowing he was doing it, he moved into a pew and sat, his hands resting on his knees.

How long he sat or what happened or even what state of consciousness he was in he did not know, but he was aware for the first time in his life of a tremendous sense of Presence, and he was completely at ease, completely at peace .... he understood that all was good and that evil existed only in the mind—and he knew that now, for these fleeting moments, he had moved into some area beyond thought.

When finally he rose and started back down the aisle, the chimes in the high tower had begun to play. He vaguely remembered the hymn from childhood, but he could not recall the words.

Out in the graveyard, a little beyond the entrance, he paused again, listening to the bells ring across the valley and looking back at the cathedral. Something had happened, something he had no way of describing, but the important thing was that it had happened and if it had, could happen again. He was sure he had a long life ahead, and one day he might be able to grasp what it had been and pull it further into the light. Until then—he turned and started along the path—until then he knew he had only to wait, even though he couldn't be sure just what he was waiting for.

And then of course his attention was diverted by the tombstone of the Hampshire Grenadier, and after reading the inscription there, he went on his way. This could have become the first great life-changing epiphany in his life, one that would have immediately changed the whole subsequent course of events in major ways, but Bill failed to follow up on it or act on it.

The first great epiphany: Ebby's visit with Bill W. in November 1934. Bill W. was not going to be pulled back again into that cathedral experience in any deep way until sixteen years later, in late November of 1918, when one of his old friends, Ebby Thacher, came to visit him, and talked about how he had turned to God and found the power to quit drinking.

In the Big Book, Bill W. told how strongly Ebby's story affected him, and how he found himself thinking about those experiences he had had of the divine Presence in earlier years. But then he explained to Ebby that the problem was that he simply could not accept the teachings about God which he heard in the churches. The problem for him with the idea of God was all the doctrines and dogmas and theological and philosophical theories about God that church people insisted on, most of which he totally rejected on rational and intellectual grounds, but also because of what he had seen in Europe of the horrible carnage and destruction produced by the First World War, which simply could not be fit in with the image of a loving and compassionate God which was taught in the churches.

> My friend suggested what then seemed a novel idea. He said, *"Why don't you choose your own conception of God?"*
>
> That statement hit me hard. It melted the icy intellectual mountain in whose shadow I had lived and shivered many years. I stood in the sunlight at last ....
>
> Thus was I convinced that God is concerned with us humans when we want Him enough. At long last I saw, I felt, I believed. Scales of pride and prejudice fell from my eyes. A new world came into view.[212]

The image of him having scales falling from his eyes makes it clear that this was the centerpiece of Bill Wilson's conversion story. The reference was to the story of the Apostle Paul's conversion to Christianity while on the road to Damascus, as it was given in the book of Acts[213] in the New Testament, in Acts 9:3-19. Paul had a vision of light which left him completely blinded for three days. But finally a devout Christian in Damascus named Ananias laid his hands on Paul and prayed, "and immediately something like scales fell from his eyes and he regained his sight" (Acts 9:18).

Now most American Protestantism during the nineteenth and early twentieth centuries was at least partially under the influence of frontier revivalism, which emphasized conversion experiences in which people who were attending a revival and listening to the preacher's voice go on and on for hours, suddenly felt themselves irresistibly compelled to come forward and kneel at some kind of altar rail, and offer their lives to Christ. But there were in fact relatively few stories of conversions in the New Testament that could be fit all that well into that kind of revivalist mode. The story of Paul's conversion was a notable exception, and could not only be used to justify the emphasis on conversion experiences in the revivalist tradition, but was also vivid and extremely memorable.

This story of the Apostle Paul's experience on the road to Damascus was therefore an important part of the standard stock of Bible stories taught to children in Protestant churches during that period. Before that point in his life Paul had in fact been battling against God and rebelling against him in every way; now he was suddenly turned into a servant of God who was willing to be obedient unto death. It was still one of the great standard stories in Sunday schools and summer bible schools in the little Protestant churches of the small towns and country areas in the United States well into the 1940's, as I remember from personal experience.

Therefore, when Bill W. spoke of the scales falling from his eyes, he was not only speaking of suddenly breaking through the barriers of stubbornness and denial which had been blocking him from God, but also stating, in a metaphor that was immediately understood by the Protestants of his time, that this was his great conversion experience. And it was a true conversion experience, satisfying all the basic criteria. Before that point, he had been hostile to the whole idea of God. Now he was suddenly anxious to learn about God, and soon found himself going to the Oxford Group's mission in New York City in order to try to find out more. The underlying psychic change was enormous and total, in terms of his basic motivation and commitment.

The psychic change did not immediately penetrate far enough and deep enough into his mind to enable him to stop him drinking, at least not right away. But the idea that any and all chronic compulsive alcoholics who had just had a conversion experience should have been able to stop drinking right on the spot is a misconception that can sometimes arise in the popular revivalist mind. This is the misguided belief that somehow or other, a genuine religious conversion will automatically and immediately, right on the spot, allow that person to stop drinking, gambling, and cigarette smoking, and stop committing all major sins. According to that popular myth (which is totally false but is nevertheless found among many of the uneducated), people who "give their lives to Christ" and are "saved" at a revival, immediately turn into sinless angels. Any good evangelist knows better than that, going all the way back to the beginnings of the modern evangelical movement in the early eighteenth century.

And in particular, people who have saving faith and are believing Christians, can nevertheless be alcoholics who are destroying their lives with their drinking and unable to stop. To see examples of this, all we need to do is look at Alcoholics Anonymous experience over the years. Father Ralph Pfau, the first Roman Catholic priest to get sober in A.A., certainly had saving faith in God when he came into the program, but lacked knowledge of how to use his faith to stop drinking. And over the years, any number of other Catholic priests and nuns and Protestant ministers of all sorts came into A.A. the same way. They had a saving faith in God, but no one had ever told them how to use that faith to free themselves from the compulsion to drink.

For some alcoholics, coming back to God and stopping drinking is a one-step process. Both are accomplished in the same dramatic experience. For Bill Wilson however, it had to be a two-step process: he first had to first make his peace with God and break through all his stubborn skepticism and hostility in that area, so that then, a couple of weeks or so later, he could make the kind of special additional commitment to God that would enable him to stop drinking.

CHAPTER 10

Bill Wilson's Second Great Epiphany: December 1934

His vision of the light at Towns Hospital on December 14, 1934.
Bill W. was admitted to Towns Hospital once in the autumn of 1933, and three more times in 1934 (around July probably, and then on September 17 and December 11).[214] It was most likely during the first 1934 stay that Bill W. met Dr. William Duncan Silkworth for the first time. As Bill describes this in the Big Book (on page 7):

> I was placed in a nationally-known hospital for the mental and physical rehabilitation of alcoholics. Under the so-called belladonna treatment my brain cleared .... Best of all, I met a kind doctor who explained that though certainly selfish and foolish, I had been seriously ill, bodily and mentally.

Bill Wilson employed an odd phrase here: "the so-called belladonna treatment." Why did he use the word "so-called"? Was it because even though ordinary people in New York still referred colloquially to "taking the belladonna treatment at Towns," patients were no longer necessarily being given belladonna? Or was it because even if they were, they were not given very much belladonna, and only for as long as they seemed on the verge of going into delirium tremens?

The reader needs to be strongly warned that a good many of the statements in A.A. histories about the medical treatment which Bill W. was given when he was admitted to the hospital are still based on what is known about the bizarre early theories held by Charles B. Towns, the man who had founded the hospital in 1901, along with journal articles written in 1909 and 1912 by Dr. Alexander Lambert,[215] a physician whom Towns brought in to give medical credence to his strange ideas. The original Towns-Lambert treatment was quite appalling: every hour, day and night, for fifty hours (that is, for a little over two days) the patient was given a mixture of belladonna, henbane, and prickly ash. Every twelve hours, the patient was given carthartics (medicines that accelerate defecation), and after abundant stools were being produced, castor oil was administered to completely clean out the intestinal tract. The doctor gave the patient very small amounts of the belladonna mixture until the first symptoms of belladonna poisoning began to appear, that is, "when the face becomes flushed, the throat dry, and the pupils of the eye dilated." The doctor then stopped the belladonna until the symptoms had disappeared, then began giving the belladonna again until the symptoms reappeared, in an endless cycle through the first fifty hours. It was quite literally a witches brew, because belladonna and henbane had been used for centuries by witches, sorcerers, and shamans to produce scary drug-induced mental states.[216]

But it was now 1934, a whole generation later. Towns' theories had fallen out of popularity, Lambert had broken his association with Towns, and a totally new figure, Dr. William Duncan Silkworth, was now the hospital's medical director. Towns had insisted vociferously that the medical doctors were wrong, and that alcoholism was not a disease. Silkworth on the other hand insisted that alcoholism was an illness, "an obsession of the mind that condemns one to drink and an allergy of the body that condemns one to die," and he had devised an entirely different method of treating incoming patients, which he described in 1937.

The first phase of the Silkworth treatment was as follows, and even this was used only for those who were at an acute crisis stage where delirium tremens was imminent, and was used only for as long as the patient seemed to still be in danger:[217]

1. About an ounce of alcohol every four hours, with an occasional ounce in between if symptoms are growing worse.
2. "To relieve the pressure in the brain and spinal cord (unless spinal puncture is contemplated), dehydration

must be begun at once" by using a carthartic (a substance that accelerates defecation) and a purgative (a laxative to loosen the stool and ease defecation). If there is enlargement of the liver, high colonic irrigations of warm saline should be used instead. Dehydration is continued for from three to four days.

3. Sleep must be induced. Morphine should be avoided if at all possible. And what must be especially avoided is a combination of alcohol and sedative which results in a state of mental confusion leading to hallucinosis. Sedatives should be "given in moderation ... not enough to cause a sudden 'knock-out.'"

4. "On about the fourth day the alcohol can be entirely withdrawn, as by this time the crisis has been avoided or safely passed through and, hence, the patient is in the second phase of the treatment."

Silkworth did not say what kind of sedatives he used, except to note that he never used morphine except as a last resort. And whatever sedative he employed in any particular case, he stressed the fact that he administered only the minimum amount necessarily to calm the patient down and make the patient drowsy so he could gently drift off to sleep. You were not trying to knock the patient out, he warned, and you wanted to avoid anything that would produce mental confusion or hallucinations.

In my own reading of the literature from that period, the commonest sedatives used to calm down alcoholics were paraldehyde, barbiturates (colloquially called goofballs), bromides, chloral hydrate (colloquially called a Mickey or Mickey Finn), and codeine. Belladonna was normally spoken of as a "sedative" only in certain specialized cases (such as whooping cough and Parkinson's disease). Nevertheless, at Knickerbocker Hospital in New York City (where Dr. Silkworth was also involved), even as late as 1952, we read of alcoholics who showed signs of going into delirium tremens being given "bromides and belladonna for [their] jagged nerves."[218]

But even if Dr. Silkworth was still giving some of his patients belladonna (those who showed symptoms of going into violent delirium tremens) the dosage could not have been very high. Belladonna was, quite literally, a standard ingredient in witch's brews, and was not something that you gave people to make them gently and pleasantly drowsy, so they could drift off to sleep. Giving people belladonna could sometimes knock them out for a while, but the delirium it produced was even more apt to make them disruptive and uncontrollable. They would often compulsively repeat bizarre actions, and frequently could not even be made to sit still. This was what Dr. Silkworth was trying to prevent.

The object, as Silkworth explained in his 1937 article, was to *normalize* the alcoholics' mind and mood, so you could then start to talk sense to them, and attempt to get them to make a rational decision (with full intellectual commitment) to stay away from alcohol permanently from that point on. Drug-crazed patients, hallucinating and imagining things, swearing mighty oaths that they were never going to drink again just to impress the doctor with how "sincere" they were, in Dr. Silkworth's experience, just went back to drinking again the moment they left the hospital. Dr. Silkworth knew all these things. He refused to play the role of a snake oil salesman peddling a quack "cure" for alcoholism.

At any rate, on December 11, 1934, Bill W. went to Towns Hospital for the fourth and last time. As he says in the Big Book, "treatment seemed wise, for I showed signs of delirium tremens."[219] But his condition was apparently not all that serious, because once he had been checked into the hospital, Dr. Silkworth seems to have done little more than give him enough of some sort of sedative to make him drowsy. As Bill reported later, the diagnosis was that "I was not in too awful a condition. In three or four days I was free of what little sedative they gave me, but I was very depressed."[220] This was from Bill W.'s own account of what happened, as given by him in 1955, which has to serve as the standard for judging later secondary accounts.

Was he then given belladonna? As we have seen, he may have been, or he may not have been. We just do not know for sure. But if he was given belladonna, it would not have been very much, because Dr. Silkworth (as opposed to Charles Towns and Dr. Alexander Lambert a generation earlier) was simply trying to relax and calm his patients.

But suppose belladonna was administered to Bill W.? The next major confusion in the modern literature on his Vision of Light arises from the fact that belladonna is listed in medical sources as a "hallucinogen." People who know very little about the pharmacology and symptomatology of mood-altering drugs do not realize that what are called hallucinogenic drugs fall into three quite different categories, and that belladonna and henbane do not give you joy-filled visions of glorious divine light that leave you feeling at peace with yourself and the world:

1. **Dissociatives** are one class of hallucinogens which produce a feeling of being unreal or totally disconnected from oneself, or a kind of derealization in which the outside world seems completely unreal. This is not a pleasant or life-affirming experience, but is extremely unnerving and disturbing to the person undergoing it.

2. **Psychedelics** have a very different effect. These drugs include LSD, psilocybin from magic mushrooms, and mescaline from peyote buds. At low doses, the effects can be similar to those produced by meditation and trance states. At higher doses, the drug takers can experience the warping and distorting of shapes and surfaces, and strange alterations in color. Some people see repetitive geometric shapes. Some people may experience what they believe to be higher spatial-temporal dimensions. People who take psychedelics claim on some occasions that the drug put them in contact with God, the Infinite, or some other kind of divine realm, and that it was a profound and inspiring religious experience.

If Bill Wilson had been given a psychedelic at Towns Hospital in December 1934, it is possible that his Vision of Light could have been drug-induced. But Sandoz Laboratories did not start producing LSD as a psychiatric drug until thirteen years later (in 1947) and Bill W. himself did not take LSD until August 29, 1956.

3. ***Deliriants*** are not at all like psychedelics; they produce a state of delirium. Deliriants include belladonna (deadly nightshade), Hyoscyamus niger (henbane), and Datura stramonium (Jimson weed), which contain the alkaloids atropine, scopolamine, and hyoscyamine.

In the case of the deliriants, the drug takers fall into a stupor, or a state of complete mental confusion. They may be unable to recognize their own image in a mirror. They may start mechanically taking their clothes off, or plucking at themselves. Sometimes they hold long conversations with completely imaginary people. Some of the things they experience inside their heads can be terrifying and extremely unpleasant. People who have taken drugs in this category sometimes describe the experience as being like going insane—going totally mad—in a very bad and unpleasant way. Governments do not pass laws against people taking deliriants, because it is unnecessary. The effects are so unpleasant that no one would use any of these drugs repeatedly for recreational purposes.

There were also Native American shamans who swallowed large amounts of raw tobacco to produce the same kind of effects. Nicotine, at high enough dosages, is also a deliriant. But again, getting sick on tobacco does not cause people to experience visions of standing on mighty mountain tops surrounded by glorious light, nor do they relax into a peaceful and satisfied state of mind after the experience is over! In shamanism, things like this were done, not to produce pleasant contact with the divine world, but as unpleasant initiation rituals, and/or to render new disciples frightened, obedient, and pliable.

It should also be remembered that in popular myth, one turns people into zombies by giving them datura (which contains the same psychoactive drugs as belladonna): that is because people who have taken deliriants are left totally psychologically wasted by the experience.

So what happened to Bill W. on December 14, 1934 was as unexpected to Dr. Silkworth as it was to Bill. If Bill had been given belladonna and then had been psychologically turned into a numb and stumbling zombie, Dr. Silkworth would have said, "Oops, I gave him a bit too much of the belladonna, all I wanted to do was to stop him shaking so much." But that was not what happened at all.

Bill Wilson spoke of this extraordinary experience only briefly in the Big Book:

> There was a sense of victory, followed by such a peace and serenity as I had never known. There was utter confidence. I felt lifted up, as though the great clean wind of a mountain top blew through and through. God comes to most men gradually, but His impact on me was sudden and profound.[221]

He did not give the full account of what happened, including in particular his Vision of the Divine Light filling all things, until sixteen years later, when he was speaking to the A.A. International Convention in St. Louis in 1955. As he told the story there, he says that "in three or four days I was free of what little sedative they gave me, but I was very depressed." After a brief visit from Ebby, Bill said that

> My depression deepened unbearably and finally it seemed to me as though I were at the bottom of the pit .... All at once I found myself crying out, "If there is a God, let Him show Himself! I am ready to do anything, anything!"
>
> Suddenly the room lit up with a great white light. I was caught up into an ecstasy which there are no words to describe. It seemed to me, in the mind's eye, that I was on a mountain and that a wind not of air but of spirit was blowing. And then it burst upon me that I was a free man. Slowly the ecstasy subsided. I lay on the bed, but now for a time I was in another world, a new world of consciousness. All about me and through me there was a wonderful feeling of Presence, and I thought to myself, "So this is the God of the preachers!" A great peace stole over me and I thought, "No matter how wrong things seem to

be, they are still all right. Things are all right with God and His world." [222]

There was another reference here to the book of Acts in the New Testament, not to the conversion of Paul in this case, but to the story of the first Pentecost in Acts 2:1-4. In the New Testament story, this was the occasion on which the disciples were given the power and the mission to spread the message to people of all the languages of the world; in Bill W.'s story, it was the occasion on which he felt the sense of being sent by God to spread the healing message to alcoholics of all the languages of the world. As it says in the book of Acts:

> When the day of Pentecost had come, they were all together in one place. And suddenly a sound came from heaven like the rush of a mighty wind, and it filled all the house where they were sitting. And there appeared to them tongues as of fire, distributed and resting on each one of them. And they were all filled with the Holy Spirit and began to speak in other tongues, as the Spirit gave them utterance.

Bill Wilson said in yet another account that he felt at "one with the universe."[223] And the account given in *Pass It On*, the 1984 biography of Bill W., is also useful to look at, because it gives a bit more detail about his mental state after the vision was over:[224]

> "Savoring my new world, I remained in this state for a long time. I seemed to be possessed by the absolute, and the curious conviction deepened that no matter how wrong things seemed to be, there could be no question about the ultimate rightness of God's universe. For the first time, I felt that I really belonged. I thanked my God, who had given me a glimpse of His absolute self. Even though a pilgrim upon an uncertain highway, I need be concerned no more, for I had glimpsed the great beyond."
>
> Bill Wilson had just had his 39th birthday, and he still had half his life ahead of him. He always said that after that

experience, he never again doubted the existence of God. He never took another drink.

What Bill Wilson experienced was a sense of the divine Presence even more intense than the one he had had in Winchester cathedral, when he had stood gazing at a bright beam of sunlight shining through the top of one of the stained glass windows. This time the light appeared to be supernatural and otherworldly. It was an incredible experience, but one which we read about numerous times in the history of spirituality. We hear about men and women having visions of the divine Light in the Roman Catholic and Eastern Orthodox monasteries and convents of the middle ages, and also among the ancient pagan Neo-Platonic philosophers (who called it the Vision of the One).

Bill's paternal grandfather, William C. ("Willie") Wilson, had had a serious drinking problem. But he climbed to the top of Vermont's Mount Aeolus one Sunday morning, and while praying to God, "saw the light" in some sort of life-changing way. He walked the mile back to East Dorset, and

> When he reached the East Dorset Congregational Church, which is across the street from the Wilson House, the Sunday service was in progress. Bill's grandfather stormed into the church and demanded that the minister get down from the pulpit. Then, taking his place, he proceeded to relate his experience to the shocked congregation. Wilson's grandfather never drank again. He was to live another eight years, sober.[225]

In Bill Wilson's own native New England Puritan tradition, one can find the great authoritative statement on the nature of this vision in Jonathan Edwards' famous sermon on "A Divine and Supernatural Light, Immediately Imparted to the Soul by the Spirit of God."[226] Edwards observed that when the true divine light shone on the human soul, the impact was so enormous, that the human imagination might be overwhelmed with what seemed to be the sensation of a powerful physical light. But that part of the experience was purely imaginary:

This spiritual and divine light does not consist in any impression made upon the imagination. It is no impression upon the mind, as though one saw anything with the bodily eyes. It is no imagination or idea of an outward light or glory, or any beauty of form or countenance, or a visible luster or brightness of any object. The imagination may be strongly impressed with such things; but this is not spiritual light. Indeed when the mind has a lively discovery of spiritual things, and is greatly affected by the power of divine light, it may, and probably very commonly doth, much affect the imagination; so that impressions of an outward beauty or brightness may accompany those spiritual discoveries. But spiritual light is not that impression upon the imagination, but an exceedingly different thing.

In my own interpretation of all this, I would prefer to say that the human mind, when powerfully contacted by the divine realm in this fashion, attempts to make better sense of the experience by "translating" it into physical images and the physical sounds of human words (or rushing wind or angelic singers or whatever). Most of the time, we apprehend these "translations" in the form of *internal* images seen in "the mind's eye," or *internal* sounds which are heard "kind of like a voice inside our heads" (as Henrietta Seiberling once described her sense of inner divine guidance). But sometimes the images and sounds are so vivid and overwhelming, that we seem to see and hear them *in the external world*, as Jonathan Edwards notes above.

The real divine and supernatural light which saves our souls and remakes our character, in its real essence, is nevertheless not seen in itself. Jonathan Edwards also says that it does not impart new information in the ordinary sense, or point out things in the Bible which we had never noticed before, or anything else of that sort. Instead it is a sense that suddenly comes upon us, that all the important things that good religious leaders had been trying to teach us all our lives, are not only absolutely true, but the most important things in the whole universe. Before we always ultimately brushed these things off. We might be emotionally titillated by them when we heard a particularly moving preacher talk about them, but their importance never sunk home in such a way as to actually change our continuing long term behavior in the real world.

A true conversion, however, had to pass the "Jonathan Edwards test." In the small New England communities where he preached his revivals, Edwards was able to observe all the details of how people who *claimed* to have been saved at his revivals were actually acting in everyday life. People who claimed to have found God, but who continued to be completely dominated by all their old anger, fear, resentment, arrogance, dishonesty, violence, and so on, were simply deluded. But those who had undergone a genuine conversion received ...

> A true sense of the divine and superlative excellency of the things of religion; a real sense of the excellency of God and Jesus Christ, and of the work of redemption, and the ways and works of God revealed in the gospel. There is a divine and superlative glory in these things; an excellency that is of a vastly higher kind, and more sublime nature, than in other things; a glory greatly distinguishing them from all that is earthly and temporal. He that is spiritually enlightened truly apprehends and sees it, or has a sense of it. He does not merely rationally believe that God is glorious, but he has a sense of the gloriousness of God in his heart. There is not only a rational belief that God is holy, and that holiness is a good thing, but there is a sense of the loveliness of God's holiness. There is not only a speculatively judging that God is gracious, but a sense how amiable God is on account of the beauty of this divine attribute.[227]

What makes Jonathan Edwards' theory so important, is that first, he and John Wesley were the cofounders during the 1730's of the modern Protestant evangelical movement, along with the kind of frontier revivalism derived from it, which swept America in the nineteenth century.[228] And second, he is the only American-born philosophical theologian whom we have had in this country so far, who can be placed in the company of the truly great Europeans. There is furthermore a direct line of development between Edwards' understanding of preaching for conversion and the Oxford Group's idea of conversion as a "life-changing" experience, and from there to the early A.A. concept of total surrender to our higher power as the only way to produce a true psychic change.

The Vision of Light which Bill W. experienced in Towns Hospital on December 14, 1934 passed the "Jonathan Edwards test." Bill Wilson not only never drank again, he made a decision to spend the rest of his life helping other alcoholics, and stuck by that decision to his life's end. At one level, there was nothing new that he learned in that experience. At some level, he had known everything he really needed to know about spirituality since he was a small child, listening to the preacher's voice from outside the church, and *knowing at some level* that he really should start acting the way the preacher was telling him, but *not yet being deeply enough impressed by it* for it to actually have any major effect on his long-term continuing behavior in the world. Now in December 1934 he finally "saw the light" and realized that this was the most important thing in the world. The proof that his change of heart was genuine was that he changed his whole life, and that the change it produced was not temporary but permanent.

What is most important of all, however, is that Bill W.'s psychic change was based upon contact with something real and external, which he could only describe as the intuited Presence of something infinite and eternal, extending into a dimension totally outside our material world, but also permeating the entire cosmos with a light which illuminated everything which was good and beautiful. No matter how desperate our situation, when we let ourselves become fully aware of this divine Presence to a great enough degree, we would abruptly cease feeling overwhelmed by the fear of death, and would find ourselves given the power to face whatever had to happen.

> AS AN ADDITIONAL NOTE: we see an excellent modern study of Bill Wilson's type of spiritual experience in William R. Miller and Janet C'de Baca, *Quantum Change: When Epiphanies and Sudden Insights Transform Ordinary Lives* (2001).[229] Miller is Emeritus Distinguished Professor of Psychology and Psychiatry at the University of New Mexico and their Center on Alcoholism, Substance Abuse and Addictions.

The book gives numerous case histories of modern American men and women undergoing profound psychological and personal transformations in sudden moments of insight. What is especially interesting for our purposes, is that these radical psychological changes are sometimes even today accompanied by phenomena like Bill Wilson's vision of light. But this sort of thing does not at all have to be present. It has nothing at all to do, either way, with the psychological verifiability and authenticity of the personal transformation.

CHAPTER 11

Bill Wilson's Third Great Epiphany: December 1940

Bill W. meets Father Ed in December 1940: Bill Wilson, in the earliest account he gave of his initial meeting with Father Dowling, spoke of encountering a powerful sense of divine Presence there also. Father Ed was one of those special men and women who function as God-bearers,[230] bringing the sense of God's holiness, goodness, and compassion to other people by something embodied in their words and bearing:

> He lowered himself into my solitary chair, and when he opened his overcoat I saw his clerical collar. He brushed back a shock of white hair and looked at me through the most remarkable pair of eyes I have ever seen. We talked about a lot of things, and my spirits kept on rising, and presently I began to realize that this man radiated a grace that filled the room with a sense of presence. I felt this with great intensity; it was a moving and mysterious experience. In years since I have seen much of this great friend, and whether I was in joy or in pain he always brought to me the same sense of grace and the presence of God. My case is no exception. Many who meet Father Ed experience this touch of the eternal. [231]

Bill W. described that evening elsewhere as being like "a second conversion experience."[232] Robert Fitzgerald in his piece in *The Catholic Digest* and W. Robert Aufill in his article on "The Catholic Contribution to the 12-Step Movement" were both struck by the aura of grace and divine presence which Bill W. sensed in the strange visitor.[233] Ernest Kurtz describes the scene in *Not-God* in even stronger terms as another vision seemingly of divine light:[234]

> As [Dowling and he] began to converse, Bill noted that his visitor's round face seemed to gather in all of the light in the room and then reflect it directly at him.

And particularly, just before departing, Dowling spoke with the voice of a prophet: he looked Bill straight in the eyes and declared, "There was a force in Bill ... that was all his own. It had never been on this earth before, and if Bill did anything to mar it or block it, it would never exist anywhere again."[235] This was a prophetic blessing, an anointing or conveying of the spirit as it were, of an extraordinary sort. Bill had been given a special mission from God, one that no one but him could carry out.

> Dowling then hobbled to the door and declared, as a parting shot, "that if ever Bill grew impatient, or angry at God's way of doing things, if ever he forgot to be grateful for being alive right here and now, he, Father Ed Dowling, would make the trip all the way from St. Louis to wallop him over the head with his good Irish stick."[236]

The concept of holy men and holy women who were special bearers of the divine went far back into the ancient world. When Christianity first appeared, this idea was utilized as a special tool for spreading the saving message, above all by teaching people about Jesus Christ as a unique embodiment of the divine Presence. But Catholicism and Eastern Orthodoxy soon realized that there are also numerous other men and women who, although hardly possessing the perfections of Christ, were nevertheless saintly souls who could give us glimpses into who and what God is, in a way which could sometimes be far more understandable (and far less frightening) to our feeble human senses than an attempt to encounter God and the infinite divine abyss directly.

Alcoholics Anonymous took this one step further. In the stories in the Big Book, and in the accounts given elsewhere of the lives of people who either were A.A. members or who worked to help the A.A. movement, we can see glimpses shining through here and there of real if imperfect saintliness, sufficient to knock us back on our heels, and sufficient to pass "the Jonathan Edwards test." That is, as a consequence of coming into contact with these good men and women, we found ourselves changing the way we lived our own lives at the concrete practical level. We already knew many things about God and the divine life which we never carried out in practice, but now we suddenly found ourselves genuinely doing these things. We quit mumbling pious but ineffective words about dedicating our lives more to God, and found ourselves actually being moved by their example to start doing some real work for God. We quit nattering ineffectively about God's all-forgiving love, and found ourselves enabled by the way these good men and women loved and accepted us, into actually starting to feel some blessed freedom from the crippling guilt and shame we had been feeling for so many years.

These people are the God-bearers: in spite of their human frailties, they carry God with them, and bring God to other people. The greater their humility and the less they vaunt themselves, the more transparent they become to God. The God-bearers become primary conveyers of the all-saving divine grace.

The first time many poor struggling alcoholics and addicts saw God smiling at them was in the faces of the people at a twelve-step meeting. The first time they felt God putting his arms around them was when a good man or woman at a twelve-step meeting gave them a loving hug. The first time they truly felt God's forgiveness was after they had made their fifth-step recital of their wrongs to a twelve-step sponsor who did not rebuke them in horror or cast them off with curses, but instead simply continued loving them.

There in December 1940, Bill Wilson would have understood this idea mostly in terms of Richard Maurice Bucke's and Emmet Fox's theories. Bucke had seen the sense of cosmic consciousness embodied in figures as diverse as Jesus, Buddha, and Walt Whitman. Fox taught about the way each individual human being was an individualization of God's consciousness, and about the way that the Wonder Child, the Inner Light or spark of the divine, could be brought to birth in the human soul and then lovingly nurtured into the fullness of its mature power.[237] But the idea that certain special human beings had been given the power to act as intermediaries in one way or another between God and ordinary human beings was part of the Catholic consciousness, and was deeply understood within the Catholic soul. In Catholic art, for centuries, the most saintly among these intermediaries had been portrayed with halos of light surrounding them, to symbolize the way in which the divine Presence could somehow be felt or sensed when you were around them.

CHAPTER 12

Richard Maurice Bucke's
Cosmic Consciousness

The sense of the divine presence: Mel Barger, the principal author of *Pass It On* (the official A.A. biography of Bill W.), tells how he asked Bill in the summer of 1956 to tell him more about his famous vision of the Divine Light at Towns Hospital some twenty-one years earlier. Bill wrote a letter back to Mel on July 2, 1956 in which he talked about three books which he said were very useful in understanding his spiritual experiences over the years, including the vision at Towns:

> Since I had mentioned William James's *The Varieties of Religious Experience*, Bill discussed that and then recommended a book called *Cosmic Consciousness*, by Richard Maurice Bucke — one that he described as having "covered the waterfront" on the subject of spiritual experience. He also referred to a book called *Heaven and Hell*, by Aldous Huxley.[238]

Of the three books, Richard Maurice Bucke's *Cosmic Consciousness*[239] seemed to be the one which Bill W. regarded as the most important. So Mel read the book, immediately saw what Bill was talking about, and many years later encouraged me also, as strongly as he could, to go read the book too. Mel believed that I also would discover that Bucke's work did in fact provide the key to understanding Bill Wilson's experience of the divine Presence, not only at Towns Hospital, but also elsewhere in his life.

Bucke was a practicing psychiatrist. It is important to note that Bucke had not only made an extensive study of comparative religions, he was also a trained psychiatrist. He earned his medical degree from McGill University's medical school in Montreal, decided to specialize in psychiatry, and went to do his internship at the University College Hospital in London, England. In 1877 he became head of the provincial Asylum for the Insane in London, Ontario, where he remained until his death twenty-five years later. He knew the difference between sanity and insanity, and also the difference between (a) the hallucinations brought on by drugs and (b) the quite different structure of the visions which illumined the minds of the world great religious, philosophical, and literary geniuses: people like Buddha, Jesus, and St. John of the Cross, the philosopher Plotinus, and poets like Dante and Walt Whitman.

If one compares Bill Wilson's account of his experience at Towns Hospital with the descriptions and analyses in Bucke's book, one can see that Bill Wilson passed the psychiatric test (his encounter with the power of God was not the hallucination of a person who was clinically insane or mentally disturbed) and matched up with the experiences of the geniuses whom Bucke discussed.

Bucke was also strongly influenced by the modern historical method and the new biblical criticism: Although it may not be immediately obvious at first glance, Bucke was in fact attempting to deal with the great problem which began to seriously disrupt the religious life of the western world in the late eighteenth and early nineteenth centuries: the discovery that the Judeo-Christian Bible was not at all infallible, but was filled with so many errors and contradictions that it could not be regarded as a guaranteed source of information about anything at all, let alone the most serious matters of life, death, and the nature of the eternal world.

The first driving force behind these increasingly more and more skeptical attacks on the Bible was the development of the modern historical method during the eighteenth and nineteenth centuries. This was a way of investigating events which stressed the importance of going back to original sources and documents, instead of uncritically accepting later legends and historical distortions which were sometimes simply credulous and ignorant, and at other times deliberately intended to further various political and religious causes even at the expense of the truth. The problem was that when this method was applied to the

Bible, it turned out that the original sources and documents were either totally lost or had never existed at all.

One of the leaders in the development of the modern historical method was the German historian Leopold von Ranke (1795-1886). In his youth, he had discovered that there were almost no dependable histories of either the sixteenth-century Protestant Reformation or anything that was going on in the Roman Catholic Church of that same era. Whether Protestant or Catholic, most of the then-existing histories of that era were little more than propaganda pieces using impossible legends and wildly improbable charges to besmear the other side in the religious disputes of that time.

Catholic historians asserted, for example, that Martin Luther was nothing but a lecherous and gluttonous man who started the Protestant Reformation to try to lure Catholic priests, monks, and nuns into believing that human sexual desires were so irresistible that no one should even attempt to follow vows of chastity. Protestant historians on the other hand responded by gleefully publishing works in which the medieval legend of Pope Joan was recited as historical truth (she pretended to be a man, but the fact that she was really a woman was revealed when she gave birth to a child while riding on horseback in a religious procession). In the more extreme versions of this tale, it was claimed that Pope Joan's election was the reason why the college of cardinals was in all later centuries compelled to meet stark naked when choosing a new pope. This was done to prevent any other women from pretending to be men and getting themselves elected to the papacy. All of this was complete historical nonsense of course, but the stories and charges were simply repeated over and over in each new history that was published.

Already in his first major historical work, which he published in 1824—it was titled *Geschichte der romanischen und germanischen Völker von 1494 bis 1514* (History of the Latin and Teutonic Peoples from 1494 to 1514)—von Ranke went to every type of written document which he could find that had been written back in the period itself. He located diaries and personal memoirs, collections of correspondence written back and forth by participants in the events, government documents (including both public documents and internal reports and analyses), and so on, looking especially for accounts (whenever possible) that had been written by actual eyewitnesses of the events. Von Ranke said, in a very famous statement, that the goal of the good historian should always be to narrate the story of what happened *wie es eigentlich gewesen,* "as it actually was," "as it actually took place."

When these new standards were applied to the Judeo-Christian Bible, many of the standard biblical narratives began disintegrating rapidly. The German scholar Johann Gottfried Eichhorn, writing in the late 1700's and early 1800's, demonstrated that, in spite of the ancient belief that Moses had written the first five books of the Bible, they were not written until long after his time.

Burke had a chapter on Moses in his book on *Cosmic Consciousness,* and used Ernest Renan's history of Israel (published in 1889-1894) for his ideas about the figure of the legendary Hebrew leader. As Burke notes, "Renan tells us that the oldest documents in which Moses is mentioned are four hundred to five hundred years posterior to the date of the Exodus, at which time Moses lived, if he lived at all."[240] That meant that the stories about the Burning Bush, the parting of the Red Sea, the giving of the Ten Commandments, and so on, were legends and fables elaborated and expanded by generation after generation of illiterate tribal storytellers for centuries before ever being put down in writing, and could not conceivably be relied upon for dependable historical information about the time of Moses.

Julius Wellhausen's *Prolegomena zur Geschichte Israels* (Prolegomena to the History of Israel) published in 1878, gave an even bleaker view of our knowledge of the earliest periods of biblical history. Wellhausen's documentary theory, which became the standard theory among biblical scholars at the major American and European universities and seminaries for most of the twentieth century, saw the first five books of the Bible (Genesis, Exodus, Leviticus, Numbers, and Deuteronomy) as made up of four earlier documents which had been interwoven in such a way that there were two or three separate and parallel accounts (at least) given of many of the major events:

> J (the Yahwist source) was written c. 950 B.C. in the Kingdom of Judah and reflected the ancient oral traditions of the two southern tribes.
>
> E (the Elohist source) was written c. 850 B.C. in the breakaway northern Kingdom of Israel and reflected the ancient oral traditions of the ten northern tribes.
>
> D (the Deuteronomistic material) was written c. 600 B.C. under the influence of King Josiah's religious reforms.
>
> P (the Priestly source) was written c. 500 by Jewish priests in the Babylonian exile camps.

The J source believes that Yahweh (God's proper name) had always been known to the Israelites since the beginning of time, whereas in E, God is called Elohim or El (the generic Hebrew word for "god") until God himself reveals the name Yahweh to Moses in the story of the Burning Bush on the top of the holy mountain. J and P refer to this mountain as Sinai, while E and D always call it Horeb instead. In some stories Moses stutters so badly that Aaron has to speak to Pharaoh for him, but in another thread of tradition, Moses has no trouble speaking for himself. The ark of the covenant is mentioned frequently in the J account, but never in the E version of the stories. God in the J tradition speaks personally with people like Adam and Abraham, but in the E tradition he speaks to people primarily in dreams, and in the P narrative, contact with God can usually only be through the priesthood.

In particular, in the Wellhausen documentary theory, Moses lived during the 1200's B.C., while the P material in the Hebrew Bible was not written down until over 700 years later in Babylonian exile camps a thousand miles from Palestine. The P account of how the world was created, which we read in Genesis 1 and which modern Protestant fundamentalists still try to defend as literally true, was simply the Jewish priests' version of the pagan Babylonian creation story, modified for Jewish ears after the Jews were marched off to Babylonian concentration camps following the fall of Jerusalem in 586 B.C.

The Babylonian creation myth, called *Enuma elish*, was discovered by Austen Henry Layard in 1849 while excavating the ruins of the Library of Ashurbanipal at Nineveh and published by George Smith in 1876. In the version which we read in Genesis 1, the Jewish priests turned the Babylonian goddess Tiamat (the goddess of the primordial ocean) into an impersonal wind-tossed sea and replaced the Babylonian storm god Marduk with their own Hebrew storm god Yahweh. But they slavishly copied the Babylonian cosmology almost unchanged: the world is flat, with a transparent hemispherical bowl over it (called the "firmament of the heavens"), holding back an infinite ocean of water. When some of the water drips down from pores in the bowl of heaven, we human beings refer to it as "rain." It should be noted that this borrowed myth was not even a faithful account of how the Israelite tribes themselves originally understood how the world began, at least back during the early days when they were still living as nomadic herders out in the desert.

Beginning in the latter years of the twentieth century, the Wellhausen documentary hypothesis began to be challenged or greatly modified by some of the biblical scholars at the major universities and seminaries, but principally in the direction of yet further increasing the skepticism about the historical accuracy of the earliest biblical material.

Major problems likewise began arising during the same period for the New Testament accounts of Jesus' life and ministry. In Germany, Gotthold Ephraim Lessing (1729-1781) wrote a work in 1778 called *A New Hypothesis on the Evangelists as merely Human Historians*. It was not published until 1784, after his death, because it was still quite dangerous to challenge Christian doctrines and dogmas in public. Lessing saw that the only possibility of reconstructing an accurate account of the life of the real historical Jesus would have to involve solving what is called the synoptic problem, that is, the relationship between the differing accounts of Jesus' life and ministry given in Matthew, Mark, and Luke.

In America, Thomas Jefferson (third President of the United States, from 1801-1809) put together a book around 1820 called *The Life and Morals of Jesus of Nazareth* (sometimes referred to as *The Jefferson Bible*). Applying the same kind of modern historiographical principles which would have been used in writing, say, a history of the French and Indian War, or a history of the founding and early years of the colony of Virginia, he took passages which he had cut from the pages of all four gospels and pasted them together to form a continuous story of

Jesus' life. He included Jesus' references to God and to "our heavenly Father," but he omitted all references to miracles, angels, the fulfillment of prophecies, claims that Jesus was divine or that he had risen from the grave on Easter, or anything else that involved the supernatural in that sense.

By the beginning of the twentieth century, it had been established by New Testament scholars that the three synoptic gospels (Matthew, Mark, and Luke) were not written until after the great Jewish-Roman War of 66-73 A.D., probably between 80 and 90 A.D.

> Just as a parenthetical side note: the gospel of John was written slightly afterwards. John does not fit in smoothly with the other three gospels, and presents so many special problems, that we will avoid talking about it here. It seems to have been, not a real historical account of Jesus' life and words in the ordinary sense, but a commentary on Jesus' life and teaching revealed to the gospel writer by the spirit of the eternal Christ Principle, which he refers to in the first chapter of his gospel as the divine Logos. Or in other words, the gospel of John was probably written in a way very similar to two well known twentieth century works, *God Calling* by Two Listeners, and *A Course in Miracles* by Helen Schucman; that is, it was dictated to the author of the gospel by a spiritual being who spoke to him in Christ's name. The speeches in John were not the words of the historical Jesus.

Since Jesus was executed by the Romans around 30 A.D., this means that roughly fifty to sixty years had passed before Matthew, Mark, and Luke were written, which means that only a very small number of people would have still been living who could have seen and heard Jesus preaching, when they were old enough to understand what they were seeing and hearing. (These would be people who would have had to have been at least 65 to 75 years old, more or less, at the time the gospels were being written, in a world where average life expectancy at birth was no more than twenty-five to thirty years. And only someone a hundred years old or more — which in that world effectively meant no one — could have been around at the time Jesus was born.)

For many years there has been a kind of book entitled "gospel parallels" or "gospel harmony" or "synopsis of the gospels" which prints Matthew, Mark, and Luke in parallel columns, so that whenever they tell the same story or recite the same saying of Jesus, one can read both accounts, or all three accounts, and compare them. Famous early ones included Johann Jacob Griesbach's 1776 synopsis and W. G. Rushbrooke's 1880 *Synopticon*. This is not some startling new discovery. My grandfather, who taught history and religion a hundred years ago, at a little Methodist college in a small town in Kentucky, had his students purchase copies of one of the early twentieth century gospel harmonies for use in the course he taught on the life of Jesus.

Now the majority of the congregation in a great number of Protestant fundamentalist churches, and a majority even of the pastors in some fundamentalist groups, have only a high school education at best. But understanding what is going on in a gospel harmony does not require advanced knowledge of history and ancient languages. All it really requires is a basic knowledge of how to read and write, sufficient to read a standard English translation of the Bible. There is no excuse for the fundamentalist movement.

What do we discover from a gospel harmony? First of all, it turns out that the gospels disagree on the order in which events took place during Jesus' active ministry, so if your gospel harmony follows the basic order given in Mark let us say (which is common nowadays), one will find oneself jumping around quite a bit in Matthew and Luke to find the appropriate parallels. Secondly, it turns out that in almost no case will one find Jesus saying exactly the same words in the different versions. Usually the underlying meaning of what Jesus says is basically the same. That is, there are no passages in which Jesus tells us to hate our enemies, hold grudges, commit adultery every chance we get, and worship the Roman gods and goddesses like Mars and Venus. The differences, instead, are the kind one would expect with oral traditions which had been passed down from person to person for fifty to sixty years, or with several people sixty-five or seventy-five years old trying to remember things they had heard Jesus say or seen him do back when they were fifteen years old.

But one of the centuries-old Christian arguments for believing in God, life after death, and so on, was based on the belief that the entire Bible was literally true and completely inerrant, and that we knew Jesus' words with absolute word-for-word accuracy. According to that belief, this kind of total infallibility was God's warranty that the biblical text was supernaturally guaranteed. So the reason for believing in the existence of God, a life after this one, eternal rewards and punishments for good and evil behavior in this life, and so on, was not because these things could be proved rationally or known first hand, but because they came from a biblical text which was supernaturally and miraculously guaranteed to be totally flawless and infallible.

And on the other hand, the existence of any contradictions at all would mean that the Bible was not supernaturally infallible, and could no longer be used to try to prove the truth of statements about God and eternal life which clearly contradicted all normal common sense. That was the fundamental problem. Documents which gave us a "reasonably good idea" of what Jesus said were not the same as a text which was believed to be dictated word for word by God and his Holy Spirit.

The new science, the skepticism it produced about life after death, and the problems raised by Darwin's theory of evolution: In addition to the new critical historical methods, the rise of modern science had a strong effect on Richard Maurice Bucke and other educated people of his era. Even as a child, Bucke believed that if a conscious personal God existed—and that in itself was a big "if" for him—he was willing to believe that God "meant well in the end to all," but he still remained almost totally skeptical about whether human consciousness and personal identity could survive death.[241] Modern science based its findings on things we could experience directly for ourselves, or on the first-hand experiences of dependable observers whose superior intelligence, honesty, observational skills, and ability to see through fraud and deception, were all well established. If as the young Bucke believed, there was no way we could directly experience the world beyond (the realm in which our souls would reside after death), so that *we could see it and feel it for ourselves*, there was no point in appealing to the Bible.

And the Judeo-Christian Bible was no longer a believable source of information on issues of this sort. No intellectually honest person who had any education at all could believe in a completely infallible Bible. And only a Bible which was absolutely infallible down to the last word and phrase could provide strong enough evidence all by itself for believing in an idea like everlasting life.

Later on, while he was in college in the late 1850's and early 1860's, Bucke was enormously impressed by Charles Darwin's newly published book *On the Origin of Species* (which came out at the end of 1859) and also read deeply in the writings of the famous physicist John Tyndall (1820-1893), who was one of Darwin's major British defenders.[242] Here again, one could see that the Bible was just plain wrong. All the living species of the earth were not created in a few days' time in 4004 B.C., but over thousands of millions of years. We could see the fossils with our own eyes, and the stratified layers of rock from different geological eras displayed in rocky hillsides and cliffs.

Darwin did however give Bucke an important clue into a new and different way the young man could start looking for answers to his spiritual questions. If there has been a process of evolution among the species inhabiting the planet Earth, involving massive changes in physical attributes such as the evolution of gills, fins, legs, lungs, hair, feathers, horns and antlers, wings, brain size, and the like, WHY COULD THERE NOT ALSO BE AN EVOLUTION GOING ON AMONG THE CREATURES LIVING HERE ON THIS PLANET EARTH IN THE FUNDAMENTAL WAY THEIR THINKING PROCESSES WERE CARRIED OUT? And this belief was to lie at the heart of Bucke's work, where the subtitle of his book revealed the guiding Darwinian principle of his approach—*Cosmic Consciousness: A Study in the Evolution of the Human Mind*. Evolution was still at work, Bucke believed, and the small but increasing number of human minds which had developed the ability to sense the divine Presence was an evolutionary advance taking place right now among a tiny exceptional class of people. SUCH A MIND WAS AS FAR SUPERIOR TO THE MIND OF AN ORDINARY HUMAN BEING, AS THE ORDINARY HUMAN BEING'S MIND WAS SUPERIOR TO THAT OF A CHIMPANZEE.

Influence on Bucke of the English Romantic poets and New England Transcendentalists: Richard Maurice Bucke did not devise his idea of Cosmic Consciousness totally out of the blue. The new awareness that the Judeo-Christian Bible was a very human book, filled with numerous contradictions and historical errors, and hence not very dependable as a source of information about God and the life to come, had begun to affect a number of educated people in Europe and America during the latter eighteenth century. The end of that century was roughly the time of the American and French revolutions, and as part of the revolutionary ethos of those years, the basic strategy of tossing the Bible to one side and appealing instead to some sort of direct human awareness of the divine, began appearing very early, among the English Romantic poets on one side of the Atlantic, and among the New England Transcendentalists on the American side.

Now the belief that the human mind could have some kind of direct experience of God had already been affirmed by many Christian, Jewish, and Muslim thinkers during the ancient and medieval period. Modern religious scholars call these people "mystics." It was a way of looking at the relationship between God and the world which originally came out of the pagan Neo-Platonist tradition, which meant that their desire to come into direct contact with the realm of the divine was coupled with a deep suspicion of anything having to do with material things, or the human body, or the world of sense perception. So when ancient and medieval Christian spiritual writers attempted to explain how to have a direct mystical experience of God, they followed their pagan Platonic predecessors and characteristically spoke about the need to abandon the physical world of the five senses and block it completely out of the mind. And after shutting out all awareness of the external material world, we then had to devise techniques, these writers said, for also shutting off our imaginations and the continuous inner dialogue which usually went on in the human mind, so that we ceased thinking about worldly things in any kind of fashion at all, and stopped the flow of the stream of consciousness which had us continually worrying over all our fears and resentments, and plotting how to do this and that.[243]

But over the course of the latter eighteenth century and early nineteenth century, some of the major currents of western thought began undergoing a profound shift. We can see this especially vividly in the English Romantic poets, where there is no longer any attempt at all to find God by blocking off the world of sense impressions. Quite the contrary, they turned various parts of the material world into the principal focal points for becoming aware of the immediate presence of God. The English Romantic poet William Wordsworth (1770-1850) referred to this in *My Heart Leaps Up* as "natural piety," that is, the feeling of awe and reverence which sometimes came upon us when we were beholding a scene of great natural beauty and magnificence, a powerful feeling of the infinite hidden within the finite, which made us aware that the hand of an all-powerful divine Creator lay behind the beauty that so enthralled us. Wordsworth's poetry was filled with numerous attempts to describe this feeling. In his *Ode on Intimations of Immortality*, for example, he began with the lines:[244]

> There was a time when meadow, grove, and stream,
> The earth, and every common sight,
>   To me did seem
>   Apparelled in celestial light,
> The glory and the freshness of a dream.

Or in his poem, *The Excursion*, Wordsworth gave a more specific description (Book I, lines 198-200, 203-207, 211-213), involving a scene very similar to Bill Wilson's account of his awareness of the divine Presence when he was approaching the coast of England and witnessed the sunrise at sea:[245]

> What soul was his, when from the naked top
> Of some bold headland, he beheld the sun
> Rise up, and bathe the world in light! He looked—
>
> Beneath him:—Far and wide the clouds were touched,
> And in their silent faces could he read
> Unutterable love. Sound needed none,
> Nor any voice of joy; his spirit drank
> The spectacle ....
>
> In such access of mind, in such high hour
> Of visitation from the living God,
> Thought was not; in enjoyment it expired.

Richard Maurice Bucke admired Wordsworth up to a point, but regarded the New England Transcendentalists as yet more highly evolved thinkers. In his book on *Cosmic Consciousness*, Bucke gave Wordsworth only a brief mention in Part V (a subsidiary section at the end of the book), and made it clear that he did not regard the English poet as having obtained the fullness of this consciousness. He admits that Wordsworth's "mind ... in his loftier moods attained a very close neighborhood to Cosmic Consciousness," even though "he did not actually enter the magic territory of the kingdom of heaven." But Bucke insisted that what Wordsworth portrayed was the "mental condition, which may be properly called the twilight of Cosmic Consciousness," not its full dawning. He cited a passage from Wordsworth's "Lines written above Tintern Abbey" (written in 1798) as an example:[246]

> I have felt
> A presence that disturbs me with the joy
> Of elevated thought; a sense sublime
> Of something far more deeply interfused,
> Whose dwelling is the light of setting suns,
> And the round ocean and the living air,
> And the blue sky, and in the mind of man—
> A motion and a spirit, that impels
> All thinking things, all objects of all thought,
> And rolls through all things.

Bucke however believed that Ralph Waldo Emerson (1803-1882), one of the great New England Transcendentalists, did better than the English Romantic poets. "He was perhaps as near Cosmic Consciousness as it is possible to be without actually entering that realm. He lived in the light of the great day, [even though] there is no evidence that its sun for him actually rose."[247]

Ralph Waldo Emerson published his famous essay on "Nature" in 1836, laying out the foundation of the Transcendentalist movement. The divine is diffused through all of nature, he said, and human beings must learn to feel this spirit of nature, and recognize it as the Universal Being. Emerson told his readers that if they wished to think of nature in terms of some kind of visual metaphor, they should think of her as being like a woman standing in solemn prayer: "The aspect of nature is devout. Like the figure of Jesus, she stands with bended head, and hands folded upon the breast. The happiest man is he who learns from nature the lesson of worship." Nevertheless, nature's spirit by itself is mute. It must express itself in and through the emotional response of human beings who stand in awe before her. "Therefore, that spirit, that is, the Supreme Being, does not build up nature around us, but puts it forth through us."[248]

> The lover of nature is he whose .... intercourse with heaven and earth, becomes part of his daily food. In the presence of nature, a wild delight runs through the man, in spite of real sorrows .... In the woods too, a man casts off his years, as the snake his slough, and at what period soever of life, is always a child .... In the woods, we return to reason and faith. There I feel that nothing can befall me in life, — no disgrace, no calamity, (leaving me my eyes,) which nature cannot repair. Standing on the bare ground, — my head bathed by the blithe air, and uplifted into infinite space, — all mean egotism vanishes. I become a transparent eye-ball; I am nothing; I see all; the currents of the Universal Being circulate through me; I am part or particle of God.

Bucke seems to have liked Emerson's essay on "The Over-Soul" (1841) best of all, a piece in which Emerson expanded further on his ideas about the divine power which is immanent in nature. "That great nature in which we rest, as the earth lies in the soft arms of the atmosphere" is in fact, Emerson proclaimed, "that Unity, that Oversoul, within which every man's particular being is contained and made one with all other."[249]

> We live in succession, in division, in parts, in particles. Meantime within man is the soul of the whole; the wise silence; the universal beauty, to which every part and particle is equally related; the eternal ONE. And this deep power in which we exist, and whose beatitude is all accessible to us, is not only self-sufficing and perfect in every hour, but the

> act of seeing and the thing seen, the seer and the spectacle, the subject and the object, are one. We see the world piece by piece, as the sun, the moon, the animal, the tree; but the whole, of which these are the shining parts, is the soul.

Richard Maurice Bucke, in his book on cosmic consciousness, gave a more carefully thought out and systematic account of this sort of Emersonian vision of the divine shining through the natural world. But it is important to note that Ralph Waldo Emerson and the Transcendentalists (a group which included such other famous authors as Henry David Thoreau, Amos Bronson Alcott, Louisa May Alcott, William Henry Channing, George Ripley, and Emily Dickinson) had already worked out many of the underlying ideas.

It is especially important to note, in this regard, that Richard Maurice Bucke's book on *Cosmic Consciousness* was not an aberrant or idiosyncratic work which could be written off as a historically insignificant piece of eccentricity. It was a logical development of one of the most important cultural themes of the nineteenth-century English-speaking world. He stood on the shoulders of both the English Romantic tradition and the New England Transcendentalists. And the influence on him of Goethe and nineteenth-century German idealism made his work an understandable development of contemporary continental European ideas as well.

It is vitally necessary to fit the history of the early Alcoholics Anonymous movement into its proper place within the major cultural currents of that era. This is not always being done at present. When some contemporary Alcoholics Anonymous historians attempt to describe the nature of Bill Wilson's and Dr. Bob Smith's religious roots in New England, they talk exclusively about the most conservative parts of the religion of that area: early New England Congregationalism and the colonial Puritan tradition, the Christian Endeavor youth movement of the 1880's, and so on. But Dr. Bob (who went to college at Dartmouth), his wife Anne (who went to college at Wellesley), Bill W., and Richmond Walker (the second most-published A.A. author, who graduated second in his class from exclusive Williams College in Massachusetts) in fact came from a world of expensive private schools and Ivy League colleges, where religious discussion regularly involved the New England Transcendentalists, Goethe, nineteenth-century German idealism, Unitarianism, and the atheistic ideas of the First Humanist Manifesto.

And in particular, if you do not reach a good understanding of the New England Transcendentalists, you will never understand important dimensions of the religious milieu in which Bill W., Dr. Bob, Anne Smith, and Richmond Walker were raised.

CHAPTER 13

Characteristics of Cosmic Consciousness

Cosmic consciousness and human evolution: Richard Maurice Bucke saw the development of consciousness in strongly evolutionary and developmental terms. He explained the three basic stages at the beginning of his famous book, which we remember was subtitled *A Study in the Evolution of the Human Mind.*

(1) "Simple consciousness" was the first form to develop, first appearing on the planet Earth many millions of years ago. Dogs and horses are modern creatures who have a strongly developed simple consciousness. They are clearly aware of various objects in the world about them, and react to them in logical fashion. They can reason things out, and adapt means to ends, sometimes in quite devious fashion. They also are conscious of the various parts of their bodies—legs, tails, ears, and so on—and react strongly to anything that touches these or affects these.[250]

(2) "Self consciousness" was a higher form of consciousness which did not appear until much more recently in biological history, during the course of the last few million years, as part of the evolution of the modern human species. Human beings are not only conscious of their external environment and their own bodies, but are also capable of standing back, as it were, within their own minds, and regarding their own mental states as objects of consciousness. We human beings evolved as creatures who are capable of self-transcendence. That is, we can think reflectively about our own thought processes and ask ourselves questions such as "how could I have thought about that differently?" and "what would happen if I did such-and-such instead?" Human language is the form in which our minds engage in higher forms of self-reflection and self-transcendence. Our minds, when we are thinking at this level, think

by means of words and conscious concepts arranged into complicated sentences and statements.[251]

> As a side note: I wrote an entire chapter on this topic in my book on *God and Spirituality*, because it is so important, especially because it provides the key to understanding the true nature of human free will, which is not opposed to the realm of scientific explanation, but builds upon it in ways which permit these scientific explanations to be put to concrete, practical use.[252]

The famous Swiss learning psychologist Jean Piaget (1896-1980) carried out years of careful studies showing how this kind of higher consciousness developed over the course of our childhood. With the very bright Swiss children whom he observed, the process took place over the following age ranges, with what Bucke called "self consciousness" developing fully by age eleven (although we, alas, had some students at Indiana University where I taught, who in spite of being young adults, still had difficulty at times in analyzing situations where two different causes or dimensions had to be balanced against one another):[253]

> Sensorimotor stage: birth to age 2 (children experience the world through movement, manipulation of objects, and sense perception, and learn object permanence)

> Preoperational stage: ages 2 to 7 (acquisition of a sophisticated understanding of space and an elementary understanding of causality, but initially in a totally preverbal way, and throughout without any strong self-analytical capability)

> Concrete operational stage: ages 7 to 11 (children learn to think more logically about concrete events, but still in an oversimplified way, where they have difficulty in analyzing situations in which two different causes or two different dimensions of the situation are affecting the outcome simultaneously)

> Formal operational stage: after age 11 (full development of abstract reasoning)

(3) "Cosmic consciousness" was a further evolutionary advance which, Bucke believed, had only begun to appear among a few exceptional human beings during the past 2,500 to 3,000 years. As Bucke describes this new and higher way of perceiving:[254]

> The prime characteristic of cosmic consciousness is, as its name implies, a consciousness of the cosmos, that is, of the life and order of the universe .... To this is added a state of moral exaltation, an indescribable feeling of elevation, elation, and joyousness, and a quickening of the moral sense .... With these come, what may be called a sense of immortality, a consciousness of eternal life, not a conviction that he shall have this, but the consciousness that he has it already.

It came in an act of inner illumination which in its strongest forms would be accompanied by what Bucke called the "subjective light," an overpowering sense of standing in a great light or gazing at a powerful light, which might sometimes appear to be outside the self, but was in fact inside oneself. Bucke usually only labeled his case studies as authentic experiences of the full cosmic consciousness if the subjective light was perceived. But he did list a number of cases where no light appeared to the subject, which he nevertheless regarded as near-instances or partial instances of the full consciousness.

He began his book with a third-person narrative describing how he himself first experienced this cosmic consciousness in a very vivid fashion during a visit to England in 1873:[255]

> It was in the early spring, at the beginning of his thirty-sixth year. He and two friends had spent the evening reading Wordsworth, Shelley, Keats, Browning, and especially Whitman. They parted at midnight, and he had a long drive in a hansom (it was in an English city). His mind, deeply under the influence of the ideas, images and emotions called up by the reading and talk of the evening, was calm and peaceful. He was in a state of quiet, almost passive enjoyment.
>
> All at once, without warning of any kind, he found himself wrapped around as it were by a flame-colored cloud. For an

instant he thought of fire, some sudden conflagration in the great city; the next, he knew that the light was within himself. Directly afterwards came upon him a sense of exultation, of immense joyousness accompanied or immediately followed by an intellectual illumination quite impossible to describe. Into his brain streamed one momentary lightning-flash of the Brahmic Splendor which has ever since lightened his life; upon his heart fell one drop of Brahmic Bliss, leaving thenceforward for always an aftertaste of heaven.

Among other things he did not come to believe, he saw and knew that the Cosmos is not dead matter but a living Presence, that the soul of man is immortal, that the universe is so built and ordered that without any peradventure all things work together for the good of each and all, that the foundation principle of the world is what we call love and that the happiness of every one is in the long run absolutely certain.

He claims that he learned more within the few seconds during which the illumination lasted than in previous months or even years of study, and that he learned much that no study could ever have taught. The illumination itself continued not more than a few moments, but its effects proved ineffaceable; it was impossible for him ever to forget what he at that time saw and knew; neither did he, or could he, ever doubt the truth of what was then presented to his mind.

After many further years of study, Bucke says that he finally came to understand that Darwinian evolution was still taking place, and that the first representatives had now appeared of a new race of beings whose bodies still looked like human bodies, but whose minds had evolved into something far higher than human beings possessed:[256]

There exists a family sprung from, living among, but scarcely forming a part of ordinary humanity, whose members are spread abroad throughout the advanced races of mankind and throughout the last forty centuries of the world's history.

The trait that distinguishes these people from other men is this: Their spiritual eyes have been opened and they have seen. The better known members of this group who, were they collected together, could be accommodated all at one time in a modern drawing-room, have created all the great modern religions, beginning with Taoism and Buddhism, and speaking generally, have created, through religion and literature, modern civilization .... These men dominate the last twenty-five, especially the last five, centuries as stars of the first magnitude dominate the midnight sky.

A man is identified as a member of this family by the fact that at a certain age he has passed through a new birth and risen to a higher spiritual plane .... The object of the present volume is to teach others what little the writer himself has been able to learn of the spiritual status of this new race.

As a skilled psychiatrist, Bucke was of course aware that human beings can have hallucinations, and imagine that they have seen things that are not real. But as he explained, in the case of a hallucination, the only person who can see it is the one having the hallucination. That is the way a psychiatrist can tell if a patient is having a hallucination, and it is extremely simple and not hard to understand.

If several people, on the other hand, all said that they had seen a tree standing half a mile off in the middle of a field, and the descriptions of the tree which they gave afterward all matched in general outline, we would judge that the tree actually existed, even though some of the details in their accounts were different. "Just in the same way," Bucke explained, "do the reports of those who have had cosmic consciousness correspond in all essentials."[257]

I might add to Bucke's arguments that if the tree were at a great enough distance, only those few observers who had the sharpest sight might in fact be able to see it. It would be easy to establish however, that these few had keener eyes than other people, that they were consistently able to spot things that other people had missed, and that closer investigation invariably showed that if these especially keen-eyed observers said they could see something off at an enormous distance, and enough other people finally agreed to walk the distance and make a closer inspection, some of the latter group would eventually be able to verify that the sharp-sighted ones were in fact right.

Cosmic consciousness: seven characteristics. In his book, Bucke studied a number of people who had developed this kind of cosmic consciousness—people living at many different eras of history, and in many different parts of the globe—and developed a list of characteristics which regularly appeared in their accounts of this experience. If I might put his list of attributes partly into my own words:[258]

1. Suddenly and without warning, they experience the *subjective light* and feel themselves to be standing in front of a flame or great light, or they feel themselves to be standing in a cloud or filled with a haze or mist.

2. They are filled with an enormous sense of *ecstasy*: they are overwhelmed by joy, assurance, and what they may describe as a sense of salvation. But this word is not quite correct, because what they feel is not some sense of being freed at last from condemnation, but an awareness that they and everyone else are already accepted. "It is not that the person escapes from sin; but he no longer sees that there is any sin in the world from which to escape."

3. An intellectual *illumination* sweeps over their minds: the cosmos is not a collection of dead matter with occasional life forms here and there, but is in its totality a living presence, "an infinite ocean of life."

4. They suddenly see and understand that they are *immortal*, "that the life which is in man is eternal, as all life is eternal; that the soul of man is as immortal as God is." This does not come to them in the form of a rational proof or convincing argument. It is rather that they suddenly sense at first hand that the core of their own being is an intrinsic part of the same realm as the eternal Godhead, and made of the same deathless substance. Or to put it another way, as long as they can sense themselves standing in that divine light and immortal presence, the fear of death completely vanishes.

5. They sense a *cosmic order built on love*, which provides for all things to "work together for the good of each and all" in such a way that the true "happiness of every individual is in the long run absolutely certain."

6. People who have achieved this cosmic consciousness will usually have a powerfully *charismatic* effect on the other people around them. Without understanding why, other people will be charmed by them and want to be around them. They will automatically turn to them for leadership, reassurance, or consolation. They will sense at some level that these people who radiate the illumination of their cosmic consciousness have a wisdom and knowledge that can guide others.
7. The one who has achieved cosmic consciousness may sometimes appear to have actually been *transfigured* or *transhumanized* into a divine being.

Bill Wilson's use of these ideas: losing the fear of death. With respect to the fourth item—realizing that they are themselves immortal beings and feeling their fear of death somehow drop away—one must note how Bill Wilson made a point of that when he described the sense of the divine Presence, both when talking about his own experiences, and also when talking about his grandfather. In the latter case (this was the grandfather who could hear the music of the spheres) Bill's account in the Big Book emphasized the old man's fearlessness as he faced his own approaching death.[259]

When Bill W. spoke about his journey to England on the troopship in 1918, and described how his fear that he might die at sea was lifted when he saw the sun rise over the coast of England, one might assume that a major portion of this release from fear came from seeing land up ahead. But as he reminisced about it later, there was also a sense that the dawning of the physical sunlight somehow pointed symbolically to a different kind of dawning of the light—a dawn which he could somehow sense (down at some deep, mostly subliminal level of his mind) had not yet arrived but was out there waiting for him. When he visited Winchester Cathedral not long afterward, the fear that he might die in battle over in France was threatening to overwhelm him until, seeing the shaft of sunlight coming through the stained glass window, he came even closer to seeing the inner light at a fully conscious level. This hint of the true divine light—still not fully separable in his mind from the physical sensation of the English sunlight coming through the top of the window-glass—was nevertheless enough to instantly wash away all of his death-fear.[260]

Ebby's visit to his apartment sixteen years later prompted Bill to remember all those feelings once again, but this time there was the sense that the blockage had suddenly dropped away: the barrier, that is, which had kept Bill from becoming fully and consciously aware of the eternal realm. It turned out that it was an overwhelming fear of God which was blocking him from seeing the divine light which would lift away his fear of death. But fear of God and fear of death are closely related in most people's minds, so this is totally understandable. For many people (particularly back in earlier centuries) the fear of God arises from the terrifying belief that God will condemn us because of all the sins that we have committed. In Bill Wilson's case, however, he was being paralyzed by an overwhelming terror whenever he realized that he would have to break with so many orthodox and conventional beliefs about God in order to become true to his own vision.

At any rate, just a short time later he checked himself into Towns Hospital and experienced the fullness of the vision of the eternal light, the one which sweeps away the fear of death, for as Bill phrased it later, as he beheld that divine light he realized that "even though a pilgrim upon an uncertain highway, I need be concerned no more, for I had glimpsed the great beyond."[261]

Cosmic consciousness and the charismatic messenger: Father Dowling and Bill W. The sixth item in the list above points to the fact that those who have achieved cosmic consciousness are so often powerfully charismatic figures. Other people are charmed and fascinated by them. They want to listen to them, be with them, and follow them. Even brief contacts with these charismatic individuals remain unforgettable years later. This is the source of the power of a number of major religious and literary figures. Some—like Jesus, Buddha, Muhammad, and the Apostle Paul—appeared among the sacred founding figures in one or another great world religion. Others—like St. John of the Cross (Juan de Yepes Álvarez), the Neo-Platonic philosopher Plotinus, and Walt Whitman—founded no separate world religion of their own but set a powerful mark on the thought world of many following generations.

Even the less famous members of this group have some portion of this charismatic power, which can be seen in their strong effect on other people. From the way that Bill Wilson described his first meeting with Father Ed Dowling in 1940, it seems clear that he believed the good priest was one of those special people who had attained cosmic consciousness. In terms of its effect on Bill, he commented that it was like undergoing "a second conversion experience." The priest's impact on him was completely overwhelming:[262]

> He brushed back a shock of white hair and looked at me through the most remarkable pair of eyes I have ever seen. We talked about a lot of things, and my spirits kept on rising, and presently I began to realize that this man radiated a grace that filled the room with a sense of presence. I felt this with great intensity; it was a moving and mysterious experience. In years since I have seen much of this great friend, and whether I was in joy or in pain he always brought to me the same sense of grace and the presence of God. My case is no exception. Many who meet Father Ed experience this touch of the eternal.

One of the things that we need to remember, of course, is that if Bill Wilson had himself already attained the fullness of cosmic consciousness on December 14, 1934, this visit was a powerful meeting of like with like. This helps us to understand how Father Ed, during the course of just one evening's talk with Bill, became totally committed to the A.A. cause, and became convinced that God had called Bill to perform a divine task that no one other than him would be able to carry out.

Cosmic consciousness: transhumanization and discovering the divine within ourselves. The seventh item on the list of characteristics of cosmic consciousness involved the rather startling claim that the one who has achieved cosmic consciousness may appear to have actually been transfigured or transhumanized into a divine being. To begin with, let us remember that Bucke included men like Jesus and Buddha in his list of famous people who had attained cosmic consciousness, and countless men and women throughout history have regarded those two religious figures as divine beings.

But Bucke also cited figures like Dante, who was clearly an ordinary human being, who lived during the Italian Renaissance and was the author (during the early 1300's) of a great epic poem called the *Divine Comedy*. In the last part of that work, the *Paradiso*, Dante spoke in Canto 1 of his "transhumanization" or divinization when the eternal light shone upon him in his own personal experience of cosmic consciousness.

Now to explain the role played by the figure of Beatrice in this passage, it should be noted that the process through which the eternal light was able to shine forth and illuminate us in the depths of our minds was often personified, with the agent or messenger or process being portrayed as a heavenly figure who was given a name and a distinct character. For the Apostle Paul, it was Christ who appeared to him on the road to Damascus; for Muhammad it was the angel Gabriel who spoke to him. For other authors the messenger or source was sometimes pictured as a divine double:[263] a sort of second self who dwelt in heaven, or was born within our hearts and spoke to us from within our hearts.

At the beginning of Canto 1 of the *Paradiso*, Dante personified the bringer of light as a symbolic figure named Beatrice. There had been a real person by that name—Beatrice di Folco Portinari (1266-1290)—but Dante had only met her twice, the first time when he was nine years old and she was eight, and the second time nine years later. She was only 24 when she died. When Dante began writing his great epic some twenty years or so later, he turned her into a completely symbolic figure. In a play on her name Beatrice, he portrayed her as the incarnation of beatific love, who led the poet into a version of the *beatific vision* in which, even though he was still in this life, he was allowed to see the Divine Light of God shining forth in the transcendent heavenly realm.

In the dazzling vision which he described, Dante said that he found himself standing at the entrance to the heavenly realm which hung suspended above the earth. Up above shone the sun, and staring at the sun was the figure of Beatrice (*Paradiso* 1.46-63). Suddenly the heavenly fire and light leapt from the sun to Beatrice, and then Dante also looked at the sun, and then the three of them were linked together—the sun,

Beatrice, and Dante—in coruscating sparks of liquid, burning fiery light (1.58-60):

> *Io nol soffersi molto, né sì poco,*
> *Ch'io nol vedessi sfavillar dintorno,*
> *Com' ferro che bogliente esce del foco.*

> I could not bear it much, just for a brief moment,
> in which I could see sparks fly around it,
> like droplets of molten iron thrown out from the fire.

And suddenly the sun was turned into the Eternal Wheels of Light (God as the Unmoved Mover who caused everything else to happen in the universe) and Beatrice was transformed into a second heavenly sun or Second God. And then Dante found himself also being transfigured and being turned into a divine being. He referred in *Paradiso* 1.67-69 to the Greek myth of Glaucus, a fisherman who was turned into a sea-god by eating a magic herb (there is a famous modern statue of Glaucus in the middle of the Fountain of the Naiads in the Piazza della Repubblica in Rome). Dante said that he found himself also being turned into a god (1.70-71) in an experience which surpassed all human language: *Trasumanar significar per verba non si poria*, "being transhumanized cannot be described in words."

CHAPTER 14

Panentheism, Nature Mysticism, and Walt Whitman

Pantheism or panentheism: God as the life and order of the universe. Bucke's book on *Cosmic Consciousness* influenced some of the top thinkers of the early twentieth century. Albert Einstein, in an article he wrote in 1930, developed a version of Bucke's ideas centered on what he called "cosmic religious feeling." In that article Einstein rejected any kind of anthropomorphic conception of a personal God as being unscientific: the idea of gods who acted like human beings was no more than primitive superstition. In his interpretation, we could stand in awe at the sublime grandeur of the universe and its order, without trying to turn it into a deity made in the human image. And going even further, Einstein's God was certainly not "alive" in the sense in which human beings were alive.[264]

Bucke in similar manner clearly rejected any notion of a highly personified God who thought and reacted like a human being. Bucke certainly never talked about God becoming angry with a particular human being, or feeling jealous, or deciding to strike someone with a lightning bolt or anything like that. Bucke also never suggested praying to God to try to get him to change the course of events or work a miracle.

In my reading of Bucke, however, he also completely rejected the idea that either God or the universe were something dead and mechanical. In fact, the vision or illumination of which he spoke revealed the exact opposite:[265]

> This consciousness shows the cosmos to consist not of dead matter governed by unconscious, rigid, and unintending law; it shows it on the contrary as entirely immaterial, entirely spiritual and entirely alive … it shows that the universe is God and that God is the universe ….

The belief "that the universe is God and that God is the universe" is called pantheism or panentheism, from the Greek words *pan* = "all," *theos* = "God," and *en* = "in." Bucke held that the universe itself was a living being of some sort, and that God was simply another name for that marvelous universe. Although Bucke sometimes expressed this idea in slightly more complicated form, he more frequently simply equated God and in the universe in fairly naive fashion, as in the above quotation.

Bill Wilson: a Catholic God instead of Bucke's pantheism. In the Big Book, Bill Wilson broke with Bucke on this point, and avoided any kind of simple minded pantheism. He sometimes spoke of the higher power as the "Spirit of the Universe" or "Spirit of Nature," a kind of phraseology which could be interpreted as the panentheistic doctrine that God was to the material universe as the human soul was to the human body.[266] But one of Bill W.'s commonest names for God was "Creator," a term which implied a fundamental ontological and metaphysical difference between God (the creator) and the universe (that which was created).[267] When using that language, the universe could still be construed as a derivative part of God, but God would clearly be the more powerful and active partner, while the universe was seen as comparatively much less powerful, and rather more apt to be the passive object of God's actions. One should especially note how Bill W. continually stressed that it was God himself who miraculously removed the compulsion to drink and produced the psychic change in the alcoholic's character, not the universe or any natural force.[268] God and nature were *not* simply two different terms for the same thing.

Even more importantly, modern scientists have calculated that the universe we live in came into existence in the Big Bang some 13.7 billion years ago. Before that time, the universe did not exist. So if God was simply the World Soul or Spirit of the Universe in a simplistic sense, we would have to have God also being created 13.7 billion years ago. This kind of God—a so-called God who had a beginning in time—would no longer be either the Creator or the eternal ground of all reality. Bill W. clearly did not believe in that kind of God: as he said on page 10 of the Big Book, God was a being "who knew neither time nor limitation."

Bill Wilson's God had a strongly intellectual aspect (at one level) which was very different from Bucke's God. The chemists, astronomers, and biologists were among Wilson's great heroes. They portrayed a universe built on a foundation of immutable laws of nature: "The prosaic steel girder is a mass of electrons whirling around each other at incredible speed. These tiny bodies are governed by precise laws, and these laws hold true throughout the material world."[269] But natural laws which were basically ideas necessitated a Creator which was a source, not just of matter, but also of *ideas* which could be fit together into a rationally coherent system of thought. This implied a God who was some sort of "Creative Intelligence," as Bill Wilson termed it.[270] Or in other words, even though he believed that human beings could sense the divine Presence in the way that Bucke had described, Bill Wilson's God was a Catholic God in a way that Bucke's God was not, the kind of God whose existence was demonstrated in the traditional Argument from Design: that is, God was some kind of pre-existent ground of all reality, which existed before the physical universe came into being, and which had something analogous to a human mind or human intelligence. By the word analogous, I mean that the Being of God was able to generate purely intellectual concepts in some fashion where they had *meaning*. A purely impersonal source could be used to obtain phrases and equations which were simply words and numerical relationships: one could draw slips of paper out of a box, for example. But these words and numbers would have no meaning, that is, there would be no way of learning how to apply them to anything real.

The ownmost Being of the God whom Bill Wilson talked about in the Big Book dwelt in a totally different realm from that in which our present physical universe was located. In two different passages Bill described this divine realm as a kind of *fourth dimension* and he said that it could not be perceived directly by the ordinary five senses, but could only be perceived by a sort of *sixth sense*.[271] We cannot take either of these phrases literally. In Einstein's special theory of relativity there were three spatial dimensions, connected to a fourth dimension which was time, but Bill W. was not referring to time. Likewise, whatever the faculty was whereby we could sense the divine Presence, it was not simply another kind of physical sense. Homing pigeons are able to find their way home because they have something in their brains which is sensitive to the earth's magnetic field and functions like a tiny compass, and electric eels are able to detect the presence of other objects around them by sensing changes in the electrical fields which their bodies generate. But when Bill Wilson talked about us becoming aware of the divine Presence through a sort of "sixth sense," he was not referring to some kind of unusual homing-pigeon-like or eel-like way of physically sensing things in the material universe which still made use of the ordinary this-worldly laws of physics.

Bill Wilson believed in a kind of two-story universe, where the lower level was made up of matter and physical energy following the scientific laws of physics, chemistry, and biology. Our human bodies existed at that level (including the cells and electrical currents in our brains), as well as all the material objects in the world around us.

But in Bill Wilson's two-story universe there was also an upper level which was totally different from the ground floor. He referred to this higher divine world as "the Realm of Spirit" in one place, and in another well-known passage in the Big Book described it as "a New Land" which we could cross over to (at least part of the way) via "the Bridge of Reason." That bridge did not reach all of the way however, so at the end of the bridge we had to take a leap of faith and (metaphorically speaking) jump out over the void which separated that world from ours.[272]

This "Realm of Spirit" was what traditional Catholic Christianity called the heavenly realm. Bill Wilson stood with Emmet Fox (and the Christian tradition as a whole) in regarding that heavenly region as an immaterial realm filled with supernatural light (not this-worldly physical light) which continually coexisted as a kind of parallel universe operating with its own kind of internal processes, above and behind the material universe.

In this two-story universe, the lower story was built of ordinary material things, while the upper story was filled with divine light, angels, and human spirits (including the spirits of those human beings who had died and were no longer living on this physical earth).

Along with Emmet Fox, Bill Wilson also seems to have believed that each this-worldly self had a kind of divine double: a sort of second self who dwelt in heaven. (Some passages in Bucke's book also spoke in that way.[273]) Or perhaps, to change the metaphor a bit, we could say that Bill W. believed in two-story human beings: on the upper level lived a being of light who was immortal and would never die, while down on the lower level a shadow or image or this-worldly double of that being of light would be born and live a material existence for a while, and then eventually die and be no more, while the immortal being of light continued on forever. That did not mean that our brief earthly existence was unimportant: God sent us to this planet Earth to carry out goals that were of vital importance to him, and our earthly responsibilities should not be neglected. Or as Bill W. put it on page 130 of the Big Book, "We have come to believe He would like us to keep our heads in the clouds with Him, but that our feet ought to be firmly planted on earth."

The great 18th-19th-20th century shift in the western view of God and nature. We have already spoken briefly of the influence on Bucke of the English Romantic poets and New England Transcendentalists. But we need to speak of this at greater length now, because Bucke was one of the first western thinkers to explicitly identify the great metamorphosis which was taking place in western thought during his lifetime.

> As a side note: if we go back to the beginning of history, there have actually been two great watersheds in the development of western thought. The first took place during the second through fourth centuries B.C., roughly speaking. The old mythological worldview of the Ancient Near East was replaced by a new way of talking about how and why things occurred, based on detailed philosophical systems, organized rational explanations, and the beginnings of modern naturalistic scientific thought. The fundamental way that people looked at the world underwent a major change. The Old Testament, along with the surviving ancient Egyptian

and Mesopotamian writings and the earliest stratum of ancient Greek literature (Hesiod and so on), shows how the old world thought: one explained things by telling a myth. If you were Greek, earthquakes were produced when the god Hephaestus began hammering away at his blacksmith's forge down below the surface of the earth, while if you were an ancient Hebrew, the earthquake was caused by a supernatural dragon or water monster called Leviathan who lived down below the flat earth that we live on. Leviathan was a mythological doublet of the Babylonian goddess Tiamat, the great Mesopotamian chaos monster, and "caused the pillars of the earth to tremble" whenever he grew restive and swished his tail. We can see the change to the new way of thought already beginning in many parts of the New Testament, and taking fully-developed form in the writings of people like the great Jewish philosopher Philo (first century A.D.), and the earliest Christian philosophical theologians like Justin Martyr (second century) and Origen (third century)

The only other watershed in western thought that has been of equal magnitude was the one that took place at the beginning of the modern era, the one that we need to talk about now.

It was actually a double shift that took place as the world moved into the modern period, one beginning in the eighteenth century and the other joining in during the early twentieth century, forcing us today to make two fundamental changes at philosophy's foundational level, if we wish to take the ideas of ancient Platonism and Aristotelianism (and the rest of the traditional ancient and medieval heritage) and restructure these ideas into a new architectonic philosophical system which will work in the modern world.

(1) From God as Unmoved Mover to God as dynamic source of energy. In one of these two modern shifts in thought — this one took place primarily in the twentieth century — God began to be seen, not as an Unmoved Mover who pulled all of the rest of reality towards him by teleological attraction, but as a dynamic source of energy who filled

the rest of reality with the power and energy to create new things and fill the universe with unending novelty. Henri Bergson, Alfred North Whitehead, and Charles Hartshorne were among the key figures who began expressing the earliest forms of this new, process-oriented kind of philosophy. I have written about this in my book on *God and Spirituality* in enough detail that I do not believe I need to write more about it here.[274]

(2) From other-worldly mysticism to nature mysticism. The other great modern shift in thought took place slightly earlier, in the eighteenth and nineteenth centuries, and involved a change from *other-worldly mysticism* (where people who were seeking contact with God and the sacred world attempted to block off everything having to do with the material world) and what I have called *nature mysticism*, which involved learning how to apprehend the presence of God and the sacred, both in and through our sense perceptions of the physical world.

This also involved a major shift in sexual attitudes: instead of portraying the ideal goal as that of virginity, chastity, and total abstinence from any kind of sexual practices at all, people now began to see how sexuality could be incorporated as a positive and blessed part of a warm human relationship between two people.

I talked about this shift in a book I wrote in 1984, and wrote what I think is the best explanation I can give of what happened during the eighteenth and nineteenth centuries. Since I am not sure I can do any better than this, it seems to me that the best thing to do is simply to repeat what I said back then.[275]

The tradition of other-worldly mysticism has been of enormous importance in Christian history. This was particularly the case in the Middle Ages, and in that formative period between the council of Nicaea in 325 and Chalcedon in 451, when the basic framework of orthodox, Catholic Christian theology was being laid down. It is still very much alive today, although no longer in the dominant mainstream.

What we need to do now, however, is to look at a more recent development, the appearance of what one might call "nature mysticism." The English Romantic poet Wordsworth, in *My Heart Leaps Up*, called it "natural piety," as distinguished from the piety derived from the reading of the Scriptures. It began to appear in authors with strong evangelical leanings in the eighteenth century,[276] and became fully developed in nineteenth-century Romanticism. It is so different from the classical Oriental and Platonic variety of mysticism that it should certainly be divided off and discussed as a second major stream of thought, a second kind of way in which people have sought to obtain a direct awareness of God's presence.

In classical Oriental mysticism, in Neo-Platonism, and in medieval Eastern Orthodox and Catholic mysticism, the language which is used speaks of abandoning the physical world of the five senses and blocking it completely out of the mind. One is taught how to move away from the world of the five senses and up to the level of abstract thought, and then how to move even beyond that, into a vision of the divine abyss which is beyond all human concepts and sense perceptions.

But in the new tradition of "nature mysticism" or "natural piety" which began to appear in the eighteenth and nineteenth centuries, there is no talk of "shutting out" the world of the five senses. One sees a beautiful clump of bushes as one comes around a bend in a country road, or one gazes in awe at the sight of a magnificent mountain peak or a multicolored sunset, and then — while continuing to see these natural objects as integral parts of the world of nature — one somehow apprehends God directly in and through them. It is the divinization somehow of the finite world itself. There is no talk of having to shut off our sense perceptions and move to higher, more removed levels, (as e.g. in Bonaventure's *The Mind's Pathway to God*, to give a typical example of medieval Catholic beliefs about how to obtain a mystical experience of God).

In the early eighteenth century, the English theologian John Wesley, using an ancient Jewish and Christian technical term, spoke of this as nature suddenly revealing God's "glory" (Hebrew *kabod*, as in Exod. 33:18 and Isaiah 6:3).[277] In the twentieth century, C. S. Lewis (1898-1963), drawing upon the tradition of the English poetry of the Romantic period, called this same momentary revelation, the experience of "joy." The great English historian Herbert Butterfield (1900-1979), in his essays on the Christian understanding of history, also used the same imagery in speaking of his sense of God.

One can find innumerable examples in the poetry of Wordsworth. In his *Ode* on *Intimations of Immortality*, he begins with the lines:

There was a time when meadow, grove, and stream,
The earth, and every common sight,
   To me did seem
   Apparelled in celestial light,
The glory and the freshness of a dream.

Or in his poem, *The Excursion*, Wordsworth gives a more specific description (Book I, lines 198-200, 203-207, 211-213):

What soul was his, when from the naked top
Of some bold headland, he beheld the sun
Rise up, and bathe the world in light! He looked—

Beneath him:—Far and wide the clouds were touched,
And in their silent faces could he read
Unutterable love. Sound needed none,
Nor any voice of joy; his spirit drank
The spectacle ....

In such access of mind, in such high hour
Of visitation from the living God,
Thought was not; in enjoyment it expired.

The Romantic tradition in literature, in its attempt to understand this kind of vision of God at the theoretical level, tended to emphasize the role of feeling and emotion (as in Wordsworth's famous definition of poetry as "the spontaneous overflow of powerful feelings" and "emotion recollected in tranquility"). And the German theologian Friedrich Schleiermacher, the nineteenth-century founder of modern liberal Protestant theology, then tried to create a theological system based upon "feeling" (*Gefühl*) in the Romantic sense.

(It should be remembered that early Alcoholics Anonymous, from 1935 to 1948, used the *Upper Room* as its main source of readings for group prayer and private meditation. These little booklets, published by the old Southern Methodist Church in Nashville, Tennessee, were beautiful examples of the way in which a spirituality based upon feeling — what the Methodists referred to as the "language of the heart" and the "religion of the heart" — could be used to build a spirituality which combined a love of nature with a warm-hearted and all-forgiving compassion and care for the other human beings around us.)

Bucke's great hero: the poet *Walt Whitman*. Richard Maurice Bucke placed himself clearly on the side of the new nature mysticism. For him, the Romantic poets had not gone nearly far enough. The New England Transcendentalist Ralph Waldo Emerson had almost achieved the ability to see God clearly and fully in the natural world. When Emerson published his famous essay on "Nature" in 1836 — the work which laid the foundation for the new Transcendentalist movement — he talked about the way that the divine is diffused through all of nature. Human beings, he said, must learn to feel this spirit of nature, and recognize it as the Universal Being.

But even this did not go far enough, Bucke said. The true representative of the fullness of cosmic consciousness was the great American poet Walt Whitman, the author of *Leaves of Grass*. Whitman (1819-1892) was only eighteen years older than Bucke (1837-1902). To a great extent they are part of the same generation, that era of U.S. and Canadian history which immediately preceded the twentieth century, and laid the foundations for it.

Whitman was one of the most influential poets in American literary history. He stands with Edgar Allen Poe and Emily Dickinson as one of the formative and innovative authors who gave first voice to what was going to become the creative new style of the country's national literature. It is important to stress that the roots from which the Twelve Step movement drew its ideas were not the trivial ideas of scattered cranks, isolated eccentrics, and temporary cults.

The Twelve Step program was linked directly to several of the mainstreams of modern American thought. And it was especially the history of American literature and the thought of the major east coast American colleges and universities which provided the foundation of the early Alcoholics Anonymous writings. This meant the New England Transcendentalists, Walt Whitman, Harvard University, William James, Dartmouth, Wellesley College, and Williams College in Massachusetts, as well as the people who had influenced them: Immanuel Kant and nineteenth-century German idealism, as well as the more esoteric

New Thought movement, and the first major incursion of Hindu philosophical ideas into American thought during the nineteenth century.

But Walt Whitman was above all Richard Maurice Bucke's great hero, the one who gave "the best, most perfect, example the world has so far had of the Cosmic Sense,"[278] and the one who represented the fullness of what the Canadian praised as a healthy, red-blooded, robustly physical (and sometimes almost alarmingly sexual) view of God and the universe.

So we see Bucke talking at great length of Walt Whitman's love of natural beauty and the simple things of nature:[279]

> [Whitman's] favorite occupation seemed to be strolling or sauntering about outdoors by himself, looking at the grass, the trees, the flowers, the vistas of light, the varying aspects of the sky, and listening to the birds, the crickets, the tree-frogs, the wind in the trees, and all the hundreds of natural sounds. It was evident that these things gave him a feeling of pleasure far beyond what they give to ordinary people. Until I knew the man it had not occurred to me that anyone could derive so much absolute happiness and ample fulfillment from these things as he evidently did.
>
> He was very fond of flowers, either wild or cultivated; would often gather and arrange an immense bouquet of them for the dinner-table, for the room where he sat, or for his bed-room; wore a bud or just-started rose, or perhaps a geranium, pinned to the lapel of his coat, a great part of the time; did not seem to have much preference for one kind over any other; liked all sorts. I think he admired lilacs and sunflowers just as much as roses. Perhaps, indeed, no man who ever lived liked so many things and disliked so few as Walt Whitman. All natural objects seemed to have a charm for him; all sights and sounds, outdoors and indoors, seemed to please him.

It was important to note, Bucke said, that Whitman was not just talking about what the philosopher Kant called the feeling of the Sublime, that is, the special feeling which one might have while standing in a safe place on shore and watching a violent storm at sea, or standing on the lip of the Grand Canyon and staring down into the depths below, or some other situation of that sort in which the normal run of nature seemed to go to almost infinite extremes:[280]

> He said, one day, while talking about some fine scenery and the desire to go and see it (and he himself was very fond of new scenery): "After all, the great lesson is that no special natural sights—not Alps, Niagara, Yosemite or anything else—is more grand or more beautiful than the ordinary sunrise and sunset, earth and sky, the common trees and grass." Properly understood, I believe this suggests the central teaching of his writings and life — namely, that the commonplace is the grandest of all things; that the exceptional in any line is no finer, better or more beautiful than the usual, and that what is really wanting is not that we should possess something we have not at present, but that our eyes should be opened to see and our hearts to feel what we all have.

Whitman's love affair with the universe extended to everything he encountered. He seemed to like everyone he met, for example — men and women, young and old. Small children in particular seemed to like and trust him at once. He never disparaged or made fun of people of any race, nationality, or social class, nor did he ever belittle other periods of the world's history or other lands. He never criticized nor made negative comments about "any animals, insects, plants or inanimate things, nor any of the laws of nature, or any of the results of those laws, such as illness, deformity or death. He never complained or grumbled either at the weather, pain, illness or at anything else."[281]

Whitman sometimes spoke of his experiences of cosmic consciousness in a manner very similar to the way that Bucke had described his encounter with the flame-colored cloud during his visit to England in 1873, or the way Bill Wilson had talked about the great white light which he saw in Towns Hospital in New York on December 14, 1934. So we read Whitman saying at one point:

As in a swoon, one instant,
Another sun, ineffable full-dazzles me,
And all the orbs I knew, and brighter, unknown orbs;
One instant of the future land, Heaven's land. [282]

Or as Whitman said elsewhere, the person of "cosmical artist mind, lit with the infinite, alone confronts his manifold and oceanic qualities." This person obeys "the prophetic vision ... the gesture of the god, or holy ghost, which others see not, hear not."[283]

Only here and on such terms, the meditation, the devout ecstasy, the soaring flight. Only here communion with the mysteries, the eternal problems, whence? whither? ... and the soul emerges, and all statements, churches, sermons, melt away like vapors. Alone, and silent thought, and awe, and aspiration — and then the interior consciousness, like a hitherto unseen inscription, in magic ink, beams out its wondrous lines to the sense. Bibles may convey and priests expound, but it is exclusively for the noiseless operation of one's isolated Self to enter the pure ether of veneration, reach the divine levels, and commune with the unutterable. [284]

In this experience, the soul realizes that it is a ship, sailing forever through Nature, the All, and the eternal — and sailing through the physical world of matter as well — in a divine journey that will have no end. For death has no power to destroy the soul:[285]

Lo! Nature (the only complete, actual poem) existing calmly in the divine scheme, containing all, content, careless of the criticisms of a day, or these endless and wordy chatterers .... That something is the All and the idea of All, with the accompanying idea of eternity, and of itself, the soul, buoyant, indestructible, sailing Space forever, visiting every region, as a ship the sea. And again lo! the pulsations in all matter, all spirit, throbbing forever — the eternal beats, eternal systole and dyastole of life in things — wherefrom I feel and know that death is not the ending, as we thought, but rather the real beginning — and that nothing ever is or can be lost, nor even die, nor soul nor matter.

Walt Whitman's first experience of cosmic consciousness: the raw sexual component. But what made Whitman's vision of cosmic consciousness new and different from anything which had ever been seen before, was the raw sexuality and earthiness which appeared in his account, starting from his description of his first encounter with the transcendental realm. This took place in June of either 1853 or 1854 (when Whitman was either thirty-four or thirty-five), and was described vividly in "Song of Myself" in *Leaves of Grass*, beginning with the first edition of that work in 1855.[286]

> I believe in you my soul, . . . the other I am must not abase
>   itself to you,
> And you must not be abased to the other.
> Loaf with me on the grass, . . . loose the stop from your throat,
> Not words, not music or rhyme I want, . . . not custom or
>   lecture, not even the best,
> Only the lull I like, the hum of your valved voice. I mind
>   how we lay in June, such a transparent summer morning;
> You settled your head athwart my hips and gently turned
>   over upon me,
> And parted the shirt from my bosom-bone, and plunged
>   your tongue to my bare-stript heart.
> And reached till you felt my beard, and reached till you held
>   my feet.
> Swiftly arose and spread around me the peace and joy and
>   knowledge that pass all the art and argument of the earth;
> And I know that the hand of God is the elder hand of my own,
> And I know that the spirit of God is the eldest brother of
>   my own,
> And that all the men ever born are also my brothers, . . . and
>   the women my sisters and lovers,
> And that a kelson of creation is love.

Most modern scholars believe that Whitman was either gay or bisexual. The important point here is that he made no bones about there being a powerful sexual component in the Eros which led human beings to God. Even the ancient Platonic philosophers of the classical Greek period, although acknowledging that it was a kind of Eros which drew human beings to God in love, believed that the sexual components of desire had to be suppressed in order to live a good and holy life. But Whitman proclaimed that the kelson of the entire created universe (the kelson or keelson was a stout timber that ran along the keel of a ship to give it strength along the direction of its course through the waves) was a kind of love that incorporated every kind of desire, from the naked Eros of human sexuality stripped bare, to the highest and most refined search for goodness, beauty, and the holy.

If some readers are shocked by this, let them not forget that the only way to pull the universe and the transcendent Godhead into a unity is to understand that the third hypostasis within the Godhead — the Energetikos — has to represent an energy which can run the whole gamut from the extraordinary physical explosion of energy in the Big Bang at the beginning of the present universe, to all the various kinds of human love (from Eros to Philia and Agapê) which drive our lives, to the most sacred experiences of the power of the Holy Spirit in the spiritual realm.[287]

I remember, when I read *Alcoholics Anonymous* for the first time in September of 1990, being truly amazed — though in a totally positive fashion — by the fact that it was the first great book on spirituality I had ever read which talked in detail, in a positive fashion, about the major role of sexual feelings and desires in the human psyche.

> **RAYNOR C. JOHNSON, THE IMPRISONED SPLENDOUR** — As an additional note, A.A. historian Jay Stinnett at the Sedona Mago Retreat Center in Sedona, Arizona, tells me that he discovered when he was reading Bill Wilson's letters in the archives at Stepping Stones, that by the end of his life, Bill was recommending another book instead of Richard Maurice Bucke's *Cosmic Consciousness* for those who wished to understand what he had experienced at Towns Hospital. This newer book, published in 1953, was entitled *The*

Imprisoned Splendour.[288] Its author, Raynor C. Johnson (1901-1987), was an Englishman who held an M.A. from Oxford University and a Ph.D. in physics from the University of London. He was Master of the Methodist Queen's College at the University of Melbourne in Australia from 1934 to 1964. He brought into his book many ideas drawn from new discoveries in twentieth century physics: the uncertainty principle and so on. A study of Raynor Johnson's book will help make it even clearer why I am reading Bill Wilson's ideas in the way that I am, including the picture of two-story human individuals living in a two-story universe.

CHAPTER 15

Father Dowling's Version of Cosmic Consciousness

Father Dowling had a kind of cosmic consciousness, including the positive attitude toward the physical dimension of existence. To those who are familiar with Richard Maurice Bucke's ideas, it is immediately apparent that the kind of language which Bill Wilson used to describe his encounter with Father Dowling in December 1940 at the A.A. clubhouse in New York employed the special terminology which Bucke used *to describe people who had experienced cosmic consciousness.* Meeting Father Ed was like "a second conversion experience,"[289] Bill W. said. The strange priestly figure who walked into the room was immediately recognizable as one of the mysterious God-bearers:

> He brushed back a shock of white hair and looked at me through the most remarkable pair of eyes I have ever seen .... I began to realize that this man radiated a grace that filled the room with a sense of presence. I felt this with great intensity; it was a moving and mysterious experience. In years since I have seen much of this great friend, and whether I was in joy or in pain he always brought to me the same sense of grace and the presence of God. My case is no exception. Many who meet Father Ed experience this touch of the eternal. [290]

So the first reason for suggesting that Father Dowling may have himself been gripped by some kind of experience of cosmic consciousness, lies in the wording that Bill Wilson used to describe the priest's powerful charismatic presence. This was something that everybody noticed, but

Bill W. immediately recognized what had to lie behind that kind of charisma.

We also notice, almost immediately, that one of the aspects of Father Dowling's thought in which we see a parallel to Bucke's view of life, lies in Dowling's positive attitude toward the physical dimension of existence. We are in no way implying, of course, that Father Dowling was involved in any of the open, lascivious sexuality that was a component in Walt Whitman's experience of the divine realm. But otherwise, the earthiness and untidiness and love of ordinary human beings of all sorts and sheer physicality which was part of Whitman's persona, was obviously also a part of Father Dowling's way of relating to the world. For Dowling, the thwack of a bat hitting a baseball and the sight of the hot, sweaty, dusty baseball players running and straining every muscle was a pleasure and a delight. He enjoyed talking with garbage men and taxicab drivers just as much as conversing with mayors and governors. He enjoyed his food — too much, alas, for his own health — but this made him the total opposite of the sort of Catholic saints and Hindu holy men who gloried in the physical pain and torture they suffered while almost starving themselves to death.

During the twenty years in which Dowling and Bill Wilson were friends — from 1940 to Dowling's death in 1960 — the Roman Catholic Church, at the official level, was still very much upholding St. Augustine's old understanding of human sexuality. Sex was bad because it arose from a kind of lust and produced a kind of physical pleasure that seemed nasty and obscene. As Augustine said, we human beings felt "shame" over it. In his *City of God*, Augustine claimed that in the Garden of Eden, before the Fall, the first man Adam would have been able to achieve an erection and penetrate the first woman Eve, and even have an ejaculation, all without feeling any lust or overwhelming physical pleasure. Augustine claimed that Adam was able to achieve an erection without lust in the same way that a human being today can lift a finger into the air without any sexual arousal.

> The man, then, would have sown the seed, and the woman received it, as need required, the generative organs being moved by the will, not excited by lust. For we move at will

> not only those members which are furnished with joints of
> solid bone, as the hands, feet, and fingers, but we move also
> at will those which are composed of slack and soft nerves: we
> can put them in motion, or stretch them out, or bend and
> twist them, or contract and stiffen them, as we do with the
> muscles of the mouth and face.[291]

If that seemed difficult to believe, Augustine argued, it should be noted that even in this present fallen world, there were human beings who had quite remarkable control over various parts of their bodies: "There are persons who can move their ears, either one at a time, or both together." There were people in his part of Africa, or so he claimed, who could fart with such precision as to produce tunes: "Some have such command of their bowels, that they can break wind continuously at pleasure, so as to produce the effect of singing."[292]

The kind of hostile attitude toward sex which we see in Augustine was part of a covert Gnosticism which began seeping into Christianity during the second and third centuries. Augustine himself belonged to a Gnostic cult called the Manicheans before he converted to Christianity. Like many Gnostic sects, the Manicheans believed that no human beings could go to heaven after death if they were involved in any kind of sex at all, even sex within marriage. Men and women who were still involved in sexual relations, no matter how pious they were otherwise, would be condemned to be reincarnated in bodies here on earth over and over again.

St. Augustine set out what was to become the official Roman Catholic position on this issue. Human beings in today's fallen world had to engage in sexual relations which arose out of lust and resulted in physical pleasure, because that was the only way they could produce children. And if no children were born, the human race would not survive. But lustful sexual activities were allowable only as long as it was done *solely* for the purpose of getting women pregnant. Augustine quite literally put sexual activity in exactly the same category as killing your enemies during warfare. If Adam and Eve had not eaten the forbidden fruit and gotten the human race cast out of Paradise, sexual lust and sexual pleasure would still be totally evil and sinful under any circumstances whatever, and killing enemy soldiers and civilians and little innocent children in battle would likewise be damnable sins which would condemn those who committed those evils to everlasting hellfire, no matter what the circumstances of the war.

In the ancient Gnostic theologies, physical pleasure was often portrayed as one of the major traps which had been devised by the evil god who created this physical universe in order to keep us prisoners. Our spirits would be forced to be reincarnated in physical bodies over and over again, until we finally turned away from all physical pleasure and material lusts, and made ourselves fit to return once more to the pure realm of the spirit from which our spirits had originally come.

By the fourth and fifth century A.D., the official doctrines of the Roman Catholic church finally began to condemn many Gnostic beliefs as heresy. Both the Nicene Creed and the Apostles' Creed condemned the Gnostic doctrine that the material world was created by a second god who was evil or incompetent. Both creeds insisted that all things, whether spiritual or material, had been created by the one good God. And both of these doctrinal statements insisted that Jesus Christ was born in a physical human body. The savior was not some bodiless phantom or super-angel come down from heaven, who was incapable of pain, fear, or physical suffering, as was taught by so many Gnostic sects.

But through the whole length of the middle ages, and even down into the twentieth century, we can see how everyday popular belief, even at many times among the Roman Catholic hierarchy, still clung to various kinds of Gnostic prejudices about the ideal spiritual life. This especially applied to attitudes toward human sexuality. One of the most important reasons for early twentieth century Roman Catholic hostility to all forms of artificial birth control, was that it would allow people to have sex simply for physical pleasure, or simply as an expression of affection, warmth, and closeness between husband and wife.

But Father Dowling stood on the same side as Richard Maurice Bucke: we could never arrive at the highest kind of spiritual life if we started talking about spirituality in language which proclaimed that the spiritual world was good while the material world was evil. That was the ancient Gnostic heresy, still partly alive and deadly, creeping around through the spiritual underbrush.

In opposition to the crazed Gnostic belief that all material things were intrinsically and inescapably evil, the Hebrew Bible presented a totally different vision of the world. So for example, in the account of Creation in the first chapter of the book of Genesis at the very beginning of the Bible, we see how the one God created everything, including not just spiritual things, but also water and dirt, trees and bushes, birds and crocodiles, antelopes and earthworms. And this physical world was not an evil one. Because in the first chapter of Genesis, we read how over and over again, at each stage in the evolution of our cosmos, the same phrase is repeated: "And God saw that it was good."

This is important, because in numerous ways we can see Father Ed Dowling, over his entire adult life, taking his stand in defense of the true biblical God, the God of the book of Genesis, against the Gnostic tendency that so often crept back into Christian teaching.

So Father Dowling, for example, had a lifelong friendship with a man named Pat Crowley, who married a woman named Patty Crowley, who joined with another married couple, Burnie and Helene Bauer in South Bend, Indiana, to found the Christian Family Movement. As we mentioned earlier, Patty came within a hairsbreadth of getting the Vatican to change the official Roman Catholic position on birth control, and was only done in by some unscrupulous political maneuvering on the part of the old Catholic conservatives in Rome. Many years later, in 1994, she stated her position in the *Chicago Tribune*: "I think women should have the choice to use contraception. They want to have children, but they want to have them responsibly." That is, sexual attractiveness (along with being a female who has the power to bear children) should no longer be regarded as a shameful thing, but as simply an area where we human beings need to learn to practice *responsible* behavior.

And Father Dowling was one of the founders of the Cana Conference, which during his lifetime supplied a place for married Catholics to learn about the physical and material dimensions of marriage in the kind of positive fashion which rejected all the old Gnostic prejudices. (Reports I have heard about more recent Catholic versions of the Cana program suggest that the old shame-filled attitudes towards sex may have crept back in again.)

And Father Ed was also a staunch supporter of the new Catholic self-help group called Divorcées Anonymous, which would (as part of their program) lecture Catholic women quite sternly about some of the questions they needed to be asking themselves if their husbands were straying. Had they, out of a misguided Gnostic zeal, worked as hard as they could to be sexually unattractive and unresponsive, thinking that this made them "good Christian women"? A modern-day feminist might bristle at that piece of advice, but one can hardly describe a Catholic like Father Dowling who associated himself with strong, powerful prophetic women like Patty Crowley — a woman who was far more courageous in challenging the overreach of papal authority than ninety-nine percent of the male Catholic priests of that period of history — as an anti-feminist figure.

And let us not forget that the old heretical Gnostic spirituality tended to not only condemn any experience of sexual pleasure as sinful, but could easily develop into an extreme position in which all physical pleasure of any kind was regarded as totally evil. That was because the old second and third century Gnostic cults taught that there were two gods: the good God had created the spiritual realm, but then a second god (the fallen Sophia, or her henchman the Demiurge, or some other god or goddess like that) had come along and created the material world, and then stolen little sparks of divine light (our human spirits) from the spiritual realm and imprisoned them in material bodies here on earth.

The Catholic Church officially condemned the Gnostics, but Gnostic beliefs and assumptions nevertheless remained embedded in numerous common beliefs and practices within the church. So we can still today look with horror at some of the French and Spanish Catholic holy men from the seventeenth and eighteenth centuries — Bill W. would have read about them in William James' *Varieties of Religious Experience* — who wore scratchy haircloth garments, slept on the stone floors of churches, nearly starved themselves to death, and otherwise tried to obtain some perverted notion of "holiness" by playing the self-torture game to the hilt. Or we can look at the flagellants of the latter middle ages who marched through medieval towns whipping one another on the back. Or the Irishman Matt Talbot, in the latter nineteenth century, who used deliberate self-torture as part of his spiritual program for trying to control his alcoholism.

But Father Ed Dowling was not one of those. And so he and Richard Maurice Bucke both tried to teach Bill Wilson that learning to fully appreciate the common joys and pleasures of the everyday physical world was a necessary part of the path that led to the highest spiritual experience of God.

Modern psychiatry teaches us that playing the self-torture game in any of its forms is a way to try to cope with an unbearable sense of shame and guilt (that is, feelings of "being a bad person" which are too painful to stand, whether conscious or subconscious). The problem of shame and guilt, and trying to deal with it through self-torture and punishment, has long been an issue in Catholic thought. The best Roman Catholic thinker in A.A.'s second generation of major authors, Ernest Kurtz, explored this subject in an extremely thoughtful and perceptive little volume simply entitled *Shame & Guilt.*[293]

Many Christians down through the centuries tried the self-torture route. But punishing ourselves was a very poor way of trying to deal with the shame and guilt, because even if self-torture seemed to give temporary local relief, it did not deal with the true underlying problem. As a result, the person simply continued to grow psychologically sicker and sicker over the long haul. Now Bucke was a trained psychiatrist, and seems to have realized — even though modern psychiatry was just beginning to develop at that period — that self-torture games were not good ways of trying to achieve the highest spiritual life.

And Father Dowling seems to have agreed with that approach at the basic level: it was *humility*, he argued, which needed to be the virtue at the heart of the true spiritual life in a traditional Catholic understanding of how that life should be led. Practicing humility might sometimes require me to accept pain and suffering when they fell my way, but deliberately inflicting pain on myself was bad if I did it simply in order to make myself suffer.

The flagellants employed a faulty logic: "If I can punish *myself* enough, then maybe God will change his mind and love me again."

But the great Catholic teacher St. Thomas Aquinas said the same thing as the great Protestant teachers Martin Luther and John Calvin: when God forgives me, he does it as a free unmerited act of grace. I cannot do anything to "deserve it" or "earn it." And that is also what the Big Book of Alcoholics Anonymous preaches, and proclaims in such pure fashion that Father Ed Dowling was willing to travel all the way to New York City to meet the author of that book, so he could bolster him up and support him, and tell him in the strongest possible way that he was doing a piece of God's work that was of truly extraordinary importance in the divine scheme of things.

CHAPTER 16

The Radical Wing of the Jesuits

The radical wing of the Jesuits: liberation theology. From their beginning in the sixteenth century, the Jesuits were known for making their own theological decisions and charting their own course to a far greater degree than most Roman Catholic religious orders. They often ignored many of the official positions being decreed by the Papal Curia, and at various points in their history were involved in rebellious struggles with many of the other Catholic religious orders and guardians of theological propriety, who continually sought to bring the Jesuits more closely in line with papal pronouncements and conservative doctrinal standards. Jesuit theologians had often played key leadership roles in the quiet underground spirit of revolution in the Catholic Church which started in the early twentieth century and eventually led to the reforms of the Second Vatican Council in 1962-1965.

Father Jean-Baptiste Janssens, S.J., who was Superior General of the Jesuits from 1946 to 1964, issued an official proclamation in 1949 urging Jesuit schools and universities all over the world to uproot any idea of privileged social "castes" among the Jesuits and their students. The Jesuits were not in any way to seem "allied with the rich and the capitalists," and should at all times show "an interest and concern for the proletariat that is equal to, or even greater than, that shown to the rich."[294] We can imagine how delighted Father Ed Dowling must have been with this proclamation: we have seen him working continuously to try to help the poor and powerless. But many of the younger and most radical Jesuits eventually came to feel that even the sorts of things that Father Dowling had supported did not go nearly far enough.

So when Father Pedro Arrupe, S.J., was elected Superior General of the Jesuits five years after Father Dowling's death (Arrupe held that post from 1965 to 1983), he moved toward an even more radical position, and openly supported the Jesuit priests in Latin America who had started teaching what was called "liberation theology." These priests saw all too many of the Latin American countries of that historical era suffering under the control of dictators who were in fact brutal fascists. But because these dictators proclaimed themselves to be anti-Communist, they were being supported with money and weapons from the United States. What made matters worse was that the Papal Curia in Rome was aiding and abetting these fascist dictators by ordering Catholic priests all over the world to preach against Communism and — in Latin America — in favor of these oppressive rightwing dictatorships. The liberation theologians argued that it was time for the Catholic Church in Latin America to start making friends with the communists and socialists, and that it was above all time for the Christian Church to start siding with the poor and downtrodden peasants.

Fellow travelers: Dorothy Day and the Catholic Worker Movement. Although Dorothy Day (1897-1980) and the people involved in the Catholic Worker Movement were not Jesuits, this is a good topic to look up for any modern researcher who wants to learn more about the general character and flavor of the radical wing of American Catholicism during the early twentieth century. During the 1910's, Day became close friends with many important American Communist leaders and never did truly disavow them, even after she converted to Roman Catholicism in 1927. In 1932, she met a man named Peter Maurin, and the two of them combined forces to start a publication called the *Catholic Worker*, whose first issue appeared on May 1, 1933. During the years that followed, this newspaper gave rise to the widespread Catholic Worker Movement.

Father Dowling's political ideas were not as radical as Day's or the revolutionary ideas proclaimed by Jesuit liberation theology in Latin America: Dowling fought for more moderate causes like proportional representation (and versions of this in fact ended up being implemented here and there within the American political tradition). Day on the other hand developed a far more revolutionary mixture of anarchism and distributism, and supported people later on like Cesar Chavez (the leader of the California farm workers movement) and Cuban revolutionaries Fidel Castro and Ernesto "Che" Guevara. But Dowling and Dorothy Day would have frequently been basically on the same side when it came to social causes like raising the status of black people and married women.

Father Dowling's political crusades, from the St. Louis Housing Authority to Proportional Representation: Father Dowling was active in St. Louis politics, and served as the first president of the St. Louis Housing Authority, which still operates today, sixty years later. (In its present form, it has ninety employees and serves as a federally funded agency, helping provide public housing for people living in St. Louis, including not only low and moderate-income families, but also the elderly and people with disabilities.) He was also of a member of the famous St. Louis Public Questions Club, described at the time as "a cross section of erudite St. Louisans who discuss current problems,"[295] and the Old Baden Society, which Dowling led in announcing on November 26, 1956 that it was mounting a campaign to erect a monument over the unmarked grave of Dred Scott, the black slave whose attempt to gain his freedom was a precipitating factor in starting the American Civil War. Scott's body was interred at that time in Calvary Cemetery in Baden, the suburb of St. Louis where Father Dowling had lived as a child.[296] At the national and international level, Father Dowling was a member of the American Political Science Association and the Proportional Representation Society of Great Britain.[297]

He also received the rare honor of being named honorary vice-president of the National Municipal League, which was founded in 1894 in Philadelphia at a convention of major American political figures, makers of public policy, journalists, and educators including Theodore Roosevelt, Louis Brandeis, Frederick Law Olmsted, and Marshall Field. Known today as the National Civic League, the group continues to fight for the kind of progressive ideas in city and county governments that produce transparency, openness, fairness and professionalism.[298]

In an obituary for Father Dowling, a journalist friend gave a long list of some of his political crusades over the years:[299]

His opinions and ideas were often unconventional. He was long a proponent of proportional representation as a means of defeating corrupt political machines. He once urged that Missouri's governors be replaced by state managers with powers similar to those of city managers on the municipal level. As early as 1941, he advocated more democracy in labor unions to protect "the rank and file against the usurpations of their self-styled leaders." He advocated a new St. Louis city charter in 1936 and in 1958 called for a "complete united merger of the entire area of city and county" with the exception of those areas which vote to stay out.

Father Ed was also a member of the American Proportional Representative League. Proportional representation is a system of counting votes used in many modern democracies — for example, Belgium, Finland, Latvia, Sweden, Israel, and the Netherlands — in which the political party which receives twenty percent of the vote, for example, is given twenty percent of the delegates to the legislature or assembly, while the party which receives forty percent of the votes is given forty percent of the delegates, and so on. This is as opposed to the "winner takes all" plurality (also called the "first-past-the-post" system) which is used in electing representatives to so many legislatures and city and county councils in the United States. The advantage of proportional representation is that even a small minority group — blacks, Hispanics, labor union members, people advocating for a particular political or social cause, and so on — can have some representatives speaking up in their behalf in the legislature or council. Even if the minority representatives usually cannot win a vote in that body, simply having a voice can nevertheless help to make the outcome more democratic, and can sometimes force the majority (when it gets split on an issue) into adopting compromises which take the minority's interests more seriously.

This was of special interest in St. Louis, which started being governed in 1915 by a single-chamber legislature composed of twenty-eight aldermen elected at large. It quickly became clear that no minority groups whatever would ever be elected to the city council in that system. In November 1916, a vote was held in which the progressive forces in the city attempted to change this to a system which used the list system of proportional representation, one of the earliest attempts in American history to bring in this new method. They failed to win this vote, and the conservative system of majority-take-all continued to be the governing principle of the city, but the progressives got enough support to establish that this was a topic which could be seriously debated in the United States.[300]

This is very relevant to later Alcoholics Anonymous history. We must remember how important it is, in the A.A. system of government, to allow even the smallest minority group to stand up and speak out, even after they have just lost a vote. One cannot help but wonder if this feature of A.A. polity was not a creative adaptation by Bill Wilson of Father Dowling's continual concern for minority rights.

In the *National Municipal Review* which was published by the National Municipal League we can see, in the issues for January and February 1949, for example, a long list of the kind of extremely high-powered and nationally prominent people with whom Father Dowling was associating. To pick out a few names from that list:[301]

Charles Edison (son of the inventor Thomas A. Edison), who served as Governor of New Jersey and U.S. Secretary of the Navy

Charles P. Taft, president of the Federal Council of the Churches of Christ in America (now called the National Council of Churches, the group which produced the famous Revised Standard Version and New Revised Standard Version Bible translations)

Belle Sherwin, president of the National League of Women Voters

U. S. Senator Paul H. Douglas (Illinois)

Harold W. Dodds, president of Princeton University

Professor Arthur N. Holcombe, Harvard University

J. Henry Scattergood, former commissioner of Indian Affairs of the U. S. Department of the Interior

Congressman Herbert Pell, former minister to Portugal and Hungary

Senator George Wharton Pepper (Pennsylvania)

C. A. Dykstra, chancellor of the University of California at Los Angeles, former president of the University of Wisconsin and former city manager of Cincinnati

The radical wing of the Jesuits: Teilhard de Chardin S.J. The progressives among the Jesuit order not only became involved on many occasions in social causes which were doing battle against the conservative establishment, they could become quite radical on theological issues too. The kind of teaching, for example, which we see in Richard Maurice Bucke's *Cosmic Consciousness*, was in fact not at all strange to them. They had their own versions of Bucke.

One of the best known was Father Pierre Teilhard de Chardin, S.J. (1881-1955), who was deeply loved and respected by Catholic thinkers all over the world during the 1920's, 30's, and 40's. He was a French Jesuit priest, a famous geologist and paleontologist, who spent many years working in China. He helped discover Peking Man and establish that these early hominins were in fact able to make stone tools and use fire.

The first fossil remains of Peking Man (*Homo erectus pekinensis*) were discovered in 1923–27 near Beijing in China (Beijing was written "Peking" in Roman characters at that period). These creatures, who lived around 750,000 years ago, had sloping foreheads and heavy brow ridges, so their faces looked like apes. But they stood upright and were about as tall as modern human beings, and although their average brain size was smaller on average than the modern human average, their brains nevertheless overlapped the lower range of modern brain size.

It eventually became very clear to Father Teilhard, as a result of his many years of work in the field, that the fact of evolution was an undeniable reality. Modern human beings are descended in a series of gradual stages from a primitive form of ape which was the ancestor of chimpanzees, bonobos, gorillas, and orangutans, as well as human beings. But this meant that there was no separate creation of human beings, in which a man and a woman named Adam and Eve were created out of nothing and placed in a Paradise called the Garden of Eden. That story was a myth.

Teilhard believed that what he called the Law of Complexity/ Consciousness caused the planet Earth first to evolve from a lifeless geosphere into a biosphere, made up of countless varieties of plants and animals forming complex interconnections of mutual dependency. Then, as a second stage, a noosphere began to develop. Creatures having a complex *nous* (mind or intellect) began to evolve. Animals *know*, but the developing human intellect comes *to know that it knows*. As our ancestors evolved higher and higher consciousness (that is greater self-awareness and self-reflective abilities), they became more and more human. In the process, they also began to assemble together in greater and greater degrees of social organization. The noosphere is a kind of planetary thinking network, in which all human minds are now interconnected.

> As a side note, we can note the partial similarity between Teilhard de Chardin's idea of the noosphere and Carl Jung's theory of a collective human unconscious binding the whole human race together at the unconscious archetypal level of our thoughts.

At a certain critical threshold, Teilhard said that the human race will finally reach such a pinnacle of advanced consciousness that it will arrive at what he called the Omega Point, and completely break through the boundaries of space and time. We will enter a higher kind of existence. This will be the second coming of the Logos or Christ, with whom we will then be one. All will be joined together into one supernatural order in which evil has now completely disappeared.[302]

One can easily see the similarity of this to Richard Maurice Bucke's theories about the evolution of cosmic consciousness. And just like Bucke, Teilhard insisted that the material world was not intrinsically bad or evil. In fact, in its own way, it participated in the divine world. Its history and evolution was grand, glorious, and full of positive value. As one commentator noted:

> Père Teilhard … both accepts and practices the Christian doctrine of detachment. He realizes that the consummation of the world can be achieved only through a mystical death, a dark night, a renunciation of the whole being ….
> But when he begins to look further into what constitutes

renunciation … he dissociates himself from ascetical practices hitherto accepted. His aim is to try out a new formula which, if it should prove effective, will enable men (already increasingly conscious of the tremendous impetus of technology) to look on Christianity not as a doctrine of impoverishment and diminution, but of expansion, and so to live as real Christians without ceasing to be artificers of the creative force.[303]

Teilhard had no sympathy for those who were hostile to human material progress. He denounced all the forces of backwardness who tried to romanticize poverty, pain, ill health, and starvation, and who fought every attempt to make human physical life more pleasant and filled with material good and beauty. As he wrote to a businessman whose business was prospering:

How, you ask, can the success of a commercial enterprise bring with it moral progress? And I answer, in this way, that since everything in the world follows the road to unification, the spiritual success of the universe is bound up with the correct functioning of every zone of that universe and particularly with the release of every possible energy in it. Because your enterprise … is going well, a little more health is being spread in the human mass, and in consequence a little more liberty to act, to think, and to love.[304]

But above all, to Father Teilhard, we were not being asked to choose between the love of God and the love of the world. He was rejecting the stark antithesis set up by St. Augustine in his *City of God*, and with that, the controlling assumption of a good deal of medieval spirituality. Teilhard proclaimed that we move towards the vision of God through immersing ourselves in a physical world lit up by the brilliance of the divine light:

"I am not speaking metaphorically," he wrote, "when I say that it is throughout the length and breadth and depth of the world in movement that man can attain the experience and vision of his God."[305]

Like the process philosophers,[306] Teilhard insisted that we recognize, not only that the physical universe is not static, but that God himself is intimately involved in the world of time.

> In [Father Teilhard's] own self the integration of life had been achieved; if he loved God, it was through the world, and if he loved the world it was as a function of God, the animator of all things. "The joy and strength of my life," he wrote a month before his death, "will have lain in the realisation that when the two ingredients — God and the world — were brought together they set up an endless mutual reaction, producing a sudden blaze of such intense brilliance that all the depths of the world were lit up for me."[307]

As any good Thomistic philosopher would agree — look for example at St. Thomas Aquinas's understanding of efficient causality in his classic five proofs for the existence of God — the real cause of a series of causes and effects is the first cause in that series. If someone balances a set of dominos on end, in such a way that tipping the first domino over causes the second domino to topple, which in turn makes the third domino fall, and so on, it does not matter how many dominos there are in the series — ten dominos or a thousand — the finger that tipped the first domino over was the real reason why the last domino fell. St. Thomas did not believe in chance or accident. A mind which knew all the laws of nature and all the starting facts could have predicted, from the very creation of the universe, exactly what was going to happen at each subsequent moment in time.

And so, Teilhard argued in *The Divine Milieu*, because our human souls live in a physical universe made of matter and following scientific laws, our roots go back to the very origins of the physical universe:

> Where are the roots of our being? In the first place they plunge back and down into the unfathomable past. How great is the mystery of the first cells which were one day animated by the breath of our souls! How impossible to decipher the welding of successive influences in which we are for ever incorporated! In each one of us, through matter, the

whole history of the world is in part reflected. And however autonomous our soul, it is indebted to an inheritance worked upon from all sides — before ever it came into being — by the totality of the energies of the earth ....[308]

First the raw matter of the universe exploded into being, and then galaxies and stars came into existence, including our own sun. Planets coalesced, including our own planet Earth. The first single-celled organisms appeared; and then sponges, corals, crustaceans and the like; then fish, amphibians and so on; and down through the evolutionary chain through reptiles, dinosaurs, birds, and mammals; to monkeys, apes, and hominins: *Australopithecus, Homo habilis, Homo erectus, Homo heidelbergensis*, and modern humans.

The totality of the divine milieu in which our souls live in their existence here on earth, includes not only the totality of the evolutionary and geological past, but also the totality of all the various parts of the material universe in which we live here and now, from the far off stars to the other human beings living around us. What we learn from this world of matter, what we take from it, and how we use it, will help determine the spiritual progress of our souls. We can learn love and unselfishness, or greed and avarice, or fear and soul-destroying anxiety. But everywhere we see

> ... the flow of cosmic influences which have to be ordered and assimilated. Let us look around us: the waves come from all sides and from the farthest horizon. Through every cleft the world we perceive floods us with its riches — food for the body, nourishment for the eyes, harmony of sounds and fullness of the heart, unknown phenomena and new truths, all these treasures, all these stimuli, all these calls, coming to us from the four corners of the world, cross our consciousness at every moment. What is their role within us? What will their effect be, even if we welcome them passively or indistinctly, like bad workmen? They will merge into the most intimate life of our soul and either develop it or poison it. We only have to look at ourselves for one moment to realise this, and either feel delight or anxiety. If even the most

humble and most material of our foods is capable of deeply influencing our most spiritual faculties, what can be said of the infinitely more penetrating energies conveyed to us by the music of tones, of notes, of words, of ideas?[309]

And as Teilhard pointed out, the all-encompassing divine *milieu* in which my soul dwells is made up not just of the entire past and present, but also of the future. In good Thomistic fashion, Teilhard portrays the true spiritual life as teleological — that is, goal directed — to its very core. God's perfections — his love, compassion, truthfulness, and so on — serve as the bright and shining goals towards which we strive to grow, pulled by a compelling Eros which wants to possess the beloved and make it ours. And this was one of the core ideas, not just in St. Thomas Aquinas, but for a vast number of other theologians in the ancient Catholic theological tradition.

So the future of the universe is like a cone, Teilhard said, in which everything leads into a central point located at some point in the distant future, when the whole universe will have returned to God. So everything I do in this material world that is good and worthwhile — which means not just giving a piece of bread to someone who is starving, but building a bridge or a house, sweeping a floor, playing a song on a piano to entertain a child, tending a field filled with cotton which will be used to make clothes — will become an intrinsic part of a world which will be made eternal when the Omega Point is reached.

> The divinisation of our endeavour by the value of the intention put into it, pours a priceless *soul* into all our actions .... will not the work itself of our minds, of our hearts, and of our hands — that is to say, our achievements, what we bring into being, our opus — will not this, too, in some sense be 'eternalised' and saved?... A thought, a material improvement, a harmony, a unique nuance of human love, the enchanting complexity of a smile or a glance, all these new beauties that appear for the first time, in me or around me, on the human face of the earth — I cherish them like children and cannot believe that they will die entirely in their flesh .... If I believed that these things were

to perish for ever, should I have given them life? The more I examine myself, the more I discover this psychological truth: that no one lifts his little finger to do the smallest task unless moved, however obscurely, by the conviction that he is contributing infinitesimally (at least indirectly) to the building of something definitive — that is to say, to your work, my God.[310]

How will the Lord bring about the final transfiguration which will allow our earthly eyes and hearts to see the vision of God which will absorb our whole being? That is a miracle which our natural minds cannot explain. But in that mystic vision, we shall be the limbs in the Mystic Body of which Christ shall be the head. The communion of the saints will encompass all our souls into the Heavenly Jerusalem, the New Heaven and the New Earth, the Pleroma or fullness of all things, in whose center God and Christ shall sit eternally enthroned.[311]

Psychoanalysis teaches us that our perceptions of the purely material enter into every level of our souls, including the most spiritual levels. And from the first explosion of the physical universe into being 13.7 billion years ago, down to that future point when everything will finally be linked into the supreme center of all things, "we must ... recognise that in the whole process which from first to last activates and directs the elements of the universe, *everything forms a single whole.*"[312]

By the mid-1920's (when Teilhard was in his mid-forties), he was being banned from teaching in Catholic universities, both by the Church authorities in Rome and by the administrators who headed his own Jesuit order, and he was being blocked from publishing his theories about the doctrine of evolution, the story of Adam and Eve, and the doctrine of original sin. As a result, *Le Milieu Divin* was written in 1926–27, but was not published until 1957. *Le Phénomène Humain* was written in 1938–40, but was not published until 1955. (The English translations — *The Divine Milieu* and *The Phenomenon of Man* — came out in 1960 and 1959 respectively).

Teilhard's ideas therefore did not begin to achieve widespread public notice until after his death in 1955. His ideas were well known however within the Jesuits, and even outside the order, among the better educated Catholic theologians and scholars all over the world, in the form of mimeographed copies circulated privately.

So already at the time when Father Ed Dowling and Bill Wilson first met in December 1940, Father Dowling would certainly have known something of Teilhard's ideas, either from reading some of his writings in mimeographed form or through hearing some of the other Jesuits talking about them. Many educated Catholics of that period felt a good deal of sympathy for Teilhard, and felt that the Church authorities were treating him unfairly. And by the time of Father Dowling's death in 1960, Teilhard's books were being openly published and discussed all over the world.

The radical wing of the Jesuits: Jean Daniélou S.J. The rise of atheistic and anti-Catholic movements in Europe during the late eighteenth and nineteenth centuries eventually produced a reactionary backlash within the Roman Catholic Church. Many of the church's leaders wanted no more of the new ideas, and became increasingly hostile to many aspects of modern science, democracy, and freedom of thought. Pope Pius IX convened the First Vatican Council to help strengthen the pope's ability to simply declare on his own authority that a particular doctrine or dogma was true, and had the council declare the doctrine of papal infallibility on July 18, 1870. The Baltimore Catechism was imposed as the standard Roman Catholic school text in the United States in 1885, and continued to be used all across the country until the Second Vatican Council tossed it out during the 1960s. This catechism, in spite of its claims, did not in fact give an adequate picture of "what has been believed everywhere, always, and by all" within the Catholic tradition (*quod ubique, quod semper, quod ab omnibus creditum est,* the famous Vincentian Canon). In particular, it not only rejected the modern world, it also largely ignored or distorted the Catholic teaching of the early Christian centuries.

As part of this reactionary response, Pope Leo XIII in his encyclical *Aeterni Patris* issued on August 4, 1879, declared that from henceforth the theology taught by the medieval Italian scholar St. Thomas Aquinas (1225-1274) was to provide the official philosophy of the Roman Catholic Church. And carrying this yet further, in 1914 Pope Pius X, in his encyclical *Doctoris Angelici*, declared that all

Catholic universities, seminaries, and schools had to use St. Thomas Aquinas' *Summa Theologica* as the basis of their classes on theology and philosophy, or they would not be given the power to grant degrees. The papacy, deeply frightened by the ideas of the modern world, wanted to put a wall around the Catholic Church and retreat back to the thirteenth century.

But as the twentieth century progressed, the more radical Catholic theologians began doing more and more research into the New Testament and patristic period (that is, going back before the Middle Ages to the ideas taught in the first five or six centuries of the early Church). A good deal of research had to be secret or at least fairly private, and even those works which were published openly had to be kept rather low key, with their more radical implications being more suggested than worked out in detail.

But these liberal Catholics finally got their chance to carry out an open rebellion against medieval Thomist theology and the old conservative Catholic establishment at the Second Vatican Council in 1962-1965. At this gathering, begun only two years after Fr. Dowling's death, the assembled bishops carried out a drastic remake of the Roman Catholic Church. And what is of special importance to us here, is that the overwhelming majority of the citations listed in the decrees of that Council were taken from Biblical sources and especially *patristic* sources, not from medieval scholastic sources.

For a young radical, the advantage of going into the study of patristic theology (that is, the study of the Catholic theology of the first five or six centuries of Christian history) was that one had, during that period, a number of first rate philosophical theologians who took a theological approach very different indeed from the complex logic-chopping that was typical of the professors in the medieval Catholic universities of the thirteenth century. One found theological positions which were often much more compatible with the modern world of Kantian and post-Kantian philosophy. But nevertheless, these patristic theologians were impeccably catholic and orthodox. If early twentieth-century Catholic scholars wrote carefully about these patristic thinkers, they might be told that their research could not be used as textbooks in general courses on Catholic theology at a good Catholic academy or university, but the church authorities could not refuse them permission to publish their books, nor could they forbid good Catholics to read them.

One of the up-and-coming Catholic scholars who made especially good use of this strategy was a young Jesuit named Jean Daniélou (1905-1974). Now to understand how I am going to be using his ideas in this work, we need to begin by being clear about dates. Daniélou came along too late to have much direct influence on Father Dowling. If we look at some of the comparative dates we can see this quickly:

> 1940 — Bill W. and Father Dowling first met.
>
> 1956 — Bill W. met with Aldous Huxley and took LSD in California under the guidance of Gerald Heard and Sidney Cohen. Eventually Father Ed Dowling also took LSD.
>
> 1960 — Father Edward Dowling died.
>
> 1942 — the young Jesuit scholar Jean Daniélou S.J. completed his doctoral thesis on the great fourth-century theologian St. Gregory of Nyssa and received his doctoral degree.
>
> 1944 — Daniélou was named Professor of Early Christian History at the Institut Catholique in Paris.
>
> 1944 — he published *Platonisme et théologie mystique: doctrine spirituelle de saint Grégoire de Nysse.*
>
> 1948 — he published *Origène*, on the great third century theologian.
>
> 1958 — he published *Philon d'Alexandrie*, on the first-century Jewish philosopher whose ideas lay behind so much early Christian theology.
>
> 1961 — Daniélou and Father Herbert Musurillo S.J. published *From Glory to Glory: Texts from Gregory of Nyssa's Mystical Writings*, making that author's ideas more available to readers who were not experts in patristic theology.

The new interest in the patristic period had already begun to appear however within French and German Catholic theological circles well before Daniélou came along. The man who taught Daniélou theology, for example, the noted French Jesuit scholar Henri de Lubac, S.J., had published his famous book *Catholicisme* in 1938. De Lubac was also eventually able to publish books and articles defending and explaining Teilhard de Chardin's ideas and redeeming that man's name.

There were in fact a large group of notable Catholic theologians involved in this twentieth-century movement, which eventually came to be referred to as the *Nouvelle Théologie*, that is, the "New Theology." Four of its leaders were Jesuits — Pierre Teilhard de Chardin, Henri de Lubac, Karl Rahner, and Jean Daniélou — and Hans Urs von Balthasar started off as a Jesuit. Other prominent Catholic theologians and philosophers who were part of this group were Yves Congar, Hans Küng, Edward Schillebeeckx, Marie-Dominique Chenu, Louis Bouyer, Étienne Gilson, and Jean Mouroux. As can be seen, this list was like a Who's Who of major twentieth century Roman Catholic theologians.

So in the pages which follow we will be looking at Daniélou primarily as one example (and an especially clear and thoughtful representative) of a major strand in twentieth-century Catholic theology: the so-called *Nouvelle Théologie*, which had already begun before Daniélou finished his doctorate in 1942, and which continued after his death in 1974. This movement was especially influential within the radical wing of the Jesuit order, which was most definitely where Father Ed Dowling found his own theological identity.

It should be explained that in the United States and Britain, as we all know, full professors at universities like Harvard, Oxford, or Edinburgh are extremely important personages just by virtue of their academic positions. In the German university system, full professors have even greater relative power and prestige compared to scholars who bear such lesser titles as *außerordentlicher Professor*, *Privatdozent*, or *Dozent*. But in France, the small handful of scholars who hold the professorial chairs at the major universities are far more dominant in their fields than even the German professors, and have almost absolute power to make or break the careers of lesser academic figures and faculty at lesser institutions.

So when Daniélou — who was still quite a young man, not yet forty years old — was given one of the most important academic positions in France in 1944, it meant that some of the most powerful academic leaders within the French Catholic Church had decided that it was time to start making some radical changes in Catholic theology, and that they wanted to give him the power to carry that out. And eventually, in 1962, Pope John XXIII appointed Daniélou as a *peritus* (expert consultant) to the Second Vatican Council, where he able to use the principles of the *Nouvelle Théologie* to help create a new and different kind of Catholic Church.

> As a side note: I first became acquainted with the movement at that time, when Albert C. Outler, one of my earliest teachers and mentors, was made an official observer at the Second Vatican Council. Outler (who was a very competent patristics scholar in addition to his vast knowledge of modern theology) played a major role in interpreting the *Nouvelle Théologie* to the American Catholic bishops, who at the time the council began were for the most part totally unaware of the great debates going on in European Catholic theology. For many years, they had been used to automatically following orders from Rome without ever questioning the wisdom of those orders. My understanding is that Outler came to be respected by the American bishops as an honest broker who could explain both the new theology and the old-fashioned conservative Catholic position to which it was opposed, and what was really at stake in all of the debates.

Although the conservatives in the papal curia remained bitterly opposed to Daniélou, popular support among Catholic bishops all over the world as well as among the faculty at the major Catholic universities, eventually forced Rome to name him as a cardinal in 1969, and finally give him full honors as one of the most formative Catholic theologians of the twentieth century.

We are therefore looking at the Jesuit theologian Daniélou in this section because he was one of the most important standard bearers in the early twentieth century Catholic intellectual rebellion that began turning to patristic theology in order to escape what had become the intellectual prison of later medieval Catholic dogmatism.

And we are also looking at him because the patristic theologian upon whom he centered so much of his research — St. Gregory of Nyssa

(c. 335 - c. 395) — taught a kind of theology which fits smoothly into the world of modern science and Kantian and post-Kantian philosophy.

When reading St. Gregory, one often feels as though one were studying a modern existentialist philosopher like Sartre, Camus, Heidegger, or Paul Tillich. And St. Gregory also fits in smoothly with much of the underlying worldview of the New England Transcendentalists, Emmet Fox, Richard Maurice Bucke, and Aldous Huxley, which means that he also fits in smoothly with the ideas held by Bill Wilson and so many of the other early members of Alcoholics Anonymous.

It should also be said that Daniélou's theological program did not die with his passing, but was still alive and flourishing in the later 1970's and 1980's. My good friend Jean Laporte (1924-2006) was part of that continuing movement. A priest originally from the south of France, Jean was educated at the Institut Catholique (where Daniélou held his professorship) and later came over to the United States and became Professor of Patristic Theology at the University of Notre Dame in Indiana. Laporte wrote an important book on the great first-century Jewish philosopher Philo[313] (who had been a major influence on the next several centuries of Christian theology, including such major figures as Origen, St. Gregory of Nyssa, and the first Christian historian Eusebius of Caesarea).

Jean Laporte arranged for me to publish my own first book, which dealt principally with the early patristic theologian and historian Eusebius of Caesarea (c. 260-339), and served as my editor during the period when I was rewriting my initial manuscript. It first came out as Glenn F. Chesnut, *The First Christian Histories: Eusebius, Socrates, Sozomen, Theodoret, and Evagrius* (Paris: Editions Beauchesne, 1977). The book was good enough that I was subsequently given the opportunity, extremely rare in patristic studies, to come out with a second edition, revised and enlarged, which was published by Mercer University Press in Macon, Georgia in 1986, and is still in print to this day. Eusebius, who was a devoted follower of the third-century patristic theologian Origen, was one of the most important theological figures of the generation which came immediately before St. Gregory of Nyssa.[314]

In addition, during the latter 1970's, Jean Laporte and I acted as the American agents for Editions Beauchesne, which was the top

French theological press and one of the major publishing organs of the *Nouvelle Théologie* movement. We helped the press start publishing titles in English as well as French, so we could spread these new ideas more actively in American Catholicism as well.

So in fact, I would have been regarded at that time as being myself a rather minor member of the *Nouvelle Théologie* movement.

CHAPTER 17

Jean Daniélou S.J. and St. Gregory of Nyssa

At the center of Eastern Orthodox Christian theology lie the great Cappadocian theologians. The province of Cappadocia, where they lived and worked, lay in that part of what is now central Turkey where they raised the best horses in the ancient Mediterranean world, the noble steeds which made the Byzantine cavalry the most effective military force in that part of the world for many centuries. It was the ancient world's equivalent to Kentucky, a land in part of wealthy estates and fine ladies and gentlemen who spoke an old-fashioned and highly formal Greek, surrounded by hill country inhabited by notably rough and primitive hillbillies. Because of the latter, crude ethnic "Cappadocian jokes" were told throughout the Greek-speaking world.

The leader of the Cappadocian theologians was St. Basil the Great (329 or 330 - 379), who came from one of the wealthy landed families. Basil wrote the first detailed formal liturgy for the Christian mass, which is still used on special occasions even to this day by the Eastern Orthodox Church. He wrote the first detailed guidelines, the Rule of St. Basil, for Orthodox monasteries, which is still the basis of Orthodox monasticism to this day, and which was later adapted for western Catholic use by St. Benedict of Nursia in Italy in the sixth century in the form of the Benedictine Rule. Basil also ended the Arian controversy which was paralyzing the fourth-century Christian church, by negotiating peace between the elderly St. Athanasius (who had been defending the Nicene creed against all comers) and the majority of the eastern bishops who (like Eusebius of Caesarea) were demanding a doctrine of the Trinity with real metaphysical distinctions between the three members of the Trinity.[315]

Basil's best friend was a fellow Cappadocian known as St. Gregory of Nazianzus (c. 329 - 389 or 390), who was sometimes referred to in the ancient texts simply as "St. Gregory the Theologian" for his importance to Eastern Orthodox theology. The two of them went to the University of Athens c. 349 and spent six years studying there, at the place where the first Western European university, Plato's Academy, had been founded over seven centuries earlier. In a symbolic way, Basil and Gregory of Nazianzus wanted to "touch base" as it were with the roots of the western intellectual tradition. For six years, they could walk through the city and look up at the temple of Athena on the Acropolis, and walk the same streets, and see the same great buildings that Socrates, Plato, Aristotle, and the Stoic philosophers Zeno of Citium and Chrysippus, had once gazed upon. And to add an additional ironic note to the symbolism, one of Basil and Gregory's fellow students was the young man who would later reign from 361 to 363 A.D. as Julian the Apostate, the last pagan Roman emperor.

St. Gregory of Nyssa (c. 335 - c. 395) was a younger brother of St. Basil the Great. Although he was married (to a woman named Theosebia) he eventually became a bishop, which was permitted in the early Christian church. After Basil died at a relatively young age (he was only forty-nine or fifty), Gregory of Nyssa felt called upon to take Basil's ideas and work them out all the way, and write them up in a set of brilliant theological tracts.

The western intellectual heritage had originally been formulated in ancient Athens in an extremely static form — clinging to an eternal and never changing world, and fearful of all change, novelty and temporal process. Gregory of Nyssa used the new ideas he had been taught by the Christian theologians Origen and Basil, and the Jewish philosopher Philo, and created a different kind of world view: a transcendental process philosophy that would give the world of time equal honor with the world of eternity, and give full respect to human growth, changeability, and creativity. The goal of human life for Gregory of Nyssa was to continue growing spiritually forever, "from glory to glory," continuing from this life even into the next, world without end.

At the center of Gregory of Nyssa's new view of God and the universe lay two major biblical texts: one was the story of Moses' ascent up into the

Cloud of Darkness at the top of Mt. Sinai, and the other was a peculiar episode in the ancient Hebrew love poem called the Song of Songs.

Symbol and allegory: Now to understand how he made use of these two pieces of scripture, it must be explained that early Christians read most of the Bible primarily in symbolic fashion. They were not greatly interested in the literal meaning of the biblical text. They were in that sense totally different from modern Protestant Fundamentalist theologians. This was partly because the early Christians knew enough about history and modern science to know that parts of the Bible were simply wrong if read at the literal level. Educated people in the Roman empire knew that the world was not flat, earthquakes were not caused by a monster named Leviathan who lived down below the surface of the earth and lashed his tail, and so on. Eusebius of Caesarea (c. 260-339) had laid out detailed charts called the Eusebian Canons showing how the words and deeds of Jesus were recounted in different (and sometimes contradictory fashion) in the four gospels.

Early Christians during the first few centuries were also led to read most of the Bible as a set of metaphors, symbols, and exemplars because that was the way the New Testament authors back in the first century had used the Old Testament. And both the Jewish rabbis and in particular the great first century Jewish philosopher Philo had read the Old Testament in the same way.

But the most important reason why the Bible was read as symbolic and not literal by the fourth century patristic theologians (especially the Cappadocians and St. John Chrysostom) was because they recognized that a good deal of the Bible is poetry (including Psalms and Proverbs, and the books of the prophets), and that a large portion of the remainder is either written in the form of something much like prose-poems, or has to be read (when reading it as literature) in much the same way that we read poetry in modern times, or in the way that social anthropologists, scholars of comparative religion, and Jungian psychiatrists interpret ancient myths (whether they come from the ancient Greeks and Romans, Native American tribes, African tribal religion, the literature of India, or wherever else).

This way of reading the biblical text symbolically was referred to in the ancient and medieval world as "allegorical" interpretation.

A brief note on the English and Greek of Gregory's writings: In the following discussion, I am taking the English translation of Gregory of Nyssa's works from the Jesuit translation done by Herbert Musurillo S.J., which he carried out at the direction of Jean Daniélou S.J. in the book of selections from the writings of Gregory of Nyssa called *From Glory to Glory.*[316] For the Greek original, I am going to Migne *Patrologia Graeca* vols. 44-46,[317] which was the Greek text that Daniélou and Musurillo used.

Climbing up the mountain step by step: The first biblical story that Gregory of Nyssa focused on (Exodus 19:9, 19:16-19 and 20:1-17) was the one that told how Moses — after leading the Israelites out of their bondage in Egypt — came to Mount Sinai, where he climbed to the top and experienced at certain times the fiery light of God's glory, but spent most of his time immersed in cloud and smoke so dark and black inside that he could see nothing at all.[318] But Gregory was not interested in writing about the history of the thirteenth century B.C., and the literal meaning of this story. As a symbolic or metaphorical tale, "Moses" is simply myself, and the encounter with the strange mountain represents my attempt to find God. As Gregory explained:

> Moses' vision of God began with light (Exod. 19:18); afterwards God spoke to him in a cloud (Exod. 20.21). But when Moses rose higher and became more perfect, he saw God in the darkness (Exod. 24.15-18) .... Our initial withdrawal from wrong and erroneous ideas of God is a transition from darkness to light. Next comes a closer awareness of hidden things, and by this the soul is guided through sense phenomena to the world of the invisible. And this awareness is a kind of cloud, which overshadows all appearances, and slowly guides and accustoms the soul to look towards what is hidden. Next the soul ... goes on higher, and as she leaves below all that human nature can attain, she enters within the secret chamber of the divine knowledge, and here she is cut off on all sides by the divine darkness. Now she leaves outside all that can be grasped by sense or by reason, and the only thing left for her contemplation is the invisible and the incomprehensible. And here God is, as

the Scriptures tell us in connection with Moses: But Moses went to the dark cloud wherein God was (Exod. 20.21).[319]

Gregory's picture of the dark and frightening world of the atheist:
As Gregory continued to develop this story of the soul's search for God, he talked about the way that our attempts to find God could seem to plunge us instead into a frightening and horrifying atheism, symbolized by cloud and darkness. Light symbolized knowledge — we wanted to know who God was, and we wanted to be able to explain how he did things — so any failure to find God right away, at any point in the soul's quest for God, could throw us into what was called the "Cloud of Unknowing" or "Dark Night of the Soul."

Atheists try to create a safe and secure world for themselves, where everything is built upon a firm foundation of logic and scientific fact. This will give them a world which (they believe) they will be able to control: in such a world, any time we want such-and-such, all we have to do is apply our intelligence and our reasoning power. We will discover some technique, some trick, some gimmick which we can use where — by merely performing some simple act of ordinary will power — we will be able to obtain all that we want.

But external reality does not cooperate. Do matter how hard we reason and use our intellect, and no matter how hard we try, bad things continue to happen to us. The more we try to think and plan, the more we see illness, death, and destruction coming at us from every corner. Criminals menace us from one direction, while enemy armies threaten us with guns and bombs from the opposite side. Time and time again we wake in the night from terrifying nightmares, until the time comes when we wake to some horror which is not a nightmare, but is actually happening, and we find ourselves able to do nothing but scream as we fall helplessly into the abyss of total destruction.

The more we study the world philosophically, the more we come to realize that the external surface of reality is only a continually changing illusion. To Gregory of Nyssa, there were in fact no solid material objects which would rest there unchanging while the human mind thought whatever it wanted to. Using the basic Aristotelian philosophical doctrine of substance and accident, Gregory pointed out that weight or mass was an idea in my mind, length and width and position in space were ideas in my mind, color was an idea, and so on. As a result, every time I changed my inner mental framework, these ideas shifted and changed, and the whole appearance of the world around me changed. We never, even at best, understood more than a trifling amount about the things that were really there external to our minds. Gregory pointed out that the human mind could never exhaustively know everything about even something like a tiny little ant, for example, crawling across the ground in front of me. Gregory was just as emphatic about the limits of our human knowledge as Immanuel Kant, the eighteenth-century German philosopher who later on became the father of modern philosophical skepticism. And to Gregory of Nyssa, the more we thought about all this, the more the surface of everything around us would seem to ripple even more with unreality.

The twentieth-century French and German atheistic existentialists pushed this view of the subjectivity of reality even further, as Daniélou well knew. Martin Heidegger (1889-1976) for example warned us that even something apparently heavy and solid, like a hammer, is not really all that substantial. To an accomplished carpenter, that hammer represents a tool for which he knows many uses. It can be used to build the door frame for a beautiful house, or lay down a hardwood floor. To a young and completely inexperienced person who has just gone out in the world and is suddenly confronted with the task of hanging a picture on the wall, the hammer may instead appear as an awkward and frightening thing. A skilled sculptor will see it as a tool to be used for chiseling out a fine marble statue. A homicidal maniac in a rage and looking for something to bludgeon his victim to death will see the hammer through yet different eyes.

The atheistic existentialists who wrote in twentieth-century France and Germany were Jean Daniélou's contemporaries. As he was well aware, their description of the modern atheistic world view was almost identical to Gregory of Nyssa's account of what the human mind perceived and felt when it fell into the Dark Night of the Soul. But that of course was the reason why Daniélou believed that Gregory of Nyssa could speak so effectively to the modern world. Gregory was not living in some naïve, credulous, primitive world where the real theological problems would never even have entered his mind. When God became silent and dropped from view, and our minds fell into the existential abyss, the journey back to faith was just as hard in the fourth century as it was in the modern world.

The atheistic existentialist Albert Camus (1913-1960) was another of Daniélou's French contemporaries. As Camus explained in 1942 in *Le Mythe de Sisyphe* (The Myth of Sisyphus), a man with a sword is not absurd, and a machine gun nest is not absurd, but a man armed only with a sword charging a machine gun nest is totally absurd. We try to control everything around us and live forever, but this is an absurd task in a universe which is eventually going to kill us and destroy everything we have built. Five years later, in 1947, Camus wrote a novel called *The Plague* in which the central character, a French doctor, works night and day to try to help his patients in a small city in Algeria struck by bubonic plague, even though he knows that, no matter what he does, all of them will end up dying. But this is at heart no different from what any physician or medical researcher does anywhere else in the world: they spend their own lives trying to save the lives of other human beings who are all going to die eventually anyway. What is the point of even trying to scientifically figure out the nature of reality and control it? And yet, if I am to live at all, I must summon up the courage and fortitude to attack life bravely, in spite of the fact that my life will always ultimately go down in doom.

From Camus' work there arose a movement called the *Théâtre de l'Absurde*, that is, the Theater of the Absurd. If human existence has no logical, sane meaning or purpose, then ultimately all communication breaks down. Dialogue between human beings becomes increasingly irrational and illogical, until finally it collapses into silence. Some of the famous playwrights who wrote plays in this genre included Samuel Beckett, Eugène Ionesco, Jean Genet, Harold Pinter, Tom Stoppard, Friedrich Dürrenmatt, and Edward Albee. In the development of modern atheism, it is important to remember that, by the middle of the twentieth century, some of the most important atheistic authors had themselves admitted — no, more than that, were proclaiming enthusiastically — that atheism ultimately resulted in the collapse of all human value, including the ability to engage in rational discourse, and act logically.

The German existentialist philosopher Martin Heidegger (1889-1976) proclaimed that we had to act in spite of the ultimate futility of all our actions. In *Sein und Zeit* ("Being and Time," published in 1927) he said that the only way to live an authentic existence — that is, to put aside denial and pretense, and stop lying to ourselves — was to project our lives resolutely upon the ultimate necessity of our own deaths. Each human being had to invent his own morality — his own ethic — and the only requirement for a sane existence was that it be made up of a set of logically consistent moral imperatives. There were no external objective standards of moral right and wrong to which we could appeal, because there was no underlying moral ground to the universe. Heidegger himself was a Nazi who was an ardent supporter of the unspeakable cruelties of Adolf Hitler. There was no God or higher power which was going to come to save us. We had to fight on our own against the great existential anxieties: the anxiety of death and destruction, the anxiety of condemnation and abandonment, and the anxiety of emptiness and meaninglessness. Down underneath, at all times, lay only *das Nichts*, the existential abyss, a bottomless chasm of nonbeing and No-thing-ness.

The French existentialist Jean-Paul Sartre (1905-1980) was another of Daniélou's contemporaries. Sarte explained how ordinary people run away from seeing reality as it really is, falling into *mauvaise foi*, "bad faith," a kind of denial based on continual acts of self-deception. We and the other people around us lie to ourselves over and over, inventing an entire imaginary world and then insisting that this fantasy world is the real one. We lie to ourselves for so long that we finally come to believe our own lies. We invent an authoritarian and legalistic set of supposed moral "laws," rigid and inflexible and inhumane, and then force ourselves fearfully to live by all these laws. The result is that we fall into *ressentiment*, pent-up anger and rage inside, which is actually anger at having to follow all the silly rules. The way to escape the resentment is to simply realize that I am the one making myself follow those mechanical rules — those laws do not really come from God or angels or divine men — which means that all I have to do is quit following them, and go do what I actually want to do. But if I continue to drive myself to follow all these legalistic rules, my resentment will be displaced onto something else — usually innocent people around me who have the misfortune of being weaker or more marginal than me.

In reality, Sartre insisted, the physical world is indifferent to the human beings who dwell in it. There is no God out there, and the world is neither moral nor immoral. It is simply uncaring. There is no way I will be able to "figure it all out" and gain more than a partial and temporary control over my own life. When a person first starts to become aware of this, it produces a sense of *nausea*, Sartre said.[320] I am going to die, everyone else is going to die, there is no God, there is no higher moral order, there are no angels or higher powers which will save me, and whenever I look at it head-on, it makes me sick at my stomach.

Gregory of Nyssa and the view into the existential abyss: Gregory of Nyssa was as well aware as any modern atheistic existentialist of what you saw when you had to look at a world without God. It did in fact make your stomach queasy. You found yourself overcome with vertigo, staring down into a view of total nothingness that left you hopelessly disoriented, and clutching at yourself involuntarily in an attempt to keep yourself from falling forward headlong into its unending horror.

See for example one passage in particular in Gregory's *Commentary on Ecclesiastes*, in which he talks about the vision down into the primordial abyss:[321]

> Imagine a sheer, steep crag, of reddish appearance below, extending into eternity; on top there is this ridge which looks down over a projecting rim into a bottomless chasm. Now imagine what a person would probably experience if he put his foot on the edge of this ridge which overlooks the chasm and found no solid footing nor anything to hold onto. This is what I think the soul experiences when it goes beyond its footing in material things, in its quest for that which has no dimension and which exists for all eternity. For here there is nothing it can take hold of, neither place nor time, neither measure nor anything else; it does not allow our minds to approach. And thus the soul, slipping at every point from what cannot be grasped, becomes dizzy and perplexed.

And Gregory also used what was basically the same image in his *Commentary on the Beatitudes*, as he gave his interpretation of Matthew 5:8, "Blessed are the pure in heart, for they will see God."[322]

> Along the sea-coast you may often see mountains facing the sea, sheer and steep from top to bottom, while a projection at the top forms a cliff overhanging the depths. Now if someone suddenly looked down from such a cliff to the depths below he would become dizzy. So too is my soul seized with dizziness now as it is raised on high .... Blessed are the clean of heart, for they shall see God .... But no man hath seen God at any time .... This then is the steep and sheer rock that Moses taught us was inaccessible, so that our minds can in no way approach it.

That is, even if I obey the Bible and try to gain some kind of real knowledge of God, the first thing I discover is that, since "no person has seen God at any time," I do not at first view find the comfort of a God of love who will be my bulwark and defender, but instead find myself staring down into an existential abyss of total emptiness. It is impossible to "know" God in the way in which I know material things, so the first thing I encounter when I try to find God is "no thing," that is, nothing at all.

Two kinds of atheism: So we see here at the beginning, by looking at Gregory and the modern atheistic existentialists, two kinds of atheistic belief. One the one hand we have the atheists who live in a fantasy world of inauthentic existence and *mauvaise foi*, who cling to the delusion that human beings can totally control their lives and destinies simply by acting logically and rationally, and using the power of modern science to solve all our problems. After all, they point out, modern science gave us cures for both tuberculosis and leprosy. It enables us to replace faulty hip and knee joints, and do open-heart surgery. It allows us to fly through the air like birds, and even visit the surface of the moon. We have developed medications that enable people who are bipolar and even severe schizophrenics to live on their own, without having to be permanently institutionalized.

One day, according to this fantasy, we will be able to send a serial killer to a good psychiatrist, who will cure him in a few sessions by using some kind of clever talk therapy, or give him a pill which will instantly make his brain start functioning like a normal human being's once again. Science will one day fix it so that human beings will never have to die, and scientists will somehow manage to keep the sun from running out of nuclear fuel, so that we will all live forever. Even if a runaway asteroid the size of the moon is suddenly spotted hurtling straight at the earth, we will somehow manage to build enough space rockets and nuclear weapons to blast the asteroid into powder. Hollywood movie producers know how to play to these pseudo-scientific fantasies.

The second kind of atheism arises when these fantasies break down. In western Europe in the early and mid-twentieth century, as people were assailed by the collapse of national economies, the rise of Nazism and fascism, and the horrors of the First and Second World Wars, the delusion that modern science was going to solve everything began to collapse fairly quickly. And as western Europeans experienced sitting helplessly, for example, as the bombs fell on your city, and the hopeless feelings that overwhelmed you when you were, let us say, digging the body of your dead child out of the ruins of your own demolished home, the notion that modern medicine, psychiatry, chemistry, and technological advancements would be able to cure all our problems collapsed like a house of cards. And so this second kind of atheism — the type we see in the atheistic existentialists — proclaimed that we just had to accept that death and destruction would eventually annihilate everything, and face the world with "resolution" and "fortitude" and true existentialist "courage."

This existentialist variety of atheism speaks to a phase in human psychological development which usually reaches its peak around the age of thirteen for girls, and around the age of sixteen for boys. But some people get locked into that phase and stop developing emotionally and intellectually past that point, so that in my experience, one can even find a certain number of university students in the eighteen to twenty-two year old range who will respond enthusiastically when you assign them atheistic existentialist articles and novels in the readings for a course you are teaching. Anyone past the age of thirty, however, who is still attempting to live on the basis of that kind of adolescent existentialist bravado, needs serious help.

A third kind of atheism, the rejected lover: As we noted before, there were two major biblical texts which lay at the center of Gregory of Nyssa's view of God and the universe: one, as we have seen, was the story of Moses' ascent up into the Cloud of Darkness at the top of Mt. Sinai.

The other was a peculiar episode in the ancient Hebrew love poem called the Song of Songs. A young woman is in love with a young man, and he in turn seems to be passionately in love with her, and begs her to come run away with him, and become his beloved (Song of Songs 2:3, 2:8-10, and 2:14).

> As an apple tree among the trees of the wood,
>   so is my beloved among young men.
> With great delight I sat in his shadow,
>   and his fruit was sweet to my taste ....
> Behold, he comes, leaping upon the mountains,
>   bounding over the hills.
> My beloved is like a gazelle,
>   or a young stag.
> Behold, there he stands behind our wall,
>   gazing in at the windows,
>   looking through the lattice.
> My beloved speaks
>   and says to me:
> "Arise, my love, my fair one,
>   and come away ....
> O my dove, in the clefts of the rock,
>   in the covert of the cliff,
> let me see your face,
>   let me hear your voice,
> for your voice is sweet,
>   and your face is comely."

But then everything plunges into a terrifying nightmare. Evening arrives, it grows dark, and the young woman undresses (that is, renders herself completely naked and vulnerable), and then falls asleep on her bed. She hears someone knocking at her window, and innocently and naively unlocks her door and goes out into the darkened city to throw herself into the arms of her lover. But he is not there. He seems to have completely rejected and abandoned her, for no reason she can understand. Had she not given herself totally to him? And then the real horror begins, as the policemen who walk the city streets at night — watchmen who have sworn oaths to protect the helpless and the innocent — fall upon her, and begin beating her savagely as though she were the criminal instead of the victim, ripping away the coat she had thrown around her shoulders, as she lies there bleeding, sobbing, and stripped naked. The poem tells the story simply and bleakly (Song of Songs 5:2-8).

> I slept, but my heart was awake.
>> Hark! my beloved is knocking.
> "Open to me, my sister, my love,
>> my dove, my perfect one;
> for my head is wet with dew,
>> my locks with the drops of the night."
> I had put off my garment,
>> how could I put it on?
> I had bathed my feet,
>> how could I soil them?
> My beloved put his hand to the latch,
>> and my heart was thrilled within me.
> I arose to open to my beloved,
>> and my hands dripped with myrrh,
> my fingers with liquid myrrh,
>> upon the handles of the bolt.
> I opened to my beloved,
>> but my beloved had turned and gone.
> My soul failed me when he spoke.
>> I sought him, but found him not;
>> I called him, but he gave no answer.
> The watchmen found me,
>> as they went about in the city;
> they beat me, they wounded me,
>> they took away my mantle,
>> those watchmen of the walls.

I adjure you, O daughters of Jerusalem,
if you find my beloved,
that you tell him I am sick with love.

If I may give my own interpretation, this is the story of people who, when they were children, loved God and believed that God loved them back. But then something terrible happened. It could have been any of a variety of things. Maybe their mother or father died. Perhaps a family member began sexually abusing them — or worse, the abuser was a religious official like a priest or Sunday School teacher. Perhaps they went off to war and both saw and participated in horrifying things in some far-off place like Korea, Vietnam, or Iraq — or they were innocent civilians in some place like Korea, Vietnam, or Iraq who were shot and bombed and torched with napalm simply because they happened to be standing in the wrong place at the wrong time.

Their minds were left permanently seared by these memories. And it was easy for something inside them to ask: where was God in all this? And worse yet, if they dared to question out loud what was happening to them, all too often the watchmen who were supposed to be protecting them — their parents, their school teachers, their pastors, the police — would suddenly start accusing them and attacking them, and calling them liars and trouble-makers, and enemies of true religion.

Atheists of this third kind are bitterly angry at God. Down underneath, it is not that they really disbelieve in God's existence, but are instead filled with rage at a God whom they once loved, but who now seems to have disappeared and totally abandoned them, just when they needed him most.

A synergistic doctrine of grace: How can atheists of any kind get out of the dead end trap in which they have been ensnared? It tends to be a self-perpetuating state of mind in which people, left to the thoughts inside their own heads, will spend the rest of their lives dodging and denying, and refusing to ask any of the specific questions that would free them from the trap. Or they will turn away and refuse to accept the only kinds of outside help which can heal them of their wounds.

The only way out of the dead end of atheism is through the power of divine grace.[323] But we must be careful here, because Gregory of

Nyssa never says that we can just sit back passively and wait for God to do all the work. God and the human being have to "work together" or "co-operate" in working out that person's salvation. The word for "work" in classical Greek was *ergon*, so the Greek word *synergia* meant "working together," from which we get the English word synergism. Gregory of Nyssa taught what is called a synergistic doctrine of grace: we need the help of God's grace, but human beings have free will, so we not only have to freely choose to accept that grace and make use of it, but we must use every ounce of our will power and courage and commitment to carry out our share of the work.

In fact most of the Greek-speaking patristic theologians in the eastern end of the Mediterranean believed in free will and a synergistic doctrine of grace. It was not just Gregory of Nyssa, and it went all the way back to the second-century theologians who began writing at the close of the New Testament period: people like St. Justin Martyr, St. Irenaeus, and Clement of Alexandria.

In the western, Latin-speaking half of the Mediterranean world, the situation was however more complicated. Two quite different teachings eventually arose, first appearing just a little after Gregory of Nyssa's time. One of these alternate theories came from Pelagius, a Celtic Christian monk from the British isles (or possibly Brittany on the other side of the English Channel), who came to Rome around 380 A.D. and began teaching that sinful and destructive behaviors were just bad habits, and that to conquer them, all we needed to do was to use our free will, and start thinking about the problem logically and rationally, and using more will power.

The figure who then arose to combat Pelagius was a man named Augustine (354-430), who was the greatest and most influential of all the early Latin-speaking patristic theologians. Before being converted to Christianity, Augustine had been a member of a Gnostic cult called Manichaeism, which may have affected his response to Pelagius. The Gnostic movement (or at least some parts of it) had been the first religious group in the ancient world to develop a doctrine of predestination. And Augustine had read deeply in ancient Stoic philosophy and was strongly affected by their fatalism. Augustine said bluntly in his *City of God* that he agreed exactly with what the Roman

Stoic philosopher Seneca had said about the way that *Fatum* (Fate) completely controlled all human events. Augustine said that the only reason he did not use that word, was because in the popular mind the word fate was all too frequently linked with astrology, which he thought was superstitious nonsense.

So instead of using the word Fate, Augustine and his followers used the word predestination, and bequeathed it to the following centuries. John Calvin picked up the idea from Augustine (and was equally strongly influenced by Stoic fatalism, since Calvin's first published work was a commentary on one of the writings of the Stoic philosopher Seneca). Calvin's followers then carried the idea to various parts of Europe, including Switzerland, southern Germany, the Netherlands, Scotland, and parts of England. And from there the doctrine of predestination was transmitted across the Atlantic to colonial New England, to the Dutch Reformed church of colonial New York, and to all the English-speaking American colonies where Calvinist groups like the Baptists and Presbyterians became established.

The important thing to remember here is that St. Gregory of Nyssa was neither a Pelagian nor an Augustinian: he taught instead *a synergistic doctrine of grace.* Had either Pelagius or Augustine appeared in central Cappadocia teaching their doctrines, Gregory would have rejected both of those positions. You could not save yourself by free will and will power alone — you needed some kind of saving contact with the transcendent realm. But you also could not just sit there passively and wait for some God or angel to come down and save you, without you having to do any work. You had to summon up all your courage and will power, and begin the process of working out your salvation by identifying all of your sins and character defects, and then using meditation and disciplined effort to start purifying your life.

The first shining of the light: the knowledge of God in the mirror of the soul.[324] In order to follow in the spirit of Gregory's synergistic doctrine of grace, I have to begin by cleaning up my life, insofar as I can, by the use of my own effort and will power. I can make myself act toward another human being, in my outward actions, in the way that I would act if I genuinely loved and honored and respected that person. I can use my will power to hold my tongue and not speak words of insult or anger. I can make myself act as though I were generous and compassionate, even if these are not my real feelings.

But then the power of God's grace gradually starts working in my life, acting *in cooperation* with me, in more and more amazing fashion. Whereas at first it took all my will power to avoid screaming and yelling at other people when they made me angry, now I find myself speaking in calm and measured fashion without even having to work at it. Things that used to make me furiously angry, now hardly bother me at all.

And then — and this is what is truly extraordinary — I find this new spirit spilling over into other areas of my life, without me having to make any great effort at it. To give a modern example, when alcoholics come into Alcoholics Anonymous and begin to use their will power to show more control over their anger and their speech, and begin making themselves tell the truth at all times, and begin trying to show a little kindness and compassion to other people — to their surprise, from the moment they honestly and sincerely commit themselves to doing all of this for God (which is what the Third Step is in the Twelve Step program) — they find that their irresistible compulsion to drink has simply disappeared. Drug addicts have the same kind of experience in Narcotics Anonymous. People who join Gamblers Anonymous lose their compulsion to gamble, and so on.

And people who undergo this experience find that it is as though a great light begins to shine on their lives, metaphorically speaking. The future no longer "looks dark" but full of hope. The world around them becomes increasingly filled with things that fill them with joy instead of dragging them down into a dark and miserable sadness. Their own motives increasingly start to make sense to them, and other people's reactions start to make a whole lot more sense as well. Instead of feeling like they are stumbling in the dark all the time, everything going on around them starts making more and more sense. Here at the beginning of the true spiritual life, this is the first way that God's light shines on us and in us.

This "knowledge of God in the mirror of the soul" is a real knowledge of God, that slowly grows greater and greater over time. The more we turn our will and our lives over to the care of God, the more loving and forgiving and generous we become. That is what we mean when we say that God is loving and forgiving and generous — we mean that God is a power whose action is to produce love, forgiveness, and generosity. Likewise, the more we devote ourselves to regular prayer and meditation, the more we find love and joy and peace filling our lives. Therefore we similarly say that God is that power whose action is to produce love, joy, and peace when we allow it to totally permeate our souls.

And as Daniélou puts it, "The knowledge of God in the mirror of the soul is truly knowledge of God and not of the soul," even though "it is not a direct knowledge, inasmuch as God's *presence* is known by and through His *activity* in the soul" [my italics]. And it serves as a light shining out (even if only metaphorically speaking) where once we had seen only darkness. As Daniélou explains it, "in contrast with the darkness of sin, the supernatural life is an illumination." As we work to produce "the purification of the soul ... the restoration of the image of God" takes place within our souls, and our lives and minds are filled with light.[325]

Process theology and panentheism: It is important to remember that Gregory of Nyssa distinguishes at all times between God's eternal essence (*ousia*) and his activities or operations or energies (or however you wish to translate the Greek word *energeia*) which act in time. So Gregory of Nyssa taught what is called in our world today a kind of *process theology* or *process philosophy*. That is one of the things which makes his theology seem so amazingly *modern*, if we may use that word. It often feels as though he was living, not in the fourth century, but in the latter twentieth or early twenty-first century, and speaking directly to us, right where we are today. It is similar in many ways to such modern philosophical doctrines as those taught by Alfred North Whitehead and Charles Hartshorne, and some of the ideas laid out in my own work on *God and Spirituality*.[326]

Creation is one of God's energies, so the created world is contained within God, and is, in a certain fashion, part of God. But the created world is not part of God's eternal essence, so if I start saying that the maple tree in front of my house "is God" or the St. Joseph river quietly flowing a short walk away "is God," this is a misuse of language, or at least apt to be dangerously misleading in many contexts.

What Gregory teaches is a kind of panentheism (to use modern philosophical terminology), a word which means "all in God." That is, God in some sense *contains* everything else in the universe within his being. It is a very biblical concept, stated explicitly in the famous passage in Acts 17:28 where the Apostle Paul, when speaking about God to the Greek philosophers gathered in the Areopagus in Athens, says simply "In him we live and move and have our being."

The modern process philosopher Charles Hartshorne likewise said that we had to include both panentheism and temporal process within our doctrine of God, if we were going to be able to (1) talk about a God who knew individual human beings as individuals, and (2) talk about human beings exercising free will.

Grace likewise is one of God's energies, so the new shape given to my soul by God's grace working within it and taking up residence within it, puts a little spark of the divine within my soul, which then "shines out" (so to speak) and enlightens my soul. And if I let it, it will enlighten those around me too. But this does not mean that my humanity becomes a direct and indistinguishable part of the eternal divine essence.

Perhaps we could put this in modern terms by viewing God's energies as operating like powerful electric currents. If I plug an electrical device into an electric outlet, the current can flow in and through the device and make it work, whatever it is: a table lamp, a vacuum cleaner, a pair of electric clippers, a computer, or an x-ray machine. Likewise, 13.7 billion years ago all the energy in the created universe exploded out of the Big Bang, erupting into existence out of an abyss of apparent absolute nothingness. God is whatever it was that existed before the Big Bang. The energies that make the physical universe operate, all derive their energy from that primordial event. And some physicists believe that even now, in what is apparently completely empty space, matter and energy can still spontaneously erupt into being out of that primordial ground of being.

If I am pursuing the spiritual life in an effective manner, God's grace likewise will be flowing through me like an electric current, empowering me with that higher octave of energy called Eros or divine Love. If I concentrate, I can sometimes actually feel it flowing through me, at least in the sense of feeling its *power* flowing through me. And sometimes it can feel like a river of divine light flowing through me, and turning my soul into a Man of Light or Woman of Light. This is not ordinary physical light, of course, but sometimes it can be apprehended as something much stronger than a merely a metaphor. Sometimes, when other human beings encounter a person who is extremely advanced in the spiritual life, they too, even from the outside, can feel or sense something which they can only describe as light shining from the person.

Divinization as the goal of the spiritual life: This was what was meant by the patristic theologians when they spoke of divinization or deification (*theôsis*) as the goal of the spiritual life. It was the divine energy (*energeia*) which filled my soul, not the divine essence (*ousia*) — my soul would always retain an identity separate from that of God's ownmost being — but as my soul made progress in the spiritual life, it would become more and more involved in a real participation in the divine life, where I was *part of God* at the level of God's temporal energies, that is, God's involvement in the realms of process, change, and novelty (both above and below).[327]

CHAPTER 18

Gregory of Nyssa: the Transcendent Realm

The spiritual senses: Sometimes we become aware of the operation of God's grace within our souls and minds only gradually, by pragmatic external observation: when we look at the external shape of our lives, we slowly come to discover that the way we act and behave has undergone enormous changes. But sometimes these changes are so striking, that we find ourselves trying to describe them by using metaphors and similes drawn from the world of physical sensation: "I *saw* the light." "I suddenly *heard* what the great spiritual teacher had been trying to tell me." "I *felt* as though my life had turned upside down."

And sometimes the impact of God's grace on us is even more vivid and compelling, so much so that we feel ourselves experiencing things that are almost like sense perceptions, even though we know that they are not physical perceptions received by the eyes, ears, and other sense organs in the ordinary physical way.

It was the great third-century Christian theologian Origen who first began trying to give an adequate philosophical analysis of the "spiritual senses," if we may call them that. In the fourth century, Gregory of Nyssa (who regarded himself as Origen's disciple) carried this discussion even further. St. Bonaventure in the thirteenth century and (in particular) Jonathan Edwards in the eighteenth century made significant contributions.

The twentieth-century Swiss theologian Hans Urs von Balthasar, who received his early training from the Jesuits, has written about this problem in the modern era. How could so many people over the past three thousand years talk about being able to see, hear, touch, smell and taste God? What do people who are pursuing the spiritual life mean

226

when they speak of seeing God with the "eyes of the mind" or "the eyes of the inner man" or "inner woman"? What does Jesus mean in the Sermon on the Mount when he says that the pure in heart will be able to "see God"? What do people mean by developing "internal ears which are purified" so they can learn how to hear with their "spiritual ears"? What do they mean when they speak of "the good odor of righteousness and the bad odor of sins" or talk about "breathing Christ in everything"?[328]

The feeling of presence (parousia) in the luminous darkness: Gregory of Nyssa points out one way in which the spiritual senses come into play, which is very subtle at one level, but nevertheless gives an enormous confidence and security to the person involved. It is a spiritual version of a kind of physical awareness which we can sometimes have in the material world. In its everyday physical and material form, I might (for example) be living in a house which I usually share with another person. But then the other person goes away on a trip, and when I wake the next morning, I am struck by how "empty" the house "feels." Then the other occupant returns, and I wake the next morning and somehow instantly feel, with relief, the other person's *presence* in the house once again. The Greek word for presence, *parousia*, combines the word *ousia* (the participle of the verb to be) with the preposition *para*, which means beside or alongside of.

Gregory of Nyssa discusses this in his commentary on Song of Songs 3:1, where (in the biblical story) the young woman who represents the human soul finds herself

> ... encompassed by a divine night, during which her Spouse approaches but does not reveal Himself. But how can that which is invisible reveal itself in the night? By the fact that He gives the soul some sense [*aisthêsin*] of His presence [*tês parousias*], even while He eludes her clear apprehension, concealed as He is by the invisibility of His nature.[329]

So atheists and people who are leading an advanced spiritual life both see darkness when they stare down into the divine abyss, but for the two groups of people, it is a different kind of darkness. Atheists look at the material universe around them and apprehend — lying underneath it and looming behind it — what feels to them like an abyss of total darkness and complete nothingness, an empty void containing nothing they could grasp intellectually or perceive with the five physical senses, a bottomless pit holding nothing they could clutch in order to keep from falling. People who are leading an advanced spiritual life, on the other hand, look around them and also see darkness and night lying beneath the surface of the world — because no matter how spiritual people become, God still surpasses all human knowledge — but Gregory of Nyssa says that the darkness which they perceive is a kind of "luminous darkness." That is an odd sort of phrase, but any attempt to describe our experience of a God who is in fact beyond all normal human theory and sense perception, must of necessity involve language which at times has a very paradoxical quality.

So for example, Gregory of Nyssa used this phrase "luminous darkness" at one place in his *Life of Moses*, as he was drawing parallels between Moses' ascent into the vision of God at the top of Mount Sinai, and the evangelist John's description of God's light shining out of the darkness in the prologue (1:5) to the gospel of John. As Gregory asked:

> What now is the meaning of Moses' entry into the darkness and of the vision of God that he enjoyed in it?... as the soul makes progress ... the more it approaches this vision, [by] so much the more does it see that the divine nature is invisible. It thus leaves all surface appearances [*pan to phainomenon*], not only those that can be grasped by the senses [*hê aisthêsis*] but also those which the mind itself [*hê dianoia*] seems to see [*dokei blepein*], and it keeps on going deeper until by the operation of the spirit it penetrates the invisible and incomprehensible, and it is there that it sees God [*ton Theon idê*]. The true vision and the true knowledge [*hê alêthês ... eidêsis*] of what we seek consists precisely in not seeing, in an awareness that our goal transcends all knowledge and is everywhere cut off from us by the darkness of incomprehensibility. Thus that profound evangelist, John, who penetrated into this luminous darkness [*en tô; lamprô; gnophô; toutô;*], tells us that no man hath seen God at any time.[330]

The gospel of John begins by talking about the initial creation of the universe, which occurred in what we would today call the Big Bang, some 13.7 billion years ago. The physical world exploded into being out of what appeared to be an abyss of nothingness. But it could not have been nothing at all, or there would have been nothing to produce the Big Bang. In particular, this abyss of apparent nothingness must have had, hidden within it, what John called the power of the *Logos*. This Greek technical term referred to the archetypal act of insight in which new scientific discoveries and paradigm changes, or a new awareness of profound moral and ethical imperatives, or other new ways of looking at all the beings in the world around us, suddenly sprang into existence in our minds and changed the way we thought about the world in a sort of massive quantum leap.

Whenever the Logos acts on our minds, it gives us new insights into the *logical structure* of the universe. That is why we can study the universe scientifically — it is logically and rationally constructed down to its core. The names of many of our sciences still contain the word *logos*: geology, biology, psychology, and so on. It was the ancient Greeks, we must remember, who provided us the foundation for the modern scientific study of the world.

And the *logos* was the sudden illuminating power of creative insight and new discovery, not just within the natural sciences, but within all of our human cognitive processes, including the development of our moral goals and principles, and our reasons for living. The *logos* was the power that stripped away our denial systems, and all our old alibis and excuses, and confronted us with the Truth. It was for this reason that the *logos* was one of the principal vehicles through which God communicated to us: the way God "spoke his word" in our ears, so to speak, and "shone his light" on the solutions to our problems.

So the divine ground of being was an abyss of darkness — that was true — but as the Gospel of John said (1:1-13), it also shone with light:

> In the beginning was the Logos, and the Logos was with God, and the Logos was God. He was in the beginning with God. All things came into being through him, and without him not one thing came into being. What has come into

being in him was life, and the life was the light of all people. The light shines in the darkness, and the darkness has not overcome it …. The true light, which enlightens every man and woman, was coming into the world …. [and] to all who received him … he gave power to become children of God, who were born, not of blood or of the will of the flesh or of the will of man, but of God.

Atheists see a pit of darkness threatening to swallow them up forever. Moses and John saw instead a *luminous darkness*, so to speak, something that appeared to be dark, but was filled with some kind of *living presence*, from which acts of *grace* emerged and transformed their souls and minds over and over again — consoling them, comforting them, loving them, healing them, teaching them, and filling their souls with a wonderful kind of *divine light*.

Ekstasis and the two-story universe: the phenomenal realm and the transcendent realm. We live in a universe with two levels. There is a lower story, so to speak, the phenomenal world, which exists within the three spatial dimensions of Euclidean geometry — height, width, and depth — and moves steadily through chronological time as the clock ticks each moment away. This phenomenal world follows the laws of mathematical science and can for that reason be partly predicted and mechanically controlled.

But there is a higher dimension of reality: in the A.A. Big Book, Bill Wilson spoke of being "catapulted into what I like to call the fourth dimension of existence" (p. 8) and testified that, within the A.A. community, "we have found much of heaven and we have been rocketed into a fourth dimension of existence of which we had not even dreamed" (p. 25).

This is the transcendent realm to which the philosopher Kant pointed in his *Critique of Pure Reason*, written in 1781 when the rise of modern science was first beginning. The transcendent realm included that noumenal reality (as he called it) which lay outside the box of space and time in which our ordinary worldly thoughts were usually imprisoned. *The transcendent dimension was a realm in which human beings had free will and could make genuine moral judgments.* Many modern western atheists tend to forget this — that Kant wrote his great analysis of scientific reasoning in order to defend human free will (and hence human moral responsibility) — but the fact is, that the *Critique of Pure Reason*, the first great description of the modern scientific world view, carefully explained how and why it was only the lower level of reality (the phenomenal level) which had to mechanically obey the laws of science. And Kant's arguments on this topic are still basically correct even today.

Gregory of Nyssa, back in the fourth century, used Neo-Platonic philosophical language to make the same point. The lower level of reality was the "phenomenal" level (he and Kant used the same word), and the higher level of reality was the world in which the spiritual life had to be lived. And human beings likewise were two-story creatures. At a lower level, our bodies and brains lived a world of flesh and blood and bone and animalistic reflexes. But at a higher level, human consciousness was a creature of the luminous darkness, a floating center of luminous awareness which moved like a being made of transcendent light through the endless spaces of the infinite and eternal divine world.

As Daniélou explained, when people made progress in the spiritual life, they eventually began to realize that the apparent darkness of the transcendent realm did not mean that there was nothing there. Part of the problem was, what was there was so grand and glorious that it overwhelmed the mind's capacity to receive and process information. As human consciousness moves further and further into the darkness and obscurity, Daniélou said,

> ... the soul experiences the transcendence of the divine nature, that infinite distance by which God surpasses all creation. Thus the soul finds itself as it were elevated above all created things and at the same time lost in an infinite darkness wherein it loses its contact with things, though it is aware of God despite the total incapacity of its knowledge.[331]

In the mystical experience of the divine darkness, the human consciousness enters a state of *ekstasis*, which literally means to "stand outside oneself" or go out of oneself. As Daniélou explains, this ecstatic state is represented symbolically and metaphorically by Gregory of

231

Nyssa in a variety of ways: as falling madly in love or being "wounded by love" (we remember Bernini's famous statue of St. Teresa in Ecstasy at the church of Santa Maria della Vittoria in Rome), as a kind of "sober inebriation," as a feeling of inner dizziness and loss of balance, or even as a kind of *mania* or madness (the word used in classical Greek times to describe the state into which the priestess of Apollo at the Delphic oracle used to fall when she was predicting the future).[332]

As the human consciousness learns how to meditate in a way which will block out the world of sense perceptions, and "turn off" the inner dialogue which usually fills our minds with a continual flow of thoughts and arguments within ourselves, we can discover how to encounter the divine abyss in a way which Daniélou describes paradoxically as a state of "watchful sleep" in which "the soul is so carried away by God's reality and so absorbed in her contemplation of Him that she loses consciousness of everything else."[333]

The great Alcoholics Anonymous meditational book *Twenty-Four Hours a Day*, written in 1948 by the A.A. movement's second most published author, Richmond Walker, spoke of the mind's descent into the divine abyss as the entry into the Divine Silence (he probably learned this technique from the teachings of the great Hindu philosophers,[334] but it represented the same kind of meditational experience which was cultivated by the Christian theologians and monastics of the early Greek patristic tradition, as well as the later Greek Orthodox hesychastic tradition).

Daniélou, as noted above, describes this ecstatic state at one point as a kind of "watchful sleep," but Gregory of Nyssa himself used an almost diametrically opposite metaphor when he described this experience of resting in the divine silence as falling into a kind of "divine wakefulness," which I think is a much better choice of words. In Gregory's *Commentary on the Song of Songs*, for example, he talked about how the soul could block off the world of sense perception, "enjoying alone the contemplation of Being [*tê̦ theôria̦ tou ontos*]." As it does this, the soul "receives the vision of God [*tou Theou tên emphaneian*] in a divine wakefulness [*dia tês theias egrêgorseôs*] with pure and naked intuition [*gymnê̦ te kai kathara̦ tê̦ dianoia̦*]."[335]

The word *ekstasis* is used seven times in the New Testament. In four of these passages (Luke 5:26, Mark 5:42 and 16:8, and Acts 3:10), it refers to a state of awe, astonishment, wonder, and amazement bordering on fear (*phobos*). In the modern period, Rudolf Otto wrote about this in his book *The Idea of the Holy*, which still remains an enduring masterpiece, both in the field of theology and in the fields of social anthropology and comparative religion.[336] When our minds look into the divine abyss, spiritual enlightenment eventually teaches us to see it not as the totally negative absence of all things and the destruction of all things, but as an infinite well of unbelievable power and might and glory. What kind of incredible energy must be contained in the ground of being, for an entire universe of stars and galaxies to simply burst forth out of it in the Big Bang! It remains scary, but now we also see it with awe as the archetypal fount of all that is sacred and holy.

In Acts 10:10, 11:5, and 22:17, the word *ekstasis* was used to refer to the special state of consciousness into which people rose when they were seeing visions and hearing heavenly voices. The transcendent dimension of the human soul is woven from the same "fiber," so to speak, as the rest of the transcendent level of reality, and can move in it, and experience things going on in that realm, while the mind continuously "translates" what it is experiencing in that mysterious region into more familiar this-worldly physical images and sounds. Some relatively modern examples would include St. Ignatius Loyola's vision of the Virgin Mary and the infant Jesus at the shrine of Our Lady of Montserrat in March 1522, Richard Maurice Bucke's vision in 1873 of being "wrapped around as it were by a flame-colored cloud," Bill Wilson's experience of the great white light at Towns Hospital on December 14, 1934, and all the accounts that have been recorded in recent years by people who had Near Death Experiences, such as Dr. Eben Alexander's vivid description in *Proof of Heaven: A Neurosurgeon's Journey into the Afterlife.*[337]

What is the human consciousness actually experiencing? As noted, as long as we still maintain some kind of connection to our present physical bodies, apparently the only way we can "think" these experiences is by translating them into sights and sounds and other physical experiences of the sort which we have in the material world. So we need to think of these physical sensations, no matter how vivid and realistic, as functioning like symbols or metaphors or religious icons (that is, like the painted images of the saints displayed on the walls of an Eastern Orthodox church). As Kant explained in his *Critique of Pure Reason*, the human mind (at least in this present world) cannot even imagine a reality which is not composed of three-dimensional material phenomena located in Euclidean space and time.

The transcendental realm as the world of the archetypes: On the one hand we must never forget that even those who are very advanced in the spiritual life still apprehend — at least at one level, some of the time — the same abyss of nothingness which causes atheists like Sartre to feel sick at their stomachs with dread and horror. Nevertheless, many valuable things are secretly contained within that darkness, including the archetypes which enable our minds to make sense of the phenomenal world.

The ancient Greek philosopher Plato called them the Ideas. Gregory of Nyssa in the fourth century and Carl Jung in the twentieth century called them the archetypes.

In the stories, myths, and works of art found in religions all over the world (as Jungian theory explains) we can see over and over again the depiction of certain standard archetypes: the Child, the Hero, the Great Mother, the Sage (the Wise Old Man or Wise Old Woman), the Damsel in Distress, the Trickster, the Evil Demon, the Mentor, and the Warrior. From 1945 to 1949, Bill Wilson was seeing a Jungian psychotherapist named Dr. Frances Weeks once a week, and presumably learning something about the role these archetypes can play in the mind's dreams and subconscious imaging.

Joseph Campbell was an especially influential twentieth-century author who used the Jungian understanding of the archetypes to write about religions and mythologies from all periods of history and all parts of the globe. Campbell's first major book, *The Hero with a Thousand Faces* (1949), came out while Father Dowling and Bill Wilson were working closely together (this was shortly before Bill began writing the *Twelve Steps and Twelve Traditions*). Campbell's later four-volume work entitled *The Masks of God* (1962-1968) came out after Dowling's death but while Bill W. was still around.

The first century Jewish philosopher Philo — one of the major influences on Gregory of Nyssa — wrote biographies of some of the major biblical figures in which the central character was treated as an archetypal figure, representing a particular virtue. So for example, Philo's lives of Abraham, Isaac, and Jacob portrayed the three Paths to Perfection, and his life of Joseph described the archetypal image of the Political Man (the good person put in a position of political power). Moses was portrayed by Philo as the archetypal image of the ideal King, who also had to embody the religious functions of the Priest in order to intercede for his people before God, and in addition, also had to represent the archetype of the Prophet in order to receive divine guidance in his decisions.[338]

Around a century later, the Middle Platonic author Plutarch (c. 46-120 A.D.), in his *Parallel Lives*, carried out the same kind of project at even greater length in a set of over two dozen biographies. Each pair of biographies (the life of one famous Greek paralleled with the life of one famous Roman) was intended to present the archetype of a specific virtue or vice.[339]

Gregory of Nyssa copied Philo by portraying Moses as an archetypal figure. But Gregory treated Moses as a very different type of archetype, that of the good human being climbing further and further into the Divine Darkness in the quest to find God. He did this so that we would be able to use Moses as a model for the highest part of our own spiritual lives.

The archetypes of the Good and the Beautiful: But the two archetypes with which we are most concerned here are the archetypes of the Good Itself and the Beautiful Itself. Plato called them the *Ideas* or *Forms* of the Good and the Beautiful.

It should be remembered, in this regard, that the most important of the Platonic Ideas functioned in ways similar to the twelve Kantian categories of the pure understanding,[340] particularly as Kant was reinterpreted by Jakob Friedrich Fries (1773-1843) and then Rudolf Otto (1869-1937). The latter figure (Rudolf Otto) argued that the Good, the Beautiful, and the Holy represented three aspects of an additional category — one which Kant had failed to include in his list — which could be schematized in three different ways, depending on context. When speaking and thinking about ethics and morality, we schematized this category as the Good; in making aesthetic judgments, we schematized this category as the Beautiful; and in the sphere of religion and spirituality we schematized this category as the Holy or Sacred.[341]

As Carl Jung explained, we cannot perceive or describe an archetype as a specific sense object in itself. The archetype of God, for example, which in Jungian theory is the archetype of the Self viewed from the outside, can be represented in art as a mandala composed of circles or squares. But even then the mandala itself is also an archetypal concept, so there is no one mandala which is the "correct" form — any mandala which can be drawn on paper or carved into stone is only one of many possible representations of the mandala archetype which lies behind it. So in this regard, the underlying archetype of the Self (or God or the Whole) is sometimes portrayed as a quarternity, that is, a fourfold mandala depicting the four elements of the alchemists and astrologers (Earth, Air, Fire and Water), or the four humors of ancient medical theory (Blood, Phlegm, Yellow Bile and Black Bile), or in the form of some other fourfold arrangement. But mandalas can also be drawn in numerous other kinds of ways. In Christianity, for example, all of the various kinds of crosses are mandalas, as also are the kind of stained glass windows called rose windows, halos around saints' heads, and Jesus's crown of thorns. A Jewish Star of David is a mandala, and so are a Hindu depiction of a lotus blossom, the circular arrangement of the pillars at Stonehenge, the A.A. symbol of the Circle and Triangle, and the famous Aztec Calendar Stone

The same underlying archetype can therefore be portrayed in thousands of different ways. So we cannot actually define or visualize either the archetypal idea of the Good or the archetypal idea of the Beautiful as a specific, individual item. An archetype is (as Gregory of Nyssa said) in a certain manner *atypôtos*, "unformed, shapeless," because the archetype is that preexisting reality which stamps a particular kind of shape in all sorts of different ways on *other things*. But we can learn to *understand* a particular archetype better by looking at its various instantiations, and Gregory of Nyssa described one way that we could do this, in a reference to the early Hebrew patriarch Abraham:

> Abraham surpassed in understanding his native wisdom, that is, the philosophy of Mesopotamia, which rested merely on

the surface appearance of phenomena [*tôn phainomenôn*]; he went far beyond that which can be perceived by the senses [*dia tês aisthêseôs*], and from the beauty that he saw around him and from the harmony of the heavenly phenomena he gained a yearning to gaze upon the archetypal Beauty [*to atypôton kallos idein*]. So too, all the other qualities which are attributed to the divine nature, such as goodness, omnipotence, necessity, infinity and the like, Abraham ... [began] using ... as steps.[342]

Plato's Parable of the Cave: To more fully understand the archetypes of the Good and the Beautiful, it is necessary to go back eight centuries or so before Gregory's time, to an important piece of classical Greek literature, called the Parable of the Cave. This was a symbolic tale which the ancient Greek philosopher Plato included in his *Republic*.[343] In that story, Plato asked us to imagine a group of human beings who had been chained from birth in a dark cave, so that they could only look in one direction, towards one wall. Behind these prisoners was a large fire, and walking between the flames and the captives' backs were other people holding up various pieces of wood and other materials shaped like human beings and animals and ducks and trees and so on, so that the shadows of these objects were cast as black silhouettes against the wall the prisoners were compelled to gaze at.

Since all they had ever seen were the shadows of these objects (and their own shadows intermingled with them) the people in chains believed that this was the real world which they apprehended. If somehow two or three of these prisoners managed to free themselves from their chains and discover a way out of the cave, it would take time for their eyes to get used to the intensity of the light outside the cave, but they would gradually begin to realize that the real world was not the sad, two-dimensional world of black and white stereotypes which they used to live in, but this marvelous realm they now saw, made up of three-dimensional objects in brilliant colors and textures. Now they were no longer looking just at shadows of models of real things, but at the real things themselves.

In Plato's explanation of this extended metaphor, the world of the shadows is the place where most human beings live. It is a realm of *doxa*, mere "opinion" — a Greek noun that comes from the verb *dokeô*, which means to suppose or imagine, to seem so, or merely appear so. And we also must not forget another Greek noun which came from the same verbal root, the word *dogma*, meaning an arbitrarily decreed doctrine set forth by some authority figure whom we were never allowed to question or challenge.

The shadow world is therefore the mental realm of denial, illusion, and introjected parental admonitions (Freud's superego) simply accepted as dogmatic truths about the world: "Good boys always do this, and good girls never do that." "Are you going to let him get away with talking to you that way?" "You're stupid and clumsy, you'll never make good." We perpetuate the shadow realm when, as a member of a dysfunctional family, we maintain the family lie by refusing to talk about or acknowledge in any way what really happens in our family. We strut about pompously trying to make our shadows appear bigger than other people's. We torture ourselves about shadows from the past, or throw ourselves into frenzied panic as our overactive imaginations project baleful shadows into the future. Some of the shadows are truly nightmarish boogiemen, with long teeth and claws and knives and instruments of torture. In the real world, we fail over and over again to accomplish what we set out to do, because no matter how carefully we analyze the shadows and no matter how hard we try to control these fleeting images, we end up grasping nothing, and we cannot discover why.

The shadowy realm of the cave is a world of black and white, like one of the old black-and-white American cowboy movies where the hero (who is absolutely pure and can do no wrong) always wears a white cowboy hat, while the villain (who is absolutely bad through and through) always wears a black cowboy hat. The leaders among the cave dwellers enjoy inventing hundreds of complicated so-called moral and religious rules, and telling the other people in chains that if they violate even a single one of these rigid dogmas, that they will be automatically blackened by sin to the core and become completely evil. All the dogmas invented by these authoritarian leaders — all their legalistic "shoulds" and "oughts" — are regarded as absolute and their followers are ordered to follow them to the letter, blindly and mechanically, and without a single failure or omission, no matter how small.

Up above in the real world, on the other hand, we behold things by the light of the sun up in the sky. Plato said that the sun in his tale stood metaphorically for "the idea of the Good," that which enables us to see what is right and beautiful, to recognize truth and intelligible meaning, and to act in a manner which is sane and sensible.[344]

We observe the vision of the Good being apprehended in a very pure (although extremely primitive) fashion in very young infants, who see the world around them with awed and delighted fascination, and attempt to grasp it and taste it in eager curiosity and sheer joy. The goal of good education is to inform this primitive vision of the Good while still retaining its openness and spirit of eager delight in the world. In some areas the infants' parents do need to teach them that certain things are dangerous to explore (for example, no matter how fascinating the electrical plug is, trying to pull it out of the wall outlet may seriously injure or kill a crawling child). In other areas, children need to learn about levels of goodness that require more knowledge and intellectual structuring in order to be appreciated, which is one of the things that higher education accomplishes (in literature, art, music, science, and so on).

Plato pointed out that young people particularly find it especially difficult to rise above the gross physical level when it comes to appreciating goodness, and then only in rather spotty fashion in certain restricted areas of their lives. Johnnie wants to go out with Margie because Margie has beautiful hair and a good figure; Margie in turn wants to go out with Johnnie because he has a nice car, and clothes that match all the current teenage fads. This is a crudely materialistic approach to life, which will never bring ultimate happiness, because it is blind to all the higher kinds of goodness. Even as adults, many people never rise much above the ability to appreciate the goodness of certain kinds of material things like automobiles, houses, clothes, and so on. So they are consciously aware of only tiny fragments of the goodness which surrounds them. At the very least, this gravely limits their lives and their enjoyment. Unfortunately, it is also usually apt to cause them to act in ways which are both self-destructive and destructive to others, because they fail to see the higher kinds of goodness in the world around them, and go around destroying good things without ever being consciously aware at the time of all the horrendous damage they are causing. At the end they are left crying out piteously, "Why is my life so terrible? I never did anything wrong."

But good education, along with experience, can teach us to expand our horizons and learn how to enjoy kinds of goodness that we were previously blind to. We can learn to appreciate good music and art and literature, and the fascination of ideas, and we can learn how to delight in the pure joy of learning itself. We can above all learn how to recognize what Plato called "justice," the difference between right and wrong at a higher level, which appears only when we look at issues in the Light of the Good.

The Platonic tradition particularly stressed one aspect of this metaphor of the sun and the cave. If we try to look directly at the sun, its light is so intense that it blinds us. The way we ordinarily determine whether we are outside in the sunshine (rather than being someplace in the dark) is not to look directly at the sun, but to look around and see if we can clearly distinguish other objects around us. If we look around and see green trees, and blue ripples on the surface of the nearby river, and red geraniums growing in a flowerbed nearby, then we know that we are in the sunlight. If we see only darkness around us, then we know that we have lost the sunlight.

In medieval Jewish, Christian, and Islamic theology all three, it was believed that the Good of which Plato spoke was one of the central archetypes contained within the being of the transcendent higher power whom the people of the book called God. His goodness was so bright that no human being could gaze on it without being blinded, so that it was impossible to paint a picture of what God looked like, or form any image in our minds of exactly what he was.

But I know that God is present in my own personal mental world, first of all, whenever I can look around me and see a world filled with things that are so good and beautiful that I am overcome with gratitude.

Those on the other hand who have left the sunlight of the spirit, and instead gone as far as possible into the darkness, see a world around them that is filled overwhelmingly with evil, failure, futility, hate, resentment, pain, and confusion. They are no longer able to feel true good-hearted joy and delight at anything. The closest they can feel to this is an evil delight at defeating someone else, or doing someone else harm — a sick kind of pleasure (*Schadenfreude* in German) which will only lead us further and further into the realm of darkness.

But God is still there, as a fountain of light — the light of goodness and beauty — so intense that our eyes cannot bear its full radiance. And everything in the universe which is good and decent and intelligent and rational came ultimately from that divine source. At the time of the Big Bang, as we have mentioned before, out of that explosion of fiery light there sprang the origins of all the good and beautiful things that would eventually appear in this material world.

And likewise, it was that same divine ground of being which contained in advance all the noetic structures of the phenomenal universe, including all the ideas and archetypes which shape the material things around us. As our minds alternate between studying the material world around us, and peering into the divine abyss, we can gradually improve our knowledge of these ideas and archetypes, which will in turn increase the richness and detail which we will be able to apprehend in the material world. And in the process, our spirits will grow and soar to greater and greater spiritual heights.

The presence of evil and the problem raised by a fourth kind of atheism: One kind of modern atheists started out as children believing in a kind of Santa Claus god. If they were good little children and obeyed all their parents' rules, they would get presents under the Christmas tree, and nothing bad would ever happen to them. Or in a more manipulative way, they thought of God as a kind of brain-damaged genie in a bottle. If they learned the right rituals and the right magic phrases, the genie would work miracles for them. If they put enough money in the collection plate at church, their business ventures would all prosper and make them an enormous profit. Their family members would never get sick and die. That is, they turned their childhood religion into what social anthropologists call a "cargo cult."

Then at some point they discovered that these fantasies were nothing but fairy tales. In reality, there was no Santa Claus god, no magic genie in a bottle. At some point they finally started noticing that in the real world, cruel wars are fought in which innocent people suffer and are maimed and die. People starve to death. Bullies gang up on the weak and beat them to death. Crooks and scoundrels grow wealthy by stealing from the helpless poor. Little children die in senseless accidents, and their mothers die young from incurable diseases.

After seeing all these things, rather than admit that they had been very foolish and credulous, they then became atheists, and went around attacking anybody and everybody who believed in any kind of higher power and accusing these people of being ignorant fools. "There is no God," they would angrily proclaim, "because a good God [that is, the kind of fantasy God we foolishly believed in when we were children] would never allow such things to happen. Therefore there is no reason to believe in God, and no way that praying to God could help us with anything at all."

It is extraordinarily difficult to comprehend how atheists of this variety can accuse the Christian church of teaching a fantasy God who never allows the innocent to suffer and who rewards everyone who worships him by giving them all the material rewards that they desire. Christianity in fact puts at the center of its religion an innocent man named Jesus, who owned nothing except the clothes on his back, and was tortured to death after being accused of crimes which he had not committed. His earliest followers traveled from town to town without property or worldly goods and were stoned to death, beheaded, thrown to the lions in public arenas, and so on.

And in particular, St. Gregory of Nyssa was born c. 335, into a world that had known great suffering. The Great Persecution of Christians in the Roman empire had begun only a generation before his birth, in 303 A.D. Gregory's maternal grandfather was a Christian martyr. The first round of persecution did not end until the emperor Constantine marched down into Italy and won the battle of the Milvian bridge in 312, and then legalized the practice of Christianity in the areas he controlled. But the eastern half of the Roman empire — the part where Gregory's family lived — was still under the control of a pagan emperor, and in 320 Licinius renewed the persecution of Christians there. It was not until 324 that Constantine was able to defeat Licinius and become sole ruler of the entire Roman empire. And even then, the possibility of a renewal of persecution was not ended. Gregory's older brother Basil had gone to the same university which Julian the Apostate was attending, and had known him personally. Julian later ruled the Roman empire from 361 to 363 A.D. as the last pagan Roman emperor, and had already begun tightening up the screws against the Christians when he was killed in battle. The Persian spear which pierced Julian the Apostate in the liver was the only thing that had prevented a renewal of persecution and suffering for the Christians. Gregory of Nyssa was about twenty-eight years old at the time.

Gregory and his family were aware of other kinds of human suffering as well. His older brother Basil, who was bishop of the city of Caesarea (modern spelling "Kayseri," in central Turkey), built a huge complex just outside the city made up of a hospital, a hospice, and a home for the poor and totally destitute. Basil conducted public campaigns against the wealthy landowners who were loaning money to poor farmers in years of drought, taking the farmers' land as collateral for the loan, and then foreclosing on the mortgages and seizing the poor farmers' little plots of land. This was taking place all over the Roman empire in the third and fourth century A.D., and was the beginning of the process which, by the time of the Middle Ages, had reduced nearly all the free farmers of the western world to helpless serfs bound for life to work the fields of the great feudal aristocracy. If there had been more spiritual leaders like St. Basil, perhaps the Middle Ages would not have had to have happened.

But the important thing to note here, is that, just like St. Ignatius Loyola's image of the Two Battle Flags a thousand years later, Sts. Gregory and Basil saw human suffering not as a proof that God did not exist, but as a call to fight evil and bring help and comfort to the suffering.

So did St. Gregory of Nyssa believe that there was real evil and suffering lying in the darkness of the divine abyss? Indeed he believed so. Just like Origen, Eusebius of Caesarea, and others within his theological tradition, Gregory personified these forces of evil as "the demons who hate the good" and "the demons who love evil." These demons were real to him — they were not just metaphors or symbols.[345]

Both creation and destruction flow out of the divine ground. The symbolism of the book of Revelation is not talking in restricted fashion about just a few events at the very end of this earth's history, but like all biblical imagery is speaking allegorically about the world right now. The cosmic Christ principle (the eternally generated messianic royal power of the *Melekh ha-'Olam*, the Eternal King) is sent out from the throne of God every day to come into the world to save human beings, but at the same time the Four Horsemen of the Apocalypse (Revelation 6:1-8) are also sent forth from the throne of God to afflict them with war, slaughter, starvation, and death:

> Now I saw when the Lamb opened one of the seven seals, and I heard one of the four living creatures say, as with a voice of thunder, "Come!" And I saw, and behold, a white horse, and its rider had a bow; and a crown was given to him, and he went out conquering and to conquer. When he opened the second seal, I heard the second living creature say, "Come!" And out came another horse, bright red; its rider was permitted to take peace from the earth, so that men should slay one another; and he was given a great sword. When he opened the third seal, I heard the third living creature say, "Come!" And I saw, and behold, a black horse, and its rider had a balance in his hand; and I heard what seemed to be a voice in the midst of the four living creatures saying, "A quart of wheat for a denarius, and three quarts of barley for a denarius; but do not harm oil and wine!" When he opened the fourth seal, I heard the voice of the fourth living creature say, "Come!" And I saw, and behold, a pale horse, and its rider's name was Death, and Hades followed him; and they were given power over a fourth of the earth, to kill with sword and with famine and with pestilence and by wild beasts of the earth.

It was not all that different from Carl Jung's vision of God and the realm of the transcendent archetypes. There are real forces of death and destruction in the world around me, in my Self, and in the transcendent divine realm. Carl Jung said that one of the first thing his patients had to do was to quit pretending that evil did not exist. It was real and it was really there, both within themselves and within God's transcendent realm. My job is not to deny the existence of this dark force, but to figure out ways of integrating it into my Self, and ways of taming it or harnessing it in some fashion which will ultimately work for good and minimize its destructiveness. My job is to search within the godhead and identify the forces and powers of goodness and beauty which I can call to my aid, and then use them to combat and domesticate all the forces of destruction, insofar as is within my power.

CHAPTER 19

Gregory of Nyssa: The Spiritual Life as Perpetual Progress, from Glory to Glory

Taking on the classical tradition: change can be growth instead of deterioration. In the classical Greek world, as we can see from a quick study of Plato and Aristotle, change was regarded in totally negative terms. Changeable beings, as Aristotle put it, were necessarily involved in the realm of "coming to be and passing away." Such beings, because they changed and mutated, would always eventually fall into deterioration and destruction. Salvation was therefore seen as searching for some way to enter a totally unchangeable and hence immortal realm. In order for God to exist forever as a secure source of help, it was therefore necessary that God be totally unchangeable, dwelling all alone in an eternal realm where nothing ever changed and time did not exist. And Christian theology has often bought into that old Platonic and Aristotelian assumption over the past two thousand years.

But not St. Gregory of Nyssa, who was the first Christian thinker to make a full and complete break from that classical world view. Change did not have to be a matter of deterioration and decline. It could also become a process of continual growth and the perpetual ascent to higher and higher stages.

Gregory did acknowledge that God had to be eternal in his inmost "essence" (*ousia* in Greek, a term which referred to the inner core of that which made him God). And if God's essence was eternal, then God could never fail to exist, or cease to be more powerful than anything else that existed.

But God also had temporal *energeiai*, that is, energies, acts, or operations which entered the world of time, and were structured in terms of past, present, and future events. The created world was one of God's temporal energies, and the realm of grace was another. Our human spirits exist now, and always will exist, in a transcendent dimension in which we will be conscious of sequences of events, ordered in terms of before and after and what I am experiencing right now. And this will be a realm where God's divine energy will move through and in us, and we will talk back and forth with him (in conversations consisting of series of events taking place in time), and he will be our friend.

As Jean Daniélou put it in his introduction to the book *From Glory to Glory*:[346]

> For the Platonist ... change can only be deterioration; for the spiritual and the divine are identical, and the divine is unchangeable. But once we establish the transcendence of the divine with respect to the created spirit, another sort of change becomes possible, the movement of perpetual ascent .... the soul is conceived as a spiritual universe in eternal expansion towards the infinite Darkness.

A doctrine of the evolution of the soul: It is the destiny of the human soul to be involved in continuous *evolution*. Gregory of Nyssa's Greek word for this was *epektasis* (*epi* + *ek* + *tasis*) which means evolution, development, or extension over time.[347]

> My note: we need to be careful here, this is not the same word as the word *epekstasis* with an "s" in the middle, a Greek word which in fact does not exist, but would have to mean something like standing outside oneself in ecstasy. The word Gregory uses, *ep-ek-tasis*, does not come from the root *sta* meaning to stand, but from the roots *teinô* (to stretch) and *tasis* (a stretching or tension).[348]

Gregory of Nyssa got the word from Philippians 3:13, where Paul says, "Forgetting those things that are behind, and reaching forth [*epekteinomenos*] unto those things which are before, I press towards the mark."[349]

In his *Life of Moses*, Gregory said that just as material bodies have a natural, automatic tendency to fall downwards under the pull of gravity unless something blocks their fall, so the human soul tends naturally and automatically to rise upward into the transcendent realm, moving toward the transcendent archetype of Goodness Itself:[350]

> All heavy bodies that receive a downward motion ... are rapidly carried downwards of themselves, provided that any surface on which they are moving is graded and sloping, and that they meet no obstacle to interrupt their motion. So too, the soul moves in the opposite direction, lightly and swiftly moving upwards once it is released from sensuous and earthly attachments, soaring from the world below up towards the heavens. And if nothing comes from above to intercept its flight, seeing that it is of the nature of Goodness to attract those who raise their eyes towards it, the soul keeps rising ever higher and higher .... And thus the soul moves ceaselessly upwards, always reviving [*ananeazousa*] its tension [*ton ... tonon*] for its upward flight by means of the progress it has already realized.

The word *ana-nea-zousa* means the "re-newal" of the soul's "life" (its *zôê* or eternal life force, see John 1:4), each time an incident occurs in which the soul successfully grows spiritually. What makes the soul a living thing is an inner *tonos*, a word that comes from the verb *teinô*, which as was noted means to stretch or put under tension. A human soul which is filled with life is not slack and passive and depressed, and filled with self-pity, and resigned to its fate. A soul which is fully alive has a vigorous inner *tonos*, a tension or tightness like the tension in a harp string which takes a limp and lifeless piece of cord and stretches it until it can express the brilliant "tone" of a beautiful musical note whenever it is plucked with a loving hand. The *tonos* or "tone" of a lively human soul is like the tension in the sinews and tendons of an Olympic athlete, crouched and ready to run a winning race the moment the word "go" is shouted.

(We are reminded quite a bit here of the concept of the *élan vital* which was developed by the French philosopher Henri Bergson in his 1907 book *Creative Evolution*. Bergson's ideas were extremely important in French thought during the first half of the twentieth century, and were spread to the English speaking world by William James, who was one of his strongest supporters.)

St. Gregory likens Moses's ascent up Mount Sinai to the angels climbing up Jacob's Ladder, the set of sacred steps that lead us from earth to heaven:[351]

> [Just like climbing Jacob's Ladder] Moses, moving ever upwards, did not stop in his upward climb. He set no limit to his rise to the stars. But once he had put his foot upon the ladder on which the Lord had leaned … he constantly kept moving to the next step; and he continued to go ever higher because he always found another step that lay beyond the highest one that he had reached.

Eros (love) as the dynamic driving power behind the healthy soul's activities: That which "tunes the strings," as it were, of the healthy soul, and gives that soul its vital tension, is an inbuilt drive — an Eros — for continually new and creative expressions of Goodness and Beauty. The soul which is fully alive looks into the dark abyss of what the atheist sees only as nothingness, destruction, meaninglessness, and death, and sees, instead of those negative things, the delight of fresh puzzles to be solved and new things to be learnt and mastered. It sees the opportunity to gain the rich satisfaction that comes from helping people who would otherwise have died, from comforting those who were suffering, and from bringing new hope to those who had given up. It sees a world in which real novelty and creativity can be brought into being. So as a result, the soul which is filled with the eternal life force looks into the existential abyss and feels, not paralyzing fear, but that Love or Eros which casts out all fear (1 John 4:18). The soul loves the dark abyss, because it sees, not an empty pit of nothingness, but an overflowing reservoir of bright-new-being-which-is-yet-to-be. The soul sees the dark abyss with the pleasure of a Michelangelo looking at a fine new uncarved marble block: it is not a rude chunk of featureless stone to him, but an opportunity to create a new statue of David or Moses that will delight the eyes of millions of other people for centuries to come.

For the truly good soul, the love which provides the driving force and tension is an Eros for God, because it is God-as-the-ground-of-being who is the source not only of the darkness but also of the opportunities for new light, new insight, new satisfactions, new rejoicings, and the constant appearance of ever-new divine consolations whenever we are feeling down. As Daniélou puts it,[352]

> Eros [for St. Gregory of Nyssa] denotes the surge of love which sweeps the soul out of itself in proportion to its awareness of God's infinite loveliness .... as God's adorable presence becomes more and more intense, the soul is, as it were, forced to go out of itself by a kind of infatuation.
>
> Eros expresses the experience of the soul as the infinite beauty of God becomes more and more present to it. The more the soul is aware of this beauty, the more it sees that it is inaccessible. And then it realizes that it attains this beauty more by desire than by actual possession, just as it comprehends it rather by darkness than in the light.

Gregory of Nyssa used this observation to provide a happy ending to an otherwise horrifying tale in the Song of Songs. A young woman, we remember, was in love with a young man, and he in turn seemed to be passionately in love with her, and begged her to run away with him, and become his beloved (Song of Songs 2:3, 2:8-10, and 2:14). But then everything plunged into a terrifying nightmare. Evening arrived, and after it grew totally dark, the young woman thought she heard someone knocking at her window. She went out into the darkened city to throw herself into the arms of her lover. But he was not there, and all she could see was the darkness, which in places was a pit of horrors with evil people falling upon her and beating her savagely as though she were a criminal, and tearing off her clothes as she lay there bleeding and sobbing (Song of Songs 5:2-8).

How do we provide a happy ending for that poor soul? For St. Gregory of Nyssa (and St. John of the Cross and Hannah Hurnard[353] and all the other theologians who wrote commentaries on the Song of Songs), the human soul finds that if it keeps on trudging — through the darkness, the deserts, the mountains, the Slough of Despond, the briar patches, or whatever other kind of difficult terrain falls temporarily in its way — it always eventually finds God again in an effulgence of divine light and sweeping insight and glorious triumph which makes the whole struggle worth it. And the good soul eventually comes to love the hard parts of the journey just as much as the easy parts, in the same paradoxical fashion as a skilled mountain climber relishing the struggle up a particularly difficult peak, or an accomplished guitarist enjoying the effort that finally enables the performance (to speed) of a particularly challenging instrumental piece. Succeeding at the task would not have been nearly so enjoyable if it had been too easy. So Gregory of Nyssa, in his *Commentary on the Song of Songs*, says:[354]

> The soul, having gone out at the word of the beloved, looks for Him but does not find Him .... But the veil of her grief is removed when she learns that the true satisfaction of her desire consists in constantly going on in her quest and never ceasing in her ascent, seeing that every fulfillment of her desire continually generates a further desire for the Transcendent [*tou hyperkeimenou* = that which lies yet further beyond] .... the bride realizes that she will always discover more and more of the incomprehensible and unhoped for beauty of her Spouse throughout all eternity. Then she is torn by an even more urgent longing .... For she has received within her God's special arrow, she has been wounded in the heart by the arrow-point of faith, she has been mortally wounded by the bowmanship of love.

Gregory of Nyssa was mixing in a pre-Christian classical reference here. In its Roman form, the goddess of love was named Venus, and her son was named Cupid (Latin *cupido* = "desire"). Cupid had the power to make human beings fall in love by shooting them in the heart with one of his magical golden arrows. But in its classical Greek form — the version that Gregory was using, because he lived in the Greek-speaking eastern half of the Roman empire — the goddess was named Aphrodite and her son was named Eros, one of the ancient Greek words for Love.

The Greek word Eros meant, in particular, a kind of Love that was a burning desire to hold and possess the Beloved, or if that was impossible, to enjoy simply being in the presence of the Beloved for all time, so that one could look upon the Beloved and delight in all the Beloved's words and gestures forever.

Perfection as perpetual progress — Gregory of Nyssa as process philosopher. As it says in 1 John 4:18, "There is no fear in love, but perfect love casts out fear." But to make sense of a doctrine of salvation which defined salvation as *perfection in love*, Gregory had to reinterpret the idea of perfection itself, and proclaim a doctrine of *perfection as perpetual progress*. And to do this, as was noted earlier, he had to attack one of the fundamental assumptions made by Plato, Aristotle, and most of the other members of the classical Greek philosophical tradition:[355]

> Gregory's notion of perfection implies a positive idea of the process of change which is a most important contribution to the Christian theology of man. For the Platonist, change is a defect …. Change is always thought of as a degeneration from a state of initial perfection; and the transformation wrought by Christ [for the pure Christian Platonist] has for its sole purpose to destroy change and restore immutability.

> But change, after all, is essential to man's nature [and] …. If change is essential to the human condition, and change is essentially degeneration, then it follows … that good can never be secure …. Now to overcome this difficulty Gregory had to destroy the equation: good = immutability, and evil = change. And consequently he had to show the possibility of a type of change which would not merely be a return to immobility — that is, to the mere negation of change.

What is today called "process philosophy" first appeared in the modern world at the very end of the nineteenth century in the writings of the French philosopher Henri Bergson (1859-1941). His 1907 book

Creative Evolution was especially important. He subsequently met the Harvard philosopher William James in London in 1908, and James immediately became one of Bergson's strongest supporters, and helped spread his ideas in the English-speaking world, including both America and Britain.

The two greatest architectonic philosophical systems of the twentieth century were Martin Heidegger's *Being and Time* (1927) and Alfred North Whitehead's *Process and Reality* (1929). As one can note immediately from the titles, a new realization was emerging within western philosophy of the importance of *time* and *process*. With this new realization there frequently came, however, a rebellion against all traditional philosophy. The standard patristic and medieval Roman Catholic authors, from St. Augustine to St. Thomas Aquinas, were derided as outmoded and irrelevant.

Jean Daniélou however, as one of the most important continental European Catholic scholars of the twentieth century, was one of the earliest Christian scholars to realize that there was a tradition of early Judeo-Christian thought which could stand up to these modern criticisms, an ancient and worthy tradition which included Philo Judaeus, Origen, and especially St. Gregory of Nyssa.

The famous Aristotle scholar Werner Jaeger had also noted this in a book entitled *Two Rediscovered Works of Ancient Christian Literature: Gregory of Nyssa and Macarius*,[356] which came out in 1954, around seven years before Daniélou and Musurillo's book on Gregory of Nyssa. Jaeger, although primarily famous for his work on Aristotle and on classical Greek educational theory, devoted a significant part of his life to producing scholarly critical texts of Gregory of Nyssa's works, so that this theologian would be better appreciated, including in particular the synergistic process in which God and the human soul co-operated in raising the soul to higher and higher levels of divine understanding.

In my own first major published work (published in 1977 by the French theological press Editions Beauchesne in Paris) I showed how process concepts were also included in the doctrine of time and free will which was taught by Origen's disciple Eusebius of Caesarea, the first Christian historian and the ancient counter-balance to Augustine's fatalism.

St. Gregory of Nyssa not only incorporated time and change into God, by distinguishing between God's eternal essence and God's temporal energies, but as we see here, also put time and change at the very heart of the soul's being by defining salvation as a *perfection in love* involving a concept of *perfection as perpetual progress.*

Gregory's teacher Origen (184/185 – 253/254, the greatest Christian theologian of the third century) had taught a doctrine of transmigration, in which spirits could be reincarnated as either angels, human beings, or demons depending on their behavior. Origen's disciple Eusebius of Caesarea (c. 260-339) in the next generation had rather pointedly condemned only doctrines of transmigration which claimed that human souls could be reincarnated as irrational creatures like worms and goats, which of course Origen had never taught. There are good modern scholars who insist that Gregory of Nyssa, who represented the next generation after Eusebius, rejected any idea of our human souls pre-existing before they were born into their present bodies here on earth. But it seems clear that Gregory believed that after our deaths, our souls would continue to grow in the love and knowledge of God for all eternity, in life without end. It was not just life here on earth, but also the life of that transcendent realm which lay beyond the material world, which had to include change, novelty, and creativity in order to be considered any kind of genuine "life" at all. There had to be the possibility of new experiences and new adventures or we would not be living at all.

From glory to glory: The soul's movement into the transcendent realm may be marked at times by long periods of wandering in what seems apparent darkness, relying on faith alone, like Abraham traveling with his flocks of sheep and goats through the wilderness regions of the Palestinian hill country, as described in Genesis 15:6, where it says "and he believed the LORD; and he reckoned it to him as righteousness." But this journey of faith is certainly not all darkness. It is punctuated again and again by experiences of the most extraordinary sort, where we are overwhelmed by some new insight or discovery or realization, or (in the case of those who are spiritual adepts) we may even receive the consolation of glorious visions of light or angels or saints appearing to us, or hear them speaking in our spiritual ears).[357]

Ecstasy, which is ultimately the experience of God's presence, is not, for Gregory, a phenomenon which recurs in the same way each time; rather, it involves a process of infinite growth. Though God never ceases to remain the Darkness, the soul advances farther and farther into this Darkness .... we have here what is Gregory's most characteristic doctrine: perfection considered as perpetual progress. We find it developed especially in his *Life of Moses*.

The Greek word *rhopê* meant an inclination dragging downwards, a force that pulled us into sinking and falling, a weight which (placed upon that side of a scale) dragged that side of the balance inexorably downwards. And there was such a factor at work inside the human soul, repeatedly presenting us with the temptation to fall into evil. That was the dangerous side of human mutability. But there was also a countervailing force which we could learn to foster, the power of Love, which could turn human changeability into the opportunity for perpetual spiritual growth:[358]

For man does not merely have an inclination to evil; were this so, it would be impossible for him to grow in good, if his nature possessed only a downwards inclination (*tên rhopên*) towards the contrary. But in truth the finest aspect of our mutability (*tês tropês*) is the possibility of growth in good; and this capacity for improvement transforms the soul, as it changes, more and more into the divine (*epi to theioteron*). And so ... what appears so terrifying (I mean the mutability of our nature) can really be a pinion in our flight towards higher things .... let us change in such a way that we may constantly evolve (*alloioumenos*) towards what is better, being *transformed from glory to glory* (*apo doxês eis doxan metamorphoumenos*), and thus always improving and ever becoming more perfect (*aei teleioumenos*) by daily growth, and never arriving at any limit of perfection (*to peras ... tês teleiotêtos*). For that perfection (*teleiotês*) consists in our never stopping in our growth in good, never circumscribing our perfection (*tên teleiotêta*) by any limitation.

The biblical quote in Gregory's commentary is from a famous passage in 2 Corinthians 3:15-18, in which the Apostle Paul was explaining how biblical literalists block themselves off from the Law of Liberty which flourishes when people allow themselves to stand in the sunlight of the Spirit:

> But even unto this day ... the veil is upon their heart. Nevertheless when it shall turn to the Lord, the veil shall be taken away. Now the Lord is that Spirit: and where the Spirit of the Lord is, there is liberty. But we all, with open face beholding as in a mirror the glory of the Lord, are changed into the same image from glory to glory, even as by the Spirit of the Lord.

These biblical literalists, with their rigidity and terrified close-mindedness, actually prevent themselves from obtaining any real spiritual growth. They read all the biblical passages which speak about "the glory of God" but have almost no personal experience of standing in awe and wonder before that divine glory. Only when they become willing to look continually, not at the dead letter of the words, but at the God who shines forth out of the darkness which lies beyond, will they apprehend the true glory.

But when we become willing to journey into the unknown darkness, and we begin to experience these occasions of greater and greater joy and insight — we not only learn to apprehend the true glory of God everywhere around us, but our own lives start becoming, ever more and more, mirror images and reflections of that glory. Like the icons on the walls of an Eastern Orthodox church, even if in a much lesser way, people look at our lives and are impressed with the glow (as it were) of serenity and compassion and sincerity which they see shining forth in our lives. And this becomes the most accurate and helpful "picture of God" which many people will ever see.

And so, if we can develop the courage and learn to fight the good fight, "we all, with open face beholding as in a mirror the glory of the Lord," will be "*changed into the same image from glory to glory.*" And life will just keep on getting better and better, the longer we pursue the true spiritual life:[359]

Each stage is important: it is, as Gregory says, a "glory"; but the brilliance of each stage is always being obscured by the new "glory" that is constantly rising. So too the sun of the new creation, the New Testament, obscures the brightness of that first sun, the Old Law. And the laws of the soul's growth are parallel with those of man's collective history. And yet this is by no means to depreciate the value of each particular stage—all are good, all are stages of perfection. But the mistake would be to try to hold on to any one of them, to put a stop to the movement of the soul. For sin is ultimately a refusal to grow.

Penetrating layer by layer, deeper and deeper into the central core of reality: In the modern twelve step program, after people have worked through all the steps for the first time, they find that they have only "peeled the outer layer of the onion," as it is put in today's parlance. Their worst sins and character defects have been searched out and handed over to God, and their lives have become filled with a joy and happiness they never ever experienced before. But then with sharper eyes, they begin to see deeper, more subtle character defects which they had never consciously noticed before, and find that they can still find things going on in their lives (even if much lesser things) which produce a certain amount of resentment and fear. So they have to reapply the twelve steps and "peel off the next layer of the onion." And in fact, as long as we continue living the spiritual life, this process of peeling away at still deeper layers of the onion will never end. As Daniélou puts it:[360]

> It would seem … that human nature is, as it were, made up of a series of spheres or layers of reality, each one inside the other. The successive removal of the "tunics" or the outer layers allows a gradual penetration into man's interior life. And all these successive deaths and resurrections bring the soul in intimate contact with God Who dwells at its center, though ever inaccessible; the spheres or levels of intensity are infinite, and thus perfection consists in this perpetual penetration into the interior, a perpetual discovery of God.

***Progress not perfection: why striving to live by moral "absolutes"
would cripple spiritual growth.*** The idea of the "Four Absolutes"
was first developed by a Presbyterian minister named Robert E. Speer
(1867-1947). He had no theological training other than a year of
seminary, but became secretary of the American Presbyterian Mission
and in his spare time wrote dozens of inspirational books. During the
fundamentalist-modernist disputes of the 1920's and 30's, he was pulled
both directions: he had two articles published in the Fundamentals, but
he also helped run fundamentalist leader John Gresham Machen out of
the faculty position Machen held at Princeton Theological Seminary.
According to the theory which Speer laid out in 1902 in one of his little
inspirational books (*The Principles of Jesus*, pp. 33-35), the heart of the
New Testament message lay in Jesus's requirement of Absolute Purity,
Absolute Honesty, Absolute Unselfishness, and Absolute Love.[361]

This theory was later developed in greater detail in 1909 by Henry
B. Wright (1877-1923) in a book called *The Will of God and a Man's
Lifework*. Wright was Professor of Theology at Yale University from
1903 until his death at an early age in 1923 (he was only in his mid-
forties).[362] He had no real training in New Testament studies however —
there were no references in his book to any of the great New Testament
scholars of that time, or the important discoveries that were being made
in New Testament theology — so his book in fact was no more than
a compendium of rather simple-minded Victorian and Edwardian era
moralisms having little or nothing to do with the world of first-century
Palestine or the real teaching of the historical Jesus.

The idea of these "absolutes" was not picked up by any of the real
New Testament scholars of the period, because the theory of the Four
Absolutes was simply not a useful way of looking at the teaching of
Jesus. It flew in the face of Jesus's insistence (in his parables for example,
but many other places as well) that self-righteousness was the greatest
danger to true spirituality. Jesus made it clear that the prayer of the
tax collector ("God have mercy on me a sinner")[363] was the only safe
prayer to utter if we wished to avoid falling into self-righteousness and
maintain a proper attitude of humility, and this was later elaborated as
the Jesus Prayer of the hesychastic Eastern Orthodox monks of Mount
Athos ("Lord Jesus Christ, Son of God, have mercy on me, a sinner").

And not just in terms of good New Testament scholarship, but in terms of the basic history of Christian doctrine, it is clear that the teaching of the Four Absolutes was simply a version of the Pelagian heresy, and had to be rejected by Roman Catholics and any Protestants who wished to adhere to the principles of the classical sixteenth-century Protestant Reformation (Martin Luther, John Calvin, Archbishop Thomas Cranmer, and so on).

But Frank Buchman, the founder of the Oxford Group, discovered the theory of the Four Absolutes, and was so delighted with it that he turned it into a major part of Oxford Group teaching. And although the New York A.A. members broke with the Four Absolutes at a fairly early date, there were people in Akron who were still clinging to them for a while longer, and some of the Cleveland A.A. members still kept pushing the idea of the Four Absolutes long after 1939. Richmond Walker, the second most published A.A. author, continued to speak in *Twenty-Four Hours a Day* about the importance of practicing purity, honesty, unselfishness, and love, but he wisely refused to speak of them as "absolute," which was the most dangerous part of the theory.

Bill Wilson, while writing the Big Book in 1938-1939, knew nothing about St. Gregory of Nyssa or the later figures in his tradition (such as St. John Climacus and the *Ladder of Divine Ascent* in the sixth century or St. Gregory Palamas and the hesychastic monks of Mount Athos in the fourteenth century). But Bill W. did have a good deal of spiritual wisdom and realized the dangers of the Four Absolutes. So in the great passage in the A.A. Big Book at the beginning of Chapter 5 ("How It Works"), the two and a half page statement read at the beginning of so many Alcoholics Anonymous meetings contains the key sentence: "We claim spiritual progress rather than spiritual perfection."

And Father Ed Dowling, who served as Bill Wilson's spiritual director and sponsor for so many years, was certainly not going to be encouraging him to reject two thousand years of Christian teaching and start preaching Robert Speer's naive idea of the Four Absolutes. Roman Catholic priests were required to have more than one year of seminary training!

There are many reasons for rejecting this idea of the Four Absolutes. St. Gregory of Nyssa however makes it especially clear why foolishly trying to live by the Four Absolutes would eventually cripple a person's spiritual growth. The truth is that there is no "absolute" righteousness which a human soul could achieve. In the true spiritual life, each time we are able to "peel off one of the layers of the onion," we will be able to glory in the new joy and happiness we have been given, but we will also soon afterwards discover yet another layer to the onion. At that point, if we continue pursuing the higher spiritual life as we ought, we will have to realize that we are being called upon to devise some yet further kind of spiritual discipline through which we can learn how to carry out this next phase in our spiritual growth. And this will go on forever — even, according to St. Gregory of Nyssa, in the life to come, which will be a series of unending new adventures of which our present earthbound minds cannot even truly imagine.

CHAPTER 20

Two Kinds of Catholicism

It has been said that there are two different kinds of Roman Catholicism: the Catholicism of the parish church and the Catholicism of the monastic tradition. To give an oversimplified account of the difference, the first kind tends to concentrate on teaching a fairly mechanical set of religious rules to ordinary lay people, and leading them in the performance of certain appointed religious rituals. The second kind however encourages people to delve deeply into their inner thoughts and feelings, spend time each day in high quality prayer and meditation, become sensitive to matters of the heart, and develop an awareness of the divine transcendent world which will enable them to sense God's presence all around them and — in the case of those who are spiritually adept — experience visions, hear heavenly voices, and feel God's spirit flowing through them in thrilling and overwhelming fashion.

This is an oversimplification — the more devout Catholic laypeople might do the Stations of the Cross, meditate on the Mysteries of the Rosary, make a long trip to pray at a famous pilgrimage site, or engage in some other practice to develop their higher spiritual feelings — but there are still strong differences between the life of the normal everyday parish church and the life of the cloistered monastery and convent.

In rather paradoxical fashion, St. Gregory of Nyssa, whom we are using as one of our prime examples of the Catholicism of the early monastic tradition, was himself a married man and never lived in a monastery. But he was part of that tradition nevertheless, and was looked upon for centuries following as one of the greatest Orthodox and Catholic teachers of the inner spiritual life.

261

We can make a long list of great spiritual authors from later centuries who belonged to that particular monastic tradition. There was Gregory of Nyssa's disciple Evagrius Ponticus (345-399), followed by another even more famous figure who was also deeply influenced by Gregory: a theologian and philosopher called St. Denis (an anonymous author who wrote under the symbolic pseudonym of "Dionysius the Areopagite" c. 500). This theologian in turn was one of the three most often quoted authors in Thomas Aquinas' *Summa Theologica*.

Other famous monastic theologians in this particular tradition included Benedict of Nursia (c. 480-547), John Climacus (c. 600), John Scotus Eriugena (c. 815 – c. 877), Symeon the New Theologian (949-1022), and Bernard of Clairvaux (1090-1153). Roughly contemporary with St. Bernard we also have Hugh of Saint Victor (c. 1096-1141) and Richard of Saint Victor (died 1173), whom the twentieth century theologian Paul Tillich regarded as the real sources of his fundamental ideas — Tillich put the Victorine teaching of God as the ground of being into modern existentialist language and showed that it was just as relevant in the modern period as it was in the middle ages. Later on in the medieval period we had Meister Eckhard (1260-1327), Gregory Palamas (1296-1359), Julian of Norwich (c. 1342-1416), St. Catherine of Siena (1347-1380), the *Theologia Germanica* (anonymous mid-14th century) and *The Cloud of Unknowing* (anonymous latter 14th century). In the early modern period we had Teresa of Ávila (1515-1582) and St. John of the Cross (1542-1591) continuing this tradition of monastic spirituality, extending down into modern times with authors like Thomas Merton (1915-1968), who we remember was a monk at Gethsemani Abbey — a quiet and peaceful place built among the woods and rolling meadows of the Kentucky Bluegrass, just an hour's drive south from where I lived as a teenager.[364]

We have given this long exposition of Gregory of Nyssa's spiritual teachings simply AS ONE EXAMPLE of this important kind of Catholic theology.

And Jean Daniélou's work on St. Gregory was also given *as one example* of an important kind of twentieth century Jesuit theological interest. As we mentioned before, there were a large group of notable Catholic theologians involved in this twentieth-century movement, which eventually came to be referred to as the *Nouvelle Théologie* or "New Theology." Four of its principal leaders were Jesuits — Pierre Teilhard de Chardin, Henri de Lubac, Karl Rahner, and Jean Daniélou — and Hans Urs von Balthasar started off as a Jesuit. Other prominent Catholic theologians and philosophers who were part of this group were Yves Congar, Hans Küng, Edward Schillebeeckx, Marie-Dominique Chenu, Louis Bouyer, Étienne Gilson, and Jean Mouroux, who between them, made up what was probably the most important single block of twentieth century Roman Catholic theologians.

But again, I do not believe that most Catholic laypeople in the United States and Canada are very aware of this kind of Catholic spirituality. For them, the Catholic religion has meant mostly the rules, sermons, and rituals of the local parish church. And I do not believe that most ordinary American parish priests — the kind who were trained in local diocesan seminaries — have any very deep knowledge of the theologians in this long and distinguished tradition. Father Ralph Pfau, the first Roman Catholic priest to get sober in A.A., went to a seminary run by the Benedictine monks of St. Meinrad Archabbey, but it was designed to function (in those days at least) as a diocesan seminary to train parish priests for the Catholic churches of southern Indiana. As a result, although Father Ralph knew some interesting things about St. Augustine (things the normal parish priest would not know about), and somewhere along the way developed a good grasp of the spiritual teachings of the cloistered Carmelite nun St. Thérèse of Lisieux, I have found nothing beyond that in his writings which would indicate any familiarity with the great monastic spiritual tradition as a whole.

In 1940, when Bill Wilson first met Father Dowling, he had had a little bit of contact with that kind of spiritual teaching in the most general sense, through the New England Transcendentalists and English Romantic poets whom he had read in his schoolboy days, as well as Emmet Fox's books and sermons, and Richard Maurice Bucke's book on *Cosmic Consciousness*. But meeting Father Dowling put Bill W. in much more direct contact with a two-thousand-year-old tradition of great Christian spiritual authors, as well as with contemporary Christian theologians who were still studying those great classics and teaching their principles. This has to have been like a breath of fresh air to a small town New England Protestant like Bill Wilson. It was not so much that this new set of Catholic authors taught him anything brand new, as it was that it made him realize that he was not alone in trying to find God in the way he had been striving.

CHAPTER 21

Aldous Huxley and the Perennial Philosophy, Gerald Heard and the LSD experiments

Gerald Heard: The Anglo-Irish religious philosopher Gerald Heard (1889-1971) was the one who first introduced Bill Wilson (and subsequently Father Ed Dowling) to an approach to spirituality which combined the Catholicism of the monastic tradition with the teachings of the great Asian religions, in particular Hinduism.

Gerald Heard's book, *The Ascent of Humanity* (1929), was similar in ways to Richard Maurice Bucke's 1901 book on *Cosmic Consciousness.* In his 1929 book, Heard portrayed human consciousness as evolving through five evolutionary stages during the centuries since the first human beings had appeared on this earth. In the fifth stage, which was just now beginning to appear, some human beings had evolved a kind of super-consciousness in which they could identify themselves with the Life Force which pervades and contains the universe.

Heard, who had been educated at Cambridge University, came over from England to the United States in 1937 along with his friend Aldous Huxley, to give some lectures at Duke University, and both of them eventually decided to stay in America rather than go back to the British Isles. Heard and Huxley eventually moved to Hollywood, where in 1939 Heard met Swami Prabhavananda, the founder of the Vedanta Society of Southern California. Vedanta is a kind of Hindu religious philosophy based on three of the great classical works of ancient India: the *Upanishads*, the *Brahma Sutras* and the *Bhagavad Gita*. It teaches us how to contact Brahman (the eternal, ultimate ground of the universe) by quieting the mind and the ego.

Heard, who was a great popularizer, played a major role in spreading knowledge of this kind of Hindu religious philosophy in the English-speaking world. In 1942, he founded Trabuco College, in the Santa Ana Mountains about forty miles southeast of Los Angeles, California, as a place to study comparative world religions, including Asian religions, with a special emphasis, of course, on Vedanta.

Bill Wilson and Dr. Bob had both been reading Gerald Heard's books, which they found fascinating, so when Bill made a trip to California and found that an A.A. member from Palo Alto named Dave D. had been to Trabuco and knew Heard, he got him to arrange an introduction. In January 1944, Bill W. and Gerald Heard met for the first time, there at Trabuco, and began "a personal friendship and collaboration that would continue over the next two decades."[365] In all, Bill made three visits to Trabuco College between 1944 and 1947. Tom Powers is reported to have said that Heard became in effect one of Bill's sponsors.

There were numerous links between Heard and the people who traveled in A.A. circles. Gene Exman, the religion editor at Harper & Brothers, may have been the one who first got Bill Wilson reading Heard's books. One of these, *A Preface to Prayer*, was part of Dr. Bob's library. Gerald Heard even wrote an article for the A.A. *Grapevine*, called "The Search for Ecstasy."

There is a fascinating recent book by Don Lattin, called *Distilled Spirits: Getting High, Then Sober, with a Famous Writer, a Forgotten Philosopher, and a Hopeless Drunk* (2012), which describes in great detail the close relationship between Gerald Heard (the philosopher), Aldous Huxley (the writer), and Bill Wilson (the man who was once a drunk but who quit when he became the co-founder of Alcoholics Anonymous).[366] Lattin, who still lives in the San Francisco Bay area, was a religion reporter for the *San Francisco Chronicle*, and himself traveled in many of the same circles as Heard and Huxley.

Aldous Huxley: It was Gerald Heard who introduced Bill Wilson to Aldous Huxley. The latter's grandfather had been Thomas Henry Huxley, the English biologist whose famous 1860 debate at Oxford

University with Anglican Bishop Samuel Wilberforce played a key role in gaining wider public acceptance for Darwin's theory of evolution.

Aldous Huxley (1894-1963) had done a degree in English literature at Balliol College, Oxford University, and had first gained fame with a novel called *Brave New World* (1932), which portrayed a nightmarish future world created by the dehumanizing aspects of scientific progress, the factory system, and the government's use of behaviorist psychology to control everyone caught in the system. As mentioned, he came to the United States with Gerald Heard in 1937, and the two of them eventually drifted to Hollywood, California. There Huxley, like his friend Heard, became involved with Swami Prabhavananda and the Vedanta Society's form of Hindu religious philosophy. At the same time Gerald Heard was building his college in Trabuco Canyon, forty miles southeast of Los Angeles, Aldous Huxley began renovating a farmhouse at Llano del Rio, forty miles northeast of Los Angeles, on the edge of the Mojave Desert.

In 1945, based on the new things he had learned about the ancient religions of India and China, Huxley published a book called *The Perennial Philosophy*.[367] In this book, he argued that the great authors of the western Catholic monastic tradition and the teachers of the religions of Asia had all been teaching the same basic thing. We live normally in a mental world which is locked inside a closed box created by the limitations of our five physical senses. But by cultivating the proper kinds of meditational and spiritual practices, we can learn how to contact and experience the transcendent spiritual reality which lies outside that box. On the Christian side, the important fourteenth century Catholic theologian Meister Eckhart was the most quoted figure in Huxley's book, but he also had numerous quotes from St. Thomas Aquinas, St. Augustine, St. Bernard of Clairvaux, St. Catherine of Siena, St. Francis de Sales, St. John of the Cross, and the *Theologia Germanica*.

With the exception of St. Augustine, these were basically fairly late figures, who lived in the twelfth through seventeenth centuries. But these particular spiritual teachers, even though they came later in Christian history, were all basically continuators of the great teachers of the first through fourth centuries A.D. — the Jewish philosopher Philo, the Christian theologians Origen and Gregory of Nyssa, and so on — who had fascinated Jean Daniélou and the other members of the *Nouvelle Théologie* movement.

Huston Smith and Alan Watts: An additional figure involved in the Trabuco College/Llano del Rio group, albeit more peripherally, was Huston Smith, who hitchhiked from Denver, Colorado to Trabuco College in 1947, just to meet Gerald Heard. In 1958, Huston Smith authored a book called *The Religions of Man* (later entitled *The World's Religions*), a work which sold over two million copies, and still remains a popular introduction to comparative religion. From 1947 to 1958, Smith taught at Washington University in St. Louis, and became friends with Swami Satprakashananda, who had founded the Vedanta Society of St. Louis in 1938, and was an important figure in the twentieth century Vedanta movement in both India and America. Since Washington University and the Jesuit-run St. Louis University were the two principal academic institutions in St. Louis — both of them top-drawer national research universities — Father Dowling might well have met Huston Smith during those years. Smith then went to teach at M.I.T. in Cambridge, Massachusetts (where he had close contact with the people at Harvard), and subsequently at Syracuse University, where he taught until his retirement in 1983.

Alan Watts, another Englishman who came to the United States in 1937, should also be regarded as at least a peripheral member of this movement. While living and working in the San Francisco Bay area, he wrote *The Way of Zen* in 1957, and became an important interpreter of Buddhism to the American world until his death in 1973.

This was an important American religious movement: The point to be noted here is that Aldous Huxley, Gerald Heard, Huston Smith, Alan Watts, and their circle — a group of major authors in the field of world religions — formed the core of an important American religious movement during the 1940's, 50's, and 60's. It captured the interest of students on many American college campuses. The approach which these authors took made it clear that people did not have to believe in things like biblical infallibility, virgin births, and men walking on water in order to be religious.

Heard attracted Bill Wilson's attention because he taught a theory of spiritual evolution similar to the one found in Richard Maurice Bucke's book on *Cosmic Consciousness*. And Aldous Huxley had written on the kind of ancient Catholic authors who had attracted the attention of the radical wing of the Jesuits, which must have struck a responsive chord in Father Dowling. These convergences and parallelisms undoubtedly formed some of the reasons why Wilson initially decided to become involved in their circle. During these years Bill began increasingly to use Gerald Heard and Father Dowling as sort of "co-sponsors" in one important portion of his own personal spiritual quest.

The psychedelic experiments and LSD: On May 5, 1953 Huxley took some mescaline (the active ingredient in peyote cactus buds) provided to him by a Canadian psychiatrist named Humphry Osmond. In 1954 he wrote a book called *The Doors of Perception* talking about his psychedelic experiences that afternoon. Then on December 24, 1955 he took LSD for the first time.[368]

Humphrey Osmond had performed experiments in which he initially seemed to have had considerable success in treating alcoholics by administering LSD to them. He originally thought that the hallucinogen was producing symptoms which were enough like delirium tremens to frighten the alcoholics into wanting to quit. But then between 1954 and 1960, when he and his colleagues gave the drug to two thousand alcoholics and still consistently achieved a very high success rate in getting them into recovery, they began to realize that it was not a fear reaction which the drug was causing. The new theory they devised was that it was the spiritual insights which the LSD experience produced which were enabling the alcoholics to stop drinking.[369]

On August 29, 1956 Bill Wilson took LSD for the first time, joining Gerald Heard and Aldous Huxley in California and taking the psychedelic drug under the supervision of Dr. Sidney Cohen, a psychiatrist at the Veterans Administration Hospital in Los Angeles. A.A. member Tom Powers was also there.[370] According to Don Lattin, "Wilson was blown away by the drug and said the experience was a dead ringer for the famous night in the 1930s when he fell down on his knees and had an epiphany about founding his twelve-step program."[371]

Bill Wilson wanted to check his own perceptions, however, against those of a person who knew much more than he did about the world of traditional Catholic monastic spirituality: someone who had had his own spiritual experiences of a higher order in a manner unaided by drugs, and who was a genuine "insider" within the living Catholic spiritual tradition, rather than just being an outside observer (like Aldous Huxley and Gerald Heard essentially were). So he got Father Ed Dowling to visit, and as *Pass It On* describes it, "the result was a most magnificent, positive spiritual experience. Father Ed declared himself utterly convinced of its validity."[372]

The four key people, it should be noted, were not crazed young hippies in their teens and twenties, with long hair and headbands and flowers in their hair, wearing love beads and riding around in old VW minibuses painted with psychedelic designs. In August 1956, Father Dowling was almost 58 years old, Bill Wilson was 60, Aldous Huxley was 62, and Gerald Heard was 66.

Aldous Huxley also gave LSD to Jesuit theologian John Courtney Murray, S.J. (1904-1967), another figure from the more radical wing of the Jesuit order.[373] Murray was editor of the Jesuit journal *Theological Studies* and taught at the Jesuit theologate in Woodstock, Maryland, and was, like Cardinal Jean Daniélou, S.J., one of the formative influences on the declarations of the Second Vatican Council. Murray and Dowling would have shared many basic political principles, since Murray was someone who was devoted to bringing real democracy into both government and the church. He and Reinhold Niebuhr were considered the two most influential American theologians at that time, in the area of the application of Christian ethics to politics.

Nell Wing, Mrs. Marty Mann, and Lois Wilson also tried LSD at Bill Wilson's urging.[374] These were not crazed young hippies.

The impact of modern chemistry on medicine: We need to remember the great defining currents of that period of history, that is, the revolutionary era that ran from the 1840's down to the 1950's. The discovery of mind-altering chemicals which could be used medically to enormously improve human life was a radical new development. In fact the modern science of chemistry really began only a century and a half ago — it is one of the newest of our sciences — but some of the medical advances of that period rapidly began producing almost miraculous benefits for the human race. We need to look at some dates, to realize what an explosion of discoveries was going on. Dr. Bob was born in

1879. Mendeleev had developed the Periodic Table, the basis of modern chemistry, only ten years previously. The first major applications of modern chemical discoveries in medicine had begun only a generation before Dr. Bob's birth: the first surgery using ether as an anesthetic, for example, was not carried out until 1842, and chloroform was not discovered until 1847. The first time nitrous oxide was used for an anesthetic was for a dental extraction in 1844, but it did not come into general use until after 1863. What an incredible boon to the human race these discoveries were!

Between 1910 and 1941, it was discovered that a whole series of chemicals called "vitamins" could have an enormous effect on human health and mental states, and cure a long list of illnesses. Every year, newspapers and magazines seemed to be trumpeting yet another new vitamin which could be used to successfully treat some disease (like pellagra, beriberi, or rickets) which had long afflicted the human race: Vitamins A, C, D, K, and a long list of B vitamins (in order of discovery Thiamine, Riboflavin, Vitamin B$_{12}$, Pantothenic acid, Biotin, Pyridoxine, Niacin, and Folic acid).

Antibiotics were another early twentieth-century discovery. The first sulfonamide drug was developed in 1932-1935, that is, about the same time the A.A. movement began. Sulfa drugs, as the first and only effective antibiotic available in the years before penicillin, were literally lifesavers for wounded soldiers and sailors during the early years of World War II. Penicillin was discovered by Scottish scientist and Nobel laureate Alexander Fleming in 1928, but it did not begin to receive serious attention until the later World War II period: on March 14, 1942, John Bumstead and Orvan Hess saved a dying patient's life using penicillin, and later that year it was used to treat victims of the famous November 28, 1942 Cocoanut Grove fire in Boston.

Then science began to discover medications which could be used to treat mental problems: chlorpromazine (Thorazine) was given its first clinical tests in 1951-1952 and was soon being used all over the United States to treat schizophrenia, mania, psychomotor excitement, and other psychotic disorders. Its use finally brought an end to the practice of using electroconvulsive therapy (shock treatment) and psychosurgery (prefrontal lobotomy) to treat mental patients, and was one of the driving forces behind the deinstitutionalization movement which allowed thousands of people to be released from insane asylums and live in the outside world once again. Bill Swegan (the most important A.A. author from the atheistic and agnostic wing of early A.A.) began using tranquillizers quite effectively in the treatment of alcoholics during the middle 1950's, and published a widely read journal article on it in 1958.[375] Then in 1958, haloperidol (Haldol) was discovered by a Belgian pharmaceutical company and quickly proved in clinical trials to also be quite successful in treating schizophrenia.

The tranquillizer chlordiazepoxide was first sold in 1959 under the brand name Librium, and then in 1963 diazepam came on the market under the brand name Valium. By 2003 in the United States, an estimated 3.21 million patients were receiving antipsychotics.

In 1929, just two weeks before the stock market crash, an American soft drink company came out with a lemon-lime flavored "Lithiated Lemon-Lime Soda" which eventually came to be called "7 Up." It is still a very popular soft drink in America today. In 1950, they finally stopped putting lithium citrate in their beverage, under pressure from the U.S. government, because of the dangers of getting an overdose of lithium if taken without fairly continuous medical supervision, but also because of government fears that lithium was only "quack medicine" that actually helped no one. Ironically however, at almost the same time, an Australian psychiatrist named John Cade demonstrated in 1949 that lithium salts were in fact quite excellent for treating mania — the first thing that psychiatrists had been able to devise in fact, that was a truly successful and workable treatment. By the 1970's lithium was regularly being used for mental patients who were bipolar, that is, who suffered from manic depression cycles, and was for many of them the only thing that really worked well.

So it was not surprising that sensible and thoughtful people might believe, in the 1950's, that LSD could possibly be another of the new wonder drugs which could revolutionize the practice of medicine and restore countless suffering men and women to full health. At the very least, experiments needed to be performed to test it on human subjects.

Putting LSD to the religious test: But Bill Wilson needed someone whose judgment he could completely trust *on the religious side* to join him in experimenting with this new medicine, and Father Dowling seemed like the ideal person to go to. Bill Wilson recognized, the first time he met him, that the Jesuit priest had had extraordinary spiritual experiences like the ones described in Richard Maurice Bucke's book on *Cosmic Consciousness*. Father Dowling started every morning with an extended period of meditation and — from the way he and Bill W. talked back and forth — must have had some of the extraordinary spiritual experiences which St. Teresa of Ávila described in her book *The Interior Castle*. (This book is well worth reading, by the way, for anyone who is interested in these aspects of the spiritual life. It is one of the greatest catalogs of various kinds of spiritual experiences, systematically distinguished and recorded, ever put together in a single volume.)

When did Father Dowling have these spiritual experiences, and what was their nature? His decision to enter the Jesuit seminary in 1919 when he was twenty-one showed signs of having been the product of some kind of extraordinary spiritual experience. Something at least has usually gone on when young men and women make that kind of abrupt decision to give themselves to the church — Protestants will often speak of "receiving the call to preach," for example. And c. 1920, after he was in the seminary, young Ed began to suffer through two years of doubt and flirting with atheism before he experienced something that put him back on the road of faith. We can only guess at the nature of these spiritual experiences, but it should be noted that Father Dowling never showed any great astonishment at Bill Wilson's accounts of having seen the great white light, or having held long conversations with a dead saint. In the history of the Jesuit order over the centuries, there were many who had experienced encounters with the divine light, heavenly voices, visitations of the Blessed Virgin Mary, and so on.

And after his initial encounter with LSD, Dowling concluded (just like Bill Wilson) that this chemical did in fact put the human mind in genuine contact with the transcendent realm that the great spiritual teachers of the past had spoken about. In order to make such a statement, Dowling must have had extraordinary spiritual experiences earlier in his life which he could now say that the LSD psychedelic trip at times mimicked or duplicated. Father Ed, going back long before he and Bill Wilson met, must have been something far more than an ordinary Catholic priest with an ordinary cleric's simple piety.

So Dowling and Wilson both began by praising LSD, and certifying that it could in fact produce a vital spiritual experience. The problem is that numerous experiments over the years that followed have taken some of the glow out of the enthusiastic evaluations of those who first tried the drug during the 1950's. It would surely be safe to say that today, over fifty years later, the overwhelming majority of the people in A.A. and N.A. — although still not one hundred percent of them — do not believe that the LSD experience leads to permanent, long-term spiritual growth. But on the other hand, there are still today some A.A. and N.A. members who continue to insist that LSD produced a vital and genuine spiritual experience when they took it.

Timothy Leary and the later drug culture of the 1960's: An often morbid fascination with this topic seems to arise among some A.A. historians today, because when the term LSD is heard, they all too often think primarily of the use of that substance later on within the psychedelic drug subculture that developed during the 1960's, the one that involved Timothy Leary, Ken Kesey, and a number of popular rock musicians. Tom Wolfe's *The Electric Kool-Aid Acid Test* (1968) gives a first-hand look at that world.

Timothy Leary (1920-1996) had begun teaching as a lecturer at Harvard University in 1959. On August 9, 1960, he ate some psilocybin mushrooms at Cuernavaca in Mexico, and went on his first psychedelic trip. Returning to Harvard, he and Richard Alpert (later known as Ram Dass), began a research program known as the Harvard Psilocybin Project, using a synthesized form of the psychedelic drug. Beat poet Allen Ginsberg, after hearing about the Harvard research project, asked to join the experiments. In the Spring of 1963, Harvard fired both Leary and Alpert. In 1964, Leary coauthored a book with Alpert and Ralph Metzner called *The Psychedelic Experience*, using the Tibetan Book of the Dead as a guide to that kind of drug trip.[376]

And past that point, psychedelic drugs became principally identified as a part of the world of hippies, college dropouts, drug-addicted American military personnel returning from the Vietnam war, and a whole host of well-known rock musicians. When people heard the term LSD, they thought of Beatles songs like "Lucy in the Sky with Diamonds" (which came out in 1967, the title being an anagram for LSD) and their film "Yellow Submarine" (1968), along with Creedance Clearwater Revival's "Looking Out My Back Door" (1970), and the music of a large number of other groups like the Grateful Dead (formed in 1965), and so on. That is, psychedelic drugs seemed part of a package of addictive behaviors that was leading more and more people into A.A. and N.A. with hopelessly unmanageable lives.

Father Ed Dowling died in April 1960, before any of the hippie and rock-and-roll drug cult involvement had begun. Bill Wilson lasted down to 1971, but in those last years he was an elderly man gravely weakened by emphysema, and was not in any shape to be involved in any way with people like Timothy Leary, and Jerry Garcia and the Grateful Dead.

CHAPTER 22

The Intersection of Four Major Religious Movements

In the preceding chapters, we tried to sketch out the way in which Bill Wilson and Father Ed Dowling stood at the intersection of four of the most important religious movements of their period, and concluded with a chapter especially devoted to Aldous Huxley and Gerald Heard, two of the major teachers within the last of these movements.

(1) TRANSCENDENTALISM AND COSMIC CONSCIOUSNESS: Bill had initially been an enthusiastic supporter of the religious movement that began with the New England Transcendentalists of his native region, as further developed by Richard Maurice Bucke in his book on *Cosmic Consciousness* and by the formative American poet Walt Whitman. Albert Einstein, the greatest scientist of the early twentieth century, was also part of that mix, with his ideas about a humanistic religion based on "cosmic religious feeling."

(2) THE NOUVELLE THÉOLOGIE: As a Jesuit, Father Ed Dowling cannot fail to have known something at least about some of the twentieth century Catholic theologians of this important movement. Teilhard de Chardin S.J. and Cardinal Jean Daniélou S.J. were both well known in Jesuit circles.

(3) NEW THOUGHT: This was a religious movement with deep roots in New England, but Bill Wilson had come into contact with it through a teacher named Emmet Fox, who had been born and brought up as a Roman Catholic in Ireland, and educated by Jesuits in London, before coming to New York City. Fox in fact had incorporated a number of theological ideas from medieval Catholic figures like John

Scotus Eriugena and Meister Eckhart, who were continuators of the early Catholic theology which had so fascinated many of the *Nouvelle Théologie* authors.

(4) THE PERENNIAL PHILOSOPHY: Aldous Huxley, Gerald Heard, Huston Smith, and their circle — a group of major authors in the field of world religions — formed the core of yet another important religious movement during the 1940's, 50's, and 60's. Huxley in particular combined an interest in (a) Asian religions, particularly Vedanta Hinduism, with (b) medieval Catholic authors who gave later versions of the patristic Catholic theology which had so fascinated the *Nouvelle Théologie* authors.

The way in which these four major religious movements intersected and overlapped gave Bill Wilson and Father Ed Dowling a common vocabulary which they could use to talk about vital spiritual matters.

It was one of the most important developments in early A.A. history, and achieved even greater importance after 1948, when A.A.'s second most published author, Richmond Walker, published a little meditational book called *Twenty-Four Hours a Day* which incorporated many of these same ideas. Its use rapidly spread all over America until more A.A. members owned copies of this book than owned copies of the Big Book itself. Rich's little black book taught a version of the kind of entry into the divine Silence found in the ancient gnostic[377] and later Christian hesychastic tradition (a method of meditation which developed among the medieval followers of Gregory of Nyssa), along with overtones of Vedanta style Hinduism. The Twenty-Four Hour book even began with a quotation from an ancient Hindu author.

Plus the continuing importance of two further twentieth-century religious movements: Alcoholics Anonymous had been born of course out of elements drawn from two rather more conventional groups within the modern Protestant tradition, and some of these foundational ideas continued to play an absolutely central role in A.A.'s spiritual message.

(5) THE OXFORD GROUP'S VERSION OF THE PREACHING OF THE EIGHTEENTH CENTURY EVANGELICAL MOVEMENT: The central gospel message of conversion by faith alone, apart from works of the law,[378] had been combined by the Oxford Group with a theory of one-on-one

individual evangelism developed by the Protestant foreign missionary movement during the early twentieth century, involving the 5 C's: Confidence, Confession, Conviction, Conversion, and Continuance. The Oxford Group's insistence that we had to "make restitution" or make amends to the people we had harmed by our past actions was also emphasized in a distinctive fashion, in a way that went beyond the formal system laid out by any other previous Christian group of which I know. Between 1935 and 1939, the A.A. movement worked out its own creative adaptation of these ideas, where the 5 C's and the idea of making amends ended up worked into the basic structure of the twelve steps, but after that point A.A. broke all of its ties to the Oxford Group.

(6) PROTESTANT LIBERALISM: During that same period, the early A.A. people resolutely turned their backs on the early twentieth century Protestant Fundamentalist movement, with its emphasis on biblical infallibility and its denial of the theory of evolution, and instead embraced the kind of tolerant liberal Protestantism represented by people like Harry Emerson Fosdick and writings like the Southern Methodist meditational booklet called *The Upper Room.*

Ideas from all of these major religious movements were combined in a number of novel and creative ways during the 1940's and 1950's, the period of A.A.'s greatest growth. This was the era which saw A.A. expand almost explosively from no more than a hundred or so members in early 1939 into a large and successful world movement over the course of the next two decades. This was also the twenty-year period during which Father Ed Dowling served as Bill Wilson's sponsor and spiritual guide.

Aldous Huxley's Heaven and Hell and Bill W.'s letter to Mel B. We find an extremely important document for understanding Bill Wilson's position on a good many of the issues that we have been talking about in this section of the book, in the letter he wrote to the young Mel B. on July 2, 1956, a little over fifteen years after Bill W.'s first meeting with Father Ed Dowling.

(Many years later, Mel — the man who received this letter — was going to be the principal author of *Pass It On*, the official conference-sponsored biography of Bill Wilson.)

Mel, who had served in the U.S. Navy in an LST (landing ship tank carrier) in some bloody landings on Pacific islands during the Second

World War, had gotten sober several years after the war was over, and had traveled to Akron, Ohio, in the summer of 1956 to hear and see Bill Wilson speak. He approached Bill after his talk to ask him some probing and interesting questions about spirituality. Bill pleaded that he was too tired at that point, and asked Mel to write him in New York, laying out those questions in detail, and promised that he would write him back and do his best to answer them. Mel tells us in *My Search for Bill W.* that one of these questions dealt with Bill's

> ... remarkable spiritual experience, which he had related in his personal story and had since told many times. I wanted to get his exact understanding of it, because I felt deeply that this experience marked the true beginning of A.A. I even felt that without such an experience as a new departure point, Bill might have faltered along the way.

Bill wrote back to him on July 2, 1956, and Mel included the text of this letter in a book he wrote many years later — Mel B., *My Search for Bill W.*[379] In the letter, Bill Wilson initially explains his vision of the Divine Light at Towns Hospital in language reminiscent of that used by Jonathan Edwards in 1734 in his sermon entitled "A Divine and Supernatural Light, Immediately Imparted to the Soul by the Spirit of God, Shown to be Both Scriptural and Rational Doctrine." This was a sermon which Edwards had preached at Northampton in colonial Massachusetts, where he had been ordained as a pastor of the Congregationalist Church in 1727.[380]

Edwards was the founder of the modern Protestant evangelical movement, whose ideas were the foundation of the American frontier revivals which spread Christianity west across North America in the first and second Great Awakenings during the eighteenth and nineteenth centuries. We must remember that Bill Wilson was a child of New England and the Congregationalist Church, born and brought up in Vermont, only ninety miles north of Northampton, which meant that he had had the ideas contained in Edwards' sermon on "A Divine and Supernatural Light" ingrained into the deepest level of his mind since his youngest years.

There is a modern A.A. author, who is neither a professional historian nor a trained theologian or biblical scholar, who has been writing books claiming that the secret to understanding the spirituality of both Bill W. and Dr. Bob lies in the study of a young people's Christian group called the Christian Endeavor Society, which was founded in 1881 by the Rev. Francis E. Clark, who served as pastor first of a church in Portland, Maine, and later of a church in South Boston, Massachusetts. But Christian Endeavor literature was basically written at a Sunday Schoolish level, and is not particularly helpful in understanding any of the great spiritual geniuses or major religious movements of New England — people such as Jonathan Edwards and the founders of the First Great Awakening, the New England Unitarians, Ralph Waldo Emerson and the New England Transcendentalists, Phineas Parkhurst Quimby (the founder of New Thought), Mary Baker Eddy (the founder of the Christian Scientist Church), William James, and many of the key authors of the First Humanist Manifesto (including John Dewey and Joseph Walker, the father of Richmond Walker, the second most-published early A.A. author, who wrote *Twenty-Four Hours a Day*) — a set of religious thinkers covering a tremendous spread of belief, but also with certain common New England religious assumptions.

Bill Wilson and Dr. Bob were not Sunday School teachers, and they were not trying to conduct local youth groups for exuberant adolescents who were often more interested in laughing and partying and having a good time. The whole idea that the A.A. movement which Bill W. and Dr. Bob founded is best understood as just a kind of noncritical teenage youth movement seriously demeans Bill and Bob both.

If we want to see the real roots of the A.A. understanding of religious conversion, we can best do this by going back to Jonathan Edwards and his seminal piece, the sermon on "A Divine and Supernatural Light," which basically "translates" (as it were) St. Justin Martyr's second-century concept of the Logos as the saving Word of God, St. Augustine's fourth-century illuminationist doctrine of truth, and St. Thomas Aquinas's thirteenth-century concept of God as Being Itself into impeccably doctrinally sound Protestant evangelical language.

But let us look here at the way Bill Wilson explained his vision of the Divine Light at Charles B. Towns Hospital[381] in his letter to Mel B. in 1956:

I talk about the experience more freely nowadays than I used to. In the light of all that has happened, people receive such an account better nowadays. Of course these spiritual experiences are as old as man himself. In fact, I know of several sudden ones in A.A. that quite eclipse my own for intensity. In talking about my flash of reality, I often fail to make the point that every A.A. who has the program, gets the same thing. The only difference that I can see is that most experiences are strung out over a long period of time. In these sudden events, I think the ego gives way at depth in complete collapse, at least momentarily. This permits a huge inrush of Grace that brings a vision. In most cases, the Grace leaks in little by little. Therefore, I can't hold with most theologians that these sudden experiences are something very special and unique. If you were to take the sum of your own transformation since you have been in A.A. and condense the whole business into six minutes, you, too, would see the stars—and more!

Mel B. went on to say that three important books were mentioned in the letter Bill W. wrote to him:

Since I had mentioned William James's *The Varieties of Religious Experience*, Bill discussed that and then recommended a book called *Cosmic Consciousness*, by Richard Maurice Bucke — one that he described as having "covered the waterfront" on the subject of spiritual experience. He also referred to a book called *Heaven and Hell*, by Aldous Huxley.

Huxley had just published *Heaven and Hell* that year, so Bill W. had presumably just finished reading it.[382] In that book, Huxley explained that he had not only had visions of a blissful and heavenly transcendent world, but that he had also on occasion had other kinds of visions: horrifying views into frightening and nightmarish regions in the world beyond. One is reminded a bit of *The Tibetan Book of the Dead*, where the human soul at death can see some divine figures offering us bliss and freedom, but also devilish supernatural figures representing the dark forces that were already driving us to desperation in this world.

Bill Wilson told Mel B. that in the years "since his spiritual experience" at Towns Hospital, "he had been subject to an immense amount of psychic phenomena of all sorts."

> So much so, that immortality is no longer a question of faith — to me, it has the certainty of knowledge through evidence. In the course of innumerable experiences of this sort, the negative has appeared as often as the positive. In this layer of consciousness, I have had a good look at what the theologians call "hell" also. My total experience seems to confirm the argument in Huxley's book — namely, that reality, which must include both absolute and relative, is arranged in several layers. We have the conscious, the unconscious or subconscious, the world of psychic phenomenalism which suggests our Father's house of many mansions, and finally the ultimate reality, glimpses of which all mystics seem to have had. To me, this makes good theological sense. We appear to be in a day at school, a relative state of affairs that slowly progresses toward a meeting with the Absolute. When the doors of perception are opened widely enough by ego deflation, we get these fleeting glimpses of ultimate destiny.[383]

Perhaps partly through his contact with Aldous Huxley, who was so fascinated with Hinduism and other Asian religions, Bill Wilson now believed that there were many paths to the vision of this ultimate reality. As Bill said in his letter to Mel:

> Nor are these experiences confined by any means to adherence to the Christian religion. Even a little reading in the field of comparative religion would convince anybody of that. Christ is, of course, the leading figure to me. Yet I have never been able to receive complete assurance that He was one hundred percent God. I seem to be just as comfortable with the figure of ninety-nine percent. I know that from a conservative Christian point of view this is a terrific heresy. But it must be remembered that I had no childhood conditioning in religion at all. I quit Congregational Sunday School at eleven because they asked me to sign a Temperance pledge. So, what

shall I do? Of course I don't know — except to try to be open-minded. In any case, though, I do think it imperative that neither my theological views nor those of Dr. Bob ever have any appreciable influence on A.A. That would only create another competing religion. Of these, we certainly have enough already.[384]

Bill W. then talked about his bouts of depression:

In the last twelve years of life, despite all my blessings and opportunities, I have spent eight in depression, sometimes very severe ones. However, there has been profit for A.A., even in this state of affairs. The depressions kept me off the road and from making speeches. In fact, I was forced to sit home and ask what would become of A.A. and what would become of me. The result was the Twelve Traditions of Alcoholics Anonymous and the present world service structure. And maybe I grew up a little myself, also — at any rate, let's hope.[385]

Was Bill saying here that his depressions might have been produced by visions of the divine world which had sometimes led him into hellish and horrifying portions of the world beyond? It is worthwhile noting that after reading Huxley's *Heaven and Hell* in 1956, Bill Wilson quit having crippling depressions. Perhaps it was a simple matter of him realizing, after reading Huxley, that he could simply choose to back out of the hellish visions and transfer his attention over instead to those parts of the transcendent realm that shone with goodness, beauty, peace, and light. He did not have to let the hellish visions, when they sprang up, lead him deeper and deeper into realms of hopelessness and despair. This would have been what Teresa of Avila and any number of other Catholic visionaries would have advised him in this matter: if you find yourself, while praying and meditating, moving into demonic regions, do not let yourself be pulled in! Do whatever is necessary to pull your mind back into the realms of goodness and light.

CHAPTER 23

Ignatian Spirituality

It is well-known that when Father Ed Dowling first read the Big Book, he and some of his fellow Jesuits surmised that the author must have been involved in deep study of the *Spiritual Exercises*, a work which had been written by St. Ignatius Loyola (1491-1556), the founder of their religious order. But to the best of my knowledge, no modern historian of the A.A. movement has yet been able to determine exactly why Father Ed and his fellow priests might have been led to that conclusion.

In this regard, I would like to offer the following hypotheses, citing some of the interesting parallels that might have suggested a possible Ignatian connection to a Jesuit priest who had lived and breathed these spiritual exercises for many years.

It should be said at the very outset, of course, that I have found no evidence anywhere that either Bill Wilson nor anyone else strongly involved in the writing of the Big Book or playing any important role in early A.A. prior to the writing of that book, was trained in the *Spiritual Exercises*. Although Sister Ignatia and Dr. Bob knew one another, they did not start working with one another in treating alcoholics until A.A. member Walter Bray had to be admitted to St. Thomas Hospital for an alcoholic relapse on August 16, 1939 (Walter's story in the first edition of the Big Book was appropriately titled "The Back-Slider").[386] And then in January 1940, Sister Ignatia negotiated a working agreement between Dr. Bob, St. Thomas Hospital, and her superior, Sister Clementine, which subsequently became the model for Roman Catholic participation in Alcoholics Anonymous across the board. But all of that was too late to affect anything written in the Big Book, which was sent to press in March 1939.

Pride vs. Humility in the Two Standards passage and in the A.A. Big Book: We have already spoken at length about St. Ignatius's powerful image of the Two Standards (the Two Battle Flags, *Las Dos Banderas*) in the meditation in the Spiritual Exercises which comes on the fourth day of the second week.[387] The Christian life is portrayed as a war between elemental Good and elemental Evil, a battle in which the distinguishing feature marking the difference between the two sides is the presence of sinful Pride on the part of the evil combatants and true Humility on the part of the good people.

Now these two words — pride and humility — do not actually show up explicitly that many times in the main part of the Big Book. The word pride appears on pages 8, 12, 25, 65, 75, 104, 105, 116, and 125, and the words humility or humble show up on pages 12, 13, 73, and 83. But the underlying concepts, and the contrast between these two qualities, is so central to the message of the Big Book, that I still remember that one of the first things I thought after my own first reading of that book was, "This is pure St. Augustine through and through!"

That great African saint was the original source of the Pride vs. Humility dichotomy when used in that way. St. Augustine (354-430) was one of the two most formative Christian figures[388] outside the New Testament. His most famous book was *The City of God*, a work which he began writing shortly after 410 when the German tribe called the Visigoths invaded Italy and sacked the city of Rome. The western Roman empire's total inability to defend itself adequately against such a comparatively small body of German barbarians, most of them marching on foot carrying only axes for weapons, and followed by a train of poorly defended covered wagons carrying their families, made it clear to any thoughtful political observer that the western half of the Roman empire had now fallen into irremediable collapse, and that the beginning of the long Dark Ages was now coming upon the west.

In the book which St. Augustine now began to write, he said that since the beginning of history, human beings had been divided into two basic types or categories. He referred to each of these two groups as a *civitas*, that is, a "city" in the sense of a community or group holding a common citizenship. The two groups were divided by what he called the

Two Loves. The City of God was made up of all those men and women who loved God above all other things, that is, all those whose ultimate concern in life centered on God. The Earthly City on the other hand was made up of all those who, when the chips were down, were not concerned with God at all, but were concerned only with something less than God: money, or prestige, or sex, or a king or dictator or political cause, or simply with saving their own skins.

St. Augustine pointed out to the frightened people of the western Roman empire, who were now seeing civilization beginning to crumble around them, that power-hungry, despotic Visigothic kings and power-hungry, despotic Roman emperors were both alike members of the Earthly City. Living under the rule of either kind of tyrant was not that much different. The fundamental decisions that good and decent human beings were going to have to make after the fall of the Roman empire would be no different under Visigothic rule than under Roman rule.

The members of the Earthly City were marked above all, St. Augustine said, by *superbia* (pride, hubris, the out-of-control desire to be SUPERior and SUPERhuman at all costs) and as a closely associated vice, were driven by the *libido dominandi* (the lust to dominate and control other people and SUPERimpose your will on them). The members of the City of God, on the other hand, were marked by what would be called *humilitas* (humility) in medieval Christian writings.

Now the works of St. Augustine were by far the biggest influence outside of the New Testament on Roman Catholic theological writings during the whole course of the Middle Ages, so it is clear that if St. Ignatius did not get the Pride vs. Humility dichotomy from reading St. Augustine directly, there were numerous other works of Catholic theology from which he could just as well have gotten it. The image of the Two Standards (the Two Battle Flags) was simply the doctrine of the Two Cities and the Two Loves as explained by a Spanish knight to a much later audience.

But Protestants were just as much affected as Catholics by St. Augustine's ideas. The sixteenth century Protestant Reformation was for the most part simply an attempt by a number of Catholic priests, bishops, and university scholars — Martin Luther, John Calvin,

Archbishop Thomas Cranmer, and so on — to return the Church's teaching to ancient Augustinian standards, in opposition to some unfortunate trends which had begun to increasingly affect the teaching of Europe's Catholic universities during the fourteenth and fifteenth centuries. So St. Augustine — whom the reformers had turned to in order to discover the shape of authentic early Christian teaching — was the only medieval theologian whom the classical Protestants still continued to read and praise without hesitation.

And what made Augustine especially important in the Protestantism of the 1920's, 30's and 40's, was the rise of what was called the Neo-Orthodox movement. It began with the publication of a book called *The Epistle to the Romans* by a Swiss theologian named Karl Barth in the period right after the First World War. In this volume, Barth emphasized the great Augustinian theme that it was our human attempt to set ourselves up as our own gods which the prime source of evil. Pride was the great underlying vice which tempted us down the path to destruction. The two most important American representatives of Neo-Orthodoxy — Reinhold Niebuhr and Paul Tillich — both taught at Union Theological Seminary in New York City (the former taught at Union from 1928 to 1960 and the latter taught there from 1933 to 1955). So Augustinian ideas were very much alive and well in New York City during the 1934-39 period when A.A. was first being formed.

I do not believe it very likely that Bill Wilson had ever read St. Augustine's *City of God.* But he was the sort of man who could read or hear a fragment or two of a large system of thought and — to an often amazing degree — reconstruct the entire system in his mind, and make good use of those ideas in his own writing and speaking. I believe that — in the case of the Pride vs. Humility dichotomy — what most likely happened was that Bill W. either worked backwards from what were obvious Augustinian presuppositions in the preaching and teaching of both the Lutheran theologian Rev. Frank Buchman and the Anglican theologian Rev. Sam Shoemaker, or that he learned about the Protestant Neo-Orthodox movement from hearing various theologians in the New York City area talk in passing about this controversial new position. And in fact, it was not just professional theologians, but many prominent American writers, thinkers, politicians, and political commentators who eventually began reading Reinhold Niebuhr's writings and being affected by his ideas, so Bill W. could have picked up these ideas from any number of different sources.

Now in the United States in the 1930's and 40's, even the very best Roman Catholic theologians knew very little about real Protestant theology, particularly at the level of reading authors like Reinhold Niebuhr or Paul Tillich. So it seems clear enough to me why a group of Jesuits, reading the Big Book in 1940 and knowing nothing about its author, would have instantly wondered if this book was not written by someone who had studied Loyola's *Spiritual Exercises.* The similarities would have seemed almost uncanny.

The general moral inventory in the A.A. Fourth Step. The twelve steps spoke of a detailed general moral inventory that was in fact very different from anything that I have observed over the years in the most common varieties of Protestantism during that period. Some have tried to trace the A.A. practice back to the Oxford Group, citing the passage where V. C. Kitchen, in *I Was a Pagan* (the book he wrote in 1934 describing his Oxford Group experiences) spoke of

> ... a version of the game of "truth" taught me by a member of the Oxford Group. You write down the five things you honestly like most in life. And you write down the five things you most hate. Then—if any change has come into your life—you write them down again to show the comparison between your old life and the new.[389]

But this was in fact not anything at all like a true Fourth Step inventory, and was done for a totally different purpose.

One could argue that the A.A. practice was derived from the Oxford Group's 5 C's — Confidence, Confession, Conviction, Conversion, and Conservation — where you confessed your own sins openly to the person whom you were trying to convert, so the other person would hopefully eventually come to feel enough confidence in you to make a similar confession back the other way. But what the Oxford Group was usually after here, was to push the would-be convert into finally admitting the one great secret sin that he or she had been hiding and trying to keep secret for years. They were not trying to get the man or woman to make a general across-the-boards confession of every sin the person had ever committed and every moral flaw the person was holding locked inside.

So if one wants to argue that the A.A. Fourth Step was derived from the Oxford Group's 5 C's, then one has to acknowledge, I believe, that they made some very creative innovations in it, and in fact turned it into something very different: a comprehensive list of the most important problems the person was going to have to start working on in order to begin leading a better spiritual life.

Or in other words, as far as I can see, the kind of general moral inventory described in the Big Book was devised by Bill Wilson and Dr. Bob and the early A.A. members themselves, in quite creative fashion. And without a doubt, the A.A. Fourth Step was not in fact derived from anything in the life of St. Ignatius Loyola or in his *Spiritual Exercises*.

Nevertheless, it is easy to see how a Jesuit reading the Big Book in 1940 would have assumed that it came from the Ignatian tradition, or at least from some obviously Roman Catholic spiritual tradition. So for example, in the life of St. Ignatius, one reads how, when he was at Manresa, he spent three whole days writing out a detailed general confession prior to turning his life totally over to God.[390] St. Francis de Sales (1567-1622) had a famous section in his *Introduction to the Devout Life*, Part I, Chapters 19 ff., on "How to make a General Confession." One could go on and on, citing various Catholic authors.

In the early twentieth century, Roman Catholic laypeople could easily obtain multi-page "laundry lists" of sins to check through before going to confession, itemizing sometimes literally hundreds of specific sins that the penitent might have committed. The tendency in the Roman Catholic Church today seems to be to get rid of the super-detailed lists, and concentrate on the Ten Commandments, listing ten or twelve items under each commandment that the penitent ought to think about. But in 1940 that was not so, which meant that Father Dowling and his fellow Jesuits simply assumed that the A.A. Fourth Step was derived from general Roman Catholic practice if not from some specifically Jesuit source.

St. Ignatius's Daily Examen and the A.A. Tenth and Eleventh Steps. What would have particularly struck a Jesuit, however, was that the twelve steps not only required a general confession at the beginning of the process, but also insisted that we take a further daily inventory every day from that point on, so that we might be able to continue working every day at weeding out our most troublesome character defects. This was Step Ten in the Big Book: "Continued to take personal inventory and when we were wrong promptly admitted it," and Step Eleven: "Sought through prayer and meditation to improve our conscious contact with God *as we understood Him,* praying only for knowledge of His will for us and the power to carry that out."

G ═══════════════════════

G ═══════════════════════

G ═══════════════════════

G ═══════════════════════

G ═══════════════════════

G ═══════════════════════

G ═══════════════════════

In the First Week of the *Spiritual Exercises,* the Particular and Daily Examen provided for three regular periods of prayer every day. To make better sense of Loyola's instructions for carrying out these prayers, it should be explained that he wanted each person to take a small piece of paper at the beginning of each week, with the letter G written down seven times in a row, listing them down the left hand side of the page.

The top G was supposed to be bigger and stood for Sunday, the next G was smaller and stood for Monday, the next G was yet smaller and stood for Tuesday, and so on. Each G was followed by two parallel lines extending over to the right hand side of the page. No one knows why he chose the letter G, but that was what he did.[391]

St. Ignatius explained the details of these three prayers to us as follows:

> The first time is in the morning, immediately on rising, when one ought to propose to guard himself with diligence against that particular sin or defect which he wants to correct and amend.

> The second time is after dinner,* when one is to ask of God our Lord what one wants, namely, grace to remember how many times he has fallen into that particular sin or defect, and to amend himself in the future. Then let him make the first Examen, asking account of his soul of that particular thing proposed, which he wants to correct and amend. Let him go over hour by hour, or period by period, commencing at the hour he rose, and continuing up to the hour and instant of the present examen, and let him make in the first line of the G————— as many dots as were the times he has fallen into that particular sin or defect. Then let him resolve anew to amend himself up to the second Examen which he will make.

> The third time: After supper, the second Examen will be made, in the same way, hour by hour, commencing at the first Examen and continuing up to the present (second) one, and let him make in the second line of the same G————— as many dots as were the times he has fallen into that particular sin or defect.

> > *This referred to the major meal in Spanish and Italian culture, which was eaten around noon time and was followed by a siesta or nap of one or two hours during the hottest part of the day.

One can easily see how smoothly the twelve steps and the Daily Examen can be fitted together. In the Fourth Step, I work out a list of all the major character defects that I find in myself. In the Fifth Step, I discuss that list and refine it with a confessor or spiritual guide (the necessity of a competent spiritual guide to mentor me while I am doing the exercises would be taken for granted wherever Jesuits were leading people through them).

In the Sixth Step, I need to do whatever it takes to become "ready to have God remove all these defects of character," and then I need to ask him in the Seventh Step to actually remove them.

I could then, if I so wished, start with any one of the character defects which I identified in the Fourth Step, and start using the seven lines laid out on the little sheet of paper to monitor my progress on eliminating it from my life. Looking back at the end of the week, I should be able to see the number of dots per line (each dot representing an instance in which I fell into that character defect on that particular A.M. or P.M.) growing less over the course of the week.

No wonder Father Ed and his fellow Jesuit priests initially thought that Bill Wilson must have been one of them!

The Daily Examen as part of a disciplined approach, not to some static concept of perfection, but to continual spiritual progress and growth. In discussing this, it is of the greatest importance to note that the *Spiritual Exercises* and the twelve steps both assume three important things:

(1) That there is no static concept of perfection that we can arrive at. There are no moral absolutes that we can totally embody in our lives. In all Catholic spiritual systems, this statement is regarded as unquestionably true in this world and this life. There is no this-worldly perfection. Most Catholic spiritual teachers (including St. Augustine and St. Thomas Aquinas for example) believed that our souls were elevated to a level of sinless perfection once we died and went to heaven. But St. Gregory of Nyssa and some other teachers in the early Origenist tradition believed that we would continue to grow spiritually for all eternity in the life of the world to come, and the same thing was believed by John Wesley in the eighteenth century, Fyodor Dostoyevsky in the nineteenth century (by the end of his life), and C. S. Lewis in

the twentieth century. Bill Wilson, in the way he described the "many mansions" of the world beyond,[392] may have been in the same camp as these latter thinkers. That seems likeliest to me, in the way that I read him — that is, Wilson believed that we could continue to move upward from one heavenly realm to even higher realms as we continued to grow spiritually — but it is difficult to be sure.

(2) <u>What we are called to instead is a life of continual spiritual progress and growth</u>. We can be free of mortal sin, but in good Catholic theology we can never be free of venial sin as long as we are in this life. And although we may be automatically forgiven for certain kinds of unconscious venial sins, a venial sin committed through ignorance is no longer venial once we have become consciously aware of its wrongness. Then it becomes a mortal sin, and then we become fully responsible for it. So as our knowledge of the world grows over the years, we have to keep on growing spiritually to adjust our regular forms of behavior to each significant new piece of knowledge.

(3) <u>And to best carry out this continual spiritual progress, we need to take a systematic and disciplined approach, doing certain things at the same time every day, and taking notes on paper, and going at things stepwise, *methodically*, and in order</u>. Most of the early A.A. people, from 1935 to 1948, started off their mornings by reading the meditation for that day in the Methodist publication called *The Upper Room*. John Wesley, the founder of the Methodist movement, was fluent in both Spanish and French, and had read the great seventeenth and eighteenth century Spanish and French spiritual writers. He had originally intended his Methodist traveling preachers to play much the same role in the Church of England that the Jesuits did in the Roman Catholic communion, that is, to serve as a kind of Special Forces detachment whom one could send into places so dangerous that no other pastors were willing to go there. Wesley had a concept of perfection (*teleiôsis*) as perpetual progress (carried out methodically, which was why his people were nicknamed the "Methodists") which he based on both the early Catholic and Orthodox teachers of the early church (theologians like St. Gregory of Nyssa whom we talked about earlier) and also on more recent Roman Catholic spiritual teachers like Thomas à Kempis (verbal echoes of whom appear continually in his

sermons), St. Ignatius Loyola, and St. Francis de Sales. So the basic Jesuit idea of the need to work out a methodical set of spiritual exercises in order to grow spiritually had already been imparted to the early A.A.'s via the indirect intermediary of the Methodists and *The Upper Room*.

The important thing to note is that the following words from the Big Book could be applied to those who practice St.Ignatius's *Spiritual Exercises* just as much as they apply to those who attempt to live by the twelve steps: "The point is, that we are willing to grow along spiritual lines. The principles we have set down are guides to progress. We claim spiritual progress rather than spiritual perfection."

But whichever system people follow — the Ignatian exercises or the twelve steps — they are called to lives of continual creativity and new discovery as they work in organized fashion to grow continually in grace and joy and peace without end.

Jesuits vs. Jansenists: a spirituality of decision-making based on introspective moral awareness vs. a spirituality based on rigidly following external rules. There is another, more subtle factor in the spirituality of the Big Book which probably would not have been noticed by most people who were not Jesuits themselves. It involved an issue which went back to the seventeenth century, when there was a great dispute between the Jesuits and a rival group of Roman Catholic theologians popularly called the "Jansenists." One of the great French literary works of that period was Blaise Pascal's *Lettres provinciales* (written in 1656-57), which represented the Jansenist point of view. In that work, Pascal accused the Jesuits of moral laxity, and claimed that their specialty was using fancy, circuitous rationalizations to give people excuses for failing to carry out their clear moral duties.

The Jesuit attitude, on the other hand, was made especially clear to me on one occasion by an important French Jesuit theologian in the *Nouvelle Théologie* movement (see the earlier material in this book on Father Jean Daniélou S.J. *et al.*). This theologian explained to me (as an American) in rather scoffing tones that the Jansenists were simply the French equivalent of the kind of New England Puritans described in the infamous American literary classic by Nathaniel Hawthorne, *The Scarlet Letter* (1850). That is, the Jansenists (to his mind) were basically just rigid, puritanical, unforgiving people who loved to draw up long lists of what they regarded as absolute moral rules — unbreakable, unmodifiable, incapable of being adapted to circumstances — and then using these legalistic rule books to attack and condemn other people without mercy, without generosity, and without compassion. Their desire was to feed their own unfocused inner rage and guilt, and make themselves feel morally superior, by taking other poor unfortunate souls and publicly disgracing them and driving them to destruction.

To give more recent examples of the two different approaches to moral issues, in the past hundred years of Roman Catholic history, the use of the Baltimore Catechism in American parochial schools was sometimes converted by sick and disturbed teachers into the worst kind of Jansenist psychological abuse of innocent and vulnerable children. On the other hand, the present Roman pontiff (the liberal Jesuit Pope Francis) is a good example of the kind of Jesuit spirit which was embodied in Father Ed Dowling and the priests who were his closest friends: a spirit of generosity and tolerance, and concern for the poor and powerless regardless of whether the rule-mongering legalists believed that these suffering people "deserved" our help.

The purpose of the *Spiritual Exercises* was NOT to draw up lists of moral absolutes and long catalogues of supposedly unbreakable rules, so that we could scold other people and preach long sermons about how wicked and sinful they were, and how they would surely go to hell when they died — and praise ourselves and pompously puff our chests up with pride because we set such incredibly high moral standards for ourselves (at least verbally, even if in actual practice we failed miserably to meet those standards). *The purpose of the exercises was to teach us how to become more and more sensitive to the deeper levels of moral awareness, and how to make better moral decisions as a result.*

Since it was a spirituality for decision makers, many major Catholic heads of state over the centuries, along with many other major government figures and business leaders have chosen a Jesuit priest as their confessor. At that level, there can often be several different ways of dealing with a given social or political or economic problem, none of which would violate normal understandings of Catholic doctrine. A good political decision has to decide which one of these will best promote the highest values for all the people in that particular society at that particular point in history. Should someone who has demonstrably broken a certain state law be put on probation, be sent to a halfway house for a year, or be given a prison sentence? And if the latter, how long a sentence? Or should the law itself be taken off the books, because it is creating more violence and turmoil and human misery than it is fixing? Most people in the United States finally agreed to remove the laws against the sale or consumption of beverage alcohol after seeing the problems that efforts at enforcing Prohibition had actually produced. Attempting to follow a simple-minded set of legalistic rules, whether taken from a Catholic parochial school catechism or from the Bible itself, will not actually give us a mechanical way of deciding these issues.

One place where the modern Jesuit order places special emphasis on the spiritual exercises as a discipline for decision-making is in helping young men decide whether they should become Jesuits. And some other Roman Catholic religious orders are now using that method as well, such as the Sisters of the Holy Cross, who run St. Mary's College just outside of South Bend, Indiana, located just three blocks from where I live. When young people are thinking about making a decision to take permanent vows to enter a particular religious community for the rest of their earthly lives, this is not a light decision to make. And yet there are no mechanical religious rules which can be invoked. It does not make a young man or young woman less a good Catholic if the person decides to live in the secular world instead, and get married, and have a family.

God's Eros and human desiring: In the Jesuit understanding, all of our good human desires arise out of God's own Eros, that is God's own passionate desiring. For each human being, God desires certain things that will advance the kingdom of God and make God's glory shine forth even more brightly upon the face of the earth. Since this is what each of us was created for, we will discover that our own deepest desires for ourselves will be automatically fulfilled when we carry through God's desire for our lives.

Or in other words, sinful people believe that their own personal desires will always be in automatic conflict with the will of God, so they interpret coming to God as a process of surrendering all their personal wants and desires at great pain to themselves, and bowing down to the will of some tyrannous heavenly tyrant.

But that is not so. When we come to realize what our ownmost desires are actually directed towards, we come to feel greater and greater personal satisfaction when we live in the way for which God created us, and a feeling that we are finally, at last, able to live the way we have always really wanted to live. In general, when people learn how to stop leading lives filled with continual resentment, and start learning how to lead lives filled with serenity and inner peace, they feel that they are now in heaven by contrast. That was what they really wanted all along. The problem was that they did not know how to attain that kind of serenity and peace.

Someone whom God really designed from birth to become a priest or nun will flower unbelievably in that way of life. But someone who instead wants to raise a family, or who is inherently a loner who does not work well in groups, will find living in a religious order is a kind of hell on earth. God made these people too. There is nothing evil or immoral about a good Catholic who would be happiest living as an isolated lighthouse keeper, or sitting in a fire tower in a lonely part of a national forest. But someone of that personality type is never going to be happy living in a close-knit monastery or convent where the individual members are never truly alone.

The Big Book lays out no complicated sets of moral rules. This is one of the most important parts of the spiritual system laid out in the main text of Alcoholics Anonymous. There are no long lists of "sins" for which an A.A. will be damned. We do not do a Fourth Step on the basis of the rules laid out by any particular religion, or any particular religious book. We must set aside what our mothers and fathers told us, and our grandmothers and grandfathers, and our church leaders, and our school teachers, and all the other authority figures who had perhaps dominated our lives during our youth. The Fourth Step is all about what I, and I alone, regard as my own internal moral standards. Can I live inside my own head afterwards, with my own thoughts, without being filled with continual guilt and shame? If I start trying to live instead by some set of preexisting legalistic religious rules forced on me from the outside, I will undo all the good work of the twelve steps.

A group of liberal young Jesuits back in 1940, having already decided after having read the Big Book, that the author was probably a Jesuit, or was at least a Roman Catholic who had received some training in the spirit of the *Spiritual Exercises*, would have immediately concluded at that point, that the author of the Big Book had obviously been trained by some very liberal Jesuit teachers. They would have been wrong, but we can easily see how they could have jumped to that conclusion.

Learning to practice discernment, which becomes the core of a new kind of spirituality, one which rejects the idea of trying to make moral decisions by drawing up absolute lists of rigid rules. In both Akron and New York, the early A.A. members began by trying to work their spiritual programs while attending meetings of the Oxford Group, which had already come to the awareness that many of our most important moral decisions could not be made by simply following a mechanical set of dogmatic rules.

The Oxford Group had developed a technique for going to God for *guidance* whenever we needed to make decisions of this sort. After first having a Quiet Time, where we tried to turn our minds off and simply sit without thinking about anything, we took a pencil and a piece of paper, and starting writing down all the thoughts which appeared in our minds. This was called *automatic writing*, and was one of the methods used by mediums and spiritualists to try to come into contact with the spirit world.[393]

The way to actually live our daily lives smoothly and well, the Oxford Group taught, was to learn to ask God for guidance by one means or another whenever we had to make a decision as to what to do next: what to spend my time working on this afternoon (where I had to choose between two or three different projects, all good and worthwhile endeavors), how best to respond to a small child who was behaving in totally obnoxious fashion (should I scold the child and threaten the child with punishment? or suggest something else for the child to do, which he or she would greatly enjoy and be entertained by?), what to actually say to a spouse or a coworker who was angrily criticizing me (regardless of the angry and abusive words I *wanted* to say back to the person), whether I should buy such-and-such even though I had a limited amount of money at this point (so it would mean that I would not be able to pay for certain other things that needed to be taken care of), and the host of other decisions which make up our daily lives.

The most important source of Oxford Group teaching here was F. B. Meyer's book, *The Secret of Guidance*.[394] Meyer (1847-1929) was a liberal English Baptist preacher who had a B.A. from the University of London. He was deeply opposed to the new Protestant Fundamentalist movement: they were violent, divisive people, as far as he was concerned, who placed entirely too much emphasis on doctrines and dogmas.

And although a Baptist, there was notable Quaker influence in his background, which was one possible reason for his interest in learning to listen for God's voice and influence inside our minds. One of his grandmothers was a Quaker, and he was also influenced by an American woman named Hannah Pearsall Smith who had Quaker roots.

Meyer's great importance was that, between 1887 and 1928, he addressed twenty-six Keswick Conventions, and was a major spokesman for the Keswick Holiness movement, which combined evangelical theology with elements drawn from Roman Catholic mystical theology (especially St. John of the Cross and Johann Tauler). The Keswick Convention is a very important religious gathering which has been held annually ever since 1875 in the small resort town by that name, which is located in the beautiful Lake District on the northwest coast of England (about two hours north of Liverpool and Manchester, and two hours south of Glasgow). It was at the Keswick Convention of 1908 that Frank Buchman had the religious experience which gave birth to the Oxford Group.

Although the early A.A. members in Akron originally participated in the automatic writing sessions at the Oxford Group meeting there, by the time the Big Book had been published they had decided to simplify their techniques for obtaining guidance. We see no statements in that book about them taking out pencil and paper and automatically writing down every idea that popped into their minds. Instead we see on pages 86-88 of the Big Book the simple suggestions:

> In thinking about our day we may face indecision. We may not be able to determine which course to take. Here we ask God for inspiration, an intuitive thought or a decision. We relax and take it easy. We don't struggle. We are often surprised how the right answers come after we have tried

this for a while. What used to be the hunch or the occasional inspiration gradually becomes a working part of the mind.

Being still inexperienced and having just made conscious contact with God, it is not probable that we are going to be inspired at all times. We might pay for this presumption in all sorts of absurd actions and ideas. Nevertheless, we find that our thinking will, as time passes, be more and more on the plane of inspiration. We come to rely upon it ....

As we go through the day we pause, when agitated or doubtful, and ask for the right thought or action. We constantly remind ourselves we are no longer running the show, humbly saying to ourselves many times each day "Thy will be done."

St. Ignatius's guidelines for practicing discernment: consolations and desolations. At the very end of the *Spiritual Exercises*, two long sets of guidelines are given to aid us in making moral decisions. They show us how to go down deeply into our own hearts and emotions, and distinguish between one group of feelings and emotions which are called "consolations," and another variety which are called "desolations."[395]

In a simple experience of consolation, I feel good about the decision I have just made, or what I have just done, perhaps even to the extent of enormous joy and elation. Or I come to the end of a long and difficult day, but realize that I did my best to do the right thing, in spite of hostility and provocation, and I feel that "the day has been satisfied." Suddenly becoming aware, with awe and gratitude, of the beauty and glory of God's universe, or of something God has just accomplished, is a consolation. But even partially negative emotions can be consolations — for example, weeping over my sins, while simultaneously being filled with gratitude that God has forgiven them, as well as feeling (with gratification) a powerful growth in my own sense of humility.

Desolations are the opposite of consolations, and ultimately leave our souls mired in overpowering resentments, constant anxiety and fear, feelings of futility and despair, hopelessness, guilt, and feelings of doom. But let us give St. Ignatius's own definition of these two terms, from sections 316 and 317 of his *Spiritual Exercises:*[396]

... I call it consolation when some interior movement is caused in the soul, through which the soul comes to be inflamed with love of its Creator and Lord, and, consequently when it can love no created thing on the face of the earth in itself, but only in the Creator of them all. Likewise when it sheds tears that move to love of its Lord, whether out of sorrow for one's sins, or for the passion of Christ our Lord, or because of other things directly ordered to his service and praise. Finally, I call consolation every increase of hope, faith and charity, and all interior joy that calls and attracts to heavenly things and to the salvation of one's soul, quieting it and giving it peace in its Creator and Lord.

... I call desolation all the contrary of the third rule, such as darkness of soul, disturbance in it, movement to low and earthly things, disquiet from various agitations and temptations, moving to lack of confidence, without hope, without love, finding oneself totally slothful, tepid, sad and, as if separated from one's Creator and Lord. For just as consolation is contrary to desolation, in the same way the thoughts that come from consolation are contrary to the thoughts that come from desolation.

Note how much space Loyola gives here to desolations. St. Ignatius and Father Dowling and the Jesuit understanding of the world recognized that the spiritual life was certainly not made up exclusively of sweetness and light and comforting divine consolations. This was very different from the view of the world which was presented in Richard Maurice Bucke and Emmet Fox. Bucke — and Fox in particular — had tended to focus almost exclusively on positive things.

Later on, in the speech he gave at the A.A. International in St. Louis in 1955, Father Ed quoted extensively from the passages about anguish and torment from Francis Thompson's poem, "The Hound of Heaven." We shall look in more detail at this talk later. But he used this poem as an example of the way that even our most negative experiences could also be experiences of God, or could be transformed into experiences of God.

"The Hound of Heaven" poem tries to teach us that excessive love of the things of this world will cause us to devote ourselves to causes which will always ultimately betray us, to cling frantically to people who will always eventually flee from us and abandon us, to seek protection from forces which can never permanently shelter us, and to try to find contentment in worldly goods (which never results in true happiness) instead of asking how we could make God content with us. But the fear and anguish and grief which we end up feeling, when we insist on learning these things the hard way, will nevertheless lead us straight to God if we draw the correct conclusions from all the tears and misery we suffer when we try to flee from God. Desolations of this sort teach us that to end our misery, we merely need to turn away from the things of this world and turn to God instead.

In the terminology of Ignatian spirituality therefore, desolations can be just as important as consolations in moving us along the path which God knows our souls need to take.

CHAPTER 24

Consolations: Feelings, Visions, Voices, and Contact with Saints

Consolations can be simple emotions and feelings which have been implanted in our hearts by God's grace, but when the limitless power of the divine realm suddenly explodes inside our souls, it can sometimes produce far more spectacular effects. So consolations can also involve intense physical sensations, and can even include seeing heavenly visions, such as Bill Wilson's experience at Towns Hospital of the divine light shining around him, or even visions of a saint or the Blessed Virgin Mary. They can also include hearing the *Bath Qol* (the Heavenly Voice) speaking to us, or words spoken by one of the saints or some other worthy person from the world beyond.

Bob Firth, an A.A. old timer from South Bend, Indiana, a good Irish Catholic, told me before he died, that when he first came into the program, and could not stay sober no matter what he did, he finally went out in an empty field one day in 1974 and got down on his knees and cried out, "God, please, all I want is some peace of mind." And then, he told me, all at once a warm feeling filled his whole body, and he became totally calm and free of fear. He still had some spiritual struggles left to go through, Bob told me, but this was the turning point, and he knew that he was going to eventually be all right.

Another South Bend old timer told me once about something that happened to him shortly after he joined A.A. and quit drinking. He had just gotten a new job, as a salesman, and was driving his automobile through the Indiana countryside on his way to make his first sales call. He was so anxious to make a success of this new job and pull himself out of the chain of failures that had marked his drinking years, that he started coming to pieces, and finally cried out, "Lord, all I want to do is find a place of peace!" And then he heard a heavenly voice speaking and saying to him, "You're already there." And he calmed down instantly, and realized that it was so. And he kept on driving, and paid his sales call on the businessman he was supposed to see, and did not attempt any aggressive sales pitch, but simply gave the man a copy of his company's catalogue, and offered to explain any parts that were not clear, or give additional details if necessary. And eventually, he said, the man became a good customer and bought many things from him.

Mrs. Marty Mann (her story is in the Big Book as "Women Suffer Too") first started down the path to sobriety in the Spring of 1939, while she was staying in a psychiatric hospital in Greenwich, Connecticut. At first she regarded the A.A. program as nonsense and refused to try going to meetings or working the steps. But one day, while storming around, overwhelmed with a crazed, uncontrollable, murderous anger at a member of the hospital staff, she looked down at a prepublication multilith copy of the Big Book which was lying open on her bed, and saw a line standing out high above the rest, as if carved out in big, black raised letters: "We cannot live with anger." Suddenly all her resistance to God and to the A.A. program collapsed, and she found herself staring through tears of joy and relief at a new world filled with color and beauty.[397]

St. Ignatius's fellow Spanish saint (and rough contemporary) St. Teresa of Avila wrote the first comprehensive study of the more flamboyant and spectacular kinds of consolations (see her *Interior Castle* and also her autobiography, both written in the last half of the 1500's). The modern systematic study of Christian spirituality begins with St. Teresa's writings. But going back long before that century, for what is now almost two thousand years, the Catholic Church has recognized that many of those who pursue the spiritual life with real passion and dedication are granted quite extraordinary spiritual experiences at certain points in their life. St. Teresa reported how some of her Spanish nuns would sometimes collapse on the floor during a religious service and just lie there on their backs compulsively crying out "Praise Jesus, praise Jesus" over and over, just like in a modern American Pentecostal revival. Others of her nuns had experienced what a modern American New Age or hippy type of person would call out-of-body-soul-travel.

What are today called out-of-body-near-death experiences, where people are taken up into a realm of heavenly light and lose their fear of dying, would fall into this category, I believe. Back in the Middle Ages, the Hesychast monks of Mount Athos developed a meditational technique involving constant repetition of the Jesus Prayer to achieve visions of this same divine light. Eastern Orthodox Christians refer to the Hesychastic experience as a vision of the Uncreated Light, and say that it was the same light which the apostles saw shining around Jesus at the Transfiguration — see Matthew 17:1–9, Mark 9:2-8, Luke 9:28–36, and 2 Peter 1:16–18.[398] One of the two examiners who gave me my oral examination on my doctoral dissertation at Oxford in 1970 was the Archimandrite of an Eastern Orthodox monastery where the monks still in the 1970's were regularly spending long periods every day reciting the Jesus Prayer.

Father Dowling's contemplative experiences: Circa 1920, in the second year of his Jesuit novitiate, young Ed Dowling underwent a major crisis of faith which took him two years to work himself out of. As he later described it, in his own words, in 1944:

> But here tonight, I am discussing a problem to which I am not entirely alien. Up to the age of 21 my spirituality, my religion, my faith was a comfortable, unchallenged nursery habit. Then over a course of some months, the most important months of my life saw that faith, that religion, drift away. It began to make demands. And as it ceased to be comfortable and comforting to big and important I, when it ceased to "yes" my body and soul, I found that I moved away from it. I am not utterly unacquainted with atheism. I know and respect agnosticism and I have been a bed-fellow with spiritual confusion, not merely the honest and sincere kind, but the self-kidding kind.[399]

But he eventually underwent spiritual experiences of some sort which enabled him to work himself out of that skepticism and doubt, and in later years spent part of every morning engaged in the kind of contemplation which St. Teresa, for example, had recommended for the nuns at the Carmelite convent in Spain where she was the Mother Superior. At home in St. Louis, Father Ed began every morning by celebrating the eucharist at the St. Louis College Church, and then would sit afterwards in the sacristy and silently contemplate the crucifix on the wall. Only after this period of deeply focused meditation would he go to the telephone and start arranging his day's business.[400] Some of St. Teresa's nuns had quite extraordinary spiritual experiences as the result of this kind of meditation and contemplation, and it was almost certain that Father Ed had undergone some of those experiences himself. It can be guaranteed that — as a result of practicing the *Spiritual Exercises* on a daily basis — he had experienced consolations of the ordinary sort on numerous occasions, but there are many indications that he had also probably undergone far more spectacular spiritual experiences as well.

Father Ed certainly expressed no skepticism when Bill Wilson told him the story of how he saw the Realm of Light and felt the rushing wind of the Spirit moving through him at Towns Hospital on December 14, 1934. The indications are that Father Ed had encountered his own visions of light or visions of the saints, if not exactly like Bill Wilson's experience of the Divine Light at Towns Hospital, then something of that general kind — the sort of encounter with the higher realm which Richard Maurice Bucke described in his book on *Cosmic Consciousness*. Bill W. says that he recognized Father Dowling at their very first meeting as a charismatic figure who possessed the full aura of true cosmic consciousness:

> He lowered himself into my solitary chair, and when he opened his overcoat I saw his clerical collar. He brushed back a shock of white hair and looked at me through the most remarkable pair of eyes I have ever seen. We talked about a lot of things, and my spirits kept on rising, and presently I began to realize that this man radiated a grace that filled the room with a sense of presence. I felt this with great intensity; it was a moving and mysterious experience. In years since I have seen much of this great friend, and whether I was in joy or in pain he always brought to me the same sense of grace and the presence of God. My case is no exception. Many who meet Father Ed experience this touch of the eternal. [401]

Bill W. described that evening elsewhere as being like "a second conversion experience,"[402] and Ernest Kurtz describes the scene in *Not-God* in even stronger terms as another vision seemingly of divine light.[403]

In his speech to the St. Louis International A.A. Convention in 1955, Father Ed made the only critical remark about A.A. which he ever made (or at least the only one I have encountered anywhere in print): "I still weep that the elders of the movement have dropped the word 'experience' for 'awakening'" in the wording of the Twelfth Step.[404] Father Ed was referring to the decision made, when preparing the second printing of the Big Book, to change the wording of the Twelfth Step on page 72 to eliminate the reference to special religious experiences (altered wording underlined by me):

> 1st PRINTING (APRIL 1939): Having had a spiritual <u>experience</u> as the result of <u>these</u> steps, we tried to carry this message to alcoholics, and to practice these principles in all our affairs.

> 2nd PRINTING (MARCH 2, 1941): Having had a spiritual <u>awakening</u> as the result of <u>those</u> steps, we tried to carry this message to alcoholics, and to practice these principles in all our affairs.

Father Ed went on to explain to the A.A. audience in St. Louis that, in his interpretation, "experience can be of two kinds." The commonest kind are gentle consolations sent to us by God, such as those "routine active observations" which can nevertheless strike us suddenly with an experience of deep pleasure: "I am sober today" as opposed to the misery and suffering I endured for so many years. But the other kind of religious experience is of a spectacular and overwhelming sort, Father Ed explained, "like Bill's experience and like the *Grapevine* story of that Christmas Eve in Chicago," or what happened to the Apostle Paul "as he was struck from his horse on the road to Damascus." Had Father Ed undergone religious experiences of this latter sort? He certainly defended both kinds of spiritual experience, and affirmed that not only Bill Wilson, but others in A.A. as well, had in fact seen and felt things of a profoundly supernatural and scientifically unexplainable sort.[405]

When Bill Wilson began experimenting with LSD, he not only took the mind-altering chemical himself, but also got Father Dowling to take it. The most obvious explanation for why he asked him to do this, was because Father Dowling (like Aldous Huxley, Gerald Heard, and Bill Wilson) had had spiritual experiences without the use of drugs which seemed similar to LSD-induced experiences (at least in terms of second-hand reports), and could therefore give a useful judgment as to whether they were in fact the same thing.

Bill Wilson speaks with St. Boniface and other spirits of the dead: When we are looking at the more spectacular sorts of consolations which one could receive when pursuing the spiritual life, we must not forget all the accounts of pious Christian men and women over the past two thousand years who reported having heard words spoken to them personally by Jesus or Mary Our Mother, or who talked and prayed to one of the many saints who dwelt up in the heavenly realm, and insisted that they had actually received concrete help from these saints.

By 1952, Bill Wilson was pushing the frame on this a bit. He said that he had actually had conversations with one of the major early medieval saints, a famous figure named Boniface (c. 675? – 5 June 754). This individual was born in Anglo-Saxon England in the kingdom of Wessex, but crossed the English Channel and became a missionary spreading Christianity in the German-speaking Frankish Empire. Boniface became the patron saint of Germany, and is called the "Apostle of the Germans." He was the first archbishop of the important Catholic city of Mainz on the river Rhine. In 754, Boniface was killed in Frisia (a Low German speaking area along the North Sea coast of Germany and the Netherlands). His remains were taken to the Benedictine monastery of Fulda in Hesse in central Germany, where they rest in a sarcophagus which subsequently became a great pilgrimage site.

In a letter which Bill Wilson wrote to Father Dowling on July 17, 1952, Bill said that he had been especially helped in writing the *Twelve Steps and Twelve Traditions* by one particular spirit from "over there," a man

> ... calling himself Boniface. Said he was a Benedictine missionary and English. Had been a man of learning, knew missionary work and a lot about structures. I think he said

this all the more modestly but that was the gist of it. I'd never heard of this gentleman but he checked out pretty well in the Encyclopedia. If this one is who he says he is—and of course there is no certain way of knowing—would this be licit contact in your book?

Father Dowling wrote back to Bill on July 24, 1952, and — most interestingly — did NOT say that this was sinful OR that it was a superstitious delusion. Father Ed was a Jesuit, and well trained in conventional Catholic orthodoxy, but was also clearly an extremely liberal and free-thinking person, who was willing to entertain the possibility that various kinds of psychic phenomena might be real. He simply advised Bill (as any wise spiritual director would do) to show caution:

> Boniface sounds like the Apostle of Germany. I still feel, like Macbeth, that these folks tell us truth in small matters in order to fool us in larger. I suppose that is my lazy orthodoxy. [406]

But it was especially interesting that his caution did not involve the denial that the human mind could contact beings such as saints, angels, spirit guides, or what American Indian shamans called "allies." He simply advised Bill Wilson to be aware that supernatural beings could include *real* demonic spirits as well as *real* angelic spirits and *real* souls of saints and holy men and women.

And Father Ed made a strange statement when he was speaking to the St. Louis International A.A. Convention in 1955. He was talking about his belief that we are called to continually grow in our knowledge of God, not only in this present material existence but also in our life after death as spirits dwelling in the transcendent world, and he told the crowd of 5,000 people gathered before him that:

> I am sure that Bill, sitting in that chair, and Dr. Bob, whose angel is probably sitting on that oddly misplaced empty chair, are growing in the knowledge of God. [407]

Was this simply a humorous or joking remark? — that is, his statement about Dr. Bob's spirit having literally come down from heaven to sit enthroned on the stage at Kiel Auditorium in St. Louis? Father Dowling's way of putting it was a safe way of talking about it, because it could easily be interpreted by anyone who wanted to, as merely humorous or symbolic or metaphorical. And some of the A.A. people gathered there would have been both skeptical and uncomfortable with the idea of people here on Earth being able to communicate with the souls of those from the spiritual realm, or being able to sense the presence of a departed soul in the room or building where they were sitting.

But Father Ed's reference to the "oddly misplaced empty chair" up there on the stage was a bit too concrete and specific for a casual metaphor or bit of jocularity. Just as with Carl Jung's references to synchronicity, there is customarily an uncanny specificity to things that play the role of divine signs or messages or indications that something from the other world has temporarily crossed over into our present physical world — that is the way we recognize them. I think that Father Ed meant his statement literally, or at least knew good and well that Bill Wilson would hear it literally.

And Father Ed spoke of Dr. Bob's "angel" sitting up on the stage. Orthodox Catholic teaching distinguished between angels and human souls — they were not the same kind of thing. On the other hand, Bill Wilson had learned, through his contact with his wife Lois and her family, to make use on occasion of Swedenborgian terminology, and Swedenborg had taught that human souls after death literally became angels. Father Ed had undoubtedly heard Bill talking that way on many occasions. So Father Ed's use of this kind of terminology was specifically directed toward Bill Wilson's way of talking about the world after death.

I think it likely that Bill Wilson heard Father Ed as much as saying, "Look Bill, if you use your deeper spiritual senses, you can see or feel Dr. Bob's angel (or spirit or ghost) sitting right there in that chair — literally and in fact — come here today to cheer everybody on and rejoice with us in this celebration of our success as a movement." And I think that Father Ed cannot have failed to understand that this was what Bill W. would have heard him saying.

CHAPTER 25

Bill W. Does His Fifth Step
with Father Dowling: 1940

Ernest Kurtz reports how Bill Wilson did his first real Fifth Step with Father Dowling on that cold winter night in December 1940 when the priest came to visit him at the 24th St. Clubhouse in New York:

> Not since his earliest days in the Oxford Group had Wilson felt himself in the loving presence of such a receptive listener. Then, Bill had unburdened himself especially to Ebby. But it was only now, as this evening with Father Dowling wore on, that the man who had written A.A.'s Fifth Step came to feel that he himself was finally "taking his Fifth." He told Dowling not only what he had done and had left undone — he went on to share with his new sponsor the thoughts and feelings behind those actions and omissions. He told of his high hopes and plans, and spoke also about his anger, despair, and mounting frustrations.[408]

Robert Thomsen made the same statement, that this was when Bill Wilson made his full Fifth Step confession to another human being, and Nell Wing likewise affirmed that Bill "took his Fifth Step with his spiritual sponsor, Father Ed Dowling."[409]

Kurtz talked more about what he had come up with in his research, in a note to the A.A. History Lovers on January 19, 2010:[410]

> In the long recording that Bill did to help Robert Thomsen in his research, Bill mentions after his long conversation

with Dowling, he "felt for the first time completely cleansed and freed." At the time of my research, I discussed this with several of the then-surviving old-timers, and they agreed that given the time and circumstances — remember [that when Bill was talking with Ebby at the beginning, and discussing alcoholism at great length with Dr. Bob in 1935], the 12 Steps had not yet been formulated and all they had to go on was Oxford Group practice — this "must have been Bill's first 'Fifth Step.'" "That is one of the things you should get from a real Fifth Step." Over time and listening to more of Bill and reading more of his correspondence about the Steps and Father Dowling, I came to agree with the historical certainty of that understanding.

Bill Wilson was 45 years old when he made this detailed Fifth Step confession, and Father Dowling was only 42 — but wise far beyond his years.

The A.A. concept of a sponsor began to be influenced by the Catholic idea of the spiritual director: In the original Oxford Group program (which was based on the idea of the 5 C's), an extremely close and personal one-on-one contact was necessary between the missionary and the person that missionary was trying to convert to a life-changing version of Christianity. But once converted, there was no real equivalent in the Oxford Group to the *continuing* extremely close relationship which developed in the A.A. program, a relationship which bound the newcomer to a more experienced member of the fellowship in unbroken fashion over the many years that followed.

At the beginning of A.A. history, the word "sponsor" referred to the member of the A.A. group who guaranteed to pay the hospital bill of a new drunk who was sent into the hospital to be detoxed and given his initial introduction to the A.A. program. After the newcomer got sobered up and got back on his feet again, he was expected to pay that hospital bill himself, but if he went back to drinking again, and never paid his bill, the sponsor was supposed to reach into his own pocket and give the hospital the money which it was owed.

Even Clarence Snyder's *Sponsorship Pamphlet*, which he wrote in 1944, talked almost exclusively about making the initial contact with a new alcoholic, and getting the person to his or her first few meetings. It was still heavily dependent on the Oxford Group teaching of the 5 C's.[411]

Nevertheless in Akron, from the beginning, there was a special relationship between Dr. Bob and the people who came to his and Anne's house to get sober, which contributed strongly to the later A.A. idea of the sponsor, even though the actual word "sponsorship" was not explicitly used to describe what Dr. Bob and Anne were doing. Or in other words, some of the most important parts of the later, more developed A.A. idea of sponsorship were clearly attempts to mirror the special love and individual care which Dr. Bob and Anne Smith had given to alcoholics who got sober under their supervision.

At one level therefore, we do not have to look outside early A.A. practice itself to find the basic origins of the concept of the sponsor. Nevertheless, we should not ignore the profound effect on A.A. understanding and practice when large numbers of Roman Catholics began coming into the program. They came with their own set of presuppositions and their own deep wisdom, based on centuries of Church teaching, about how the good spiritual life needed to be led.

After the Akron A.A. group made its break with the Oxford Group in October 1939, and Dr. Bob promised Sister Ignatia in January 1940 that he would keep his A.A. program non-sectarian, Roman Catholics began pouring into the A.A. movement. By October 1940, Bill Wilson estimated that the fellowship was now 25% Roman Catholic.[412]

There was a long Catholic tradition of choosing someone to be your spiritual director when you set out upon the spiritual life. That person, if a priest, was sometimes called your "confessor," as we see in the case of St. Teresa of Avila for example, but this was a completely different role from that of the parish priest who heard routine confessions from parishioners where they confessed to committing specific sins for which they wished to receive absolution.

And in particular, the Jesuits recommended that anyone attempting to carry out the *Spiritual Exercises* do so only under the supervision of a competent spiritual director. Some of the meditations could become so intense, and involved psychological issues that probed so deeply into our most primordial fears and anxieties, that a person could sometimes be pushed over the edge into psychosis and even suicidal behavior.

So in A.A. during the early 1940's, as I interpret what happened, the fourth step — under this new Roman Catholic influence — was made far more detailed and began to go far deeper, and along with this, it became clear that most of those who were making the most spiritual progress, had the greatest serenity, and got in the least psychological trouble, were those who linked up with someone who could serve, at least in part, as a good spiritual director of the traditional Roman Catholic sort.

So the early A.A. idea of the sponsor evolved into the concept of a person who could, when necessary, play the role of a good spiritual director, and the quality of the sobriety and serenity that started emerging quickly convinced most A.A.'s, whether they came from Catholic backgrounds or not, that this was the best way to work the program.

Father Dowling's Later Life: 1940-1960

CHAPTER 26

Bill Wilson and A.A. from 1941 to 1945

After December 1940: the doors begin to open for A.A. As a conclusion to the story of the priest who came out of the snow and sleet to visit the struggling author of a book about addiction and redemption, there in December 1940, perhaps at the very time when Father Dowling was making his trip to New York City to meet Bill Wilson for the first time, the *Saturday Evening Post* was assigning a reporter named Jack Alexander to write a story about A.A. The reporter went first to Bill Wilson and the New York A.A. members, but did not believe them. He next went to visit the A.A. people in Akron and Cleveland but did not believe them either. He then went to Chicago and took these A.A. people a little more seriously, but still remained skeptical.

It was not until Jack Alexander went home for Christmas — home for him was St. Louis — and met Father Dowling and the St. Louis A.A. group which Dowling had founded, that he finally became a believer.

In March 1941, Jack Alexander's article came out in print, and the story of the astonishing nationwide spread of A.A. truly began. Over 6,000 inquiries were sent to the New York A.A. office during 1941 because of the piece, and the Big Book finally began selling in large numbers. In anticipation, a second printing of the Big Book was brought out on March 2, 1941. By the end of the year, A.A. membership had grown from around 2,000 to over 8,000. In April 1941, Bill and Lois Wilson were finally able to obtain their own home (Stepping Stones), a seven-room house on almost two acres of land in Bedford Hills, New York.

In more ways than one, the story of Bill Wilson's encounter with Father Ed Dowling lay at the heart of one of the most important turning points in early A.A. history.

1936-1941 — huge changes sweep through the Oxford Group while the lead-up to the Second World War begins: In terms of the A.A. movement's external surroundings, the years 1936-41 formed a tumultuous period.

In 1936, Adolf Hitler reoccupied the Rhineland, sent German troops to Spain to help General Franco, and entered into pacts with both Italy and Japan. He took over Austria in March 1938, and then he ordered the German army to invade Poland on September 1, 1939, the date which is normally taken as the formal beginning of World War II. The strain and tension were felt all across America during these years as powerful political forces fought one another, one side attempting to bring the United States into the war which was developing, and the other struggling to keep it out.

Finally on December 7, 1941, the American port and air field at Pearl Harbor in Hawaii was bombed by Germany's ally Japan, and the United States found itself forced to join in the worldwide fighting, which lasted all the way down to the summer of 1945. We should never forget, when studying the history of A.A. in the years 1941 to 1945, that during that period it was not the problem of alcoholism, but this war which was dominating the thoughts and imaginations of the majority of people in the United States.

Meanwhile, within the Oxford Group — the Christian evangelical organization out of which A.A. had originally emerged — Frank Buchman came up with a new name for the movement in 1938 and began referring to it as "Moral Re-Armament" (MRA). Also the nature of the group itself began to change: in response to the war tensions that were building up all over Europe and America, Buchman started increasingly reframing the group's purpose in terms of working to bring about world peace. Any major interest in helping alcoholics started withering away.

In the United States, the Rev. Sam Shoemaker, the rector of Calvary Episcopal Church in New York City, had allowed the Oxford Group to make use of Calvary House (a nine-story building which belonged to the church) as a place for their American headquarters during the 1930's. Shoemaker himself was serving as the American head of the movement when A.A. was first coming into being. Bill Wilson in later years gave him a good deal of credit for teaching him many of the things which became part of the spiritual foundation of Alcoholics Anonymous and the twelve step movement. (At the A.A. International in St. Louis in 1955, Bill asked the Rev. Sam Shoemaker and Father Dowling to share the stage together as the two most-honored religious teachers of A.A.[413])

But in the spring of 1937, the leaders of the Oxford Group in New York ordered alcoholics staying at Calvary Episcopal Church's Rescue Mission to stop going to the meetings for alcoholics which were being held at Bill and Lois Wilson's home, and in August 1937, Bill and Lois themselves stopped attending Oxford Group meetings.

On May 10-11, 1939 the Cleveland contingent pulled out of the Oxford Group meeting held in Akron on Wednesdays at the home of T. Henry and Clarace Williams, and set up their own weekly meeting at the home of Albert (Abby or Al) and Grace Golrick. In October 1939, most of the rest of the alcoholics who were attending the Oxford Group meeting at the Williams' home, agreed to begin meeting at Dr. Bob's house instead, and severed all their remaining connections with the Oxford Group.

Things then fell further apart. In 1940, the relationship between Shoemaker and Frank Buchman began growing more and more strained, and in November 1941, Moral-Re-Armament was asked to leave Calvary House. Shoemaker formed his own fellowship, which he called "Faith at Work."

There was no longer any working relationship between A.A. and the Oxford Group during the 1940's. This was the case even in Akron: the beginner's manual which was published in Akron in 1942 (called *A Manual for Alcoholics Anonymous*) listed no Oxford Group publications at all in its recommended reading list for newcomers to A.A.[414] The works on that list were mostly a mix of classical liberal Protestantism and New Thought.

In the 1940's, A.A. instead embarked on an ever-increasing involvement with the Roman Catholic Church: The reading list in the 1942 Akron Manual excluded all of the older Oxford Group works which some A.A.'s had read during the later 1930's. But it did have one recommended set of publications that seems to have represented an overture to Roman Catholics: a reference to a series called *The Unchanging Friend* which was published by a Roman Catholic press, the Bruce Publishing Co. in Milwaukee. This publishing firm, which was founded in 1891 by William George Bruce (1856-1949), operated for seventy-seven years until it was bought in 1968 by Crowell Collier and Macmillan. During some of that period it was the largest Roman Catholic publisher in the world, publishing two thousand books as well as magazines, journals and pamphlets. And the highest levels of Catholicism in turn gave great public honors to Bruce for his service to the Church: he was made a Knight of St. Gregory in 1920 by Pope Benedict XV, an award given to laypeople for extraordinary services to the Papacy and the Roman Catholic Church, and he received the Laetare Medal in 1947 from the University of Notre Dame in South Bend, Indiana, which was possibly the best known Catholic university in America.[415]

And then past that point, we can see A.A. progressively being pulled deeper and deeper into the Roman Catholic orbit during the 1940's and 50's. Sister Ignatia's alcoholism treatment ward at St. Thomas Hospital, located just across the hall from the balcony entrance to the hospital's Catholic chapel, had a profound influence on all the many alcoholics who passed through there. And as of 1940, as we have just seen, a Jesuit priest (Father Ed) began serving as the spiritual director and moral guide for Bill Wilson, one of the co-founders.

In 1943, Father Ralph Pfau, a diocesan priest in Indianapolis, was the first alcoholic Roman Catholic priest to get sober in A.A., and became over the course of the next twenty-some years one of the four most-published A.A. authors. The well-known American mystery writer Austin Ripley got sober in 1942, and attempted to start the first treatment center at Hazelden in 1947, which he intended at that point to be used exclusively for the treatment of alcoholic Roman Catholic priests.[416]

In 1947, Bill W. took instruction in the Catholic faith from the Venerable Fulton J. Sheen, professor at the Catholic University of America and host of the nationally broadcast radio program, the Catholic Hour. In 1952, Father Ed and another Jesuit priest (Father John C. Ford, S.J., America's most famous Catholic moral theologian of that time) were allowed to vet the manuscript, before it was printed, of the A.A. movement's second most important book, the *Twelve Steps and Twelve Traditions*.

The twenty-year-long association between Father Dowling and Bill Wilson was an important part of this story of A.A.'s mid-century love affair with the Roman Catholic Church.

Trouble in Cleveland and Akron developed in 1940-1941: In May/June of 1940, Hank Parkhurst (who had started back drinking again eight or nine months earlier) went to Cleveland and claimed that Bill Wilson was taking large amounts of money from the sales of the Big Book and putting it in his own pocket. At one point Hank was married to the sister of Clarence Snyder's wife Dorothy, and Clarence eventually became involved in the attacks on Bill W. also.

Then Clarence Snyder organized a Dr. Bob Smith Dinner which was set for October 5, 1941, and held at the Hotel Statler in Cleveland, Ohio. There were around 850 to 900 people present at the huge affair. Bill Wilson was invited to attend, and came from New York.[417]

Clarence said that he had not known that Bill Wilson and Dr. Bob were both supposed to be receiving royalties from the sale of the Big Book until that point. It came out when he went to meet Bill at the Cleveland railroad depot to welcome him to the city.

> "He told me then," said Clarence. "I was stunned. I thought it was a labor of love — no one was supposed to get any royalties. But Bill didn't make any bones about it. People in New York knew, and he assumed that Dr. Bob would tell them in Akron."[418]

Some of the Cleveland A.A.'s brought Bill W. and Dr. Bob back a second time, ostensibly for another dinner in their honor, but in fact they dragged the two of them before a private meeting of the chairmen or secretaries of all the Cleveland A.A. groups, with both a lawyer and a certified public accountant present. They accused Bill and Dr. Bob of splitting $64,000 in profits from the sale of the Big Book in 1941.[419] As Bill Wilson described it, "They believed that I, the Wall Street promoter, had my truck backed right up to Mr. John D. Rockefeller's strongbox and had persuaded him to fill it with coin for me and my friends."[420]

At the time, in fact, Bill was receiving $25 a week from the publishing sales. In addition, both he and Dr. Bob were receiving $30 a week, supplied by contributions from well-to-do non-A.A.'s friendly to the fellowship .... Records show that Dr. Bob received a total of $1,000 during 1941; evidently, even their weekly $30 was not always forthcoming.[421]

Bill, who had been forewarned of what was going to happen, had brought along a certified audit of the movement's financial affairs. After the Cleveland people had read that, they apologized for the attack. And in fact, even though sales of the Big Book increased during the next year, 1942, Bill W. and Dr. Bob still only received $875 in royalties apiece that year.[422]

As Bill Wilson explained fourteen years later at A.A.'s Second International Convention in St. Louis, that experience back in 1941 obliged Dr. Bob and himself "to carefully re-examine our status."

This was one of the test cases out of which A.A.'s Tradition respecting professionalism and paid workers was evolved. It was certain that I could not continue full time nor Bob devote more than half his working hours to A.A. unless we both had some definite source of steady income. We could not expect our [Rockefeller] dinner guests to bolster us up indefinitely. That would be contrary to the then-forming Tradition of no contributions from the outside world. Neither could he and I receive group funds, which were already pledged to the support of the Headquarters office ....[423]

Royalties from the sale of the Big Book seemed to Bill to be the best answer. He had put enormous time into writing and editing the book and organizing the publishing company, and Dr. Bob had furnished some of the most important ideas found in the book.

Shortly after the financial investigation episode, Father Ed Dowling, our Jesuit friend from St. Louis, turned up in New York. Still puzzled, I put the case up to him. He asked, "Do you think A.A. requires your full-time efforts?" I replied, "Yes, I think it does, perhaps indefinitely." Then he inquired, "Could you become a paid therapist, taking money for Twelfth Step work?" I told him that this issue had been settled long since. Most emphatically I could not, regardless of the consequences, nor could any other A.A. member.

"Well, Bill," said Father Ed, "if you were the only one concerned, you could certainly start wearing a hair shirt and take nothing. But what about Lois? Once upon a time you made a marriage contract to support her. Suppose you put her on the charity of friends so that you can do a service organization job for A.A. free. Would that be the kind of support your marriage contract called for? I should think the royalties would be the best bet."

That meant that Dr. Bob and I must certainly never accept money for Twelfth Step work but that we could be recompensed for special services. We both accepted Father Ed's down-the-middle advice and have stuck by it ever since, and I am glad to say this status for Dr. Bob and me was later accepted as correct in principle by our entire fellowship.[424]

Jesuit casuistry vs. the Jansenist attempt to make moral decisions on the basis of rigid, mechanical rules: We remember how, earlier in this book, we discussed the great controversy which pitted Jesuits against Jansenists in European Catholicism during the seventeenth and eighteenth centuries. Blaise Pascal's defense of Jansenism in his *Provincial Letters* (written in 1656-57, and still considered one of the great French literary classics), denounced what was called Jesuit "casuistry." In Catholic moral theology, casuistry employed case-based reasoning, as opposed to the kind of rigid rule-based reasoning which Jansenism stressed.

Clarence Snyder (although not a Catholic) had applied what was a rigid Jansenist-type, rule-based critique of Bill Wilson's taking royalty payments from the sale of the Big Book: "I was stunned" Clarence exclaimed, "I thought it was a labor of love — no one was supposed to get any royalties." [425] That is, first one established a mechanical rule — perhaps something like "no A.A. members are ever supposed to take any money for anything which they do for A.A." — and then applied that rule rigidly and legalistically to all situations, no matter what the context.

I have encountered some modern-day Jansenist-type A.A.'s who wanted to argue that A.A. people should never be asked to pay for anything they were involved in as part of their A.A. activities — anything at all — and who as a consequence objected to charging people a registration fee (for example) for attending an A.A. conference. But that is an extraordinarily extreme position, and back then, even someone like Clarence Snyder did not go that far: A.A. members who attended the banquet Clarence organized to honor Dr. Bob on October 5, 1941 at the Statler Hotel in Cleveland — the place where the whole controversy over Bill W. and Dr. Bob receiving royalties had actually started — were charged $1.35 to defray the cost of the meal and renting the hotel banquet room.

In various ways, legalism and absolutism tend to crop up in Alcoholics Anonymous over and over again, and various kinds of works righteousness, and situations where pompous, self-important alcoholics start making grandiose proclamations in the attempt to seem more moral than anyone else around them.

Father Dowling however showed Bill Wilson how to analyze this particular moral issue in a different kind of way, using Jesuit casuistry, that is, practical, pragmatic, case-based reasoning. The first practical aspect of the actual case at hand, was that A.A. in its early years could not have survived without Bill Wilson's diplomatic skills and constant work writing endless letters, talking on the telephone and traveling all over the country calming down alcoholics who were getting ready to tear the movement to pieces over various resentments and hostilities. That was the central issue Bill talked about later on in his chapter on the First Tradition in the *Twelve Steps and Twelve Traditions*: "In the world about us we saw personalities destroying whole peoples. The struggle for wealth, power, and prestige was tearing humanity apart as never before." That was the whole purpose of the Twelve Traditions, to help keep one fairly small group within A.A. — the angry, ego-driven promoters and "stage directors" — from tearing everything apart as they attacked other people or tried to force their way on everybody else. But in the earliest days of A.A., the program also needed the full-time services of

Bill Wilson and his people skills, in order to keep the movement from fragmenting and breaking apart.

Then Father Ed reminded Bill W. of another actual case from not long before: in 1936, Charles B. Towns had offered Bill a very well-paying job as an alcoholism counselor at Towns Hospital. The members of the fellowship had decided, however, that the A.A. program could not have a class of professional, salaried therapists running the movement. So it had already been decided, in an actual practical case, that Bill's living expenses could not be provided for in that manner.

Next Father Ed referred to another kind of practical case, which was surely (to a certain extent) lying at the back of people's minds: great holy men and women who, like St. Francis of Assisi, had lived in a cave and survived by begging for their food, while they did great deeds to help the rest of the human race. But then Father Ed immediately pointed out the severely practical matter which made that kind of approach not applicable here: Bill had a wife. How could he possibly abandon Lois and throw her out, and force her to once again go around living off the charity of their friends — people who would give her a spare room to sleep in perhaps, and some of their cast-off clothes to wear?

The specific answer to the practical problem, Father Ed suggested to Bill, was for him and Dr. Bob to be given enough of the royalties from the sale of the Big Book to enable them to live, not in a mansion waited on by a crowd of servants, but each in a modest middle class house, with food on the table, and some clothes of their own for Bill and Bob and their wives to wear. But this was a specific answer to the problem of dealing with a specific case, and was not intended to establish a general rule for the permanent establishment of some supposed governing elite in A.A.

This was the way Jesuit casuistry operated. The majority of A.A. members in subsequent years have tended to use a similar approach to dealing with thorny organizational and moral issues. Jesuit spirituality specialized in dealing with what they called the practice of "discernment," that is, devising ways of deciding what God really wanted us to do, and what decisions we ourselves should take in dealing with practical moral issues. This included the discernment of spirits, and learning how to interpret consolations and desolations in our daily lives.

We should also notice the way this good Jesuit advice has affected the ethos of ordinary, everyday A.A. meetings. People are discouraged from trying to criticize other people at a meeting by accusing them of breaking one or another mechanical and absolutistic moral "rule," and in particular, they are advised not to start using mechanical rules and comparisons to make themselves appear superior to the other people at the meeting. Saying to myself, "I am not an alcoholic because I never did that terrible thing which so-and-so did," in fact keeps me from realizing that I need help myself. So does saying to myself, "Thank goodness I never did that immoral thing which so-and-so did, which proves that I am clearly a much better person than that degenerate wretch."

Casuistry on the other hand — which looks at real cases from the past, and searches for parallels and similarities which can help illuminate what is at stake in our present situation — listens to the other people at the twelve-step meeting and tries to *identify* rather than *compare*. How much of what those other people reported about what they did and felt was in fact similar at some level to things which I have also done and felt? And another piece of traditional A.A. advice — "take what you want and leave the rest" — is also part of the basic casuistic methodology. If another person, in a similar case, did such-and-such and it worked, then it would be wise for me to think about ways that I could use a similar strategy for dealing with my own case in my own life situation. But this cannot be done mechanically: I may also discover, as I think about it a bit longer, that the other person's way of dealing with the problem would not be appropriate for me at all.

Above all — this is so very important to note — the Jesuit method of discernment keeps me sane, non-neurotic, and free of resentment. Because if I try instead to solve all of my moral and personal problems by devising dozens of mechanical, legalistic rules and following them slavishly — "NEVER do such-and-such, ALWAYS do thus-and-so, good boys ALWAYS do this, and good girls NEVER do that" — the best psychiatrists and psychologists tell us that this is a guaranteed pathway to chronic depression and/or deep resentments poisoning all my relationships with other people.

Father Ed's New Year's 1942 visit to Stepping Stones: On April 11, 1941, Bill and Lois moved into their new home, Stepping Stones, where they would live for the remainder of their lives. Bill subsequently asked Father Dowling to spend the next New Year's with them. Several days after this visit (on January 6, 1942), Father Ed wrote Bill a thank you note saying, "I want to thank Lois for seconding your efforts to make that New Year's Day one of the happiest I've ever spent." We do not know what they talked about, but another letter from Father Ed, written four years later, made it clear that the historical event which was hanging over their heads during that visit was the recent Japanese bombing of Pearl Harbor on December 7, 1941. In that letter, Dowling wrote, "I often recall our New Year's together just after Pearl Harbor."[426] The Japanese attack three weeks earlier had destroyed most of the U.S. Navy's Pacific Fleet, and had left America totally vulnerable to further attacks on Hawaii, on the Philippines, on the Panama Canal, or ultimately anywhere on the coast of California, Oregon, or Washington state. Everyone in the United States was waiting with dread and fear to see what would happen next.

But as we see — and as St. Ignatius and Carl Jung both tried to teach us — Good and Evil can both surround us on every side in this world and this life, all mixed together. We don't try to deny that both are real.

February 1942 — Father Dowling asked to be a trustee: One of Bill Wilson's first reactions, after he and Lois had both gotten to know Father Ed well, was to try to put the priest into a key governing role in Alcoholics Anonymous. So just a month after the three of them had their New Year's visit, Bill wrote a letter on February 3, 1942, and asked Father Ed if he would be willing to be one of the Trustees of the Alcoholic Foundation.[427]

The Alcoholic Foundation had been set up as a charitable trust on August 5, 1938 (it was later given its present name, the "General Service Board of Alcoholics Anonymous," in 1954). In its original form, the Alcoholic Foundation was supposed to have five Trustees, the majority of whom were required to be non-alcoholics. The original non-alcoholic Trustees were Willard Richardson, Frank Amos, and an attorney named John Wood (a friend of Frank Amos who only served until December 1939). The two original alcoholic trustees were Dr. Bob and William J. "Bill" Ruddell (a man from New Jersey whose story was put in the Big Book as "A Businessman's Recovery").

They had problems at first, however, finding alcoholic trustees who could stay sober for very long. As one device for obtaining more stability in this vital governing body, its size was therefore increased from five to seven Trustees in January 1939. Bill Wilson's brother-in-law Dr. Leonard V. Strong was added as a non-alcoholic Trustee, giving them a hard core of four board members they could count on. And then in February 1940, Bert Taylor (who owned a fashionable clothing business on 5th Avenue in New York City) and Horace Chrystal (who first suggested printing the Serenity Prayer on little cards, and effectively turned it into the official A.A. prayer) were appointed as alcoholic Trustees, and served long and well.

On March 16, 1940, the Alcoholic Foundation moved its office to 30 Vesey St., Room 703, in Lower Manhattan (the mailing address was Box 658, Church St. Annex Post Office). Ruth Hock served as secretary to the Alcoholic Foundation and carried out the major correspondence with A.A. groups all over the world.

A position as Trustee would have given Father Dowling a good deal of control over the future course of Alcoholics Anonymous, and how its central headquarters was run. If Dowling had been put in that position, it might well have had a powerful effect on the organizational structures which A.A. adopted during the 1940's and 50's, as well as the design and goals developed within its publishing arms. (Father Ed was after all one of the editors at a very important and successful Catholic publishing house.)

But on February 18, 1942, Father Ed wrote back to Bill W., and told him that he had asked the Provincial who was head of his Jesuit Province for permission to serve as a Trustee, and was told that it would have to be a bishop, not a priest, for a post as important as that one.[428]

There was no Catholic bishop who knew enough about A.A. to fill that role, so Bill Wilson was forced to remain in the position of having to work full time as the one person at the national level who had the diplomatic and people skills to keep what were now increasingly large numbers of alcoholics from tearing the movement apart with resentments, ego trips, and loudly expressed out-of-control temper tantrums. This was the period of A.A.'s most explosive growth, as we can see from the figures below, which trace the growth of the fellowship from 1,400 members in 1940 to 102,177 members in 1951:[429]

1940	1,400
1941	5,500
1942	6,000
1943	8,000
1944	10,000
1945	14,000
1946	29,000
1947	40,000
1948	60,000
1949	73,218
1950	96,475
1951	102,177

1943 to 1955 — Bill Wilson starts going to psychiatrists in addition to working with Father Dowling, as he continues trying to find some more effective way to deal with his chronic depression — first to Dr. Tiebout: For myself, I believe that trying to keep the peace between what were eventually thousands of quarrelsome alcoholics was one of the factors that drove Bill Wilson into long-term chronic clinical depression during this period. I believe that this was enough to pull anyone's spirits down, and does not require an elaborate theological or psychiatric explanation (that is, as to its cause).

But at any rate, in mid-1944 Bill's depression became so crippling that he began going twice a week to Dr. Harry M. Tiebout, M.D., for treatment. Tiebout had been trained as a psychiatrist at the Johns Hopkins University School of Medicine (in a kind of eclectic approach with what were nevertheless heavy Freudian components), and wrote some famous articles on the psychiatry of alcoholism, with titles like "The Act of Surrender in the Therapeutic Process, "Surrender Versus Compliance in Therapy," and "The Ego Factors in Surrender in Alcoholism."[430] (Tiebout was the one who brought Mrs. Marty Mann into the A.A. program in April 1939 by repeatedly insisting that she read in a prepublication copy of the A.A. Big Book.)

Bill Wilson fairly quickly found that he was not being helped by an approach which presumably saw his depression as repressed rage arising from unwillingness to totally surrender his ego and cease trying to control or manage anything around him. In fact, A.A.'s very survival depended on his being willing to play a strong leadership role in the movement, in highly directive fashion when necessary. And he had to do this in spite of the fact that part of the membership of the A.A. program was made up of deeply disturbed people with personality disorders (antisocial personality disorder, borderline personality disorder, psychopaths, and so on) along with others who were openly psychotic, so that telling him to practice total surrender was not going to keep the fellowship from being destroyed by this small but extremely disruptive handful of trouble makers.

1945 — Jungian psychology vs. Loyola's Spiritual Exercises on the underlying nature of moral evil. So in 1945, Bill switched to a Jungian therapist named Dr. Frances Weeks, whom he saw once a week on Fridays for several years, all the way down to 1949.[431] Carl Jung was in his seventies by this time, and had worked out all the basic features of his mature psychiatric doctrine, so we are presumably talking about a fully developed Jungian system of ideas being available to her in her sessions with Bill.

> <u>As a side note</u>: We need to remember, on the other hand, that when Rowland Hazard went to Carl Jung, it was the year 1926, and many of the most distinctive ideas associated with Jungian psychiatry had not yet been developed, to such a degree that it is in fact difficult to work out exactly what kind of treatment strategies Jung would have attempted in his sessions with Hazard. We know from a letter which Hazard wrote that he was telling the psychiatrist about his dreams, for example, but we do not know exactly what Jung would have been looking for in those dreams in 1926.[432]
>
> So if we are looking for the possible influence of classical Jungian psychiatry on twelve step thought, we need to forget about Rowland Hazard's visit to Jung in 1926, and start looking more at things like possible influences

from Bill Wilson's psychoanalysis with Dr. Frances Weeks in 1945-1949.

And of course even before that, Bill Wilson, Dr. Bob, and many other A.A.'s eagerly read Carl Jung's *Modern Man in Search of a Soul,* which came out in 1933.[433]

The object of Jungian analysis was to take the "shadow," that is those parts of the patient's personality which were locked in the unconscious, and *integrate* them into the conscious self in such a way as to produce a well-functioning whole. Jung also referred to this process of integration as individuation. Some of the dark parts might be made up of what were originally very negative parts of the personality, but the shadow also contained the reservoir of the forces that could produce real creativity.

There were profound differences between this kind of Jungian approach and the ideas taught in the section on the Two Battle Standards in St. Ignatius Loyola's *Spiritual Exercises.* In Loyola, the forces of wickedness were pure evil, and our duty as good people was to fight against them unceasingly and work to totally destroy them. In Jung, the forces which could produce such wickedness did not come from an external power of evil, attacking us from the outside, but were in residence within our own souls and could not be totally eradicated; our job therefore was to figure out ways of *restructuring* them and *domesticating* them in ways which converted them into forces which could be used for eventually positive purposes.

The position which Bill Wilson took in 1953 in the chapter on the Fourth Step in the *Twelve Steps and Twelve Traditions* was more like Jung's than it was like Loyola's. The natural instincts — the sex drive, the drive to achieve physical and emotional security, and the desire for human companionship (which included being given a meaningful and appropriate place within the social hierarchy) — were not evil in and of themselves, although they could push us into doing very evil things if we failed to bring them into balance and let them run riot. Just as with Jungian psychology, the goal was to integrate the natural instincts, not eradicate them or pretend that they were really "not us." This kind of approach was part of a long western tradition that went back thousands of years, to originally pagan roots: Plato's tripartite division of the soul and Aristotle's *Nicomachean Ethics*.

One could argue that once Bill Wilson's mind had totally assimilated the approach which he worked out in writing the *Twelve Steps and Twelve Traditions*, he was able to start applying this theory, with the result that his depressions disappeared within two or three years. But this is a complicated issue, and there were other possible contributory factors for these bouts of depression, one of them being Bill W.'s psychic sensitivity.

When Aldous Huxley wrote his little work entitled *Heaven and Hell* in 1956, and Bill read it and began thinking about those aspects of his own spiritual experiences, he was made aware of the fact that some of his problems with what he was labeling as *depression* may in fact have come from his attempts to explore deeper and deeper into the spiritual world. Huxley's book, along with the teachings of the ancient Gnostics and the *Tibetan Book of the Dead*, made it clear that when we penetrated deeply enough through the veil that separated our everyday world from the transcendent world, we encountered not only good spiritual realities but also spiritual realms filled with anger, murder, envy, lust, greed, and so on. Some of the beings encountered in the visions in the *Tibetan Book of the Dead* for example were terrifyingly demonic, but we had to experience them — without nevertheless being pulled into their grasp — in order to escape the negative consequences of the law of karma in our lives later on.

But perhaps the most important thing to note is, that when Bill W. finally pulled out of the worst of these depressions around 1955 or 1956, he had not found the teachings of Loyola's *Spiritual Exercises* to be very helpful in terms of dealing with his depression, although he did indicate at one point in the mid-1950's that the St. Francis Prayer had been useful.[434]

Father Dowling did not supply Bill Wilson with all the answers to all his problems. But he did continue to provide Bill with the kind of emotional support which the love and concern of a good sponsor can provide someone working through the twelve steps and walking the path to serenity.

CHAPTER 27

Making Moral Decisions: An Ignatian Pro vs. Con List in Father Ed's 1945 *Queen's Work* article

In the June 1945 issue of *The Queen's Work*, the Catholic magazine where he worked as an editor and writer, Father Ed gave an example of an actual analysis which a woman alcoholic had made, using what was in fact one of the standard Jesuit techniques for making moral decisions, a method St. Ignatius described in his *Spiritual Exercises* for "'reckoning up, how many advantages and utilities follow for me . . . and . . . on the contrary, the disadvantages and dangers' that would come from making a certain decision."

There is no heavy handed moralism here. The woman does not say, "if I do thus-and-so I would break the Church's rule against such-and-such and commit a mortal sin which would send my soul to eternal hellfire after my death." She does not use words like always, never, absolute, and perfect. In fact, she does not give lists of moral rules at all.

But there is nevertheless a deep moral underlay to her analysis. A "false feeling of superiority" is something she considers as bad, for example, along with hanging around with worthless people. "False courage" is recognized as dangerous when it comes to decisions about one's sex life. "Loss of real friends" is seen as a negative value, along with sitting around at work constantly hating your boss. Being continuously dishonest is seen as evil at some deep level. These are things which she clearly feels are unworthy of herself and the kind of person she would like to be.

The woman's self-analysis does not deal with spiritual issues in the narrow sense — there is no explicit reference to things such as losing the vital sense of God's presence or feeling excluded from the company of God's people — but as Father Dowling pointed out, the spiritual dimension is in fact there, deep underneath, and was the driving force behind creating the table.

There are interesting parallels between this chart and what the Oxford Group called "the Game of Truth," described in 1934 in V. C. Kitchen's book *I Was a Pagan*.[435]

There are even more parallels between the items this A.A. woman was tabulating and the ones on what was called the Jellinek Curve or Jellinek Chart. This diagram was drawn up by the famous early alcoholism researcher E. M. [Elvin Morton] Jellinek in the same year that Father Dowling published his article in *The Queen's Work*. Jellinek put a questionnaire in the April 1945 issue of the A.A. *Grapevine*, and used the responses which he received to create a chart called "The Progressive Disease of Alcoholism." One side of the curve displayed the descent of the alcoholics into graver and graver problems as their alcoholism progressed, while the other side of the curve showed the gradual recovery of health and a workable life style.

Alcoholics Anonymous

by Father Edward (Ed) Dowling

The Queen's Work Magazine (June 1945), page 13

St. Ignatius in his rules for making a good decision recommends "Reckoning up, how many advantages and utilities follow for me . . . and, consider likewise, on the contrary, the disadvantages and dangers" that would come from making a certain decision.

One of the groups of the Alcoholics Anonymous has a chart made by a woman alcoholic, which chart conforms fairly well to the suggestions that St. Ignatius makes. While it ignores the specifically spiritual motivation, this spiritual motivation was the basis for this self-evaluation.

The Alcoholics Anonymous are much more successful with people over forty than they are with people under thirty. They find very few high-bottom alcoholics. A high-bottom alcoholic is one who can see the bottom before he hits it. A low-bottom person is one who has to splash on the bottom before he is convinced that it exists.

On this page we give an analysis by a woman alcoholic who has completed ten years of complete abstinence. The analysis was made before she stopped drinking. It is hoped that some alcoholic novices may use her experience and become high-bottom.

Factual Gain and Loss Chart
on Uncontrolled Drinking

ASSETS	LIABILITIES
New Feeling of Maturity.	Silly and Foolish.
Disappearance of Self-Consciousness. Pleasure of Disregarding Conventions.	Pseudo Maturity, Pulling Boners, *Penalty of Indiscretions.*

Magnified Feelings of Friendships for "pals."	Indifference to Feelings of Others.
	Temporary Depression.
False Feeling of Superiority, Grandeur.	Inferiority Reactions.
	Hangovers.
Mental Elations — Good Parties.	Unfavorable Publicity.
Temporary Elimination of Business and Family Worries.	Loss of Real Friends. Disruption of Family Affections. Divorce? Boss Hatred.
Source of Companions of No Import.	Auto Accidents. Serious Trouble; Loss of Self-Respect. Debts.
Self-Esteem in "Going on the Wagon."	Disregard of Honesty. Fear of Society, other than Drunks.
Wishful Thinking!	Increasing Resentments.
Compensations of Feeling of Inferiority.	Sapped Vitality—Worry about Health.
	Loss of Memory—Gradual or Serious.
Temporary Physical and Mental Well-Being.	Business Losses (Timed out?) (Fired?).
	Worry, Relative to Reputation and Dependency, and Size of Liquor Bills.
False Courage Relating to Social, Sex and Business Life.	Disintegration of Central Nervous System. Fear of Wasted Life.
	Dissipated Appearance.

Satisfying Flight from Reality.	Jails — Hospitals — Continuous Borrowing or Pan-handling — Mooching — Fear of Insanity.
	Fear of being Sober Enough to See Depleted Self in True Light.
	Chronic Insomnia—*Horror—Dreams.*
	Alcoholic Illness — Bitterness — Melancholy
Satisfying a Craving and Addiction.	Loss of Zest for Life—Chronic Illness.
	Contemplated Suicide. Accentuation of Insanity Characteristics.
	Wet Brain. Institutions. Death !!!
ASSETS	LIABILITIES

A.A.

Humiliation leading to humility leading to God's promised help to the humble has prospered the growth of the Alcoholics Anonymous (Post office box 459, Grand Central Annex, New York 17). Their most recent report shows that they have 19,000 members in 535 centers in every state of the Union and Canada, Honolulu, Australia, Mexico and Brazil. Archbishop Cushing of Boston recently spoke to the A.A.'s of Dorchester, Massachusetts, on their first anniversary. Archbishop Murry of St. Paul has addressed them many times.

CHAPTER 28

Bill W. Takes Instructions in Catholicism from Fulton J. Sheen: 1947

As the bond between Father Ed and Bill W. grew ever tighter, we can see Father Ed becoming willing to go public in stronger and stronger fashion in support of Alcoholics Anonymous, and Bill beginning to explore converting to Roman Catholicism.

January 1946 — Father Dowling provided a quote to go on the dust jacket of the Big Book: The first time most A.A. members heard Dowling's name was when he wrote a blurb to go on the book jacket for the ninth printing of the first edition of *Alcoholics Anonymous:*[436]

> "God resists the proud, assists the humble. The shortest cut to humility is humiliations, which A.A. has in abundance. The achievements of A.A., which grew out of this book, are profoundly significant. Non-alcoholics should read the last nine words of 12th step, page 72." —Edward Dowling, S.J., The Sodality of Our Lady, St. Louis, Mo.

Writing this took some bravery on Father Ed's part. By 1946, there were members of the Roman Catholic hierarchy who were beginning to support A.A. quietly in various ways, but there were also those who were quite hostile.

Among the pro-A.A. figures was Archbishop Joseph Ritter, who was transferred from Indianapolis to St. Louis in 1946. Ritter had already become a quiet supporter of A.A. through his dealings with one of his parish priests, Father Ralph Pfau, who had been the first Roman Catholic priest to get sober in A.A. (Pfau had come into A.A. in

Indianapolis on November 10, 1943). Ritter served as Archbishop of St. Louis from 1946 until his death in 1967, so Father Dowling could count on strong support for A.A. from the head of the Catholic hierarchy in St. Louis during the last fourteen years of his life. Ritter (who was made a cardinal in 1961) was later one of the leading reformist bishops at the Second Vatican Council in 1962–1965, and was throughout this period a very powerful and respected figure in the American Catholic hierarchy.

But Father Dowling would not have known anything about all of this in January of 1946, so he was taking a real risk when he wrote those words of praise for A.A. The Catholic hierarchy of that era kept rigid control over everything the clergy said in public. If Dowling offended the wrong person, he could have easily found himself removed from his position at *The Queen's Work* and sent off into permanent exile at a punishment post somewhere else.

And there were members of the Catholic hierarchy who were extremely hostile to A.A., such as James Cardinal McIntyre, the Archbishop of Los Angeles from 1948 until 1978. So for example, a Jesuit named Father John C. Ford, S.J., asked Cardinal McIntyre to allow him to speak at the Third A.A. International in Long Beach, California, in 1960. Father Ford was an alcoholic who came into A.A. and got sober c. 1947; he had quickly become a prominent figure within A.A.'s innermost circles (although, until the very end of his life, he kept his membership in A.A. not only secret from the outside world, but hidden even from the general A.A. membership). The Cardinal immediately and brusquely told Ford that he would absolutely not allow him to speak.

Fr. Ed Dowling himself also wrote McIntyre, and asked whether he would be permitted to address the conference. The Cardinal wrote back saying that he would allow him to do so since he was not an alcoholic, but only provided that he follow the ideas set out in the pamphlet "Help Your Alcoholic Friend" by Rev. William Kenneally. In his letter to Fr. Dowling, Cardinal McIntyre said furthermore that he did not want any priests talking who were themselves alcoholic; and that he totally objected to A.A.'s disease theory of alcoholism.[437]

Cardinal McIntyre, who was an arch-traditionalist, as we know later deeply opposed many of the changes made by the Second Vatican Council (1962–1965), especially the changes in the liturgy. After he retired as archbishop and took on the duties of a parish priest at St. Basil's Church in downtown Los Angeles, he celebrated the old Tridentine Mass on its side altars as a rebellion against the new liturgy.

Father Dowling nevertheless took a chance, and wrote four sentences publicly praising Alcoholics Anonymous to go on the dust jacket of the Big Book. The heart of his little blurb was the statement that "God resists the proud, assists the humble. The shortest cut to humility is humiliations, which A.A. has in abundance." This was obviously a short statement of one of the crucial sections in St. Ignatius Loyola's *Spiritual Exercises*, the passage on the Two Standards or Battle Flags: the forces of evil rally around the principle of destructive Pride, while the forces of good are marked by their deep Humility.

The twelve steps are of universal significance: The "last nine words of the Twelfth Step," which Father Ed referred to in the little statement he wrote for the Big Book, said "and to practice these principles in all our affairs." This emphasized one of Father Ed's most prominent and oft-recurring themes. The basic principles of the twelve step program laid out a system for spiritual growth and healing, which could be applied by ordinary people who were not alcoholics at all, to all sorts of different spiritual problems and life problems. The twelve steps were not just for alcoholics, not just for Roman Catholics, not just for Protestants. THEY WERE AN INSPIRED GIFT OF DIVINE GRACE GIVEN TO THE ENTIRE WORLD.

1947 — Bill Wilson went to Fulton J. Sheen to learn more about the Catholic faith: Fulton and Grace Oursler, two famous friends of A.A., introduced Bill Wilson to Sheen in the summer of 1947, and for about a year thereafter, Bill visited Sheen every Saturday to learn about the theology and doctrine of the Catholic Church. Lois Wilson said that the two men in fact became good friends, and "their discussions were more like debates than conversations."[438]

Fulton J. Sheen was not only famous across the entire United States for most of his life, he continued to be greatly admired within the Roman Catholic Church even after his death in 1979. The formal process towards eventually being made a saint was started in 2002, and in 2012 the Pope granted Sheen the honorary title of Venerable, the stage right below saint.

Fulton J. Sheen, born in 1895 (he was the same age as Bill W.), was a Roman Catholic priest who taught at the Catholic University of America in Washington, D.C. Sheen was not a Jesuit. Brought up in Peoria, in the middle of the flat plains and endless corn fields of central Illinois, he received his initial theological education at a diocesan seminary in St. Paul, Minnesota, where he was trained, not for the more rarified levels of higher scholarship, but for the everyday parish priesthood. He nevertheless went on to earn a doctorate in philosophy at the Catholic University of Leuven in Belgium, where he was put in contact with the new radical theology which was developing within European Catholicism. But he then went on to further studies in Rome, where he earned a Sacred Theology Doctorate, which was much more reassuring to the American Catholic hierarchy of that time. American Catholic bishops, prior to the Second Vatican Council (1962-1965), knew very little about the new currents that were sweeping northern European Catholicism, and preferred to stick with the official doctrinal positions coming out of the Papal Curia in Rome.

His European experiences put a polish on Sheen. In spite of his simple Midwestern roots, by the time Sheen was appearing on television, he conveyed an urbane, sophisticated, cosmopolitan, aristocratic air. In his full ritual regalia, which he donned to go before the cameras, he came across as a true Prince of the Church.

Sheen, who eventually received the titles of monsignor, bishop (1951), and archbishop (1969), quickly became one of the best-known Catholic figures in America after he began hosting an evening radio program called the Catholic Hour, which was on the air from 1930 to 1950, followed by additional years in which he broadcast his program on television. A polished, smooth, and witty orator, Sheen has been described as one of the first modern televangelists, making him the twentieth-century Catholic equivalent in some ways to the Protestant revivalists who influenced America so much in the nineteenth century. Like them, his method tended to stress emotion over logic, or perhaps it would be better to say that his style of presentation often took the form of a kind of emotional logic, where the capstone of the logical argument was an emotional appeal in which he presented his conclusion as the one which would clearly satisfy our deepest emotional desires.

It was hoped that Bill Wilson would be impressed by him, and hopefully impressed enough to join the Roman Church. Many Catholics were praying for this.

Now it should also be noted, that although Monsignor Sheen gave the air of being extremely conservative and doctrinally proper on theological issues, he could also at times take surprisingly liberal and controversial positions on moral and political issues. In a sermon on April 7, 1946 at St. Patrick's Cathedral in New York City, he spoke out against America's dropping of the atomic bomb on Hiroshima in Japan eight months earlier on August 6, 1945. He quoted the Pope's denunciation of atomic warfare which was made at the opening of the Pontifical Academy of Science on February 21, 1943: atomic bombs, with their wholesale destruction of thousands of innocent civilians, were immoral because they did away with the moral distinctions which had to be made in warfare. Sheen's condemnation of the bomb was filled with deep outrage: "The worst evil the world has witnessed since the crucifixion of Jesus was the dropping of the atomic bomb on Hiroshima."

Many years later, Sheen also took a strong stance against the Vietnam War. In July 1967 he begged President Lyndon Johnson to make the simple announcement: "In the name of God, who bade us love our neighbor with our whole heart and soul and mind, for the sake of reconciliation I shall withdraw our forces immediately from southern Vietnam." So Sheen was certainly much more than simply a conservative television evangelist preaching to the lowest common denominator among the American populace.

One of Bill Wilson's problems with the Roman Catholic Church: the body and blood of Christ in the mass. As we have seen, Bill W. was deeply attracted to the medieval Catholic monastic theologians who wrote about the spiritual life — authors whom he had read about in Richard Maurice Bucke's book on *Cosmic Consciousness* and Aldous Huxley's book *The Perennial Philosophy*. And he remembered for all his life that moment in 1918 when he stood beneath the medieval arches of Winchester Cathedral and gazed at the rays of light streaming in through the gem-like reds and blues and yellows of the ancient stained glass windows, and felt the divine presence there. That primordial awareness of the sacred and the holy which Bill Wilson felt on that day — that sense of contact with a fourth dimension of existence which continued to lie at the heart of his later more developed spirituality — had a distinctly medieval Catholic hue to it almost from the beginning.

In a letter to Father Dowling on September 3, 1947, Bill Wilson said:

> I'm more affected than ever by that sweet and powerful aura of the Church; that marvelous spiritual essence flowing down by the centuries touches me as no other emanation does, but when I look at the authoritative layout, despite all the arguments in its favor, I still can't warm up. No affirmative conviction comes . . . P. S. Oh, if only the Church had a fellow-traveler department, a cozy spot where one could warm his hands at the fire and bite off only as much as he could swallow. Maybe I'm just one more shopper looking for a bargain on that virtue— obedience![439]

But he had the same two qualms which most American Protestants had about the Roman Catholic Church during the first half of the twentieth century: the doctrine of transubstantiation (the belief that the bread and wine of the mass literally turned into the body and blood of Christ) and even more importantly, the doctrine of the Pope's infallibility.[440]

At the Last Supper, when Jesus blessed the bread and wine before passing them to his disciples, he said of the bread, "This is my body," and of the wine, "This is my blood" (Matthew 26:26-28, compare Luke 22:19-20, John 6:53-56, 1 Corinthians 10:16 and 11:25-27). By the eleventh century A.D., the Catholic Church in western Europe was using the word "transubstantiation" and taking this idea of the body and blood of Christ quite literally at the deepest philosophical level. After the priest spoke the words of institution during the mass, even though the little wafers of unleavened bread continued to look and taste like bread, and even though the wine in the chalice continued to look and taste like wine, they had really — at the level of their inner substance or essence — been transformed into the body and blood of Jesus. And yet Catholic theologians argued that church goers who partook of the bread and wine were not committing cannibalism, and that a church mouse which ate a left-over piece of communion bread would most definitely NOT have eaten the body and blood of Christ. It was not a simple doctrine, and it seems to many modern people to fly in the face of direct observation and common sense.

By the end of the Middle Ages, most Christians in northwestern Europe were no longer finding this idea believable, and in the sixteenth century, the various Protestant groups which rebelled and turned against Rome and set up their own independent churches within that region, all rejected this belief (in whole or at least in part) and argued that there was no way to make that overall set of claims logically coherent. The more radical Reformed theologians (like Zwingli) insisted that Jesus' words had merely been intended to be symbolic or metaphorical, in the same way as when he said "I am the door," or when he advised his disciples to "reject the leaven of the Pharisees," referring metaphorically to their ideas and teachings, not to the yeast they used to make their bread. Some Protestants (including many of the Calvinists) believed that the Real Presence of Christ in the communion service occurred through the presence of the Holy Spirit, which raised the participants' souls up to heaven to commune directly with Christ there. John and Charles Wesley taught in their Methodist communion hymns that the Real Presence was the redeeming and healing power of the Cosmic Christ which flowed through the bread and wine like water through a pipe (or like electricity through a power cable, to use a modern metaphor). The Lutherans (ever conservative) did teach that the body and blood of Christ were truly present "in, with, and under" the bread and wine in a literal fashion, but even they nevertheless insisted that the bread and wine themselves still remained as real bread and wine — there was no transmutation of elements going on.

We have no way of knowing which (if any) of those alternate explanations Bill Wilson would have accepted, but at any rate, he was definitely Protestant enough that he simply could not accept the Roman Catholic doctrine of transubstantiation. This was one major block to converting to Catholicism, no matter how compelling Fulton Sheen's explanation of this Roman doctrine must have been.

And there were important issues at stake here, in terms of the basic understanding of the connection between the everyday material world and the transcendent divine world. In the extreme Zwingian/ Calvinist position which more than half of Americans held in the first half of the twentieth century, there was no quality of enchantment filling the material world in which we lived. The physical realities around us — trees, hills, rocks, chemicals, atoms — were regarded as impersonal and mechanical things, while God dwelt off in a totally separate realm. He might work an occasional miracle, but God and the divine world otherwise did not interpenetrate or interleave itself directly and immediately into the physical world.

Since over half of the Americans who come into A.A. still think that way when they first start attending meetings, this is one of the major obstacles to getting them to regard God as anything real and imaginable. How do we surrender our will and our lives to something which appears to have nothing at all to do with the concrete physical world around us?

There were other Americans however, such as those who had read the New England Transcendentalists and the Romantic poets, who had learned how to see a sacred and holy dimension shining through the world of nature. For them the world could still be enchanted. Romantic literature was still being widely read in schools and universities during the early twentieth century, and Bill Wilson certainly believed with these authors that the divine presence could be seen and felt while gazing upon a Spring flower blossoming at the bottom of a wall, or while looking up at the starry heavens at night, or while standing in a medieval Catholic church (as he did at Winchester Cathedral in 1918), observing the sunlight falling through the stained glass windows upon the ancient stone carvings and arches.

> As a side note: for those who would like a deeper taste of this view of the interpenetration of the divine and the everyday physical world, the romantic authors being read in America and Europe in the early twentieth century included such figures as William Wordsworth, Percy Bysshe Shelley, and Elizabeth Barrett Browning from England; Goethe, Heinrich Heine, Novalis, and Friedrich Hölderlin from Germany; and Aleksandr Pushkin from Russia.

The problem for Bill Wilson was that most American Roman Catholics during the first half of the twentieth century, went far beyond the Romantic tradition, and believed in a far more literalistic notion of the intrusion of the sacred realm into the ordinary earthly realm. This included both Archbishop Fulton J. Sheen and Father Ed Dowling.

In Roman Catholic practice at that time, it was believed (for example) that a vision of an angel or a saint (like the Blessed Virgin Mary) could be so solid and concrete that it could be seen by more than one person simultaneously (as at Fatima in Portugal in 1917, and Knock in Ireland in 1879). By the twentieth century there were once more healing shrines like the famous one at Lourdes all over Catholic Europe, to replace the ones which had been shut down in the Protestant parts of Europe during the sixteenth century Protestant Reformation. American parochial school children, during their religion classes, were sometimes shown photographs of people who had the raw, bleeding wounds of the stigmata in the palms of their hands.

From that perspective, there was no problem in believing that bread and wine could be transformed quite literally into human flesh and blood, in the same way that Jesus was reported to have turned water into wine at the wedding feast at Cana.

Another of Bill Wilson's problems with the Roman Catholic Church: the divinity of Christ. And as we shall discuss in more detail further along, it seems as though Father Dowling believed that in the Incarnation, God (or a part of God) surrendered its deity in quasi-kenotic fashion and quite literally turned into a flesh and blood human being — but while still in some fashion nevertheless remaining God, for Pope Pius XII declared in 1951 that good Catholics had to believe that the divinity of Christ still in some essential way remained within the incarnate Christ.

And there too Bill Wilson had problems, for just as he could not understand how a piece of bread and a chalice of wine could be transformed into Jesus' body and blood, he could not see how a human being — even Jesus of Nazareth — could be a genuine god, through and through. We have this not only from one of Bill's letters to Father Dowling, but also from the memoirs of Francis Hartigan, who knew Bill well,[441] and from a letter which Bill wrote to Mel Barger on July 2, 1956:[442]

Christ is, of course, the leading figure to me. Yet I have never been able to receive complete assurance that He was one hundred percent God. I seem to be just as comfortable with the figure of ninety-nine percent. I know that from a conservative Christian point of view this is a terrific heresy. But it must be remembered that I had no childhood conditioning in religion at all. I quit Congregational Sunday School at eleven because they asked me to sign a Temperance pledge.

Now Bill, oddly enough, had no problem in accepting the New Testament accounts of Jesus's resurrection from the dead on Easter morning and his resurrection appearances to his disciples later on, nor did he have a problem believing in Jesus's healing miracles. But that was probably because Bill had himself had many personal experiences, during séances, of speaking with the souls of the dead, and because he could see at first hand that Alcoholics Anonymous — which was a form of faith healing — unquestionably worked.

But he had problems with some of the other Catholic beliefs about Christ, such as the doctrine of the Virgin Birth. As Bill related in a letter which he wrote to Father Dowling on October 14, 1947, he believed in miracles, but only (as Fitzgerald explains)[443]

those "confirmed by experience — the Resurrection and return, the healing miracles, spiritual experiences themselves." He did not believe in what was beyond human experience: the Virgin birth, Christ's blood and body in the Mass, infallibility.

Alcoholics Anonymous taught a pragmatic faith which Bill Wilson refused to surrender. In my own belief, that was fortunate for the movement. People who came into the twelve-step program were not asked to take someone else's word for things — there were no appeals to authority figures from the past, whose ideas we simply had to accept on faith. We were not asked to accept ultimately unverifiable claims, such as whether or not Mary was still a virgin at the time she became pregnant with Jesus. Our final evaluation of the spiritual beliefs of the program had to be based solely on what we could verify within our own personal experience.

As a result, Bill Wilson was willing to go partway into the Roman Catholic understanding of the world, but in the end he drew back, and refused to go the whole distance. He could handle Richard Maurice Bucke, Emmet Fox, Aldous Huxley — and even seemed to have no problem with the Swedenborgian beliefs held by Lois Wilson and her family — but Monsignor Fulton Sheen went too far for him.

The spirit of the Enlightenment vs. the infallibility of the pope: The problem raised for Bill Wilson by the Roman Church's claim of the pope's infallibility was even more basic than those other two theological problems and was from the start doomed to be non-negotiable.

In the seventeenth and eighteenth centuries, a movement called the Enlightenment swept across Western Europe and the English colonies of North America, a movement in the history of ideas which was closely tied to the rise of modern science. It was a rebellion against the Middle Ages, and a rebellion against dogmatic religion and authoritarianism of all kinds. One of the best summaries of its spirit was contained in an oft-quoted essay written by Immanuel Kant towards the end of the eighteenth century. (Kant in Germany and John Locke in England were the two greatest and most influential of the Enlightenment-era philosophers, and Locke would certainly have agreed, I feel sure, with Kant's rebellious spirit in this essay.)

In this little piece — published in 1784 and entitled "What Is Enlightenment?" — Immanuel Kant explained in blunt and colorful terms what the spirit of his age was all about. If I may give my own translation of its opening lines:

> Enlightenment is the exit for human beings from their self-imposed status as minor children. Lack of adulthood is represented in the inability to use one's own intelligence without direction from someone else. This lack of adulthood is self-imposed if the cause lies not in lack of intelligence, but in lack of the decisiveness and courage to use it without direction from someone else. *Sapere aude!* — "Have the courage to use your own intelligence" — is therefore the motto of the Enlightenment.

Laziness and cowardliness are the reasons why so great a number of human beings, even after nature has long declared them free from outside direction — *naturaliter maiorennes* [for they have legally come of age] — nevertheless gladly continue to act like children all their lives, and their laziness and cowardliness are the reason why it becomes so easy for others to raise themselves up as their guardians.

It is so comfortable being childlike! If I have a book whose intelligence I can put in place of mine, a pastor whose conscience I can put in place of mine, a physician who can evaluate my diet instead of me, and so on, I do not need to put myself to any bother at all. I have no need to think, as long as I can pay: other people will take over that miserable business for me.[444]

Any historian who wishes to write about the origin and history of Alcoholics Anonymous should first be compelled to read one key book about the Enlightenment, a book by Carl Becker written back in 1932. One feels the absence of this knowledge particularly in some of the sillier A.A.-bashing literature written during the past several decades, the kind that tries to portray A.A. as an authoritarian and coercive organization which demands the surrender of all our native intelligence, and the abandonment of the will to take control of our own lives. The real nature of A.A. is in fact the exact opposite: by this point in the early twenty-first century, the twelve step program is one of the last major representatives and defenders of the spirit of the Enlightenment, which is now under continual attack by conservative political, social, and religious forces.

Carl L. Becker was Professor of History at Cornell University, the Ivy League university in upstate New York. The famous book he wrote, *The Heavenly City of the Eighteenth-Century Philosophers* (1932), was originally put together as four lectures on the Enlightenment delivered at Yale University. Peter Gay, who taught at Columbia University and then at Yale, famously attacked Becker later on for making the Enlightenment itself look too authoritarian and traditional, and this point is undoubtedly well-taken — the Enlightenment was certainly not just a repeat of medieval dogmas phrased in a new terminology. But

Becker still gives the best summary in one place of the leading ideas of the great Enlightenment thinkers, and phrases them in ways that allow us to see instantly how A.A. and the Big Book enthusiastically took up all the major Enlightenment themes.

The Enlightenment rejected all claims that some religious book or other was directly written by God's own hand, and was infallible, and had to be obeyed blindly and without question. It did not matter whether it was the Christian New Testament, the Hebrew Bible and Talmud, the Koran, the great religious writings of Asia, or what have you. From a modern scientific perspective, these ancient writings were filled with what was to a great extent simply myth, legend and primitive superstition.

We should instead draw our ideas of God and morality, the Enlightenment said, from what they called "the great book of nature" (that is, from what ancient and medieval philosophers had called natural law). To give some examples, it was clear to any thinking person that no society could allow any of its members to murder anyone else in that society who simply annoyed or offended them for any reason at all. A community that allowed this would quickly rip itself apart. All stable human societies therefore had laws against murder. In like manner, laws against burglary, fraud, and rape were necessary for the smooth running of a society. You did not need to consult a divine holy book to figure this out — all it required was common sense and simple everyday observation.

It seemed obvious to most Enlightenment thinkers that the physical universe had to be built upon some sort of logical and rational ground, an intellectual system of some sort embodying the laws of nature which the scientists studied and the moral principles which human societies had to follow to be successful. As Becker pointed out, most Enlightenment thinkers were a bit uncomfortable referring to this as "God," because that word was just too much associated with the world of ancient myths and superstitions, and also made this ground seem a bit too personal. There was no giant personal being in the sky, wearing a beard and sitting on a throne, who had the magical power to change anything in my own world, no matter how small or large, if I simply pleaded with him using the right ritual phrases.

So Enlightenment-era literature often tried to avoid using the word God, and instead used circumlocutions like "Architect of the Universe" or "Author of All Things." In the same fashion, in good Enlightenment spirit, the A.A. Big Book would sometimes refer to God as "Spirit of the Universe" (p. 10), "Creative Intelligence, Universal Mind or Spirit of Nature" (p. 12), a "Power greater than myself" (p. 12), and so on. Building off of that last phrase, A.A. members quickly began to use the phrase "Higher Power" far more often than they did the word God.

The most important and decisive thing that Ebby Thacher said when he was talking to Bill Wilson in his kitchen, was the little suggestion he finally made to the angry, rebellious man: he simply asked Wilson, "Why don't you choose your own conception of God?" The basic idea lying behind this suggestion became the keystone of Bill's theology. This was the spirit of the Enlightenment at its best, the point Immanuel Kant was trying so hard to establish in his explanation of that attitude toward life. We have to stop trying to be good little obedient children, blindly doing whatever we are ordered and believing whatever we are told. We have to start acting like adults, and going to work to figure out what kind of power underlies the physical universe, and what kind of personal code of behavior we can follow and still live with ourselves. We have to quit being deliberately stupid and start becoming intelligent; we have to quit sitting up and performing meaningless tricks like trained poodles and start thinking for ourselves.

The great Enlightenment thinkers of the seventeenth and eighteenth centuries were horrified by organized religion, because their ancestors had just lived through the merciless wars of religion which had swept over Europe in the aftermath of the sixteenth century Protestant Reformation, culminating in the wholesale bloodshed of the Thirty Years' War (1618-1648). Catholics and Protestants burnt one another at the stake, tortured one another to death, and massacred whole cities. And then the Protestants began killing other Protestants who did not agree with them on some theological issue (Lutherans against Baptists, Calvinists against Unitarians, Anglo-Catholic English armies marching through Calvinist Scotland, while in England itself Anglo-Catholic armies fought armies filled with Congregationalists and Baptists who held to more strongly Protestant beliefs). And during this whole period,

Spanish Catholics continued to torture and murder Muslims and Jews in Spain, and destroy the religions which were followed by the Native American tribes of the New World by killing any of these stone age tribesmen who refused to learn Spanish and attend Catholic mass.

By the latter part of the seventeenth century, sensitive and intelligent people all over northwestern Europe (and in the English colonies of North America as well) were sick at their stomachs with disgust at the hideous slaughter being carried out by organized religion. The Enlightenment was a rebellion against any and all authoritarian religious systems where one group of people went around telling other people what they were supposed to believe about the nature of God.

The British parliamentary system, as it began developing in the English Civil War (1642-1651), the Cromwellian Republic, the Glorious Revolution (1688), and the appointment of Sir Robert Walpole in 1721 as the first modern prime minister, came increasingly to be built on basic Enlightenment principles. And then at the end of the eighteenth century, two famous revolutions — the American Revolution and the French Revolution — created governments with Enlightenment ideals built into their most basic structure. Over the two centuries which have followed, those basic understandings of government — the forms developed in the seventeenth and eighteenth century British parliamentary system, the American Revolution and the French Revolution — have been used as the model for new democracies all over the globe.

The American Revolution embodied many of the best Enlightenment principles. Thomas Jefferson, in his introduction and preamble to the Declaration of Independence which sparked off the American Revolution (July 4, 1776), defended the Americans' act of revolt in pure Enlightenment terms. The opening appeal was not made to biblical verses or rules proclaimed by medieval popes, but instead referred only to natural law and the concept of a higher power which could be derived by a thoughtful and intelligent person who looked at the natural world in light of the laws of science, that is, what Jefferson called "the Laws of Nature and of Nature's God."

Jefferson appealed to common sense, to things about the world which any intelligent person could observe, and above all to the kind of plea which Immanuel Kant was going to repeat over in Germany eight years later: it was time for the American colonists to start acting like adults, and start taking responsibility for their own lives, instead of waiting for some all-powerful government or church leader to run their lives for them.

> We hold these truths to be self-evident, that all men are created equal, that they are endowed by their Creator with certain unalienable Rights, that among these are Life, Liberty and the pursuit of Happiness. That to secure these rights, Governments are instituted among Men, deriving their just powers from the consent of the governed, That whenever any Form of Government becomes destructive of these ends, it is the Right of the People to alter or to abolish it, and to institute new Government, laying its foundation on such principles and organizing its powers in such form, as to them shall seem most likely to effect their Safety and Happiness.

The French Revolution and Italian Unification subsequently carried out the principles of the Enlightenment in what were sometimes far more radical ways: the attack on the Roman Catholic Church. In the French Revolution (1789-1799), the hostility to organized religion and authoritarian religious leaders which had built up over much of the continent of Europe during the Enlightenment, finally erupted in a violent upheaval which destroyed many parts of the structure and social underpinnings of the Roman Catholic Church in France. Most Catholic Church property ended up being taken over by the French government, and the remains of the Catholic hierarchy in France were left nearly powerless and more and more unpopular as the years passed. A series of other revolutions swept Catholic Europe during the period which followed, modelled in whole or in part on the French Revolution, and the Roman Catholic Church came more and more under siege.

In the 1860's and 70's, the Pope himself came under direct attack in Italy itself. There at the beginning of the modern era, the part of southern Europe which we now call the country of Italy was divided up into a number of separate states, some maintaining their independence under the control of small local governments, while others continually fell prey to conquest by Spanish, French, or Austrian armies. The Papal States, a continuous band of small areas stretching from coast to coast across the center of the Italian peninsula, was composed of secular states which the Pope controlled with large armies of mercenary soldiers: Latium (the area around the city of Rome), Umbria (which lay immediately to the north), Marche (on the east coast), and Romagna (the area around Bologna).

But in the 1800's, a movement for the unification of Italy began, called the *Risorgimento*. In 1860 Giuseppe Garibaldi, with an army of one thousand men called the *Camicie Rosse* (Red Shirts), took over the island of Sicily and then crossed the Straits of Messina and conquered Naples, which controlled the entire southern third of the mainland of Italy. Meanwhile up in the north, King Victor Emmanuel II, who originally controlled only a few areas, principally Piedmont in northwestern Italy and the island of Sardinia off the west coast of Italy, had been expanding his control over the rest of northern Italy. Garibaldi and his men — political radicals who upheld the ideals of the Enlightenment with zeal and enthusiasm — wanted a French-style revolution to take over and modernize Italy, and produce a country without king or aristocracy, and with the Catholic Church either abolished or rendered totally powerless. But Garibaldi realized that Victor Emmanuel's army was needed to unify all of Italy — he could not do it all by himself — so he voluntarily relinquished his own claim to rulership and proclaimed Victor Emmanuel II as King of Italy.

By 1861, the King had taken over most of the rest of northern Italy except for the area immediately around Rome. All of Italy was now unified under his kingship except for the great capital city itself, which was defended by an army of mercenary soldiers under the command of the Pope.

In September 1870, King Victor Emmanuel II sent his army into the city of Rome, defeated the Pope's mercenary soldiers, and added it to his kingdom. In June 1871, Rome was declared as the new capital of the Kingdom of Italy.

Only one concession was made to the pope. The Vatican hill, a small area of a little over a hundred acres within the boundaries of the modern city (the hill is located on the west bank of the Tiber river, directly across from the old part of the city of Rome) was allowed to remain as an independent sovereign state, with the Pope effectively imprisoned within its walls. All of the Catholic Church's property in Italy was taken over by the new government, except for buildings used for immediate ecclesiastical purposes. The popes who followed over the next century were strongly discouraged from traveling any great distance from the Vatican. Pope Paul VI (1963-1978) was the first pope to travel outside Italy in the period after the new Italian government's takeover of the city of Rome in 1870-71.

The infallibility of the pope was proclaimed at the First Vatican Council in 1870. During the entire long period when Italy was being unified, the head of the Roman Catholic Church was Pope Pius IX, a determined and inflexible figure who reigned as pope for nearly thirty-two years, from 1846-1878. Being aware of the way events in Italy were moving, Pius IX had already called all of the bishops of the Roman Catholic Church in June 1868 to meet at the papal court for the First Vatican Council. The assembled bishops opened their council on December 8, 1869 and Pope Pius IX told them to begin drafting a statement proclaiming the infallibility of the pope. The final vote ratifying this new doctrine was held on July 18, 1870, following which the bishops were allowed to adjourn for a summer break. King Victor Emmanuel II's Italian army then entered the city of Rome and annexed it on September 20, 1870. The bishops were clearly not going to be allowed to return, so on October 20 Pope Pius IX suspended the council indefinitely. He tried pressuring the Italian government first by barring any Catholic from communion who held any post in the new government, and then tried barring any Catholic from communion who even voted in Italian elections, but majority of the people in Italy ignored him.

In medieval Catholic theological disputations, a debater could score major points by quoting relevant Bible verses and formal statements made by the great general church councils of the past, such as the Council of Nicaea in 325 A.D. or the Council of Chalcedon in 451 A.D. (In these councils, bishops were gathered together from all over the Catholic Church and voted on what position the Church was going to take on a disputed issue.) Both scripture and the decrees of church councils were regarded as infallible.

A debater could also score a few points by quoting from statements made by one of the great Catholic theologians of the past, like St. Augustine or St. Jerome, or by finding a supporting statement made by a pope, but to win the dispute on these grounds, the debater had to come up with more statements supporting his view than the opposing debater could cite, or find statements made by theologians or popes who were considered more famous or impressive.

The new doctrine of papal infallibility as defined in 1870 meant that an official statement by a pope could now be used as a trump card, so to speak, to end any theological argument. A papal statement could, at the practical level, be regarded as a new revealed truth equal to the Bible as a source of divine revelation, and in fact, by the early twentieth century the Vatican was issuing lists of specific bible verses with orders as to how each of those biblical passages was to be interpreted, so that in practice pronouncements made by the Pope and the members of his Curia trumped even the Bible.

Back a century earlier, in the most radical phase of the French Revolution, the Roman Catholic Church in France had been dissolved and abolished. On October 21st, 1793, an anticlerical law was passed ordering that Catholic priests be executed on the spot wherever they were found in France, and on November 10th the Cathedral of Notre Dame in Paris was re-dedicated to the ceremonies of the new atheistic Cult of Reason which the revolutionary government was supporting. This extremely radical phase soon passed, but in the years which followed, the Roman Catholic Church never came even close to recovering its old power in France.

Pope Pius IX was clearly afraid that the new Italian government which had taken over the city of Rome might decide to do the same thing to him. He seems to have believed that declaring the infallibility of the pope would strengthen his hand in Italy. Even if the new Italian government with its Enlightenment ideas was going to strip away all of his secular powers, including his army and most of his enormous sources of revenue, the office of pope would not be completely abolished, he hoped, as long as it was needed to resolve ecclesiastical disputes and define points of doctrine.

During the century that followed, the Roman Catholic Church fell more and more under attack in ever larger sections of the world (Bismarck's *Kulturkampf* against the Catholic Church in Germany during the 1870's, the Mexican revolutions of 1860 and 1910, the killing of almost seven thousand Catholic clergy during the Spanish Civil War in the 1930's, and so on). In the process, the Roman Church fell into a kind of fortress mentality, adopting more and more authoritarian rules and policies.

On August 4, 1879, Pope Leo XIII issued an encyclical declaring that the theology of the medieval scholar St. Thomas Aquinas (1225-1274) was to be used as the basis of all Catholic teaching. There was to be no more free spirit of inquiry or toleration of differing points of view. In the United States, in accordance with this new authoritarian mindset, what was called the Baltimore Catechism was drawn up to outline a rigid and detailed set of doctrines and rules to be studied and memorized by parochial school students.

The Roman Catholic Church during the Middle Ages was not nearly so rigid. This was something new, which I suppose one could argue had begun developing as early as the Council of Trent (1545 and 1563) and the French Revolution (1789-1799), but it certainly was not the way the medieval church operated.

The new total rigidity completely took hold, however, at the First Vatican Council in 1869-1870, and there was no break in this authoritarian way of running the Church until the Second Vatican Council in 1962-1965 carried out a successful rebellion against many of the old strictures. But this did not take place until Father Ed Dowling had already died, and Bill Wilson was an old man whose lungs were giving out (Dowling died in 1960 and Wilson in 1971).

CHAPTER 29

Bill W. and Father Ed on Papal Infallibility: 1947-1948

Bill Wilson rejected the First Vatican Council's authoritarian view of the church: Father Robert Fitzgerald describes a letter which Bill W. wrote to Father Dowling on September 14, 1947, in which "he said as an ex-drunk he was not scandalized by the sins of the Church but by 'the inability of the Church to confess its own sins.' 'Did I not think so seriously of joining, I wouldn't even think of raising the question.'"[445] Or in other words, in Bill Wilson's eyes, the problem with the pope's claim of infallibility was that it allowed the Church to evade looking at all those places where the Church was regularly acting in ways (or historically had all too frequently acted in ways) that were dishonest, cruel, and self-serving. Institutions were no different from individual human beings — if they pretended that they could never be in error or make mistakes, they would never be able to identify their own sins, or take measures to correct those sins. A Church which claimed to be infallible would never be able to take the equivalent of a Fourth Step and make a truly searching moral inventory of its own behavior and policies.

On October 14, 1947, Bill wrote another letter to Father Ed, stressing that point even more strongly:

> I seem congenitally unable to believe that any human beings have the right to claim unqualified authority and infallibility about anything, whether dogma, morals, or politics. I suppose my Yankee ancestry is showing up here ....

His *Yankee ancestry* as he puts it — two small but very important words — point us to the source from which Bill Wilson had derived some of his most deeply held beliefs. Bill came from Vermont: he was a New England Yankee born and bred, and that included a zealous commitment to the core foundational beliefs of the Calvinist world view. It was true that he stopped attending the Congregationalist church's Sunday School classes in his home town when he was eleven years old, because he refused to sign their required temperance pledge.[446]

Nevertheless, all over New England, the original background of belief among the European colonists during the area's early history had been shaped by the Calvinist religious principles of the little Congregationalist churches which still dotted its landscape. These were the "Puritans," as they were called, men and women who had fled England for the New World, where they wanted to create a "purified" Christianity and a "purified" society in all the towns and villages of the land. And the word "pure" to them meant a church and society built on the principles laid out by the great religious leader John Calvin in a book he wrote in 1536 called the *Institutes of the Christian Religion*, a work which laid out the basic principles of the variety of Protestantism referred to as "Calvinism" or the "Reformed tradition."

And as Bill Wilson admitted, there was no way he could totally escape his Yankee heritage. Even if some people had quit going to church, the basic Calvinist assumptions about the nature of the world and human society and the way the human mind worked, still permeated all of life in the small towns and rural areas, which was where he had been brought up.

It was a core belief in Calvinism that no man or woman in this world and this life could be totally free of sin, which meant that there were no human beings on earth who would not in some circumstances fool themselves into believing that there were logical reasons for believing that certain religious propositions were true, when in fact all they were doing was rationalizing their own most selfish and self-serving desires.[447] Any religious or spiritual institution which declared that one of its leaders (or one of its governing bodies) was infallible and could make statements about matters of spiritual beliefs or moral behavior which were infallible and could not possibly be wrong, was guaranteeing that it as an institution would be taken over in fairly short order by people operating on selfish, greedy, dishonest, power-mad, vanity-filled desires.

> <u>As a side note</u>: this was also the reason why the U.S. Constitution was designed with checks and balances, limited terms of office, guaranteed freedom of speech for minority groups, and so on. The majority of church goers in the Thirteen Colonies were members of Calvinist denominations, and shared the general Calvinist belief in the danger of giving unlimited power to anyone at all, no matter how virtuous that person (or group of people) at first appeared: these denominations and religio-ethnic groups included the Congregationalists, Baptists, Presbyterians, and Dutch Reformed, as well as all the originally French-speaking colonists from the Protestant Huguenot areas of France and the originally German-speaking colonists from the Calvinist parts of Switzerland and from the Heidelberg Catechism region of western Germany (over near the German border with the Netherlands and Switzerland).

Feel like a Catholic but think like a Protestant: On the other hand, there was a side of Catholicism which pulled at Bill Wilson just as deeply as his Calvinist cynicism about human nature. He felt the power of the Roman Catholic Church's rituals and sense of the sacred, and wanted to immerse himself in it ever more deeply. Old-fashioned Catholic worship pulled at all five senses: the stained glass windows and sacred statues, the hymns and chants, the wetness of the holy water when you dipped your fingertips into the font and the hardness of the stone floor under your knees, the taste of the communion wafer in your mouth and the scent of the incense in your nostrils when you breathed in. The most important parts of the service did not try to convince you with reason and logic, but appealed nakedly to your most basic feelings and emotions. Bill Wilson had found that his highest spiritual experiences invariably had a profoundly aesthetic and emotional component. You did not just "see" heavenly light and have the tactile sensation of wind rushing through your being, you were overwhelmed with the most powerful emotions of joy and relief, and stood in open-mouthed awe before the magnificent beauty of the heavenly realm, and felt a courage arising within you that gave you the emotional strength and burning passion which would enable you to take on a task which would have been far too frightening before.

And Catholicism also recognized a dimension of reality which went far beyond even that world of sense impressions and powerful emotions. To a far greater extent than most forms of Protestantism, the historical Catholic faith did not deny the higher dimensions of true spirituality but celebrated them, and gave honor to those great saints from the past who had most deeply apprehended these things. As Bill Wilson put it in the letter to Mel Barger which he wrote on July 2, 1956:[448]

> Reality, which must include both absolute and relative, is arranged in several layers. We have the conscious, the unconscious or subconscious, the world of psychic phenomenalism which suggests our Father's house of many mansions, and finally the ultimate reality, glimpses of which all mystics seem to have had. To me, this makes good theological sense. We appear to be in a day at school, a relative state of affairs that slowly progresses toward a meeting with the Absolute. When the doors of perception are opened widely enough by ego deflation, we get these fleeting glimpses of ultimate destiny.

Bill did not want to relinquish that part of Catholic teaching — the part which was at the heart of so much of his own spirituality. He is said to have told Bishop Fulton Sheen and others "that he wished the Church would open a division for fellow travelers" — people who were not card-carrying Roman Catholics so to speak, but were more like Catholic sympathizers or partial believers — "which was where he thought he would feel most at home."[449]

Bill wrote Sheen at one point and said:[450]

> Your sense of humor will, I know, rise to the occasion when I tell you that, with each passing day, I feel more like a Catholic and reason more like a Protestant!

But Father Ed called Bill Wilson on that one, in a letter he wrote him on November 26, 1947. That was a very misleading way of describing where Bill really was.[451]

> As you say, you feel like a Catholic. This I know. But I doubt if you think like a Protestant. If you did, you would be at Sunday services at a Protestant church and subscribing to that code and creed. Protestant with a capital P is not only negative but also positive. I think you may be a protestant, spelled with a small p, which is happy, but semi.

The major Protestant denominations, particularly the ones (like the Lutherans and Presbyterians) which went back to the sixteenth century, had complicated statements of doctrine and dogma which went into just as much detail as anything the Roman Catholic Church had ever drawn up. Bill Wilson was not going to join the Presbyterian Church or Dutch Reformed Church and embrace the doctrine of predestination, or join the Lutheran Church and agree to Martin Luther's doctrine of the bondage of the will. He would certainly not have been able to stomach the ordination vow that Methodist ministers had to make in those days, where they had to swear that they believed that a state of Christian perfection was achievable in this life, and that they would teach this to all their parishioners.

The truth of the matter was that the twelve-step program represented something that spoke deep truths about the spiritual life in ways that went far deeper than any specific religion. The twelve steps were not Christian *per se*, any more than they were Buddhist, Vedanta Hindu, Jewish, Muslim, Sikh, Taoist, or any other of the traditional religions of the earth.

Father Dowling's attempt to defend the doctrine of papal infallibility: To begin with, it had to be explained to Bill that no one was claiming that every word spoken by the Roman pope was filled with infallible truth. That would be absurd. The doctrine applied only to *ex cathedra* statements, that is, those very rare and infrequent proclamations made by the pope "from the throne," meaning the papal throne, as an official statement of church policy, to clarify a matter which had been under discussion within the church and give the final official word on what position the church was going to hold on that issue from henceforth. And it did not apply to questions such as the square root of the number two, or the speed of light in a vacuum, or the correct spelling of the Roman poet Virgil's name (Virgil or Vergil). It applied only to weighty matters of Catholic theological and moral teaching.

And in a letter which Father Ed wrote to Bill on October 1, 1947, he tried to make an even further distinction between what the doctrine of papal infallibility did, and did not, mean:

> As I understand it, it does not mean that the teaching body of the Church will talk horse sense but that it is protected from formally teaching moral nonsense. [452]

Now Father Dowling believed that the way in which Bill Wilson had been given the twelve steps, which just popped into his mind and flowed forth from his pen in a few minutes time, showed that they had to be divinely inspired.[453] God intervened and put those words in his head — Bill already knew that. But he had to ask a further question about this: *Why* did God intervene here with an act of direct inspiration? Bill had had to struggle to write the rest of the Big Book. But God had to act directly in the case of the steps, because they were going to be too important to the divine work to which the twelve step movement had been assigned. God could not stand aside and allow an incorrect statement of the moral teaching contained in the steps to become officially established.

Why then, Father Ed asked, was it so difficult for Bill Wilson to believe that in something as important as the moral teaching of the Catholic Church (which has over a billion members all over the earth), God would not likewise intervene and make sure that the pope got the words right when he proclaimed what the church needed to teach about a particular moral issue? As he went on to say in that same letter of October 1, 1947:

> You are so right that "it is ever so hard to believe that any human beings are able to be infallible about anything." Infallibility is

more than human. It calls for an intervention by a Power greater than ourselves .... Even as you in the hospital witnessed a superhuman intervention for the sake of a relatively unimportant quantity of people, so the point you correctly make that human infallibility, as hopeless, would seem to force a merciful and just Father to intervene. Historically, there have been superhuman interventions — yourself, Horace Crystal, The Incarnation. [454]

Unfortunately, in his next letter to Bill, on October 4, 1947, Father Ed went on to give what he (and many other contemporary pious Roman Catholics of that era) regarded as an excellent example of how the concept of papal infallibility should be used:

In one of the few formal uses of it that I can recall at the present the Papacy ... proclaimed the doctrine of the Immaculate Conception, the exemption of Christ's mother from the taint of original sin. It was years later at Lourdes that the apparition of Mary announced, "I am the Immaculate Conception," and then as now at Lourdes the blind see and the lame walk. [455]

Pope Pius IX had tested the waters — fifteen years before he got the First Vatican Council to declare the doctrine of papal infallibility — by making a formal proclamation on December 8, 1854 of the doctrine of the Immaculate Conception. This was the doctrine that held that the Virgin Mary was conceived in her mother Anne's womb without original sin. That meant that the only two human beings who had been born without the taint of original sin, after Adam and Eve's expulsion from the Garden of Eden, had been Jesus and his mother Mary.

Three years and two months after Pope Pius IX proclaimed this new doctrine, on February 11, 1858 a fourteen-year-old peasant girl named Bernadette Soubirous began seeing apparitions of the Blessed Virgin Mary. Bernadette lived in the little isolated mountain town of Lourdes in southern France, just twenty miles from the Spanish border, in the foothills of the Pyrenees mountains. The apparitions took place in front of a small grotto next to a field. On February 25, the vision of Mary instructed Bernadette to dig in the dirt at the bottom of the grotto until a spring came up and began filling the hole with water. Still today, five to six million pilgrims visit Lourdes every year to drink the water and bathe in it, because of what is believed to be its miraculous healing power.

When the visions first began to appear, Bernadette knew only that the figure she was seeing was that of a beautiful lady standing with her hands joined in prayer, and surrounded by a glow of supernatural light. The ghostly apparition was dressed in a long white robe tied at the waist with a blue ribbon; over this she wore a long white veil which covered her head and shoulders and cascaded down nearly to the ground.

On March 25, 1858 when Bernadette went to the grotto and the vision appeared to her, she asked the woman who she was, and the vision answered, "I am the Immaculate Conception."

Now Roman Catholic priests trained in the first half of the twentieth century usually knew little or nothing about Protestantism. It was not part of their training. So Father Dowling can be excused for having used an example which, almost more than anything else he could have mentioned, was guaranteed to raise the hackles of any Protestant listening to him. In the sixteenth century, when the Protestant Reformation began, the rebellion against late medieval Catholicism took a wide variety of different forms — Lutherans, Calvinists, and sixteenth-century Anglicans, along with Radical Reformation sects like Baptists and Unitarians, and later on, Congregationalists, Quakers, and German Pietists — but the one thing they all had in common was the total rejection of any notion of praying to Mary or glorifying Mary.

The Protestants noted that the figure of Mary was never prayed to in the New Testament, nor in the first six or seven centuries following. In the New Testament, it was always Jesus Christ whom people were told to look to for their salvation, and Jesus whom they were told to pray to for help. Venerating the figure of Mary and putting statues of her in churches was a medieval development. To critical Protestant eyes, the cult of Mary seemed to represent the worst of medieval superstition and legend-mongering, and stood out as one of the major ways in which medieval Catholicism had — from their Protestant point of view — completely obscured the original New Testament message.

Most importantly of all, there was no mention anywhere in the New Testament of anything even remotely like a belief in the Immaculate Conception. Again, in Protestant eyes, Pope Pius IX seemed to be trying to elevate himself to the same status as the divinely inspired authors of the New Testament, and present himself as a purveyor of new extra-scriptural revelations.

So Father Dowling's argument did have the positive effect which he desired, and neither he nor Bishop Fulton Sheen were able to persuade Bill Wilson to accept the doctrine of the infallibility of the pope and convert to Roman Catholicism.

Bill Wilson was called, NOT to preach Christianity, but to preach the Twelve Steps: In the interpretation of Father Dowling's letters given by Father Robert Fitzgerald, S.J. —which I believe is correct — Father Ed eventually changed his stance and took the very startling step of telling Bill Wilson to quit trying to be a Christian. God did not intend Bill to be either a Catholic or a Protestant. Wilson had been called by God to preach his message to all the religions and peoples of the earth, and had been given the Twelve Steps — the heart of his message — in a special divine revelation straight from God.

As Fitzgerald put it, Dowling eventually gave up on trying to turn Bill Wilson into a Roman Catholic, and "pulled back to a wider frame. He ... emphasized instead a larger God who came for sinners," and pleaded with Bill Wilson to "surrender to the action of God's grace, intervening in you, now."[456] The Twelve Steps were the words not of man, but of God. This meant that the divine call to preach them was far bigger than organized religion.

As Dowling phrased it in a letter he wrote Bill on September 8, 1947:

> The road to truth has never been better charted than Christ charted it. "Live in My way and you will know the truth." I believe that for you that way is lodemarked by the 12 steps; especially for those who can pray by the 7th step; for the more privileged who cannot pray easily, by the 6th step.[457]

This may seem like a very surprising statement indeed, coming from a Roman Catholic priest. How could Father Ed remain true to his ordination vows while advising Bill Wilson to quit trying to be a Christian and to carry out the task which God had actually assigned him?

There is no mention of praying to Jesus by name in the Twelve Steps, or using him by name as our source of grace, or as our teacher. A scholar of comparative religions who looked at the Twelve Steps would have to describe them as a non-Christian spiritual system, in terms of their essential core. In a university course on world religions, a Christian religious system, by definition, would be one which assigns some central role to the figure of Jesus somewhere in the system.

But the Sixth Step, which Father Ed talks about above, tells us to become "entirely ready to have God [*not Jesus Christ*] remove all these defects of character," and the Seventh Step speaks of the way we "humbly ask Him [*meaning God, not Jesus Christ*] to remove our shortcomings." How can a Roman Catholic priest remain faithful to his ordination vows while advising someone else to take up and preach a spirituality which entirely removed Jesus Christ (in any explicit fashion) from the language of prayer and ritual invocation?

But we should look at the words in quotation marks in the letter above, where Father Ed seems to be giving, not a verbatim quote *per se*, but at least a condensed version of the message contained in the fourteenth chapter of the Gospel of John in the New Testament. As Father Ed phrases it in his shorthand version, "Live in My way and you will know the truth." If I may cite the most important verses in chapter 14 (using the Douay-Rheims translation which American Catholics were ordered to use during that period of history), I think the rationale Father Ed used for adopting his position will quickly become clear:

> (2) In my Father's house there are many mansions. If not, I would have told you: because I go to prepare a place for you.

> (6) Jesus saith ... I am the way, and the truth, and the life. No man cometh to the Father, but by me.

> (15-17) If you love me, keep my commandments. And I will ask the Father, and he shall give you another Paraclete, that he may abide with you for ever. The spirit of truth, whom the world cannot receive, because it seeth him not, nor knoweth

> him: but you shall know him; because he shall abide with you, and shall be in you.

> (26) But the Paraclete, the Holy Ghost, whom the Father will send in my name, he will teach you all things, and bring all things to your mind, whatsoever I shall have said to you.

"In my Father's house are many mansions" is frequently interpreted as teaching that there are many different regions within the heavenly realms, with each one designed as a home for a different kind of good soul. This was a particularly highly developed concept within Lois Wilson's Swedenborgian religion.

In John 14:6, Jesus says "No man cometh to the Father but by me," but the gospel of John is here referring to the Cosmic Christ Principle (called the Logos or Word of God in the first chapter of John) which has been in existence since before the foundations of the earth. It most definitely does NOT require that we engage in the mere mechanical recitation of the human name of Jesus of Nazareth before we can be saved, as some extreme Protestant Fundamentalists claim. See the stiff warning that Jesus gives at the end of the Sermon on the Mount, in Matthew 7:21-23 (Douay-Rheims translation):

> Not every one that saith to me, Lord, Lord, shall enter into the kingdom of heaven: but he that doth the will of my Father who is in heaven, he shall enter into the kingdom of heaven. Many will say to me in that day: Lord, Lord, have not we prophesied in thy name, and cast out devils in thy name, and done many miracles in thy name? And then will I profess unto them, I never knew you: depart from me, you that work iniquity.

In John 14:15 above, Jesus says "If you love me, keep my commandments." Now at that point, we have to look around a bit to see what that means, because in this book of the Bible, Jesus gives no commands at all until we are over halfway through the gospel, and then he only gives one command. This is to make sure we take it seriously, because it represents the heart and soul of everything that is embodied in the Cosmic Christ Principle. In the Gospel of John, Jesus announces it for the first time at the Last Supper, after washing his disciples' feet as an example of total humility, and then passing the bread which he has blessed to nourish their souls on the Bread of Eternal Life. This is in chapter 13, and then the author of the Gospel of John repeats it again two chapters later in exactly the same words, to make sure we did not miss it:

> (John 13:34-35) A new commandment I give unto you: That you love one another; as I have loved you, that you also love one another. By this shall all men know that you are my disciples, if you have love one for another.

> (John 15:12) This is my commandment, that you love one another, as I have loved you.

If we learn to keep that commandment, then the Gospel of John says that God will send the Paraclete into our hearts. This is John's word for the Holy Spirit — the sunlight of the spirit — which is the divine power that enters into our hearts, and heals our souls, and grants us redeeming grace, and raises us up to even higher visions of the God who dwells beyond the world.

But this is what the Twelve Step program does. As Father Dowling said in his letter to Bill Wilson on April 15, 1948:

> ... anyone who sincerely tries to apply the 12 steps is following in Christ's footsteps with the result which Christ promised when he said, "Dwell in My way and you will know the truth."[458]

We come to our first Twelve Step meetings hating ourselves and everyone around us, but the people at the meetings love us in spite of ourselves, just as we are. And if we keep on coming back and actually work the steps, we too will eventually learn how to love our fellow human beings in the same way. And the love which now fills our hearts is the divine proof that the Holy Spirit and the Cosmic Principle of All-Filling Love have now raised us to the realm of the good angels and blessed saints, where we will receive the fullness of salvation.

Bill Wilson was not called to receive sacramental grace through the Catholic Mass, but through his marriage to Lois: In that letter of September 8, 1947, Father Ed says something that is even more startling. He knows that Bill Wilson yearns for some kind of saving infusion of sacramental grace, but finds that he cannot accept the Catholic doctrine of the bread and wine of the communion service turning into the body and blood of Christ. So Father Ed turns to a totally different sacrament, and tells Bill that his source of salvation is going to have to come from that instead:

> I believe there is a priesthood of husband to wife and wife to husband. The Catholic Church teaches that on their wedding day the minister or priest of the sacrament of matrimony is the couple themselves. As for other priestly functions, Lois is the important key to the solution of your worries these days. Give her my love.[459]

This is radical, startling, jaw-dropping. But he is saying that, given where Bill Wilson is coming from, if he wants to be saved, he is going to have to turn to his wife Lois as the priest of God who will act as the agent by which God's grace will be able to reach him. And it works vice versa as well. Father Ed accurately sees that Lois has always needed Bill just as much as he has needed her.

Father Dowling had helped start a campaign to bring more love and less fear into Catholic marriages, by founding the Cana Conference marriage enrichment program. He set up the first gathering in St. Louis in or before 1942, and devised the name for the program. He gathered some marvelous Catholic married couples around him, ordinary Catholic laypeople like Pat and Patty Crowley, who met another Catholic couple, Helene and Burnie Bauer, at the Cana Convention in August 1948, and laid the foundations of the Christian Family Movement. These devoted people came very close to revolutionizing (in a positive way) the role of women and the understanding of marriage in the Roman Catholic Church. It was only the early and untimely death of Father Ed, I believe — he was only 61 years old when he passed away — which caused the movement to eventually lose its energy and power.

In a Catholic sacrament, an extraordinary power of divine grace is mediated to human beings by what at first glance are grossly materialistic things and sometimes grossly physical functions. We stuff our mouths with bread, or wash the grime and sweat off our bodies with water. Olive oil, used in the ancient Mediterranean world as a lotion to soothe our skins, is converted sacramentally into a gesture of love to help comfort the dying.

And in his letter of September 8, 1947, Father Ed points out that, in the teaching of the Catholic Church, marriage is a sacrament just like communion, baptism, and last rites. Marriage is an extremely physical and materialistic relationship: Husband and wife dig in the soil and get sweaty and dirty together; they cook food (sticky and greasy) and eat it out of the same pot; they sleep in the same bed at night, have sex (a grossly physical act in all its tastes, smells, and sensations), and go through childbirth helping one another. A host of material things — from the house they live in to the crying child with the dirty diaper sitting on their laps — bind them together. But in a good marriage, this is the way true love is shown and received. In a good marriage, wives and husbands support one another emotionally, comfort one another, defend one another, and exhort and encourage one another. In an ideal world, this is the way children will learn the true nature of the divine love — from the example their parents set for them. Men and women serve equally as priests and distributors of sacramental grace. Father Dowling, through the Cana Conference marriage enrichment program, was trying to teach this to the contemporary American Catholic Church.

It is also probably no accident that only three and a half years after he wrote this letter to Bill and Lois about the sacramental nature of marriage, Lois Wilson (along with her friend and neighbor Anne Bingham) held the first organizational meeting for what would become Al-Anon Family Groups on April 21, 1951.

We also see a kind of echo of this sacramental view of the world — a reminder that there is a continual interchange going on between the life of the eternal realm and the physical life of this world — in the prayer which Bill and Lois Wilson wrote and recited together every morning when they first woke up. [460] This prayer assumed the doctrine of the transmigration of souls (or at least a doctrine of preexistence) for it stated that *before* our present incarnation in physical bodies on this planet, all of our human spirits were *already* in existence. And beyond that, the prayer says not only that all of our individual human spirits have always existed in some realm or other, but always would exist for all eternity, and would continue to have fresh experiences and adventures. The prayer may have implied a belief that our spirits would be reincarnated in future lives on this planet Earth (or in material existences on other planets in other parallel multiverses, in the way that C. S. Lewis describes in the Chronicles of Narnia). But it is also possible that, in quasi-Swedenborgian fashion, the prayer simply assumed that after our deaths, we would pass through a series of different heavenly realms (the "house of many mansions" in John 14:2), in each one of which we would learn yet further new and different things about God:

> Oh Lord, we thank Thee that Thou art,
>   that we are from everlasting to everlasting ....
> Accordingly, Thou has fashioned for us a destiny
>   passing through Thy many mansions,
> ever in more discovery of Thee
>   and in no separation between ourselves.

Our most important job as human beings, Bill and Lois reminded themselves in this morning prayer, was simply to attempt to turn our will and our lives over to the care of God as best we could, while seeking continually to improve our conscious contact with him:

> May we find and do Thy will
>   in good strength, in good cheer today.

And what we found, with each new discovery which we made about God, was that the eternal Power whom we were seeking was the source of all saving Grace and the divine light of Eternal Love:

> Blessed be Thy holy name and all Thy benefactions to us
>   of light, of love, and of service ....
> May Thy ever-present grace be discovered ....
>   by men and women everywhere ....

Oh Lord, we know Thee to be all wonder,
    all beauty, all glory, all power, all love.
    Indeed, Thou art everlasting love.

That was the divine vision which Bill and Lois were pledging to try to communicate to one another. And it worked — there would have been no Bill Wilson as we know him without Lois Wilson.

Bill Wilson's additional worry: would A.A.'s governing structures be able to avoid eventually falling into a belief in their own infallibility? During that same general period in 1947 to 1948 when Bill Wilson was visiting Bishop Fulton Sheen, and worrying away at the issue of papal infallibility in the Roman Catholic Church, Father Ed sent Bill a letter reminding him of this issue:

> Bill, I do not think you seem to be as second and third step on headquarters as you are on alcoholism. Could it be that the "Power" of the second step and the God of the third, fifth, sixth, seventh and eleventh steps is not powerful enough to handle headquarters: I know this has been a worry to you.

As the A.A. movement's headquarters in New York became more and more organized, the people in the New York office (and all the apparatus of Trustees and Area Delegates which eventually built up around it) were going to be subject to the same temptations as those afflicting the people who served in the Papal Curia at the Vatican in Rome. The seeds of sinful pride which lurked (consciously or unconsciously) within all human souls could just as easily tempt the officials and delegates and trustees of a twelve step program to start grabbing for the power to strut around and wear the equivalent of scarlet cardinals' robes while they pronounced infallible truth for all the lesser members of the group.

But let us not appear to be just picking on the Roman Catholic Church here, as though it were the only religious group whose leaders seemed sometimes to have believed that they had the right and the duty to tell everyone else in their religion what to read and what to believe. Father Dowling reminded Bill Wilson rather forcibly at one point, that it was not just the Roman Catholic Church which he was rejecting — he was refusing to join any Protestant denomination either.

In the United States, for example, the Lutheran Church Missouri Synod (the eighth largest Protestant denomination in the U.S.) began imposing such strict doctrinal and dogmatic standards on Concordia Seminary (located in a suburb of St. Louis, Missouri) — including biblical inerrancy and all the detailed dogmatic statements in the Book of Concord — that in 1974, forty-five of its fifty faculty members and the vast majority of its students walked out and refused to be associated with the seminary any more. In the largest Protestant denomination in the United States, the Southern Baptist Convention, all the faculty in their seminaries and all their foreign missionaries are at present required to follow the long, detailed set of doctrines and dogmas laid out in the document called *The Baptist Faith and Message.*[461] The denomination has been torn by continuous and extremely bitter controversy since the 1970's as its fundamentalist wing has been gaining tighter and tighter control over what Southern Baptists are ordered to believe. In seminaries and colleges this includes driving out faculty who are "too moderate," and banning the reading of numerous books. The Presbyterian Church (U.S.A.) keeps its people under what are sometimes even tighter controls: members are certainly not allowed to read the Bible for themselves and form their own ideas. Instead, everyone is expected to be ruled by the *Book of Confessions*, which includes the *Westminster Confession*, the *Scots Confession*, the *Heidelberg Catechism*, the *Helvetic Confession*, and so on — an enormous body of detailed doctrines and dogmas. A religious governing body where the pastors wear long black robes can be just as doctrinaire and dictatorial as one where the pastors wear long scarlet robes.

Could A.A. governing bodies fall into the same kind of behavior? Father Dowling, in my reading of his little note above, believed that God would be powerful enough to tame down New York A.A. headquarters if they got too far out of hand. The Big Book's explanation of the Third Step in pages 60-63 expressly said that we had to quit trying to play stage director, and quit trying to tell everyone else what to do and believe, and he thought that the influence of this step would be strong enough to block these A.A. officials' inbuilt human desire to control other people. But Bill Wilson (with his New England Calvinist background) was far more fearful of the power of human pride and ego.

And in fact, by now — only eighty years after A.A.'s founding — one can already see examples of infallibist beliefs and behaviors arising within the A.A. structure at the national level. We can already see collections of conference advisories and the like being gathered together with the insistence (at least on the part of some A.A. officials) that everybody in the fellowship has to treat these as unbreakable rules, and we can observe A.A. folks acting on far too many occasions as though any opinions expressed by the Area Delegates sent to New York, are automatically to be considered as infallible and absolutely binding on all A.A. members.

Already one newly invented doctrine has appeared (a sort of A.A. equivalent of the doctrine of the Immaculate Conception, in the sense of turning a pious but not carefully thought out emotional urge into a kind of sanctimonious overkill) which proclaims the absolute rule of posthumous anonymity (which would make writing honest, responsible A.A. history practically impossible). Violators are given the A.A. equivalent of excommunication by being barred for life from ever again looking at any of the materials in the A.A. archives in New York City.

Within a religious movement, claims of infallibility can sometimes be naked and overt: that was the situation both in the First Vatican Council's proclamation of papal infallibility in 1870 and in the Protestant Fundamentalist claims of biblical infallibility and inerrancy which began with the Niagara Bible Conference in 1878–1897 and were subsequently spread all over the United States by the publication in 1910–1915 of the twelve-volume series called *The Fundamentals*. But infallibilism can also be covert and buried under layers of surface denial: so for example, people may be told that they can read any books they want to, but find that the only books available, for all practical purposes, are those supplied by the authorities (books which only present the position which the authority figures want you to take). People are told that they have freedom to disagree, but are de facto barred from all the places where ideas can truly be exchanged between members of the movement, and barred from publishing their findings in any effective way.

The decision to put the phrase "conference approved literature" on books published by A.A. World Services has had an enormous practical effect (which was fully intended by the people at the New York headquarters who pushed for that proviso, according to my contacts with insiders there) — the effect of convincing A.A. meetings and intergroups all over the United States to refuse to make any other books on A.A. available for sale or distribution, even ones (like *The Little Red Book*, *Twenty-Four Hours a Day*, and Emmet Fox's *Sermon on the Mount*) which were a traditional and essential part of A.A. teaching since the early years.

This is thought control. This is an attempt to turn 99% of the A.A. members in America into the kind of little children whom the philosopher Kant talked about — people who blindly act like tiny children because they lack the courage to stand up like adults and tell the bullies who are trying to terrorize them, that they intend to think for themselves.

This is the exact equivalent to the kind of things that were going on during that dark period in Roman Catholic history which fell between the First and Second Vatican Councils. It is the same kind of out-of-control religious tyranny which was seen breaking out in even more violent fashion in colonial New England in the village of Salem in 1692–1693, in the infamous Salem witch trials, where any villagers who spoke out against the persecution were silenced by being physically assaulted and beaten up, or were even put on trial as witches themselves (like poor Martha Corey).

And in fact the A.A. phrase "conference approved literature" is the exact equivalent of the old Roman Catholic phrases *nihil obstat* and *imprimatur* that were printed at the beginning of a book which the Roman Catholic *censor librorum* (censor of books) would allow the faithful to read. In the early twentieth century, when blind authoritarianism ruled so much of American Catholic Church practice, a truly pious Catholic would refuse to read a book on theology or morals which lacked the *nihil obstat* and *imprimatur,* for fear that some wrong idea present in that non-approved book might lead his or her soul down the path to everlasting damnation.

So the question remains of how far it is safe to go in the direction of officially established doctrines and reading lists in any spiritual movement, including twelve step programs. Bill Wilson refused to join the pre-Vatican II Catholic Church because he refused to let someone else tell him what he should believe and what books he could read (and buy and sell). Father Dowling pointed out to Bill that it wasn't just a Catholic issue — Protestant churches also told their people what to believe — which was why Bill was also refusing to sign on with any of the existing Protestant denominations.

But instead of criticizing him for that, Father Ed told Bill that he was doing the right thing, and went on to warn that it would be a betrayal of the mission to which God had appointed him in that vision of light at Towns Hospital if he allowed A.A. as such to be turned into a vehicle for propagating one and only one of the world's current religions — *any of them* — Christianity, Buddhism, Hinduism, Judaism, Islam, the Sikh religion, or whatever.

The most difficult part of this issue however, was one which Bill Wilson had already apparently begun to worry about. Was A.A. itself safe from being betrayed down the same path? Electing an alcoholic as an area delegate, or hiring an alcoholic to work in the A.A. offices in New York City, did not confer infallibility on that person any more than being elected to office did on a potentially over-zealous Roman Catholic pope or a group of naively over-literalist Protestant Fundamentalist pastors. Did God have enough power to bring the New York A.A. office back in line, if this needed to be done? Was the almighty Power who is spoken of in the second step forceful enough the bring those people back to sanity if they became power mad? Was the God of the third step strong enough to compel those people to re-surrender their wills to him, if they went astray and began yielding to the lust to tell everybody else what to believe and think and read and say and do? Or did even stronger safeguards need to be built into the A.A. organizational structure to keep the bleeding deacons from taking over and destroying the movement with their rules and quibbles and rigidly authoritarian mindset?

Bill Wilson wrote the Third Tradition in an effort to undercut any attempts by A.A. officials and leaders to tell other members what they could read, think, say, and publish. In 1946 — the year before he began visiting Fulton J. Sheen and flirting with the idea of converting to Catholicism — Bill published the original long form of the Third Tradition in the April *Grapevine*:

> Our membership ought to include all who suffer from alcoholism. Hence we may refuse none who wish to recover. Nor ought A.A. membership ever depend upon money or conformity. Any two or three alcoholics gathered together for sobriety may call themselves an A.A. group, provided that, as a group, they have no other affiliation.

In the November 1949 issue of the *Grapevine*, Bill published the short form of the traditions and made his meaning even clearer, reducing the Third Tradition to a single simple sentence: ***"The only requirement for A.A. membership is a desire to stop drinking."***

In an article which he wrote in the April 1946 *Grapevine* (reprinted in *The Language of the Heart* on pp. 32-33), Bill tried to make it clear that the Third Tradition was intended to block any attempts by A.A. officials or legislative bodies (a) to practice thought control, or (b) define "correct A.A. doctrine" about belief in God or any other religious issue, or (c) tell A.A. groups what they were supposed to teach, or (d) specify what books the members of that group could read or study, or loan or sell to other members of their group, or (e) give orders about the things which A.A. members could and could not publish in the books which they wrote about the program and its history. As Bill Wilson said in this April 1946 article:

> Point Three in our AA Tradition looks like a wide open invitation to anarchy .... It reads "... Any two or three alcoholics gathered together for sobriety may call themselves an AA group" .... In fact, our Tradition carries the principle of independence to such a fantastic length that, so long as there is the slightest interest in sobriety, the most unmoral, the most antisocial, the most critical alcoholic may gather about him a few kindred spirits and announce to us that a new Alcoholics Anonymous group has been formed. Anti-God, anti-medicine, anti-our recovery program, even anti-each

other — these rampant individuals are still an AA group if they think so!

So in fact as early as 1946, Bill Wilson had already decided down in his heart that there were no infallible human beings anywhere on the planet, which meant that there were neither individuals nor groups anywhere who could be entrusted with absolute power over other people's thoughts, beliefs, and words. Over the course of 1947-48 he came to realize that this belief would block him from joining either the Roman Catholic Church or any of the Protestant denominations that he knew of.

The A.A. fellowship does not run the Roman Catholic Church (or any other traditional religion or denomination), so at that level, the story of Bill Wilson's refusal to convert to Catholicism is now just a historical curiosity. But the question of whether modern A.A. (and the twelve step movement in general) will go back and re-read what Bill Wilson said about the real meaning of the Third Tradition — the question, that is, of whether A.A. can manage to stop and reverse its present slow slide further and further into dogmatism, thought-control, authoritarianism, and infallibilism — this is a question whose answer will determine the long-term future of the twelve step movement, for good or for ill.

Chapter 30

Ratifying of the Twelve Traditions and Dr. Bob's Death: 1950

The Twelve Traditions: The year 1950 marked a decisive turning point in A.A. history. When the Twelve Traditions were approved on Sunday, July 30, 1950 at the First International A.A. Convention in Cleveland, A.A. was given a sort of Bill of Rights, along with a set of extremely effective strategies for avoiding the most deeply disruptive disputes. And along with this, the Twelve Traditions also erected a protective fence around the fellowship to help keep it from being drawn too deeply into outside affairs. Taken all together, the Twelve Traditions functioned to guarantee the members' basic human rights, minimize internal conflicts, and keep the movement away from over-involvement with external material things.

If we lay out a time table for the writing, approval, and final publication of the Traditions in final book form, we can see that this process extended over eight years, from 1945 to 1953:

August 1945 — the *Grapevine* carried Bill W.'s first Traditions essay.

April 1946 — the *Grapevine* carried Bill W.'s essay "Twelve Suggested Points for A.A. Tradition," later known as the long form of the Traditions.

1947 — at the suggestion of Earl Treat (the founder of A.A. in Chicago), Bill W. began developing the short form of the Traditions.

November 1949 — the short form of the Traditions was published in the *Grapevine*. The wording of the traditions in this article, with two exceptions,[462] was taken over verbatim in the book called the *Twelve Steps and Twelve Traditions* when it was published in 1953.

July 28-30, 1950 — the First International A.A. Convention met in Cleveland, Ohio. The crowd gathered in the Cleveland Auditorium Music Hall gave its unanimous approval to a partly paraphrased version of the Twelve Traditions which Bill Wilson read to them.

mid-May, 1952 — Bill Wilson had finished the basic draft of the part of his book on the *Twelve Steps and Twelve Traditions* which dealt with the traditions, and sent a copy to Father Dowling.

mid-June, 1952 — Father Dowling had a retinal stroke and ended up in the hospital unable to read. Some of his friends tape recorded the twelve chapters, and his sister Anna also read him portions of the manuscript out loud, at places where he wanted to be sure he understood exactly what was being said.

1953 — the publication of Bill Wilson's book on the *Twelve Steps and Twelve Traditions*.

At the end of the process, in 1952-1953, it appears that Father Ed's eyesight was too severely compromised to allow him to give Bill Wilson any kind of detailed critiques of the final finished product. But we must remember that during the first six years in which Bill was working on the wording and interpretation of the Twelve Traditions, from 1945-1951, he was in regular communication with the good priest who was his spiritual director. It would be interesting to put together a collection of all of Father Ed's letters and writings in various publications, and compare his ideas and attitudes with those taught in the part on the traditions in the *Twelve Steps and Twelve Traditions*.

We can see Father Ed's liberal social and political ideas, and his lifelong battle against all forms of discrimination, and in defense of tolerance and compassion for the downtrodden, being reflected — in some ways even more strongly — in Bill Wilson's vision of an A.A. fellowship which extended love and support to any person who suffered from alcoholism from the minute that person walked through their doors.

The A.A. Bill of Rights: The chapter on Tradition Three in the *Twelve Steps and Twelve Traditions* laid out a strong Bill of Rights.[463] It began by assuming that people living in the United States would already be under the protection of the Bill of Rights laid out in the first ten amendments to the U.S. Constitution in 1789-1791,[464] even in matters which were totally internal to the Alcoholics Anonymous organizational structure. (Those who wish to make an even broader comparative study of Enlightenment-inspired statements of fundamental human rights should also look at the Declaration of the Rights of Man and of Citizen that was drawn up during the French Revolution in 1789.[465])

The chapter on A.A. Tradition Three assumed that the fundamental principles of Enlightenment-era freedoms applied within A.A. wherever relevant, and devoted itself instead to talking about additional guarantees of human rights which were even stronger than those mentioned explicitly in the first ten amendments to the U.S. Constitution (one cannot help but suspect that Father Dowling's influence may have been at work on Bill Wilson here):

1. You cannot be barred from A.A. because of "how low you've gone" (page 139). A.A. meetings cannot exclude "beggars, tramps" (140). "We must never compel anyone to pay anything" (141) because this would serve as a bar to the totally down and out.

2. "How grave your emotional complications" are cannot be used to discriminate against you, nor "how twisted ... you may be" (page 139). Alcoholics Anonymous cannot refuse to admit people because they are "asylum inmates" or just "plain crackpots" (140).

3. "Even your crimes," "never mind how ... violent you may be" (page 139) cannot be used to bar you from

A.A. membership. "Prisoners" (140) must be allowed to attend A.A. meetings, whether they are ex-convicts or still in prison (in which case A.A. prison groups needed to be set up, like the one formed at San Quentin in 1942 by the San Francisco A.A. group, or the one formed at Michigan City in 1944 by the South Bend, Indiana, A.A. group).

4. A.A. groups could not bar those whom they regarded as "fallen women" (page 140).

5. A.A. groups could not bar "queers" (page 140), that is LGBT (lesbian, gay, bisexual, and transgender) people. The chapter on Tradition Three had a long story about Dr. Bob's insistence in 1937 that the Akron group had to allow the man with "the double stigma" to join their group (141-142) — he was not only an alcoholic but also gay, that is, homosexual.

6. There must be no preaching about specific beliefs of specific religious denominations in A.A. meetings: "we must never compel anyone to ... believe anything" (page 141). The chapter on Tradition Three went on to tell the long story of "Ed the atheist" (143-145), who was a real person, a very famous early A.A. figure named Jim Burwell. The next chapter (on Tradition Four) went on to point out that "there would be real danger should we commence to call some groups ... 'Catholic' or 'Protestant'" (147)

7. The chapter on Tradition Four also said that there should be no talking about politics in A.A. meetings: "There would be real danger should we commence to call some groups ... 'Republican' or 'Communist'" (page 147).

8. A.A. had to "cut across every barrier of race ... and language" (page 141).

With respect to this last proviso, the possibility of Father Ed's influence on this Bill of Rights seems particularly notable: The first black groups were not started in A.A. until 1945, but in that year three successful groups were formed: The first was started on January 24, 1945 in St. Louis (where *Father Ed Dowling* had started the first

A.A. group in October 1940 and was still actively associated with the groups). The second (the Evans Avenue Group) was begun in March 1945 in Chicago (where they asked **Earl Treat**, the founder of Chicago A.A., for ninety days to see if they could make a black A.A. group work, and he agreed). What was actually the third group was then formed in either April or September 1945 in Washington, D.C. by a black physician named Dr. Jim Scott M.D.[466]

It is significant that two of Bill Wilson's major advisers and helpers in writing the *Twelve Steps and Twelve Traditions* — Father Dowling and Earl Treat — had been closely associated with the founding of the first two black A.A. groups.

This issue remained important to Bill Wilson. The story of the man who started the black group in Washington D.C. was put in the second edition of the Big Book,[467] which came out in 1955, only three years after the publication of the *Twelve Steps and Twelve Traditions*, to make the record clear and completely official: people could not be excluded from A.A. groups on racial grounds.

> Parenthetically we might note that the story of early Spanish language A.A. has not been worked out in as much detail by A.A. historians, but it appears that the first translation of the Big Book into Spanish was carried out by either Dick P. in Cleveland or Frank M. (or independently by both) in 1946 or 1947.[468] But copies of this translation were not widely distributed or easily available. So the first major spread of A.A. into Spanish speaking areas (in both North and South America) was not connected with either Father Dowling and Bill W., or with Clarence Snyder and the people in Cleveland, but with Spanish language pamphlets containing translations of sections from the Golden Books written by **Father Ralph Pfau**.[469] The fact that Ralph was a Roman Catholic priest may have given Spanish-speaking people a greater degree of trust in what he was telling them about alcoholism.

Dr. Bob's death in 1950 left Father Ed as Bill W.'s only truly reliable spiritual guide: This stretch of time that we are looking at now, the period from 1945 to 1950, also included those sad years during which Dr. Bob and Anne Smith came to the end of their journey:

> 1947 — Dr. Bob developed colon cancer.
>
> 1948 — it was diagnosed as terminal, and he retired from practice.
>
> June 1, 1949 — Anne Ripley Smith died after a heart attack (aged 68).
>
> July 30, 1950 — Dr. Bob, quite ill, made a brief appearance at the First International A.A. Convention in Cleveland, Ohio and gave his last talk.
>
> November 16, 1950 — Dr. Bob died (aged 71).

At the time of Dr. Bob's death, Father Dowling was 58 years old and Bill Wilson was almost 55. Bill had people other than Father Ed whom he could talk to about spiritual issues — Father Ed was not his only trusted friend — but it strikes me that during this period there was almost no one other than Earl Treat in Chicago who was as wise and ultimately dependable as the good Jesuit priest. During these ten years in particular — from 1950 to Father Ed's death in 1960 — the priest was absolutely vital to maintaining Bill's sanity and spiritual strength.

CHAPTER 31

Spooks and Saints

In 1956, the young Mel Barger (who later became one of the most important A.A. authors of the second generation) asked Bill Wilson to explain what had happened at Towns Hospital in the famous vision of light which he had experienced on December 14, 1934. It was after a meeting, and Bill told him he was too exhausted to get into that right at that moment, but he promised to write Mel after he got back to New York City. What Mel eventually received was a missive that contained what is probably (still to this day) the most detailed account in one place of what Bill Wilson believed on a large variety of spiritual issues. Mel says in his book, *My Search for Bill W.*[470]

> I received the following letter, which was dated July 2, 1956 .... Since I had mentioned William James's *The Varieties of Religious Experience*, Bill discussed that and then recommended a book called *Cosmic Consciousness*, by Richard Maurice Bucke — one that he described as having "covered the waterfront" on the subject of spiritual experience. He also referred to a book called *Heaven and Hell*, by Aldous Huxley. He went on to say that since his spiritual experience, he had been subject to an immense amount of psychic phenomena of all sorts, adding:

> "So much so, that immortality is no longer a question of faith — to me, it has the certainty of knowledge through evidence. In the course of innumerable experiences of this sort, the negative has appeared as often as the positive. In this layer of consciousness, I have had a good look at what

the theologians call "hell" also. My total experience seems to confirm the argument in Huxley's book [*Heaven and Hell*][471] — namely, that reality, which must include both absolute and relative, is arranged in several layers. We have the conscious, the unconscious or subconscious, the world of psychic phenomenalism which suggests our Father's house of many mansions, and finally the ultimate reality, glimpses of which all mystics seem to have had. To me, this makes good theological sense. We appear to be in a day at school, a relative state of affairs that slowly progresses toward a meeting with the Absolute. When the doors of perception are opened widely enough by ego deflation, we get these fleeting glimpses of ultimate destiny."

It was a complex view of a transcendent realm in which the spirits of the dead dwelt at various levels, experiencing some kind of afterlife suitable to their degree of spiritual advancement, and appropriate to their own temperament and personality type. Some were heavenly realms, where good spirits dwelt in peace, while others could be quite hellish, and were populated by spirits who held enormous evil locked within themselves.

Speaking with the spirits of the dead: Later on, when Mel was carrying out the research for *Pass It On* (the official A.A. biography of Bill W., which was published in 1984), he discovered additional details about Bill Wilson's beliefs about mysticism, psychic phenomena, and talking with the spirits who dwelt in the other world. As that book describes it:[472]

As early as 1941, Bill and Lois were holding regular Saturday "spook sessions" at Bedford Hills. One of the downstairs bedrooms was dubbed by them the "spook room"; here, they conducted many of their psychic experiments. Of one session with a ouija board, Bill wrote this description:

"The ouija board got moving in earnest. What followed was the fairly usual experience — it was a strange mélange of Aristotle, St. Francis, diverse archangels with odd names, deceased friends — some in purgatory and others doing nicely, thank you! There were malign and mischievous ones of all descriptions, telling of vices quite beyond my ken, even as former alcoholics. Then the seemingly virtuous entities would elbow them out with messages of comfort, information, advice — and sometimes just sheer nonsense."

Bill would lie on the couch in the living room, semi-withdrawn, but not in a trance, and receive messages, sometimes a word at a time, sometimes a letter at a time. Anne B[ingham], neighbor and spook circle regular would write the material on a pad.

Later on, in 2004, Susan Cheever gave additional details about these sessions in *My Name Is Bill*:[473]

Sometimes the Wilsons used a Ouija board .... Lois and Bill, or two or three of the other participants, rested their fingers lightly on the board, closed their eyes, and allowed the unconscious pressure from their fingers to move the triangular marker across the smooth surface. Sometimes it stopped on Yes or No; at other times it spelled out what seemed to be words.

On evenings when they decided to use the table instead of the Ouija board, they gathered around it, each person with their fingers resting lightly on the table's sharp edge. They dimmed the lights. Bill's voice would often ask the questions. "Are there any spirits in the room?" he would ask. "Are there any spirits who have a message for us?" ....

Then the people seated around the table would hear a soft, hesitant tap. Sometimes, if Bill had asked a direct question, the taps meant yes or no: one for yes and two for no. At other times the spirits had a longer message. If it tapped once, that meant the letter A, twice for the letter B and so on. In an evening the table might tap out a phrase or two. According to both Bill and Lois, on more than one occasion they succeeded in levitating the table a few inches off the floor.

At other times the Wilsons and their guests experimented with automatic writing. Bill Wilson was very good at this. He would set a pen down on a piece of paper, close his eyes and wait for the spirit to guide his hand. On some evenings Bill would relax his long frame out on the living room couch in front of the big stone fireplace and wait in a state of half-dreaming, half-consciousness, the smoke curling up from his cigarette. Lying there, he would receive messages, sometimes whole, as when he heard the Reverend Dwight Moody warning him against the past, and sometimes they would come to him letter by letter [and he would spell out the words, one by one, in a quiet voice].

For those who asked for some proof that these experiences were real, there were at least two quite spectacular examples of things that seemed impossible to explain on naturalistic grounds. Bill and Lois arrived in Nantucket in 1944 for a visit, the first time either of them had been there. Bill got up the first morning around 6 o'clock and was drinking his first cup of coffee when the spirits of several dead people began speaking to him. One was a sailor named David Morrow who said he had been killed while fighting under Admiral Farragut at the Battle of Mobile Bay during the Civil War. Another was the ghost of a man named Pettengill who said he had been master of a whaler out of Nantucket (or Martha's Vineyard). A third spirit was another master of a whaling ship, this one named Quigley (as Bill remembered it later). Bill repeated this story later at breakfast, taking pains to stress the three names that he remembered. As a result, his host later remembered all three names, although he remained belligerently skeptical about Bill's claim to have spoken with the souls of the dead. But later on Bill was invited to a picnic lunch in a circle on Nantucket's Main Street, a place with a small monument in the center, with the names chiseled on it of all the men from Nantucket who had died in the Civil War. On the list, Bill Wilson spotted the name David Morrow, which he pointed out to his host. And then the next day, Bill and Lois visited the Nantucket Sailing Museum, where he looked through a book containing the names of all of the ship captains who had commanded whaling ships during the great period of the whaling industry. There was the name Pettingill and also a ship captain named Quigley.[474]

The other event was perhaps even more spectacular, and involved a message in a language Bill did not know. As Lois Wilson told the story later,[475]

> Bill would lie down on the couch. He would "get" these things. He kept doing it every week or so. Each time, certain people would "come in." Sometimes, it would be new ones, and they'd carry on some story .... This time, instead of word by word, [the message came] letter by letter. Anne put them down letter by letter.

Lois had had three years of Latin, and it looked to her like the message was written in that language, but she did not know Latin well enough to translate it. Bill Wilson knew no Latin except for the Latin terms he had picked up in law school, like *amicus curiae, corpus delicti, cui bono, habeas corpus, in camera, mens rea,* and so on. But no one could write a long connected text with only a vocabulary of those words. Bill took the text to Willard "Dick" S. Richardson of the Rockefeller Foundation, who knew Latin well. Richardson told him that it was written in good grammatical Latin and seemed to be an account of the founding of Christianity in Italy.[476]

As Nell Wing remembered the story, [477] Willard Richardson was there at the séance where Bill Wilson received the Latin text, and it was instead a sermon written by St. Boniface, but it seems to have been the same basic story: Bill (who knew only a few words of law school Latin legal terms) nevertheless recited a long message, one letter at a time, that turned out to be written in good medieval Latin and seemed to come from someone who had lived many centuries in the past.

St. Boniface, the Apostle of Germany, gives Bill Wilson advice on his book on the Twelve Steps and Twelve Traditions: One of the most famous stories about Bill Wilson's contacts with the souls of the deceased, concerns what he said were detailed and regular conversations at one point with St. Boniface (presumably the same Boniface who, as described in the preceding paragraph, on one occasion had dictated a long passage to Bill in medieval Latin).

St. Boniface (c. 675 – June 5, 754) was the Anglo-Saxon missionary who brought Christianity to Dark Age Germany and Frisia (the Low German speaking area that runs along the coast of the North Sea). We already discussed this earlier in Chapter 24, but as part of the present discussion of Bill Wilson's attempts to speak with the spirits of the dead, the story needs to be mentioned again.

On July 17, 1952 Bill Wilson sent Father Dowling a draft version of the first four chapters of his book on the *Twelve Steps and Twelve Traditions*, the chapters on the first four steps, with a cover letter in which he said, "But I have good help — of that I am certain. Both over here and over there" in the spirit world.

> One turned up the other day calling himself Boniface. Said he was a Benedictine missionary and English. Had been a man of learning, knew missionary work and a lot about structures. I think he said this all the more modestly but that was the gist of it. I'd never heard of this gentleman but he checked out pretty well in the Encyclopedia. If this one is who he says he is — and of course there is no certain way of knowing — would this be licit contact in your book?[478]

Dowling wrote back on July 24, 1952, advising Bill to use caution: "Boniface sounds like the Apostle of Germany. I still feel, like Macbeth, that these folks tell us the truth in small matters in order to fool us in larger." [479]

Father Ed's reference was to Shakespeare's play *Macbeth* (1.3.132). The scene was a mysterious heath near Forres, on the northern coast of Scotland. The three witches were on stage when Macbeth and Banquo entered (both of these men were generals at that time in the King of Scotland's army). The witches told Macbeth he would become the thane (Scottish feudal lord) of Cawdor, and eventually would become the King of Scotland. To Macbeth's surprise, the first prediction came true almost immediately. Banquo warned him however:

> ... oftentimes, to win us to our harm,
> The instruments of darkness tell us truths,
> Win us with honest trifles, to betray 's
> In deepest consequence.

Now it is important to note, as we can see from this example, that Father Dowling was NOT trying to deny that Bill Wilson was speaking with some kind of spirits from the other world. But in orthodox Catholic belief — as well as in the *Bardo Thodol* (the Tibetan Book of the Dead), Aldous Huxley's *Heaven and Hell,* and Carl Jung's gnostic psychological theories — there are not only good spirits, but also evil, malicious, terrifying, and downright dangerous spirits in the transcendent realm.

Dr. Bob and Anne Smith were also involved in attempts to contact the spirit world: We must not fall into the mistaken belief that attempts to talk with the spirits of the dead were just idiosyncrasies and aberrations that Bill W. alone became involved in over on the East Coast, as part of an over-intellectualized and over-psychologized "New York A.A." which somehow stood in opposition to the supposed common sense and practical spirituality of Dr. Bob and good, honest "Akron A.A." Deep involvement with psychic phenomena was part and parcel of the spiritual life of both of the two founding figures of the twelve step program, in Akron as well as on the East Coast.

In fact it is possible that it was Dr. Bob and Anne who first introduced Bill to the idea of attempting to communicate with the spirits of the dead. When Bill Wilson first met Dr. Bob and Anne Smith in 1935 and spent part of the summer at their house, he wrote back to Lois in his letters about séances and other psychic events going on at Dr. Bob and Anne's house.[480]

Dr. Bob's son Smitty said that his father believed that, as modern science continued to progress, it would eventually become possible to easily make "contact between the living and the dead." And John and Elgie R.[481] said that "in the late 1930's, Doc would talk for hours to a fellow named Roland J." who was deeply involved in exploring various kinds of psychic phenomena.[482] Elgie remembered one experience in particular:

> "I had several experiences with Roland J_____, his wife, Doc and Anne, and Ruth T_____ in Toledo," Elgie recalled. "We had a spiritualist séance one night, and an amazing thing happened: I became controlled, as it were. I was telling Doc about his father, who was a judge, and I didn't know

anything about it. Afterwards, when I came to myself, Doc advised me to stay out of crowds. He told me I was sort of susceptible and liable to go into some sort of trance if there was somebody around who was upset."[483]

Elgie also told a particularly strange story about something that happened once when Roland J. was around:

"I remember another time Doc, Anne, and I were sitting in the living room over at Roland's house one Sunday afternoon. Doc was reading the paper; Anne was sitting smoking cigarettes; Dorothy was out in the kitchen getting dinner; and Roland was sitting in a chair. All of a sudden, Anne started rolling her eyes, trying to get my attention. I looked in that direction. And so help me God, Roland had created the illusion of a beard on his chin. I didn't believe what I was seeing. When he saw that I was looking, he let it disappear. Doc just sat there and laughed. He believed that was the funniest thing he had ever seen."[484]

Anne Smith had her own special abilities in this area. She was famous for receiving divine messages or impulses a day or two prior to an especially important new alcoholic coming to see her and Dr. Bob. One of these new men was J. D. Holmes, who subsequently founded the first A.A. group in Indiana (at Evansville), and in addition played a major role in helping to start or maintain groups in many other cities in that state, including the capital Indianapolis. He said,

"Dr. Bob and Anne had planned to go to Vermont two days before I came into the group. But Anne woke up in the middle of the night and said she felt they shouldn't go — that they would be needed here."[485]

Clarence Snyder's wife Dorothy told a similar story, about what happened when Archie Trowbridge was sent from Detroit down to Akron to see if Dr. Bob and Anne could help get him sane, sober, and physically healthy once again:

> "I was down spending the night with [Anne Smith], and we were all going to a picnic on Sunday. On Saturday night, Anne announced firmly that she wasn't going. Something told her it wasn't right. Sure enough, along about five o'clock in the morning, there was a call from Detroit about a man they wanted to send down."[486]

Archie Trowbridge also turned out to be one of the great A.A. founding figures. He eventually got back to Detroit, where he joined with a nonalcoholic friend, Sarah Klein, to start the first A.A. group in Detroit.

Continual visions (or hallucinations?) during the last six years of Bill Wilson's life: Father Ed died in April 1960. Bill Wilson was sixty-four years old at that point, and already beginning to show his own age. Then in the later 1960's, Bill's emphysema became worse and worse. By the time he turned seventy in 1965, his breathing had begun to become noticeably labored. By 1969, his episodes of severe bronchitis had turned into bouts with pneumonia. [487] Francis Hartigan notes:

> As the emphysema progressed, Bill's nights were frequently filled with dreams and visions. Even when awake, he sometimes fell victim to hallucinations. While many of them were pleasant, others were not pleasant at all. Bill's ravings about the things he thought he was seeing turned his existence, and that of Lois, Harriet, their housekeeper, and Nell Wing, who was a regular guest, increasingly nightmarish.[488]

As we remember, Bill went to the A.A. International Convention in Miami in July, 1970, but had to cancel all of his appearances except for a brief one at the Sunday morning breakfast (which turned out to be the last talk he ever gave). He was so exhausted afterwards, it took him a number of days in intensive care at the Miami Heart Institute before they could get him in good enough shape to make the airplane flight back to New York. And then unfortunately, once back at Stepping Stones, he had another bout with pneumonia.

"The hallucinations were a regular feature now," Francis Hartigan says, and

Bill was confined to the upstairs bedroom at Stepping Stones through the rest of the fall into the winter, attended by nurses around the clock. Most commonly, he would greet each day filled with dread at what lay in store for him.[489]

In January 1971, Brinkley Smithers chartered an airplane and had Bill Wilson flown back down to Miami, to see if he could be helped by a new breathing machine they had just obtained at the Miami Heart Institute. The aircraft was a small Learjet, where they had to remove a partition in order to lay Bill out flat.[490] He was accompanied on the plane by Lois, Nell Wing, and Dr. Ed B. from the Heart Institute.

During the flight, Bill entertained his fellow passengers with descriptions of his parents, grandparents, and his old friend Mark Whalon. They were all dead, but he could see them there with him on the plane.[491]

They arrived in Miami in the late afternoon, and Bill was put in a bed at the Heart Institute on January 24, 1971. Lois finally said good night to him, and went to bed herself. At 11:30 p.m. they found Bill dead.

Dark visions in the world's great spiritual traditions, from the Tibetan Book of the Dead to Hieronymus Bosch: Were these authentic visions which Bill was having, where he was in real contact with the transcendent spiritual realm? Or were these just meaningless hallucinations, as both Francis Hartigan and the authors of *Pass It On* characterize them?[492] Now we must acknowledge that Bill was existing on the borderline between this world and the next for that entire last year or so. He was dying and knew it, which caused the remainder of the mind's normal protective shields (always thin in his case) to drop away. So these visions could have been something very similar to out-of-body near-death experiences, which means that if you believe that experiences of that type involve real contact with the world of the dead, then the people whom Bill was seeing and hearing could also have been real inhabitants of the world after this one.

One of the classic accounts of various kinds of out-of-body near-death experiences is the book referred to in the west as *The Tibetan*

Book of the Dead. Its real title is *Bardo Thodol,* which means something more or less like "Liberation Through Hearing During the Intermediate State." It is a description of the various things which we experience after death, during the period between death and our next rebirth. Some of these visions are blissful and can bring the soul liberation from the chains of karma. (Current western accounts of near-death experiences tend to concentrate exclusively on pleasant and liberating visions of this sort, which are the kind of spiritual experiences that the methodology of the twelve steps attempts to lead the soul into.) But *The Tibetan Book of the Dead* makes it clear that there are other visions potentially lying in wait in the Intermediate State, which are horrifying and nightmarish in the extreme.

And let us also remember that the same medieval Roman Catholic cathedrals which had such beautiful sculptures and murals of angels and saints staring down at us beatifically, also had depictions of terrifying demons and gargoyles, which medieval people took equally seriously. Or one might look at the paintings of the medieval Christian artist Hieronymus Bosch (c. 1450 – 1516), whose demons and hellish figures were sometimes even more grotesque and frightening than the figures of the darker deities from ancient India and Tibet (where Hindu and Buddhist art often portrayed beings who wore necklaces of human skulls, carried bloody swords, and rode on the backs of sharp-fanged lions and tigers, or stood astride the corpses of their victims).

Dr. Bob's angel and the empty chair at the St. Louis International: And where did Father Dowling stand on all these things? We remember already mentioning the strange statement that Father Ed made when he was speaking to the St. Louis International A.A. Convention in 1955. He was talking about his belief that we are called to continually grow in our knowledge of God, not only in this present material existence but also in our life after death, when we will become spirits dwelling in the transcendent world, and he told the crowd of 5,000 people gathered before him that:

> I am sure that Bill, sitting in that chair, and Dr. Bob, whose angel is probably sitting on that oddly misplaced empty chair, are growing in the knowledge of God. [493]

I do not myself believe that this was simply a joking or metaphorical statement. I think that Father Ed was saying something to Bill Wilson that we could paraphrase as follows: "Look Bill, if you use your deeper spiritual senses, you can see or feel Dr. Bob's angel (or spirit or ghost) present right here with us today. You could easily form a mental image of him sitting right there in that chair, in effect, hearing and seeing everything we are doing up here on this stage. And you and Dr. Bob are both still involved in making spiritual progress, and learning more and more about God, in a process which will go on forever in a huge eternal cosmic fellowship which includes both those of us here on this earth and those who have gone on to the next world."

The Catholic faith never denied that people in this world could talk and be in contact with the spirits of the dead. The Catholic Church however felt much more comfortable if the dead person whom we were talking to was certified by the Church as a saint, and was even happier about these contacts if the dead person and the person who was still alive were both saints. So for example, the Church had no problem when the story was told by Augustin Poulain, S.J. in *The Graces of Interior Prayer* (a much approved Catholic work on this subject) about how St. Teresa saw Jesus continually walking with her on her right side for two whole years, while St. Peter and St. Paul walked with her at her left side (*Life*, ch. 27.3 and ch. 29.6).

The question here is whether — in Father Ed's eyes — Bill W. and Dr. Bob were both saintly enough for it to be safe to talk openly about Bill possibly being able to converse with the ghost of Dr. Bob up in heaven and feel his presence come down here on earth. You who read this present book will have to decide for yourselves on this issue.

And Bill Wilson certainly did complicate the matter when he spoke with a dead saint — St. Boniface, the Apostle to the Germans — and the dead saint started giving him copious and detailed help in writing his book on the *Twelve Steps and Twelve Traditions*. That was not at all what was usually meant by speaking with the saints in the medieval Roman Catholic tradition!

CHAPTER 32

Spiritual Experience and Poulain's Graces of Interior Prayer

To the best of my knowledge, the only critical remark which Father Dowling ever made in public about the A.A. movement was one comment in his speech to the St. Louis International A.A. Convention in 1955: "I still weep that the elders of the movement have dropped the word 'experience' for 'awakening'" in the wording of the Twelfth Step.[494] Father Ed was referring to the decision made when preparing the second printing of the Big Book, to revise one sentence on page 72 by changing the wording of the Twelfth Step (altered wording underlined by me):

> **First printing (April 1939):** Having had a spiritual experience as the result of these steps, we tried to carry this message to alcoholics, and to practice these principles in all our affairs.

> **Second printing (March 2, 1941):** Having had a spiritual awakening as the result of those steps, we tried to carry this message to alcoholics, and to practice these principles in all our affairs.

Father Ed went on to explain to the A.A. audience in St. Louis that, in his interpretation, "experience can be of two kinds":

(1) The commonest kind are gentle consolations sent to us by God, such as those "routine active observations" which can nevertheless strike us suddenly with an experience of deep pleasure: "I am sober today" as opposed to the misery and suffering I endured for so many years.

(2) But the other kind of religious experience is of a spectacular and overwhelming sort, Father Ed explained, like Bill's experience of the divine light at Towns Hospital on December 14, 1934, or "like the *Grapevine* story of that Christmas Eve in Chicago," where a shaking, convulsive alcoholic underwent a near instantaneous conversion and physical rehabilitation, or like what happened to the Apostle Paul "as he was struck from his horse on the road to Damascus."[495]

Poulain, The Graces of Interior Prayer: Father Ed had quite detailed ideas about the various kinds of things which should and should not be included under the heading of good and worthwhile spiritual experiences. At one point, replying to a letter which Wilson sent him on March 20, 1943, Dowling suggested that Bill get a copy of Poulain's book *The Graces of Interior Prayer*, and "page over the last third of it and you will recognize some familiar situations, which a good many Catholics would find strange."[496]

The author of that book was Father Augustin François Poulain, S.J. (1836-1919). He was born in France, became a Jesuit in 1858, and became deeply involved in the higher spiritual life. In 1901, when he was in his mid-sixties, he published the book for which he became so famous. Based on his previous forty years of research and personal experience, it was entitled *Des Graces d'Oraison*, or in its English translation, *The Graces of Interior Prayer: A Treatise on Mystical Theology.*[497]

It contained five hundred pages of detailed accounts of visions, apparitions, and other spiritual experiences which had been recorded in the lives of Catholic saints down through the centuries. It included stories of angelic visitations, levitation, religious convulsions, ecstatic paralysis and blindness, knowledge of events taking place hundreds of miles away, out-of-body soul travel, and any number of other strange phenomena. It gave detailed accounts of saints who entered into the depths of the bottomless divine abyss and lost all sense of personal selfhood, or who were transfixed by the brilliant white light of glory shining out from the highest heavenly realm, or who entered into what was called the spiritual marriage with God.

As Father Ed said to Bill in his 1943 letter, Poulain's book described a world of extraordinary experiences totally different from anything talked about in the ordinary Catholic parish church. And yet, Poulain's book was impeccably orthodox and had the approval of the most conservative Roman Catholic authorities. In 1904 and 1907, it received the blessing of Pope Pius X and the Cardinals of the Papal Curia in Rome:

> "Now, thanks to you, directors of consciences possess a work of great worth and high utility. You ... rely on the incontestable doctrine of the old masters who have treated this very difficult subject."

> "Directors of souls and the masters of the spiritual life will draw from it abundant supplies of enlightenment and the counsels necessary to enable them to solve the many complicated questions that they will encounter."

Now in light of some of the things we have already discussed, an interesting question to ask at this point is: what are the major differences between Poulain's *The Graces of Interior Prayer* and Aldous Huxley's *The Perennial Philosophy?* Which author is the true radical, Huxley or Poulain? Huxley at one level appears far more the rebel against the conservatism of established thought. He mixes medieval Roman Catholic authors with not only Protestant Christian authors, but also with numerous figures like the Sufi Muslim poet Jalal-uddin Rumi, the Hindu Vedanta philosopher Shankara, the Taoist philosophers Lao-Tzu and Chuang Tzu, the ancient Jewish philosopher Philo of Alexandria and other non-Christian sources, including numerous quotes from the Hindu scripture called the *Bhagavad-Gita*. And yet in many parts of his book, Poulain was describing a world of spiritual experiences which were far more exotic and bizarre than anything described in Huxley's book.

Poulain reaffirmed the validity of good spiritual experience, but also gave full details of all the fraud and self-delusion in this area: It seems that, at one level, Father Dowling wanted to be sure that Bill Wilson was taking some of his own spiritual experiences with deadly seriousness. In Bill's extraordinary vision of the divine light at Towns Hospital in 1934, he was given a special mission by God, and Father Ed wanted Bill to understand that as the most important thing in his entire life, the task for which he must, if necessary, sacrifice everything else. Father Ed also believed that the way Bill received the twelve steps — appearing in his mind over the course of just a few minutes time, in perfect order, without any great conscious effort on his part — was a clear indication that the steps were a divine revelation inspired directly by God. As Father Ed said in a speech to the National Clergy Conference on Alcoholism:

> To a priest who asked Bill how long it took him to write those twelve steps he said that it took twenty minutes. If it were twenty weeks, you could suspect improvisation. Twenty minutes sounds reasonable under the theory of divine help.[498]

(Just as a side note, the Rev. Sam Shoemaker held the same opinion, and likened the way Bill Wilson received the twelve steps to the way in which he believed that Moses must have received the Ten Commandments.[499])

But Father Dowling *also* clearly wanted Bill to read all the accounts which Poulain gave of *fraud and self-deception* on the part of people who claimed to be mediums, psychics, and the receivers of special divine revelation, even within the Church itself.

So for example, one could NOT count on the one hundred percent accuracy of factual statements made in the revelations and visions even of quite saintly people: the mistakes were still there, even if they clearly involved no deliberate and conscious fraud. Poulain points out, for example, that on pp. 286-287 of "Mary of Agreda's revelations ... she declares that the earth's radius is 1251 Spanish miles."[500] A Spanish mile at that time could be as short as 4,566 to 4,842 feet or as long as 5,564 feet, that is, it could represent a distance as short at 1.39 kilometers or as long as 1.70 kilometers. This means that a radius of 1,251 Spanish miles would 1,739 to 2,127 kilometers in length. But the true radius of the earth is 6,371 kilometers (almost 4,000 modern American miles) or roughly twice as big as the figure which Mary gave, so her figure was not only off, but grossly incorrect. The moral of this story was that one could not safely go to divine visions and sacred revelations to find the answer to scientific problems.

Just as a side note, María de Ágreda (1602-1665) was an interesting figure. When Father Dowling recommended Poulain's book to Bill Wilson, he was certainly not rejecting all psychic phenomena, but in fact affirming that some occurrences of this sort seemed to be totally real. María was a nun in Ágreda in northern Spain (about fifty miles west of Zaragoza) who told people that she had been involved in frequent out-of-body soul travel between 1620 and 1623 to the Jumano Indians in what is today Texas and New Mexico. Later on, when the first Roman Catholic missionaries visited the Jumanos in 1629, the tribe reported that they had been visited by a Lady in Blue (dressed like a Spanish nun of her order) at a place south of Albuquerque near modern day Mountainair, New Mexico. They said that the Lady in Blue had told them that the "fathers" would be visiting them and would help them.

Poulain pointed to the figure of Catherine Emmerich, to show that even references to the scriptures in what were seemingly divine visions and revelations could nevertheless be wrong. The Blessed Anna Katharina Emmerick (1774-1824) was a nun from the Low German speaking area of Westphalia, near Münster, over in the part of Germany close to the Netherlands. Poulain pointed out that in the first edition of her works, "it was said that St. James the greater was present at the Blessed Virgin's death," but this clearly contradicted the chronology given in the book of Acts in the New Testament.[501]

But worse things could be found, even in what seem to be impeccably pious Roman Catholic circles. Poulain gave examples of deliberate fraud, such as the false claims made by Magdalen of the Cross (1487-1560) in Cordova.[502] And in the case of Catherine Emmerich whom we mentioned in the preceding paragraph, in the period after Poulain wrote his book, the best Catholic scholars (along with the Catholic authorities at the Vatican) came to the conclusion that most of the material published by the famous poet Clemens Brentano, who claimed to have written down detailed accounts of Catherine's vision and revelations, seems to have been made up by him, and was totally undependable. It was even worse — much worse — than Poulain suggested.

Hélène Smith, the popularizer of automatic writing: In the late nineteenth and early twentieth century, this psychic from the French-speaking part of Switzerland became famous for her use of automatic writing to communicate with the spirit world.[503] She was called "the Muse of Automatic Writing" by the Surrealist movement in painting and literature, that is, people like Salvador Dalí, Max Ernst, Man Ray, Hans Arp, and Joan Miró, who believed that they were bringing the images they painted and described directly up out of the subconscious.

> As a side note, one can see a much more sophisticated version of this attempt to draw images directly out of the unconscious in *The Red Book*, written and illustrated during that same general period, c. 1914-1930, by the Swiss psychiatrist Carl Jung. He believed that this sort of imagery drawn from the unconscious did in fact put us in some kind of contact with God and the divine world, via the collective unconscious and its archetypes.

The most famous proponents of automatic writing within the A.A. tradition, we remember, were the people of the Oxford Group, including those who attended the Oxford Group meeting at T. Henry and Clarace Williams' home in Akron, Ohio, where Dr. Bob and the other early Akron A.A. members were still involved in automatic writing as late as 1938 and afterward.

At any rate, Hélène Smith (1861-1929, real name Catherine-Elise Müller) began to show abilities as a medium in 1892. At the beginning of her career, she began by doing simple things like producing rapping sounds and table-tipping during séances, and later on began going into trances where she could do various things but claimed she could remember nothing afterwards. During one period of her life, she claimed that she was visiting a civilization on the planet Mars while she was in her trance states. She would use automatic writing to write out messages in what she said was the Martian language, using a form of writing which she claimed was the Martian alphabet. The problem with this was, that when the "Martian" message was translated by her, it followed the syntax and grammar of a small child speaking French, with what seemed to be a made-up word replacing what would have been the French word in each instance. And the "Martian alphabet" corresponded letter for letter with the Roman alphabet, simply using a different made-up symbol to stand for each sound. All told, her "Martian language" seemed less like an unconscious imaginary invention arising during a genuine trance state, and much more like an elaborately devised, laboriously practiced, and carefully organized fraud.

Poulain's complaint is that most of these people give us nothing but trivialities, banalities, and parlor games. The popular mediums and psychics give us no information which would actually be *useful for our salvation.*[504]

> We see ... prophetesses who pretend to speak in the name of an angel or of a saint, and who at all hours and to all comers give audiences, during which inquiries are made regarding births, marriages, legal proceedings, diseases, the outcome of political events, etc. In spite of the religious *mise en scène*, they are simply fortune-tellers ....
>
> In spiritualist meetings the spirits are often occupied with mere trifles. They condescend to reply to idle questions or to provide a drawing-room game. They push furniture about, cause vibrations in musical instruments, and introduce small objects from outside. The medium will amuse you in this way for a whole evening, just as conjurors will do at a fair. Would spirits who have our eternal welfare at heart consent to lend themselves to such childish things? How far removed is all this from the office attributed by theology to our Guardian Angel!
>
> These puerilities become still more distressing when the spirits pose as being our deceased relations, or great philosophers. For if they endeavour to be serious, it is to dictate an appalling tirade of platitudes. Such are the high thoughts that occupy these beings immersed in the light of eternity!

And yet Father Dowling, like Poulain, wanted to insist on the necessity of real spiritual experience: In Poulain's book, he stressed the fact that most spiritual experience did NOT involve spectacular things like visions and levitations and heavenly voices, but was of a quiet and gentle sort. It was a kind of experience which most spiritual people, laypeople as well as clergy, had on a regular basis.

As a Jesuit, Father Dowling was especially sensitive to the fact that we had to rely on religious experience — the interplay between *consolations* and *desolations* — to practice *discernment*, and work out for ourselves what God's will was for our lives. When we did something unselfish for someone else, and then felt good about it, this was a religious experience. When we asked God in prayer, what should we do on this occasion? should we do such-and-such? — and then felt somehow that we knew what God's answer was, yes or no — this was a kind of quiet but vitally important spiritual experience of the kind that most A.A. people eventually come to depend on throughout the course of their everyday lives.

An additional danger: falling under the sway of evil spiritual powers. Although Poulain did not stress it in his book, St. Ignatius Loyola (along with the Catholic and Orthodox tradition going back for well over a thousand years before his time) had been well aware of the dangers of falling under the power of evil spirits, and Father Dowling also seems to have been concerned about Bill Wilson running into some of these wicked ghosts and demons, and coming to great harm as a result.

Even as late as 1952, Bill was still making light of this danger. In a letter to Father Dowling dated August 8, 1952 he wrote, rather airily,[505] "the spook business is no longer any burning issue so far as I am concerned. Without inviting it, I still sometimes get an intrusion such as the one I described in the case of the purported Boniface." He brushed aside any possibility of real danger by commenting that our relationships with "discarnates" (as he called the spirits of the dead) would be no different from our relationships with the spirits of the living. "Since prudent discrimination and good morality is necessary when we deal with people in the flesh, why shouldn't these be the rule with discarnate, too." Bill Wilson acknowledged that, on the one hand, some discarnates are saints and some are well-disposed, while on the other hand, some may be agents of the Devil. But remembering "all the good folks who have gone ahead of us," why should the "aperture" between them and us be narrower than for the agents of the Devil? Or in other words, we are just as likely to meet basically good and decent ghosts in the land of the dead, as we are to meet good and decent people in our everyday life here on earth. [506]

It was not until 1956, when Bill Wilson read Aldous Huxley's book *Heaven and Hell*,[507] that he began to wonder if the dangers of encountering demons and other evil powers in his visions and other encounters with the transcendent world, might not be a whole lot greater than he had assumed. Bill even began to wonder if his crippling bouts with depression might have in fact been hellish visions from the netherworld. The way to deal with visions of that sort was to quit traveling into those regions of the land of the dead, and it is worthwhile noting that after reading Huxley's *Heaven and Hell* in 1956, Bill Wilson seems to have perhaps learned how to avoid lingering in the really frightening visions, because he quit having crippling depressions.

CHAPTER 33

Father Ed Has a Retinal Stroke in 1952 and Bill W. Works on the Twelve and Twelve

On May 20, 1952 Bill Wilson wrote Father Dowling a letter to accompany some drafts that he was sending him, of what seems to have been the twelve separate chapters on the twelve traditions for the *Twelve Steps and Twelve Traditions* book.[508] He told him that he wanted Father Ed to send him any criticisms that he had of the material, and explained that at this stage, Tom Powers, Betty Love, and Jack Alexander were also taking a critical look at the chapters.

He also said in that letter of May 20 that he had just finished the first drafts of the chapters on two of the twelve steps, and for the first time in his now twelve-year-long relationship with Father Ed, asked the priest if there was anything he could read that would give a simple explanation of the *Spiritual Exercises* of St. Ignatius Loyola. He felt that he needed to know more about Ignatian spirituality in order to write better explanations of how to work the twelve steps.

Dowling wrote back on May 27, 1952 and said that he did not know of any explanatory books on the *Spiritual Exercises*, and that all that was available was just "the dry text." He did say, interestingly enough, that "The best text with an official commentary is *The Spiritual Exercises of St. Ignatius* edited by the Episcopalian clergyman, W. H. Longridge." The *Spiritual Exercises* were not only read and studied by many Roman Catholics who were not Jesuits (Sister Ignatia was one good example), but also by a surprisingly large number of Christians outside the Roman communion. And the text which Father Ed recommended in this case came from an Anglican priest: the Rev. W. H. Longridge, M.A., *The*

Spiritual Exercises of Saint Ignatius of Loyola (London: Robert Scott Roxburghe House, 1919).[509]

On June 17, 1952, Bill Wilson wrote Father Ed and said that he was writing 2,000 word chapters on each of the twelve steps, and would send all his drafts to the priest for his critique. Three days later, on June 20, 1952, Dowling wrote Bill back and said he was sending him a copy of Longridge's version of the *Spiritual Exercises*.[510]

Father Dowling's retinal stroke: But the priest also said, in that letter of June 20, 1952, that "he had been in the hospital for nearly a week with a retinal stroke that made it hard to read. Friends had taped the draft of the traditions so he could critique them." In spite of the stroke (probably caused by a blood clot or piece of plaque which had traveled up one of his carotid arteries and gotten lodged in one of the arteries in his retina) he was still planning to sail for England and Ireland on August 21.[511] His sister Anna was with him, he told Bill, and was helping by reading to him from the manuscript drafts which Bill had sent.[512]

A month later, on July 17, 1952, Bill sent Father Ed the drafts of his chapters on the first four steps, and also thanked him for the copy of Longridge's version of the *Spiritual Exercises*: [513]

> Please have my immense thanks for that wonderful volume on the Ignatian Exercises. I'm already well into it, and what an adventure it is! Excepting for a sketchy outline you folks had posted on the Sodality wall years back, I had never seen anything of the Exercises at all. Consequently I am astonished and not a little awed by what comes into sight.

We might wonder how thoroughly Bill Wilson actually studied this short but nevertheless quite difficult little text in just a few days time. On the other hand, if that person had spent almost twelve years with a very competent Jesuit priest as his primary spiritual advisor, one would expect more than a little Jesuit theology to already have been quietly absorbed into that person's soul in the process of all the hundreds of conversations and letters he had had with his advisor.

In particular, in this chapter I want to explore how Bill Wilson dealt with the problem of pain and suffering in the *Twelve Steps and Twelve*

Traditions, as an example of the kind of influence which Father Ed and his Ignatian spiritual principles ended up having on Bill.

At any rate, Dowling's letter which he wrote back to Bill a week later, on July 24, 1952, attempted to make light of his stroke, in spite of the fact that the blindness he was suffering might end up being permanent, along with the problem that a person who had blood clots and pieces of plaque floating around in his arteries was in serious danger of having some of the other fragments travel to his brain or heart, causing a fatal stroke or heart attack at some point in the near future. Father Ed however attempted to brush it all off as simply a good excuse for a brief vacation:

> My retinal stroke, sans pain and sans labor, is giving me an enjoyable loaf. I have a reader who comes in so I hope to have the Steps read .... My sister, Anna, is going to be my eyes in England and Ireland—to take dictation, etc.[514]

Dowling, as we can see, was bound and determined that he was still going to carry out the trip to England and Ireland which he had planned for August, and in his letter to Bill Wilson on August 9, 1952, he told him where he could reach Anna and him abroad later that month:

> My sister, Anna, is going to Europe with me to do my reading, etc. We will be at the Lexington Hotel August 20th and the morning of 21. We sail in the afternoon of August 21 on the America.[515]

Pain and Suffering in the Twelve and Twelve: As was noted, we know that Bill Wilson had never even looked at Ignatius Loyola's *Spiritual Exercises* until midsummer 1952, and we have no idea how carefully he read through that work even then. But Father Ed had been serving as Bill's sponsor for almost twelve years by the time Bill was writing the *Twelve Steps and Twelve Traditions*, during which time Bill could have absorbed many of the fundamental principles of Ignatian spirituality simply through all the work he had done on the spiritual state of his own soul in numerous letters and discussions with Father Ed over the course of those years.

One place where I believe that one can see this influence clearly, is in all the statements made in the *Twelve Steps and Twelve Traditions* about the positive role which suffering can play in the spiritual life.

The first edition of the Big Book had handled that issue very differently back in 1939: the words *suffer* and *suffering* were given an almost unfailingly negative connotation in the first part of the book. People entered A.A. because "they suffered from alcoholism." While they were still drinking, they "caused great suffering" to their families. The word *pain* was likewise never given any positive meaning in the first part of the Big Book.

The story by John Parr (Tuscaloosa, Alabama), "The Professor and the Paradox," said "'We A.A.s surrender to win; we give away to keep; we suffer to get well; and we die to live." But that story was not put into the Big Book until the second edition, which did not come out until 1955, two years *after* the publication of the *Twelve Steps and Twelve Traditions*. And the fact that John Parr's story was inserted in the Big Book at that time, was a byproduct, I believe, of the changed attitude toward the role of suffering which Bill Wilson had developed through his work with Father Dowling after the priest became his sponsor at the end of 1940.

One of the first places this new and different attitude appeared was actually during the early years of Bill Wilson's mentorship by Father Dowling, in Bill's Christmas Greeting for 1944.

> Nor can men and women of A.A. ever forget that <u>only through suffering did they find enough humility</u> to enter the portals of that New World. How privileged we are to understand so well the divine paradox that strength rises from weakness, that humiliation goes before resurrection; that <u>pain is not only the price but the very touchstone of spiritual rebirth</u>. Knowing its full worth and purpose, we can no longer fear adversity, we have found prosperity where there was poverty, peace and joy have sprung out of the very midst of chaos. Great indeed, our blessings![516] [My underlining.]

But the basic idea was then raised most famously in 1953 (nine years later) in the chapter on the Tenth Step in the *Twelve Steps and Twelve Traditions* in the passage which said (pp. 93-94):

Someone who knew what he was talking about once remarked that pain was the touchstone of all spiritual progress. How heartily we A.A.'s can agree with him, for we know that the pains of drinking had to come before sobriety, and emotional turmoil before serenity. [My underlining.]

The question is much debated as to who was meant by the phrase "someone who knew what he was talking about." Ernest Kurtz said that he

> ... was inclined to guess that the source was either Father Edward Dowling or Rev. Sam Shoemaker or Dr. Harry Tiebout, to each of whom Bill referred in other contexts as 'someone who knew what he was talking about.' That was my guesswork order of probability, but I was never able to get any further in that research. The phrase becomes more common in Bill's letters after 1957, as I believe an endnote in *Not-God* evidences.[517]

Shoemaker does not appear very likely to me, if the idea fails to show up in the Big Book and only appears in 1944 and afterwards (Bill W. had broken with Shoemaker by August 1937, and did not get back on friendly terms with him until much later). And I cannot find anything which Tiebout wrote prior to 1944 which could have supplied an idea of this sort.

So it would seem to me that Ernest Kurtz's first choice, Father Ed Dowling, would in fact be the only *likely* one of that group. And in particular, the linkage of suffering with humility seems to point straight at the central Ignatian teaching of the Two Standards (the two battle flags).

The 1919 edition of Bartlett's *Familiar Quotations* listed a passage which was at least partly similar, "Calamity is man's true touchstone," taken from a Beaumont and Fletcher play. And this in turn was probably a paraphrase of a line from the famous classical Roman author Seneca, who lived at the time of the Emperor Nero, and wrote in his essay *On Providence* the phrase: *Ignis aurum probat, miseria fortes viros,*[518] which could be translated as

> Fire is the test of [i.e. touchstone of] gold,
> suffering [is the test of] strong men.

At any rate, in the *Twelve Steps and Twelve Traditions*, Bill Wilson takes great pains to separate this positive component of suffering from the perverted attempt to win God's love by wearing hair cloth shirts, sleeping on the bare wooden floor, lashing ourselves with whips, and other such methods of deliberately inflicting suffering on ourselves.

And he also takes great pains to separate this positive and beneficial kind of suffering from the Self-Hate Syndrome in which we deliberately wallow in depression, guilt, and self-loathing — in his chapter on Step Four in the *Twelve Steps and Twelve Traditions* (on p. 45) he expressly warns against that kind of self-destructive behavior:

> If temperamentally we are on the depressive side, we are apt to be swamped with guilt and self-loathing. We wallow in this messy bog, often getting a misshapen and painful pleasure out of it. As we morbidly pursue this melancholy activity, we may sink to such a point of despair that nothing but oblivion looks possible as a solution. Here, of course, we have lost all perspective, and therefore all genuine humility. For this is pride in reverse. This is not a moral inventory at all; it is the very process by which the depressive has so often been led to the bottle and extinction.

Humility and true serenity in the Seventh Step: Suffering can be put to positive purposes however. Learning how to do that is the central topic in the chapter in the *Twelve Steps and Twelve Traditions* which discusses Step Seven, "Humbly asked Him to remove our shortcomings."

> Until now, our lives have been largely devoted to running from pain and problems. We fled from them as from a plague. We never wanted to deal with the fact of suffering. Escape via the bottle was always our solution. Character-building through suffering might be all right for saints, but it certainly didn't appeal to us.
>
> Then, in A.A., we looked and listened. Everywhere we saw failure and misery transformed by humility into priceless assets. We heard story after story of how humility had brought strength out of weakness. In every case, pain

had been the price of admission into a new life. But this admission price had purchased more than we expected. It brought a measure of humility, which we soon discovered to be a healer of pain. We began to fear pain less, and desire humility more than ever.[519]

As we begin healing some of our character defects, our lives become more serene and "our thinking about humility commences to have a wider meaning."

We enjoy moments in which there is something like real peace of mind. To those of us who have hitherto known only excitement, depression, or anxiety — in other words, to all of us — this newfound peace is a priceless gift. Something new indeed has been added. Where humility had formerly stood for a forced feeding on humble pie, it now begins to mean the nourishing ingredient which can give us serenity.[520]

The quite different treatment of the Seventh Step in the Big Book: Fourteen years earlier, when he was writing the Big Book, there was no talk about humility in Bill Wilson's discussion of the Seventh Step (other than the bare occurrence of the word "humbly" in the step, which applied to how we asked, not an attitude carried throughout our lives in general), nor was there any talk about any special kind of suffering being associated with that particular step. In fact, if we look at the two short paragraphs on page 76 of the Big Book, there was effectively almost no discussion at all:

... we then look at *Step Six*. We have emphasized willingness as being indispensable. Are we now ready to let God remove from us all the things which we have admitted are objectionable? Can He now take them all — every one? If we still cling to something we will not let go, we ask God to help us be willing.

When ready, we say something like this: "My Creator, I am now willing that you should have all of me, good and bad. I pray that you now remove from me every single defect

of character which stands in the way of my usefulness to you
and my fellows. Grant me strength, as I go out from here,
to do your bidding. Amen." We have then completed *Step
Seven.*

The word *humbly* was in the Seventh Step, but in the Big Book Bill
Wilson completely disregarded it, and took no interest in it. Why then
is there the lengthy sermon in the chapter on the Seventh Step in the
Twelve Steps and Twelve Traditions, on the virtues of humility and the
positive role which suffering can play in the spiritual life? To my mind,
this was Father Dowling's influence on Bill, where Wilson was getting
(via the Jesuit priest) a strong dose of the sections in Ignatius Loyola's
Spiritual Exercises on the Two Standards (contrasting humility vs. pride,
and contrasting spiritual concerns vs. preoccupation with worldly goods
and pleasures), together with continual echoes in Father Ed's words of
the priest's own lengthy meditations on the sufferings undergone by
Christ and the Virgin Mary.

Father John C. Ford, S.J. Perhaps partly because of Father Ed's
declining health, Bill Wilson asked another Jesuit priest to also help
edit the book, a man named Father John C. Ford, S.J., who was one of
the most preeminent Catholic moral theologians of that era. [521] And
Ford had the further qualification that he was a member of Alcoholics
Anonymous himself. Obtaining a positive Catholic evaluation of the
Twelve Steps and Twelve Traditions was very important to Bill W.

John Cuthbert Ford (December 20, 1902 – January 14, 1989) was
brought up as a child in Brookline, Massachusetts, a suburb of Boston.
He entered the Jesuit novitiate in 1920, and in 1935-1937 was sent to
study moral theology at the Pontifical Gregorian University in Rome,
where he earned his doctorate. From 1937–45 Ford was back in the
Boston area and serving as Professor of Moral Theology at his alma
mater, Weston College. In 1945 he was appointed Professor of Moral
Theology at the Gregorian University in Rome. But he was sent back to
Boston, and returned to teaching at Weston from 1947–48, and then
from 1948–51 taught ethics and religion at Boston College. [522]

Somewhere in the 1940's, his drinking had gotten out of hand. He
went to the same place Bill Wilson had gone, to Dr. William Silkworth

at Towns Hospital in New York. We know that in 1948 Ford took part in the summer program of Alcohol Studies at Yale University, and became a regular lecturer in that program for many years to follow, so we know that by 1948 he had gotten heavily involved with A.A.[523]

With respect to his A.A. membership, Father Ford preserved his anonymity carefully until the very end of his life, even from most people in Alcoholics Anonymous. It was felt that his reputation as America's greatest Catholic moral theologian needed to be carefully safeguarded, so that American Catholic priests and bishops would respect the works he was writing in which he showed that A.A. was compatible with the Catholic faith. Ernest Kurtz, who greatly admired the Jesuit, knew that Ford was an A.A. member — in private conversations, Kurtz has told me about the enormous help that Ford quietly gave over the years to priests who had drinking problems — but since Kurtz also was a priest who worked with alcoholics, he had a need-to-know. Bill Wilson presumably knew that Ford was an A.A. member. But the first public announcement that Father Ford was in A.A., and was himself a recovering alcoholic, did not come until Ford revealed it to Mary Darrah when she interviewed him in 1985 (when he was around 82 years old), and Darrah subsequently published that information in her book on Sister Ignatia in 1991.

As a result of Ford's desire to keep his A.A. membership private, we do not know the exact date when he joined Alcoholics Anonymous. In a phone conversation, Mary Darrah told me that Father Ford had told her that he came into A.A. before Father Ralph Pfau, and that he (not Pfau) was the first alcoholic Roman Catholic priest to get sober in A.A. But Ernest Kurtz told me that by the time Darrah was interviewing Father Ford, the elderly Jesuit's mind was getting confused about matters of dates and chronology, and that he did not believe Ford's claim should necessarily be taken seriously. And in fact, if we look at the overall sequence of events back at that time, it does not really appear to have been at all possible that Ford could have come into A.A. first.

Father Ralph Pfau telephoned A.A. in Indianapolis on his thirty-ninth birthday, on November 10, 1943, and began going to A.A. meetings in that city. He never drank again. Fr. Pfau wrote about his role as the first priest-member of Alcoholics Anonymous in a talk given fourteen years later, in 1957,[524] and also in his autobiography *Prodigal Shepherd*, which was published in 1958.[525] And the statement that Pfau was the first Roman Catholic to join A.A. was in fact made publicly on any number of other occasions as well, where no one (priests or laypeople) ever objected to his claim.

In Mary Darrah's book on Sister Ignatia,[526] Ford writes of his telephone conversation with Mary in 1985, in which "I told Mary of my own alcoholism and recovery from it some forty years earlier under the care of Dr. William Silkworth at New York's Towns Hospital," which would suggest that he joined A.A. circa 1945. But the forty year figure has to be only a very rough and approximate one, because in 1945, Father Ford was appointed Professor of Moral Theology at the Gregorian University in Rome. He went over to Italy and he did not come back to the United States until he returned to teaching at Weston again in 1947. There is no way he could have gone to Towns Hospital or undergone the laborious process of getting through those rough initial A.A. meetings, which groggy and confused newcomers have to attend for some months before they begin to get at least halfway stabilized. There were no A.A. meetings in Italy at that time.

In an interview with David A. Works in 1984, Father Ford "stated that he had a chance to learn more [about alcoholism] when, in 1947, he had met someone who was a member of A.A. and who took him to several 'meetings.'"[527] Remembering that Ford was still trying to preserve his public anonymity down to the time of his interview with Mary Darrah, I think that his phrase about meeting "someone who was a member of A.A." and going to "several meetings" at that time, was an indirect way of signaling that it was here in 1947 that he went to Dr. Silkworth, started attending A.A. meetings, and got sober. In fact, I suspect that the reason why Father Ford was removed from his position as Professor of Moral Theology at the Gregorian University in Rome and sent back to the United States in 1947 may have been because his alcoholism had gotten completely out of hand.

At any rate, in the middle of June in 1952, as we have seen, Father Dowling was left blind by a retinal stroke, and was hampered as to the amount of help he could give Bill Wilson during the finishing stages of writing the *Twelve Steps and Twelve Traditions*. But at some point in there, another Jesuit, Father John C. Ford, S.J., was brought in to help. So the one thing we can say for sure is that the process of writing the *Twelve Steps and Twelve Traditions* was very carefully vetted by two members of the Jesuit order, one of them (Father Dowling) a strong defender of the Catholic Church's mystical theology, and the other of them (Father John C. Ford) a theologian who was an expert in scholastic ways of thinking and traditional Catholic moral theology.

And Ford was eminently qualified to help Bill. During this general period, he wrote some interesting and thoughtful things about A.A. and alcoholism, such as his article on "Depth Psychology, Morality, and Alcoholism" (1951), a book called *Man Takes a Drink: Facts and Principles About Alcohol* (1955), and an article on "Pastoral Treatment" (1957), describing how the priest can best reach out to alcoholics and put them into saving contact with the grace of God.[528]

CHAPTER 34

Father Dowling's 1953 Article Comparing St. Ignatius's Ascetic Theology and the Twelve Steps

In 1953, Bill Wilson published his book on the *Twelve Steps and Twelve Traditions*, and in that same year Father Dowling put together his own first detailed comparison of St. Ignatius's *Spiritual Exercises* and the Twelve Steps of Alcoholics Anonymous.

It was a talk entitled "Catholic Asceticism and the Twelve Steps" which Father Dowling gave on April 8, 1953, at the meeting of the annual meeting of the NCCA (the National Clergy Conference on Alcoholism, an organization that Father Ralph Pfau had founded in 1949.[529] The talk was published in what was called the *Blue Book*, a volume which was published annually by the NCCA and contained all the talks given at that year's conference.[530]

Humility as the foundation of real spiritual growth: the Two Battle Standards in the Spiritual Exercises. In his talk at the conference, Dowling began with the theme that ran through so many of his speeches and writings, the necessity of learning true humility in order to achieve real spiritual growth, and the perplexing and discomfiting way that what seems to be a disgraceful plunge into total humiliation can turn out to be the beginning of the kind of humility that soon bathes us in God's healing and saving grace:

> I am sensible, as you are, of God's closeness to human humility.
> I am sensible, also, of how close human humility can come to humiliation, and I know how close that can come to an alcoholic.

418

Those clergy in his audience who had done the *Spiritual Exercises* recognized this immediately as a reference to one of the most famous parts of Loyola's guided meditations, the one which came on the fourth day of the second week: the long discourse on the Two Standards (*Las Dos Banderas*, the two battle flags), which portrayed the Christian life as a war between elemental Good and Evil.[531]

In St. Ignatius's description of the scene, Satan told the demons who were gathered around his battle flag, to tempt human beings into the deadly sins beginning with the following three, because if they could lure them into these three sins, the others would quickly follow. They were to tempt them first of all by (1) greed for material things (*avaritia*), then by (2) vainglory (*vana gloria*, the desire to be publicly praised and applauded and to be the center of everyone else's attention), and finally by (3) the sin of pride (*superbia*).

Then St. Ignatius asked us to picture Christ preaching to all the good men and women who were gathered around his battle flag, which had been planted in the beautiful green fields around the city of Jerusalem. He warned them (1) to guard themselves against the temptations of greed and avarice by learning how to stop being so fearful of poverty and financial problems.[532] He warned them (2) to protect themselves against the temptations of vainglory by learning how to stop being so afraid that they might be humiliated by things that happened to them. And finally he advised them (3) to defend themselves against the temptations of sinful pride by taking up instead a deep spirit of personal humility.

This was the great theme in the *Spiritual Exercises* to which Father Dowling wished to draw his audience's attention in the opening paragraphs of his speech. Feeling humiliated is not necessarily bad, because it can lead us to adopt the kind of genuine spiritual Humility which protects us against that kind of humiliation. And Humility is our shield and defense against Pride. That is what the *Spiritual Exercises* are about, and that is in particular what the Big Book of Alcoholics Anonymous is about: men and women who had descended into the darkest pits of personal humiliation, but who then learned how to put aside Pride, and use all of those degrading experiences — and the stigma of their own alcoholism — to gain genuine spiritual Humility and become some of the truest spokesmen and spokeswomen who had ever marched behind the battle flag of goodness and holiness.

The use of unashamedly Christian language. Now it should also be noted that Father Ed gave this particular talk to an audience made up of Roman Catholic clergy, so its language was that of a man who was a believing Christian speaking to an audience of trained Christian theologians. It was very different in style and language from the kind of carefully nonsectarian speeches which A.A. audiences had by now become more used to getting.

It should also be observed that Father Ed was typical of those young, reformist theologians like Cardinal Jean Daniélou S.J., who were going to start remaking the Roman Catholic Church at the Second Vatican Council (the great reforming Church council which was going to begin in 1962, just two years after Father Ed died). At that council, when these reformist theologians laid out what they believed to be true Catholic doctrine, they did not appeal to the decrees of medieval and Counter-Reformation popes or to the ideas of medieval Catholic theologians like St. Thomas Aquinas, but to the New Testament and to the teaching of the great patristic theologians who taught during the first five or six centuries of Christian history.

The asceticism of the ancient desert monks. In his talk on "Catholic Asceticism and the Twelve Steps" Father Dowling therefore began by turning to the Church's early patristic theologians and reminding his audience that the word "exercises" in the title of St. Ignatius's great work, the *Spiritual Exercises*,[533] was a literal translation of the ancient Greek word *askêsis*. This was the term that was used by the Catholic and Orthodox monks, nuns, and influential spiritual authors who lived in the deserts of Egypt, Syria, and Asia Minor in the fourth and fifth centuries A.D. (people like Evagrius Ponticus, Macarius the Homilist, and Gregory of Nyssa), to describe the kinds of ascetic "exercise" and "practice" that were necessary to become truly advanced in the spiritual life. This was the ancient Christian spirit which St. Ignatius worked to revive in his *Spiritual Exercises,* and which the early Alcoholics Anonymous leaders worked to revive in their teaching of the Twelve Steps. Or to put this in Father Ed's words:

Asceticism comes from the Greek word meaning the same as exercise, or better, to practice gymnastics. The concept of exercise is to loosen up the muscles to prepare them for vigorous activity. Applied to spiritual matters, it means to loosen up the faculties of the mind or soul, to prepare them for better activity. Physical exercise is gymnastics, setting-up exercises, preparing me to take steps. In the same way, asceticism is preliminary, a preparation for me to use the powers of my soul ....

One of the many different systematized forms of Christian exercises is the *Spiritual Exercises* of St. Ignatius .... "Spiritual Exercises" indicate, of course, that the thing to be exercised is the spirit. The word "exercise" indicates a releasing of the faculties or powers of the soul.

The New Testament path that leads from Hell, through the sufferings of the Passion, to the Resurrection into Heavenly Light. Father Ed further linked this kind of asceticism directly to the New Testament, the Four Gospels, and the path to obtaining the divine union with God in Christ which deifies our souls and fills them with the divine light. Again, quoting from Father Ed's article in the NCCA *Blue Book*:

> Christian asceticism is contained, of course, in the Gospel. All the teachings of Our Lord boil down to the cardinal ideas; one negative, the denial of self; the other positive, the imitation of and union with Christ .... [all] the many different systematized forms of Christian exercises ... are efforts to apply to one's life those two principal ideas of denial of self and an affirmation of Christ.

The "self" which I have to deny and reject, is the part of myself which has fallen into bondage to "sinful tendencies and addictions to the wrong things." Dowling's reference to the "wrong things" can clearly include slavery to chemical substances like alcohol and drugs, but can also include compulsive behaviors like a desire for money or power or sex which leads us to violate all the principles of honest, decent behavior; or a tendency to fly into uncontrollable anger over minor things; or a tendency to run away whenever any problems arise; or any of a thousand other forms of destructive compulsions and lusts.

The basic problem is a human problem as such, and all human beings suffer from it. Alcoholism is only one of the forms which our rebellion against God can take.

St. Ignatius therefore attacked this spiritual problem from both sides, by teaching us to meditate not only on the horrors of the descent into hell to which our addictions and compulsions were driving us, but also on the opposite patterns of behavior which we could see and admire in Christ and his followers. The latter were using the suffering of this world — the sufferings of the cross — as a tool to win a glorious resurrection at the end, where our souls rose up into the heavens and were rewarded with starry crowns of glory in the realm of eternal light. As Dowling summed it up:

> The Spiritual Exercises, therefore, work on the soul in both a negative and positive way.
>
> The first section, the consideration of my sins and of their effects in hell,[534] is the negative part. It aims by self-denial to release our wills from our binding addictions, to enable the will to desire and to choose rationally.
>
> The second part of the Spiritual Exercises, start in with a consideration of the Incarnation and going through the Passion and Resurrection, is an effort to see how Christ would handle various situations.

The first three Steps in A.A. lay down the foundation: In the Alcoholics Anonymous program, we have to begin by admitting that we have been thrown into powerlessness, unmanageability, and a kind of insanity by our refusal to acknowledge our *total dependence* on God. That admission has to be the foundation of everything else that we work on as we pursue the higher spiritual life. Saint Ignatius saw the same kind of dependence on God as universal and necessary, because all human beings (along with the rest of the universe) are a creation of God. We cannot manage the world around us in any kind of ultimately satisfying fashion without the support of God. But alcoholics have an additional kind of total dependence, because in a particular and special way, their alcoholism cannot be managed without the aid of God.

At the foundation of the *Spiritual Exercises*, Father Ed says in this talk, there lies the principle that "everything else shall be chosen or rejected in the light of the purpose that grows out of this dependence." That is, if we devote our lives now to "doing His will on earth," and thereby acknowledging our total dependence on Him, then our reward will be "sharing Him for all eternity" in the realm of the Eternal Heavenly Light.

Likewise, in A.A. the Third Step directs us "to turn our will and our lives over to the care of God." This is a perfect way of phrasing this, Father Dowling said, because it puts the emphasis on *will* rather than *feeling*. In order to live the good life, we often have to use a little will power (and sometimes even a lot of will power) to do something we do not *feel* like doing. We sometimes have to make ourselves do things that make us feel uncomfortable, or things that take unpleasant work, or even things that cause us real pain and suffering. And St. Ignatius points us in the same direction, because Ignatian spirituality is above all *a spirituality of decision making:*

> This emphasis on the will indicates that the alcoholic should direct himself by his will rather than by the feelings that have enmeshed him. The focal importance of the will is a characteristic of the *Spiritual Exercises*.

Moral inventory — Step Four: In the *Spiritual Exercises*, after committing ourselves to God, we start off our more lengthy meditations by spending a long time looking at sin, beginning with the sin of others. Father Ed was here referring us to the First Exercise in the First Week, where St. Ignatius asked us first of all to meditate — think deeply — about the sin of the fallen angels. These were the grand heavenly beings who rebelled against God even before the universe was created, and thereby lost their status as glorious heavenly angels, and were turned into devils and demons who were forced to dwell down in hell. In our meditation we are asked to think deeply about our own feelings when we hear this story. How do we really react when we regard an angelic being, shining with the heavenly glory, who gives it all up? What kind of stupid motive could such a being have been driven by? false pride? jealousy? a perverse fascination with evil? or an equally perverse hatred of things that are good? Real devils and demons are not matters for jokes, but sad, pathetic, things, who could have been great, but threw it all away for nothing.

Then as the next step in this First Exercise, St. Ignatius asked us to look seriously at the way Adam and Eve were given a Paradise on earth, and ruined it all on the whim of a moment. How stupid to give up Paradise for an apple! Or was it something deeper? The serpent told Eve that "God doth know that in what day soever you shall eat" of the forbidden fruit, "your eyes shall be opened: and you shall be as gods, knowing good and evil" (Genesis 3:5, in the Roman Catholic Douay version). Eve fell for the serpent's trickery, and believed that if she and Adam ate the apple, they would magically receive all the powers of gods, and would no longer need to be absolutely dependent on the God who was the Creator of the universe.

That (according to St. Augustine's interpretation of this story in the *City of God*) was the essence of the pride that destroyed us: pride (*superbia* in the ancient Latin) was the desire to be our own Gods. And we failed of course, because we were not Gods, merely frail human beings who were always ultimately totally dependent on the God who created us as "images" of Himself (or however we wished to describe our human status — tiny individualized hypostases formed within the massive flowing currents of God's creative energy, or tiny little sparks and glints of the divine light, or localized awarenesses within the overall divine consciousness — or whatever terminology we preferred).

The detailed Jesuit moral inventory of ourselves: But then, after meditating on the sins of the fallen angels and the sin of Adam and Eve, we finally needed to look at our own sins, and quit making excuses and refusing to look at ourselves, and start cataloguing our own misdeeds and failures. Father Ed was here referring to the Second Exercise in the First Week of the *Spiritual Exercises*, where St. Ignatius asks us (quoting from that section of the exercises):

... to bring to memory all the sins of life, looking from year to year, or from period to period. For this three things are helpful: first, to look at the place and the house where I have lived; second, the relations I have had with others; third, the occupation in which I have lived.

In the traditional fashion in which Jesuits carried out this General Confession, they spent three to ten days going over all the sins they had ever committed over the entire course of their life. They then solemnly confessed all these sins as the culmination to the First Week of their structured four-week-long program of meditation, heart searching, and spiritual rebirth.

St. Ignatius Loyola had done that himself in 1522, at the beginning of his own entry into the higher spiritual life. In his autobiography, he described "the general confessions he had made at Montserrat [which] had been quite carefully done and all in writing." After three days writing it all down, and then confessing his sins to a priest, he gave away all his expensive garments to the poor and hung up his sword and dagger at Our Lady's altar at her shrine at Montserrat. He then went to live for ten months in a cave near the town of Manresa, begging to support himself.

If I may make a parenthetic note here to what Father Ed was describing, it should be said that the kind of extremely detailed Fifth Step inventories that became the general practice in Alcoholics Anonymous during the 1940's and 50's were not part of Oxford Group teaching — in most Oxford Group accounts, the people talked about admitting one previously unacknowledged sin, or three or four at most — and the example given in the Big Book on page 65 is still extremely brief (his having an affair with another woman and his padding his expense account at work were the two main sins he was willing to admit). I cannot help wondering myself if the Roman Catholic practice of making long, detailed general confessions on certain occasions may not have influenced early A.A. to move in that direction once large numbers of Catholics began entering the program in the 1940's. (Of course this may also have happened simply because everyone, Protestants and Catholics alike, may have started discovering that a longer and fuller fourth step worked better in the long run, in terms of freeing alcoholics from their resentment and fear, and their compulsion to drink.)

Confession — Step Five: And then, Father Ed said, I have to make a confession of those sins, not only to God but also to another human being:

> ... after a moral inventory of one's life, all spiritual exercises, Catholic anyway, demand the confession of sins. It is specifically required in the *Spiritual Exercises*. In the A.A. fifth step, you have that general confession admitting my sins to myself, to God, and to another human being.

Reatus culpae and reatus poenae. Father Dowling next makes an interesting distinction in this part of his talk: when we are dealing with a *reatus*, that is, an accused person's guilt, liability, and/or the debt which that person owes, we must distinguish between (1) the crime or fault of which he or she is accused, and (2) the penalty or compensation which he or she will be asked to pay. As Father Dowling puts it:

> There are two liabilities when we commit a sin: one, *reatus culpae*, the guilt of the sin; the other *reatus poenae*, the obligation of restitution. The A.A. sixth and seventh steps cover the guilt of the sin, and the eighth and ninth steps the obligation of restitution.

What is interesting in Father Ed's analysis here, is that he sees the element of suffering primarily entering into the *first part* of this process, the *reatus culpae*, because we have to completely stop committing the sin before we can move on to the next part of our recovery, and the process of stopping a compulsive behavior will necessarily involve significant pain and suffering on our part. Now this may at first glance seem an awkward interpretation, because the word *poena* (which refers to the *second part* of this process, i.e. the *reatus poenae*) can mean "pain" and "punishment" in Latin. But it can also mean "compensation," "restitution," or "payment" of an obligation we have incurred, and Father Ed chooses to regard the *reatus poenae* primarily in that sense instead, as an action in which I simply buckle down and start paying back some debts that I owe.

Dealing with (1) the reatus culpae, the guilt of the sin: the Sixth and Seventh Steps. Father Ed began this part of his talk by making the famous statement (the underlining is mine):

> I think the sixth step is the one which divides the men from the boys in A.A. It is love of the cross. The sixth step says that one is not almost, but entirely ready, not merely willing, but ready. The difference is between wanting and willing to have God remove all these defects of character. You have here, if you look into it, not the willingness of Simon Cyrene to suffer, but the great desire or love, similar to what Chesterton calls "Christ's love affair with the cross."

This is the famous sentence which Bill Wilson repeated as the opening line of his chapter on Step Six in the *Twelve Steps and Twelve Traditions* (again the underlining is mine):

> "This is the Step that separates the men from the boys." So declares a well-loved clergyman who happens to be one of A.A.'s greatest friends. He goes on to explain that any person capable of enough willingness and honesty to try repeatedly Step Six on all his faults — without any reservations whatever — has indeed come a long way spiritually, and is therefore entitled to be called a man who is sincerely trying to grow in the image and likeness of his own Creator.

In order to accomplish great goals, we have to be able to make ourselves do things that will hurt. Climbing a mighty mountain in the Swiss alps requires pain and suffering. Spending weeks exploring the jungles of Brazil or Central Africa means endless discomfort and hardship. And yet people do these things willingly and even joyfully. Good concert musicians do not have to be forced to spend hours every day practicing the violin or the trumpet, in spite of the fact that the average human being would regard their daily regimen as impossibly painful.

Football players have to spend hours in the summer heat, doing their pre-season practice. We can go out to the practice fields and see them running through automobile tires to increase their ability to duck and dodge, hurling themselves against sand-filled tackling dummies to increase their strength in blocking and tackling, and jogging around the playing field ten or a dozen times (sweat pouring down their faces) to increase their running speed and endurance. It is painful by the end of the afternoon, so that getting to be a really good player requires a willingness to undergo genuine physical suffering. Yet good football players also get a fierce sense of enjoyment from their exertions on the practice field.

A chemist in training has to spend countless hours carrying out brute memorization of reactions and formulas, while those learning ancient languages have to spend many days laboriously memorizing things like Greek noun declensions and Hebrew verb conjugations. Pursuits of this sort involve *mental* pain and suffering, not *physical* agony, but making yourself do it requires just as much will power as boxing practice or weight-lifting. And yet some people *want* to do these things and *love* what they are doing.

Father Ed made an interesting comment on this subject. When Jesus was forced by the Roman soldiers to carry his own cross, he quickly fell under the weight, and Simon of Cyrene carried the cross the rest of the way for him. It was a heavy weight, and Simon presumably felt the unpleasantness of the burden. He showed that he was *willing* to suffer a certain amount of pain and discomfort himself in order to help another human being. But this, Father Ed said, was not the emotion that was needed to carry out the Sixth Step properly. Simon of Cyrene was *willing* to suffer if he had to, but he did not in any way show that he *wanted* to suffer.

Having God remove our defects of character will hurt. It is not enough, Father Ed is warning us, to simply sit there and say "Well, I suppose if it has to be done, I'm willing to suffer through it. But I'm not going to like what God is doing, and I'm going to complain and feel sorry for myself every step of the way." The problem is that I will never genuinely let go of those character defects as long as I constantly whine and complain and feel sorry for myself because I won't be able to do those things anymore. I will simply grab them back again the next time I am feeling particularly full of self-pity and pseudo-righteous indignation.

I have to *want* those character defects to be removed from my soul with the fierce desire of a great lover who *wants* and *desires* the struggle and combat of this battle against entrenched sin and evil.

Nevertheless, what a strange phrase Father Dowling pulled from G. K. Chesterton: "Christ's love affair with the cross." But we can see what this means if we stop and think about it. We do not see Jesus complaining about having to sleep on the bare ground and forage in the fields for his food as he makes his long journey from Galilee to Jerusalem. We do not hear him crying out from the cross that "This was all somebody else's fault — that crooked judge Pontius Pilate, the corrupt Roman legal system, that ungrateful Judas Iscariot who pretended to be my friend. Oh, I feel so sorry for myself. It's all so unfair. Oh poor me, poor me, poor pitiful me!"

No, instead Jesus "set his face to go to Jerusalem" (Luke 9:51) where his suffering on the cross would act across time and space and eternity itself to destroy the cosmic foundations of all sinfulness. He made this his life work and the love of his life. So likewise, recovering alcoholics who are working the twelve steps must take as the love of their life, the destruction of the individual foundations which underlie their own most evil personal characteristics.

Dealing with (2) the reatus poenae, the obligation to make restitution for the sin: the Eighth and Ninth Steps. In Father Ed's interpretation, the real pain and suffering came in the Sixth Step instead of here. Why would he have taken that position? Why was making amends — comparatively speaking — so much more pleasant? If I interpret him correctly, I think that he believed that having to give up our most deeply beloved character defects involved real anguish and torment, in a way that hurt far more deeply than anything we would experience when we were making amends. Becoming willing to just stand there and let God nail our character defects to a cross was torture;

making amends (on the other hand) was just paying our past due bills. Father Ed deliberately reduced the Eighth and Ninth Steps to those terms:

> In the eighth and ninth steps one makes restitution. In the eighth step the alcoholic makes a list of those people he has offended and whose bills he hasn't paid. In the ninth step he pays off these obligations, if he can do so without hurting people more.

The Positive side: Steps Eleven and Twelve and the latter part of the Spiritual Exercises. The first ten steps, Father Ed observed, described only the bare beginnings of the true spiritual life. Step Eleven, however, pointed us beyond that, to the vast world of the more advanced spiritual life which was discussed in the latter parts of St. Ignatius's *Spiritual Exercises*, in the Second, Third, and Fourth Weeks (that is, in the last three quarters of the book).

"The eleventh step," Dowling said, "bids one by prayer and meditation to study to improve his conscious grasp of God, asking Him only for two things, knowledge of His will and the power to carry it out."

The first clause of the eleventh step — learning to increase our conscious knowledge of God (and our understanding of our relationship to him) — is what the last three quarters of the *Spiritual Exercises* is about, where we are led through a variety of meditations such as the one on the Two Standards in the Fourth Day of the Second Week.

But these topics found in the latter part of the *Spiritual Exercises* also form the prime focus of all the other great pieces of western literature which devote themselves to what Father Dowling calls "the positive aspects of Christian asceticism." This includes all the important Catholic works on that topic from the past two thousand years, enough to require a lifetime and more of careful reading and meditation.

And the second clause of the eleventh step — learning how to gain a better knowledge of what God wants us to do — leads us into the long and involved subject of *discernment* and the two long lists of rules given at the very end of the *Spiritual Exercises*, at the end of the Fourth Week (sections 313-336 of the exercises). As we remember from an earlier chapter of this present book, these twenty-two rules for discernment (fourteen in the first list and eight in the second list) show us how to obtain divine guidance by going down deeply into our own hearts and emotions, and distinguishing between one group of feelings and emotions which are called "consolations," and another variety which are called "desolations."

Since this daily study and prayer enables "my growth toward Christ-like sanity and sanctity" in continuous and never-ending fashion through all the years which follow, I will discover (Father Ed says) that I will progressively become more and more "an instrument in God's hands." Or in other words, the A.A. twelfth step, which prescribes a life devoted to service both to God and to my fellow human beings, is simply a statement of the true underlying goal of the Catholic Faith.

DOWLING'S ATTACK ON 20ᵀᴴ CENTURY PSYCHIATRY

In the second half of his speech, Father Dowling seemed to change topic drastically. Suddenly and without warning, he turned the remainder of his speech into what was a trenchant assault on some of the prevailing ideas and assumptions of American psychology and psychiatry there at the middle of the twentieth century.

Sigmund Freud's attack on religion, morality, and human reason: To understand the underlying nature of the problem Dowling was attacking, it would be helpful to remember some of Sigmund Freud's especially controversial ideas. In particular, readers who have never read the famous book which Freud published in 1930 — *Das Unbehagen in der Kultur* ("Civilization and Its Discontents") — need to obtain a copy and carefully think about what is being said. In that work, Freud portrays the human race as caught in a dreadful dilemma.

There were three parts to the human psyche, Freud believed — the Ego, the Superego, and the Id — and it was the third part which represented the great danger to civilization. This was because the Id was totally evil — or perhaps put in terms Freud would have liked better, totally amoral in a senselessly destructive fashion. There was no blessed image of a loving God lying at the bottom of the human soul, in the way that Christianity traditionally taught. The natural human instincts were not fundamentally good, in the way that Bill Wilson taught in the chapter on the Fourth Step in the *Twelve Steps and Twelve Traditions*. Instead, Freud argued, the basic human instincts buried in the Freudian subconscious were raging, out-of-control desires for killing and rape. If these urges were allowed free expression, civilization would be totally destroyed by rampaging murderers, serial killers, rapists, and sexual perverts of every kind of depraved sort. Freud based this belief on what can be observed in human dreams and what was called free association, and on his analysis of what was actually done in real life by neurotics, insane people, child molesters, sadomasochists, torturers, out-of-control prison guards and policemen, and armed soldiers in times of war.

On the other side, Freud said, the only way to keep these hideously destructive subconscious urges hammered down deep into the Id where they could not emerge and hurt other people, was to create an opposing and equally irrational subconscious force called the Superego. This was called "conscience" by Christians, but Freud argued that the Superego was just a set of authoritarian and arbitrary rules, based on that particular society's ancient customs and taboos, which were indoctrinated into small children from the earliest age by the authority figures of that society (parents, teachers, and leadership figures, but above all priests, medicine men, and other professional religious functionaries). Children who were thus indoctrinated, were conditioned down to a deep subconscious level to believe that these arbitrary rules were infallible, divinely given, and absolutely unbreakable and unmodifiable. They were brainwashed into believing that anyone who broke even the slightest of their particular religious group's rules would be tortured for all eternity in a hell whose characteristics came from the darkest parts of the Id (torture, cutting instruments, fire, and the acting out of the other kinds of nightmarish subconscious urges which were seen in the behavior of depraved serial killers).

The problem was that the Superego might partially curb the Id's desires for murder and perverted sex, but only at the expense of creating subconscious guilt, which then made the person neurotic. If a proper young Roman Catholic woman from Viennese high society came to Freud to be treated for crippling neuroses, the only way he knew to ease her neurotic symptoms was to encourage her to quit being so moralistic, and let herself go a bit, and in particular to urge her to stop being so frightened of her own darker sexual fantasies and desires.

There was also, of course, a third part of the psyche in Freud's theories, called the Ego, which was the center of rational and logical thought. But there were limits to what the Ego could accomplish, because the only force which was really strong enough to control the irrational Id and create a civilized society, was the equally irrational Superego. We had to trade off violence, rape and destruction on the one side, against crippling guilt and misery-producing neurotic symptoms on the other, and work out what we might consider the least painful compromise. But life was going to be fairly wretched for most human beings no matter how we negotiated this issue, so it was perfectly natural, Freud believed, for many of these unhappy people to turn to alcohol and drugs for comfort (he was a cocaine addict during one part of his life, from around 1883 to 1896, and one of his friends, Ernst von Fleischl-Marxow, was a morphine addict). Alcohol and addiction did not ultimately bring us peace and freedom from psychological torment, as Freud pointed out in *Civilization and Its Discontents* — he had had to learn this for himself the hard way — but he knew of no really good method for countering their power to lure unhappy neurotics into addiction and dependency.

> As a further note: Another of Freud's books, which came out in 1913 — *Totem und Tabu: Einige Übereinstimmungen im Seelenleben der Wilden und der Neurotiker* ("Totem and Taboo: Resemblances between the Psychic Lives of Savages and Neurotics" — attempted to derive important parts of Christian belief from Freud's Oedipus complex (where God was the subconscious father figure who was murderously hated by the small child but also desperately needed by the child for protection). And Freud explained other parts of Christian practice on the basis of primitive totemism, where the Catholic mass was interpreted by him as the sacrificial meal in which the totem animal, who stood both for God and for the young men's fathers, was killed and eaten by the rebellious sons of the tribal chieftain (the supreme father

figure), in an act of symbolic cannibalism, which they performed so they could (at the subconscious level) enjoy the fantasy of having sex with their father's many wives, who were their mothers.

Other trends in mid-twentieth century psychiatry: It should be clear why the Roman Catholic Church quickly came to regard Sigmund Freud's theories with horror and disgust. But on the other hand, even by 1950 only a minority of American psychiatrists had become orthodox Freudians.

The Neo-Freudian reaction against some of Freud's most extreme ideas had already started in the 1920's, 30's, and 40's (e.g. Alfred Adler, Erich Fromm, and Karen Horney, with Erik Erikson, Harry Stack Sullivan, and Abraham Maslow beginning to become important in the early 1950s). Most of the Protestants in Alcoholics Anonymous who stressed the psychological side of the A.A. program, like William E. Swegan,[535] held what were basically neo-Freudian positions. And there were many other currents present in American psychiatry and psychology during that part of the twentieth century.

Early Akron A.A. was not hostile to all forms of psychiatry and psychology. In 1942 the *Manual for Alcoholics Anonymous* published by the A.A. group in Akron, Ohio, had a recommended reading list for newcomers to the program which included Ernest M. Ligon, *The Psychology of Christian Personality*. This book was first published in 1935, and was very widely read (it was in its eighteenth printing by 1950). Ligon analyzed Jesus's Sermon on the Mount and its relationship to modern psychology, particularly Neo-Freudian thought (citing authors like Alfred Adler and Gordon W. Allport's brother, the social psychologist F. H. Allport). By 1951, Sister Ignatia had a psychiatrist on the hospital staff at St. Thomas Hospital to treat any major psychiatric problems among the patients at the alcoholism treatment ward which she ran in conjunction with the Akron A.A. group.

In Boston, the first Alcoholics Anonymous group (formed in 1940) grew out of the Jacoby Club and the Emmanuel Movement, which had begun there in Boston in 1906-1909 and combined religion with a kind of psychology which combined small group therapy with the use of "suggestion" (a mild form of hypnotherapy utilizing cognitive behavioral methods to reframe the patient's attitudes and assumptions).

Nevertheless, for much of the twentieth century, the majority of mental health professionals were as hostile to religion as Sigmund Freud was. Most of them tended to regard religion of any sort as hopeless superstition held over from an ignorant and primitive world which had its origins in the Dark Ages and even earlier — in the savagery of stone age tribal culture, and the harsh world of cave men and cave women who scrabbled for seeds and roots and grubs and carrion, and died of "old age" at the age of thirty. When patients tried to talk to these mental health professionals about moral issues, they were all too often simply scolded and told that this kind of moralism and religiosity was one of the major causes of their crippling psychological problems. When patients tried to discuss "what was fair" in their attempts to balance their own needs against the demands and desires (and interpretations) of spouses, children, and parents, they were all too frequently told that psychological issues were "not a matter of right and wrong but of learning to figure out and go for what *you* really want." There was a kind of popular psychology appearing in American magazines and books which believed that the cure for all unhappiness was simply to start acting out all your repressed desires: You are a married person not getting enough sex? simply have an affair on the side. You are suffering from terrific depression? simply start dumping all your repressed anger and feelings of hurt in wild, angry tirades against everyone around you.

It was not just the hostility of these mental health professionals toward religion and traditional morality which bothered Roman Catholic theologians, but even more the way they pretended to be the defenders of rationality and logic, while in fact turning the whole psychological show over to the lowest part of the human brain, the so-called "lizard brain" where we shared the same urges as alligators, crocodiles, cobras, rattlesnakes, and snapping turtles. And these psychiatrists and psychologists in fact short-circuited and undermined the whole process of carrying out any kind of true rational evaluation which could result in the application of genuine human free will.

If the reader has never done so, I would strongly suggest obtaining a copy of an English translation of St. Thomas Aquinas's *Summa*

Theologica (originally written in 1265-1274), and reading a page or two, to understand what I am talking about here. On every page, the book's pure logic and rationality almost overwhelm you. The Catholic Church of the Middle Ages stood above all for the ability of the human mind to use logic and reason to explain every aspect of the universe. It is no accident that the rise of modern science occurred in western Europe, where men's and women's minds had been indoctrinated for centuries with the belief that human reason could explain every aspect of the universe which was in fact explainable.

Father Dowling did not deny that there was good psychiatry: Carl Jung and Abraham A. Low. Like many people who were associated with the A.A. camp, he had an appreciation for Carl Jung, whom he quoted in his talk, reciting a famous passage from Jung's *Modern Man in Search of a Soul*. In this book (which was published in 1933 and had long been popular reading in A.A. circles) the psychiatrist said:

> Among all my patients in the second half of life — that is to say, over thirty-five [years of age] — there has not been one whose problem in the last resort was not that of finding a religious outlook on life. It is safe to say that every one of them fell ill because he had lost that which the living religions of every age have given to their followers. None of them has been really healed who did not regain his religious outlook.[536]

Dowling also showed appreciation, for quite different reasons, for Dr. Abraham A. Low, the Chicago neuropsychiatrist who in 1937 founded Recovery Inc., an organization which set up small group therapy meetings all over the United States. The year before Father Ed gave this talk, the *Saturday Evening Post* magazine had an article on the doctor in its December 6, 1952, issue, which gave considerable national publicity to his ideas. What made these ideas especially important, Father Ed said, was Dr. Low's very powerful and skillful attacks on the basic assumptions of Freudian psychoanalysis:

> Its founder, Doctor Abraham A. Low, rejects psychoanalysis as philosophically false and practically ineffective. He writes: "Life is not driven by instincts but is guided by the will."

Dr. Low, who was the real founder of modern cognitive behavioral therapy, rejected the Freudian idea of the subconscious. We in fact know what the thoughts and feelings are which are constantly running through our minds — all we have to do is to stop and listen and really pay attention — which means that we can learn to analyze these thoughts, and figure out when they are wildly exaggerated, or phrased in a kind semantically loaded fashion which triggers inappropriate emotional responses, or when our thinking processes are attempting to take on too much at a time, or otherwise are driving us to desperation.

Low's groups, which are today organized under the name of the Abraham Low Self-Help Systems, are still active and effective today in the treatment of phobias, anxiety, obsessive thoughts, poor anger control, and other distressing emotions and feelings. These groups can also help people who suffer from major mental problems, so they can learn to remain calmer and more in control, even in quite distressing situations.

Abraham Low's methods and group meetings are completely compatible with the principles of the Catholic faith, and also with simultaneous membership in Alcoholics Anonymous, Al-Anon, Narcotics Anonymous, and other twelve step groups. So good and effective psychiatry and psychology does not have to attack all religious faith, or attack the foundations of morality, or undermine our human ability to think rationally and utilize free will to choose our course through life.

Why then was so much twentieth-century psychiatry and psychology mounting war on religion, morality, and human reason and free will?

The moral side of psychiatric problems: Sebastian de Grazia on the Errors of Psychotherapy. In a section of his talk subtitled "The Moral Side of Psychiatric Problems," Father Ed cited a just-published book by Sebastian de Grazia entitled *Errors of Psychotherapy: An Analysis of the Errors of Psychiatry and Religion in the Treatment of Mental Illness* (it came out in 1952).[537] De Grazia was born in Chicago and did both his undergraduate degree (1944) and a doctorate in political science (1948) at the University of Chicago. Father Dowling had extensive connections in Chicago, and may have learned about de Grazia that way. Four years after receiving his Ph.D., in 1952, de Grazia published his book on the *Errors of Psychotherapy*.

NOTE: Sebastian de Grazia (1917-2000) was a very interesting figure. During the Second World War, he worked for the OSS (the Office of Strategic Services, the clandestine espionage agency which was the predecessor of the CIA). He eventually ended up as Professor of Political Philosophy at Rutgers University (1962-1988) and received a Pulitzer Prize in 1990 for another book he wrote, entitled *Machiavelli in Hell.*

Father Ed's assessment of de Grazia's work is so important to understanding the Jesuit's own position on these issues, that it is worth quoting in full:

Errors of Psychotherapy, by Sebastian de Grazia, is a humble confession of the failure of most psychiatric efforts. Psychoanalysis, which is the dominant psychotherapy today, is impractical for most people because of the expense and because of the unavailability of psychoanalysts. Its record of cures is not much better than the rate of neglected and spontaneous cures in state mental hospitals.

De Grazia's book is replete with devastating quotations from psychiatrists on the failure and inadequacy of current therapy, though he recognizes that all therapies have a certain percentage of cures. After surveying all therapies through history and throughout the world, de Grazia says, "Moral authority, an idea widely spurned by modern healers of the soul, is the crux of psychotherapy. The crystals that remain after the distilling of the multiplicity of therapies are not many. A bewildering array of brilliants dwindles down to a few precious few: neurosis is a moral disorder; the psychotherapeutic relationship is one of authority; the therapist gives moral direction."

We must never forget that Father Dowling, although a liberal on many issues, was nevertheless still a Roman Catholic priest. He did not at all agree with the more extreme antiauthoritarian diatribes of Immanuel Kant and so many other famous spokesmen for the Eighteenth Century Enlightenment. Neurosis was fundamentally a moral disorder, Dowling argued (and we should not forget in this regard what Dr. Silkworth said in the Doctor's Opinion at the beginning of the A.A. Big Book, "We doctors have realized for a long time that some form of moral psychology was of urgent importance to alcoholics").

The psychiatrists and psychotherapists who actually got their patients better, Dowling and de Grazia argued, were those who at least covertly realized that the patient was disturbed because he or she was acting immorally, who also realized that their M.D. or Ph.D. or M.S.W. degree automatically made them authority figures, and who used that authority to quietly maneuver and talk the patient into behaving in a more morally responsible manner.

The successful therapist has to be an authority figure who gives moral direction. That means there is nothing necessarily incompatible between being a genuinely successful psychotherapist or psychiatrist (i.e. one who actually get patients well) and a genuinely good Catholic priest (i.e. one who actually helps men and women solve their life problems with compassion but also with true effectiveness).

More on the moral side of psychiatric problems: Frank R. Barta, The Moral Theory of Behavior. Father Dowling further supported de Grazia's arguments by citing another recent book, also published just the year before Dowling gave this talk: a work by Frank R. Barta, entitled *The Moral Theory of Behavior: a New Answer to the Enigma of Mental Illness.*[538] As Dowling summed up Barta's arguments:

> The theory that moral and religious treatment is the type needed for today's epidemic of psychoses and neuroses is being most effectively urged by Dr. Frank R. Barta .... In his book, "The Moral Theory of Behavior" he writes: "All extant theories of mental illness have been refuted by able critics." He feels that the virtues of charity and humility would go a great distance in many neurotic and psychotic situations.

Dowling (along with any other Jesuits in the audience) would have known of this book because Dr. Barta was the director of the department of psychiatry at Creighton University, a prominent Jesuit institution. Barta was trying to work out an alternative theory of mental illness based in good traditional Roman Catholic fashion on the understanding of sin and involuntary behavior found in the writings of St. Thomas Aquinas and the ancient Greek philosopher Aristotle (whom St. Thomas so strongly depended on). Mental illness was a kind of involuntary behavior, but it was ignorance instead of unconscious forces which produced the irrational actions. In order to get better, the patient needed to be re-educated morally and religiously. Interestingly, Barta suggested group therapy as one useful tool for this kind of Thomistic-Aristotelian psychotherapy, and argued that general physicians could supervise these groups quite effectively, even if they had no specialized psychiatric training.[539]

It is the clergyman rather than the psychologist who is the ultimate specialist in human adjustment: Father Ed then made a quite daring series of statements to the assembled group of Catholic clergy:

> In this room we may be seeing the confirmation of R. B. Cattell's statement, in his "Meaning of Clinical Psychology": "The possibility that the clergyman, rather than the psychologist or mental practitioner, is the ultimate specialist in human adjustment has been most unscientifically ignored."[540]

> The experience in this room makes it easier to see de Grazia's statement: "Were a system of psychotherapy to be built by having all secular therapies agree to harmonize their divergent criteria of cures, it would emerge as a religious enterprise, an *Imitatio Christi* [imitation of Christ]."

> Here are not only members of A.A., but priests trained by and adept in the use of Christian asceticism, priests who speak with authority because they are experienced. I cannot help feeling that there are trends and forces, human and divine, that keep rendezvous here tonight, and that the happiness and sanctity can be richer if we meet the challenge of this rendezvous.

Traditionally, one of the major roles of the Catholic priest was to carry out the *cura animarum*, the "care of souls" or "cure of souls." In that role, they had been largely replaced over the course of the late nineteenth and early twentieth centuries by a newly appeared group of professionals: the psychologists and psychiatrists.

How did Father Dowling set up a connection between the two halves of his talk? At first glance, they appear to have been devoted to entirely different subject matters. But let us look more carefully at what he was doing in each half:

In the first half of his talk, Father Ed attempted to make it clear to the clergy gathered at this meeting of the NCCA that the Twelve Steps of Alcoholics Anonymous were completely compatible with the Roman Catholic faith and its traditional *cura animarum*. In fact, the Twelve Steps simply led people through the same basic process of spiritual development and growth that one found in St. Ignatius Loyola's *Spiritual Exercises*. The steps led men and women to the point where they could go even deeper into the spiritual life, if they wished, by studying any of the advanced guides to the spiritual life that were available within the Catholic tradition.

This meant, he told these Catholic clergy, that the A.A. people were their friends — their *very good* friends — and not their enemies. And if they thought about it, it also meant that the Twelve Steps of Alcoholics Anonymous could potentially be applied to many issues in addition to alcoholism, including any of the purely spiritual problems which St. Ignatius's exercises had been intended to deal with — anger, lust, selfishness, greed, and so on.

Then in the last half of his talk, Father Dowling warned the assembled Roman Catholic clergy that the majority of the psychologists and psychiatrists, on the other hand, were NOT their friends. And he furthermore challenged the clergy at the conference to start taking more responsibility *themselves* for the pastoral counseling of the troubled souls whom they encountered.

> AND AS A SIDE NOTE: The majority of the psychologists and psychiatrists of that time were also not friends of the new Alcoholics Anonymous movement. This can be clearly seen in the battles in the U.S. Congress over the Hughes Act (the Comprehensive Alcohol Abuse and Alcoholism Prevention,

Treatment, and Rehabilitation Act of December 31, 1970).
During the period before and the period right after the
signing of this act (that is, throughout the late 1960's and the
early 1970's) the psychiatrists tried to seize both the federal
monies and the control of government policy on alcoholism
for themselves, and totally squeeze out organizations and
treatment programs which were in any way linked with A.A.
See Nancy Olson, *With a Lot of Help from Our Friends: The
Politics of Alcoholism.*[541]

CONCLUSION: FATHER DOWLING'S OWN MISSION IN LIFE

When we look at both halves of this talk, what it reveals is Father
Dowling's sense of his own mission in life — the driving purpose that
kept him traveling all over the United States for years, working with
small groups and inspiring larger audiences, in spite of the crippling
pain from his arthritis and the other severe physical problems which
beset him by the end of his life.

He founded the first A.A. meeting in St. Louis, and set up the St.
Louis group of Abraham Low's Recovery Inc. in one of the offices of
The Queen's Work (where he was on the editorial staff).[542] He helped
start the Cana conference movement, founded the Montserrat Circle
for Catholics suffering from scrupulosity, was actively involved in the
group called Divorcées Anonymous, and traveled all over the country
putting on programs for the Summer School of Catholic Action.

He mixed Twelve Step principles with techniques borrowed from
Abraham Low's Recovery Inc. and concepts derived from the *Spiritual
Exercises* of St. Ignatius Loyola, as he led what were in fact small group
therapy sessions in the other groups with which he was involved. Now
Abraham Low's methods could deal with a wide range of different
psychological problems, including phobias, general anxiety and panic
attacks, depression, obsessive-compulsive disorder, and bi-polar disorder.
It could even help in anger management and make it easier for patients
to manage schizophrenic symptoms.

This particular mix of therapies combined advanced spiritual
insights with a respect for fundamental moral principles in a manner

which encouraged both rational thought and the strengthening of human free will.

So this good priest was in fact carrying out the *cura animarum*, in his own newly retooled version of the traditional Catholic cure of souls or care of souls, with an effectiveness probably higher than well over fifty percent of the psychiatrists and psychologists of his era. The program he was describing for his audience at the National Clergy Conference on Alcoholism was not just some airy piece of theoretical speculation, but something which he had demonstrated repeatedly could heal troubled souls and remake human lives. And the Twelve Steps of Alcoholics Anonymous formed one of the foundation sections of this new kind of therapy.

CHAPTER 35

Father Ed's 1954 Article:
How to Enjoy Being Miserable

Father Ed wrote a little article at Christmas time in 1954, with the deliberately provocative and eye-catching title: "How to Enjoy Being Miserable."[543] It concluded with the paradoxical holiday greeting, "May you enjoy a miserable Christmas! No other kind can really be merry."

MY OWN NOTE: Why did Father Ed write something like this for a *Christmas* greeting, of all things? It was, I suspect, because holidays and big festive events (like Christmas and New Year's and wedding celebrations) can be such a great problem for people in A.A. and N.A. and other twelve step programs, in part because of all the little pressures and petty annoyances that result from being around family and friends in what are in fact stressful situations. Many people in twelve step groups lapse and go back to their addictive behavior, and there are always an increased number of suicides. So it was a particularly appropriate time for Father Ed to write an article about learning to deal with the *little* everyday problems of life. He points out that, in the final analysis, it is God who chooses these problems for us — but because these problems are coming at us from *outside ourselves*, we can quickly build up resentment and be plunged into depression, or out-of-control outbursts of anger, or (as we noted) go back to drinking or drugging or overeating or whatever our fundamental destructive pattern has been.

In order to learn how to cope with suffering and things going wrong in our lives, it is first of all, not deliberate acts of self-denial which cause us so much psychological difficulty, but *(1) problems brought on us by forces outside our control: "headaches, sister-in-law's temper, weather, death," and so on.*

Before trying to devise ways for handling the truly enormous calamities that can sometimes strike us, Father Ed says — things like the death of a loved one, losing our house or our job, being diagnosed with a terribly serious medical condition, or the like — we need to "practice" as it were on learning how to deal with *the little things.* The big disasters do not actually strike us that often, Father Ed notes, and in fact they tend to be so completely overwhelming, that we would never be able to get through them successfully without a good deal of advanced preparation in living the true spiritual life.

Therefore we need lots of practice first on *(2) learning how to cope with all the "petty inconveniences and annoyances [that] are a thousand times more frequent than big tragedies."* With the countless little problems like these, "usually we have only a mite of suffering, like a traffic delay or a telephone busy signal." But having things like this go wrong is "inevitable," and a daily occurrence.

> MY NOTE: Chicago psychiatrist Dr. Abraham A. Low, in his Recovery Inc. program, taught people to say, whenever things like this happened to them, "This is average." Instead of overreacting and allowing ourselves to be driven frantic by things like this, we need to remind ourselves that minor frustrations are a constant and regular part of everyday existence, and that occurrences of this sort are never going to go away.

(3) Father Ed pointed out that there were three ways we could try to deal with our sufferings. So for example we could (a) simply allow ourselves to "*be crushed* by them and jump into the river or a movie or into a debauch of self-pity, profanity, or resentment." Or we could (b) "accept them resignedly," trying to look all stoic and Spartan on

the outside, while treasuring up inside our hearts a bitter and resentful feeling of being injured and put upon and victimized.

> In A.A. much later on, in 1976 (in the 3rd edition of the Big Book), the word "acceptance" was given a positive meaning in Dr. Paul Ohliger's story (p. 449 in the 3rd edition and 417 in the 4th edition): "And acceptance is the answer to *all* my problems today. When I am disturbed, it is because I find some person, place, thing or situation — some fact of my life — unacceptable to me, and I can find no serenity until I accept that person, place, thing or situation as being exactly the way it is supposed to be at this moment." But that is a different kind of spirit of acceptance, and is not at all like the negative and grudging attitude that Father Dowling was criticizing in this little article.

There is a third way in which we can deal with our sufferings, Father Ed says, phrasing this third alternative in the most startling and unexpected way possible: (c) *"Enjoy them."* But how in the world could anyone *enjoy* feeling pain and discomfort? "To do this," Father Ed explains, "you have to be either crazy or in love." And that of course is the secret trick which resolves the apparent paradox: ***You have to be in love.*** As he says in this article:

> In everyday life we see instances of people wanting pain if it helps someone they love. In carrying a trunk upstairs with your mother, you definitely want to get the heavy end of the burden. On a winter night a mother will shiver so as to give a warm blanket to her child. Hence the psychological trick of changing from resigned willing acceptance of suffering, to grateful wanting to take up and enjoy suffering consists in finding someone we love who will be helped by our sufferings.

This third route is the best path to choose, because this is what real spirituality is about: falling passionately in love with a Great Cosmic Force called ***Love*** which for some totally unknown reason came to touch me and heal my soul when it was filled with so much hate and fear that life no longer seemed bearable. And once I have fallen in love with the one who loved me first, I will understand why I must in turn become willing to act as an agent of this great Eternal Power of Love, by undergoing suffering myself whenever necessary to free other people from helpless captivity to their sufferings.

In Father Ed's Catholic understanding of the history of the world, the formative event of world history came some two thousand years ago, when Christ (acting as God's agent) voluntarily embraced personal suffering and pain, in order to liberate us from all the suffering and pain which had enslaved us and left us so powerless that we could no longer free ourselves by our own efforts. But once we have been liberated, it becomes our turn now to take on suffering and pain in order to free the next group of people who come along. Father Ed here quotes from the Apostle Paul's letter to the Colossians to help explain the point he is trying to make: "I am now rejoicing in my sufferings for your sake, and in my flesh I am completing what is lacking in Christ's afflictions for the sake of his body, that is, the church."[544]

> MY NOTE: In Father Dowling's 1953 talk on "Catholic Asceticism and the Twelve Steps" he attempted to make a very similar point. In that talk he said, "I think the sixth step is the one which divides the men from the boys in A.A. It is love of the cross." A.A. members have to develop something "similar to what Chesterton calls 'Christ's love affair with the cross.'" We need to remember that in order to accomplish great goals of any kind, we will have to be able to make ourselves do things that will hurt. Christ took the task that was his life work and made it the love of his life. Love takes our overpowering fear of suffering and turns it into overpowering *gratitude* that God gave us the opportunity to do such great deeds for him.

(4) *This positive attitude toward pain and suffering has to be based, not on emotions and feelings, but on the use of my human will power* — the power to make decisions and do what I know ought to be done, taking so much pleasure in the deeds of love and the great accomplishments which my courage and steadfastness are enabling me to perform, that I may oftentimes barely notice the pain and hardship I am undergoing for love's sake. Father Ed emphasizes the difference — *NO to feelings* — *YES to will power* and rational decision-making — as he carefully explains:

> This grateful wanting and enjoyment of suffering is .... *NOT in our FEELINGS.* Christ in Gethsemane or a patient in a dentist's chair are examples of a person's will wanting to do things which his feelings do not want .... *BUT in our WILL* which is the essential determinant of virtue and vice, of misery and joy.

Father Dowling pointed toward two memorable sets of passages in the Bible to help illustrate his points. The first (Luke 2:1-7) dealt with the beginning of Christ's life, and was the account of Mary giving birth to the baby Jesus in the stable in Bethlehem:

> The joys of the first Christmas were accompanied by, if not rooted in, misery — the damp, cold night, the inhospitality that poor relatives always get, the discomfort and dirt of the donkey, the roads and the cave, the loneliness and awe that young mothers have always felt at the coming of their firstborn — who will say that these are not the things that have brought to a sore, sick world the merriment and the joys of Christmas?

The second set of passages which he pointed toward, were taken from the description of Jesus's sufferings at the end of his life, together with the Old Testament prophecies which explained the significance of those sufferings. We should perhaps begin by setting down the scriptural passages in question, for the benefit of those who are not biblical scholars:

> LONELINESS: (Matthew 26:36, 38, and 40) "Then Jesus went with them to a place called Gethsemane; and he said to his disciples, 'Sit here while I go over there and pray'" .... Then he said to them, "I am deeply grieved, even to death; remain

here, and stay awake with me" .... Then he came to the disciples and found them sleeping; and he said to Peter, "So, could you not stay awake with me one hour?"

DISCOURAGEMENT: (Isaiah 53:5-6) "But he was wounded for our transgressions, crushed for our iniquities; upon him was the punishment that made us whole, and by his bruises we are healed. All we like sheep have gone astray; we have all turned to our own way, and the Lord has laid on him the iniquity of us all."

FUTILITY: (Matthew 27:46, quoting Psalm 22:1) I suspect that Father Ed was thinking here of the particular verse which was called Jesus's Cry of Dereliction — when he was hanging on the cross and at the point of death, at "about three o'clock Jesus cried with a loud voice, 'Eli, Eli, lema sabachthani?' that is, 'My God, my God, why have you forsaken me?'"

Father Dowling, who was a marvelous biblical scholar himself, gave these passages what were in part startlingly unconventional and unexpected interpretations, but in light of the message he was trying to deliver in this little Christmas missive, we can see why he interpreted them this way. This is particularly the case, because in his understanding of Catholic theology, Jesus was the God-Man, in whose being God voluntarily gave up all his enormous power and majesty, and became an ordinary suffering human being. What Dowling taught was a kind of kenotic Christology, based on Philippians 2:7, where it says that in the incarnation God "*ekenôsen* (emptied) himself, taking the form of a servant."

In Dowling's kenotic Christology, God felt our human sufferings at first hand as only a real human being could feel these sufferings. Suffering was thus ennobled, and raised up to the dignity of being a Divine attribute. So we ordinary human beings could now have our lives divinized and become "like God" not only when we showed extraordinary love and compassion and forgiveness, but also when we took on suffering in the right kind of way. For this reason, Father Ed said:

449

These three sufferings — loneliness ("Couldn't you watch an hour with Me?"), discouragement (Isaiah said Christ took upon Himself the sickening responsibility for "the iniquity of us all"), the futility (What's-the-use?) engulfed God in Gethsemane in that rendezvous where Divinity came closest to me. Where God's loneliness and mine are bridged by St. Paul's union of suffering, I can find the closest approach to God, to power, to achievement, to happiness, to joy!

(5) *I must therefore practice every day, teaching myself to respond to the little pains and sufferings of life with gratitude.* But what could be there which could merit being grateful? How could *I will to be grateful* for pain and suffering? Father Dowling explains that, to begin with, in order to do this, I need to quit thinking all the time about the past and the future, and start living in the present:

> In this matter of the will's gratitude for and want of suffering, it is psychologically important to realize that our little act of gratitude for a snub or a splinter means
>
> [Not total preoccupation with the future, that is] *NOT* that I want the suffering to continue, because as far as I know I may be dead the next instant and it may be God's will that the suffering cease. Nor does it mean that I want the suffering to be worse than it is, because the amount I have is the exact amount that God wills.
>
> [But living here in the present, reminding myself that] ... in the specific instant, now, since I cannot avoid this suffering, I want to get the best possible use out of it. The Devil will try to frighten you by directing your attention to the future and pointing out how terrible it will be if this suffering continues. Tell him to go to hell.

This idea of the importance of learning how to quit living in the future and the past, and discovering how to live instead in the Eternal Now, was one of the central motifs in A.A.'s second most published work, *Twenty-Four Hours a Day*, published by Richmond Walker in 1948, six years earlier.

But Father Ed cited another source for this idea, a very wise spiritual writer named C. S. Lewis. This author was an Anglo-Catholic rather than a Roman Catholic, but Father Ed clearly admired his work. Lewis was a scholar who taught medieval literature and thought at Oxford University and had a profound knowledge of medieval Catholic belief. At one point in his life he began writing popular fiction and essays on the side, and one of his most widely read fictional pieces was a little book entitled *The Screwtape Letters*.[545] This work, written during the middle of World War II, purported to be a collection of thirty-one letters written by Screwtape, a senior demon down in hell, to his nephew Wormwood, a young demon-in-training who had been assigned the task of tempting and seducing a young man into turning his life over to Satan instead of God. The young man ended up being killed in an air raid (invoking the fear which people in England were continually living in during that period, when German bombs were raining down on their heads day after day — Lewis, a wounded First World War veteran himself, never soft-pedaled the real pains or dangers of life). But the young man in the story, who had remained loyal to God, went to heaven, and Wormwood's career as a demon came to its own disastrous end.

Father Ed seized upon one particular part of that famous book, a passage where the demon named Screwtape was advising the younger demon about one of the ways that human beings could most easily be tempted into abandoning their faith in God. Father Ed comments:

> Screwtape, the old business agent of the Devil's Union, says that since the present is the only point at which time touches eternity, humans should be tempted to live in the past or, better still, in the future, where most vices, such as fear, avarice, lust, and ambition draw their strength. According to *Screwtape Letters*, the Devil's delight is a human soul "hag-ridden by the future — haunted by visions of imminent heaven or hell on earth."

Using a kinesthetic anchor (similar to the ones used in Neurolinguistic Programming) to chain a feeling of fear about future suffering to a feeling of gratitude over some present delight. So we can best deal with *suffering*, Father Ed says, by ceasing to torment ourselves with fears of the *future*, and by turning our concentration instead toward all the causes for *gratitude* in our *present* situation. And we can help ourselves to develop the ability to turn from future-tense suffering to present-tense gratitude, by using a little trick which Father Ed devised to turn it into an automatic reflex action. He based it on the chest-tapping technique which was already regularly used in Jesuit spirituality in a slightly different context (namely, keeping tabs on how well we were doing in handling a specific character defect that we were working on).

> A little insurance against feeling that you are insincere in your will's act of gratitude for suffering can be had by momentarily placing your hand to your breast to accompany your aspiration of gratitude, since this is an external action which cannot be done without an act of the will. Even in this matter of the will's gratitude for and want of suffering, it is psychologically important to realize that our little act of gratitude for a snub or a splinter means [that I want to use this suffering for a positive purpose if possible].

Father Dowling borrowed this idea from St. Ignatius, but it was also similar to a technique which was developed later on during the 1970's by psychologist Richard Bandler and linguistics scholar John Grinder (the developers of Neurolinguistic Programming) to establish an automatic reflexive link to a particular feeling state. The therapist asks the patient to call up all the feelings associated with a specific set of circumstances, and then taps the patient on the patient's knee or shoulder or chest or knuckle. In this instance, the method is used to produce a feeling of enormous gratitude sweeping in and replacing a feeling of resentment over suffering. After the anchor has been established, whenever some resentment begins to arise, all the patient needs to do is to tap in the same place (the chest in the version used by Dowling and Loyola), whereupon by Pavlovian reflex the corrective emotion (a feeling of joyful gratitude) will flood into the patient's mind and replace the painful feeling.

Learning to enjoy even a miserable Christmas: Father Dowling's theories are well thought out, and psychologically astute. But even then, this seems at first glance to be a truly bizarre and grotesque holiday greeting from a good priest: "May you enjoy a miserable Christmas!" How could he have said such a terrible thing?

Before we start feeling too outraged, however, let us look at that message once again, reading more carefully this time. We need to keep ourselves from being taken in by commercial advertisers, greeting card publishers, and sentimental movies and television shows. Christmas will usually be like all the rest of the ordinary days of our lives. Things will happen that will in fact create pain, misery, and suffering, even though most of them — if we are honest with ourselves — will be at the level of what are no more than petty annoyances and temporary inconveniences. So in the real world, it is almost guaranteed that we will experience "a miserable Christmas" during a few parts of the day at the very least.

But we need to look at the one word we are failing to truly pay attention to in Father Dowling's Christmas greeting: "May you *enjoy* a miserable Christmas!" The joy which we speak of here is the overpowering joy of the truly grateful. At any time on Christmas day when I start feeling misery in any of its forms — pain, suffering, disappointment, annoyance, fear, anxiety, or what have you — I need to instantly start focusing on *gratitude*. Gratitude beings me back to God, gratitude returns my heart to joy, and gratitude enables me to once more find the path that I should be walking.

So my own wish for anyone reading this is, may your every sacred holiday — may every day of your life — be filled with so much gratitude that any pain or suffering which you might be undergoing pales into insignificance by comparison!

CHAPTER 36

Father Dowling in 1955: Appendix to the Second Edition of the Big Book

In 1955 the Big Book of Alcoholics Anonymous came out in a second edition. In this new edition, a quote from Father Dowling was included in Appendix V, "The Religious View on A.A." It is located on page 572 in the present fourth edition:

Appendix V
The Religious View on A.A.

Clergymen of practically every denomination have given A.A. their blessing.

Edward Dowling, S.J.,* of the Queen's Work staff, says, "Alcoholics Anonymous is natural; it is natural at the point where nature comes closest to the supernatural, namely in humiliations and in consequent humility. There is something spiritual about an art museum or a symphony, and the Catholic Church approves of our use of them. There is something spiritual about A.A. too, and Catholic participation in it almost invariably results in poor Catholics becoming better Catholics."

*Father Ed, an early and wonderful friend of A.A., died in the spring of 1960.

As we can see, Father Ed's message began by invoking one of his standard themes, derived from the meditation on the Two Battle Standards in the fourth day of the second week of St. Ignatius Loyola's *Spiritual Exercises*. This meditation described two great spiritual armies, one made up of the forces of evil who were dominated by arrogant pride, and the other made up of the forces of good who were marked above all by their great humility and their ability to rise above humiliation.

But the first sentence in that little message also included an interesting statement that touched on another very important part of Father Ed's thought. It is in fact one of the most crucial issues in the study of theology: if God dwells in a "supernatural" realm (what Bill W. referred to on pages 8 and 25 of the Big Book as a kind of fourth dimension) and God's realm lies above and beyond everything in our human "natural" realm, then where — if anywhere — do these two worlds have any point of contact? Are they separated by an infinite chasm so deep and wide that we can never "touch" God as it were? — or make immediate contact with God or truly come into God's living presence?

Father Ed says here that the divine ***contact point***, "where nature comes closest to the supernatural," lies at those places where humility and humiliation hold sway, and where God in Christ empties himself in kenotic fashion and personally takes on our human humiliation and suffering.

Although Father Ed was convinced that the Twelve Steps themselves were given to Bill Wilson by divine inspiration, he did not in any way consider the rest of the Big Book to be divine revelation in the same sense as the Bible, nor did he consider the Alcoholics Anonymous organization to be under the direct divine care in the same way as the true Catholic church. The A.A. organization and the Big Book were natural, not supernatural.

Nevertheless, Father Ed insisted, A.A. "is natural at the point where nature comes closest to the supernatural." A.A. is one of those extraordinary ***contact points*** where God reaches down to the human race and crosses over at that point of contact, in order to raise up the human beings on the other side, and carry them back across to join him in his eternal realm.[546]

And there are two other major contact points which Father Ed chooses to mention: "There is something spiritual about an art museum or a symphony, and the Catholic Church approves of our use of them." Art and music are also contact points between the natural world and the supernatural world.

During one part of the early twentieth century, a German theologian named Rudolf Otto was regarded (along with Karl Barth) as one of the two most important theologians of that era. Otto's work is still regarded with great respect today in the study of comparative religions. In his book *The Idea of the Holy*,[547] Otto pointed to the interesting overlap between the category of the holy or sacred (in theological thought), the category of the good (in ethical thought), and the category of the sublime, that is, the overwhelmingly beautiful (in the study of aesthetics). They were at some level simply three different aspects of what was fundamentally the same thing.

And the same basic observation was made in one of the earliest A.A. pamphlets, "Mr. X and Alcoholics Anonymous," which was a sermon warmly praising the new A.A. movement, preached in 1939 by the Rev. Dilworth Lupton, pastor at the First Unitarian Church in Cleveland, Ohio.[548] He noted that one of the basic principles upon which the A.A. movement was based was "the principle of universality":

> In our great museums one usually finds paintings covering several ages of art, often brought together from widely separated localities — the primitive, medieval and modern periods; products of French, American, English, and Dutch masters; treasures from China, Japan, and India. Yet as one looks at these productions he instinctively feels that a universal beauty runs through them all. Beauty knows no particular age or school. Beauty is never exclusive and provincial; it is inclusive and universal.
>
> So, too, in the field of religion .... Back of all religions is religion itself. Religion appears in differing types, but they are all expressions of one great impulse to live nobly and to adore the highest.

It seemed to make good sense to the Rev. Lupton to link Beauty and the Sacred and see a parallel between them, in part surely because when we stand before extraordinary beauty, our minds can so easily be raised up to an appreciation of all that is sacred and good. That is why Roman Catholic churches have so often stood out as magnificent works of art and architecture, containing paintings, sculptures, mosaics, and stained glass windows of enormous beauty.

But the important thing is that you do not need to be a Roman Catholic or an Anglican to be inspired by Winchester Cathedral, and in the same way, the A.A. program can lead men and women of all sorts of different backgrounds to healing contact with the God of the universe.

And finally, the very last part of Father Ed's little message refers back to one of the basic points he tried to make in his 1953 talk to the National Clergy Conference on Alcoholism, where he spoke on "Catholic Asceticism and the Twelve Steps" and argued that the first ten of the Twelve Steps basically reduplicated the First Week of St. Ignatius's *Spiritual Exercises*, and would usually lead Roman Catholics into a desire for even further growth in the Catholic faith. "Catholic participation in [Alcoholics Anonymous] almost invariably results in poor Catholics becoming better Catholics."

Should any member of the Roman Catholic hierarchy pick up a copy of the Big Book, Father Ed knew that this was a very important message to get across. A.A. is not the enemy of any religion that is true and vital.

CHAPTER 37

Father Dowling in 1955:
The A.A. International in St. Louis
— Part I

Learning to find and understand all God's personal
messages to me

On July 1-3, 1955, the Second International Convention was held in St. Louis in the Kiel Auditorium. Around 3,800 people attended. Dr. Bob had died five years previously, and Bill Wilson, who was to turn sixty in November, was sensing his own mortality. But a new system of governance had been devised for A.A., to take over from Bill and Dr. Bob, where the principal governing body would be an elected General Service Conference. The five year trial period for that system had been concluded, and it was now agreed, by the unanimous acclamation of the convention, to make it permanent. A.A.'s new circle and triangle symbol was displayed on a fifteen foot wide by twenty-five foot long banner hanging in front of the curtains at the back of the stage.

The book which Bill Wilson put together describing that historic conference was entitled simply *Alcoholics Anonymous Comes of Age.* Dowling's talk to the assembled A.A. members has been preserved on pages 254-261 of that work.[549] In both the present chapter and the two following chapters, my references to Father Ed's words will be directed to the material in those eight pages.

Two key spiritual leaders had in fact been invited to speak, two people from outside A.A. who had helped Bill Wilson at vital points along his own spiritual journey: the Anglo-Catholic (Episcopalian) priest Dr. Sam Shoemaker and the Roman Catholic priest Father Ed Dowling. The latter began his talk by saying "I asked my friend of very recent vintage, Dr. Shoemaker, to say a prayer for me and for you during this talk, and he said, "God is with you." This was a measure of Father Ed's essential humility: although he was a Jesuit priest of considerable clout and importance, he nevertheless asked a clergyman of another communion to pray for him, spontaneously and on the spot. This was also a measure of Father Ed's willingness to engage in a pointed and very public rejection of the conservative Roman Catholic hierarchy's belief that those of the Roman communion could not pray together with those whom they considered as Protestants.

God as we understand Him and the language of the heart: Father Ed had been assigned the task of speaking on the topic of "God as we understand Him." He began by warning his audience that he was not going to give a highly intellectual discourse on philosophical theology. No one ever really understood God that way. But everyone, even non-Roman Catholics, is familiar with the paintings and statues showing the Sacred Heart of Jesus flickering with holy light and flames on the front of Jesus's chest, and the similar depictions of the Immaculate Heart of Mary. To understand God, we need to turn our attention toward the deepest emotions and feelings and desires of the human heart.

> If you will listen with your hearts, as I know you have during this whole meeting, rather than with just your ears, I think God will bless us.

Remembering this will help us to understand what Father Ed was doing when he concluded his talk with extensive quotations from the various cries of panic, fear, and despair in Francis Thompson's poem "The Hound of Heaven." When we talk about the depths of the human heart, we are not just looking at pleasant feelings like love and tenderness and joy.

Psychiatry as "the id being examined by the odd." Father Ed then stuck into his talk a peculiar and at first glance puzzling little statement:

> My trying to understand God somehow reminds me of a
> definition of psychiatry which I heard just a day or two ago.
> It is "the id being examined by the odd," and I think that
> there could be our breakdown of topics: The *id* is the primary
> reservoir of power, or *God. Examined* could mean *understood.*
> And the *odd* is *us.*

For the sake of this little play on words — "the id being examined
by the odd" — Father Ed used the Freudian term "id" in this paragraph,
but we remember that he (like most Roman Catholic theologians)
regarded Freud as one of the worst enemies which the Catholic faith had
encountered in the modern period. Dowling was definitely not saying
that God was the dark sex-ridden part of the Freudian unconscious!

Carl Jung: God and the collective unconscious. We need to
remember that the only two psychiatrists whom Father Ed truly admired
among the nationally and internationally famous twentieth-century
figures were Abraham Low and Carl G. Jung. And it is Carl Jung with
whom we must be concerned here. He is still the one psychiatrist
who fascinates Catholic thinkers above all the others, in part because
his theory of archetypal images adds so much depth to the study of
the rich symbolism, present not only in the paintings and statuary
of a Catholic church, but present also in the vivid images and stories
scattered throughout the Christian Bible.

In Jung's theories, each individual human being's psyche has, below
the conscious level, a deep unconscious level. And this lower level in
turn participates in a huge collective unconscious which is shared by all
human beings around the world. This is where we find the archetypes
— the primordial ideas — which come to expression with only slightly
different surface forms in our dreams, our religious symbols, our
paintings and sculptures, and our sense of self-identity.

At times, Jung spoke as though God and the collective unconscious
were the same thing:

> For the collective unconscious we could use the word God ....
> But I prefer not to use big words, I am quite satisfied with
> humble scientific language because it has the great advantage

of bringing that whole experience into our immediate vicinity.[550]

> You all know what the collective unconscious is, you have certain dreams that carry the hallmark of the collective unconscious; instead of dreaming of Aunt This or Uncle That, you dream of a lion, and then the analyst will tell you that this is a mythological motif, and you will understand that it is the collective unconscious. This God is no longer miles of abstract space away from you in an extra-mundane sphere. This divinity is not a concept in a theological textbook, or in the Bible; it is an immediate thing, it happens in your dreams at night, it causes you to have pains in the stomach, diarrhea, constipation, a whole host of neurotic symptoms, and you know this is the collective unconscious.[551]

But whatever we call it — the God-Image or the collective unconscious — it refers to an endless realm of apparent paradoxes, contradictions, and polar opposites. It contains the ideas and potential realities of all possible creations in all possible universes. There is no way the rational human mind can wrap itself completely around this huge reality and even begin to comprehend it all.

> This most shocking defectuosity of the God-image ought to be explained or understood. The nearest analogy to it is our experience of the unconscious: it is a psyche whose nature can only be described by paradoxes: it is personal as well as impersonal, moral and amoral, just and unjust, ethical and unethical, of cunning intelligence and at the same time blind, immensely strong and extremely weak, etc. This is the psychic foundation which produces the raw material for our conceptual structures. [This God-image comes from that vast unconscious side of Nature which] our mind cannot comprehend. It can only sketch models of a possible and partial understanding.[552]

Jung in his writings can frequently refer to it by either of two names — God or the collective unconscious — implying that they are identical, or nearly so. But it is in fact more complicated than that. And we must also remember that the human Self is involved, because the psyche is made in the *imago Dei*, the image of God. So it is also the case that if my own Self were to be brought to full consciousness and complete psychological wholeness, then (1) my archetypal Self, (2) the human collective unconscious regarded as a whole, and (3) the God-Image or *imago Dei* living within me would be simply three ways of talking about the same thing, or at least three very closely related things.

> It is only through the psyche that we can establish that God acts upon us, but we are unable to distinguish whether these actions emanate from God or from the unconscious. We cannot tell whether God and the unconscious are two different entities. Both are border-line concepts for transcendental contents. But empirically it can be established, with a sufficient degree of probability, that there is in the unconscious an archetype of wholeness. Strictly speaking, the God-image does not coincide with the unconscious as such, but with this special content of it, namely the archetype of the Self.[553]

I think we can see, at least fundamentally, where Father Dowling was heading. When we go down into the bottomless depths of the human unconscious, we enter the apparently formless abyss which is the Ground of Being — that infinite and eternal reality which was responsible for everything else in the universe coming into being — or in other words, what traditional Catholic theology called God the Father.[554] Dowling did not believe that we could know God the Father directly. But according to Dowling's kenotic Christology, some two thousand years ago, the Father had "emptied" himself of his infinitude and power in order to appear to us as Jesus Christ, giving us something which could be grasped and felt emotionally by our finite, limited human minds. And in many other ways as well, the infinite divine power reached out to human beings over and over again, by turning the ordinary things of this world — bread, wine, coffee, doughnuts, marriage, the A.A. fellowship — into humble bearers of the divine grace and power.

AS A SIDE NOTE: We need to notice the similarities between Jung's theories and the ideas taught by the leading Jesuit theologian of the mid-twentieth century, a French priest (later a Cardinal) named Jean Daniélou S.J., who was already making his name known by this time. In 1944 Daniélou was named Professor of Early Christian History at the Institut Catholique in Paris and published his great book on *Platonisme et théologie mystique: doctrine spirituelle de saint Grégoire de Nysse*. We have already spoken about the radical wing of the Jesuits, about Jean Daniélou, and about his research on St. Gregory of Nyssa, talking in detail about St. Gregory's understanding of God as an abyss of apparent nothingness, a realm beyond our direct conscious grasp, which however contained all the Platonic ideas and archetypes. The human consciousness could dive down into this abyss and come up with conscious concepts which provided salvation and New Being. In the period right after the Second World War, although conservative Roman Catholic families in the Chicago area[555] sent their children to South Bend (to the University of Notre Dame and St. Mary's across the road) to study St. Thomas Aquinas, the more intellectual Catholic families sent their children to the University of Chicago, where they could learn about Jean Daniélou's ideas instead.

THE THREE MAIN DIVISIONS OF THE TALK

Father Ed noted that the topic "God as we understand Him" has three parts: "God," "we," and "understand," and as he proceeded to get into the main part of his talk, he divided it into sections on each of those three parts, changing the order a bit, so that he began with us human beings, and ended with God.

PART I. WE HUMAN BEINGS

Members of Alcoholics Anonymous, as individual human beings, are confronted by three problems which trouble their lives: (1) alcohol,

(2) the other members of the A.A. fellowship, and (3) their agnosticism and skepticism.

(1) Alcohol and what it has done to them, and could still do to them in the future, fills recovering alcoholics with *shame* and *fear*. But the *fear* can be converted into the inner motivation required to really work the program and take no chances with halfway measures. And the *shame* can also be put to good purpose: although alcoholics can never truly regain their lost innocence (just like people who were raped or left with severe PTSD from wartime horrors), nevertheless if they learn to feel shame for the terrible things they did (the things they were asked to tally up in their fourth and eighth steps), this means a recovery of the sense of how an innocent and blame-free life must be lived. As Father Ed put it:

> Alcoholic means to me that we have the tremendous drive of fear, which is the beginning of wisdom. We have the tremendous drive of shame, which is the nearest thing to innocence.

And all of this teaches us something about the nature of God and good and evil. To help make this point, Father Ed inserted a reference here to John Milton (1608-1674), the author of *Paradise Lost*, the great epic poem which told the story of how Adam and Eve lost their innocence when they ate the fruit of the forbidden tree, and how they were cast out of Paradise, and never again allowed to return to that earlier life of carefree joy. Milton's poem began with the following introductory lines. Please especially note the last line, which I have put in italics:

> Of Mans First Disobedience, and the Fruit
> Of that Forbidden Tree, whose mortal tast
> Brought Death into the World, and all our woe,
> With loss of EDEN .... Sing Heav'nly Muse ....
> That to the highth of this great Argument
> I may assert th' Eternal Providence,
> And *justifie the wayes of God to men*.[556]

Dowling made a humorous little word play on that last line, quoting someone from one of the Irish A.A. groups: "Alcohol doth do more than Milton can to make straight the ways of God to man." But we must be careful: Father Ed was often never more serious than when he seemed at first glance to just be making a little joke. Alcoholics and addicts in fact did the same thing to themselves as poor Adam and Eve, when they first began drinking and drugging. And most of the time they were like Adam and Eve, in that some wiser head had warned them in advance against taking up that kind of life. Alcohol and drugs were their forbidden fruit, and at some level, usually they knew it beforehand. They ignored the wise parent, the wise poet, the wise pastor or rabbi or priest, and as a consequence had to learn their lesson the hard way, at the hands of alcohol and drugs.

These poor souls were not the only human beings, however, who had damaged their lives by falling prey to temptation. As Father Ed tried to make clear whenever he spoke at length about alcoholism, the alcoholic's fall into a ruinous way of life was no different at heart than the fall of the human race into thousands of other different kinds of obsessive and compulsive wrongdoing and self-destructive behavior. And that meant that many people who had never been alcoholics or addicts could *also* improve their lives enormously by learning how to apply the Twelve Steps to their lives.

As the poem *Paradise Lost* went on, it described the role which Satan played in taking on the form of a serpent, and tempting Adam and Eve into eating the forbidden fruit. Satan had once been a good angel, but then had rebelled against God and formed an army composed of other angels he had talked into joining his revolt. What could possibly have motivated an Angel of Light to turn away from the goodness and glory of High Heaven itself? Milton described Satan's turn to a career of evil and destruction in a few simple words:

> Th' infernal Serpent ... whose guile
> Stird up with Envy and Revenge, deceiv'd
> The Mother of Mankinde, what time his Pride
> Had cast him out from Heav'n, with all his Host
> Of Rebel Angels ....

Satan, according to Milton, was led into warring against God by Envy, Revenge, and above all Pride. Or in other words, the Protestant Milton in his *Paradise Lost* and the Roman Catholic Ignatius Loyola in his *Spiritual Exercises*, taught the same basic thing: in the great war between good and evil which sweeps from heaven down to earth, the arrogance of overweening **Pride** leads us to rebel against God, while adopting an attitude of true **Humility** puts us on the side of the good angels.

Father Ed does not ever want us to forget that point: developing real Humility and the ability to handle humiliation without coming to pieces is the necessary starting point of all recovery from alcoholism and addiction, and the necessary starting point as well of all true spirituality. And Bill Wilson took Father Ed to heart on this point. We need to remember how Bill's chapter on Step Seven in the *Twelve Steps and Twelve Traditions* (which had been published only two years earlier) was entirely and completely one long discourse on Humility.

(2) The other members of the A.A. fellowship are also put by Dowling in his list of the three major problems which trouble the lives of recovering alcoholics. At first glance, what a strange and truly startling thing to say! Did he misspeak? Was this a typographical error?

In fact, Father Ed was entirely serious, and he put his finger on one of the biggest problems A.A. has in retaining new members, one which is for all practical purposes never even mentioned inside the A.A. fellowship itself. But if we look at the web sites which are put on the internet by A.A. bashers, we need to note how often they complain that they tried going to A.A. meetings, but found some of the older members to be incredibly bossy and opinionated people who were continually attacking them, criticizing them, and putting them down.

Now it should be noted that we occasionally find newcomers walking into their first A.A. meeting after having been sober for only two or three days, and immediately starting to lecture people with years of successful sobriety on how to treat alcoholism, and what is obviously wrong with the A.A. program. Their blind arrogance is truly astonishing. And sometimes an old timer needs to speak the truth to a newcomer, even if it hurts — you do not do anyone a favor, in the long run, by lying to that person. But my own experience is that most newcomers, on the contrary, come to their first meetings showing considerable outward respect and politeness, and demonstrating a willingness (to at least a certain degree) to listen and perhaps learn a bit.

So the first part of this problem is that newcomers are in fact sometimes treated in a manner which is rude and abusive. And among A.A. members who have been around a while longer, who has not had their serenity disturbed by obnoxious fellow members on an A.A. committee? Or by disputes when involved in service work such as putting on an A.A. picnic, or by genuinely nasty and offensive e-mails sent in when you are trying to moderate an A.A. related website on the internet?

As Father Dowling puts it, "there is an inside antagonist who is crueler" than any of the people outside A.A. who criticize the program. He does admit, however, that A.A. is not the only place where this takes place, because in fact it can occur in all sorts of different kinds of groups. As a priest, he was well aware for example, of the bitter enmities and disputes that can divide a church congregation, sometimes over the silliest things.

Part of this arises, Father Ed says, because "I think that in all groups you have the problem of people of lynx-eyed virtue." Being lynx-eyed is like being eagle-eyed — it is a metaphor referring to people who are extremely good at spotting whatever is going on around them down to the smallest detail — only there is an additional note of nastiness and cruelty to the image of the lynx, who searches out other people's flaws so he can use his razor sharp claws to rip them to shreds.

Those who wish to see examples of this kind of nastiness and cruelty within A.A. circles need only to read some of the especially offensive letters which some A.A. members sent to Bill Wilson over the years. Or they might look at the way Henrietta Seiberling talked about Bill in some of the letters she wrote Clarence Snyder just three or four years before Father Ed gave the present talk.[557]

Father Ed calls them "people of lynx-eyed virtue," while Bill Wilson (in the chapter on the Second Tradition in the *Twelve Steps and Twelve Traditions*) calls them "bleeding deacons," and talks about the bleeding deacon as someone who continually criticizes every minor detail, who tries to get power and control over everyone else in the group, "who is ...

convinced that the group cannot get along without him, who constantly connives for reelection to office, and who continues to be consumed with self-pity."

> And if I may make an additional comment: In Bill Wilson's explanation of the traditions in the 12 & 12, he warns us as strongly as possible that the greatest danger to A.A. is created by relatively small handfuls of A.A. members who would tear the groups apart if allowed to run amok. These destructive people are of several varieties, which Bill lists in the chapters on the traditions: the "bleeding deacons," the "promoters," the glory seekers, those who lust for power and control over others, the discriminatory and intolerant, and the publicity seekers who try to turn their A.A. activities into a public "vaudeville show."[558]

The term "bleeding deacon" or "bleating deacon" originated in small town Protestant churches, where every little congregation seemed to have at least one nosy fussbudget who became the self-appointed minder of everyone else's business in a hypercritical and obnoxious way. Bleeding deacons are members of the group who have the classic authoritarian personality, are overly preachy, and are continually negative and moralizing. They think they know all the answers to everything (no matter how little they actually know about the subject) and consider themselves to be the sole voice of reason. They get so over-involved in the minor details of how the organization is run that they lose sight of the group's larger goals.

And above all, the "people of lynx-eyed virtue" and "bleeding deacons" continually attack their fellow A.A. members and try to turn every A.A. meeting into a bitter argument.

Perhaps A.A. members who act that way toward other members of the fellowship will try to defend themselves by arguing, "But so-and-so is such a *phony*, pretending to be such a good A.A. member, and look at how he (or she) actually acts!" Father Ed's answer to this is simple: "Who of us is not a phony?"

(3) Agnosticism and skepticism provide the third set of problems that we, as ordinary human beings, have to deal with in the twelve step

program. Agnostics are people who do not know whether God exists or not — people who are filled with deep doubt and skepticism on that issue.

As a good Catholic priest, Father Dowling begins his response by stating simply that "I think we are all agnostic." Even the clergy, and in fact even the greatest saints, can find themselves afflicted by doubts and fears. Father Ed told his A.A. audience about

> ... a very good priest friend of mine [who] says, "I really think that the first thing we will say when we get to Heaven is, 'My God, it's all true!'"

This is not just Catholic experience. Even the most stiff-nosed of the classical Protestant theologians from the sixteenth-century Reformation, the great John Calvin himself, said bluntly in the section on Faith in his *Institutes of the Christian Religion* (1559): "There is no faith unmixed with doubt." But Calvin also said that even the faintest glimmer of genuine faith would save us, no matter how frightened and despondent we otherwise became.

And there was more than one kind of agnosticism, Father Ed pointed out. Within the A.A. fellowship, there were those who were pious in their belief in the doctrines and dogmas of their childhood religion, but were ***agnostic as to application.*** These were

> ... the devout who did not seem to be able to apply their old-line religious truths. They were agnostic as to application. They are people like the priest who passed the man in the ditch before the good Samaritan[559] helped him.

Or in other words, they have the theory, but they do not have enough faith to be able to put it into practice. That is, they may go to church regularly, and be able to recite all the doctrines and dogmas of the Church, and quote numerous passages from Scripture by memory. But when they are asked, for example, to go out of their way to aid another human being, in a situation in which helping that person will involve them in a considerable amount of work, *they do not trust God enough to realize that God really means what he is saying when he tells us that we absolutely have to give concrete help to other people who need help.* So in the example which Father Ed gives — Jesus's story of the Good Samaritan in Luke 10:25-37 — the priest and the assistant priest refuse to help their fellow Jew who is lying in the ditch after being beaten and robbed, which makes it clear that all their claims to faith and piety and correct belief are in fact bogus. The task of helping the wounded man is left to a Samaritan, who becomes the real hero of the tale even though he is a man of another tribe and another religion (a religion which denied the truth of most of the Jewish Bible).

As it says in the letter of James, "faith without works is dead." And as Father Dowling says here, no matter how much you talk about religious doctrines and dogmas and how much you love God and Jesus and so on, if it has no effect on your real actions, then somewhere down deep you are in fact *a cynic and a scoffer who does not believe that these things really matter.* You too are an agnostic and atheist; you just refuse to openly admit the secret underground current of skepticism and doubt that undermines all your ability to act.

Father Ed is humble enough to say here that "I think all of us are rusty in some phases of our application of beliefs." We all have trouble turning theory into practice in our everyday lives, and in fact all of us sometimes become *agnostics* — doubters and skeptics and scoffers and casual ignorers of our full moral responsibilities — at the level of *application.*

CHAPTER 38

The 1955 A.A. International in St. Louis — Part II

PART II. UNDERSTANDING

There is another kind of agnostic however — the skeptics and doubters and cynics who have real intellectual problems with the concept of God, problems severe enough to block them in whole or in part from being helped by the twelve step program. As Father Ed phrases it, these are "the sincere eighteen-carat agnostics who really have difficulty with the spiritual hurdle." If the assigned topic for this talk was "God as we understand Him," we therefore need to spend part of the talk discussing that word "understanding."

Our understanding of God will always be lacking to some degree. We need to begin here, Father Ed says, by reminding ourselves that there will never be any full and complete understanding of God, either in this world or the next. In a good spiritual life, our understanding of God will always be growing, for the whole length of our lives on earth. And Father Ed adds that our growth in our knowledge of God (who is infinite) will continue after our deaths, in the world to come, for all eternity.

> As we move from an obscure and confused idea of God to a more clear and distinct idea, I think we should realize that our idea of God will always be lacking, always to a degree be unsatisfying. Because to understand and to comprehend God is to be equal to God. But our understanding will grow. I am sure that Bill, sitting in that chair, and Dr. Bob, whose angel

is probably sitting on that oddly misplaced empty chair, are growing in the knowledge of God.

St. Gregory of Nyssa, back in the fourth century A.D., taught that our souls, even after death, would still continue to grow forever in their understanding of God. His fellow fourth-century figure, Eusebius of Caesarea (the first great Christian historian) implied the same thing in his teachings about time and history. The great English spiritual writer C. S. Lewis taught a similar sort of idea in his seven-book series, *The Chronicles of Narnia.* In the concluding novel in the series, called *The Last Battle* (published by Lewis in 1956, only a year after this talk by Father Dowling) the series ends with the statement that all of the adventures related in the chronicle are only the beginning of the true story, "which goes on forever, and in which every chapter is better than the one before."[560] Likewise, the prayer which Bill and Lois Wilson recited together every morning described how our souls, after death, would pass through a series of different heavenly realms (the "house of many mansions" in John 14:2), in each one of which we would learn even grander and more glorious things about God.[561]

Dr. Bob's angel sitting on the stage. Now for a real puzzle — what exactly did Father Dowling mean when he referred in the paragraph quoted above to "Dr. Bob, whose angel is probably sitting on that oddly misplaced empty chair"? Although this is speculation on my part, I cannot help but believe that, in context, he was trying to point doubters and skeptics toward one kind of possible direct experience of the supernatural realm.

For those who doubt the existence of God, and especially those who doubt the existence of the eternal world, let us look seriously at this common A.A. experience. Can we not feel the spiritual presence of some of our fellow A.A. members who have now left this material realm, when we are sitting at the table at an A.A. meeting? This feeling — which needs to be taken seriously — is a proof from direct experience. When we sit down in an A.A. meeting and feel some sort of calming and healing presence surrounding us and filling us with serenity (what is called "the spirit of the tables"), is this not direct evidence of the existence of a higher dimension of reality? It this not evidence that a part of that eternal realm can dip down to earth and fill the room where that little A.A. gathering is being held? And evidence that, vice versa, I have a two-level soul, where the upper story of my soul already extends up into that higher dimension and has its true eternal home there?

Now we still have to ask the question here, what exactly did Dowling mean when he referred in the paragraph quoted above to "Dr. Bob, whose angel is probably sitting on that oddly misplaced empty chair"? As a Catholic priest, he would obviously not deny that we could be visited by angels and by the spirits of the saints. At one point back in 1943, he had recommended that Bill Wilson read a famous and much-respected work on that general subject by a great Jesuit spiritual writer: Augustin Poulain, S.J., *The Graces of Interior Prayer* (1901).[562] I am sure that, at the very least, Father Ed believed that Dr. Bob's spirit in heaven was aware of what was going on at the A.A. International in St. Louis, and that Dr. Bob's spirit was also aware of what both Father Ed and Bill Wilson were thinking and feeling at that time. But in the way in which he phrases it here, this sounds like a rather more concrete idea — namely, that Dr. Bob's spirit was actually present there with them on stage. Of course, this could just have been Dowling being humorous, or searching for a catchy way to say something. But on the other hand, as was noted once before, it was when Father Ed seemed at first glance just to be saying something humorous, that he was often at his most serious.

The real problem with the agnostics who think that their intellectual skepticism about the existence of God is logical and reasonable, is that they think they know more than they really do. Even though most people come into A.A. with their lives obviously lying in ruins, some of these psychological wrecks still continue to be arrogant know-it-alls, convinced that they know all the answers to everything. They lecture the other people around them about how modern physics and modern psychology "prove" that belief in God is superstitious nonsense, in spite of the fact that they have no real training in either physics or psychology. "There is an old German saying that applies here," Father Dowling tells us — "'Very few of us know how much we have to know in order to know how little we know.'"

As we grow in understanding of both God and ourselves, it is strange, but the more we come to understand, the less we realize that we understand. But also the happier we become, and the more we find ourselves loving God and the other people around us, along with the world we live in. We even begin loving ourselves.

A. The negative approach to agnosticism and doubt. Father Ed began this section of his talk by quoting John 6:68, where the Apostle Peter said to Jesus, "Lord, to whom shall we go?" What point was Father Ed trying to make?

We need to look at that whole chapter in the gospel to understand the meaning of Peter's statement. In chapter six of the Gospel of John, Jesus did a number of things. He performed miracles right before the people's eyes, and he also presented his listeners and tentative disciples with some teachings that they found difficult to believe. As a result, many of these would-be disciples turned away and left him. Jesus asked the twelve apostles if they also wished to leave him and go seek some other teacher. In verse 68, the Apostle Peter answered for them all: "Lord, to whom can we go?" For anyone in Palestine at that time who wanted to find God and eternal life, Jesus was the only place to go. Even if part of Jesus' teaching left even some of his most devoted disciples feeling skeptical, their problem was the same: where else did they have left to go? And they had seen Jesus working miracles. Somehow or other, in terms of end results, his teachings clearly worked.

If we are alcoholics who find some A.A. teachings difficult to believe, leaving the program is still not an option. Seriously speaking, there is no other good place to go to get sober. Newcomers to A.A. need to remember that at the beginning, they may need to continue going to meetings and trying to work the steps for some weeks or even months, without really believing that many parts of it will work. But if they watch and listen at their A.A. meetings, they will see miracles occurring: drunks getting sober, addicts quitting drugs, angry people turning into calm and loving people, and on and on.

So if you are an agnostic who is filled with skepticism and doubt, you may need to begin by taking what Father Ed calls *the negative approach*: ask yourself seriously what other choices you have left at this point, and then stick with the A.A. program out of sheer desperation, if nothing else.

And if you cannot truly motivate yourself with positive thoughts of the beauty and goodness of God and the true spiritual life, in like manner, try motivating yourself by *the negative route*, and start thinking seriously about how terrible and awful your present drunken life is making you feel. In colorful language, Father Ed calls this **backing away from Hell**:

> I doubt if there is anybody in this hall who really ever sought sobriety. I think we were trying to get away from drunkenness. I don't think we should despise the negative. I have a feeling that if I ever find myself in Heaven, it will be from backing away from Hell. At this point, Heaven seems as boring as sobriety does to an alcoholic ten minutes before he quits.

B. The positive approach to agnosticism and doubt: direct spiritual experience in the Twelfth Step. At this point in his talk, Father Ed gave the only public criticism of Alcoholics Anonymous that I know of him ever expressing. He believed that changing the wording of the Twelfth Step was a serious mistake, and said it in no uncertain terms: "I still weep that the elders of the movement have dropped the word 'experience' for 'awakening.'" The steps were listed on pages 71–72 of the Big Book, and the changes made in the Twelfth Step were as follows (altered wording underlined by me):

> FIRST PRINTING (APRIL 1939): Having had a spiritual <u>experience</u> as the result of <u>these</u> steps, we tried to carry this message to alcoholics, and to practice these principles in all our affairs.

> SECOND PRINTING (MARCH 2, 1941): Having had a spiritual <u>awakening</u> as the result of <u>those</u> steps, we tried to carry this message to alcoholics, and to practice these principles in all our affairs.

Father Ed believed that having some kind of real spiritual experience was necessary to the program, and divided significant spiritual experiences into two kinds: (a) "sudden, passive insight" and (b) "routine active observations."

(a) Spiritual experiences and life-changing insights that suddenly fall upon us in spectacular fashion in a way totally out of our control. Dowling described this sort of experience as

> ... a sudden, passive insight like Bill's experience and like the *Grapevine* story of that Christmas Eve in Chicago. Those are all in the valid pattern of Saul's sudden passive insight as he was struck from his horse on the road to Damascus.

When Bill Wilson was at Towns Hospital in New York City, on December 14, 1934, he had an experience of the Heavenly Light, which he described in greater detail than he ever had before at one point during the St. Louis International Convention (see pages 62-63 of *Alcoholics Anonymous Comes of Age*):

> Suddenly the room lit up with a great white light. I was caught up into an ecstasy which there are no words to describe. It seemed to me, in the mind's eye, that I was on a mountain and that a wind not of air but of spirit was blowing. And then it burst upon me that I was a free man. Slowly the ecstasy subsided. I lay on the bed, but now for a time I was in another world, a new world of consciousness. All about me and through me there was a wonderful feeling of Presence, and I thought to myself, "So this is the God of the preachers!" A great peace stole over me and I thought, "No matter how wrong things seem to be, they are still all right. Things are all right with God and His world."

The mention of the Christmas Eve story in the *Grapevine* was probably a reference to "A Miracle at Christmas — a Man Re-born," in the A.A. *Grapevine*, Vol. 3, No. 7, December 1946, which began as follows:

> Would you say that a man who had been drinking for months, who had wound up in a flop house in such shape he could not get out of bed and whose "entire frame shook with convulsive-like tremors" — would you say that man could

get up the following morning "clear eyed, his complexion good and ... perfectly poised?" Of course not. But that's what happened in Chicago one Christmas five years ago. Following is an account of the strange happening, written by an A.A. member of the Chicago Group.

The mention of what happened to Saul (the Apostle Paul's original Jewish name) on the road to Damascus was a reference to the story of his conversion to Christianity, as given three times in the book of Acts in the New Testament (in chapters 9, 22, and 26).

> Saul, still breathing threats and murder against the disciples of the Lord, went to the high priest and asked him for letters to the synagogues at Damascus, so that if he found any who belonged to the Way, men or women, he might bring them bound to Jerusalem. Now as he was going along and approaching Damascus, suddenly a light from heaven flashed around him. He fell to the ground and heard a voice saying to him, "Saul, Saul, why do you persecute me?" He asked, "Who are you, Lord?" The reply came, "I am Jesus, whom you are persecuting. But get up and enter the city, and you will be told what you are to do." (Acts 9:1-7)

As Father Dowling indicates, this kind of spiritual experience is *sudden* — it strikes in an instant without any warning. Our stance before it is *passive* — it completely overwhelms us and renders us helpless in the face of its power; we definitely do not have to engage in active thought or long analysis to understand its meaning. And finally, it conveys to us a totally new *insight* into the nature of God and our relationship to him.

One classical description of this kind of spiritual experience was given in the little piece called "A Divine and Supernatural Light," written by the famous American philosophical theologian Jonathan Edwards (1703-1758). He makes it clear (I quote from the eighteenth century colonial American English of the original 1734 first printing) that, although the person's imagination may sometimes supply the impression that visible light is shining all around, this imaginary light is not what is meant when we speak about having the real "spiritual light" suddenly illuminating our minds:[563]

> This spiritual and divine light don't consist in any impression made upon the imagination. 'Tis no impression upon the mind, as though one saw anything with the bodily eyes: 'Tis no imagination or idea of an outward light or glory, or any beauty of form or countenance, or a visible luster or brightness of any object. The imagination may be strongly impressed with such things; but this is not spiritual light. Indeed when the mind has a lively discovery of spiritual things, and is greatly affected by the power of divine light, it may, and probably very commonly doth, much affect the imagination: so that impressions of an outward beauty or brightness, may accompany those spiritual discoveries. But spiritual light is not that impression upon the imagination, but an exceeding different thing from it.

In the Middle Ages, the Hesychastic monks of Mount Athos used long periods of meditation on the Jesus Prayer to have experiences of this sort, which they referred to as visions of the Uncreated Light, and regarded as the same supernatural light which the apostles had seen shining from Jesus's face at the Transfiguration (Matthew 17:1-9).

We see a truly excellent modern study of this kind of spiritual experience in William R. Miller and Janet C'de Baca, *Quantum Change: When Epiphanies and Sudden Insights Transform Ordinary Lives* (2001).[564] Miller is Emeritus Distinguished Professor of Psychology and Psychiatry at the University of New Mexico and their Center on Alcoholism, Substance Abuse and Addictions. The book gives numerous case histories of modern American men and women undergoing enormous psychological and personal transformations in sudden moments of insight, that sometimes are accompanied by phenomena like Bill Wilson's vision of light and wind, although they do not have to be.

It should also be noted that Father Dowling's description of these events as conveying *major new insights into both God and ourselves* links us to a long tradition in Christian philosophical theology: St. Justin Martyr in the second century on the role of the Logos in conversion,[565]

St. Augustine's doctrine of illuminationism in the fifth century (as part of his concept of God as Truth Itself), and St. Thomas Aquinas in the thirteenth century (along with Paul Tillich in the twentieth century) on God as Being Itself.

And when Dowling stressed the word *insight*, he may have been thinking in particular about the book by the Canadian Jesuit, Father Bernard J. F. Lonergan, S.J., entitled *Insight: A Study of Human Understanding.*[566] This book was not published until two years after Father Ed gave this talk in St. Louis, but Lonergan had to spend a long time sending his book around to a number of publishers before he could find anyone who would print it — ironic, since it quickly became a great classic — and Dowling may well have already known about it in 1955 through his contacts with his fellow Jesuits.

The cognitive behavioral therapists of the 1960's and 70's spoke of the need to "reframe" their patients' minds, so as to produce sweeping changes in the cognitive structures which provided the basic framework for those patients' thinking processes. An insight or illumination of the type which Father Ed was describing would create this kind of massive reframing of the mind's cognitive structures, although in a quite different way from anything which the cognitive behavioral therapists ever imagined. Dr. William D. Silkworth, in "The Doctor's Opinion" at the beginning of the Big Book, spoke of this as a kind of total psychological transformation which would produce "an entire psychic change."

In summary, the kind of insight we are talking about here is one which changes some of our most basic presuppositions about the world and life, in a way which changes the way that we perceive and interpret everything else going on around us. It causes us to put enormous value, at an important level of our being, on things which we never valued nearly so strongly before. And as a consequence of this, we find ourselves suddenly actually doing things which we had never been able to make ourselves do before.

This can be a valuable and powerful kind of spiritual experience. But nevertheless, *the great problem here is that the majority of A.A. members do not witness spectacular occurrences of this sort.* Most people in the twelve step program never see visions of heavenly light, or hear God speaking clear and distinct words inside their heads, or experience any other extraordinary events of that sort. So Father Dowling goes on to describe a completely different way of coming to know God, *a second kind of path to God*, in which *everyone in the twelve step program can learn to hear God speaking to us*, as it were.

(b) The spiritual experiences and messages from God which we discover in routine active observations of our own emotions and feelings, supply ways in which we can learn to hear God speaking to us clearly and distinctly, on a regular everyday basis. Dowling bases his description of this second path to God partly on the Big Book's instructions for doing the Fourth Step (which it tells us to carry out by analyzing the patterns in our more obsessive resentments and fears), and partly on the *Spiritual Exercises* of St. Ignatius Loyola (the kind of spirituality in which the Jesuits had schooled him ever since he came into the order back in 1919). Jesuit spirituality is above all *a spirituality of decision-making*, and learning how to practice *discernment* — that is, learning how to determine with greater and greater accuracy what God actually wants us to do in each of our daily decisions.

In the Jesuit method of discernment, we learn how all our emotions and feelings can be understood as messages from God. As our emotional states constantly change during the day, we can use our "routine active observations" (as Father Ed puts it) of all these little shifts in our emotions to stay involved in a continual daylong conversation with God.

Although the early Jesuits based their method of discernment on earlier Christian theories about ways to seek guidance from God and ways to "test the spirits to see if they be of God," the developed theory — realizing how many of our emotions and feelings, if evaluated properly, were shaped by our encounters with God and were messages to us from God — was regarded in Roman Catholic circles as the distinctive center of classic Jesuit spirituality.

In this kind of Ignatian spirituality, we practice *discernment* (that is, learn how to interpret these messages from God and receive guidance from them) by paying close attention to the difference between *consolations* and *desolations*:

When we are feeling enormous pleasure, joy, satisfaction, or delight, this can usually be regarded as a *consolation*. Father Ed gives an example:

an A.A. member, going through the course of the day, notes at one point that "I am sober today" and feels a glow of enormous satisfaction and appreciation. That pleasurable emotion is a message from God congratulating and rewarding the person for this accomplishment. If the A.A. member slips, on the other hand, and goes back to drinking, this will always eventually involve the person in a feeling of *desolation*. That will mean unpleasant feelings like guilt, shame, despair, and so on, each of which is a message from God trying to get us to look at — and change — a particular character defect or pattern of behavior.

Now we must be careful here: using St. Ignatius's technique for discernment smoothly and skillfully can be a little more complicated than that at times. Pleasant emotions can sometimes be temptations from an evil spirit, for example, and unhappiness does not necessarily mean that we are doing anything wrong (we may feel enormous sorrow for example when seeing another human being who is hungry or homeless or in great physical pain, or when making our Fourth Step review of some of the evil things we did before entering the good spiritual life). St. Ignatius gives us two long lists of rules (fourteen in the first list and eight in the second list) at the very end of the *Spiritual Exercises*, at the end of the Fourth Week (in sections 313-336 of the exercises), which guide us in various kinds of considerations which may need to be taken in evaluating our innermost desires and feelings.

To quickly paraphrase a few of the more important rules: We have to be careful because an evil spirit can put images of physical delights and pleasures into our minds in such a way that they appear pleasurable and tempting. Pleasurable emotions do not count as a spiritual consolation unless they act to lead us into yet another and even more powerful emotion, which is to be filled with an even more powerful love for God.

Evil spirits (pretending to be angels of light) can put what are apparently good and worthy thoughts in our mind in order to gain our confidence, so they can eventually lead us astray. The rule we need to follow here is, if the course of our thoughts is genuinely coming from God, then all parts of it — the beginning, the middle, and the end — will be completely good. We also need to look at the direction in which the overall course of our life is taking us. If it is God who is leading us, we will continually go from good to better. If it is an evil spirit which is leading us, we will continually go from bad to worse.

A state of spiritual desolation will be marked by agitation, obsessions and compulsions, loss of hope and confidence, a deep inner sadness, procrastination and laziness, and the inability to love. If our thoughts and feelings weaken, disquiet, and disturb our souls, and take away our peace, serenity, and quiet, then they are coming from an evil spirit and not from God. The touch of the evil spirit usually comes with noise and clatter, while the touch of God usually comes lightly and gently.

The section in the A.A. Big Book which describes how to write out our Fourth Step inventory uses a different terminology from the one St. Ignatius employed, but in fact is closely similar in many ways. The A.A. method uses two red flags, as it were, for identifying trouble areas in our thoughts, emotions, and feelings. If we are feeling continual *resentment* or continual *fear* over some matter, then this is God's warning message that we have a character defect in that area. We need to remember here that resentment includes not only anger and rage, but also feeling self-pity. And fear also includes all forms of obsessive worry, problems with anxiety attacks, and gnawing feelings of guilt and shame. Furthermore, we need to remember that it still counts as a resentment even if I can "prove" logically that the other person's behavior was wrong and my behavior was right. It is my own emotions, not the other person's emotions, that are going to contain the messages which God is sending me.

Father Ed points out that we can learn a great deal about God from the consolations which he sends us, but that we often learn even more from the *suffering* which fills our hearts when we are overcome by a feeling of desolation. He inserted two interesting quotes into his talk making this point, one from Bernard Smith, the Chairman of A.A.'s

Board of Trustees — "The tragedy of our life is how deep must be our suffering before we learn the simple truths by which we can live."

The other came from a rather bizarre source, the ex-Soviet spy Whittaker Chambers[567] — "And yet it is at this very point that man, that monstrous midget, still has the edge on the Devil. He suffers. Not one man, however base, quite lacks the capacity for the specific suffering which is the seal of his divine commission."

> An additional note: signs from God. In addition to consolations and desolations, the Catholic tradition (and the early Puritan tradition as well), teaches us to be continually on the watch for *signs from God*, signs which give us guidance and point us in the direction we should go. These are events which, at one level, seem to be simply coincidences. But at another level, I immediately sense that God is saying to me "I just gave you this sudden unexpected opportunity in a way designed to catch your attention, because that is the next job I am assigning you," or "the startling thing that person just said to you was designed by me as a warning, that you need to change the direction you are going, for reasons that will be apparent to you the minute you stop and think about it," or something else of that sort.
>
> The great Christian historian Eusebius of Caesarea, in the fourth century A.D., called events of this sort by the Aristotelian term *symbebêkota*, the *conjunctures* of history. We encountered what seemed at first glance to be merely the *accidental* coming together of different lines of events, but when we took a longer view, and saw the overall pattern of history at that point, we realized that this was God's providence directing the course of events.[568]
>
> The psychiatrist Carl Jung referred to an event of this sort as a *synchronicity*. On the surface it appeared to be nothing but a chance occurrence, but it immediately pushed the observer into a major new insight into his or her life in a way that had a marvelous healing effect.

So in summary, as we receive continual messages from God all day long, conveyed from him to us by means of the emotions, feelings, and desires which fill the deepest levels of our hearts (along with the signs which he sends us through the coincidences and synchronicities of our lives), and as we then learn how to respond to these messages in positive and fruitful ways, we slowly begin to realize that we are dealing with a warmly personal God who is totally real. He wipes away our tears when we are sad, delights with us whenever we rejoice over the beauty and grandeur of his creation, braces up our courage when we are afraid, guides us back onto the path we should be walking when we begin to wander into the weeds along the side — and sometimes he just sits and laughs at us. That is when we begin to truly realize that it is all real, and that God is the most genuinely personal being in all of reality, and that this God is my one true friend.

> ***A note from the author of this book: we could also describe this as learning to use our "spiritual radar."*** Some readers may be tempted to argue that these warning and guiding emotions which we feel inside us during the course of our everyday lives — the resentment and fear spoken of in the Fourth Step inventory on pages 64-68 in the Big Book, and the more complex emotions analyzed in St. Ignatius Loyola's *Spiritual Exercises* — are merely our own subjective human reactions, and could not possibly be regarded as containing messages direct from God or objective information about the way God's path leads us.
>
> If I may introduce my own attempted explanation here, perhaps it would help you to think of this as like a kind of "spiritual radar," to put it in metaphorical form. A modern riverboat pulling barges down the Mississippi river in the middle of the night has a radar antenna attached to the pilothouse, with a transmitter which beams microwave radiation out over the surrounding water. The radiation which is reflected back is used by the radar receiver to draw a picture on a computer monitor showing other boats, the shoreline, raised sandbars, any highway and railroad bridges crossing the river, and so on.
>
> When bats fly through the dark night, they emit high pitched sounds which bounce off of objects and reflect back to their ears, enabling them to avoid obstacles and locate

tiny insects by the nature of the reflected echoes. Electric eels create an electrical field in the water around them, and are capable of detecting minute changes in this field, to the point of being able to detect the presence of a rod no bigger around than a pencil inserted in the water near them.

Likewise, when we take action on the world around us, our actions are shaped by our purposes and drives, and hence loaded with the power of our emotions. The world around us is structured not only by the laws which are studied by physicists, chemists, and engineers, but also by what is sometimes simply called the moral law. This natural moral law is not based on commandments written in sacred books like the Bible and the Koran, but on the simple rational observation of what happens in the real world when certain things are done. For example, there is no human society on earth where anyone at all is allowed to kill anyone else at all at any time that he or she feels like it. Thoughtful, rational human beings at all times and places have observed that a society which allowed this would quickly destroy itself in chaotic violence. There is likewise no society where anyone at all is allowed to have sex with anyone at all at any time that he or she feels like it. That also is a rule based on reason and common sense. Likewise, in any workable human society, there will always be items or categories of personal belongings designated as belonging to particular people or appointed for the use of particular people, which other people will not in fact be allowed to simply arbitrarily walk off with whenever and wherever they choose.

I like to refer to this set of rational rules as forming *the deep moral structure of the universe*. In ancient Latin, it was called the *lex naturalis*, that is, the natural law or law of nature. In traditional Catholic theological ethics, St. Thomas Aquinas (*Summa Theologica* I-II qq. 90–106) said that the term natural law referred to what the rational human mind could work out about God's eternal moral law without having to make recourse to divine revelation. Thomas Jefferson, in the opening sentence of the U.S. Declaration of Independence, refers to these moral structures as "the Laws of Nature and of Nature's God." John Wesley (one of the key founders of modern evangelical Protestantism) referred to this moral law as "the face of God unveiled," the clearest picture we could obtain of God's true character. In Alcoholics Anonymous, it is sometimes referred to as Good Orderly Direction, abbreviated G.O.D., and recommended to newcomers searching for a meaningful higher power.

When I slam my bare fist as hard as I can into a stone wall, the laws of physics and biology specify that I will feel physical pain in my hand. Likewise, when I fly out in uncontrolled, wildly disproportionate, and poorly thought out anger against someone or something in the world around me, the *deep moral structure of the universe* dictates that my action will "bounce back" on me in a way which will ultimately make me feel some very unpleasant emotions (things like frustration, depression, self-pity, guilt, shame, anxiety, fear, or the growth of even more resentment than I had before).

As I grow in the spiritual life, I then begin to find that the *deep moral structure of the universe* refers to more than just an unchanging, static set of moral rules which apply equally to all people at all times and places. It is true that I can use this moral radar to work out the unchanging structures of the moral framework of the universe, but it is also possible to use this moral radar to see what specific directions God is guiding me in at any particular moment in time. This part of my moral duty is not based on rigidly following unchanging rules in mechanical fashion, but requires me to listen for what special job or special responsibility God wants me (and me alone) to take care of now. There is no universal moral rule saying that everyone should found a religious order like the Jesuits, or a recovery group like Alcoholics Anonymous. But Ignatius Loyola and Bill Wilson received those commands as special orders from God. In a much a more modest way, ordinary people like us also regularly receive requests from God to do special jobs for him.

So in fact, many of the emotions we feel in our hearts are being "bounced back" off of the deep moral structures of the universe. This moral framework serves as part of God's "face," the external façade which he presents to us human creatures. But just as we can use a fellow human being's facial expressions — that man or woman's outer skin as it were — to learn about that person's inner feelings, and even that person's deepest values, so too can we use the moral structures of the universe to obtain a glimpse of God's heart.

This means that if we use our spiritual radar to pay careful attention to the stream and flow of our everyday emotions, we can learn to converse all day long with God every day of our lives. "Speak to Him, thou, for He hears, and Spirit with Spirit can meet — closer is He than breathing, and nearer than hands and feet."

C. The positive approach to agnosticism and doubt: the Second Step speaks of simply accepting God's existence on faith. This step says that the beginning of the A.A. path to God lies in an act of faith or trust *in something outside ourselves*: "Came to believe that a Power greater than ourselves could restore us to sanity."

But we have to be careful about this, Father Ed warns. Most devoted Roman Catholics in the United States during the first half of the twentieth century had gone to parochial schools where they were drilled over and over in the Baltimore Catechism and made to memorize all the doctrines and dogmas of the Catholic Church. They could easily be misled into believing that this, all by itself, counted as the kind of belief in God which would save their souls and rescue them from an alcoholic death. As Father Dowling put it:

> I've known some of my Catholic friends who at that Step said, "Well, I believe already, so I don't have to do anything." And in a great burst of kindness they kept on drinking to let the Protestants catch up with them!

In fact, Protestants who have memorized hundreds of Bible verses, and people from any other kind of religious background — Jews, Muslims, or whatever — can just as easily delude themselves into thinking that they have saving belief in God simply because they have memorized all the doctrines and dogmas which their appointed leaders taught them when they were small children, and because they obey all the taboos of their religious group, know all the sacred rituals, and know how to sing and chant all the proper ceremonial hymns and prayers.

But we must remember that formal, outward religion, all by itself, will not save us. What saves us is the true inner religion of the heart.[569] Some modern A.A. people refer to the first as "religion" and the second as "spirituality." What matters in the distinction is that formal, outward religion — *when that is all that is there* — does nothing but carry out religious rituals and blindly obey religious taboos and argue about the words in the doctrines *without ever doing anything else.* As Dowling puts it, they live by the slogan that "I believe already, so I don't have to do anything."

But the true religion of the heart (real spirituality) involves the innermost levels of our hearts and souls, so that it automatically affects all our acts of will, which in turn means that it necessarily motivates us to take real, concrete actions in the outside world — actions that make a difference, as opposed to meaningless blather about rituals and taboos and abstract philosophical distinctions. For those who belong to a twelve step group, embracing some kind of real spirituality will necessarily move them to start working the steps and doing service work.

Dowling was just giving his version of a sermon on the passage in James 2:17 and 26 — "faith without works is dead" — a biblical passage that Roman Catholics had traditionally stressed much more strongly than many varieties of classical Protestantism.

What did Father Ed mean therefore by the kind of faith or belief or trust that would genuinely lead a person into a deeper understanding of God? When newcomers to A.A. first started going to A.A. meetings, those who had been sober for a while would tell them that the only thing which had gotten them sober was coming to realize that God was real, and that God had the power to get them sober, no matter how far down they had fallen. *Why not try believing what these people were saying, and trusting them just a little bit?* When newcomers first started coming to A.A. meetings, the old timers would continually tell them about things they did which seemed to help enormously in keeping them sober, and about other sorts of behavior which (in their experience) invariably ended up driving people who did them back to drink. Again, *why not try believing what these people were saying, and trusting them just a little bit?* As Father Dowling put it:

> Belief is capitalizing on the experience of others. Blessed are the lazy, for they shall find their short cuts. The world can now capitalize on the A.A. experience of two decades.

Newcomers to A.A. characteristically believe that they have no one to rely on but themselves. There is no other human being — no other power in the entire universe — who is going to help them. They have been abandoned by all. And then their minds get locked into repeating cycles of guilt, attempted rationalization, excuses, alibis, boasting and bravado — and there is no way for them to *break out* of this cycle from *within* the cycle. And they enclose themselves in a rigid shell where no outside information can get in, which means that as long as this shell remains intact, nothing can get through to divert them from their path to doom.

How then can they be saved? Dowling points to the act of faith as an action which breaks the individual out of this shell *by pointing that person's attention outside the self,* which in turn will allow the person to start breaking out of the self-perpetuating cycle which holds him or her prisoner:

> Newman says that the essence of belief is to look outside ourselves. Dr. Tiebout seems to think that, psychiatrically, the great problem is the turning of our affection away from self, outward. Faith is hard, as hard and as easy as sobriety, and has been called the greatest of our undeveloped resources.

Dr. Harry M. Tiebout (1896-1966) was the psychiatrist at Blythewood Sanitarium in Greenwich, Connecticut, who used a prepublication copy of the Big Book to get Mrs. Marty Mann started on the path to sobriety in 1939, and thenceforth became a strong supporter of A.A. in every way. He was one of the key speakers, along with Father Dowling, at the A.A. International Convention in St. Louis in 1955.[570] The famous Roman Catholic theologian John Henry Newman

(1801-1890), the other author to whom Father Ed referred, made this point in a sermon he gave back in the nineteenth century called "Saving Knowledge":

> The essence of Faith is to look out of ourselves; now, consider what manner of a believer he is who imprisons himself in his own thoughts, and rests on the workings of his own mind, and thinks of his Saviour as an idea of his imagination, instead of putting self aside, and living upon Him who speaks in the Gospels.[571]

CHAPTER 39

The 1955 A.A. International in St. Louis — Part III

PART III. GOD

Alcoholics Anonymous does not require its members to follow any particular religion's doctrine of God. Father Dowling quotes from a letter which Bill Wilson wrote to him stressing that point:

> What experience should we seek? What beliefs should we accept in our quest for God? ... Bill early wrote a letter — I have it — in which he said, "How far the alcoholic shall work out his dependence on God is none of A.A.'s business. Whether it is in a church or not in a church, whether it is in that church or this church, is none of A.A.'s business." In fact, he implied, "I don't think it's any of the members' business. It's God's business." And the A.A.'s business is charted in the Eleventh Step. Seek through meditation and prayer to find God's will and seek the power to follow it out.

Not much more than a year after Father Ed gave this talk, Bill Wilson went to California to visit Gerald Heard and Aldous Huxley. With their aid, Bill arranged to take LSD on August 29, 1956, and Father Ed subsequently tried the drug also.[572]

The LSD experiment was only a sideshow, however, compared to the real importance of Gerald Heard and Aldous Huxley. The latter had written a book in 1945 called *The Perennial Philosophy*, which

491

talked about a large number of great religious authors from all over the world who for over two thousand years, had been teaching the same fundamental idea of a Higher Power.[573]

Among the authors whom Huxley discussed were numerous Catholic figures: Meister Eckhart most of all, but also St. Thomas Aquinas, St. Augustine, St. Bernard of Clairvaux, St. Catherine of Siena, St. Francis de Sales, St. John of the Cross, and the author of the *Theologia Germanica.* He talked about far fewer Protestant authors, but did mention the Anglican spiritual writer William Law and the Quaker George Fox, and also one Jewish figure — the ancient Jewish philosopher and spiritual author Philo of Alexandria.

Huxley discussed the Sufi Muslim poet Jalal-uddin Rumi, the Hindu Vedanta philosopher Shankara, the Taoist philosophers Lao-Tzu and Chuang Tzu, and in addition, he also included numerous quotes from the Hindu scripture called the Bhagavad-Gita.

Bill Wilson said that A.A. members were allowed to try any of these various religious traditions, or any other religion which they chose, or no religion at all. And it is important to note that Father Ed Dowling heartily agreed with him.

But the place to begin looking for God is usually closest to home: Francis Thompson's poem "In No Strange Land." Father Ed, a man of great humility, began by identifying with his audience: "I believe the problem which half the people in this room have had in attaining sobriety I have had in attaining belief and faith." Or in other words, he was admitting that he had had struggles too — struggles which were in their own way as great as theirs — in his efforts to find God. But he had found that "there's something to be said about starting at the nearest manifestation of God," that is, at the point where God is nearest to me.

And in this context, he quoted from a poem "In No Strange Land" by a very interesting poet: Francis Thompson, an Englishman, who was born in 1859 and moved to London when he was around 26 years old. There Francis Thompson unfortunately became an opium addict, and ended up living on the streets at Charing Cross, which is located in the very center of London, immediately south of Nelson's Column and Trafalgar Square. He slept with the homeless and his fellow addicts by the River Thames, several blocks away. He died of tuberculosis in 1907, when he was only 47 years old.

In the poem, Francis Thompson points out that fish do not have to sprout wings and fly in order to find the ocean depths, and the eagle does not have to grow gills and dive down into the ocean to find the sky. Likewise, human beings who are trying to find God do not have to journey out into outer space, poking around among the stars and wheeling galaxies.

The pinions of the angels' wings beat on our own doors, where our mortal human clay unfortunately often shuts itself behind closed shutters, and refuses to look outside at "the many splendored thing" hovering just an arm's length away — like a fish trying to ignore the ocean in which it swims, or an eagle trying to ignore the air in which it flies. All we have to do is just open our eyes, wherever we are, and (as the poem goes on, in the part which Father Ed did not quote) even a poor addict like Francis Thompson, living on the streets in London, can in effect see Jacob's ladder[574] stretching from Charing Cross up to Heaven, with the holy angels climbing up and down, and God promising him that he will always stay with him and keep him and protect him. And a poor addict like Thompson, sleeping rough along the banks of the River Thames, does not have to journey all the way to Palestine, to the Sea of Galilee, to see Christ walking on the water. Christ can also walk on the River Thames and reach down and save one of the men in rags sleeping on its banks.

Father Ed made it clear to his audience that he had had to learn that lesson too. He had to learn how to quit looking fruitlessly for God in far away and exotic places, and start looking right at home, in the things that were closest to him.

Father Dowling's understanding of Christianity, which he sees as God's twelve steps toward the human race. This section of his talk is a little awkward and contrived in many ways, but it is nevertheless extremely important because of several little nuggets of information it gives us about Father Ed's own (often quite radical) religious beliefs. I'm going to leave this in Father Ed's own words, just putting the appropriate numbers in brackets to indicate which step he is interpreting at that point:

[1] The first step is described by St. John. The Incarnation. The word was God and the word became flesh and dwelt amongst us. He turned His life and His will over to the care of man as He understood him.

[2] The second step, nine months later, closer to us in the circumstances of it, is the birth, the Nativity.

[3] The third step, the next thirty years, the anonymous hidden life. Closer, because it is so much like our own.

[4] The fourth step, three years of public life.

[5] The fifth step, His teaching, His example, our Lord's Prayer.

[6] The sixth step, bodily suffering, including thirst, on Calvary.

[7] The next step, soul suffering in Gethsemane; that's coming close. How well the alcoholic knows, and how well He knew, humiliation and fear and loneliness and discouragement and futility.

[8] Finally death, another step closer to us, and I think the passage where a dying God rests in the lap of a human mother is as far down as divinity can come, and probably the greatest height that humanity can reach.

[9] Down the ages He comes closer to us as head of a sort of Christians Anonymous, a mystical body laced together by His teachings. "Whatsoever you do to the least of these my brethren so do you unto me." "I can fill up what is wanting in the sufferings of Christ." "I was in prison and you visited me." "I was sick and I was hungry and you gave me to eat."

[10] The next step is the Christian Church, which I believe is Christ here today. A great many sincere people say, "I like Christianity, but I don't like Churchianity." I can understand that. I understand it better than you do because I'm involved in Churchianity and it bothers me too! But, actually, I think that sounds a little bit like saying, "I do love good drinking water but I hate plumbing." Now, who does like plumbing? You have people who like sobriety, but they won't take A.A.

[11] And then, the eleventh step is several big pipe lines or sacraments of God's help.

[12] And the twelfth step, to me, is the great pipe line or sacrament of Communion. The word that was God became flesh and becomes our food, as close to us as the fruit juice and the toast and the coffee we had an hour ago.

The word "God" refers to the cosmic principle of Suffering Love. The God whom Father Ed teaches is not some cold, unfeeling tyrant who dwells in a palace located far above the universe and cares not a whit about the feelings of us human beings who live down below. We need to note his account of these steps in particular:

STEP 1. In true Christian teaching, as Father Ed understands it, God is a cosmic principle of Suffering Love who "emptied" (*ekenôsen*) himself and took the shape of a human being two thousand years ago, in the form of the Palestinian carpenter Jesus, so he could share our pain and fear with us *as one of us*. (This is called a kenotic Christology, from the use of the Greek word *ekenôsen* in this passage from Philippians 2:7.)

STEP 7. As Father Ed observes, when we read about Jesus praying in terror in the Garden of Gethsemane and begging to escape his oncoming death,[575] we realize that Jesus and the alcoholic both have known "humiliation and fear and loneliness and discouragement and futility." We are one with him and he is one with us.

STEP 8. In his commentary on this step, Dowling is referring to the famous scene which Michelangelo depicted, the marble sculpture called the Pietà, which stands in St. Peter's Basilica in Rome. It is a scene from right after Jesus's body was taken down from the cross. Mary is seated, with the body of Jesus lying on her lap, and her right arm holding up his head and shoulders. Father Ed says simply:

I think the passage where a dying God rests in the lap of a human mother is as far down as divinity can come, and probably the greatest height that humanity can reach.

If I may sum up in my own words what I think Father Dowling is saying in this extraordinarily powerful statement: in this piece of sculpture we see two things meeting and joining together:

God is humanized: the true Higher Power, the cosmic principle of Suffering Love, renounces the power it would have (we must suppose) to crush and kill and annihilate anything in the universe which got in its way. Instead it comes down and suffers and dies as a human being. This is truly Suffering Love.

Human beings are divinized: Mary, weeping over her son, clings to her continuing power to love, and turns away from the temptation to collapse into hatred, self-pity, and revenge. In this marble sculpture, Michelangelo portrays Mary rising up to the human heights of the power of Suffering Love.

STEP 9. Father Ed reminds us that all of us human beings have the power to divinize our own lives by reaching out to help and comfort anyone else who is suffering. The stained glass windows in the chapel at St. Thomas Hospital in Akron (the place where Sister Ignatia set up her A.A.-based alcoholism treatment program) portray the Seven Corporal Works of Mercy. Six of these come from Jesus's parable of the Sheep and the Goats (Matthew 25:34-46), which tells us precisely what we are going to be judged on at the Last Judgment. Jesus informs us that at the Last Judgment, he will grant eternal life to anyone who has done these six things, and that he will send into eternal punishment anyone who has not done these six things (the summary below is based on my own translation of the original New Testament Greek words):

1. We must give food *to anyone* who has no food to eat.
2. We must provide something to drink *to anyone* who is going thirsty.
3. We must make friends *with any person* who is a *xenos* (refugee, foreigner, immigrant, guest worker) in our country.
4. We must provide clothes *to anyone* who needs clothes to wear (and by extension, most real Christians believe) we must also provide a warm place to sleep and shelter from the weather, if we live in climates which are much colder (or otherwise more inhospitable) than the Palestine which Jesus lived in.

5. We must take care of *anyone* who is sick, which (again by extension in the modern world) includes providing them with doctors, hospitals and all other necessary medical care if they need these things (see Luke 10:33-35 in this regard).

6. We must "go to" *anyone* who is locked up in prison. In prisons in the ancient world, the inmates were sometimes given no food at all, and would starve to death if they had no friends or relatives to bring them something to eat. That was what "go to them" meant in Jesus's time. By extension, in the modern world, this duty includes making sure that all the jails and prisons provide adequate food and care (and personal safety) to the people who are locked up. And people in A.A. and N.A. who visit prisons to help set up and maintain twelve-step groups are fulfilling this duty in an especially meritorious way.

[7. The Roman Catholic Church eventually added an additional duty to this list to bring the number up to seven, that of burying the dead, taken from the Book of Tobit 1:17-19.]

It should be noted that at the Last Judgment, according to what Jesus said here, we are not going to be asked what doctrines and dogmas we believed in. Jesus furthermore said in his Sermon on the Mount (Matthew 7:21-23) that if we do not do these six things, it will not matter how much we recited his name over and over, and went around preaching about him to everyone else. Empty words and endless disputes over intellectual theories do not count in Jesus's book.

Father Dowling himself spent his whole career as a priest contemplating a crucifix every morning and reminding himself of the dying God of Michelangelo's Pietà, then devoting the rest of that day to seeking out people who needed help, and doing concrete things to help and comfort them.

STEPS 11 AND 12. THE SACRAMENTAL VIEW OF THE UNIVERSE. It is here at the end of the list that we encounter the truly radical part of Father Dowling's theology. In the Roman Catholic Church, in a formal sacrament — e.g. baptism with water, receiving bread and wine at the mass, or anointing of the sick with oil — God uses a physical medium to communicate his grace and his presence to the human being receiving the sacrament. The physical medium serves as *a pipeline*, Father Dowling says — I love that analogy — it is like a pipeline which can carry water, or an electrical cable which can carry electricity to whatever it is connected to, in order to make that thing do its work.

But in the Roman Church (and in the broader Catholic tradition in general, including Lutherans, Anglicans, and Methodists) it is believed that God, whenever he wishes, can use anything in the physical world to communicate his grace and presence to us. This is what is meant by "the sacramental view of the universe." We can encounter God's glory shining out in a tiny brook flowing over tumbled rocks, in the reds and purples of a vivid sunset, in the mist-shrouded hills overlooking the place where we live, in the exuberance of a small child frolicking in a play area, in the sound of the birds singing, in the aroma of a flower-covered vine, and in the taste of a peach or apple which I have just plucked off the tree.

Two thousand years ago, the true Higher Power, the cosmic principle of Suffering Love, wished to speak the word of compassion (and, where necessary, forgiveness) to human beings, so the Word of God took the human flesh and blood and soul of Jesus and used him as a pipeline (an electrical cable, a sacramental conduit) for transmitting that love and grace to us. In the Roman Catholic Church (which is a sacramental physical medium in itself), we see how the Word of God can in addition use the communion bread (a material substance) to feed the human soul (a spiritual thing) with the living presence and grace of the immaterial God.

Now comes the radical part of Father Ed's message, smuggled in almost as an aside at the very end of this section. In the Roman Catholic Church, he says, "the word that was God became flesh and becomes our food" whenever the mass is celebrated, at which time — the sacred high point of the Roman mass — *God comes "as close to us as the fruit juice and the toast and the coffee we had an hour ago" at this A.A. meeting.*

In 1955 in St. Louis, people could see a group of drunks who had assembled to form what was in fact a sacramental community, because A.A. was a powerful new pipeline devised for conducting the grace and power and living presence of God to suffering human beings. Alcoholics Anonymous was as real as the Roman Catholic Church — very different indeed, but just as concrete and real — and the sacramental grace it imparted also in its own way conveyed "the true body and blood" as it were, the true presence of God.

In traditional Catholic theology (if I might sum it up in my own words, not Father Dowling's) the formal sacraments of the Catholic Church convey three great divine gifts upon those who participate:

(1) forgiveness and absolution (and opportunity for confession if necessary),
(2) the real presence of God and his grace (which gives us the power to start actually behaving as we know we ought), and
(3) fellowship and communion with the God-bearers (the true people of God, both here on earth and in the eternal world, who have carried the message to us, comfort us and steady us, pray for us and with us, and provide us with the example of their own lives).

But Alcoholics Anonymous does the same three things. It furnishes sacramental pipelines connecting the world up above with the world down here below. When we attend A.A. meetings, we discover that the group and its members supply us with the same three kinds of sacramental powers, and the proof of it is that our lives start to be transformed positively in truly dramatic ways.

Where can we go to find God? Quit fooling around, and go to an A.A. meeting! God attends them too.

Looking for God right at home: Francis Thompson's poem "The Hound of Heaven." Father Dowling finished his talk by quoting at length from a second poem by Francis Thompson (1859-1907). Dowling took pains to note that Thompson had been helplessly addicted to opium, so that his poem reflected what were basically the same kind of feelings of fear and despair that alcoholics experienced:

The picture of the A.A.'s quest for God, but especially God's loving chase for the A.A., was never put more beautifully than in what I think is one of the greatest lyrics and odes in the English language. It was written by a narcotic addict, and alcohol is a narcotic. It's a poem by Francis Thompson called "The Hound of Heaven."

Alcoholics often come into A.A. explaining how they have spent countless years fruitlessly searching for a God who has always hidden from them and escaped them. They have tried so hard, they say, to find a God whom they could believe in, but they are so much more intelligent than most people, that they can only rebel in skepticism, doubt, agnosticism, and total rejection of the kind of things that A.A. people tell them. And this is the reason they cannot work the steps, they explain — they are simply atheists, they say, who cannot honestly accept the idea of God. First show us, they tell us, where we can find God, and prove his existence to us, and then we will begin seriously working the steps. But until you can show us how to chase God down and grasp him, you surely could not expect us to be dishonest, they protest, or to be hypocrites.

Father Ed probably remembered a famous Catholic prayer here. It came from a story which St. Augustine included in his *Confessions* (the autobiography he wrote in 397-398 A.D., eleven or twelve years after his conversion to Christianity). Augustine had been a great womanizer, who spent a good deal of his time going around starting up affairs with women and attempting to seduce them. He eventually came to acknowledge that his behavior was very disturbed and destructive — if for no other reason than that it was going to prevent him from entering into a very good marriage which his mother had arranged for him — but he confessed that for a long time, his prayers to God were basically of the form "God, give me chastity, but not yet!"

Father Ed told the audience of alcoholics that what he often seemed to hear them actually praying were evasive prayers like St. Augustine's prayer for chastity: "Lord, give me sobriety, but not yet!" "Lord, let me make that step, but not yet!"

So the first thing that Father Ed said to newcomers to A.A. who refused to work the steps because they said that they were agnostics and had *honest* doubts ("*genuinely* honest doubts" they protested) about whether God existed, was to ask them *whether they were really in fact being honest at all.* In order to get alcoholics sober, one first had to break through their alibi system. Was it really the case that they were refusing to work the steps because they doubted God's existence? Or was this just another version of St. Augustine's famous chastity prayer: "Lord, give me sobriety, but not yet!" That is, was their behavior in fact just a con game,[576] a way of wasting days, weeks, and months playing intellectual games with words and definitions, pretending to be all serious and sincere, where the real payoff was that it enabled them to keep putting off and delaying having to actually start working the program?

The long quotations from Francis Thompson's poem "The Hound of Heaven" pushes this argument one stage further. Is it really true that these self-proclaimed agnostics and atheists have spent their whole lives running everywhere trying to find God? That is what so many of them claim. But is it not *the real truth* that the pursuit has always been the other way around?

When God has important messages for us, one of the main means he uses for communicating with us, is via the ebb and flow of our own deepest feelings, emotions, and desires. That principle lies at the heart of St. Ignatius Loyola's *Spiritual Exercises* and is one of the foundation stones of Jesuit spirituality.

Perhaps I went around constantly claiming that I was on a great spiritual quest, searching for God everywhere — reading books on science and philosophy, investigating all sorts of exotic religions from other parts of the globe, and on and on. But wasn't the real truth exactly the opposite? Wasn't the truth in fact that I had spent my whole life running away from God as hard as I could?

> I fled Him down the nights and down the days;
> I fled Him down the arches of the years;
> I fled Him down the labyrinthine ways
> Of my own mind ....

What emotion was I really feeling down in my heart at the end of the day? The desperate yearning of a lover for the beloved who is late coming home? — because that is what the saints feel. Or was the emotion not instead the fear of someone fleeing from a pursuing bloodhound? Because the truth is that I could almost hear the padding feet of the divine bloodhound relentlessly coming after me, with "unhurrying chase and unperturbed pace, deliberate speed, majestic instancy."

What emotions was I actually feeling in my heart? Perhaps it was that everyone around me had betrayed me — parents, spouse, friends, employers — with me being left alone as the helpless victim of their betrayal. But the Hound of Heaven not only has feet that pad after me relentlessly, but also a Voice that repeats over and over to me the real message that is being conveyed by the emotions I am feeling. It is a warning straight from God, short and simple:

"All things betray thee, who betrayest Me."

Perhaps the emotion I am feeling is that I can find no one anywhere who will shelter me and protect me and love me. But the true divine message contained in that emotion is also a short and simple warning from the Voice of the Hound of Heaven:

"Naught shelters thee, who wilt not shelter Me."

When alcoholics, on the other hand, begin working the steps and changing the way they behave, they discover that people stop betraying them and victimizing them so much, and that they start finding people who will do their best to love them and protect them.

When people reject God, they always eventually end up finding that nothing else in life makes them happy either. Down in their hearts, they feel nothing but boredom perhaps, or a sense of meaninglessness, or constant irritation at all the things around them that annoy them. But again, what is the Heavenly Voice really saying to them via those emotions? The words are a bit more pointed and critical this time:

"Lo, naught contents thee, who content'st not Me."

And then, coming through all these terrible, unbearably painful emotions roiling around inside me, I hear the Voice of the Hound of

Heaven, and this time, it may be an actual voice, speaking these very words inside my mind. *Why should any other human being love someone like me?* It may well be that I have fallen so low, that there is no longer anything at all lovable about me — or at least not to another ordinary human being who has been given no special gift of God's grace. And I may pretend that this is just my own disturbed human thought, but in fact, these words may well be the words of God, telling me that I in fact have nothing in me to merit the love of my fellow human beings (unless they are extraordinary saints).

But then the Voice goes on — if I can build up the courage to keep on listening, instead of trying to shut it off with alcohol or opium or some other numbing drug — and the Voice informs me that there is only one person left in the universe who still loves me:

"[For] human love needs human meriting:
   How has thou merited —
Of all man's clotted clay the dingiest clot?
   Alack, thou knowest not
How little worthy of any love thou art!
Whom wilt thou find to love ignoble thee
   Save Me, save only Me?"

The Catholic Church and the A.A. program both tell fallen souls that some of the critical voices inside their heads (along with the unbearably painful emotions which accompany them, i.e. the feelings of guilt, failure, victimization, abandonment, lovelessness, and despair) *are speaking the truth*. In the twelve step program, we use the fourth and eighth steps to sort out how much of this we must in fact become responsible for.

But I am misreading the real divine message contained in my emotion of total despair, if I fail to move beyond that point and hear ALL of the divine message. Yes, I am helpless and powerless — *"But there is One who has all power — that One is God."*

The minute I really understand where all these negative emotions are coming from and the nature of the real message contained in them, I will realize that I do not have to continue searching for God any longer. I did not find him, he found me, and finally got through to me. So when I get up in the morning, I can pray at last, perhaps praying something as follows, if that is what I wish:

> You who have forced me to look at who I really am, please
> keep me sober today.

And if I have started to really take Father Ed Dowling's message to heart, I could even add something to it like the following little additional prayer:

> O cosmic power of Suffering Love,
> who comes willingly to share in my sufferings,
> teach me to love others the same way.

CHAPTER 40

Bill Wilson and
Father Dowling Take LSD: 1956

Two Englishmen — Gerald Heard and Aldous Huxley — came over to the United States together in 1937, and eventually ended up in the Los Angeles area, where they became deeply involved with Swami Prabhavananda and the group he had founded there, the Vedanta Society of Southern California, which taught a Vedanta Hindu form of Indian religious philosophy.

In 1942, Gerald Heard founded Trabuco College in Trabuco Canyon in the Santa Ana Mountains, forty miles southeast of Los Angeles, to teach these ideas.[577] (In 1949 the college was turned into a Vedanta religious center called Ramakrishna Monastery, which still exists today.) At the same time that Gerald Heard was settling himself there in Trabuco Canyon, his friend Aldous Huxley began renovating a farmhouse at Llano del Rio, forty miles northeast of Los Angeles, on the edge of the Mojave Desert.

In January 1944, Bill W. and Gerald Heard met for the first time, at Trabuco, and began "a personal friendship and collaboration that would continue over the next two decades."[578] In all, Bill made three visits to Trabuco College between 1944 and 1947.

Tom Powers often spoke of Heard as one of Bill Wilson's sponsors.[579] So by this point in A.A. history, Bill was in fact making use of two co-sponsors or spiritual directors to help him in his explorations of the higher spiritual life, one of them (Father Ed Dowling) a Roman Catholic priest, and the other (Gerald Heard) a philosopher who was deeply involved in Vedanta Hindu spirituality.

It was Heard who introduced Bill Wilson to Aldous Huxley. In 1945, Huxley published a book called *The Perennial Philosophy*,[580] where he argued that the great authors of the western Catholic monastic tradition and the great teachers of the religions of Asia had all been talking about the same basic thing. Our minds are normally locked inside a box of space and time, where we cannot be conscious of anything that is not mediated by our five physical senses and defined by conventional human words and concepts. But by cultivating the proper kinds of meditational and spiritual practices, we can learn how to break down the walls of this confining box and experience the transcendent spiritual realities which lie outside it.

Aldous Huxley's first time taking mescaline in 1953. With this as a background — extensive knowledge of the past two thousand years of the most advanced forms of religious experience in both Europe and Asia — on May 5, 1953, Huxley took some mescaline (the active ingredient in peyote cactus buds) provided to him by a Canadian psychiatrist named Humphry Osmond, and in 1954 he published a book called *The Doors of Perception* talking about the psychedelic experiences which mescaline produced.[581] The first effects which he noticed did not seem to him to be all that impressive:

> The change which actually took place in that world was in no sense revolutionary. Half an hour after swallowing the drug I became aware of a slow dance of golden lights. A little later there were sumptuous red surfaces swelling and expanding from bright nodes of energy that vibrated with a continuously changing, patterned life. At another time the closing of my eyes revealed a complex of gray structures, within which pale bluish spheres kept emerging into intense solidity and, having emerged, would slide noiselessly upwards, out of sight. But at no time were there faces or forms of men or animals. I saw no landscapes, no enormous spaces, no magical growth and metamorphosis of buildings, nothing remotely like a drama or a parable.

But Huxley eventually began to notice that — for him at least — the noteworthy effect of the drug did not lie in producing strange visions and hallucinations of things that were not there, but in the way it changed his perception of all the everyday objects in the physical world around him. He looked over at a small glass vase containing three flowers: a pink rose, a magenta and cream-colored carnation, and a purple iris. It was not what most people would have regarded as an attractive color combination.

> At breakfast that morning I had been struck by the lively dissonance of its colors. But that was no longer the point. I was not looking now at an unusual flower arrangement. I was seeing what Adam had seen on the morning of his creation — the miracle, moment by moment, of naked existence.

He believed that he was in some way actually seeing what Plato in the fourth century B.C. called the "Being" of the flowers, except that the ancient Greek philosopher had turned that idea into something hopelessly abstract, Huxley complained, and had failed to understand what the Being of a thing really was.

> Plato .... could never, poor fellow, have seen a bunch of flowers shining with their own inner light and all but quivering under the pressure of the significance with which they were charged; could never have perceived that what rose and iris and carnation so intensely signified was nothing more, and nothing less, than what they were — a transience that was yet eternal life ... pure Being, a bundle of minute, unique particulars in which ... was to be seen the divine source of all existence.

What he had encountered, Huxley said, could also be described as what Vedanta Hinduism called Brahman or *Sat-cit-ananda*, "Being-Awareness-Bliss," the experience of the boundless pure consciousness which is a glimpse of ultimate reality.

In Buddhism this was referred to as "the Dharma-Body of the Buddha," which "is another way of saying Mind, Suchness, the Void, the Godhead." In a Buddhist monastery, Huxley said, a novice once asked the Zen master, "What is the Dharma-Body of the Buddha?" and (so the traditional story goes) the master answered, "The hedge at the bottom of the garden."

Huxley admitted that he had always, up to this point, regarded that little Zen Buddhist story as more of a Marx Brothers comedy routine than serious religious philosophy. But now he suddenly realized, he said, that it was absolute truth:

> Of course the Dharma-Body of the Buddha was the hedge at the bottom of the garden. At the same time, and no less obviously, it was these flowers, it was anything that I — or rather the blessed Not-I, released for a moment from my throttling embrace — cared to look at. The books, for example, with which my study walls were lined. Like the flowers, they glowed, when I looked at them, with brighter colors, a profounder significance. Red books, like rubies; emerald books; books bound in white jade; books of agate; of aquamarine, of yellow topaz; lapis lazuli books whose color was so intense, so intrinsically meaningful, that they seemed to be on the point of leaving the shelves to thrust themselves more insistently on my attention.

If I might attempt to explain this in simpler terms: in the Big Book, Bill W. described us as living in a sort of two-story universe. Our minds are held captive most of the time down at the lower level, locked inside a box of three-dimensional Euclidean space, where we move step by step through chronological time. But in rare moments, Bill W. said, our minds find themselves standing outside the box, as it were, and becoming aware of "a fourth dimension of existence."[582] This additional dimension is the divine world, the eternal world, the realm in which God dwells. In the modern world, we can see in reports of out-of-body near-death experiences, that people whose souls move over into that heavenly realm commonly report seeing the same kind of bright light that Bill Wilson said that he saw in his extraordinary experience at Towns Hospital on December 14, 1934.

> As a side note: And as Jonathan Edwards had warned two centuries earlier, when we step outside the box of ordinary

space and time, we may speak of this as an experience in which we seem to see visible light shining forth, or the colors of ordinary things made brighter and more vivid, but this is merely the mind trying to make sense of something far greater.[583] It is certainly clear from Aldous Huxley's description that he realizes this, and is struggling with the same limitations imposed by human language which Edwards had encountered.

The crucial aspect of these experiences is that we somehow know that we are in contact with something far higher and grander than any earthly material reality. We know with an absolute certainty that this higher dimension contains the core of the divine and "the really real," compared to which everything else is temporary, partial, clouded, distorted, and illusory. And no matter how hard we try, we find that we cannot truly describe the most important part of this experience in any kind of physical terms, or fit it into a system of mathematical or philosophical logic.

So let us not become overly concerned about Huxley's report of vivid colors glowing with an inner light — if this sort of thing is the part of the psychedelic experience you are trying to reproduce and concentrate on, then you are totally missing what Huxley was really trying to point you towards, and you will turn it into a circus sideshow. That was in fact what began to happen later on in the 1960's — people taking psychedelic drugs just for amusement or as an unhealthy escapism. *What is important about Huxley's experience is the overwhelming awareness of standing before the Ultimate.*

The brain and nervous system as a "reducing valve." Huxley developed a theory about the core part of the psychedelic experience. He believed that human beings could in principle come into conscious contact with higher reality at any time or place, but that we ordinarily set up mental shields and blocks and rigid conceptual frameworks which kept most of that higher world from crossing over into our conscious awareness.

Huxley said that, as he reflected on his mescaline experience afterward, he began to consider that perhaps the Cambridge University philosopher C. D. Broad was right, and that the true center of human consciousness is far greater in capacity than most of us have ever imagined:

> "Each person is at each moment capable of remembering all that has ever happened to him and of perceiving everything that is happening everywhere in the universe. The function of the brain and nervous system is to protect us from being overwhelmed and confused by this mass of largely useless and irrelevant knowledge, by shutting out most of what we should otherwise perceive or remember at any moment and leaving only that very small and special selection which is likely to be practically useful."

The true center of consciousness in each of us is what Huxley calls "Mind at Large," but if we actually began to use this capacity to become conscious of literally everything we could potentially perceive, we would be so overwhelmed with information that we could not survive on the face of this planet. So the brain and nervous system normally acts as a "reducing valve" to decrease the pressure and quantity of information coming into the brain to manageable proportions, somewhat analogous to the reducing valves that are used to take high pressure water from a public water system and lower it to a far more moderate pressure for a house's interior plumbing.

> To make biological survival possible, Mind at Large has to be tunneled through the reducing valve of the brain and nervous system. What comes out at the other end is a measly trickle of the kind of consciousness which will help us to stay alive on the surface of this Particular planet.

It is the straightjacket of human language and conventional concepts, Huxley says, which sets up the shields preventing the larger reality from breaking in on us. It is human language which most of all creates the lower world that holds us captive by telling us that nothing can be real unless there is already a word for it, and a preexisting conceptual theory which allows it to exist.

That which, in the language of religion, is called "this world" is the universe of reduced awareness, expressed, and, as it were, petrified by language.

And yet Huxley denies that psychedelic drugs can all by themselves lead us to the ultimate goal of spirituality. At the end of *The Doors of Perception*, Huxley pulls back from claiming that taking psychedelic drugs can create ultimate enlightenment, and lead us into the final heavenly courts, or nirvana, or whatever we wish to call it:

> I am not so foolish as to equate what happens under the influence of mescalin or of any other drug, prepared or in the future preparable, with the realization of the end and ultimate purpose of human life: Enlightenment, the Beatific Vision. All I am suggesting is that the mescalin experience is what Catholic theologians call "a gratuitous grace," not necessary to salvation but potentially helpful and to be accepted thankfully, if made available. To be shaken out of the ruts of ordinary perception, to be shown for a few timeless hours the outer and the inner world, not as they appear to an animal obsessed with survival or to a human being obsessed with words and notions, but as they are apprehended, directly and unconditionally, by Mind at Large — this is an experience of inestimable value to everyone ....

So Huxley, at the point when he was writing *The Doors of Perception*, believed that taking psychedelic drugs could be helpful at some points in our spiritual growth, but could not take us all the way.

Bill W. takes LSD on August 29, 1956. Only a little over a year after the A.A. International Convention in St. Louis, Bill Wilson went to California to visit Gerald Heard and Aldous Huxley. They had access now to another psychedelic drug, lysergic acid diethylamide, often referred to simply as "LSD" or "acid." On August 29, 1956, Bill took LSD for the first time.[584] When Don Lattin (as part of the research for his book on the psychedelic drug culture of the 1960's) attempted to find out more about this, he found that:

Shortly after that acid trip, Huston Smith [the great scholar of comparative religions] accompanied Heard on a trip to Kansas City and spent two hours in a hotel room listening to Wilson and Heard talk about the acid trip. Wilson was blown away by the drug and said the experience was a dead ringer for the famous night in the 1930s when he fell down on his knees and had an epiphany about founding his twelve-step program.[585]

Bill wanted to check his impressions, however, against those of someone who knew the traditional Catholic monastic spiritual tradition, and had also himself clearly had genuine spiritual experiences of a higher spiritual order without any use of drugs. So he got Father Ed Dowling to observe an LSD session, and reported to Sam Shoemaker afterwards that "the result was a most magnificent, positive spiritual experience. Father Ed declared himself utterly convinced of its validity, and volunteered to take LSD himself."[586]

It is important to note that these people were not rebel youth, but men already getting along in years: in August 1956, Father Dowling was almost 58 years old, Bill Wilson was 60, Aldous Huxley was 62, and Gerald Heard was 66.

Wilson reported to Heard at the end of 1956 about the arrangement that was made for Father Dowling to take LSD. As Don Lattin described this in his book *Distilled Spirits*:

Wilson became so intrigued by the spiritual potential of LSD that he formed an experimental group in New York that included Father Ed Dowling, a Catholic priest, and Eugene Exman, the religion editor at Harper and Brothers. The "friend" of Powers that Wilson mentioned in his letter [to Heard on December 4, 1956] may have been a psychiatrist from Roosevelt Hospital in New York, who served as the supervising physician at Bill Wilson's psychedelic salon.[587]

Father John Courtney Murray, S.J. takes LSD. Aldous Huxley also gave LSD to the Jesuit theologian John Courtney Murray, S.J. (1904-1967), a prominent figure from the radical wing of the Jesuit order.[588]

Murray was editor of the Jesuit journal *Theological Studies* and taught at the Jesuit theologate in Woodstock, Maryland, and was, like Cardinal Jean Daniélou, S.J., one of the formative influences on the declarations of the Second Vatican Council. Murray and Dowling would have shared many basic political principles, since Murray was someone who was devoted to bringing real democracy into both government and the church. Murray and Reinhold Niebuhr were considered the two most influential American theologians at that time, in the area of the application of Christian ethics to politics.

Letter from Aldous Huxley to Father Thomas Merton. And there were other Roman Catholic theologians in the later 1950's who either took LSD or were in correspondence with those who were using it. On January 10, 1959, for example, Aldous Huxley wrote to Father Thomas Merton at the Trappist Abbey of Gethsemani. This quiet and peaceful monastery was located in the rolling hills of the Kentucky Bluegrass region, a short drive south of Louisville. (Father Ralph Pfau held an annual A.A. spiritual retreat at the Abbey.) Merton, who became world famous after the publication in 1948 of his autobiography, *The Seven Storey Mountain*, was one of the best-known Roman Catholic writers on spirituality and social justice at that time. Merton had begun combining ideas drawn from the medieval Catholic tradition of mystic theology with some new ideas he was picking up from Zen Buddhism — the reason why he and Huxley were interested in one another's work. The important part of this letter lies in Huxley's comments about "a friend of mine," who was clearly Bill Wilson:[589]

> A friend of mine, saved from alcoholism, during the last fatal phases of the disease, by a spontaneous theophany, which changed his life as completely as St. Paul's was changed on the road to Damascus, has taken lysergic acid two or three times and affirms that his experience under the drug is identical with the spontaneous experience which changed his life—the only difference being that the spontaneous experience did not last so long as the chemically induced one. There is, obviously, a field here for serious and reverent experimentation.

Bill Wilson's reports on his LSD experiences were quite positive throughout 1956 and 1957: So for example, Bill wrote to Gerald Heard in September 1956 (almost immediately after he had taken LSD for the first time, which was on August 29) and said, "I do feel a residue of assurance and a feeling of enhanced beauty that seems likely to stay by me."[590] On December 4, 1956, Bill W. wrote Heard again and gave an even more positive assessment of the long term effects the LSD seemed to have had on him: "More and more it appears to me that the experience has done a sustained good."

> My reactions to things totally, and in particular, have very definitely improved for no other reason that I can see. Tom [Powers] says he has been thinking about the possibility of visiting you soon again with a friend with the idea of trying this out some more.[591]

In a 1957 letter to Heard, Bill Wilson continued to note what he regarded as the enduring positive effect which taking the LSD had left on his soul. The vivid colors and the powerful beauty of the world of nature still seemed to meet him everywhere he looked. And the physical world still seemed almost *transparent* as it were. The boundary separating this material world from the transcendent eternal world remained so thin that it felt as though he could look right through it and apprehend the divine realm shining in all its splendor.

> I am certain that the LSD experience has helped me very much. I find myself with a heightened color perception and an appreciation of beauty almost destroyed by my years of depression. . . . The sensation that the partition between 'here' and 'there' has become very thin is constantly with me.[592]

But by the end of 1958, Bill Wilson was becoming much more guarded about the potential benefits of alcoholics taking LSD. On December 29, 1958 Wilson wrote to Father Ed Dowling:

> On the psychic front the LSD business goes on apace. . . . I don't
> believe that it has any miraculous property of transforming
> spiritually and emotionally sick people into healthy ones
> overnight. It can set up a shining goal on the positive side. . . .
> After all, it is only a temporary ego-reducer. . . . But the vision
> and insights given by LSD could create a large incentive—at
> least in a considerable number of people.[593]

And by October 26, 1959, Bill Wilson was admitting to Father
Ed that the controversy within Alcoholics Anonymous over his use of
LSD had "created some commotion." Bill attempted to joke about it:
"It must be confessed that these recent heresies of mine do have their
comic aspects." A.A. people were saying that "Bill takes one pill to see
God and another to quiet his nerves."[594] It was definitely causing real
trouble within the fellowship.

***And by November 1959, Father Dowling was clearly becoming
very negative toward the use of LSD.*** Three years had now passed
since Bill Wilson and Father Ed had taken LSD for the first time, many
more people in A.A. circles had also taken the drug, and there were now
sufficient people who had taken it a number of times, to start making
some tentative judgments about what happened with long term use.
Our main source here is a letter which Bill Wilson wrote to Father Ed
on November 23, 1959, but in reading what Bill is saying, we can come
up with some pretty good ideas about what Father Ed was saying:[595]

> Please be sure that I am very glad that you set out your
> apprehension about the LSD business. I should have
> mentioned that two members of our LSD group — have
> come to share your concern. G. had quite a negative reaction
> the second time he tried the material. He saw devils and had
> a deep sense of malignancy. With only one exception, this
> is the only case I have ever heard of where there was such
> a development. Under LSD a delinquent kid, a real bad
> boy, had a similar experience. Whether such views are to be
> construed as helpful or damaging is hard to say. If the LSD
> business is actually invested with malignancy, I would think
> it likely to be more subtle than this.

The group which you saw in operation was disbanded early this year, partly because the extension of it would have led to a lot of controversy, partly because there was little or no urge on the part of its members to return to the experience, having once had it, and partly because T and G didn't care to go on.

Since this last group experience ... I have early in this year, tried out the material again. These later results were far less of emotional intensity. They varied from the sensations of being at a retreat, to a day of sunny satisfaction at the shore, or to the joys of picnics in fine mountain scenery. Therefore there seems to be a tendency for the emotional content to subside. This had become true when I entered the experience of September 20th. Even this one didn't compare with the great cataclysm, resembling my earlier experience, which took place on the Coast when I first took the material.

Two people had had bad trips — always a possibility with LSD — and others (including Bill) were finding that the initial huge thrill of the experience wore off with repeated usage. Bill Wilson seems to have basically stopped using LSD there in 1959, although there are some A.A. historians who think that it is possible that his use of the drug continued over into the early 1960's.[596]

But once into the 1960's, Bill Wilson seems to have fairly quickly moved on to other interests: in particular, in December 1966, he began a passionate campaign for the use of vitamin B3 (niacin) to treat depression, schizophrenia, and alcoholism.

The experience of God. At one level, there was never a clear resolution to the question of whether taking LSD could in some circumstances put people into authentic contact with the higher dimension of reality — were the experiences which some people were reporting under the influence of the drug anything real at all, or were all the strange things they believed they were encountering just chemically induced illusions? And it was certainly true that no firm conclusions were reached as to whether using psychedelic drugs was *a safe or wise way* to produce the experience of the Godhead. On this score, by the end of 1959, Father Dowling had undoubtedly developed great apprehensions about doing any further work with LSD, and was doing his best to discourage Bill Wilson from any more involvement with it.

But we also have to ask why Father Dowling and Bill Wilson ever got involved with LSD in the first place. And here, the important thing to note is that both of them continued to put their highest priority on trying to help men and women gain *a real firsthand experience of God*. It was the power of God that rescued people from alcoholism, drug addiction, gambling obsessions, eating disorders, sexual addictions, the effects of living with alcoholic family members, and so on. Father Ed and Bill W. were two brave men who were simply attempting to serve God, holding nothing back and going wherever the journey seemed to lead.

CHAPTER 41

Father Dowling's Last Years: 1957-1960

DECLINING HEALTH

Father Dowling was a compulsive overeater, and eventually got up to 240 pounds — very overweight — and spent years eating too much starch, butter, salt and sugar. He eventually was made to realize the danger to his health, and finally managed to lose 60 pounds by using strategies he learned from the twelve step program, but not before permanent damage had been done to his heart and arteries.[597]

JUNE 1952: We remember that as a first sign of his developing health problems, in mid-June 1952, Father Ed had a retinal stroke (a blood clot blocking an artery in his retina) and ended up in the hospital unable to read.[598] If the blood clot had traveled the other way at the fork in his carotid artery, it would have lodged in his brain instead and could have either killed him or left him even more gravely crippled.

AUGUST 1957: He had managed to take off twenty-five pounds (see his August 9, 1957 letter to Sister Ignatia below) so he was clearly deeply involved in trying to deal with his dangerous weight problem by that point.

MAY 1958: But solving all his health problems was not going to be that simple. In a letter he wrote to Bill Wilson in May 1958, Father Ed mentioned having had two small strokes at some point prior to that.[599] This time, we might assume, some of the debris lining his arteries had traveled to his brain instead of his eye.

AUGUST 1958: Around the beginning of August 1958, a month before his sixtieth birthday, Father Ed had a heart attack, but was soon doing his best to be up and about once more.[600]

DECEMBER 1958: Nevertheless, a little over three months later, Father Ed was hospitalized for eight days, and afterwards had to carry a portable oxygen tank around with him when he went to New York to celebrate Bill Wilson's twenty-fourth sobriety anniversary in mid-December.[601]

DECEMBER 1959: A year later, Father Ed (now 61 years old) wrote and said he had been put "in the hospital for nine days because a 'conservative doctor' said he had 'over extended.'"[602] We can see Father Ed trying his best to minimize how bad a shape he was in physically.

MARCH 1960: Anna Dowling wrote to the Coordinator of the 1960 A.A. International Convention in Long Beach, California on March 17, 1960 and said "that her brother was in the hospital but would be in his office soon and would like to know how long his talk should be." Anna was informed that Father Ed had been put on the convention schedule for a thirty minute talk.[603] But his health had declined too far, and he never made it to the Long Beach International Convention on July 1-3, 1960.

APRIL 3, 1960: In fact, it was only a little over two weeks later that Father Ed — out on the road and traveling once more, and still attempting to carry the message — died in his sleep of a heart attack in Memphis, Tennessee.[604] He was only 61½ years old.

OCCASIONAL CORRESPONDENCE

This first letter was written in 1957, probably before Father Dowling suffered the two small strokes which he mentioned in the letter he wrote to Bill Wilson on May 8, 1958 (which we referred to a few paragraphs back).

Father Ed was clearly on close and friendly terms with Sister Ignatia Gavin: this is a letter between two good friends who could talk to one another freely and share their personal feelings. As we can see, Sister Ignatia was no longer working at St. Thomas Hospital in Akron — she had been moved by her order in 1952 to St. Vincent Charity Hospital in Cleveland, Ohio, to set up an alcoholism treatment ward there.

Sackville O'C. Millens was a famous Irish A.A. leader. He joined A.A. and got sober in Dublin, Ireland in 1947, five months after Conor

Flynn had started the first A.A. meeting in Ireland. Sackville's story, "The Career Officer," appeared in the 2nd and 3rd editions of the A.A. Big Book.

It is important to note the close relationship which developed early on between Father Dowling, Sister Ignatia Gavin, and Sackville — three major leaders who realized the importance of establishing a good working relationship between A.A. and the Roman Catholic Church. Sackville in particular recognized from the time he joined A.A. that the movement was going to have to win the support of the Catholic Church if it was ever going to become established in southern Ireland.

And they were eventually notably successful. There is a famous photograph showing Sackville (standing side by side with Travers, an important early English A.A. leader from Bristol) meeting in 1972 with Pope Paul VI, who blessed Alcoholics Anonymous as Sackville and Travers stood there clasping the pope's hands.

There was a lot at stake here, and Father Dowling was determined to help in every way that he could. I also think it is of enormous importance to see here that neither Dowling nor Gavin were alcoholics — it was two non-alcoholics, a priest and a nun, who played key roles in bringing Alcoholics Anonymous into the Catholic Church's set of spiritual tools.

It is also interesting to note that Father Ed, as an Irish Catholic on a pilgrimage at the end of his life, knowing that he would probably never be healthy enough to make such a journey again, traveled to Ireland *first* and then to Rome! And could any true Irishman fault him for understanding his priorities in this fashion?

And finally, in line with this, it should be observed that although Father Dowling and Sister Ignatia Gavin (and Father Ralph Pfau as well) had no objection to working with Protestant and other non-Roman Catholic alcoholics, there was no weakening in their own Roman Catholic faith, and both Dowling and Gavin were still hoping strongly that they could bring Bill Wilson into the Roman Church. Both of them cared for Bill, and seemed clearly to feel that it would be better for Bill's soul to join the Roman faith.

The August 9, 1957 letter reads as follows: [605]

The Sodality of Our Lady
The Queen's Work
3115 South Grand Boulevard
Saint Louis 18, Missouri

August 9, 1957

Sister M. Ignatia, C. S. A.
St. Vincent Charity Hospital
2222 Central Avenue
Cleveland, 15, Ohio

Dear Sister Ignatia:

I have taken off twenty-five pounds and will sail for Rome via Ireland on September 4th, on the Queen Mary.

I know Jane Murray quite well and have talked to her husband over the phone. Very worthwhile saving. She is an attractive but difficult person, has dallied with A.A. a bit. While I was in the hospital, her husband called me and said he thought that Jane really wanted to go into A.A. Centralia is fifty or one hundred miles away from St. Louis, but apparently she makes the trip here without too much difficulty. I can think of two or three women here with similar background who would probably be available if Jane herself was willing. I think that A.A. is her best hope especially if she could get a Rosary Hall conditioning.

I look forward to seeing Sackville.

I feel as you do about Bill's evolution. He seemed "closer" this time than ever.

I expect to be in Ireland about 10th to 14th, in Rome from the 15th to the 21st and then probably back thru Ireland on the way home.

[Handwritten note: Do you know anybody going over?]
Joe Diggles sent me the enclosed from St. Augustine.

Sincerely,
Edward Dowling, S. J.

The second letter is from Sackville in Ireland to Sister Ignatia Gavin in Cleveland. He mentions a book which had just appeared, written by a famous American Roman Catholic moral theologian, Father John C. Ford, S.J., *Man Takes a Drink: Facts and Principles About Alcohol*, with a foreword by Mrs. Marty Mann, which had just come out in 1955.[606] Sackville apparently approved of that book and felt that it was well done.

Father Ford, who was a Jesuit (like Father Dowling) was a kind of "secret weapon" whom the A.A. people had in their initial struggle for acceptance within the Roman Catholic Church. Father Ford was himself a recovering alcoholic who came into Alcoholics Anonymous c. 1947, but kept his anonymity intact until the very end of his life. Father Dowling almost certainly would have known that Father Ford was in A.A., and Sister Ignatia probably, but it is not certain whether a layman like Sackville would have been told.

Sackville was highly critical of Father Ralph Pfau in this letter, specifically of the two-part autobiography which Pfau had just published in *Look* magazine in March 1958. It should be noted that there were a number of full face photos of Father Ralph in the article, including a very large one of him in his full priestly regalia, preparing the communion chalice for serving mass.

Father Dowling was clearly over on the radical wing of the Jesuits, but nevertheless seems to have tried in many ways to keep a fairly low profile. Father Ralph on the other hand believed in challenging, head on, both the Church hierarchy *and* the A.A. hierarchy in New York! Which man was more important in the history of early A.A. and accomplished the most in helping recovering alcoholics? Father Ed had Bill Wilson's ear, but Father Ralph rose to become one of the four most published early A.A. authors. They both played extraordinarily important roles in the history of early A.A.

I have included this letter because it gives us a bit better picture of Sackville and the newly founded A.A. movement in Ireland (a strongly Roman Catholic country), and also because it gives us such an interesting contrast between Father Ed Dowling and Father Ralph Pfau.[607]

19.3.58.

Dear Sister Ignatia,

Thank you so much for your letter of February 18th, which got here very late. I was so very sorry to hear through Mickey and Joe Donnigan of Kay's death. R.I.P. I know how much you will feel her loss and would like you to have my very sincere sympathy.

The Vantage Press which published Reese's book keep on writing me about a European edition, but I don't think it would do well this side of the Atlantic. Even _well_-written books by alcoholics don't sell much here, I gave them the address of the publishing company that reprinted Fr. Ford's 'Man takes a Drink' in London, so perhaps they may transfer their attentions to them.

We had quite an excellent convention here this month if you care for them. I don't myself, but it was a success and I may be quite wrong about them. There will be a full account in the next Road Back, so I won't weary you with another now.

Mickey seems to be in good heart, and I hear from him frequently. I haven't made my mind up about the trip in the Fall yet, but might manage to get over. It's an expensive trip, though.

He sent me Fr. Pfau's articles in 'Look' [Pfau's autobiography in *Look* magazine in March 1958]. I thought them rather horrible. I did miss the word ADVT. at the end, but that was the impression I got from them! I didn't care for the accompanying photographs either and cannot think that this form of publicity can do much good for the Church or for A.A. Of course there are always two ways of looking at things, and perhaps once again I have got the wrong one.

The bike, thanks to St. Christopher, goes well and safely so far. The winds are rather cold for long rides at present. I hope it is warmer with you.

Must end and get to Mass. Very best wishes, and thanks for not tearing up my photograph on sight. You really are VERY tolerant...

Yours sincerely,
[signed] Sackville

––––––––––––––––––––

The third letter is a very important one. It was written on March 25, 1960 — just nine days before Father Ed died — to Sister Ignatia Gavin (someone whom he clearly trusted at a very deep level) and gives an unusually frank and unguarded look at Father Ed's own innermost goals and purposes.

Father Ed began by begging Sister Ignatia to come to the Long Beach International A.A. Convention on July 1-3, 1960 if she possibly could. He wanted to have a very strong and highly visible Roman Catholic presence up on the stage at that convention. He made a statement which at first glance may seem quite shocking:

Non-Catholic America, with Devil's help, is frightened of and irritated at Catholicity.

But we must think about what was going on in the larger currents of American history. In 1928, a Roman Catholic named Alfred E. Smith had run for the presidency (against Herbert Hoover) and lost disastrously. He was the object of vicious anti-Catholic attacks by American Protestants, particularly Southern Baptists and German Lutherans, which was one of the major reasons for his loss.

Now in 1960, this issue was being revisited once again. In January 1960, a Roman Catholic of Irish background named John F. Kennedy had entered the race for the presidency, running as a Democrat, and was successful in the early primaries against rivals Hubert Humphrey and Wayne Morse. From the beginning however, Kennedy drew some of the same kind of anti-Catholic attacks which had fallen on Alfred E. Smith a generation earlier. At the Democratic Convention in Los

Angeles in July, Kennedy received the party's nomination, but in March (when Father Ed wrote this letter) that had still not been accomplished.

So in March 1960, when Father Ed wrote this letter, virulent anti-Catholic attacks on John F. Kennedy were still going strong, and at the actual election on November 8, Kennedy only beat Richard Nixon (the Republican candidate) by two tenths of one percent of the popular vote.

During this whole ten-month period (from January to November of 1960), many Americans of Protestant background were writing open attacks on the Roman Catholic Church in the major national newspapers and magazines, and arguing that America would lose its freedom if it elected a president who took orders from Rome and imposed Roman Catholic beliefs about birth control, divorce, and all sorts of other issues on the United States.

> MY NOTE: Among other things these anti-Catholic forces feared that under a Roman Catholic president, moves would be taken to make the laws of the United States more like those in Roman Catholic countries like Italy and Ireland, if not by directly changing the laws themselves, then by imposing more and more added-on rules and restrictions until it became de facto almost impossible to obtain divorces, contraceptives, and so on. Divorce was not legal in Italy under any situation until 1970. In Ireland, divorce first became possible with great difficulty in 1997. Contraceptives could not be sold in Ireland until 1978, and could not be obtained without a doctor's prescription until 1985.

Father Ed then went on to make another set of startling comments about Americans, A.A., and the Roman Catholic Church:

> The two best approaches to Catholicity for the non-Catholic heart that I know of are marriage and alcoholism. They admire our marriages. And you know how A.A. has been a theoretical and personal introduction to Catholicity for so many.

One of these statements — "they admire our marriages" — I believe showed an odd lack of awareness on his part about actual Protestant fears and beliefs at that time.

Another of these statements — about A.A. as an "introduction to Catholicity" — showed that Father Ed regarded his work with A.A. as a kind of missionary endeavor. I think the best way to put this, is that it was rather like a Christian church sending doctors and nurses to set up a hospital in a non-Christian tribal area in some part of the globe where modern medicine had hitherto been unknown. They did in fact want to save the lives of these poor people who would otherwise die of all sorts of treatable illnesses. But they also thought of themselves as missionaries, and they had the conversion of these native people to Christianity — as many of them as possible — as their long term goal.

I believe that many A.A. members at that time would most definitely have been horrified at the idea of Alcoholics Anonymous being used as a missionary endeavor of the Roman Catholic Church, and being steered and directed (openly or covertly) by Roman Catholic agents attempting to convert people to Catholicism.

And the next paragraph of Father Ed's letter, in disconcerting fashion, highlighted the very kind of problematic attitudes which in fact affected some of the hierarchy in the Roman Catholic Church of that time period — Cardinal McIntyre in Los Angeles was issuing decrees, Father Ed said, as to which Roman Catholic figures would be allowed to speak at the A.A. International Convention in Long Beach in July and what he would force them to say about the proper treatment of alcoholism. This was the very kind of authoritarian, reactionary, highhanded, dictatorial, and dogmatic behavior which made the Protestants and other non-Roman Catholics so afraid of the Roman church.

The moralistic little pamphlet which Cardinal McIntyre was insisting that Roman Catholic speakers would have to use as the basis of any comments they made was written by the Very Reverend William J. Kenneally, C.M., of the Vincentian Fathers, who was rector of St. John's Major Seminary, in Camarillo, California (fifty miles west of Los Angeles) from 1958 to 1967. Father Kenneally was closely connected with Cardinal McIntyre, who had been working on the expanding of the seminary since 1954.

Cardinal James Francis McIntyre served as Archbishop of Los Angeles from 1948 to 1970. He was an archconservative both ecclesiastically and politically. He opposed the new simplified English-language Catholic liturgy which began being used in the United States after the Second Vatican Council, attacked the Sisters of the Immaculate Heart of Mary when they stopped wearing the traditional medieval nun's habits, sent his priests to meetings of the ultra-conservative John Birch Society to be indoctrinated about what the society believed were communist plots to destroy American society (reaching all the way to the level of President Eisenhower, whom they characterized as a Communist fellow-traveler), and used the diocesan newspaper to ask laypeople to buy subscriptions to *American Opinion* and other John Birch publications.

And Cardinal McIntyre had the power to forbid Father John C. Ford S.J., Father Ed Dowling S.J., or Father Ralph Pfau from giving a talk — anywhere within the bounds of his diocese — that actually spoke about the real way the Alcoholics Anonymous program worked.

Father Ed's letter read as follows:[608]

The Queen's Work
3115 S. Grand Blvd.
St. Louis 18, Missouri
Serving The Sodalities of Our Lady
March 25, 1960

Sister M. Ignatia, C. S. A.,
St. Vincent Charity Hospital
2222 Central Avenue
Cleveland, 15, Ohio

Dear Sister Ignatia

I must strongly urge you to attend the Long Beach convention of A.A., if your Superior gives you clearance.

Non-Catholic America, with Devil's help, is frightened of and irritated at Catholicity. America will be reached morally rather than mentally, by works rather than words.

The two best approaches to Catholicity for the non-Catholic heart that I know of are marriage and alcoholism. They admire our marriages. And you know how A.A. has been a theoretical and personal introduction to Catholicity for so many.

Bill tells me that Cardinal McIntyre refused permission for Father Ford. When I asked the Cardinal for permission to attend the Long Beach convention he wrote that he did not want an alcoholic priest talking and he objected to the disease theory of A.A. He granted me permission if I was not an alcoholic and provided that I follow the ideas of the pamphlet HELP YOUR ALCOHOLIC FRIEND by Very Reverend William J. Kenneally, C.M., rector of St. John's Major Seminary, Camarillo, California.

My talk will not touch the issue of disease or non-disease.

I suggest that you clear with Cardinal McIntyre.

I will keep your health and your intention in my daily Mass.

I have been here for about a week and feel quite well.

Sincerely
Edward Dowling, S.J.

Nine days after writing this letter, Father Ed (who was out on the road and traveling again, in spite of his failing health) died in Memphis, Tennessee.

CHAPTER 42

From Substance Abuse, Insanity, and Trauma to Gays and Gluttony: 1960

Father Dowling's last published writing about Alcoholics Anonymous was a little piece in the A.A. *Grapevine* called "A.A. Steps for the Underprivileged Non-A.A.," which came out three months after his death, in July 1960.[609] Someone (perhaps Bill W. himself) put a header on the article which announced:

> A longtime friend of A.A. shows how the Twelve Steps
> can be effectively applied to any problem in life.

"ANY problem in life" — the highest praise anyone could give the twelve step program. And in fact, Father Ed proclaimed in this article that the twelve-step methodology devised by Alcoholics Anonymous was one of the most influential and far-reaching spiritual developments of the twentieth century. It was his parting gift to A.A., to praise them, but also to remind them how consequential — how sweepingly important all the way up to the world historical level — their quiet, humble discoveries had turned out to be, not just for alcoholics, but for all human beings everywhere.

The journey across the Atlantic of the warming currents of the Gulf Stream: Father Ed opened his article with a bold metaphor, comparing A.A. to the mighty Gulf Stream. This powerful warm current starts at the mouth of the Gulf of Mexico and sweeps up past the coast of Florida, Georgia, and the Carolinas, where part of it breaks away toward Europe, as what is called the North Atlantic Drift, whose warming waters run around Ireland, England, and Scotland on all sides, and create a climate in those far northern islands that is far more moderate than their latitude would otherwise permit. Thanks to the Gulf Stream, in places like London, Oxford, and Dublin, the grass is green and flowers blossom for most of the year. Its effects are far greater and far more extended than land-based rivers, which have narrowly constrained banks and boundaries — a few hundreds of yards away from the Nile, the land of Egypt reverts back to barren desert. The Gulf Stream, on the other hand, has no banks of earth and rock hemming it in, but spreads its warming current hundreds of miles to either side:

> More influential on history than the Nile or the Mississippi, is another river — the Gulf Stream. Without it the British Isles would be as bleak as Labrador or Siberia. A.A. is like a Gulf Stream in the ocean of today's life. It is indistinguishable from its banks — but its winds, like burnt incense, whisper hope and life to human Siberias.

1. Adaptations of the twelve steps to deal with other kinds of SUBSTANCE ABUSE: Narcotics Anonymous, which was begun in 1953, had made only a handful of changes in the original A.A. wording of the steps, principally the change made in Step 1, so it read "We admitted that we were powerless over our addiction" instead of "over alcohol."

Father Ed not only approved of this new group, we can see by the way he talked about the drug problem that he was already getting in tune with the wild 1960's era, when there would be so many radical changes in American culture. He said that "Narcotics Anonymous members use the Twelve Steps" because *"alcohol* is a narcotic." In line with the methodology employed in most of the new American treatment centers which were going to be founded in the 1960's and 70's, Father Dowling argued that *if alcohol and drugs were both narcotics, then they should both be treated the same way.* This put him at odds with the position taken by one wing within A.A. which was, even as late as the 1980's and 90's, sometimes still trying to verbally abuse and drive out new A.A. members the minute they said even one word about also having used drugs. In fact, even today in 2014, this is a topic which one can sometimes hear people in A.A. meetings tiptoeing around quite gingerly and apologetically when it is brought up.

Father Dowling, however, was not afraid of drugs in the sense of being driven into any kind of hysterical and insane panic by the very idea. We remember that he had joined Bill W. in taking LSD. Father Ed had observed that alcohol, cocaine, heroin, and all the other common addictive chemicals held people prisoner in basically the same way, and that these prisoners could be freed from their chains by exactly the same twelve steps.

2a. Using the twelve steps in *THE SEARCH FOR SANITY* and the treatment of psychological disorders: The Twelve Step current, as it swept across the United States and Canada, tended to spread out more and more around its outer edges. It began to be realized that the concept of addiction could not only be applied to SUBSTANCE ABUSE (as psychologists today refer to dependence on *substances* like alcohol, heroin, cocaine, methamphetamine, tobacco, and so on) but also to BEHAVIORAL ADDICTION (the *recurring compulsion* to engage in a particular kind of activity which is harmful in itself or becomes harmful when overdone).

The wording of the Twelve Steps themselves suggested expansion of their application into areas involving harm-producing compulsive behaviors instead of addiction to a chemical substance. Father Dowling noted for example that when the A.A. version of the Second Step said "Came to believe that a power greater than ourselves could restore us to *sanity*," it was describing alcoholism as a psychiatric disorder. That is, in his own layman's terms, it is referring to alcoholism as a *psychosis*. But, he argued, that automatically suggested the possibility of using the steps to help people who had other psychiatric disorders, and had other forms in which they seemed to be almost irresistibly drawn over and over into the same repetitive harmful behaviors:

> If these steps can arrest one psychosis, why not other psychoses and neuroses? At least two groups, "Security Cloister" and "Average People" use A.A.'s Twelve Steps as a filter for spiritual and religious helps in arresting neuroses and psychoses.

Already in 1956, Bill Wilson had suggested (making reference to some of the ideas of the Neo-Freudian psychoanalyst Karen Horney) that someday a recovery group called Neurotics Anonymous needed to be put together.[610] In fact in 1964, four years after Father Dowling's death, a group called Neurotics Anonymous was formed (abbreviated N/A or NAIL) to attempt that task, and in 1971 part of their group (now called Emotions Anonymous or EA) separated from it and has now put together what is an even larger organization. These two groups follow the original twelve steps with only minor adaptations.

Father Ed mentioned one recovery group in this article called WANA, "We Are Not Alone," which was directed toward people who were totally psychotic. This group was first started in 1938, when Psychiatrist Dr. Hiram Johnson at the Rockland State Hospital in upstate New York observed the success of the new A.A. movement, and set up a self-help group for some of his mental patients there. The group later located a building in Manhattan in 1943 and began using it for a clubhouse. WANA in its original form did not continue for very long — the members were too mentally ill to be completely self-directing. The Manhattan clubhouse, however, was eventually successfully reorganized as "Fountain House," and the Fountain House organization now has around 400 clubhouses all over the world, each one run as a cooperative self-help group by men and women suffering from serious mental illnesses, who make their group decisions however with the assistance of a professional staff.[611]

Two other groups that Father Dowling mentioned in his *Grapevine* article dealt with behavioral addictions instead of substance abuse. Gamblers Anonymous, which had begun in Los Angeles in 1957, took the word alcohol in Step 1 ("we admitted we were powerless over alcohol") and replaced it with the word gambling. The other group he listed, Check Writers Anonymous, sounds like it also probably used something like the twelve steps, although all I could find out about the group came from two newspaper articles from a number of years later. Check Writers Anonymous started as a prison group, they said, formed by men who were serving long sentences for writing hundreds of thousands of dollars of bad checks.[612]

If we look at a modern list of recovery groups for men and women where the central problem is behavioral addictions instead of substance addictions, some of the organizations which have appeared after Father Ed's death would include CoDA (Co-Dependents Anonymous, 1986), DA (Debtors Anonymous, 1977), and On-Line Gamers Anonymous (OLGA, 2002).

And in addition, there are five "S" fellowships today, using different conceptions of their basic goal of freedom from sexual addiction: SA (Sexaholics Anonymous, 1979) sets the narrowest standards for acceptable sexual sobriety — for married couples, sex only with the partner, and no masturbation. For unmarried people, no sex at all. No same-sex relationships are permitted, and no unmarried-but-committed-relationships where sex is involved. The other four organizations are SLAA (Sex and Love Addicts Anonymous, 1976), SAA (Sex Addicts Anonymous, 1977), SRA (Sexual Recovery Anonymous, 1993), and SCA (Sexual Compulsives Anonymous, 1973 or 1982). This last fellowship was originally for gay or bisexual men, but now has a much broader membership.

These five groups did not exist in Father Ed's lifetime, but he was certainly aware of the possibility of using the twelve steps to deal with problems of both sexual addiction and what SLAA calls "love addiction" (that is, an infatuation with another man or woman which has become dangerous and harmful in the extreme, but which we cannot seem to make ourselves pull away from). As Father Ed says in his 1960 article in the *Grapevine*:

> I have seen, in one case, the arresting of sexual deviation and resultant normal behavior through the help of the A.A. Steps in a non-alcoholic man. I have seen a compulsive infatuation (with its sensual concomitants and addiction) yield to the A.A. Steps.

2b. THE SEARCH FOR SANITY and the treatment of psychological disorders in non-twelve-step groups: A.A.'s growth helped various other organizations gain greater support from the public, including groups which did not use the twelve steps at all, but were designed along different principles. As Father Ed put it:

> "It's like A.A." [that is, the statement that the group is similar in some ways to Alcoholics Anonymous] has been the passport to acceptance among the dignosclerotic (hardening of the dignity) for such stigma-pilloried movements.

One of the most important and useful of these self-help groups, in the eyes of both Father Dowling and Father Ralph Pfau (the two most important Roman Catholic priests involved with A.A.) was **Recovery, Inc.** This program, which had been founded in 1937 by Dr. Abraham Low, was turned into a peer run self-help group after his death in 1954, and is now called Recovery International. Dr. Low, a Chicago psychiatrist, was the founder of modern cognitive behavioral therapy. His methods had nothing to do with the twelve step program per se, but were completely compatible with the spirit of the twelve steps, and have done enormous good over the past seventy-five years for alcoholics in A.A. who were also suffering from chronic depression, phobic reactions, general nervous fragility, anxiety attacks, and other psychological disorders. It could even sometimes help people like schizophrenics deal more easily and effectively with some of their symptoms, so that they would not have to be institutionalized.

We have already discussed Father Ed's role in helping establish meetings for the Divorcées Anonymous movement which was started in 1949. This also was not a twelve-step group per se, although Father Ed encouraged the members to apply the twelve step methodology to solving some of their personal emotional problems.

3. Recovery programs for those suffering from STIGMA AND TRAUMA: During the 1940's, Mrs. Marty Mann set up the National Council of Alcoholism as an organization working partly in parallel with A.A., for the purpose of carrying out public campaigns to help reduce the enormous stigma attached to being an alcoholic.

Modern groups for those who unfairly suffer from the stigma, shame, and guilt of something that happened to them beyond their will to control include SIA (Survivors of Incest Anonymous, 1982), various support groups around the country for the survivors of rape, and so on. But the issue can sometimes involve more *trauma* than guilt. So for example we nowadays also have recovery groups for people suffering from PTSD (post-traumatic stress disorder) because of their experiences in combat while they were serving in the military.

Two groups which already existed in Father Ed's day dealt with an issue which certainly brought on considerable public stigma, and could also involve being insulted, humiliated, harassed, fired from one's job, beaten, raped, arrested, and even killed. These were groups for people who were gay (homosexual), lesbian, or transgender.

The Mattachine Society: The real rise of the modern gay rights movement, at least in full-fledged form, did not occur until after Father Ed's death: the Stonewall riots began on June 28, 1969 in Greenwich Village in New York City when a group of drag queens objected to the police department's assumption that people could automatically be arrested for gay, lesbian, and transgender appearance or behavior. A year later, on June 28, 1970, the first Gay Pride marches took place in New York, Los Angeles, San Francisco, and Chicago to celebrate the anniversary of the Stonewall rebellion.

But Father Ed made it clear in this 1960 article, which he published at the end of his life, that he completely supported two of the earliest twentieth century gay rights groups, the Mattachine Society, which had been founded in Los Angeles in 1950 by a group of gay men, led by Harry Hay, and the Daughters of Bilitis, which had been founded in San Francisco in 1955 for lesbian women.

These two movements were in many ways very different from the preceding groups. (1) They were not twelve step groups. (2) They were also not trying to "cure" something which they regarded as a disorder, illness, or sin, but were instead intended to serve as support groups for people who were determined to keep on leading a particular way of life which was deeply stigmatized in the United States at that time. (3) They were very radical groups indeed.

At that time in U.S. history, the F.B.I. kept dossiers on "homosexuals," and the U.S. Post Office kept records of those who received "homosexual literature" through the mail. The mid-twentieth-century politicians who were leading the infamous anti-Communist crusades of that period were often attacking gays as well, and getting them fired from their jobs on the grounds that they were supposedly "security risks" who could be blackmailed by Communist plotters. Gay sex was a crime, and you could also be arrested simply for wearing the clothes of the opposite sex. That was the reason why both groups — the Mattachine Society and the Daughters of Bilitis — gave themselves names that would not immediately identify their members as gays and lesbians.

But Father Dowling was a very brave man, who was not frightened by anything, and who would go anywhere and be a friend to any of God's children. He was not afraid to say here in print that he was a supporter of these two groups, both the Mattachine Society and the Daughters of Bilitis.

It must be noted at the outset that Harry Hay, the founder of the Mattachine Society, was a member of the Communist Party — anti-gay attacks on the Mattachine Society which like to stress that so strongly in their accounts of its origin, are not making that up — but ironically, the Communist Party itself was virulently anti-gay, and the other members of the Mattachine Society were embarrassed by Harry's Marxist political theories. The Communist background had nothing to do, really, with the real intent and purposes of the society, except perhaps in making Harry more willing to rebel against the anti-gay persecutors within the contemporary American political, police, and ecclesiastical establishment. All you have to do, however, to understand who Harry was, is to look at one of the many photographs of him wearing a long woman's skirt, a woman's hat with big colorful flowers on it, and the biggest grin in the world spread across his square-jawed face — obviously a man wearing women's clothes in flamboyant and garish fashion, and enjoying the looks of shock on everyone's faces — to realize that Harry was simply a rebel through and through.

Harry Hay first came up with the idea of a gay activist group in 1948. He originally planned to call it Bachelors Anonymous, and modeled it partly after Alcoholics Anonymous. *The A.A. connection and inspiration was clear.* If A.A. could successfully remove some of the stigma of being an alcoholic, then the right kind of group could work to remove the stigma of being gay, lesbian, and transgender. But the group did not really get going until 1950, when it began to call itself the Mattachine Society.

In explanation of the name, in the medieval and renaissance period, there was a form of entertainment called a "masque," in which people wearing masks to preserve their anonymity put on performances involving music, dancing, acting, and elaborate stage designs. One such group of masked performers in France was called the Société Mattachine (pronounced mah-tah-SHEEN). Jonathan Katz, in his book *Gay American History*, explains in more detail why Harry Hay's gay support group decided to take that as their name:

> One masque group was known as the "Société Mattachine." These societies, lifelong secret fraternities of unmarried townsmen who never performed in public unmasked, were dedicated to going out into the countryside and conducting dances and rituals during the Feast of Fools, at the Vernal Equinox. Sometimes these dance rituals, or masques, were peasant protests against oppression — with the maskers, in the people's name, receiving the brunt of a given lord's vicious retaliation. So we took the name Mattachine because we felt that we 1950s Gays were also a masked people, unknown and anonymous, who might become engaged in morale building and helping ourselves and others, through struggle, to move toward total redress and change.[613]

The Daughters of Bilitis: The Daughters of Bilitis (also called the DOB or just "the Daughters") was formed in San Francisco in 1955. In October of that year, Del Martin and Phyllis, a lesbian couple, joined with three other lesbian couples to form what was at first intended simply to be a social club, where lesbians could dance with one another and admit their sexual orientation openly, without being stared at by tourists, insulted, or harassed by the police (because among other things, dancing with a member of your own sex was against the law at that time).

But it was quickly realized that the group also needed to be carrying out a number of other jobs. It needed to help frightened and confused lesbians — many of them still locked in considerable denial and self-loathing — to come out and admit their sexual orientation more openly, both to other people and to themselves. Psychologists and sociologists needed to be urged to start doing better scientific studies of homosexual behavior in general. The many taboos and prejudices found among the general public needed to exposed and corrected. And campaigns had to be started in state legislatures all over the U.S. to remove all the horrendous anti-homosexual legislation which was found in the penal codes of that era.[614]

By 1959, the year before Father Dowling wrote this article, there were chapters in San Francisco, Los Angeles, New York City, Chicago, and Rhode Island. A woman who came to one of their meetings was met at the door by a greeter who said, "I'm _____, who are you? You don't have to give me your real name, not even your real first name." In 1960, the DOB held its first national convention in San Francisco, with two hundred attendees. The San Francisco police insisted on coming inside, to make sure that none of the women were wearing men's clothes, but upon finding that all the women were wearing dresses, stockings, and high heels, they had to leave them alone. (They were dressed that way deliberately, because women in the U.S. at that time could technically be arrested just for wearing blue jeans, and they did not want to give the police any excuse at all to run them off to jail.) Once the police left, past that point it was all positive, except for an Episcopal priest who was invited to be one of the speakers, who used the opportunity to deliver an angry tirade accusing all the women in the group of being damned sinners. But the women simply took that in their stride, and refused to let it ruin their gathering.[615]

The name of this group was taken from a book of erotic poems called *The Songs of Bilitis*, which had originally appeared in France in 1894. A man named Pierre Louÿs claimed that he had discovered an ancient Greek manuscript containing poems from around 600 B.C., written by a woman named Bilitis who was an acquaintance of the famous woman poet Sappho (who had lived on the Greek island of Lesbos, and wrote poetry about love between women, the name of the island being the original source of the word "lesbian"). The book which Pierre Louÿs published claimed to be a translation of a number of poems which Bilitis had written, which were often fairly sexually explicit. Some of them described young girls reaching puberty and discovering their sexuality, others described their first encounters with young men, whether simply amorous or involving overt sexual acts. But some of the poems were about lesbian sexual encounters and romantic amorous contacts between young women.[616]

In truth, it was a fraud. Pierre Louÿs had no ancient Greek manuscript, and had written all the poems himself. But they were also very good poems, of high literary value, and the fact that some of them involved very sensuous lesbian imagery gave them an enormous notoriety. It turned them into underground classics, a status they hold even to this day.

4. GLUTTONY — out-of-control sensuality — as the traditional Catholic spiritual disorder underlying alcoholism, cigarette smoking, and compulsive overeating. In the *Twelve Steps and Twelve Traditions*, in the chapter on Step Four — the step which described how we "made a searching and fearless moral inventory of ourselves" — Bill Wilson explained that this fourth step was the one where we needed to write down a list on paper of all our major personality defects, defects of character, maladjustments, and areas where we were regularly involved in serious violations of our own inner moral principles, or whatever we preferred to call the problems in our way of thinking which were sabotaging our best efforts to live in this world successfully, and blocking "any real ability to cope with life."[617] To make sure we understood how this kind of self-analysis linked back to the traditional western spiritual tradition, Wilson put it in medieval Catholic terminology at one point:

> To avoid falling into confusion over the names these defects should be called, let's take a universally recognized list of major human failings — the Seven Deadly Sins of pride, greed, lust, anger, gluttony, envy, and sloth.[618]

One of these seven deadly sins was gluttony. In medieval Latin it was called *gula*, a word which in ancient classical Latin had basically meant gullet, throat, or esophagus, but could by extension mean taste, appetite, voraciousness, gluttony, or hoggish desire for food. So gluttony as a deadly sin literally meant the out-of-control craving to swallow things down our throats. Although it primarily referred to compulsive overeating, in medieval works on moral theology, alcoholism was also regarded as a type of gluttony.

Father Dowling gave the term an even wider definition however, and described gluttony as a kind of *sensuality* in which the desire to give physical pleasure to our five material senses overrode our desire for spiritual things:

> Gluttony is a species of sensuality or inordinate body drives. Unarrested alcoholism is sensuality. Sensuality covers such situations as too many cancer-threatening cigarettes and qualitative or quantitative sex deviations.

Father Ed was not an alcoholic, but in this article he confessed to his A.A. audience that he too had fallen prey to a kind of sensuality which had almost destroyed him. And he told them frankly that the only success he had had in battling his own kind of self-destructive sensuality had come from applying A.A.'s twelve steps to it:

> Alcoholism is, when unchecked, gluttony for alcoholic drink. A.A.'s success with this type of gluttony opens new hope for the better known gluttony, which is killing many people — respectfully autopsied as obesity or overweight.
>
> My 240-pound gluttony gave me two heart attacks. An alcoholic doctor got me down toward 180 when he advised a total A.A. abstinence from starch, butter, salt and sugar. He said these four foods were probably my "alcohol." Abstinence was so much easier than temperance. The "balanced" diet often prescribed was loaded with these four "craving-creating appetizers." I was like a lush tapering off on martinis. Only after the discovery of the A.A. approach to craving-creating intake did I realize that the Jesuit Ignatius' first rule for diet in his *Spiritual Exercises* was to go easy on craving-creating food and drink.

Father Ed does not seem to have been aware of it, but earlier that very year, in January 1960, a recovery organization called Overeaters Anonymous was founded, which used the twelve steps in the treatment of overeating, and eventually other eating disorders as well (including binge eating, anorexia, and bulimia). It now has around 6,500 groups spread around the world, in over 75 different countries.

And it is of interest to note that another twelve-step group was started later on, which explicitly referred to Father Dowling's teaching in this article in the *Grapevine*, and tried to model itself very closely on his specific theories. It was originally founded in 1979 in Phoenix, Arizona, and reorganized in 1996. It is called CEA-HOW, which is an abbreviation for Compulsive Eaters Anonymous — Honesty Openmindedness Willingness.

Addiction to tobacco: Father Ed added to his confession of the serious health problem he had had with overeating, the admission that he had had another problem that also had affected his health, cigarette smoking. But here too, "some ten years ago I arrested my own nicotinic addiction with the help of the A.A. Steps."

A.A.'s mission to the world: One of the often unrecognized gifts which A.A. gave to the world came from their work as explorers, venturing out into an often wild and dangerous wilderness, and discovering ever new places to plant settlements — not A.A. meetings necessarily, but often new kinds of recovery groups embodying hundreds of novel and creative approaches:

> As Columbus, Marquette, and Lewis and Clark pushed toward the terminals of our frontier, so A.A. has advanced the frontiers of hope even in situations otherwise "powerless."

For a more recent appreciation of the vast effect Alcoholics Anonymous and the twelve step program have had on American life, one should see the beautiful book by Prof. Trysh Travis at the University of Florida, called *The Language of the Heart: A Cultural History of the Recovery Movement from Alcoholics Anonymous to Oprah Winfrey.*[619] As Travis shows, the influence of A.A. has now quietly and unobtrusively permeated down into American culture from the highest to the lowest levels.

Modern cultural historians speak automatically of the enormous impact which the Great Awakening and Frontier Revivalism had on American culture in the eighteenth and nineteenth centuries. It is considered a truism. But revivals are noisy and easy to notice, so this observation is easy to make. Little A.A. meetings, on the other hand, creep in silently and anonymously, meeting in odd little nooks without even signs on the doors indicating what kind of group is gathered inside, and spread their concepts of making amends, confessing our character defects, breaking through our denial of who we really are, searching for a kind of gentle, quiet serenity, and letting whatever kind of higher power runs this universe do its work without interference from us. I think that the impact of the twelve step movement on American culture in the twentieth and early twenty-first century has in fact been even greater than that of the frontier revivalists on our earlier history.

And in fact, I think that the twelve step movement is going to end up being even more important historically than that, and that it is already in the process of changing the whole center of gravity in western religion and spirituality. But time will tell on this.

The spread of the twelve step understanding of recovery and SPIRITUALITY from psychiatrists to physicians to the clergy: One of the first groups of people to notice the A.A. movement were the psychiatrists, or at least a small handful of them. They saw A.A. getting alcoholics sober, and they were impressed. But alcoholism was at least in part a problem which involved the physical body, the body's metabolic processes, and so on. At that point, a few wiser physicians were reminded that the effect on the body of psychosomatic influences, the placebo effect, and so on, pointed to the fact that psychological treatment could often help produce recovery from physical ailments and other kinds of physical problems. And then some of the clergy had to be reminded by A.A. that, even if some self-proclaimed "faith healers" were quacks, recovery from almost any kind of physical ailment could be speeded up or improved if the patient could be convinced to carry out a serious, disciplined, daily program of spiritual growth. As Father Dowling put it:

> The psychiatrist has alerted the non-psychiatric doctor to the psychic dimension of somatic disorders. A.A. alerted both to a third dimension, the spiritual or religious, and pioneered an

ethico-psycho-somatic therapy.[620] That means that the cure for the shakes is via the shaker's belief in God.

Psychiatrists alerted the clergy to the "cause and cure significance" of the spiritual or psychic. A.A. helped them even more by demonstrating the "cause and cure significance" of religion.

In a statement that may seem strange, coming from a Roman Catholic priest, Dowling suggested that the twelve step movement's greatest beneficiaries of all might well be the American *clergy*. Whether Catholic or Protestant or Jewish, America's religious leaders had found themselves increasingly butting their heads ineffectually against "the agnostic smog of urban materialism [which] had corroded [the] religious heirlooms" — the traditional religious beliefs and practices — of so many of the now "spiritually impoverished people" who made up their flocks. But Father Ed had found that when he was working with all sorts of different kinds of religious groups, his flock would benefit spiritually whenever he brought in a little bit of twelve step teaching, and began instructing them on how they could work some of the twelve steps in their lives. (This was part of what I meant when I commented several paragraphs back that I thought that the twelve step movement was going to end up changing the whole center of gravity in western religion and spirituality at a very basic structural level.)

Psychiatrists and priestly celebrants of the sacraments: And the way Father Ed characterizes A.A. at the end of this article may seem shocking to many. He speaks of the "psychiatric-sacerdotal role" played by the people in the program who are organizing and chairing meetings, sponsoring newcomers, and otherwise carrying the message. I referred to these people in one of my other books as "the God bearers," the humble, unassuming men and women who ask for no fancy titles or positions, but sometimes almost visibly shine with the divine light as they quietly carry out God's work.

There is a line from the last few paragraphs of this *Grapevine* article which we quoted at the very beginning of this book. I have underlined two of his very deliberate and shocking phrases in that sentence, to make sure that we notice exactly what he is saying:

> In moving their therapy from the expensive clinical couch to the low-cost coffee bar, from the <u>inexperienced professional</u> to the <u>amateur expert</u>, A.A. has democratized sanity.

But Father Ed says something even more shocking: he speaks of the "psychiatric-<u>sacerdotal</u> role" played by the people in the program who are organizing and chairing meetings, sponsoring newcomers, and so on. To speak of some of the good old timers in A.A. as people who can on occasion be filled with a kind of healing divine presence seems like a not-too-preposterous claim, but to suggest that these sometimes rather rough-and-ready and unconventional people function as priests celebrating a new kind of holy sacrament seems totally outrageous. Certainly this was not the sort of thing that most people would expect a very pious Roman Catholic priest to say. Yet in his speech at the A.A. International in St. Louis five years earlier, Father Ed proclaimed:

> And the twelfth step, to me, is the great pipe line or sacrament of Communion. The word that was God became flesh and becomes our food, as close to us as the fruit juice and the toast and the coffee we had an hour ago.[621]

Father Dowling's parting message to A.A. — seek not breadth but length and depth. In a short paragraph which, I think, is just as applicable today, Father Ed's very last words to the A.A. movement warned them not to worry so much about the "breadth" issue as though it were a separate factor all its own, that is, becoming too concerned about whether overall A.A. membership figures were growing, or declining, or getting stalled on a plateau. What they needed to be concerned about instead was A.A.'s "length" and "depth."

Length meant *going all the way* with the Twelfth Step: not only working industriously "to carry this message to alcoholics," but also doing our best "to practice these principles in all our affairs." Applying the steps to all our affairs meant learning to tame all of our destructive compulsions (our neurotic obsessions, our sex problems, and our inability to stop eating and smoking ourselves to death), as well as learning to calm our frantic worries and gnawing anxieties, and (if this applied to us) to start curbing our overuse of medications like barbiturates (which many A.A. people still used in the 1940's and 50's as "sedatives" to "calm their nerves").

Depth meant *taking the journey down into the truly profound levels* of the life of prayer and meditation which is described in the Eleventh Step, and seeking in those depths not only true knowledge but also real power:

> Possibly, if the A.A. spent less time and energy in the breadth dimension of spreading A.A. and more in the length and depth dimension, the breadth of its spread might not be limited to such a low percentage of the world's alcoholics. The length dimension means the application of these Steps to *all our affairs* — sedatives, tensions, compulsions, and so on. The depth dimension is suggested by the Eleventh Step, "sought through meditation ... for knowledge of His will for us and the power to carry that out."

Thus Father Dowling's final words of farewell were written. And at the end of this article in the *Grapevine*, Bill Wilson added his own final words of goodbye to his beloved sponsor:

> Father Ed, an early and wonderful friend of A.A., died as this last message to us went to press. He was the greatest and most gentle soul that I may ever know. Bill W.

CHAPTER 43

Death: April 3, 1960

Father Ed Dowling died in Memphis, Tennessee on Sunday, April 3, 1960. He was buried on Wednesday, April 6, 1960 in the cemetery at St. Stanislaus Seminary in Florissant, a northern suburb of St. Louis, Missouri. He was 61 years old and Bill Wilson was 64.[622]

> AS AN ADDITIONAL NOTE: The seminary was closed in 1971, and the 35 remaining acres of their property was sold to the United Pentecostal Church. In 1972, Father Dowling's body was reburied at Calvary Cemetery in St. Louis, Missouri, in Lot 33, Sec 0022, in the Jesuit section.[623]

Father Ed had flown in to Memphis, Tennessee, on Saturday, April 2, to preside over a Cana marriage conference sponsored by local alumnae of the Maryville College of the Sacred Heart in St. Louis. There were also A.A. people present, and Father Ed, as he typically did, used twelve step teachings to help the people at the Cana Conference better understand the nature of a good Catholic marriage, and their own moral responsibilities in life. After dinner on Saturday, Father Ed and his friends from the Cana Conference, along with two A.A. people, sat around until late at night, talking and having a good time, at the home of Mr. and Mrs. Frank Barzizza, where he was staying.[624] It was a wonderfully happy gathering, and as Bill Wilson said, "He would have wanted to take his leave of us in just that way."[625]

Paul K. in Memphis wrote a letter afterwards describing that Saturday evening:

I took an A.A. Gal (3 years) with me and he was very glad to show us off; the others belonged to the Cana Conferences he had originated and he wanted to emphasize how A.A.'s faced their problems and spoke about their problems and about "God directly and not as if the word were immodest like 'legs' in the Victorian age." The quotes are direct .... Those in the Fellowship were always his "pets" so to speak — you could tell that by the way his eyes lit up when we came into the room.

But Paul K. said in this letter that Father Dowling's health was obviously very fragile: "One look at him and I knew he wouldn't be with us long."[626]

At 8 a.m. the next morning, Dowling was found dead in the bed which the Barzizza's had provided for him. He had died peacefully in his sleep during the night.[627]

Father Ed's body was brought back to St. Louis. Bill Wilson came there for the funeral, and as Father James McQuade explained, in a formal visit to the Jesuit Father Superior there, Wilson "expressed the deep gratitude of Alcoholics Anonymous to the Society of Jesus, not only for the work of Fr. Dowling, but also for the generally favorable attitude toward the organization on the part of Jesuits from the beginning. He attributed this in part to the influence of Fr. Dowling."[628]

AS AN ADDITIONAL NOTE: The other key Jesuit defender of A.A. was Father John C. Ford, S.J., (1902-1989) who was considered at the time to be America's foremost Roman Catholic moral theologian. Father Ford publicly supported the A.A. kind of method, and was also a prominent figure within A.A.'s innermost circles. Ford was an alcoholic himself, and discovered the program c. 1947 when he was sent to Towns Hospital to get sober; after arriving there, Dr. Silkworth told him to go to A.A. But until the very end of his life, Ford kept his membership in A.A. not only secret from the outside world, but hidden even from the general A.A. membership. It was felt that his ability to influence the Roman Catholic hierarchy favorably towards A.A. was so important, that it was not worth having him reveal his own problems with alcohol and risk him losing some of his reputation.

The attempt to bar Dowling's friends and supporters from using the College Church for his funeral. St. Francis Xavier's is the College Church at St. Louis University. Built in 1884-1898, it is a beautiful structure, an elaborate Gothic style church: a major St. Louis City Landmark which is listed on the National Register of Historic Places.

But the Jesuit who was pastor tried to block Father Ed's funeral from being held there. He told them to just set up a small service at *The Queen's Work*, which was basically only an office building located at 3115 S. Grand Boulevard, at the corner of Tower Grove Park. It appears that the conservative wing of the Jesuits regarded Father Dowling as so far over on the radical wing, that they did not even want his funeral conducted in a proper Catholic church. Fortunately, the Provincial (the Jesuit in charge of the order's major Midwestern division, of which the state of Missouri was part) stepped in at this point and ordered the funeral held in the College Church.[629]

To keep the pastor of the church from creating other kinds of trouble, Father Fred Zimmerman, S.J., the manager of *The Queen's Work*, was allowed to supervise all the details of the funeral that Wednesday. Zimmerman reminisced about it some years later:[630]

> When we gathered near the grave at Florissant, Father Leo Brown next to me remarked, "So this is the man they would not bury from the College Church?" The cemetery and the grounds were packed with cars and people who came from all over the country. Mr. Wilson was there to give Puggy Dowling a sendoff that was rarely seen at Florissant. To distract Anna Dowling, I made her call all the Jesuit houses in the Province from St. Matthew's rectory.

Bill Wilson's obituary: Father Ed shone with the eternal light of sainthood. In the obituary he wrote in the June 1960 *Grapevine*,[631] Bill W. praised his sponsor in numerous ways: "This was one of the most gentle souls and finest friends we AAs may ever know. He left a heritage of inspiration and grace which will be with us always." Father Dowling traveled thousands of miles and spent thousands of hours helping A.A.

And Bill also expressed his own debt of gratitude for what the good priest had done for him personally, in this case simply repeating in his obituary what he had said in *Alcoholics Anonymous Comes of Age*:

> In my entire acquaintance, our friend Father Ed is the only one from whom I have never heard a resentful word and of whom I have never heard a single criticism. In my own life he has been a friend, adviser, great example, and the source of more inspiration than I can say.[632]

But above all, Bill Wilson came back in the obituary to what struck him most strongly of all at his first meeting with Father Ed on that cold winter evening at the end of 1940.

> He lowered himself into my solitary chair, and when he opened his overcoat I saw his clerical collar. He brushed back a shock of white hair and looked at me through the most remarkable pair of eyes I have ever seen. We talked about a lot of things, and my spirits kept on rising, and presently I began to realize that this man radiated a grace that filled the room with a sense of presence. I felt this with great intensity; it was a moving and mysterious experience. In years since I have seen much of this great friend, and whether I was in joy or in pain he always brought to me the same sense of grace and the presence of God. My case is no exception. Many who meet Father Ed experience this touch of the eternal.

And Bill W. repeated the simple words he had spoken when introducing his beloved sponsor and mentor to the audience at the A.A. International Convention in St. Louis in 1955:[633]

> Father Ed is made of the stuff of the saints.

NOTES

1.   Robert Fitzgerald, S.J., "Father Ed Dowling and AA's Bill W.," *The Catholic Digest*, April 1991, available online at http://www.barefootsworld. net/aafreddowling.html and http://www.cleanandsobernotdead.com/ aahistory/dowling.html

2.   As quoted in Fr. James McQuade, Obituary of Fr. Edward Dowling, S.J. (1898-1960), *News-Letter, Missouri and Wisconsin Provinces*, May 1960, Vol. 20, No. 8, available online at http://boards.ancestry.com-localities. northam.usa.states.missouri.counties.stlouis-4261-mb.ashx.

3.   Bill W. inserted this quote from Father Dowling as an appendix in the second edition of the Big Book in 1955. In the current fourth edition of *Alcoholics Anonymous*, it is Appendix V on page 572.

4.   Quoted in part in "Father Ed Dowling — Bill W.'s Confidant and Friend," *Box 459: News and Notes from the General Service Office of AA*, Vol. 52, No. 4 (August-September 2006). It may be read online at http://aa.org/ en_pdfs/en_box459_aug-sept06.pdf, which says it first began to be used with the ninth printing. I have been told by one of the experts that it also appeared on the dust jackets of the tenth, eleventh, and thirteenth printings (but not, for example, on the fifth printing).

5.   Dowling Family Genealogy in Ancestry.com, available online at http:// wc.rootsweb.ancestry.com/cgi-bin/igm.cgi?op=GET&db=dowfam 3&id=I18100.

6.   Robert Fitzgerald, S.J., *The Soul of Sponsorship: The Friendship of Fr. Ed Dowling, S.J. and Bill Wilson in Letters* (Center City, Minnesota: Hazelden, 1995), 72. Fiona Dodd in County Mayo sent me a note on August 17, 2013 giving me the contemporary Irish spelling of the address: "It's actually Ballagh, Kilroosky, Co Roscommon as Kilroosky is the post office. Easting 594533/Northing 770874 on the ordnance survey map."

7.   Fitzgerald, *Soul of Sponsorship* 13; McQuade, Obituary; also see Rev. Edward Dowling, S.J., Résumé, as reprinted in Fitzgerald, *Soul of Sponsorship*, Appendix F, pp. 138-139 — this was the résumé sent by

Fr. Dowling and his sister Anna Dowling to the coordinator of the 1960 A.A. International Convention in Long Beach, California, around three months or so before the convention (see Fitzgerald, *Soul of Sponsorship*, p. 101). See also Heywood Broun's memories of Fr. Dowling in "Religion: Conversion," *Time* magazine, 22 May 1939, available online at http://www.time.com/time/magazine/article/0,9171,761385,00.html. For the birth and death dates of Fr. Ed's parents, see "James Dowling" in Find a Grave, available online at http://www.findagrave.com/cgi-bin/fg.cgi?page=gr&GRid=51003060. Fitzgerald seems to be mistaken about Fr. Ed's mother's name— her name was Annie (born 1866 and died in 1934)—it was Annie's mother who was named Anastasia—see "Anastasia Newman Cullinane" (1826-1883) in Find a Grave, available online at http://www.findagrave.com/cgi-bin/fg.cgi?page=gr&GRid=51001061.

8   Both the 1900 census and 1910 census list his residence as 8224 Church Rd., St. Louis, Missouri, see Dowling Family Genealogy in Ancestry.com.

9   Fitzgerald, *Soul of Sponsorship* 13; Norbury L. Wayman, *History of St. Louis Neighborhoods*, Baden-Riverview Churches, available online at http://stlouis.missouri.org/neighborhoods/history/baden/churches2.htm. His baptism at Our Lady of Mt. Carmel, St. Louis, Missouri, is listed in the Dowling Family Genealogy in Ancestry.com.

10   Edward Dowling, Résumé.

11   Fitzgerald, *Soul of Sponsorship* xiii and 14. Fitzgerald seems to have had erroneous information about Anna's birthdate: he said that she was three years younger than Fr. Ed, but the dates on her grave indicate that she was not much more than a year younger (Ed born Sept. 1, 1898 and Anna born Nov. 21, 1899), see "Anna Dowling" in Find a Grave, at http://www.findagrave.com/cgi-bin/fg.cgi?page=gr&GSln=Dowling&GSiman=1&GScid=27890&GRid=51002606&. Many later historical accounts give an erroneous date (April 3, 1960) for Father Dowling's death. But April 3 was the date of his burial, not his death — he actually died on March 30, 1960, see "Fr Edward P Dowling," Find a Grave, the newer, corrected version, posted by Brian Koch, a careful researcher and good A.A. historian, available at http://www.findagrave.com/cgi-bin/fg.cgi?page=gr&GRid=73326044. See also "Mary Dowling" in Find a Grave, available online at http://www.findagrave.com/cgi-bin/fg.cgi?page=gr&GSln=Dowling&GSiman=1&GScid=27890&GRid=51003507&; "Paul Vincent Dowling," in Find a Grave, at http://www.findagrave.com/cgi-bin/fg.cgi?page=gr&GRid=51000982; and "Beatrice

F. Dowling," in Find a Grave, at http://www.findagrave.com/cgi-bin/ fg.cgi?page=gr&GRid=48185876.

12 Edward Dowling, Résumé; also see Fitzgerald, *Soul of Sponsorship* 13.

13 Edward Dowling, Résumé.

14 Fitzgerald, *Soul of Sponsorship* 14.

15 Ibid.

16 McQuade, Obituary.

17 McQuade, Obituary; Fitzgerald, *Soul of Sponsorship* 14; Edward Dowling, Résumé. In the Dowling Family Genealogy in Ancestry.com, it says "Military service 28 OCT 1918 Pvt., ASN 5268144, STUDENTS ARMY TNG C ST.LOUIS UNIVERSITY, ST. LOUIS, MO TO DISCHARGE."

18 From the Wikipedia article on the *St. Louis Post-Dispatch*, available online at http://en.wikipedia.org/wiki/St._Louis_Post-Dispatch. This oft-quoted paragraph, referred to as "The Post-Dispatch Platform," was first published in the *St. Louis Post-Dispatch* for April 11, 1907.

19 McQuade, Obituary; Fitzgerald, *Soul of Sponsorship* 14; Edward Dowling, Résumé.

20 Quoted in McQuade, Obituary.

21 *Peter John De Smet, S.J. (1801 - 1873): Life and Times of a Blackrobe in the West*, "The Museum of the Western Jesuit Missions in Florissant," p. 307, available online at http://users.skynet.be/pater.de.smet/pj-e/ pagina307.htm. Also see "St. Stanislaus Seminary, Florissant, Missouri," at Waymarking.com, available online at http://www.waymarking.com/ waymarks/WM88V6_St_Stanislaus_Seminary_Florissant_Missouri.

22 Joseph T. McGloin, S.J., *I'll Die Laughing!* (Milwaukee: Bruce Publishing Company, 1955), a humorous popular account of Jesuit formation in the first half of the twentieth century, as quoted in Joe Koczera, S.J. (Philadelphia, Pennsylvania), "Cornbread and beef stew in Jesuit life," February 22, 2006 in his weblog *Novitiate Notes: Ad Majorem Dei Gloriam* at http://novitiatenotes.blogspot.com/2006/02/cornbread-and-beef-stew-in-jesuit-life.html.

23 St. Ignatius Loyola, *The Spiritual Exercises of St. Ignatius*, trans. Anthony Mottola, introd. Robert W. Gleason, S.J. (New York: Doubleday Image Books, 1989; this Eng. trans. orig. pub. 1964).

24 "St. Stanislaus Kostka: Novice Religious," *The Jesuit Curia in Rome: The House of the Superior General,* available online at http://www.sjweb.info/jesuits/saintShow.cfm?SaintID=42; Penn Dawson, S.J., "St. Stanislaus Kostka: Patron of Jesuit Novices," *Company: The World of Jesuits and Their Friends* (Fall 2009), available online at http://www.companysj.com/v271/new-day.html. As the great Christ Hymn in Philippians (2:2-11) says in verses 5-8, "Have this mind among yourselves, which is yours in Christ Jesus, who ... emptied himself, taking the form of a servant .... humbled himself and became obedient unto death, even death on a cross."

25 *Twelve Steps and Twelve Traditions* (New York: Alcoholics Anonymous World Services, 1952, 1953), 93-94. Ernest Kurtz, "Re: Is Bill responsible for this quote?" AAHistoryLovers message no. 4395, at https://groups.yahoo.com/neo/groups/aahistorylovers/conversations/messages/ commented that "I was inclined to guess that the source was either Father Edward Dowling or Rev. Sam Shoemaker or Dr. Harry Tiebout, to each of whom Bill referred in other contexts as 'someone who knew what he was talking about.' That was my guesswork order of probability, but I was never able to get any further in that research." Compare the line in Bill W.'s 1944 Christmas greeting to A.A. "pain is not only the price but the very touchstone of spiritual rebirth," quoted in AAHistoryLovers message no. 7043, "Who was Bobbie?" at https://groups.yahoo.com/neo/groups/aahistorylovers/conversations/messages/7043.

26 Fitzgerald, *Soul of Sponsorship* 6 and 15. Ernest Kurtz, in a telephone conversation in March 2011, said he asked a Jesuit who was very close to Fr. Dowling whether this was rheumatoid arthritis, and that he was told that it was not, but some other kind of severe arthritis.

27 From a talk given by Dowling on April 18, 1944, preserved in the Dowling Archives at Maryville College, as quoted in Fitzgerald, *Soul of Sponsorship* 15.

28 Fitzgerald, *Soul of Sponsorship* 15; McQuade, Obituary; Edward Dowling, Résumé; Jesuit Vocation Office: Maryland, New England & New York Provinces at http://www.jesuitvocation.org/information/become.shtml; Dowling Family Genealogy in Ancestry.com.

29 Fitzgerald, *Soul of Sponsorship* 15; McQuade, Obituary; Edward Dowling, Résumé; Jesuit Vocations website of the New England, Maryland and New York Provinces at http://www.jesuitvocations.org/; "Loyola Academy," http://en.wikipedia.org/wiki/Loyola_Academy.

30 John N. Kotre, *Simple Gifts: the Lives of Pat and Patty Crowley* (Kansas City: Andrews and McMeel, 1979) 22; "Christian Family Movement: History," available online at http://www.cfm.org/history.html.

31 Kotre, *Simple Gifts* 22.

32 "Christian Family Movement: History." Dorothy Day, "Reflections on Work—November 1946," *The Catholic Worker*, November 1946, 1, 4.

33 "Patty Crowley: founder of the Christian Family Movement dies," *Catholic New Times*, Dec. 18, 2005, available online at http://www.highbeam.com/doc/1G1-140304355.html.

34 "Remembering Patty Crowley, Godmother of Call To Action," an article on the website of Call to Action: Catholics Working Together for Justice & Equality, at http://www.cta-usa.org/News200601/PattyCrowley.html.

35 Margery Frisbie, *An Alley in Chicago: The Ministry of a City Priest* (Lanham, Maryland: Sheed & Ward, 1991), Chapter 6, "Selling God, He Got Us," a book based on a series of interviews with Monsignor John Joseph Egan (1916-2001). In the University of Notre Dame Archives. Available online at http://archives.nd.edu/findaids/html/etext/alley006.htm.

36 The 1930 Census listed his residence as 221 N. Grand Ave., St. Louis University Dormitory, St. Louis, Missouri, but this must have been just a temporary residence at the time the census taker was passing through. See Dowling Family Genealogy in Ancestry.com.

37 Dowling Archives, as quoted in Fitzgerald, *Soul of Sponsorship* 16.

38 Fitzgerald, *Soul of Sponsorship* 17.

39 Ibid.

40 Ibid.

41 Ibid.

42 Glenn F. Chesnut, "A Century of Patristic Studies 1888–1988," in Henry Warner Bowden (ed.), *A Century of Church History* (Carbondale: Southern Illinois University Press, 1988), pp. 36–73.

43 McQuade, Obituary; Edward Dowling, Résumé; Dowling Family Genealogy in Ancestry.com.

44 Donald J. Kemper, "Catholic Integration in St. Louis, 1935-1947," *Missouri Historical Review*, October 1978, pp. 1–13; Ted LeBerthon, "Why Jim Crow Won at Webster College," *Pittsburgh Courier*, 5 Feb. 1944, p. 13; "Pressure Grows to Have Catholic College Doors Open to Negroes," *Pittsburgh Courier*, 19 Feb. 1944, p. 1; "St. Louis U. Lifts Color

Bar: Accepts Five Negroes for Summer Session," *Pittsburgh Courier*, 6 May 1944, p. 1.

45 Frisbie, *An Alley in Chicago*. Also see articles on John Joseph Egan in the *American National Biography* and the *Encyclopaedia Britannica*.

46 *Baltimore Afro-American*, November 27, 1956.

47 Adam Arenson, "Freeing Dred Scott: St. Louis confronts an icon of slavery, 1857-2007," *Common-Place* 8, no. 3 (April 2008), available online at http://www.common-place.org/vol-08/no-03/arenson/. For the photograph of Fr. Edward Dowling and Dred Scott's descendants, see this article or the original newspaper photo in the *St. Louis Globe-Democrat*, February 10, 1957, which can be found in the *St. Louis Globe-Democrat* Archives of the St. Louis Mercantile Library at the University of Missouri-St. Louis.

48 Except for the year he spent at St. Stanislaus Seminary in Cleveland as part of his tertianship. See McQuade, Obituary; Edward Dowling, Résumé. In his résumé he also referred to studies at St. Mary's College in St. Mary's, Kansas, and the Medill School of Journalism at Northwestern University in Chicago's Evanston suburb.

49 David J. Endres, "Dan Lord, Hollywood Priest," *America: The National Catholic Weekly*, December 12, 2005, article available online at http://www.americamagazine.org/content/article.cfm?article_id=4533. Also see the bibliography of Fr. Lord's pamphlets and links to those which are available online at http://en.wikipedia.org/wiki/Daniel_A._Lord.

50 Edward Dowling, Résumé; McQuade, Obituary.

51 *St. Louis Post-Dispatch*, 6 April 1960, quoted in McQuade, Obituary.

52 Fitzgerald, *Soul of Sponsorship* 18 and 118 n. 130. In note 33 (on page 109), Fitzgerald refers to the article by Rhea Felknor, "Glad Gethsemane, The Story of Father Edward Dowling, S.J.," *The Voice of St. Jude*, Fall 1960, as an important source. Back issues of that periodical can be found at the Claretian Missionaries Archives, located at the St. Jude League/Claretian Publications building at 205 West Monroe Avenue in Chicago.

53 Fitzgerald, *Soul of Sponsorship* 21.

54 Fitzgerald, *Soul of Sponsorship* 19-20, a story collected by Father Jim Egan, S.J., in his interview of Father Chuminatto in July 1986.

55 Fitzgerald, *Soul of Sponsorship* 14.

56 Fitzgerald, *Soul of Sponsorship* 20-21 and n. 41, citing a letter from Father Jim Swetnan, S.J., to Father Robert Fitzgerald, S.J., 5 June 1990.

57 Fitzgerald, *Soul of Sponsorship* 69. Fitzgerald said that Brother Malone, a Jesuit brother sacristan at the college church, was the source of this information.

58 Fitzgerald p. 111, n. 52. See also James Martin, S.J., *My Life with the Saints* (Chicago: Loyola Press, 2006), 229-230: "After two years in the novitiate a Jesuit pronounces vows of poverty, chastity, and obedience .... After vows he is no longer a novice: he may write *SJ* after his name .... Some American Jesuits, when pronouncing their vows, use a special name, following their first name, as a sign of reverence to a particular saint .... a vow name is taken to remind the person of a particular trait of the saint he wishes to emulate, to ask the saint's help in his vocation, or to remind him of a particular aspect of the saint's life."

59 Fitzgerald, *Soul of Sponsorship* 69, refers to this story as an example of the way that "Dowling, like Chesterton, [had] a love affair for the cross." The reference was to G. K. Chesterton, the famous Christian author of *Orthodoxy* (1908) and *The Everlasting Man* (1925). Edward Dowling, S.J., "Catholic Asceticism and the Twelve Steps," was published in the National Clergy Conference on Alcoholism's *Blue Book* for 1953. The article can be read on-line at AAHistoryLovers message no. 1322, September 13, 2001, at https://groups.yahoo.com/neo/groups/aahistorylovers/conversations/messages/1322 or at http://www.silkworth.net/religion_clergy/01038.html.

60 Fitzgerald, *Soul of Sponsorship* 18.

61 Fitzgerald, *Soul of Sponsorship* 18-19. See Dowling's November 1958 letter to Frank Riley. There was one other occasion where he had to be given the last rites because he had eaten so much.

62 Fitzgerald, *Soul of Sponsorship* 19. Letter from Father James McQuade to Jim Egan, 7 January 1985.

63 Fitzgerald, *Soul of Sponsorship* 19. Letter from Mary Wehner to Jim Egan, 7 January 1985.

64 Fitzgerald, *Soul of Sponsorship* 18, 55-60, 91-92, 94, 97, 101, and 122 n. 183.

65 As quoted in an article on Broun's conversion in *Time* magazine, 22 May 1939, available online at http://www.time.com/time/magazine/article/0,9171,761385,00.html

66 Ibid.

67 Letter from Fr. Ed Dowling to Bill Wilson, September 8, 1947, quoted in Fitzgerald, *Soul of Sponsorship* 47-48.

68 Fitzgerald, *Soul of Sponsorship* 57.

69 Quoted in Frisbie, *Alley in Chicago.*

70 Fitzgerald, "Father Ed Dowling and AA's Bill W.," *Catholic Digest.* A counter-claim is made in Richard P. McBrien, ed., *HarperCollins Encyclopedia of Catholicism* (San Francisco: HarperSanFrancisco, 1995), "Cana Conference," p. 214. The encyclopedia article states that "Cana began in New York in 1943 with a retreat given to eleven couples by Jesuit John P. Delaney. Delaney's description of the retreat in an article in *America* popularized the idea of a special program for the married." But the letter from Fr. Dowling to Bill Wilson which Fitzgerald cites was dated the previous year, 1942, making it clear that Dowling not only came up with the name Cana, but was the founder of the movement.

71 McBrien, "Cana Conference," p. 214.

72 Ibid.

73 A.A. *Grapevine*, May 1947 and June 1947, in the "A.A.'s Country-Wide News Circuit" section, relevant portions can be read online at AAHistoryLovers message no. 1371 and no. 1365 at https://groups.yahoo.com/neo/groups/aahistorylovers/conversations/messages/1371 and https://groups.yahoo.com/neo/groups/aahistorylovers/conversations/messages/1365.

74 Bill W., "To Father Ed—Godspeed!" [obituary of Father Edward Dowling], A.A. *Grapevine*, June 1960; repr. in AAHistoryLovers message 1731, https://groups.yahoo.com/neo/groups/aahistorylovers/conversations/messages/1731. See also McQuade, Obituary.

75 This is what Fr. Robert Fitzgerald suggested in *The Soul of Sponsorship*, see p. 43 and p. 115 n. 90. Bill W.'s letter to Fr. Ed, May 20, 1946 is in the New York Archives.

76 The Sodality of Our Lady was founded in Rome by a Belgian Jesuit priest named Father Jean Leontius (Van de Leeuw) in 1563. The first group in North America was founded in 1730 at the Ursuline School in New Orleans. A revised form of the Common Rule was established in 1910, beginning with the statement that "The Sodality of Our Lady, an association founded by the Society of Jesus and approved by the Holy See, is a religious body which aims at fostering in its members an ardent devotion, reverence, and filial love toward the Blessed Virgin." The Jesuits were given the task of spreading the use of the Rule, through a magazine called *The Queen's Work*, begun in 1913. Father J. Garesche,

S.J., was the first editor. He was succeeded by Father Daniel Aloysius Lord, S.J. (1888-1955), who in 1926 became national director of the Sodality of Our Lady and editor of their publication, *The Queen's Work*; the movement rapidly grew and flourished under his direction. In 1931, Father Lord established summer schools for Catholic Action to train sodality leaders. By 1963, at least 250,000 Catholics had taken part in these summer schools. During the 1930's and 1940's, Father Lord in his writings was seeking a middle way between socialism and capitalism for Catholics to follow. Father Lord stepped down from the editorship in 1948, but continued to write for *The Queen's Work* all the rest of his life. After the Second Vatican Council, the name of the Sodality was changed to "Christian Life Communities" and the Common Rule was revised into a set of "General Principles." See the article on Daniel Aloysius Lord, S.J., at http://en.wikipedia.org/wiki/Daniel_A._Lord, also *Jesuits of the Missouri Province: Brief Chronology of the Missouri Province* at http://www.jesuitsmissouri.org/iden/chronology.cfm, and the history of the Sodality at http://www.sodalityadw.org/History.html. Also see: Daniel A. Lord, *Played by Ear: The Autobiography of Daniel A. Lord, S.J.* (Chicago: Loyola University Press, 1956), which may be read online at http://archive.org/details/playedbyear001277mbp. Also see Mary Kathryn Barmann, *Father Daniel A. Lord, S.J.* (St. Louis, Missouri: St. Louis University, 1953) and Joseph T. McGlin, S.J., *Backstage Missionary, Father Dan Lord, S.J.* (New York: Pageant Press, 1958).

[77] Quoted from Fitzgerald, *Soul of Sponsorship* 31; see also McQuade, Obituary; Edward Dowling, Résumé.

[78] McQuade, Obituary.

[79] Letter from Fr. James McQuade (one of the other Jesuits on the staff of The Queen's Work) to Jim Egan, 4 October 1984, as quoted in Fitzgerald, *Soul of Sponsorship* 31.

[80] William E. Swegan with Glenn F. Chesnut, Ph.D. *The Psychology of Alcoholism*, Hindsfoot Foundation Series on Alcoholics Anonymous History (Bloomington, Indiana: iUniverse, 2011; orig. pub. 2003 as Sgt. Bill S. with Glenn F. Chesnut, *On the Military Firing Line in the Alcoholism Treatment Program*). On his response to Cadle's radio sermons on the old Cowper hymn—"There is a fountain filled with blood drawn from Emmanuel's veins; and sinners plunged beneath that flood lose all their guilty stains"—see p. 33 and p. 312 n. 3.

81   *Pass It On: The Story of Bill Wilson and How the A.A. Message Reached the World* (New York: Alcoholics Anonymous World Services, 1984), pp. 290 (Bill W.'s mother) and 334-335 (Dr. Frances Weeks). On Karen Horney, see Bill W., letter to Ollie in California, January 4, 1956, as cited in Fitzgerald, *The Soul of Sponsorship* 41.

82   Jack Alexander, "Alcoholics Anonymous," *Saturday Evening Post* (March 1, 1941).

83   Swegan and Chesnut, *Psychology of Alcoholism.*

84   Glenn F. Chesnut, *The Factory Owner & the Convict: Lives and Teachings of the A.A. Old Timers,* 2nd ed., Hindsfoot Foundation Series on Alcoholics Anonymous History (New York: iUniverse, 2005).

85   The photograph can be seen in Glenn F. Chesnut, "In Memoriam: Nancy Moyer Olson," obtainable online at http://hindsfoot.org/nomem1.html. For an account of her years in Washington, D.C. (1970-1980) as a powerful political figure in the U.S. Senate, see Nancy Olson, *With a Lot of Help from Our Friends: The Politics of Alcoholism,* ed. Glenn F. Chesnut, Hindsfoot Foundation Series on the History of Alcohol Treatment (New York: iUniverse / Writers Club Press, 2003).

86   Glenn F. Chesnut, *The Higher Power of the Twelve-Step Program: For Believers & Non-believers,* Hindsfoot Foundation Series on Spirituality and Theology (San Jose: iUniverse / Authors Choice Press, 2001), see e.g. Ch. 6, "Resentment."

87   See Chesnut, *The Factory Owner & the Convict* pp. 18-24 for extended excerpts from the article. Kenneth G. Merrill wrote it c. 1954 under the pseudonym Junius Senior, under the title "Drunks Are a Mess." It was reprinted in 1965 (two years after his death) in a magazine called *Barless* (written for recovering alcoholics in prison, as part of a program for alcoholic convicts which he had himself helped start). In this article he lays out, in layman's terms, his own theory of the ways in which early childhood trauma, and becoming blocked in one's normal psychological growth at a certain point, could result in alcoholic behavior in adulthood. He also explains his own conviction that the three things which gives the A.A. program such a miraculous healing power are (1) unconditional love, (2) a higher power who grants self-forgiveness, peace, and freedom from fear, and (3) the end of personal isolation from other human beings, which finally allows us to begin "growing up" emotionally. Ken Merrill's article can also be read online at http://hindsfoot.org/nsbend2.html.

88   Ernest Kurtz, *Shame & Guilt*, second edition, revised and updated, Hindsfoot Foundation Series on Treatment and Recovery (Lincoln, Nebraska: iUniverse, 2007). May be read online at http://hindsfoot.org/eksg.html.

89   By the Neo-Freudians we mean psychiatrists like Erich Fromm, Karen Horney, and Erik H. Erikson, who emigrated from Germany to the United States in the 1930's, as well as the Austrian physician Alfred Adler. See Swegan and Chesnut, *Psychology of Alcoholism*. Swegan, who got sober in 1948 on Long Island, New York, and was a protégé of Mrs. Marty Mann, served as the principal spokesman for the wing of early A.A. which emphasized the psychological side of the A.A. program instead of the spiritual side. See also Merrill, "Drunks Are a Mess." For more about Merrill, the South Bend factory owner who started A.A. in 1943 in northern Indiana and southwest Michigan, see Chesnut, *The Factory Owner & the Convict*.

90   Fitzgerald, "Father Ed Dowling and AA's Bill W.," *Catholic Digest*.

91   The book that is presently used as the major study work in Recovery, Inc. is Abraham Low, *Mental Health Through Will-Training: A System of Self-Help in Psychotherapy as Practiced by Recovery, Inc.* (Boston: Christopher Publishing House, 1950). The earlier work was Abraham A. Low, *The Technique of Self-Help in Psychiatric Aftercare*, 3 vols., (Chicago: Recovery, Inc., 1943), including *Lectures to Relatives of Former Patients* (Boston: Christopher Publishing House, 1967).

92   Edward Dowling, "Catholic Asceticism."

93   Edward Dowling, "Catholic Asceticism."

94   McQuade, Obituary.

95   "Father Ed Dowling — Bill W.'s Confidant and Friend," *Box 459*. Also see McQuade, Obituary.

96   And also in other places, see e.g. Ralph Pfau, *The Golden Book of Sanity* (Indianapolis: SMT Guild, 1963), 47n.

97   Kurtz, Linda Farris, DPA, *Self-Help and Support Groups: A Handbook for Practitioners, Sage Sourcebook for the Human Services*, Vol. 34 (Thousand Oaks, California: Sage Publications, 1997); Linda Farris Kurtz, DPA, and Adrienne Chambon, Ph.D., "Comparison of Self-Help Groups for Mental Health," *Health and Social Work* 12 (1987): 275-283.

98   McQuade, Obituary.

99 McQuade, Obituary. Telephone conversation with Ernest Kurtz in April 2012 about the possible linkage with the later group called Emotions Anonymous. Neurotics Anonymous (N/A) was officially founded in 1964 in Washington, D.C. by Grover Boydston. In 1971 Marion Flesch in Minnesota led a breakaway movement within N/A that eventually took the name Emotions Anonymous (EA), which is now the larger group within the English-speaking world.

100 The *Blue Book* published annually by the National Clergy Council on Alcoholism (today called the National Catholic Council on Alcoholism and Related Drug Problems), Vol. V, 167; as quoted in Fitzgerald, *Soul of Sponsorship* 69.

101 As quoted in Fitzgerald, *Soul of Sponsorship* 73.

102 See the attorney's own description of the program in Samuel M. Starr, "'Divorcées Anonymous' a Remarkable Success," *Virginia Law Weekly: Divorce and Family Relations*, 50-52. Also see the detailed study in Kristin Celello, *Making Marriage Work: A History of Marriage and Divorce in the Twentieth-Century United States* (Chapel Hill: University of North Carolina Press, 2009), Ch. 3 "They Learned to Love Again: Marriage Saving in the 1950s," pp. 72-102. In the earlier part of the 1950s, the group obtained a good deal of attention in popular American magazines. See for example A. Prowitt, "Divorcées Anonymous," *Good Housekeeping* 130 (Feb. 1950): 35; Joseph Millard, "Divorcées Anonymous," *Reader's Digest* 56 (May 1950): 15-18; "They Mend Broken Marriages," *American Magazine* 149 (June 1950): 107; "Divorcées Anonymous," *Time* 66 (Sept. 26, 1955): 64; and Vance Packard, "New Cure for Sick Marriages," *American Magazine* 161 (May 1956): 30-31, 96-100.

103 See McQuade, Obituary.

104 Fitzgerald, "Father Ed Dowling and AA's Bill W.," *Catholic Digest.*

105 *A.A. Bulletin* No. 1 (November 14, 1940), published by the Alcoholic Foundation, National Headquarters—Alcoholics Anonymous, available online at http://hindsfoot.org/bullno1.pdf.

106 Bob Pearson, *A.A. World History 1985* (unpublished draft), Chapt. 5. "Father Ed Dowling — Bill W.'s Confidant and Friend," *Box 459* puts all this slightly earlier, and claims that Father Ed learned about Alcoholics Anonymous in late 1939 and attended his first A.A. meeting in Chicago in March 1940.

[107] Don B., *History of the Chicago Group*, available online at http://hindsfoot. org/chicago1.pdf. Jack Alexander, when he was researching the *Saturday Evening Post* article that was published on March 1, 1941, was also deeply impressed when he "visited the Chicago group and met several members who were newspaper people, and he said these guys talked my language."

[108] Marty Mann, "The Pastor's Resources in Dealing with Alcoholics."

[109] Ibid.

[110] Bill Wilson, "To Father Ed—Godspeed!"

[111] Nancy Olson, Brief biographies.

[112] *Dr. Bob and the Good Oldtimers* 179-181.

[113] Nancy Olson, Brief biographies.

[114] Don B., *History of the Chicago Group*.

[115] Jack Alexander, "Alcoholics Anonymous," *Saturday Evening Post* (March 1, 1941).

[116] Bob Pearson, *A.A. World History 1985* (unpublished draft), Chapt. 5. The date is corroborated by Renee (Eastern Missouri District 51 Archivist), "From Golden Moments of Reflection: 1st A.A. meeting in Missouri at Gibson Hotel on Enright October 30, 1940," available online at http:// health.groups.yahoo.com/group/AAHistoryLovers/message/5881. *A.A. Bulletin* No. 1 (November 14, 1940)—published by the Alcoholic Foundation, National Headquarters Alcoholics Anonymous, available online at http://hindsfoot.org/bullno1.pdf —does not list the newly formed St. Louis group among the twenty-two well established A.A. groups but does include St. Louis in its list of sixteen additional cities "where there are isolated A.A. members who have recovered either through the book alone or through brief contact with established centers." The St. Louis group did in fact survive and continue to grow: *A.A. Bulletin* No. 2 (January 15, 1941)—published by the Alcoholic Foundation, National Headquarters Alcoholics Anonymous, available online at http://hindsfoot. org/bullno2.pdf —said that "St. Louis, Mo., which two months ago was virtually 'without benefit of A.A.,' now has ten members who meet every Wednesday evening." An early A.A. document dated less than a year later ("List of A.A. Groups—as of Dec. 31, 1941," available online at http://hindsfoot.org/dec1941.pdf) said that St. Louis now had 75 A.A. members. The A.A. *Grapevine* for Feb. 1946, in the News Circuit column (as quoted in AAHistoryLovers message no. 1229, https://groups.yahoo. com/neo/groups/aahistorylovers/conversations/messages/1229), said that:

"The 400 members of the eight St. Louis, Mo., Groups have held their fifth anniversary meeting," presumably dating St. Louis' anniversary, not from the first gathering on October 30, 1940, but from January 8, 1941, when the second person got permanently sober.

117   *Pass It On* 245.

118   Born in St. Louis, see "Jack Alexander Gave A.A. Its First Big Boost," *Box 4-5-9*, February/March 2008—available online as AAHistoryLovers message no. 6218 at https://groups.yahoo.com/neo/groups/aahistorylovers/conversations/messages/6218. Date of birth given in AAHistoryLovers message no. 2182 — available online at https://groups.yahoo.com/neo/groups/aahistorylovers/conversations/messages/2182 — where the excellent A.A. historian Jared Lobdell notes that the Social Security Death Index gives the name of a man who must have been our Jack as "John Alexander," born February 8, 1903; died September 17, 1975 in St. Petersburg, Florida.

119   Jack Alexander's obituary, *New York Times* (September 20, 1975), a short summary may be read online in AAHistoryLovers message no. 6211 at https://groups.yahoo.com/neo/groups/aahistorylovers/conversations/messages/6211.

120   Jack Alexander, "Jack Alexander of Saturday Evening Post Fame Thought A.A.s Were Pulling His Leg," *A.A. Grapevine* (May 1945), with a copy of the article in AAHistoryLovers message no. 1814, available online at https://groups.yahoo.com/neo/groups/aahistorylovers/conversations/messages/1814. See also "Jack Alexander Gave A.A. Its First Big Boost," *Box 4-5-9* (February/March 2008); there is a copy in AAHistoryLovers message no. 6248, which can be read online at https://groups.yahoo.com/neo/groups/aahistorylovers/conversations/messages/6218. The date of Sunday, December 15, 1940 for the visit to Philadelphia is from a letter which Bill Wilson (in New York City) wrote to Jimmy Burwell on December 9, 1940 (see AAHistoryLovers message no. 1705, available online as https://groups.yahoo.com/neo/groups/aahistorylovers/conversations/messages/1705): "Jack Alexander expects to be in Philadelphia all day next Sunday [which would have been December 15, 1940]. He would like to see Drs. Hammer and Saul and also the man in charge of alcoholics at the Philadelphia General Hospital. Will let you know just when he will arrive and may come down myself, proceeding with him, Sunday night to Akron where he will also take in the Cleveland group, going from there to Chicago and finally writing his article at St.

Louis, which is his home town. This schedule is still tentative so will keep you posted."

[121] Alexander, "Jack Alexander of Saturday Evening Post Fame."

[122] Alexander, "Jack Alexander of Saturday Evening Post Fame." Alexander, "Alcoholics Anonymous," *Saturday Evening Post*, said (probably referring to his Chicago visit) "On one of the most influential newspapers in the country, I found that the city editor, the assistant city editor, and a nationally known reporter were A.A.s, and strong in the confidence of their publisher." See also Don B., *History of the Chicago Group*.

[123] See Wilson, letter to Jimmy Burwell on December 9, 1940.

[124] Pearson, *A.A. World History 1985* (unpublished draft), Chapt. 5.

[125] We see the story of the founding of the Washington D.C. black A.A. group appearing in print for the first time ten years afterwards, in "Jim's Story" in the Big Book (2nd, 3rd, and 4th eds.). This is the story of Jim Scott M.D., a black physician from Washington, D.C., who is described as "one of the earliest members of A.A.'s first black group." In that story Jim tells how he attended a meeting at the home of a woman named Ella G., which "was the first meeting of a colored group in A.A., so far as I know" (Big Book 4th ed., pp. 232 and 244). Bob Pearson, *A.A. World History 1985* (unpublished draft), Chapt. 3, says that "The Washington Colored Group was founded in April '45 by Jimmy S. It later changed its name to the Cosmopolitan Group to convey the fact that it was 'a group for all people, all races; it doesn't matter who you are.'"

Dr. Jim S. was asked to speak at the Second A.A. International Convention in St. Louis in 1955, where Bill Wilson repeated the claim that this was the first black A.A. group and—such was the speed at which human memories faded—even the people in St. Louis seem to have forgotten (or never been told) that the first black A.A. group was established in their city, not Washington D.C. See *Alcoholics Anonymous Comes of Age* (New York: Alcoholics Anonymous World Services, 1957), p. 37, where Bill W. said: "'Dr. Jim S. ... re-enacted for us his own struggle to start the very first group among Negroes, his own people.'"

And in fact, the Washington D.C. group was not even the second black A.A. group formed. That honor went to Chicago, whose first black A.A. group was started in March 1945, a month before the Washington D.C. group got off the ground. This was the famous Evans Avenue Group, still active and going strong in Chicago today. You can see photographs of the great early black A.A. leaders on the walls of their building. It was started by Earl Redmond, who was eventually joined by Bill Williams (in December 1945) and other strong and self-possessed men who became leaders in the black A.A. movement, not only in Chicago, but also in two of the big industrial cities of Indiana (Gary and South Bend) further east. See Glenn Chesnut, "Chicago in 1945: The first black people to join A.A.," containing my interview in July 17, 1999 of Bill Williams (who was by then 96 years old) and Jimmy Hodges, another great black A.A. leader from Chicago, at http://hindsfoot.org/nblack3.html.

[126] Arthur S. (Arlington, Texas), *A Narrative Timeline of AA History*, see Sept. 1936 and Apr. 26, 1939 — available online at http://hindsfoot.org/aatimeline.pdf, also at http://silkworth.net/timelines/timelines_public/timelines_public.html. *Pass It On* 175. Robert Thomsen, *Bill W: The absorbing and deeply moving life story of Bill Wilson, co-founder of Alcoholics Anonymous* (New York: Harper & Row, 1975) 288.

[127] Thomsen, *Bill W.* 288.

[128] Arthur S., *A Narrative Timeline of AA History*. On p. 172 of *Alcoholics Anonymous Comes of Age*, it says that Bill and Lois moved out of Clinton Street not on April 26 but on May 1. (Thomsen, *Bill W.* 288, said however that May 1 was the bank's deadline, not the date they actually moved out.)

[129] Arthur S., *A Narrative Timeline of AA History* and *Pass It On* 239. The latter says that Bill and Lois stayed in the upstairs bedroom at 334½ West 24th St. not for a year, but for only five months.

[130] *Pass It On* 238-9; Francis Hartigan, *Bill W.: A Biography of Alcoholics Anonymous Cofounder Bill Wilson* (New York: St. Martin's Press, 2000) 129.

[131] Hartigan, *Bill W.* agrees that Father Dowling had already started the first A.A. group in St. Louis before he made his first visit to Bill W., and has Dowling visiting the Chicago A.A. group early in 1940, during the Spring.

[132] Bill Wilson's account on page 38 of *Alcoholics Anonymous Comes of Age* (1957).

[133] The figure of a million dollars was remembered by Hank's son, see *Pass It On* 195.

[134] Thomsen, *Bill W.* 305-7.

[135] For some of the details on the Hindu contribution see Philip Goldberg, *American Veda: From Emerson and the Beatles to Yoga and Meditation— How Indian Spirituality Changed the West* (New York: Three Rivers Press, 2010), Chapt. 3, "New Thought in Old Wineskins," pp. 47-66.

136   See AAHL Message 9505 from Glenn Chesnut, "Buddhist quote on karma in James Allen," at https://groups.yahoo.com/neo/groups/aahistorylovers/ conversations/messages/9505. The message notes that in James Allen, *As a Man Thinketh*, there is an extended quote from the Buddhist scripture called the Dhammapada at the beginning of Chapter 1, "Thought and Character":

> Thought in the mind hath made us. What we are
> By thought was wrought and built. If a man's mind
> Hath evil thoughts, pain comes on him as comes
> The wheel the ox behind . . . . If one endure in purity
> Of thought, joy follows him as his own shadow — sure.

This is the classic Buddhist description of karma. A translation of the original Buddhist work may be read at: http://www.sacred-texts.com/bud/ sbe10/sbe1003.htm

137   See also Mel B., *New Wine: The Spiritual Roots of The Twelve Step Miracle* (Center City, Minnesota: Hazelden, 1991), p. 105. Mel, who attends Unity Church and is a devout believer in the power of New Thought spirituality, is one of the two or three most important A.A. thinkers from the second generation (he and Ernest Kurtz represented two different sides of the A.A. movement during that period, Mel's the more intuitive side and Ernie's the more intellectual).

138   Emmet Fox, *The Sermon on the Mount: The Key to Success in Life* and *The Lord's Prayer: An Interpretation* (New York: Grosset & Dunlap, 1938; orig. pub. New York: Harper & Brothers, 1934). Emmet Fox, *Power Through Constructive Thinking* (New York: Harper & Brothers, 1940; the individual articles which make up the volume were copyrighted from 1932 to 1940).

139   Available online as AAHistoryLovers message 1705 from Nancy Olson (Mar 13, 2004). Bill W. spoke of receiving a copy of Jim's historical narrative in a letter he wrote back to Jim on December 11, 1947, so the account was necessarily written before that date: "From what I can remember, Bill's only special preparation for [writing the Big Book] was confined to the reading of four very well known books, the influence of which can clearly be seen in the A.A. Book. Bill probably got most of his ideas from one of these books, namely James' 'Varieties of Religious Experience.' I have always felt this was because Bill himself had undergone such a violent spiritual experience. He also gained a fine basic insight of spirituality through Emmet Fox's 'Sermon on the Mount,' and a good

portion of the psychological approach of A.A. from Dick Peabody's 'Common Sense of Drinking.' It is my opinion that a great deal of Bill's traditions [which he first wrote about in the *Grapevine* in 1945-6] came from the fourth book. Lewis Browne's 'This Believing World.' From this book, I believe Bill attained a remarkable perception of possible future pitfalls for groups of our kind for it clearly shows that the major failures of religions and cults in the past have been due to one of three things: Too much organization, too much politics, and too much money or power."

140 Mel B., commentary on Emmet Fox's "Making Your Life Worthwhile," available online at http://hindsfoot.org/fox1.html. See also Mel B., *New Wine* 105.

141 Doug B. (Riverside, California), AAHistoryLovers message 4003 (January 7, 2007), "Re: Emmet Fox's secretary and Al S." available online at https://groups.yahoo.com/neo/groups/aahistorylovers/conversations/messages/4003.

142 Igor I. Sikorsky, Jr., *AA's Godparents: Carl Jung, Emmet Fox, Jack Alexander* (Minneapolis: CompCare Publishers, 1990) 23, as cited in Mel Barger, AAHistoryLovers message 4001 (January 5, 2007), "Emmet Fox's secretary and Al Steckman (correct spelling)," available online at https://groups. yahoo.com/neo/groups/aahistorylovers/conversations/messages/4001.

143 *Dr. Bob and the Good Oldtimers: A Biography, with Recollections of Early A.A. in the Midwest* (New York: Alcoholics Anonymous World Services, 1980), 310.

144 Mel B., *New Wine*, p. 105.

145 William (Barefoot Bill) Lash, "Tex B. (Sober 2/6/47)," describing early A.A. in the Chicago area, AAHistoryLovers message no. 1881 (June 22, 2004), at https://groups.yahoo.com/neo/groups/aahistorylovers/conversations/messages/1881.

146 Mel B., "Re: Conference Approved Literature," his gratitude for Emmet Fox's book on *The Sermon on the Mount*, AAHistoryLovers message no. 1861 (June 15, 2004), at https://groups.yahoo.com/neo/groups/aahistorylovers/conversations/messages/1861.

147 Harold A. "Al" Steckman (December 9, 1903-February 1978), worked in advertising and film, came into A.A. in March 1944. Al Steckman, *Bert D.: Hardhat, Inebriate, Scholar* (Memphis: Harbor House, 1976). See Jared Lobdell, "Re: Emmet Fox's secretary," AAHistoryLovers message no. 7249 (March 19, 2011) at https://groups.yahoo.com/neo/groups/

aahistorylovers/conversations/messages/7249 and "Re: Can anyone tell me a little more history about Al S.," AAHistoryLovers message no. 6761 (Jul 29, 2010) at https://groups.yahoo.com/neo/groups/aahistorylovers/conversations/messages/6761; and Arthur S. (Arlington, Texas), "Re: Responsibility Declaration," AAHistoryLovers message no. 2485 (June 12, 2005) at https://groups.yahoo.com/neo/groups/aahistorylovers/conversations/messages/2485. His sobriety date of 1944 is also given in Arthur S. (Arlington, Texas), *Timelines in A.A.'s History* (the earliest version of his timeline) at http://silkworth.net/timelines/timelines.html. See also Nell Wing, *Grateful to Have Been There: My 42 Years with Bill and Lois, and the Evolution of Alcoholics Anonymous,* 1st ed. (Park Ridge, Illinois: Parkside Publishing, 1993), page 87. The Declaration of Unity which was recited in Miami in 1970 was "This we owe to A.A.'s future; to place our common welfare first; to keep our fellowship united. For on A.A. unity depend our lives and the lives of those to come," see "A Declaration of Unity," AAHistoryLovers message no. 278 (June 11, 2002) at https://groups.yahoo.com/neo/groups/aahistorylovers/conversations/messages/278.

[148] Arthur S., "Re: Responsibility Declaration," AAHistoryLovers no. 2485.

[149] See under Al S. in the A.A. People section at http://www.barefootsworld.net/aapeople.html.

[150] Arthur S. (Arlington, Texas), Tom E. (Wappingers Falls, New York), and Glenn C. (South Bend, Indiana), *Alcoholics Anonymous (AA) Recovery Outcome Rates: Contemporary Myth and Misinterpretation* (October 11, 2008), page 30. Available online at http://hindsfoot.org/recout01.pdf.

[151] *A Manual for Alcoholics Anonymous,* commonly referred to as *The Akron Manual* — the earliest known version of this booklet can be read online at http://hindsfoot.org/akrman1.html and http://hindsfoot.org/akrman2.html. This, the first surviving edition of the *Akron Manual,* came out circa June 1942, see Glenn Chesnut, "Re: More than one edition of the Akron Manual?" AAHistoryLovers message 7516 (July 26, 2011) at https://groups.yahoo.com/neo/groups/aahistorylovers/conversations/messages/7516. The cover of the pamphlet talks about members with five, six and seven years of sobriety and on page 15 it states that the Akron Group has been in existence for seven years. Dr. Bob and Bill Dotson both got sober in June 1935, which meant that they would have had seven years of sobriety in June of 1942, and the Akron Group would likewise have been in existence for seven years in June 1942. The printed version which

is currently available for sale at Dr. Bob's house in Akron, on the other hand, is a later revised edition with some material removed, including the reading list.

152 The first Beginners Meeting in Detroit was conducted by the North-West Group at 10216 Plymouth Road on Monday night, June 14, 1943. The pamphlet is available online at http://hindsfoot.org/detr0.html.

153 The version in the *Detroit Pamphlet* can be read online at http://hindsfoot.org/detr4.html.

154 Fox, *Sermon on the Mount* 13.

155 Ibid. 24-25.

156 Ibid. 8.

157 Ibid. 10.

158 Ibid. 21, 37, 44-45, and 50-51.

159 Ibid. 22.

160 Ibid. 35, 109; Fox, *Constructive Thinking* 165. Glenn F. Chesnut, *God and Spirituality: Philosophical Essays*, Hindsfoot Foundation Series on Spirituality and Theology (New York: iUniverse, 2010), see Ch. 14 (pp. 258-281) on "The Three Primal Hypostases," especially the second hypostasis, which I here termed the *Logos*, but is the same as what is called *Nous* or *Intellectus* in other ancient and medieval philosophical systems.

161 The term "Creative Intelligence" is used in the book *Alcoholics Anonymous* on pp. 12 and 46, note also p. 10.

162 Fox, *Constructive Thinking* 3, 165, 136, 166. Chesnut, *God and Spirituality*, see Ch. 13 (pp. 238-257) on the new dynamic concept of God found in the Boston Personalist philosophers and the philosophers Rudolf Herman Lotze, Alfred North Whitehead, and Charles Hartshorne; and Ch. 14 (pp. 258-281) on "The Three Primal Hypostases," especially the *Energetikos* (the third hypostasis). The ancient Greek philosopher Aristotle famously talked about what he called the "four causes," using the example of a carpenter building a bed. In Aristotelian terminology, medieval Christian philosophers and theologians were mainly concerned with the "final cause" or "teleological explanation," that is, the goal the carpenter had when he decided to build the bed. Modern science confines itself instead to investigating the "efficient cause" or "moving cause," which in this case is the carpenter, who supplies the source of energy and furnishes the agency through which the bed is built. (The material cause

is the wood out of which the bed is constructed, and the formal cause is the idea or plan for what the bed should be which the carpenter had in his head before he began building.)

[163] Fox, in his commentary on the Lord's Prayer in *The Sermon on the Mount* 129 and *Power Through Constructive Thinking* 165.

[164] Fox, *Constructive Thinking* 2.

[165] Étienne Gilson, *The Elements of Christian Philosophy* (New York: New American Library, 1960), 208. The great Catholic scholar Étienne Gilson (1884-1978), after teaching the history of medieval philosophy at the University of Paris from 1921 to 1932, set up the Pontifical Institute of Medieval Studies in Toronto, where he was Director of Studies, in addition to serving as a member of the Pontifical Academy of Saint Thomas Aquinas in Rome.

[166] Bernard J. F. Lonergan, *Insight: A Study of Human Understanding* (London: Longmans, Green & Co., 1957). Compare this with St. Augustine's doctrine of illuminationism and his concept of God as Truth Itself, that is, God as the divine power to break through our denial structure and strip off all our alibis and excuses and fraudulent attempts at self-justification, and reveal to us the truth about who we truly were.

[167] Fox, *Constructive Thinking* 3.

[168] Ibid. 4-5.

[169] *Alcoholics Anonymous*, 4th ed. (New York: Alcoholics Anonymous World Services, 2001; orig. pub. 1939) 12, 46.

[170] Ibid. 49.

[171] Ibid. 55.

[172] Ibid. 55.

[173] See Dick B., "'God as We Understood Him'—The A.A. Story," at http://www.dickb.com/aaarticles/AA-Story.shtml, who cites Samuel Shoemaker, *Extraordinary Living for Ordinary Men: Excerpts Selected from the Writings of Sam Shoemaker* (Grand Rapids, Michigan: Zondervan, 1965), p. 76; also Samuel Moor Shoemaker, Jr., *Children of the Second Birth: Being a Narrative of Spiritual Miracles in a City Parish*, (New York: Fleming H. Revell, 1927), pp. 25 and 47. Dick B. also cites Oxford Group author Stephen Foot, *Life Began Yesterday* (London: William Heinemann, 1935), pp. 12-13 (cf. 175), "Life began for me with a surrender of all that I know of self to all that I knew of God."

174 Fox, *Constructive Thinking*, see both the chapters on "Life After Death" (pp. 195-223) and "Reincarnation" (pp. 227-256).

175 Fox, *Constructive Thinking* 227-229.

176 *Pass It On* 276-280.

177 Lois Wilson, as we all know, came from a Swedenborgian background, and Emanuel Swedenborg had certainly believed that he had been in regular contact with the spirits of the dead, but the idea that we had valid memories of past lives or that our souls would be reincarnated into other lives here on earth were not part of Swedenborgian belief. He held that human souls were immortal in the sense that they survived death and would continue to live for all times to come. But based on my reading of Swedenborgian sources, he also seems to have believed that souls, when they appeared, were created out of nothing, and had not always existed from infinite times past.

178 See http://en.wikipedia.org/wiki/Matt_Talbot, http://savior.org/saints/talbot.htm, http://www.catholicassociates.com/leaflets/A%20Man%20for%20our%20Times_Rev1.pdf, and http://www.frgabrielburke.com/2011/01/venerable-matt-talbot.html.

179 Ibid.

180 Ibid.

181 Ibid.

182 See the article on Matt Talbot at http://en.wikipedia.org/wiki/Matt_Talbot.

183 *Dr. Bob and the Good Oldtimers* 210-211.

184 Glenn Chesnut, "Re: What was the Matt Talbot Club circa December 1939?," AAHistoryLovers message no. 7692, at https://groups.yahoo.com/neo/groups/aahistorylovers/conversations/messages/7692. The original first printing Golden Book in the Indianapolis A.A. office, instead of using the initials SMT, says "Copyright 1947, The Sons of Matt Talbot, Indianapolis."

185 Rita Akerman, "Matt Talbot — A Man for Our Times," available at http://www.catholicassociates.com/leaflets/A Man for our Times_Rev1.pdf.

186 Thomsen, *Bill W.* 308.

187 Loyola, *Exercises* 136. My English translation is based on San Ignacio de Loyola, *Los Ejercicios Espirituales* (the Spanish text of Loyola's *Spiritual Exercises*) available online at http://www.librear.com/archivosebookstres/Loyola%20Ignacio%20de-Ejercicios%20Espirituales.pdf. My translation

has been compared with one of the standard English versions: *The Spiritual Exercises of St. Ignatius of Loyola*, trans. from the autograph by Father Elder Mullan, S.J. (New York: P.J. Kennedy & Sons, 1914), available online at http://www.nwjesuits.org/JesuitSpirituality/SpiritualExercises.html or http://www.sacred-texts.com/chr/seil/index.htm.

188   Loyola, *Exercises* 138.

189   Ibid. 140-142.

190   Ibid. 146.

191   The folk singer Pete Seeger was a famous singer of this song. When I hear the lines "my daddy was a miner, and I'm a miner's son," this turns it into more than just a folk song for me, because my father was in fact a coal miner in Harlan Country when they were unionizing, and what was at stake for him was my future well-being even more than his: would his young son have food to eat and a roof over his head? For Pete Seeger's version, go to You Tube and call up https://www.youtube.com/watch?v=msEYGql0drc or https://www.youtube.com/watch?v=5iAIM02kv0g.

192   Marian T. Horvat, "Let None Dare Call it Liberty: The Catholic Church in Colonial America," available online at http://www.traditioninaction. org/History/B_001_Colonies.html. Also see (as cited in that work) Mary Augustina Ray, *American Opinion of Roman Catholicism in the Eighteenth Century* (New York: 1936), 27 and Thomas Hughes, *The History of the Society of Jesus in North America: Colonial and Federal*, Vol. 1 (London, New York, Bombay, and Calcutta: 1907, 2nd ed. 1970).

193   *Twelve and Twelve* 74-75.

194   Glenn F. Chesnut, "The Pattern of the Past: Augustine's Debate with Eusebius and Sallust," in John Deschner, Leroy T. Howe, and Klaus Penzel (eds.), *Our Common History as Christians: Essays in Honor of Albert C. Outler* (New York: Oxford University Press, 1975), pp. 69-95: on the City of God vs. the Earthly City, original sin, and providence in Augustine's theology of history.

195   Ernest Kurtz, *Not-God: A History of Alcoholics Anonymous*, expanded edition (Center City, Minnesota: Hazelden, 1991; orig. 1979).

196   *Alcoholics Anonymous Comes of Age* 258.

197   Thomsen, *Bill W.* 307-308.

198   One exception among Protestant commentators was that very Catholic theologian John Wesley (along with the following Methodist tradition)

where "having the mind which was in Christ Jesus" was one of the standard phrases which Wesley used to explain what he meant by *teleiôsis* or "Christian perfection," that is, the goal (*telos*) to which the spiritual life was directed.

199   *Twelve and Twelve*, chapter on Step Four, p. 45.

200   *Dr. Bob and the Good Oldtimers* 75.

201   Thomsen, *Bill W.* 309. See also Robert Fitzgerald's comments on this in his article on "Father Ed Dowling and AA's Bill W.," *Catholic Digest*.

202   Ernest Kurtz and Katherine Ketcham, *The Spirituality of Imperfection: Modern Wisdom from Classic Stories* (New York: Bantam Books, 1992).

203   This was at Perkins of School of Theology at Southern Methodist University. I was asked to read this paper to the entire seminary, including both students and faculty, the only time during those years that a student was ever asked to read a scholarly paper to the whole body. The seminary professors were especially interested in my paper, because I also did a comparison with the way the concept of Christian perfection was taught by John Wesley, the founder of the Methodist movement.

204   *An Explanation of the Baltimore Catechism of Christian Doctrine*, No. 4, Annotated Edition for Teachers (1891), available online at http://www. gutenberg.org/cache/epub/14554/pg14554.html. The problem with the Baltimore Catechism in practice was that an authoritarian and overly strict parochial school teacher could terrorize and even permanently traumatize young children by over-emphasizing things like the warning in Question 53: "'Venial' sin does not drive out all the grace; it wounds the soul, it weakens it just as slight wounds weaken the body. If it falls very frequently into venial sin, it will fall very soon into mortal sin also; for the Holy Scripture says that he that contemneth small things shall fall by little and little. (Ecclus. 19:1). A venial sin seems a little thing, but if we do not avoid it we shall by degrees fall into greater, or mortal, sin. Venial sin makes God less friendly to us and displeases Him. Now if we really love God, we will not displease Him even in the most trifling things." There are many alcoholics from Roman Catholic backgrounds who still come into the A.A. program explaining how, as young people, this kind of teaching style convinced them that they were going to hell anyway—that leading a life free of sin was impossible for them, for they had tried repeatedly and failed to achieve those absolutist standards—so that they had simply abandoned themselves to every kind of sin, and fallen deeper and deeper into evil and degradation.

205 The so-called Four Absolutes did not come out of any ancient Christian tradition, and had nothing to do with the traditional teaching of either the Roman Catholic Church or the Protestant movement. The over-simplified idea that one could sum up all of Jesus's message in commandments to practice four "absolute" virtues appeared originally in a book by Robert E. Speer (1867-1947) called *The Principles of Jesus* (New York: Fleming H. Revell, 1902). Speer had only a year of seminary, and missed most of the points in Jesus's preaching, but there were people who read his books because of his important role in the foreign missionary work of the American Presbyterian missionary society. Two of his articles were published in *The Fundamentals*, and he is in most ways best considered as a Fundamentalist, but he ultimately ended up abandoning the Fundamentalist Presbyterian leader John Gresham Machen when the northern Presbyterian church removed Machen from his position as Professor of New Testament at Princeton Seminary. That is, if I may be excused for putting it this way, Speer was not a devoted enough Fundamentalist to lose his own position in the Presbyterian church over it. The idea of the Four Absolutes was then expanded further in a book by Yale University Professor Henry B. Wright (1877-1923), called *The Will of God and a Man's Lifework* (New York: The Young Men's Christian Association Press, 1909), from where the idea was picked up by Frank Buchman (the founder of the Oxford Group).

206 *Alcoholics Anonymous* 10.

207 A more conventional English translation of the Cherubic Hymn would read: "We who mystically represent the Cherubim and sing to the Life-Giving Trinity the thrice-holy hymn. Let us now lay aside all earthly cares that we may receive the King of all, escorted invisibly by the angelic orders. Alleluia, Alleluia, Alleluia."

208 Thomsen, *Bill W.* 116-117.

209 See the section on nature mysticism in Glenn F. Chesnut, *Images of Christ* (San Francisco: Harper & Row, 1984) 57-62, where these three poems by Wordsworth are cited and discussed.

210 *Alcoholics Anonymous* 1.

211 Thomsen, *Bill W.* 118-119.

212 *Alcoholics Anonymous* 12.

213 With parallel accounts in Acts 22:6-21 and 26:12-18.

214 Arthur S. (Arlington, Texas), *Narrative Timeline of AA History*; Kurtz, *Not-God* 15 and 310 n. 26.

215 Alexander Lambert, M.D. "Care and Control of the Alcoholic," *Boston Medical and Surgical Journal* [now called the *New England Journal of Medicine*] 166 (April 25, 1912): 615-621 and Alexander Lambert, "The Obliteration of the Craving for Narcotics," *Journal of the American Medical Association* LIII, 13 (1909): 985-989—both as cited in Bill Pittman, *The Roots of Alcoholics Anonymous* (Center City, Minnesota: Hazelden, 1999; orig. pub. as *A.A.: The Way It Began* by Glen Abbey Books in 1988) 164-169.

216 From Alexander Lambert, "Care and Control of the Alcoholic," as cited in Pittman, *The Roots of Alcoholics Anonymous* 164.

217 William D. Silkworth, "Reclamation of the Alcoholic," *Medical Record* (April 21, 1937), available online at http://www.aa-nia-dist11.org/Documents/silk.pdf.

218 Anonymous, "I'm a Nurse in an Alcoholic Ward," *Saturday Evening Post* (Oct. 18, 1952), written by a nurse who worked in the A.A. ward at Knickerbocker Hospital in New York City. "We give them vitamins to re-establish nutritional balance, fruit juices to combat dehydration, and bromides and belladonna for jagged nerves."

219 *Alcoholics Anonymous* 13.

220 *Alcoholics Anonymous Comes of Age* 62.

221 *Alcoholics Anonymous* 14.

222 *Alcoholics Anonymous Comes of Age* 62-63.

223 Bill W., "Re: Bill's spiritual experience -- belladonna induced?" an excerpt from his 1958 talk to the New York City Medical Society, AA History Lovers message no. 6281, at https://groups.yahoo.com/neo/groups/aahistorylovers/conversations/messages/6281.

224 *Pass It On* 121.

225 Hartigan, *Bill W.* 11.

226 Jonathan Edwards, "A Divine and Supernatural Light, Immediately Imparted to the Soul by the Spirit of God," available online in the Christian Classics Ethereal Library, http://www.ccel.org/ccel/edwards/works2.iii.i.html.

227 Ibid.

228 I trace all this out in detail in Glenn F. Chesnut, *Changed by Grace: V. C. Kitchen, the Oxford Group, and A.A.*, Hindsfoot Foundation Series on Spirituality and Theology (New York: iUniverse, September 2006).

229 William R. Miller and Janet C'de Baca, *Quantum Change: When Epiphanies and Sudden Insights Transform Ordinary Lives*, afterword by Ernest Kurtz (New York: Guildford Press, 2001).

230 Chesnut, *God and Spirituality*, Chapter 12. "The God-Bearers and the Analogy of Being," pp. 221-237.

231 Bill Wilson's account on page 38 of *Alcoholics Anonymous Comes of Age* (1957).

232 *Pass It On* 242.

233 Fitzgerald, "Father Ed Dowling and AA's Bill W.," *Catholic Digest*. See also W. Robert Aufill, "The Catholic Contribution to the 12-Step Movement," in *This Rock* magazine in October, 1996 (now *Catholic Answers Magazine*, published by Catholic Answers, Inc., based in El Cajon, near San Diego, California); this article is available online at http://www.catholicculture.org/culture/library/view.cfm?recnum=703.

234 Ernest Kurtz, *Not-God.*

235 Fitzgerald, "Father Ed Dowling and AA's Bill W.," *Catholic Digest*.

236 Fitzgerald, "Father Ed Dowling and AA's Bill W.," *Catholic Digest*. Also Thomsen, *Bill W.* 10.

237 Richard Maurice Bucke, *Cosmic Consciousness: A Study in the Evolution of the Human Mind* (Philadelphia: Innes & Sons, 1901). Emmet Fox, in his commentary on the Lord's Prayer in *Sermon on the Mount* 129 and *Constructive Thinking* 165. Also *Constructive Thinking* 3.

238 Mel B., *My Search for Bill W.* (Center City, Minnesota: Hazelden, 2000), pp. 20-22, in which he cites at length from the letter which Bill Wilson wrote him.

239 Bucke, *Cosmic Consciousness*.

240 Bucke, *Cosmic Consciousness* 257, citing Ernest Renan, *Histoire du Peuple d'Israel*, 5 vols. (Paris: Calmann Levy, 1889–1894) Vol. I. p. 160.

241 Bucke, *Cosmic Consciousness* 8-9.

242 Ibid.

243 Chesnut, *Images* 58.

244 Ibid. 57-62.

245 Ibid.

246 Bucke, *Cosmic Consciousness* 285-286.

247 Ibid. 290-291.

[248] The full text of Ralph Waldo Emerson's essay on "Nature" is available online at http://oregonstate.edu/instruct/phl302/texts/emerson/nature-emerson-a.html#Introduction.

[249] Bucke, *Cosmic Consciousness* 291. Quotations from Ralph Waldo Emerson's essay on "The Over-Soul" are taken from the online version at http://www.emersoncentral.com/oversoul.htm.

[250] Bucke, *Cosmic Consciousness* 1-2.

[251] Ibid. 1-2.

[252] Chesnut, *God and Spirituality*, Chapter 21 "Self-Transcendence," 402-426.

[253] Chesnut, *God and Spirituality* 416, based on the excellent book by John H. Flavell, *The Developmental Psychology of Jean Piaget* (Princeton, New Jersey: D. Van Nostrand, 1963).

[254] Bucke, *Cosmic Consciousness* 2-3.

[255] Ibid. 9-10.

[256] Ibid. 11.

[257] Ibid. 71.

[258] Ibid. 72-75.

[259] *Alcoholics Anonymous* 10.

[260] Thomsen, *Bill W.* 116-119. *Alcoholics Anonymous* 1, 10, 12.

[261] *Alcoholics Anonymous* 12-13. *Alcoholics Anonymous Comes of Age* 62-63. *Pass It On* 121.

[262] "Second conversion experience" in *Pass It On* 242; Bill Wilson's long account is in *Alcoholics Anonymous Comes of Age* 38. This same account is also given in Wilson, "To Father Ed — Godspeed!"

[263] See for example Bucke, *Cosmic Consciousness* 61, "The duplex personality of men having cosmic consciousness will appear many times as we proceed and will be seen to be a constant and prominent phenomenon" and 63-64, his long quotation from William Sharpe, *The Dual Image* (London: H. A. Copley, 1896).

[264] Chesnut, *God and Spirituality*, Ch. 11, "Tillich and Einstein," pp. 200-220, see espec. pp. 213-214.

[265] Bucke, *Cosmic Consciousness* 17.

[266] *Alcoholics Anonymous* 10, 12, and 46.

[267] Ibid. 13, 25, 28, 56, 68, 72, 75, 80, 83, 158, and 161.

268   Ibid. 25.

269   Ibid. 10 and 48-49.

270   Ibid. 12, 46, and 49.

271   Ibid. 8, 25, and 85.

272   Ibid. 46 and 53.

273   See e.g., the reference in Bucke, *Cosmic Consciousness* 63-64 to Sharpe, *Dual Image*:

> ... for henceforth by his side
> A radiant being stood, his guiding light
> And polar star, that as a magnet held
> Him in the hold of ever-during love!
> ... she seemed to say:
> "Thou art mine own, mine equal and my spouse,
> My complement, without whom I were nought;
> So in mine eyes thou art more fair than I,
> For in thee only is my life fulfilled."
> [And] with her presence she endowed
> Him with new senses, faculties and powers,
> That far surpassed the limits of the old.

274   I do not believe that any modern philosopher worked out a system which fully and totally embodied this metamorphosis — a shift from viewing God as teleological cause to viewing God as efficient cause — until I published Glenn F. Chesnut, *God and Spirituality*, see Chapter 13. "Modern Personalist Philosophies of God" (http://hindsfoot.org/g13pers.pdf), Chapter 14. "The Three Primal Hypostases," and Chapter 15. "A Personal God: Love and Energy" (http://hindsfoot.org/g15energy.pdf).

275   The six paragraphs which follow are mostly taken verbatim from Chesnut, *Images* 57-59.

276   Hoxie Neale Fairchild, *Religious Trends in English Poetry*, Vol. III. *1780-1830, Romantic Faith* (New York: Columbia University Press, 1949).

277   See John Wesley's *Standard Sermons*, Sugden ed., Vol. 1, p. 361.

278   Bucke, *Cosmic Consciousness* 225.

279   Ibid. 220-221.

280   Ibid. 224.

281   Ibid. 221-224.

282 Walt Whitman, as quoted in Bucke, *Cosmic Consciousness* 228.

283 Ibid. 228-229.

284 Ibid. 228-229.

285 Ibid. 229-230.

286 Walt Whitman, *Leaves of Grass* (1855 edit.), page 15, as quoted in Bucke, *Cosmic Consciousness* 227-228.

287 Chesnut, *God and Spirituality* — the three primal hypostases in the Godhead are the Arbitrarium, the Logos or Sophia, and the Energetikos (what the ancient pagan Neo-Platonists called the One, Nous or Intellect, and Psyche or Soul) — on the Third Hypostasis, the Energetikos, see 264-265, 301-306. Also see the section on pp. 307-308 on St. Teresa of Avila and the spiritual marriage. Roman Catholic spirituality, in commentaries on the Song of Songs in the Old Testament, was always willing to accept male-female sexuality as a *metaphor* for the higher love between God and the human soul. But a real Platonist — or so I would argue — would always point out that in a Platonic image, the image *participates* in that of which it is the image, so that the sexual desires portrayed so vividly in the Song of Songs have to be understood as sharing in the transcendent divine love, albeit at a lower ontological level.

288 Raynor C. Johnson, *The Imprisoned Splendour: An approach to reality, based upon the significance of data drawn from the fields of natural science, psychical research and mystical experience* (London: Hodder & Stoughton, 1953).

289 *Pass It On* 242.

290 Bill Wilson's account on page 38 of *Alcoholics Anonymous Comes of Age* (1957). See also Fitzgerald, "Father Ed Dowling and AA's Bill W.," *Catholic Digest*; and Aufill, "Catholic Contribution to the 12-Step Movement."

291 Augustine, *City of God*, bk. 14, ch. 24, from the well-known 1887 Marcus Dods translation, now available online at New Advent Fathers of the Church, http://www.newadvent.org/fathers/120114.htm.

292 Ibid.

293 Ernest Kurtz, *Shame & Guilt*.

294 As quoted in the Wikipedia article on Jean-Baptiste Janssens at http://en.wikipedia.org/wiki/Jean-Baptiste_Janssens.

295 See the *Linden Bark* (published at Lindenwood University in the St. Charles suburb north of St. Louis), Vol. 27, No. 8 (February

27, 1947), p. 4, column 5, in the article titled "C. C. Clayton Bark Romeo," available online at http://library.lindenwood.edu/archive/docs/lindenBark/1940-1949/1946-1947/1947-02-27.pdf.

296 *Baltimore Afro-American*, November 27, 1956.

297 McQuade, Obituary.

298 Ibid.

299 As quoted in McQuade, Obituary.

300 *National Municipal Review*, Volume 30, Issue 7, pages 450–454, July 1941, photocopy available online at http://onlinelibrary.wiley.com/doi/10.1002/ncr.4110300716/abstract.

301 *National Municipal Review*, January and February 1949, available online at http://www.archive.org/stream/nationalmunicipa38natirich/nationalmunicipa38natirich_djvu.txt.

302 His idea of the noosphere appeared already early in the 1920's, see Pierre Teilhard de Chardin, "Hominization" (1923), in the collection of his essays called *The Vision of the Past* (New York: Harper & Row, 1966) p. 63.

303 Pierre Leroy, S.J., "Teilhard de Chardin: The Man," in Pierre Teilhard de Chardin, *The Divine Milieu* (New York: Harper & Row, 1968; this Eng. trans. first pub. 1960, orig. pub. in French as *Le Milieu Divin* in 1957) 13-42, see espec. pp. 34-35.

304 As quoted in Leroy, "Teilhard de Chardin: The Man," p. 36.

305 Ibid.

306 Chesnut, *God and Spirituality*, see Chapter 13 "Modern Personalist Philosophies of God" on the modern process philosophers Alfred North Whitehead and Charles Hartshorne, and Chapter 20 "Why the Future Cannot Be Totally Predicted," available online at http://hindsfoot.org/g13pers.pdf and http://hindsfoot.org/g20future.pdf.

307 As quoted in Leroy, "Teilhard de Chardin: The Man," p. 37.

308 Pierre Teilhard de Chardin, *The Divine Milieu* 59.

309 Ibid. 59-60.

310 Ibid. 55-56.

311 Ibid. 57-58 and 61.

312 Ibid. 61.

313 Jean Laporte, *La doctrine eucharistique chez Philon d'Alexandrie* (Paris: Editions Beauchesne, 1972).

314   Glenn F. Chesnut, *The First Christian Histories: Eusebius, Socrates, Sozomen, Theodoret, and Evagrius*, 2nd ed., rev. and enlarged (Macon, Georgia: Mercer University Press, 1986; orig. pub. in Paris by Éditions Beauchesne in 1977).

315   The Council of Nicaea in 325 had inserted the word *homoousios* (of one substance or essence, consubstantial) into a traditional baptismal creed, which made it clear that the Godhead always remained a single *ousia* (essential reality). But the Anathemas of the Council of Nicaea forbade people from speaking of a plurality of either *ousiai* or *hypostaseis*, which meant that the only way left philosophically for speaking of a Trinity would have been to speak of God in three *prosôpa*, that is, portraying God as a single actor wearing three different actors' masks or external façades. That meant a God who could appear outwardly as a human being, and give the external illusion that one was dealing with a real flesh-and-blood human being, but something which only appeared to be a man on the surface could not meaningfully suffer and die on the cross for our salvation. St. Basil talked St. Athanasius into letting him quietly explain away the Anathemas of the Council of Nicaea, so that theologians would be able to talk about the Trinity in terms of one *ousia* and three *hypostaseis*. This would not only satisfy the objections of the vast majority of anti-Nicene Christian bishops, but would put Christian theology back in contact again with the central Neoplatonic philosophical teaching of the three primal hypostases within the Godhead.

316   Gregory of Nyssa, *From Glory to Glory: Texts from Gregory of Nyssa's Mystical Writings*, selected and with an introduction by Jean Daniélou S.J., trans. Herbert Musurillo S.J. (Crestwood, New York: St. Vladimir's Seminary Press, 1979; orig. pub. by Charles Scribner's Sons, 1961).

317   Gregory of Nyssa, Vols. 44-46 of Migne *Patrologia Graeca* (the full series is 166 vols., 1857-66). Available online at http://archive. org/details/patrologiaecursu44mignuoft, http://archive.org/details/ patrologiaecursu45mignuoft, and http://archive.org/details/ patrologiaecursu46mignuoft.

318   Page 247 in Greg. Nyss., *From Glory to Glory* (see the next two notes), which is a translation from Gregory of Nyssa, *Commentary on the Canticle*, Migne *Patrologia Graeca* 44, 1000C-1004C.

319   Gregory of Nyssa, *Commentary on the Canticle*, Migne *Patrologia Graeca* 44, 1000C-1004C in Greg. Nyss. *From Glory to Glory* p. 247.

320 Jean-Paul Sartre's philosophical novel *La Nausée* — the title means "Nausea" — (Paris: Gallimard, 1938) was one of his earliest and most famous published works.

321 Gregory of Nyssa, *Commentary on Ecclesiastes*, Sermon 7, Migne *Patrologia Graeca* 44.729D-732A — translated into English as selection 17 pp. 122 ff. of Greg. Nyss. *From Glory to Glory*.

322 Gregory of Nyssa, *Commentary on the Beatitudes*, Sermon 6, Migne *Patrologia Graeca* 44.1264C, English translation from pp. 122 ff. of Greg. Nyss. *From Glory to Glory*.

323 On the topic of grace, see Chapter 19 "The Nature of Grace" in Chesnut, *God and Spirituality*.

324 On the knowledge of God in the mirror of the soul, also see Chesnut, *Higher Power* 11-12.

325 Jean Daniélou, Introduction (pp. 1-78) to Gregory of Nyssa, *From Glory to Glory: Texts from Gregory of Nyssa's Mystical Writings*, ed. Herbert Musurillo (New York: Scribner, 1961), pp. 23-25.

326 Chesnut, *God and Spirituality*, see especially Chapter 13 on Whitehead and Hartshorne, and Chapter 20 "Why the Future Cannot Be Totally Predicted."

327 That is, both down here in this present earthly realm, and up above in the Land of the Living, that transcendent realm where growth and change and new adventures still occur, but where death no longer holds power. See Psalm 27:13 — "I believe that I shall see the goodness of the Lord in the Land of the Living" — the verse numbered as 26:13 in the Latin Vulgate (*credo videre bona Domini in terra viventium*) and the Greek Septuagint (*pisteuô tou idein ta agatha kyriou en gê, zôntôn*).

328 See Paul L. Gavrilyuk (University of St Thomas, Minnesota) and Sarah Coakley (University of Cambridge), eds., *The Spiritual Senses: Perceiving God in Western Christianity* (Cambridge: University of Cambridge Press, 2012).

329 Gregory of Nyssa, *In Cantica Cantic.* Homilia XI, as trans. in Greg. Nyss. *From Glory to Glory* p. 248; the original Greek text can be found at Migne *Patrologia Graeca.* 44.1001B.

330 Gregory of Nyssa, *Life of Moses*, Migne *Patrologia Graeca* 44, 376C-377A, as quoted in Daniélou, Introd. to Greg. Nyss. *From Glory to Glory*, p. 29; see also Selection 15 at p. 118.

331 Daniélou, Introd. to Greg. Nyss. *From Glory to Glory*, p. 30.

332 Ibid. p. 33. On sober inebriation see p. 39 on Acts 2:15.

333 Daniélou, Introd. to Greg. Nyss. *From Glory to Glory*, pp. 39-41 on Song of Songs 5:2.

334 See e.g. *Twenty-Four Hours* for January 7: "In silence comes God's meaning to the heart . . . . God's word is spoken to the secret places of my heart." He would probably have been at least introduced to Hindu philosophy in college, in English translation or even German translation (since the curriculum at Williams College was set up to get a good many of its students to learn German). Richmond Walker's knowledge of Hinduism may also have been mediated in whole or in part through Ralph Waldo Emerson and the New England Transcendentalists, who obtained copies of the Bhagavad Gita and Vishnu Purana in 1845, the Upanishads and Vedic Samhitas in 1850, and the *Shakuntala* of Kalidasa in 1855. Richmond Walker put a quotation from that last work at the beginning of *Twenty-Four Hours a Day*. The dates at which Emerson and his associates obtained copies of those works is taken from a chart listing the Asian books known to have been in the hands of Emerson and his circle and the date acquired, in Todd Lewis and Kent Bicknell, "The Asian Soul of Transcendentalism," available online at http://www.asian-studies.org/eaa/EAA-16-2-Lewis-Bicknell.pdf.

335 Gregory of Nyssa, *Commentary on the Canticle*, Migne *Patrologia Graeca* 44.993D; see Greg. Nyss. *From Glory to Glory*, selection 67, pp. 240-243.

336 Rudolf Otto, *The Idea of the Holy: An Inquiry into the Non-Rational Factor in the Idea of the Divine and Its Relation to the Rational*, 2nd ed., trans. John W. Harvey (Oxford: Oxford University Press, 1950). Original German published 1917: *Das Heilige: Über das Irrationale in der Idee des göttlichen und sein Verhältnis zum Rationalen*. For more on Otto's ideas, see Chesnut, *God and Spirituality*, Chapter 4 on learning to see the sacred dimension of reality and Chapter 5 on the seven faces of the experience of the divine reality.

337 Dr. Eben Alexander, *Proof of Heaven: A Neurosurgeon's Journey into the Afterlife* (New York: Simon and Schuster, 2012).

338 Chesnut, *First Christian Histories*, pp. 156-160 and 163.

339 Ibid. pp. 149-153 and 233.

340 QUANTITY: unity, plurality, totality. QUALITY: reality, negation, limitation. RELATION: substance and accident, cause and effect, community or reciprocity. MODALITY: possibility, existence, necessity.

[341] On Rudolf Otto, see Chesnut, *God and Spirituality*, Chapters 4 and 5.

[342] Gregory of Nyssa, *Against Eunomius*, Book 4, original Greek in Migne, *Patrologia Graeca* 940CD, English trans. based on Greg. Nyss. *From Glory to Glory* p. 120.

[343] Plato, *Republic*, 2 vols., trans. Paul Shorey, Loeb Classical Library (London: William Heinemann, 1935–7), 7.1.514A-3.518B. My description here of the teaching of the Parable of the Cave is copied fairly much verbatim from Chesnut, *Changed by Grace*, Chapter 7, see espec. pp. 119-124.

[344] See Plato, *Republic*. In 7.3.517B–C Plato said that the sun stood metaphorically for "the idea of the Good" (*hê tou agathou idea*), which was that which enabled us to see what is right (*orthos*) and beautiful (*kalos*), to recognize truth (*alêtheia*) and intelligible meaning (*nous*), and to act in a manner which was sane and sensible (*emphrôn*). This central concept therefore linked together the Good (and Truth and Beauty), and the establishment of the noetic realm (the realm in which the cognitive structures of our minds enable us to think intelligibly).

[345] Chesnut, *First Christian Histories*.

[346] Daniélou, Introd. to Greg. Nyss. *From Glory to Glory*, pp. 56-57.

[347] Ibid. p. 57.

[348] J. Glenn Friesen, *Studies relating to Herman Dooyeweerd: Linked Glossary of Terms*, available online at http://members.shaw.ca/jgfriesen/Definitions/Epektasis.html.

[349] Ibid.

[350] Gregory of Nyssa, from p. 57 of Daniélou, Introd. to Greg. Nyss. *From Glory to Glory*. For the original Greek, see Gregory of Nyssa, *Life of Moses*, Migne *Patrologia Graeca* 44.400D-401B. For an English translation of the entire section see Greg. Nyss. *From Glory to Glory*, Selection 21, pp. 142-148.

[351] Gregory of Nyssa, from p. 58 of Daniélou, Introd. to Greg. Nyss. *From Glory to Glory*. For the original Greek, see Gregory of Nyssa, *Life of Moses*, Migne *Patrologia Graeca* 44.400D-401B. For an English translation of the entire section see Greg. Nyss. *From Glory to Glory*, Selection 21, pp. 142-148.

[352] Daniélou, Introd. to Greg. Nyss. *From Glory to Glory*, pp. 43 and 45.

[353] Hannah Hurnard, *Hind's Feet in High Places* (Wheaton, Illinois: Tyndale House Publishers, 1975; orig. pub. 1955).

354 Gregory of Nyssa, *Comm. on the Cant.*, Migne *Patrologia Graeca* 44.1037C, my English trans. based on the quotation in Jean Daniélou, Introd. to Greg. Nyss. *From Glory to Glory* on p. 45. For an English translation of the full passage, see Greg. Nyss. *From Glory to Glory*, Selection 75, pp. 263 ff.

355 Daniélou, Introd. to Greg. Nyss. *From Glory to Glory*, p. 47.

356 Werner Jaeger, *Two Rediscovered Works of Ancient Christian Literature: Gregory of Nyssa and Macarius* (Leiden: E. J. Brill, 1954).

357 Daniélou, Introd. to Greg. Nyss. *From Glory to Glory*, p. 46-47.

358 Ibid., pp. 51-52, quoting from Gregory of Nyssa, *On Perfection*, Migne *Patrologia Graeca* 46.285B-C. The entire section is translated into English as Selection 2 in Greg. Nyss. *From Glory to Glory* pp. 83 ff.

359 Daniélou, Introd. to Greg. Nyss. *From Glory to Glory*, pp. 59-60.

360 Ibid. pp. 60-61.

361 Speer, *Principles of Jesus*, pp. 33-35.

362 Henry B. Wright, *The Will of God*, pp. 167-218.

363 Luke 18:10-14, "Two men went up into the temple to pray, one a Pharisee and the other a tax collector. The Pharisee stood and prayed thus with himself, 'God, I thank thee that I am not like other men, extortioners, unjust, adulterers, or even like this tax collector. I fast twice a week, I give tithes of all that I get.' But the tax collector, standing far off, would not even lift up his eyes to heaven, but beat his breast, saying, 'God, be merciful to me a sinner!' I tell you, this man went down to his house justified rather than the other; for every one who exalts himself will be humbled, but he who humbles himself will be exalted."

364 Father Ralph Pfau, who was the first Catholic priest to get sober in A.A., led a famous A.A. weekend spiritual retreat at Gethsemani Abbey once a year for many years. He probably knew of Merton, but does not seem to have been affected by any of that writer's ideas.

365 Don Lattin, *Distilled Spirits: Getting High, Then Sober, with a Famous Writer, a Forgotten Philosopher, and a Hopeless Drunk* (Berkeley: University of California Press, 2012), pp. 140 and 167.

366 Lattin, *Distilled Spirits*.

367 Aldous Huxley, *The Perennial Philosophy* (New York: Harper & Brothers, 1945).

368 Lattin, *Distilled Spirits*, pp. 184-185. Aldous Huxley, *The Doors of Perception* (London: Chatto and Windus, 1954).

369 Don Lattin, *The Harvard Psychedelic Club: How Timothy Leary, Ram Dass, Huston Smith, and Andrew Weil Killed the Fifties and Ushered in a New Age for America* (New York: HarperCollins, 2010), p. 66.

370 *Pass It On*, Chapter 23, pp. 368-377; on Tom Power's presence see p. 371. See also Ernest Kurtz, "Drugs and the Spiritual: Bill W. Takes LSD," in Ernest Kurtz, *The Collected Ernie Kurtz* (Wheeling, West Virginia: The Bishop of Books, 1999; republished by the Hindsfoot Foundation through iUniverse in Bloomington, Indiana, in 2008), can be read online at http://hindsfoot.org/tcek03.pdf.

371 Lattin, *Harvard Psychedelic Club*, p. 67.

372 *Pass It On*, p. 371.

373 Don Lattin, "What Bill W. told Carl Jung About his Awesome LSD Trip," Blog Post by Don Lattin, Oct. 16, 2012, see http://redroom.com/member/ don-lattin/blog/what-bill-w-told-carl-jung-about-his-awesome-lsd-trip.

374 "Bill Wilson's Fight With Depression," in the West Baltimore Group's *Let's Ask Bill* section at http://www.westbalto.a-1associates.com/ LETS_ASK_BILL/Fightwithdepression.htm.

375 Neville Murray, M.D., and M/Sgt William Swegan, USAF, "To Tranquillize or Not to Tranquillize," *Quarterly Journal of Studies on Alcohol* 19, no. 3 (September 1958): 509-510. Excerpts reprinted in the 1958 yearbook of the *American Peoples Encyclopedia* (a popular set of volumes distributed by Sears Roebuck). See also Swegan and Chesnut, *Psychology of Alcoholism*.

376 The whole story is told in great detail in Lattin, *Harvard Psychedelic Club*.

377 Carl Jung was fascinated by ancient Gnostic teaching because he felt it did more justice to the reality and pervasive presence of evil — that is, evil *as well as* good — both in the world and in ourselves. And perhaps because they are aware of Jung's interest in this ancient religious movement, A.A. people in turn seem to quickly become fascinated by Gnosticism whenever the topic comes up.

378 The two classical biblical statements of the Gospel message are Romans 3:28 — "For we hold that a person is justified by faith and not by works of the law," and Galatians 2:16 — "we know that a person is justified not by works of the law but through faith in Jesus Christ."

379 Mel B., *My Search for Bill W.* (Center City, Minnesota: Hazelden, 2000), 18-22.

380 Jonathan Edwards, "A Divine and Supernatural Light," pp. 123-134 in Jonathan Edwards, *Basic Writings*, ed. Ola Elizabeth Winslow (New York: New American Library, 1966).

381 Arthur S. (Arlington, Texas) dates this to December 14 (possibly but less likely December 13), 1934. See "Re: Date of White Light Experience at Towns," AA History Lovers Message #4235 posted on April 13, 2007 — http://health.groups.yahoo.com/group/AAHistoryLovers/message/4235.

382 Aldous Huxley, *Heaven and Hell* (New York: Harper & Brothers, pub. in 1956 along with *The Doors of Perception*, which had orig. been pub. by itself in 1954).

383 Bill Wilson's letter to Mel B. dated July 2, 1956, in Mel B., *My Search for Bill W.* (Center City, Minnesota: Hazelden, 2000), 20-21.

384 Ibid. 21.

385 Ibid. 22.

386 Mary C. Darrah, *Sister Ignatia: Angel of Alcoholics Anonymous* (Center City, Minnesota: Hazelden, 2001; orig. pub. Loyola University Press 1991), 299-300.

387 Loyola, *Spiritual Exercises*.

388 The other one was the great Egyptian theologian Origen (184/185 – 253/254), whose influence on later centuries was mediated through his numerous extremely important disciples, including St. Athanasius, Eusebius of Caesarea, St. Basil the Great, St. Gregory of Nyssa, and St. Gregory of Nazianzus.

389 V[ictor] C[onstant] Kitchen, *I Was a Pagan* (New York: Harper & Brothers, 1934), ch. 9, pp. 89–90, as cited in Chesnut, *Changed by Grace*, pp. 20-21.

390 Michael A. Mullett, *The Catholic Reformation* (Abingdon, Oxfordshire: Routledge, 1999), 80.

391 Louis J. Puhl, S.J., *The Spiritual Exercises of St. Ignatius: Based on Studies in the Language of the Autograph* (Chicago: Loyola Press/Newman Press, 1951): "We are not certain why St. Ignatius used the letter G. The editor of the volume on the Exercises in the *Monumenta Historica* thinks it is an abbreviation for the subject of the Particular Examination, for example, *gula*."

392 On p. 265 of *Pass It On*, it is reported that Bill and Lois recited a prayer together every morning which said: "We are from everlasting to everlasting .... Accordingly, Thou has fashioned for us a destiny passing

through Thy many mansions, ever in more discovery of Thee and in no separation between ourselves."

393   It has also long been believed that highly spiritually attuned people called dowsers can obtain contact with the spiritual realm by using different kinds of devices, such as a small pendulum swinging on a string held in their fingertips. It has also long been believed — for thousands of years in fact — that people who are now called channelers can use various methods for coming in contact with spirit guides from the higher realm who are able to speak directly in and through the channeler.

394   F[rederick] B[rotherton] Meyer, *The Secret of Guidance* (New York: Fleming H. Revell, 1896). The text is available on the internet at http://www.ccel.org/m/meyer/guidance/guidance.htm. The other major source for Buchman's understanding of guidance was Henry B. Wright, *The Will of God* (1909), but this book had been heavily influenced by F. B. Meyer's ideas, so the latter still stands in the background as a dominant source of Oxford Group beliefs about divine guidance.

395   The guidelines are contained in sections 313-336 of Loyola's *Spiritual Exercises*, at the very end of the Fourth Week, after "The Mysteries of the Life of Christ Our Lord," in the long section on Rules. There is first a set of fourteen "Rules for Perceiving and Knowing in Some Manner the Different Movements Which Are Caused in the Soul: the Good, to Receive Them, and the Bad to Reject Them," followed by a set of eight "Rules for the Same Effect with Greater Discernment of Spirits." If the reader is using a translation of the *Spiritual Exercises* where the sections and divisions are marked differently from the text I have used here — since it can sometimes be confusing for newcomers trying to find their way around St. Ignatius's book — this is the way to tell if you have located the part we are discussing here: In the first list of rules, the first rule (*Spiritual Exercises* section 314) reads "In persons who are going from mortal sin to mortal sin, the enemy is ordinarily accustomed to propose apparent pleasures to them, leading them to imagine sensual delights and pleasures in order to hold them more and make them grow in their vices and sins. In these persons the good spirit uses a contrary method, stinging and biting their consciences through their rational power of moral judgment." In the second list of rules, the last and eighth rule (*Spiritual Exercises* section 336) reads "When the consolation is without cause, although there is no deception in it, since it is of God our Lord alone, as has been said, nevertheless the spiritual person to whom God gives such a consolation

should, with much vigilance and attention, look at and distinguish the time itself of such an actual consolation from the time following, in which the soul remains warm and favored with the favor and remnants of the past consolation; for frequently, in this second time, through his own reasoning by associating and drawing consequences from ideas and judgments, or through the good spirit, or through the bad, he forms different proposals and opinions which are not given immediately by God our Lord; and therefore they must be very well examined before entire credit is given them or they are put into effect."

396   St. Ignatius's explanation (in his own words) of the kinds of human experiences which the words consolation and desolation refer to, as translated by Fr. Timothy Gallagher, O.M.V. in his book *The Discernment of Spirits: An Ignatian Guide for Everyday Living* (New York: The Crossroad Publishing Company, 2005).

397   See Chesnut, *Changed by Grace* p. 17 and Sally Brown and David R. Brown, *A Biography of Mrs. Marty Mann: The First Lady of Alcoholics Anonymous* (Center City, Minnesota: Hazelden, 2001), pp. 107-108.

398   Some Roman Catholic theologians of the last few centuries have argued that the Hesychastic vision was not one of the true Uncreated Light, but was a vision only of a lesser kind of divine light shining forth at a lower ontological level. Fortunately, Bill Wilson never made any claims as to whether he did or did not believe it to have been Uncreated.

399   From a talk given by Dowling on April 18, 1944, preserved in the Dowling Archives at Maryville College, as quoted in Fitzgerald, *Soul of Sponsorship* 15.

400   Fitzgerald, *Soul of Sponsorship* 69, describing Father Dowling's regular morning meditation as reported by Brother Malone, a Jesuit brother sacristan at the college church.

401   Bill Wilson's account on page 38 of *Alcoholics Anonymous Comes of Age* (1957).

402   *Pass It On* 242.

403   Kurtz, *Not-God*.

404   Edward Dowling, S.J., in *Alcoholics Anonymous Comes of Age*.

405   Ibid. The mention of the Christmas Eve story was probably a reference to "A Miracle at Christmas — a Man Re-born," in the A.A. *Grapevine*, Vol. 3, No. 7, December 1946: "Would you say that a man who had been

drinking for months, who had wound up in a flop house in such shape he could not get out of bed and whose 'entire frame shook with convulsive-like tremors' — would you say that man could get up the following morning 'clear eyed, his complexion good and ... perfectly poised?' Of course not. But that's what happened in Chicago one Christmas five years ago. Following is an account of the strange happening, written by an A.A. member of the Chicago Group." The famous story of the Apostle Paul on the road to Damascus came from the New Testament, see Acts 9:3-19, 22:6-13 and 26:12-18.

406 Both Bill's and Father Ed's words quoted from Fitzgerald, *Soul of Sponsorship* 59.

407 Edward Dowling, S.J., in *Alcoholics Anonymous Comes of Age*, p. 255.

408 Kurtz, *Not-God*, pp. 98-99.

409 Thomsen, *Bill W.*, p. 309; Nell Wing, *Grateful to Have Been There: My 42 Years with Bill and Lois, and the Evolution of Alcoholics Anonymous*, 2nd ed., revised and expanded (Center City, Minnesota: Hazelden, 1998), 81.

410 Ernest Kurtz, "Re: How quickly should the twelve steps be taken?" AAHistoryLovers Message #6252 (Jan 19, 2010), may be read online at http://health.groups.yahoo.com/group/AAHistoryLovers/message/6252.

411 For the text of Clarence Snyder's *Sponsorship Pamphlet*, see http://www.barefootsworld.net/aasponsorship1944.html.

412 Bill Wilson, 30 October 1940 letter to a member in Richmond, Virginia, as quoted in *Pass It On*, see espec. 173.

413 *Alcoholics Anonymous Comes of Age*, Section V, "Religion Looks at Alcoholics Anonymous," pp. 253-271.

414 *A Manual for Alcoholics Anonymous*, often referred to as *The Akron Manual* — the original 1942 version can be read online at http://hindsfoot.org/akrman1.html and http://hindsfoot.org/akrman2.html. The printed version which is currently available for sale at Dr. Bob's house in Akron is a later revised edition with some material removed, including the reading list.

415 See http://en.wikipedia.org/wiki/William_George_Bruce.

416 When others among Hazelden's supporters insisted that this was too narrow a focus, Ripley had to back away from that and Hazelden went its own separate way, but he later successfully founded Guest House in

Lake Orion, Michigan, in 1956, an institution which is still dedicated exclusively to the treatment of alcoholic Roman Catholic clergy.

417 Mitchell K., *How It Worked*, typescript for the 2nd revised ed. (2014), Chapt. 6, Sect. 3, p. 230. The first edition is Mitchell K., *How It Worked: The Story of Clarence H. Snyder and the Early Days of Alcoholics Anonymous in Cleveland, Ohio* (Washingtonville, New York: AA Big Book Study Group, 1999).

418 *Dr. Bob and the Good Oldtimers* pp. 265-268.

419 Ibid. pp. 268-269.

420 *Alcoholics Anonymous Comes of Age* p. 193.

421 *Dr. Bob and the Good Oldtimers* pp. 268-269.

422 Ibid.

423 Bill Wilson, in *Alcoholics Anonymous Comes of Age*, p. 194.

424 Ibid. p. 195.

425 *Dr. Bob and the Good Oldtimers* pp. 265-268.

426 Fitzgerald, *Soul of Sponsorship* 23, citing letters from Father Dowling written on January 6, 1942 and December 7, 1945.

427 Fitzgerald, *Soul of Sponsorship* 24-25, letter from Bill W. to Fr. Ed Dowling, 3 February 1942.

428 Fitzgerald, *Soul of Sponsorship* 24-25, letter from Fr. Ed Dowling to Bill W., 18 February 1942.

429 Arthur S., *Counts of AA Groups and Members*, http://hindsfoot.org/aatimeappend1.pdf.

430 Harry Tiebout, *The Collected Writings* (Center City, Minnesota: Hazelden, 1999). Also see Arthur S., *Narrative Timeline of AA History*, for the year 1944.

431 Arthur S. (Arlington, Texas), *Narrative Timeline of AA History*, for the year 1945.

432 Cora Finch, "Stellar Fire: Carl Jung, a New England Family, and the Risks of Anecdote" (2006), available online at http://hindsfoot.org/jungstel.pdf. Also see Amy Colwell Bluhm, Ph.D., "Verification of C. G. Jung's analysis of Rowland Hazard and the history of Alcoholics Anonymous," in the American Psychological Association's journal *History of Psychology* (November 2006). It was Dr. Bluhm who pointed out to me in a conversation several years ago, that most of the classical Jungian

psychiatric motifs had not yet been developed in 1926, and that there was almost nothing in Jung's publications prior to that date to indicate what his theories might have been about the best kind of psychiatric treatment for alcoholics.

433   C. G. [Carl Gustav] Jung, *Modern Man in Search of a Soul*, trans. W.S. Dell and Cary F. Baynes (New York: Harcourt, Brace & Company / Harvest Books, 1933). See Cora Finch, "Additional Notes to Stellar Fire," available online at http://www.hindsfoot.org/jungnote.pdf, p. 7, where Finch says: "Bill Wilson ... and other early AA's read Jung's popular book, *Modern Man in Search of a Soul*, a fact Bill mentioned later in a letter to Jung (part of this letter, sent March 20, 1961, is reproduced in *Pass It On*, (New York: AAWS, 1984), pp. 383-4. [And in addition to Bill Wilson's psychoanalysis with Dr. Frances Weeks in 1945-1949] ... over the years he corresponded with others who were familiar with Jung's work." Dr. Bob had a copy of *Modern Man in Search of a Soul* in his library, see Dick B., *Dr. Bob and His Library*, 3rd ed. (Kihei, Hawaii: Paradise Research Publications, 1998), p. 55. Bill Wilson thought so highly of Jung's book that at one point he gave a copy to Henrietta Seiberling, see Dick B., *The Akron Genesis of Alcoholics Anonymous* (Kihei, Hawaii: Paradise Research Publications, 1992 and 1998), p. 88.

434   Bill W., "A Letter From Bill W. on Depression," excerpts quoted in the memoirs of Tom Pike, an early California A.A. member, see http://www.silkworth.net/aahistory/billw_depression.html.

435   Chesnut, *Changed by Grace*, Chapt. 1, pp. 20-21; quoting from Kitchen, *I Was a Pagan*, pp. 89-90.

436   See "Father Ed Dowling — Bill W.'s Confidant and Friend," *Box 459*. For the full quotation, see Tom Hickcox, "Re: Quote from Father Dowling on Big Book jacket," AAHistoryLovers Message 9395, available online at https://groups.yahoo.com/neo/groups/aahistorylovers/conversations/messages/9395.

437   Contents of a letter from Fr. Ed Dowling to Sister Ignatia, dated 25 March 1960, as related by Sr. Mary Denis Maher, CSA, Archivist, Sisters of Charity of St. Augustine, in a note dated 25 September 2008.

438   Hartigan, *Bill W.*, p. 174.

439   Fitgerald, *Soul of Sponsorship* p. 47 and Aufill, "Catholic Contribution to the 12-Step Movement."

440 Aufill, "Catholic Contribution," states that "the simplest explanation" for Bill Wilson's ultimate decision not to join the Roman Catholic Church "is that Wilson remained profoundly ambivalent about organized religion and its doctrines. Just as he had shied away from the 'Absolutes' of the Oxford Group, so he could not see his way to accepting Catholicism's own absolutism."

441 Hartigan, *Bill W.*, p. 175 — Bill W. admitted "that he was never 'able to receive assurance that He [Christ] was one hundred percent God.'"

442 Letter from Bill Wilson to Mel Barger, dated July 2, 1956, as transcribed in Mel B., *My Search for Bill W.*, pp. 18-22.

443 Fitzgerald, *Soul of Sponsorship*, p. 51.

444 The Latin phrase *sapere aude* was a quote from the ancient Roman author Horace (65-8 B.C.), and literally meant "dare to be wise," "dare to know." Kant probably intended the Latin phrase *naturaliter maiorennes* to mean "having attained the natural age of majority." Under the current laws of the United States and the United Kingdom, this would usually mean having reached eighteen years old or twenty-one years old (depending on the locality and the legal issue), at which age young men and women became legally able to take on various full adult responsibilities. The original German text, which appeared in the *Berlinische Monatsschrift*. Dezember-Heft 1784. S. 481-494, is available online at https://www.uni-potsdam. de/u/philosophie/texte/kant/aufklaer.htm. It reads as follows: *Aufklärung ist der Ausgang des Menschen aus seiner selbstverschuldeten Unmündigkeit. Unmündigkeit ist das Unvermögen, sich seines Verstandes ohne Leitung eines anderen zu bedienen. Selbstverschuldet ist diese Unmündigkeit, wenn die Ursache derselben nicht am Mangel des Verstandes, sondern der Entschließung und des Mutes liegt, sich seiner ohne Leitung eines andern zu bedienen. Sapere aude! Habe Mut, dich deines eigenen Verstandes zu bedienen! ist also der Wahlspruch der Aufklärung. Faulheit und Feigheit sind die Ursachen, warum ein so großer Teil der Menschen, nachdem sie die Natur längst von fremder Leitung freigesprochen (naturaliter maiorennes), dennoch gerne zeitlebens unmündig bleiben; und warum es anderen so leicht wird, sich zu deren Vormündern aufzuwerfen. Es ist so bequem, unmündig zu sein. Habe ich ein Buch, das für mich Verstand hat, einen Seelsorger, der für mich Gewissen hat, einen Arzt, der für mich die Diät beurteilt usw., so brauche ich mich ja nicht selbst zu bemühen. Ich habe nicht nötig zu denken, wenn ich nur bezahlen kann; andere werden das verdrießliche Geschäft schon für mich übernehmen.*

445 Fitzgerald, *Soul of Sponsorship*, p. 49.

446 Letter from Bill Wilson to Mel Barger, dated July 2, 1956, as transcribed in Mel B., *My Search for Bill W.*, p. 21.

447 This was called the doctrine of Original Sin, a theological concept which could be traced all the way back to St. Augustine at the time of the Fall of the Roman Empire in the fifth century A.D. In addition, the Calvinist tradition all over Europe (in Switzerland, western Germany, the Netherlands, Scotland, and many parts of England) eagerly translated and reprinted Machiavelli's *The Prince*, the Renaissance Italian political treatise which explained how would-be tyrants could easily manipulate ordinary people, through their temptation to be selfish and self-seeking, and turn even a dedicated democracy into a dictatorship.

448 Letter from Bill Wilson to Mel Barger, dated July 2, 1956, in Mel B., *My Search for Bill W.*, pp. 21-22.

449 Hartigan, *Bill W.*, pp. 174-175.

450 Aufill, "Catholic Contribution to the 12-Step Movement."

451 Letter from Father Dowling to Bill Wilson on November 26, 1947, in Fitzgerald, *Soul of Sponsorship*, p. 52.

452 Dowling's letter to Bill W. on October 1, 1947, in Fitzgerald, *Soul of Sponsorship*, p. 50.

453 In Edward Dowling, "Catholic Asceticism and the Twelve Steps," Father Ed commented: "To a priest who asked Bill how long it took him to write those twelve steps he said that it took twenty minutes. If it were twenty weeks, you could suspect improvisation. Twenty minutes sounds reasonable under the theory of divine help." See also Fitzgerald, *Soul of Sponsorship* 67-68 and note 122.

454 Dowling's letter to Bill W. on October 1, 1947, in Fitzgerald, *Soul of Sponsorship*, p. 50.

455 Letter from Father Dowling to Bill Wilson on October 4, 1947, in Fitzgerald, *Soul of Sponsorship*, p. 51.

456 Fitzgerald, *Soul of Sponsorship*, p. 49.

457 Letter from Dowling to Bill Wilson on September 8, 1947, as quoted in Fitzgerald, *Soul of Sponsorship*, p. 48.

458 Fitzgerald, *Soul of Sponsorship* p. 49.

459 Letter from Dowling to Bill Wilson on September 8, 1947, as quoted in Fitzgerald, *Soul of Sponsorship*, p. 48.

460 *Pass It On*, page 265.

461 The version approved in 2000 by the Southern Baptist Convention may be read online at http://www.sbc.net/bfm2000/bfm2000.asp.

462 The phrase "primary spiritual aim" in Tradition Six was changed to "primary purpose," and the phrase "principles above personalities" in Tradition Twelve was changed to "principles before personalities."

463 I discussed this at greater length in a symposium held at the auditorium in the public library at Fort Wayne, Indiana, on January 14, 2012, during which Mel Barger and I talked about the Third Tradition.

464 Passed by Congress September 25, 1789. Ratified December 15, 1791.

I. Congress shall make no law respecting an establishment of religion, or prohibiting the free exercise thereof; or abridging the freedom of speech, or of the press; or the right of the people peaceably to assemble, and to petition the government for a redress of grievances.

II. A well regulated Militia, being necessary to the security of a free State, the right of the people to keep and bear Arms, shall not be infringed.

III. No Soldier shall, in time of peace be quartered in any house, without the consent of the Owner, nor in time of war, but in a manner to be prescribed by law.

IV. The right of the people to be secure in their persons, houses, papers, and effects, against unreasonable searches and seizures, shall not be violated, and no Warrants shall issue, but upon probable cause, supported by Oath or affirmation, and particularly describing the place to be searched, and the persons or things to be seized.

V. No person shall be held to answer for a capital, or otherwise infamous crime, unless on a presentment or indictment of a Grand Jury, except in cases arising in the land or naval forces, or in the Militia, when in actual service in time of War or public danger; nor shall any person be subject for the same offence to be twice put in jeopardy of life or limb; nor shall be compelled in any criminal case to be a witness against himself, nor be deprived of life, liberty, or property, without due process of law; nor shall private property be taken for public use, without just compensation.

VI.   In all criminal prosecutions, the accused shall enjoy the right to a speedy and public trial, by an impartial jury of the State and district wherein the crime shall have been committed, which district shall have been previously ascertained by law, and to be informed of the nature and cause of the accusation; to be confronted with the witnesses against him; to have compulsory process for obtaining witnesses in his favor, and to have the Assistance of Counsel for his defence.

VII.   In Suits at common law, where the value in controversy shall exceed twenty dollars, the right of trial by jury shall be preserved, and no fact tried by a jury, shall be otherwise re-examined in any Court of the United States, than according to the rules of the common law.

VIII.   Excessive bail shall not be required, nor excessive fines imposed, nor cruel and unusual punishments inflicted.

IX.   The enumeration in the Constitution, of certain rights, shall not be construed to deny or disparage others retained by the people.

X.   The powers not delegated to the United States by the Constitution, nor prohibited by it to the States, are reserved to the States respectively, or to the people.

465   The Declaration asserted that "All the citizens, being equal in the eyes of the law, are equally admissible to all public dignities, places, and employments, according to their capacity and without distinction other than that of their virtues and of their talents," and then went on to list seventeen articles:

1.   Men are born and remain free and equal in rights. Social distinctions may be founded only upon the general good.

2.   The aim of all political association is the preservation of the natural and imprescriptible rights of man. These rights are liberty, property, security, and resistance to oppression.

3.   The principle of all sovereignty resides essentially in the nation. No body nor individual may exercise any authority which does not proceed directly from the nation.

4.   Liberty consists in the freedom to do everything which injures no one else; hence the exercise of the natural rights of each man has no limits except those which assure to the other members of the society the enjoyment of the same rights. These limits can only be determined by law.

5. Law can only prohibit such actions as are hurtful to society. Nothing may be prevented which is not forbidden by law, and no one may be forced to do anything not provided for by law.

6. Law is the expression of the general will. Every citizen has a right to participate personally, or through his representative, in its foundation. It must be the same for all, whether it protects or punishes. All citizens, being equal in the eyes of the law, are equally eligible to all dignities and to all public positions and occupations, according to their abilities, and without distinction except that of their virtues and talents.

7. No person shall be accused, arrested, or imprisoned except in the cases and according to the forms prescribed by law. Any one soliciting, transmitting, executing, or causing to be executed, any arbitrary order, shall be punished. But any citizen summoned or arrested in virtue of the law shall submit without delay, as resistance constitutes an offense.

8. The law shall provide for such punishments only as are strictly and obviously necessary, and no one shall suffer punishment except it be legally inflicted in virtue of a law passed and promulgated before the commission of the offense.

9. As all persons are held innocent until they shall have been declared guilty, if arrest shall be deemed indispensable, all harshness not essential to the securing of the prisoner's person shall be severely repressed by law.

10. No one shall be disquieted on account of his opinions, including his religious views, provided their manifestation does not disturb the public order established by law.

11. The free communication of ideas and opinions is one of the most precious of the rights of man. Every citizen may, accordingly, speak, write, and print with freedom, but shall be responsible for such abuses of this freedom as shall be defined by law.

12. The security of the rights of man and of the citizen requires public military forces. These forces are, therefore, established for the good of all and not for the personal advantage of those to whom they shall be entrusted.

13. A general tax is indispensable for the maintenance of the public force and for the expenses of administration; it ought to be equally apportioned among all citizens according to their means.

14. All the citizens have a right to decide, either personally or by their representatives, as to the necessity of the public contribution; to grant this freely; to know to what uses it is put; and to fix the proportion, the mode of assessment and of collection and the duration of the taxes.

15. Society has the right to require of every public agent an account of his administration.

16. A society in which the observance of the law is not assured, nor the separation of powers defined, has no constitution at all.

17. Property being an inviolable and sacred right, no one can be deprived of it, unless demanded by public necessity, legally constituted, explicitly demands it, and under the condition of a just and prior indemnity.

[466] Ernest Kurtz, *Not-God*, p. 361 n. 33 — "The first 'Negro' A.A. group was organized in St. Louis on 24 January 1945; others followed in Washington, DC, and Valdosta, GA, in September 1945 — Torrence S. (St. Louis) to Secretary, Alcoholic Foundation, 20 October 1945; Margaret B. (New York) to Torrence S., 25 October 1945." Bob Pearson, *A.A. World History 1985* (unpublished draft), Chapt. 5, has the same date for the foundation of the St. Louis group, but dates the beginning of the Washington D.C. group in April 1945. Information on the Chicago group comes from my interview of Bill Williams (who joined the group in December of 1945 and was later Area Delegate from Chicago Area 19 for 1969-70), together with another major black old timer in Chicago, Jimmy Hodges, on Saturday, July 17, 1999 at the lakeside home of Frank Nyikos near Syracuse, Indiana — see Glenn F. Chesnut, *The Stories and Memories of Early Black A.A. Leaders Told in Their Own Words*, including his talk on "Early Black A.A. Leaders" (Jimmy Miller, Bill Williams, and others) given on July 26, 2014 at Serenity House in Gary, Indiana — available online at http://hindsfoot.org/blackaa.html and http://hindsfoot.org/gary2014.doc. The same dates and facts are also recorded in the lengthy and detailed "History of the Evans Avenue Group" at http://evansavenuebanquet.org/?page_id=4. Also see the excerpts taken from Henry L. Hudson's article, "How and Why Alcoholics Anonymous Works for Blacks," in Frances Larry Brisbane and Maxine Womble, eds., *Treatment of Black Alcoholics*, published as *Alcoholism Treatment Quarterly*, Vol. 2, Nos. 3/4 (Fall 1985 / Winter 1985-86 (New York: Haworth Press, 1985), pp. 11-30 — this gives an account of Dr. Jim Scott, M.D., and the black AA group started in Washington

D.C. in 1945, together with material on early black AA members in the New York City area (Greenwich Village and Harlem) — available online at http://hindsfoot.org/blackwashdc.doc. See also AAHistoryLovers Message 5754 from Tom C., June 3, 2009, "Re: First black A.A. group was in Washington D.C. — or Chicago?" at https://groups.yahoo.com/neo/groups/AAHistoryLovers/conversations/messages/5754.

467 "Jim's Story," in the Big Book, second edition, pp. 471-484.

468 See Barefoot Bill L., *People In A.A. History Mentioned In The Literature: Who Were They? What Did They Do?* — available online at http://www.barefootsworld.net/aapeople.html — where it notes that *Dr. Bob and the Good Oldtimers* (p. 249) says that "Dick P. — perhaps first Spanish speaking A.A. member, joined Cleveland A.A. in early 1940, achieved citizenship 1963, manager of Cleveland Central Office, translated Big Book into Spanish, finished 1946 ... and gave Bill the book." But *Alcoholics Anonymous Comes of Age* (p. 200) says that Frank M. translated the Big Book into Spanish about 1946 or 1947 so "maybe both did independently."

469 See Juan Rodriguez, "Ralph Pfau instead of Big Book in early Spanish language AA" in Message 5584 (February 23, 2009) in the AAHistoryLovers, available online at https://groups.yahoo.com/neo/groups/aahistorylovers/conversations/messages/5584.

470 In Mel B., *My Search for Bill W.*, pp. 18-22.

471 Aldous Huxley, *Heaven and Hell* (published 1 January 1956).

472 *Pass It On*, p. 278.

473 Susan Cheever, *My Name Is Bill: Bill Wilson — His Life and the Creation of Alcoholics Anonymous* (New York: Washington Square Press, 2004), p. 204.

474 *Pass It On*, pp. 278.

475 Ibid. p. 279.

476 Ibid.

477 See Nell Wing, *Grateful to Have Been There*, pp. 83-84; also Susan Cheever, *My Name Is Bill*, p. 204.

478 Fitzgerald, *Soul of Sponsorship*, p. 59.

479 Ibid.

480 *Pass It On*, p. 275.

481 Presumably John T. Reese, W. North St., Akron, Ohio. See "First 226 Members Akron, OH AA Group" as transcribed by Tommy H. (Baton

Rouge, Louisiana), at http://hindsfoot.org/akrn226.doc. John Reese's wife's name was Elgie, see *Dr. Bob and the Goodoldtimers* p. 128. Also see Brian Koch, AAHistoryLovers message no. 10046, available online at https://groups.yahoo.com/neo/groups/aahistorylovers/conversations/messages/10046 — "Elgie M. (Russell) Reese, born 14 August 1912, died 5 March 1989, and John T. Reese, born 26 Dec 1902, died 20 Jan 1989, are both buried in Rose Hill Cemetery, Akron Ohio. Section 40, lot 138, graves 5 and 6. Amazing that in those early days of AA, Elgie was only in her 20's."

[482] Presumably Roland Jones, 1614 Glenmount Ave., Akron, Ohio. See "First 226 Members Akron, OH AA Group" as transcribed by Tommy H.

[483] *Dr. Bob and the Good Oldtimers*, pp. 311-312.

[484] Ibid. p. 312.

[485] Ibid. pp. 114-115.

[486] Ibid.

[487] Hartigan, *Bill W.*, pp. 208-209.

[488] Ibid. p. 209.

[489] Ibid. p. 210.

[490] *Pass It On*, pp. 402-403.

[491] Hartigan, *Bill W.*, pp. 210-211; *Pass It On*, p. 403.

[492] *Pass It On*, p. 401.

[493] Edward Dowling, S.J., Alcoholics Anonymous International Convention in St. Louis (1955), the text of his talk in *Alcoholics Anonymous Comes of Age* (New York: A.A. World Services, 1957), pp. 254-261; see espec. p. 255.

[494] Ibid. p. 256.

[495] Ibid. The mention of the Christmas Eve story was probably a reference to "A Miracle at Christmas — a Man Re-born," in the A.A. *Grapevine*, Vol. 3, No. 7, December 1946. "Would you say that a man who had been drinking for months, who had wound up in a flop house in such shape he could not get out of bed and whose 'entire frame shook with convulsive-like tremors' — would you say that man could get up the following morning 'clear eyed, his complexion good and ... perfectly poised?' Of course not. But that's what happened in Chicago one Christmas five years ago. Following is an account of the strange happening, written by an A.A. member of the Chicago Group."

496 Fitzgerald, *Soul of Sponsorship*, p. 33.

497 The edition I have worked from is A. Poulain, S.J., *The Graces of Interior Prayer: A Treatise on Mystical Theology*, translated from the 6th edition by Leonora L. Yorke Smith (London: Kegan Paul, Trench, Trubner & Co., 1921).

498 As Father Dowling put it in his talk on Catholic asceticism, "To a priest who asked Bill how long it took him to write those twelve steps he said that it took twenty minutes. If it were twenty weeks, you could suspect improvisation. Twenty minutes sounds reasonable under the theory of divine help." See Edward Dowling, "Catholic Asceticism"; see also Fitzgerald, *Soul of Sponsorship* 67-68 and note 122.

499 From the Wikipedia online article on Sam Shoemaker (Samuel Moor Shoemaker III) as accessed on August 3, 2014: "Rev. Shoemaker ... addressed an A.A. group in Charlotte, North Carolina, June 17, 1962 saying: 'To set the record straight, that there has gotten going in A.A., a kind of rumor, that I had a lot to do with the 12 steps. I didn't have any more to do with those 12 steps other than that book had, those twelve steps, I believe came to Bill by himself, I think he told me they came to him in about 40 minutes and I think it's one of the great instances of direct inspiration that I know in human history, inspiration which doesn't only bring material straight down outta heaven, but brings rather I think from God the ability to interpret human experience in such a way that you distill it down into transmissible principles, I compare it to Moses going up on a mountain and bringing down Ten tables of the Law, I don't think that's the first time Moses ever thought about righteousness, but I'm glad he went up there and got those ten and brought 'em down and gave 'em to us.'"

500 Poulain, *Graces*, Yorke Smith trans. p. 275.

501 Ibid. p. 289.

502 Ibid. p. 293.

503 Ibid. p. 299-300.

504 Ibid. p. 307-309.

505 Fitzgerald, *Soul of Sponsorship* 61, letter from Bill W. to Fr. Dowling, 8 August 1952.

506 Ibid.

507 Huxley, *Heaven and Hell*.

508 If I am reading correctly what Father Fitzgerald is saying in *The Soul of Sponsorship* on pp. 55-56.

509 Fitzgerald, *Soul of Sponsorship* 56 and 116 n. 101.

510 Ibid. 57-58.

511 Ibid. 57.

512 Ibid. 55-56.

513 Ibid. 58.

514 Ibid. 59-60.

515 Ibid. 62-63.

516 The full text of Bill W.'s 1944 Christmas Greeting can be read at Bill W., "Christmas greetings from Bill W. in 1944," AAHistoryLovers message no. 5441, available online at https://groups.yahoo.com/neo/groups/aahistorylovers/conversations/messages/5441; also at "Who was Bobbie?" AAHistoryLovers message no. 7043, available online at https://groups.yahoo.com/neo/groups/aahistorylovers/conversations/messages/7043.

517 Ernest Kurtz, "Re: Is Bill responsible for this quote?" AAHistoryLovers message no. 4395 (June 24, 2007), available online at https://groups.yahoo.com/neo/groups/aahistorylovers/conversations/messages/4395.

518 Seneca, *De Providentia*, v. 9 — one modern English translation is "Fire is the test of gold; adversity, of strong men." The Latin word *miseria* means suffering, distress, unhappiness, or affliction.

519 *Twelve and Twelve*, Step 7, pp. 74-75.

520 Ibid. p. 74.

521 Aufill, "Catholic Contribution to the 12-Step Movement."

522 See "Biography of John C. Ford, S.J.," taken from the website "The Way of the Lord Jesus" at http://www.twotlj.org/Ford.html and also William P. Fischer, *John C. Ford, S.J.: A Mid-Century Reformer Revisited, 1937–1969* (Ph.D. dissertation, Catholic University of America, 2004).

523 Ibid.

524 From the book *Alcoholism: A Source Book for the Priest* (National Clergy Council on Alcoholism, 1960), as cited in Monsignor William J. Clausen, "Historical Perspective of Father Ralph Pfau and the NCCA," adapted from a talk given by Msgr. William J. Clausen at the fiftieth anniversary celebration of the NCCA in 1999. It can be found in the NCCA Blue Book Archives, and is also available online at the Venerable Matt Talbot

Resource Center, see http://venerablematttalbotresourcecenter.blogspot.
com/2008/02/historical-perspective-of-father-ralph.html.   (When
originally founded by Fr. Ralph Pfau in 1949, the NCCA was called
the National Clergy Council on Alcoholism. His niece — who served
as his assistant in his work with the council — told me when I went to
Indianapolis to interview her, that when membership was opened up to
laypeople as well as clergy, the name was changed to the National Catholic
Council on Alcoholism. It is today called the National Catholic Council
on Addictions, see http://nccatoday.org/ for more information.)

525   Ralph Pfau (Father John Doe) and Al Hirshberg, *Prodigal Shepherd*
(Indianapolis: SMT Guild, orig. pub. 1958.

526   Darrah, *Sister Ignatia*, p. ix.

527   Interview with David A. Works at the Campion Center in Weston,
Massachusetts, on June 26,1984, pp. 1-2, as cited on p. 34 and in note
13 of Oliver J. Morgan, "'Chemical Comforting' and the Theology of
John C. Ford, SJ: Classic Answers to a Contemporary Problem," *Journal
of Ministry in Addiction & Recovery*, Vol. 6(1) 1999: 29-66.

528   John C. Ford, "Depth Psychology, Morality, and Alcoholism" (Weston,
Massachusetts: Weston College, 1951), an article from the *Proceedings Of
The Fifth Annual Meeting Of The Catholic Theological Society Of America*,
June 26-28, 1950. John C. Ford, *Man Takes a Drink: Facts and Principles
About Alcohol* (New York:, P. J. Kenedy, 1955). John C. Ford, S.J., "Pastoral
Treatment," *Institute of Pastoral Theology* (1957), available online at http://
www.silkworth.net/religion_clergy/01044.html.

529   Today called the National Catholic Council on Addictions, their central
office is now located at 1601 Joslyn Road, Lake Orion, Michigan, at
one of the two national centers for Guest House, a treatment facility for
Catholic priests, deacons, brothers, seminarians, and women religious
who suffer from alcoholism, other chemical dependencies, and food and
gambling addictions. Guest House was founded in 1951-1956 by Austin
Ripley, a famous mystery writer and recovering alcoholic who was one of
the major Roman Catholic figures in early Alcoholic Anonymous.

530   Edward Dowling, "Catholic Asceticism"; see also Fitzgerald, *Soul of
Sponsorship* 67-68 and note 122.

531   See Loyola, *Spiritual Exercises* 136, 140-142.

532   Compare the Twelve Promises on pp. 83-84 of the Big Book: "Fear of ...
economic insecurity will leave us."

533 The title was *Ejercicios espirituales* in the Spanish.

534 In the Fifth Exercise during the First Week of the Spiritual Exercises, this is carried out in vivid detail as St. Ignatius asks me to "see with the sight of the imagination the length, breadth and depth of Hell .... to ask for interior sense of the pain which the damned suffer .... to see with the sight of the imagination the great fires, and the souls as in bodies of fire .... to hear with the ears wailings, howling, cries, blasphemies against Christ our Lord and against all His Saints .... to smell with the smell smoke, sulphur, dregs and putrid things .... to taste with the taste bitter things, like tears, sadness and the worm of conscience .... to touch with the touch; that is to say, how the fires touch and burn the souls."

535 Swegan and Chesnut, *Psychology of Alcoholism.*

536 This quote comes from Carl G. Jung, *Modern Man in Search of a Soul*, Chapter 11, "Psychotherapists or the Clergy" p. 229.

537 Sebastian de Grazia, *Errors of Psychotherapy: An Analysis of the Errors of Psychiatry and Religion in the Treatment of Mental Illness* (New York: Doubleday & Co., 1952).

538 Frank R. Barta, *The Moral Theory of Behavior: a New Answer to the Enigma of Mental Illness* (Springfield, Illinois: Thomas, 1952), 35 pages.

539 See the review of Barta's book in *California Medicine*, available online at http://www.ncbi.nlm.nih.gov/pmc/articles/PMC1531949/.

540 Raymond B. Cattell, "The Meaning of Clinical Psychology," in L. A. Pennington and Irwin A. Berg, eds., *An Introduction to Clinical Psychology* (Oxford and New York: Ronald Press, 1948), pp. 3-16.

541 Nancy Olson, *With a Lot of Help from Our Friends.*

542 "Father Ed Dowling — Bill W.'s Confidant and Friend," *Box 459.*

543 Edward Dowling, S.J., "How to Enjoy Being Miserable," *Action Now*, Vol. 8, No. 3, Dec. 1954; reprinted in Fitgerald, *Soul of Sponsorship*, Appendix B, pp. 128-130.

544 Colossians 1:24 in the New Revised Standard Version. Father Dowling would have read this either in the Douay-Rheims version "Who now rejoice in my sufferings for you, and fill up those things that are wanting of the sufferings of Christ, in my flesh, for his body, which is the church," or in the Latin Vulgate version "*qui nunc gaudeo in passionibus pro vobis et adimpleo ea quae desunt passionum Christi in carne mea pro corpore eius quod est ecclesia.*"

545   C. S. Lewis, *The Screwtape Letters* (London: Geoffrey Bles, 1942).

546   Mircea Eliade, *The Sacred and The Profane: The Nature of Religion*, trans. Willard R. Trask (New York: Harcourt, Brace & World, 1957) is the classic description in the modern comparative study of religions, of the way the sacred manifests itself in a hierophany at contact points where the sacred realm touches and overlaps into the secular realm.

547   Rudolf Otto, *Idea of the Holy*. For more on Otto's ideas, see Glenn F. Chesnut, *God and Spirituality*, Chapter 4 on learning to see the sacred dimension of reality and Chapter 5 on the seven faces of the experience of the divine reality.

548   "Mr. X and Alcoholics Anonymous," a sermon preached on November 26, 1939 by Dilworth Lupton at the First Unitarian Church, Euclid at East 82nd Street, Cleveland, Ohio. Can be read online at http://silkworth.net/aahistory/mr_x.html.

549   Father Edward Dowling, his talk at the Alcoholics Anonymous International Convention in St. Louis (1955). A transcription of the talk is given in pp. 254-261 of *Alcoholics Anonymous Comes of Age* (New York: A.A. World Services, 1957).

550   Carl G. Jung in a 1933 seminar, as quoted in Edward Edinger, *The Creation of Consciousness* (Toronto: Inner City Books, 1984), p. 66.

551   Carl Gustav Jung, *Visions: Notes of the Seminar Given in 1930-1934 by C. G. Jung*, ed. by Claire Douglas, Volume 1 (Princeton, New Jersey: Princeton University Press, 1997), p. 1030.

552   Letter from Carl G. Jung to the Rev. Morton T. Kelsey, 3 May 1958, in Edward F. Edinger, *The New God-Image: A Study of Jung's Key Letters Concerning the Evolution of the Western God-Image* (Willimette, Illinois: Chiron Publications, 1996), p. 170.

553   Carl G. Jung, *Psychology and Religion: East and West*, in his *Collected Works*, Vol. 11, Bollingen Series (Princeton, New Jersey: Princeton University Press, 1970), pp. 468 ff.

554   In one of the analogies which St. Augustine used to illustrate the doctrine of the Trinity, he said that the Logos (the second member of the Trinity, which formed the logical structure of the universe including all the laws of nature and the natural moral law) was like a logically constructed idea which a human mind was thinking about. The Holy Spirit (the third member of the Trinity) was then the act of intentionality by which the mind was keeping that particular idea within its conscious attention. And

the Father (the first member of the Trinity) was analogous to *memoria*. This latter concept of course referred to the mind's memory banks, where the mind had stored all its stock of conscious ideas and recollections, and ALSO *all the unconscious content of the human mind.*

555 As noted by the Chicago Roman Catholic novelist and sociologist Father Andrew M. Greeley (1928-2013) in *A Christmas Wedding* (New York: Forge Books, 2000).

556 John Milton, *Paradise Lost* I, 1-4, 6, 24-26.

557 See for example the letters from Henrietta Seiberling to Clarence Snyder dated February 9, 1951; September 1951; and July 31, 1952.

558 In the last half of the *Twelve and Twelve*, where Bill Wilson writes about the traditions, he makes it clear that the greatest danger to A.A., in his view, is created by relatively small handfuls of people who would tear the groups apart if given full rein. In the chapter on the First Tradition, he likens the A.A. group to a lifeboat afloat on a trackless sea, filled with shipwreck survivors who must cooperate with one another at all costs if they are going to survive at all. Who are the dangerous ones who are most apt to tip the lifeboat over and dump everyone into the sea to drown? They are the people, Bill W. says in that chapter, who are driven by out-of-control "ambition" and the desire to grab "wealth, power, and prestige" at the expense of all the other people around them. In the chapter on the Second Tradition, he warns of the further dangers created by the "bleeding deacons," who display one particularly destructive form of the desire to dominate and demean others. The chapter on the Third Tradition lays out an A.A. Bill of Rights in an effort to ward off the additional dangers created by intolerance and prejudice (whether based on race, religion, sexual and gender persuasion, wealth and worldly success, political beliefs, or what have you). The chapter on the Fourth Tradition warns of the danger to the group which is created by "the promoter." And most of the rest of the traditions are designed to make it more difficult for the **bleeding deacons** and the **promoters** to destroy the A.A. fellowship. The chapters on the Eleventh Tradition and Twelfth Tradition (both dealing with anonymity) make it clear that the principal danger which the anonymity principle is designed to help counteract, is the danger created by "the promoter instinct in us," where a small handful of self-aggrandizing individuals would, if they were allowed, go out and set up their own personal publicity programs in the public media. In their search for public fame and notoriety, these publicity seekers would turn

A.A. into something more like a "vaudeville circuit," Bill W. said, where self-proclaimed A.A. experts competed against the pop singers, standup comedians, talk show hosts, and television stars to see who could get the biggest audience in the public media.

559   See Jesus' parable of the Good Samaritan in Luke 10:30-37.

560   In fact, as we see particularly in *The Magician's Nephew* (London: Bodley Head, 1955), C. S. Lewis taught that we live in a multiverse made up of many worlds, some of them just beginning, and others ending. There are small gateways — a wardrobe, a ring, a woodland, a pool — which can provide links between different worlds. And there also seems to be something like transmigration of souls taking place at some points, or something very close to it.

561   The text of Bill and Lois's prayer is given in *Pass It On* p. 265. This prayer assumed the doctrine of the transmigration of souls, for it stated that all of our human spirits had preexisted before their incarnation in physical bodies on this planet in the present era. Indeed, the prayer says that all of our individual human spirits had always existed in some realm or other, and always would exist for all eternity, and would continue to have fresh experiences and adventures. And in quasi-Swedenborgian fashion, as we have noted, the prayer stated that our future incarnations or embodiments would ultimately involve passing through a series of different heavenly realms (the "house of many mansions" in John 14:2), in each one of which we would learn yet new and different things about God.

562   Augustin Poulain, S.J., *The Graces of Interior Prayer.*

563   Jonathan Edwards, "A Divine and Supernatural Light," section I.2.

564   William R. Miller and Janet C'de Baca, *Quantum Change.*

565   Justin Martyr, *Dialogue with Trypho*, trans. George Reith, Ante-Nicene Christian Library (Edinburgh: T. & T. Clark, 1867-1873) chapters 3-8.

566   Bernard J. F. Lonergan, S.J. *Insight: A Study of Human Understanding* (London: Longmans, Green & Co., 1957).

567   Whittaker Chambers (1901-1961) was a member of the Communist Party and a Soviet spy until he defected somewhere around 1937 or 1938. In 1948, he was called to testify before the House Un-American Activities Committee against Alger Hiss, who was being accused of being a Soviet spy. California congressman Richard Nixon, who later (in 1969) became President of the United States, was an important member of that committee. Then in 1955, Whittaker Chambers (who by now had

switched to the completely opposite wing politically) went to work as a senior editor at William F. Buckley, Jr.'s new magazine, the *National Review*. Buckley had become the standard bearer in American politics of the intellectual wing of the American Conservative movement.

568 Chesnut, *First Christian Histories*, pp. 12, 41-42, 44-50, 59, 190, 210, 255.

569 This was the terminology used by John Wesley, who along with Jonathan Edwards, was one of the two great theorists of the Protestant evangelical movement back in the early eighteenth century, when it first began. See Wesley's *Standard Sermons* for continual examples of the contrast he made between "formal outward religion" and "the true inner religion of the heart."

570 Harry M. Tiebout's talk is in *Alcoholics Anonymous Comes of Age* on pp. 245-251.

571 John Henry Newman, Sermon 14, "Saving Knowledge," pp. 151-161 in *Parochial and Plain Sermons*, Volume 2 (London: Longmans, Green, and Co., 1908), quote taken from pp. 161-162. Available online at http://www.newmanreader.org/Works/parochial/volume2/index.html.

572 *Pass It On* p. 371.

573 Huxley, *Perennial Philosophy*.

574 For the biblical reference, see the story in Genesis 28:10-22 of Jacob's dream at Bethel.

575 Matthew 26:36-46, Luke 22:39-46, Mark 14:32-42.

576 See Eric Berne, M.D., *Games People Play: The Psychology of Human Relationships* (New York: Grove Press, 1964). In further explanation, Father Dowling is talking here about *rationalization*, which is a psychological defense mechanism in which a whole series of spurious but seemingly rational and logical objections and arguments are given in order to avoid having to speak about how the rationalizer is really feeling and thinking. Self-styled intellectuals of a certain sort like to use non-stop rationalization to block psychotherapists when painful truths threaten to surface.

577 The monastery grounds spread over 40 acres of rolling hills at 19961 Live Oak Canyon Road, Trabuco Canyon, California.

578 Lattin, *Distilled Spirits*, pp. 140 and 167.

579 See social psychologist Fraser Trevor's blog for May 1, 2013, entitled "One man who influenced Bill Wilson greatly was Gerald Heard. Tom Powers often said that Heard was one of Bill's sponsors." In *Dream Warrior*

Recovery, at http://dreamwarriorrecovery.blogspot.com/2013/05/one-man-who-influenced-bill-wilson.html.

580 Huxley, *Perennial Philosophy*.

581 Huxley, *Doors of Perception*.

582 Big Book pp. 8 and 25.

583 Edwards, "A Divine and Supernatural Light," section I.2.

584 *Pass It On*, Chapter 23, pp. 368-377; on Tom Power's presence see p. 371. See also Ernest Kurtz, "Drugs and the Spiritual: Bill W. Takes LSD."

585 Lattin, *Harvard Psychedelic Club*, p. 67.

586 *Pass It On* p. 371; Hartigan, *Bill W.*, p. 178.

587 Lattin, *Distilled Spirits*, p. 205, citing a letter written from Wilson to Heard on December 4, 1956. The group which included Dowling and Eugene Exman is also mentioned in Amelia Hill, "LSD could help alcoholics stop drinking, AA founder believed," *The Guardian* (Thursday 23 August 2012), available online at http://www.theguardian.com/science/2012/aug/23/lsd-help-alcoholics-theory.

588 Lattin, "What Bill W. told Carl Jung About his Awesome LSD Trip."

589 Letter from Aldous Huxley to Father Thomas Merton, 10 January 1959, as quoted in Ernest Kurtz, "Drugs and the Spiritual: Bill W. Takes LSD."

590 Letter from Bill Wilson to Gerald Heard on September 1956, as quoted in Amelia Hill, "LSD could help alcoholics stop drinking, AA founder believed."

591 Letter from Bill Wilson to Gerald Heard on December 4, 1956, as quoted in Lattin, *Distilled Spirits*, p. 205. Also quoted in Amelia Hill, "LSD could help alcoholics."

592 Letter from Bill Wilson to Gerald Heard in 1957, as quoted in Don Lattin, Interview in *Points: The Blog of the Alcohol and Drugs History Society* at http://pointsadhsblog.wordpress.com/2012/10/15/the-points-interview-don-lattin/. Part of this quote is also cited in Amelia Hill, "LSD could help alcoholics."

593 Letter to Father Ed Dowling from Bill Wilson on December 29, 1958 as quoted in Don Lattin, *Distilled Spirits*, p. 207. The same paragraph is also given verbatim in Don Lattin, as interviewed by Ron Roizen in *Points: The Blog of the Alcohol and Drugs History Society* (October 15, 2012) at http://pointsadhsblog.wordpress.com/2012/10/15/

the-points-interview-don-lattin/. It is also cited in Amelia Hill, "LSD could help alcoholics stop drinking, AA founder believed."

594   Letter to Father Dowling from Bill Wilson on October 26, 1959 as quoted in Lattin, as interviewed by Ron Roizen in *Points* (October 15, 2012).

595   Letter from Bill W. to Father Ed Dowling on November 23, 1959, in Fitzgerald, *Soul of Sponsorship* 96-97.

596   Arthur S. (Arlington, Texas), *Narrative Timeline of AA History*, under the year 1956: "Bill had several experiments with LSD up to 1959, perhaps into the 1960's."

597   Fitzgerald, *Soul of Sponsorship* 92 and 126.

598   Ibid. 55-57.

599   Letter from Bill Wilson to Father Ed Dowling on May 8, 1958 in Fitzgerald, *Soul of Sponsorship* 91.

600   See Fitzgerald, *Soul of Sponsorship* 92 and 122 n 183, letter from Bill W. to Joe Diggles (one of Father Ed's former students) on September 2, 1958: "He has recently been here, by the way. He has had a heart attack only a month since; nevertheless he carries on as usual."

601   See Fitgerald, *Soul of Sponsorship* 92 and 94, citing letter from Bill W. to Fr. Ed on December 29, 1958.

602   Letter from Father Dowling on December 14, 1959 in Fitzgerald, *Soul of Sponsorship* 97.

603   Letter from Father Dowling's sister Anna Dowling on March 17, 1960 in Fitzgerald, *Soul of Sponsorship* 101.

604   Fitzgerald, *Soul of Sponsorship* 92.

605   A transcript of a photocopy (in an Irish A.A. archival source) which had been made of the original letter, which I was told was preserved in the archives of the Sisters of Charity of St. Augustine (Sister Ignatia Gavin's order) in the United States.

606   John C. Ford, S.J., *Man Takes a Drink: Facts and Principles About Alcohol*, with a foreword by Mrs. Marty Mann (New York: P. J. Kenedy, 1955).

607   A transcript of a photocopy (found in an Irish A.A. archival source) which had been made of the original letter, which I was told was preserved in the archives of the Sisters of Charity of St. Augustine (Sister Ignatia Gavin's order) in the United States.

608 Also a transcript of a photocopy (found in an Irish A.A. archival source) which had been made of the original letter, which I was told was preserved in the archives of the Sisters of Charity of St. Augustine (Sister Ignatia Gavin's order) in the United States.

609 Edward J. Dowling, S.J., "A.A. Steps for the Underprivileged Non-A.A.," *Grapevine* (July 1960), reprinted in Fitzgerald, *Soul of Sponsorship*, Appendix A, pp. 125-127.

610 Bill W., letter to Ollie in California, January 4, 1956, as quoted in Fitzgerald, *Soul of Sponsorship* 40-42.

611 Linda Farris Kurtz, DPA, *Recovery Groups: A Guide to Creating, Leading, and Working with Groups for Addictions and Mental Health Conditions* (New York: Oxford University Press, 2015), p. 30.

612 See the Toledo, Ohio, *Blade* for Tuesday, December 5, 1967 and the Chariton, Iowa, *Herald-Patriot* for Thursday, October 12, 1972.

613 Jonathan Katz, *Gay American History: Lesbians and Gay Men in the U.S.A.* (New York: Thomas Y. Crowell, 1976). This French group had named itself after Mattaccino, the name given to a famous court jester figure in the Italian theater, who would speak out boldly and tell the truth to the king when everyone else was afraid to do so. The *mutawajjihin* ("mask-wearers" in Arabic) were originally Moorish sword-dancers.

614 See the four-part statement of the organization's purpose which appeared on the inside cover of their publication, *The Ladder*.

615 Lilian Faderman, *Odd Girls and Twilight Lovers: A History of Lesbian Life in Twentieth Century America* (New York: Penguin Books, 1991), chapters 6 and 7, pp. 148-149 and 179-186; and Marcia Gallo, *Different Daughters: A History of the Daughters of Bilitis and the Rise of the Lesbian Rights Movement* (New York: Carrol & Graf Publishers, 2006).

616 Pierre Louÿs, *The Songs of Bilitis* translated from the Greek, trans. into English by Alvah C. Bessie, privately printed for subscribers by Macy-Masius Publishers in New York, 1926.

617 *Twelve and Twelve* p. 48.

618 Ibid.

619 Trysh Travis, *The Language of the Heart: A Cultural History of the Recovery Movement from Alcoholics Anonymous to Oprah Winfrey* (Chapel Hill, North Carolina: University of North Carolina Press, 2009).

[620] The *Grapevine* has "ethnic-psycho-somatic," but ethnic (which makes no sense) is surely a misspelling for the word ethico, by simply exchanging an o for an n.

[621] *Alcoholics Anonymous Comes of Age* p. 259.

[622] One researcher gives Father Ed's date of death as March 30, 1960 (and his date of burial as April 3, 1960) — see the older Find a Grave page on Rev. Edward Patrick Dowling at http://www.findagrave.com/cgi-bin/fg.cgi?page=gr&GRid=16958125. But a number of excellent sources certify that April 3rd was the date of death. Only a month after his death, for example, we read in an official Jesuit publication that Father Ed "had flown to Memphis, Tenn., on Saturday, Apr. 2 .... He was found dead in bed at 8:00 A.M. the following day" — see McQuade, Obituary. The official Alcoholics Anonymous obituary, which appeared only two months after his death, says the same thing: "Early Sunday morning, April 3rd, Father Edward Dowling died peacefully in his sleep" — see "To Father Ed — Godspeed!" the obituary of Fr. Ed Dowling by Bill W., A.A. *Grapevine* (June 1960), available online at https://groups.yahoo.com/neo/groups/aahistorylovers/conversations/messages/1731 (AAHistoryLovers Message 1731from William Lash, April 1, 2004). The well-researched biography of Father Ed by Fitzgerald, *Soul of Sponsorship* 101, likewise says "Early on Sunday morning, April 3, [1960] Father Ed died peacefully in his sleep." Brian Koch, a careful researcher and A.A. historian, also gives Dowling's date of death as April 3, 1960, see "Fr Edward P Dowling" on the Find a Grave website, at http://www.findagrave.com/cgi-bin/fg.cgi?page=gr&GRid=73326044. We are told that his burial was on "6 APR 1960 Florissant, St. Stanislaus Cem., St. Louis, MO" on the Rootsweb website, see http://wc.rootsweb.ancestry.com/cgi-bin/igm.cgi?op=GET&db=dowfam3&id=I18100.

[623] But Brian Koch, a very careful researcher, says that "there is some dispute, especially among the local Jesuit Historical Society that no bodies were actually moved." See the Find a Grave website at http://www.findagrave.com/cgi-bin/fg.cgi?page=gr&GRid=73326044. Also see the Rootsweb website at http://wc.rootsweb.ancestry.com/cgi-bin/igm.cgi?op=GET&db=dowfam3&id=I18100.

[624] McQuade, Obituary. Bill W., "To Father Ed — Godspeed!" Fitzgerald, *Soul of Sponsorship* 124 n. 206.

[625] Bill W., "To Father Ed — Godspeed!"

[626] Letter from Paul K. in Memphis to Lyb in St. Louis on April 4, 1960, as quoted in Fitzgerald, *Soul of Sponsorship* 102-103.

[627] McQuade, Obituary.

[628] Ibid.

[629] Fitzgerald, *Soul of Sponsorship* 103-104.

[630] Father Fred Zimmerman, S.J., letter of July 16, 1986 to Father Jim Egan, S.J., as quoted in Fitzgerald, *Soul of Sponsorship* 103.

[631] Bill W., "To Father Ed — Godspeed!" In this obituary, Bill W. quoted from some of his introduction of Father Dowling at the A.A. International in St. Louis in July 1955, see *Alcoholics Anonymous Comes of Age*, p. 254.

[632] *Alcoholics Anonymous Comes of Age*, p. 254.

[633] Again see Bill W., "To Father Ed — Godspeed!" and Wilson's introduction of Father Dowling at the A.A. International in St. Louis in July 1955, as recounted in *Alcoholics Anonymous Comes of Age* on page 254.

BIBLIOGRAPHY

AA HISTORY LOVERS WEB GROUP: The AAHistoryLovers web group may be found at https://groups.yahoo.com/neo/groups/aahistorylovers/conversations/ messages. All the messages from 2002 to 2012 are also available at http:// hindsfoot.org/aahl.html and can be read as text files (.txt), as Microsoft Word files (.docx), or as Microsoft Access database files (.mdb files). They are also available on the Silkworth.net website at http://silkworth.net/aahistorylovers/ aa_history_lovers_messages.html where they can also be read in either of two additional file formats, as .html files or as .pdf files.

BOX 4-5-9: NEWS AND NOTES FROM G.S.O. This is a quarterly newsletter from the Alcoholics Anonymous General Service Office in New York City. See online at http://www.aa.org/pages/en_US/box-4-5-9-news-and-notes-from-gso.

A.A. Bulletin No. 1 (November 14, 1940). Published by the Alcoholic Foundation, National Headquarters—Alcoholics Anonymous. Available online at http://hindsfoot.org/bullno1.pdf.

A.A. Bulletin No. 2 (January 15, 1941). Published by the Alcoholic Foundation, National Headquarters—Alcoholics Anonymous. Available online at http:// hindsfoot.org/bullno2.pdf.

"A.A.'s Country-Wide News Circuit" section. A.A. *Grapevine*, May 1947 and June 1947. The relevant portions can be read online at AAHistoryLovers message no. 1371 and no. 1365, see https://groups.yahoo.com/neo/groups/ aahistorylovers/conversations/messages/1371 and https://groups.yahoo.com/ neo/groups/aahistorylovers/conversations/messages/1365.

Akerman, Rita. "Matt Talbot — A Man for Our Times." At http://www. catholicassociates.com/leaflets/A Man for our Times_Rev1.pdf.

Akron Manual, see *A Manual for Alcoholics Anonymous*.

Alcoholics Anonymous. 4th ed. New York: Alcoholics Anonymous World Services, 2001.

Alcoholics Anonymous Comes of Age. New York: Alcoholics Anonymous World Services, 1957.

Alexander, Dr. Eben. *Proof of Heaven: A Neurosurgeon's Journey into the Afterlife.* New York: Simon and Schuster, 2012.

Alexander, Jack. "Alcoholics Anonymous." *Saturday Evening Post* (March 1, 1941).

_____. "Jack Alexander of Saturday Evening Post Fame Thought A.A.s Were Pulling His Leg." *A.A. Grapevine* (May 1945), There is a copy of the article in AAHistoryLovers message no. 1814, available online at https://groups.yahoo.com/neo/groups/aahistorylovers/conversations/messages/1814.

Alexander, Jack. Obituary. *New York Times* (September 20, 1975), a short summary may be read online in AAHistoryLovers message no. 6211 at https://groups.yahoo.com/neo/groups/aahistorylovers/conversations/messages/6211.

Arenson, Adam. "Freeing Dred Scott: St. Louis confronts an icon of slavery, 1857-2007." *Common-Place* 8, no. 3 (April 2008). Available online at http://www.common_place.org/vol_08/no_03/arenson/.

Arthur S. (Arlington, Texas). *Counts of AA Groups and Members.* Available online at http://hindsfoot.org/aatimeappend1.pdf.

_____. "Re: Date of White Light Experience at Towns." AA History Lovers Message #4235 posted on April 13, 2007 — http://health.groups.yahoo.com/group/AAHistoryLovers/message/4235.

_____. *A Narrative Timeline of AA History.* Available online at http://hindsfoot.org/aatimeline.pdf, also at http://silkworth.net/timelines/timelines_public/timelines_public.html.

_____. "Re: Responsibility Declaration." AAHistoryLovers message no. 2485 (June 12, 2005) at https://groups.yahoo.com/neo/groups/aahistorylovers/conversations/messages/2485.

_____. *Timelines in A.A.'s History* (the earliest version of his timeline). At http://silkworth.net/timelines/timelines.html.

Arthur S. (Arlington, Texas), Tom E. (Wappingers Falls, New York), and Glenn C. (South Bend, Indiana). *Alcoholics Anonymous (AA) Recovery Outcome Rates: Contemporary Myth and Misinterpretation* (2008). Available online at http://hindsfoot.org/recout01.pdf.

Augustine. *City of God.* Marcus Dods 1887 translation. New York: Random House, 1950. Now available online at New Advent Fathers of the Church, http://www.newadvent.org/fathers/120114.htm.

Aufill, W. Robert. "The Catholic Contribution to the 12-Step Movement." In *This Rock* magazine in October, 1996 (now *Catholic Answers Magazine*, published by Catholic Answers, Inc., based in El Cajon, near San Diego, California). This article is available online at http://www.catholicculture. org/culture/library/view.cfm?recnum=703. It may also be read online as AAHistoryLovers message no. 347, "The Catholic Contribution to the 12 Step Movement," at https://groups.yahoo.com/neo/groups/aahistorylovers/ conversations/messages/347.

Barger, Mel = Mel B.

Barefoot Bill L. *People In A.A. History Mentioned In The Literature: Who Were They? What Did They Do?* Available online at http://www.barefootsworld.net/ aapeople.html.

Barmann, Mary Kathryn. *Father Daniel A. Lord, S.J.* St. Louis, Missouri: St. Louis University, 1953.

Barta, Frank R. *The Moral Theory of Behavior: a New Answer to the Enigma of Mental Illness.* Springfield, Illinois: Thomas, 1952. 35 pages. See also the review of Barta's book in *California Medicine*, available online at http://www. ncbi.nlm.nih.gov/pmc/articles/PMC1531949/.

Berne, Eric, M.D. *Games People Play: The Psychology of Human Relationships.* New York: Grove Press, 1964.

Big Book = *Alcoholics Anonymous*. 4th ed. New York: Alcoholics Anonymous World Services, 2001.

"Biography of John C. Ford, S.J." On the website "The Way of the Lord Jesus" at http://www.twotlj.org/Ford.html.

Bill W. = Wilson, Bill

Bill W. "Christmas greetings from Bill W. in 1944," AAHistoryLovers message no. 5441, available online at https://groups.yahoo.com/neo/groups/aahistorylovers/conversations/messages/5441; also at "Who was Bobbie?" AAHistoryLovers message no. 7043, available online at https://groups.yahoo.com/neo/groups/aahistorylovers/conversations/messages/7043.

_____. "A Letter from Bill W. on Depression." Excerpts quoted in the memoirs of Tom Pike, an early California A.A. member, see http://www.silkworth.net/aahistory/billw_depression.html.

_____. Letter to Jimmy Burwell on December 9, 1940. See AAHistoryLovers message no. 1705, available online at https://groups.yahoo.com/neo/groups/aahistorylovers/conversations/messages/1705.

_____. Letter to Mel B. dated July 2, 1956. Pp. 20-22 in Mel B., *My Search for Bill W.* Center City, Minnesota: Hazelden, 2000.

_____. "Re: Bill's spiritual experience — belladonna induced?" An excerpt from his 1958 talk to the New York City Medical Society. AA History Lovers message no. 6281, at https://groups.yahoo.com/neo/groups/aahistorylovers/conversations/messages/6281.

_____. "To Father Ed — Godspeed!" Obituary of Fr. Ed Dowling. A.A. *Grapevine* (June 1960), available online at https://groups.yahoo.com/neo/groups/aahistorylovers/conversations/messages/1731 (AAHistoryLovers Message 1731 from William Lash, April 1, 2004).

"Bill Wilson's Fight With Depression." In the West Baltimore Group's *Let's Ask Bill* section at http://www.westbalto.a-1associates.com/LETS_ASK_BILL/Fightwithdepression.htm.

Bluhm, Amy Colwell, Ph.D. "Verification of C. G. Jung's analysis of Rowland Hazard and the history of Alcoholics Anonymous." The American Psychological Association's journal *History of Psychology*. November 2006.

Box 4-5-9: News and Notes from G.S.O. This is a quarterly newsletter from the Alcoholics Anonymous General Service Office in New York City. See online at http://www.aa.org/pages/en_US/box-4-5-9-news-and-notes-from-gso.

Brown, Sally and David R. Brown. *A Biography of Mrs. Marty Mann: The First Lady of Alcoholics Anonymous.* Center City, Minnesota: Hazelden, 2001.

Bucke, Richard Maurice. *Cosmic Consciousness: A Study in the Evolution of the Human Mind.* Philadelphia: Innes & Sons, 1901.

Cattell, Raymond B. "The Meaning of Clinical Psychology." Pp. 3-16 in L. A. Pennington and Irwin A. Berg, eds., *An Introduction to Clinical Psychology.* Oxford and New York: Ronald Press, 1948.

Celello, Kristin. *Making Marriage Work: A History of Marriage and Divorce in the Twentieth-Century United States.* Chapel Hill: University of North Carolina Press, 2009.

Cheever, Susan. *My Name Is Bill: Bill Wilson — His Life and the Creation of Alcoholics Anonymous.* New York: Washington Square Press, 2004.

Chesnut, Glenn F. "Buddhist quote on karma in James Allen." AAHistoryLovers message no. 9505 at https://groups.yahoo.com/neo/groups/aahistorylovers/conversations/messages/9505.

_____. "A Century of Patristic Studies 1888–1988." In Henry Warner Bowden (ed.). *A Century of Church History.* Carbondale: Southern Illinois University Press, 1988.

_____. *Changed by Grace: V. C. Kitchen, the Oxford Group, and A.A.* Hindsfoot Foundation Series on Spirituality and Theology. New York: iUniverse, September 2006.

_____. "Chicago in 1945: The first black people to join A.A." His interview in July 17, 1999 of Bill Williams (who was by then 96 years old) and Jimmy Hodges, another great black A.A. leader from Chicago, at http://hindsfoot.org/nblack3.html.

_____. "Early Black A.A. Leaders." A talk (about Jimmy Miller, Bill Williams, and others) given on July 26, 2014 at Serenity House in

Gary, Indiana — a full transcript is available online at http://hindsfoot.org/gary2014.doc.

_____. *The Factory Owner & the Convict: Lives and Teachings of the A.A. Old Timers.* 2nd ed. Hindsfoot Foundation Series on Alcoholics Anonymous History. New York: iUniverse, 2005.

_____. *The First Christian Histories: Eusebius, Socrates, Sozomen, Theodoret, and Evagrius.* 2nd ed., rev. and enlarged. Macon, Georgia: Mercer University Press, 1986; orig. pub. in Paris by Éditions Beauchesne in 1977.

_____. *God and Spirituality: Philosophical Essays.* Hindsfoot Foundation Series on Spirituality and Theology. New York: iUniverse, 2010.

_____. *The Higher Power of the Twelve-Step Program: For Believers & Non-believers.* Hindsfoot Foundation Series on Spirituality and Theology. San Jose: iUniverse / Authors Choice Press, 2001.

_____. *Images of Christ.* San Francisco: Harper & Row, 1984.

_____. "In Memoriam: Nancy Moyer Olson." Available online at http://hindsfoot.org/nomem1.html.

_____. "The Pattern of the Past: Augustine's Debate with Eusebius and Sallust." In John Deschner, Leroy T. Howe, and Klaus Penzel (eds). *Our Common History as Christians: Essays in Honor of Albert C. Outler.* New York: Oxford University Press, 1975.

_____. *The Psychology of Alcoholism.* See under: Swegan, William E.

_____. *The Stories and Memories of Early Black A.A. Leaders Told in Their Own Words.* Available online at http://hindsfoot.org/blackaa.html.

_____. "The Third Tradition." Mel Barger and I talked about the Third Tradition at a symposium held in the auditorium of the public library at Fort Wayne, Indiana, on January 14, 2012.

_____. "Re: More than one edition of the Akron Manual?" The first surviving edition of the *Akron Manual* came out circa June 1942.

AAHistoryLovers message 7516 (July 26, 2011) at https://groups.yahoo.com/neo/groups/aahistorylovers/conversations/messages/7516.

_____. "Re: What was the Matt Talbot Club circa December 1939?," AAHistoryLovers message no. 7692, at https://groups.yahoo.com/neo/groups/aahistorylovers/conversations/messages/7692.

_____, ed. *With a Lot of Help from Our Friends.* See under: Olson, Nancy.

"Christian Family Movement: History." Available online at http://www.cfm.org/history.html.

Clausen, Monsignor William J. "Historical Perspective of Father Ralph Pfau and the NCCA." Adapted from a talk given by Msgr. William J. Clausen at the fiftieth anniversary celebration of the NCCA in 1999. It can be found in the NCCA Blue Book Archives, and is also available online at the Venerable Matt Talbot Resource Center, see http://venerablematttalbotresourcecenter.blogspot.com/2008/02/historical-perspective-of-father-ralph.html. (When originally founded by Fr. Ralph Pfau in 1949, the NCCA was called the National Clergy Council on Alcoholism. His niece — who served as his assistant in his work with the council — told me when I went to Indianapolis to interview her, that when membership was opened up to laypeople as well as clergy, the name was changed to the National Catholic Council on Alcoholism. It is today called the National Catholic Council on Addictions, see http://nccatoday.org/ for more information.)

Cullinane, Anastasia Newman (1826-1883). Find a Grave. Available online at http://www.findagrave.com/cgi-bin/fg.cgi?page=gr&GRid=51001061.

Daniélou, Jean. Introduction (pp. 1-78) to Gregory of Nyssa, *From Glory to Glory: Texts from Gregory of Nyssa's Mystical Writings.* Ed. Herbert Musurillo. New York: Scribner, 1961.

Darrah, Mary C. *Sister Ignatia: Angel of Alcoholics Anonymous.* Center City, Minnesota: Hazelden, 2001; orig. pub. Loyola University Press 1991), 299-300.

Dawson, Penn, S.J. "St. Stanislaus Kostka: Patron of Jesuit Novices." In *Company: The World of Jesuits and Their Friends* (Fall 2009). Available online at http://www.companysj.com/v271/new-day.html.

Day, Dorothy. "Reflections on Work—November 1946." *The Catholic Worker*, November 1946, 1, 4.

de Grazia, Sebastian. *Errors of Psychotherapy: An Analysis of the Errors of Psychiatry and Religion in the Treatment of Mental Illness*. New York: Doubleday & Co., 1952.

"A Declaration of Unity." AAHistoryLovers message no. 278 (June 11, 2002) at https://groups.yahoo.com/neo/groups/aahistorylovers/conversations/messages/278.

Detroit / Washington D.C. Pamphlet, also called the *Tablemate* or *Table Leaders Guide* (c. June 14, 1943). At http://hindsfoot.org/detr0.html.

Dick B. *The Akron Genesis of Alcoholics Anonymous*. Kihei, Hawaii: Paradise Research Publications, 1992 and 1998.

_____. *Dr. Bob and His Library*. 3rd ed. Kihei, Hawaii: Paradise Research Publications, 1998.

_____. "'God as We Understood Him'—The A.A. Story." At http://www.dickb.com/aaarticles/AA-Story.shtml.

"Divorcées Anonymous." *Time* 66 (Sept. 26, 1955): 64.

Dr. Bob and the Good Oldtimers: A Biography, with Recollections of Early A.A. in the Midwest. New York: Alcoholics Anonymous World Services, 1980.

Don B. *History of the Chicago Group*. Available online at http://hindsfoot.org/chicago1.pdf.

Doug B. (Riverside, California). "Re: Emmet Fox's secretary and Al S." AAHistoryLovers message 4003 (January 7, 2007), available online at https://groups.yahoo.com/neo/groups/aahistorylovers/conversations/messages/4003.

Dowling, Anna. Find a Grave. Available online at http://www.findagrave.com/cgi-bin/fg.cgi?page=gr&GSln=Dowling&GSiman=1&GScid=27890&GRid=51002606&.

Dowling, Beatrice F. Find a Grave. Available online at http://www.findagrave.com/cgi-bin/fg.cgi?page=gr&GRid=48185876.

Dowling, Edward, S.J. "A.A. Steps for the Underprivileged Non-A.A." *A.A. Grapevine* (July 1960). Reprinted in Appendix A, pp. 125-127, in Fitzgerald, *Soul of Sponsorship.*

_____. "Catholic Asceticism and the Twelve Steps." National Clergy Conference on Alcoholism, *Blue Book* (1953). Dowling's article is available online in AAHistoryLovers message no. 346, "Religion & AA – N.C.C.A. 'Blue Book' an anthology," at https://groups.yahoo.com/neo/groups/AAHistoryLovers/conversations/topics/346. Also as AAHistoryLovers message no. 1322, 'Rel. & AA. - The "Blue Book", 1953,' at https://groups.yahoo.com/neo/groups/aahistorylovers/conversations/messages/1322. And also at http://www.silkworth.net/religion_clergy/01038.html.

_____. His talk at the Alcoholics Anonymous International Convention in St. Louis (1955). A transcript is given in pp. 254-261 of *Alcoholics Anonymous Comes of Age.* New York: A.A. World Services, 1957.

_____. "How to Enjoy Being Miserable." *Action Now*, Vol. 8, No. 3, Dec. 1954; reprinted in Appendix B, pp. 128-130 of Fitgerald, *Soul of Sponsorship.*

_____. Résumé. Reprinted as Appendix F, pp. 138-139, in Fitzgerald, *Soul of Sponsorship.*

Dowling Family Genealogy in Ancestry.com. Available online at http://wc.rootsweb.ancestry.com/cgi-bin/igm.cgi?op=GET&db=dowfam3&id=I18100.

Dowling, Fr Edward P. Find a Grave. The newer, corrected version, posted by Brian Koch, a careful researcher and good A.A. historian. At http://www.findagrave.com/cgi-bin/fg.cgi?page=gr&GRid=73326044.

Dowling, James. Find a Grave. Available online at http://www.findagrave.com/cgi-bin/fg.cgi?page=gr&GRid=51003060.

Dowling, Mary. Find a Grave. Available online at http://www.findagrave.com/cgi-bin/fg.cgi?page=gr&GSln=Dowling&GSiman=1&GScid=27890&GRid=51003507&.

Dowling, Paul Vincent. Find a Grave. At http://www.findagrave.com/cgi-bin/fg.cgi?page=gr&GRid=51000982.

Dowling, Rev Edward Patrick. Find a Grave. The older, partially incorrect entry, posted by Karl Kleen. At http://www.findagrave.com/cgi-bin/fg.cgi?page=gr&GRid=16958125.

Edinger, Edward. *The Creation of Consciousness*. Toronto: Inner City Books, 1984.

_____. *The New God-Image: A Study of Jung's Key Letters Concerning the Evolution of the Western God-Image*. Willimette, Illinois: Chiron Publications, 1996.

Edwards, Jonathan. "A Divine and Supernatural Light." Boston: S. Kneeland and T. Green, 1734), section I.2. Reprinted in "A Divine and Supernatural Light," pp. 123-134 in Jonathan Edwards, *Basic Writings*, ed. Ola Elizabeth Winslow (New York: New American Library, 1966). Also available online as Jonathan Edwards, "A Divine and Supernatural Light, Immediately Imparted to the Soul by the Spirit of God," in the Christian Classics Ethereal Library, http://www.ccel.org/ccel/edwards/works2.iii.i.html.

Eliade, Mircea. *The Sacred and The Profane: The Nature of Religion*. Trans. Willard R. Trask. New York: Harcourt, Brace & World, 1957.

Emerson, Ralph Waldo. "Nature." Available online at http://oregonstate.edu/instruct/phl302/texts/emerson/nature-emerson-a.html#Introduction.

_____. "The Over-Soul." Available online at http://www.emersoncentral.com/oversoul.htm.

Endres, David J. "Dan Lord, Hollywood Priest." *America: The National Catholic Weekly*, December 12, 2005. Article available online at http://www.americamagazine.org/content/article.cfm?article_id=4533.

An Explanation of the Baltimore Catechism of Christian Doctrine. No. 4. Annotated Edition for Teachers (1891). Available online at http://www.gutenberg.org/cache/epub/14554/pg14554.html.

Faderman, Lilian. *Odd Girls and Twilight Lovers: A History of Lesbian Life in Twentieth Century America*. New York: Penguin Books, 1991.

"Father Ed Dowling — Bill W.'s Confidant and Friend." *Box 459: News and Notes from the General Service Office of AA.* Vol. 52, No. 4 (August-September 2006). May be read online at http://aa.org/en_pdfs/en_box459_aug-sept06.pdf.

Fairchild, Hoxie Neale. *Religious Trends in English Poetry.* Vol. III. *1780-1830, Romantic Faith.* New York: Columbia University Press, 1949.

Felknor, Rhea. "Glad Gethsemane, The Story of Father Edward Dowling, S.J." *The Voice of St. Jude*, Fall 1960. Back issues of that periodical can be found at the Claretian Missionaries Archives, located at the St. Jude League/Claretian Publications building at 205 West Monroe Avenue in Chicago.

Finch, Cora. "Additional Notes to Stellar Fire." Available online at http://www.hindsfoot.org/jungnote.pdf.

_____. "Stellar Fire: Carl Jung, a New England Family, and the Risks of Anecdote" (2006). Available online at http://hindsfoot.org/jungstel.pdf.

"First 226 Members Akron, OH AA Group." Transcribed by Tommy H. (Baton Rouge, Louisiana). Available online at http://hindsfoot.org/akrn226.doc.

Fischer, William P. *John C. Ford, S.J.: A Mid-Century Reformer Revisited, 1937–1969.* Ph.D. dissertation, Catholic University of America, 2004.

Fitzgerald, Robert, S.J. "Father Ed Dowling and AA's Bill W." *Catholic Digest* (April 1991). Available online at http://www.barefootsworld.net/aafreddowling.html and http://www.cleanandsobernotdead.com/aahistory/dowling.html

_____. *The Soul of Sponsorship: The Friendship of Fr. Ed Dowling, S.J. and Bill Wilson in Letters.* Center City, Minnesota: Hazelden, 1995.

Flavell, John H. *The Developmental Psychology of Jean Piaget.* Princeton, New Jersey: D. Van Nostrand, 1963.

Foot, Stephen. *Life Began Yesterday.* London: William Heinemann, 1935.

Ford, John C., S.J. "Depth Psychology, Morality, and Alcoholism." Weston, Massachusetts: Weston College, 1951. An article from the *Proceedings of the*

Fifth Annual Meeting of the Catholic Theological Society of America, June 26-28, 1950.

_____. *Man Takes a Drink: Facts and Principles About Alcohol.* With a foreword by Mrs. Marty Mann. New York:, P. J. Kenedy, 1955.

_____. "Pastoral Treatment." *Institute of Pastoral Theology* (1957), available online at http://www.silkworth.net/religion_clergy/01044.html.

Fox, Emmet. *Power Through Constructive Thinking.* New York: Harper & Brothers, 1940; the individual articles which make up the volume were copyrighted from 1932 to 1940.

_____. *The Sermon on the Mount: The Key to Success in Life* and *The Lord's Prayer: An Interpretation.* New York: Grosset & Dunlap, 1938; orig. pub. New York: Harper & Brothers, 1934.

Friesen, J. Glenn. *Studies relating to Herman Dooyeweerd: Linked Glossary of Terms.* Available online at http://members.shaw.ca/jgfriesen/Definitions/Epektasis.html.

Frisbie, Margery. *An Alley in Chicago: The Ministry of a City Priest.* Lanham, Maryland: Sheed & Ward, 1991. Chapter 6, "Selling God, He Got Us." In the University of Notre Dame Archives. Available online at http://archives.nd.edu/findaids/html/etext/alley006.htm.

Gallagher, Timothy, O.M.V. *The Discernment of Spirits: An Ignatian Guide for Everyday Living.* New York: The Crossroad Publishing Company, 2005.

Gallo, Marcia. *Different Daughters: A History of the Daughters of Bilitis and the Rise of the Lesbian Rights Movement.* New York: Carrol & Graf Publishers, 2006.

Gavrilyuk, Paul L. and Sarah Coakley, eds. *The Spiritual Senses: Perceiving God in Western Christianity.* Cambridge: University of Cambridge Press, 2012.

Gilson, Étienne. *The Elements of Christian Philosophy.* New York: New American Library, 1960.

Goldberg, Philip. *American Veda: From Emerson and the Beatles to Yoga and Meditation—How Indian Spirituality Changed the West*. New York: Three Rivers Press, 2010.

Greeley, Andrew M. *A Christmas Wedding*. New York: Forge Books, 2000.

Greg. Nyss. — see Gregory of Nyssa.

Gregory of Nyssa. *Against Eunomius*. In Migne *Patrologia Graeca* Vol. 45.

_____. Commentary on the Beatitudes. In Migne *Patrologia Graeca* Vol. 44.

_____. Commentary on Ecclesiastes. In Migne *Patrologia Graeca* Vol. 44.

_____. Commentary on the Canticle. In Migne *Patrologia Graeca* Vol. 44.

_____. *From Glory to Glory: Texts from Gregory of Nyssa's Mystical Writings*. Selected and with an introduction by Jean Daniélou S.J. Trans. Herbert Musurillo S.J. Crestwood, New York: St. Vladimir's Seminary Press, 1979; orig. pub. by Charles Scribner's Sons, 1961.

_____. *In Cantica Cantic*. Homilia XI. In Migne *Patrologia Graeca* Vol. 44.

_____. *Life of Moses*. In Migne *Patrologia Graeca* Vol. 44.

_____. *On Perfection*. In Migne *Patrologia Graeca* Vol. 46.

_____. Vols. 44-46 of Migne *Patrologia Graeca*. (The full series is 166 vols., 1857-66.) Available online at http://archive.org/details/patrologiaecursu44mignuoft, http://archive.org/details/patrologiaecursu45mignuoft, and http://archive.org/details/patrologiaecursu46mignuoft.

Hartigan, Francis. *Bill W.: A Biography of Alcoholics Anonymous Cofounder Bill Wilson*. New York: St. Martin's Press, 2000.

Hickcox, Tom. "Re: Quote from Father Dowling on Big Book jacket." AAHistoryLovers Message 9395. Available online at https://groups.yahoo.com/neo/groups/aahistorylovers/conversations/messages/9395.

Hill, Amelia. "LSD could help alcoholics stop drinking, AA founder believed." *The Guardian* (Thursday 23 August 2012). Available online at http://www.theguardian.com/science/2012/aug/23/lsd-help-alcoholics-theory.

Horvat, Marian T. "Let None Dare Call it Liberty: The Catholic Church in Colonial America." Online at http://www.traditioninaction.org/History/B_001_Colonies.html.

Hudson, Henry L. "How and Why Alcoholics Anonymous Works for Blacks." Excerpts from this article in Frances Larry Brisbane and Maxine Womble, eds. Pp. 11-30 in *Treatment of Black Alcoholics*. Published as *Alcoholism Treatment Quarterly*, Vol. 2, Nos. 3/4 (Fall 1985 / Winter 1985-86. New York: Haworth Press, 1985. Gives an account of Dr. Jim Scott, M.D., and the black AA group which was started in Washington D.C. in 1945, together with material on early black AA members in the New York City area (Greenwich Village and Harlem) — available online at http://hindsfoot.org/blackwashdc.doc.

Hughes, Thomas. *The History of the Society of Jesus in North America: Colonial and Federal*. Vol. 1. London: Longmans, Green, and Co., 1907.

Hurnard, Hannah. *Hind's Feet in High Places*. Wheaton, Illinois: Tyndale House Publishers, 1975; orig. pub. 1955.

Huxley, Aldous. *The Doors of Perception*. London: Chatto and Windus, 1954.

_____. *Heaven and Hell*. New York: Harper & Brothers and London: Chatto & Windus, pub. in 1956 along with *The Doors of Perception*, which had orig. been pub. by itself in 1954.

_____. *The Perennial Philosophy*. New York: Harper & Brothers, 1945.

Ignatius — see Loyola.

"I'm a Nurse in an Alcoholic Ward." *Saturday Evening Post* (Oct. 18, 1952).

"Jack Alexander Gave A.A. Its First Big Boost." *Box 4-5-9* (February/March 2008). There is a copy in AAHistoryLovers message no. 6248, which can be read online at https://groups.yahoo.com/neo/groups/aahistorylovers/conversations/messages/6218.

Jaeger, Werner. *Two Rediscovered Works of Ancient Christian Literature: Gregory of Nyssa and Macarius.* Leiden: E. J. Brill, 1954.

Janssens, Jean-Baptiste. Wikipedia article at http://en.wikipedia.org/wiki/ Jean-Baptiste_Janssens.

Jesuit Vocations website of the New England, Maryland and New York Provinces at http://www.jesuitvocations.org/.

Jesuits of the Missouri Province: Brief Chronology of the Missouri Province. At http://www.jesuitsmissouri.org/iden/chronology.cfm.

Johnson, Raynor C. *The Imprisoned Splendour: An approach to reality, based upon the significance of data drawn from the fields of natural science, psychical research and mystical experience.* London: Hodder & Stoughton, 1953.

Jung, C. G. [Carl Gustav]. *Modern Man in Search of a Soul.* Trans. W. S. Dell and Cary F. Baynes. New York: Harcourt, Brace & Company / Harvest Books, 1933.

_____. *Psychology and Religion: East and West.* In his *Collected Works.* Vol. 11. Bollingen Series. Princeton, New Jersey: Princeton University Press, 1970.

_____. *Visions: Notes of the Seminar Given in 1930-1934 by C. G. Jung.* Ed. by Claire Douglas. Volume 1. Princeton, New Jersey: Princeton University Press, 1997.

Justin Martyr. *Dialogue with Trypho.* Trans. George Reith. Ante-Nicene Christian Library. Edinburgh: T. & T. Clark, 1867-1873.

Katz, Jonathan. *Gay American History: Lesbians and Gay Men in the U.S.A.* New York: Thomas Y. Crowell, 1976.

Kemper, Donald J. "Catholic Integration in St. Louis, 1935-1947." *Missouri Historical Review*, October 1978, pp. 1–13.

Kitchen, V[ictor] C[onstant]. *I Was a Pagan.* New York: Harper & Brothers, 1934.

Koczera, Joe, S.J. (Philadelphia, Pennsylvania). "Cornbread and beef stew in Jesuit life." February 22, 2006 in his weblog *Novitiate Notes: Ad Majorem Dei Gloriam* at http://novitiatenotes.blogspot.com/2006/02/cornbread-and-beef-stew-in-jesuit-life.html.

Kotre, John N. *Simple Gifts: the Lives of Pat and Patty Crowley*. Kansas City: Andrews and McMeel, 1979.

Kurtz, Ernest. *The Collected Ernie Kurtz*. Wheeling, West Virginia: The Bishop of Books, 1999; republished by the Hindsfoot Foundation through iUniverse in Bloomington, Indiana, in 2008. Can be read online at http://hindsfoot. org/ktcek1.html.

_____. "Drugs and the Spiritual: Bill W. Takes LSD." In Kurtz, *The Collected Ernie Kurtz*.

_____. *Not-God: A History of Alcoholics Anonymous*. Expanded edition. Center City, Minnesota: Hazelden, 1991; orig. 1979.

_____. "Re: How quickly should the twelve steps be taken?" AAHistoryLovers Message no. 6252 (Jan 19, 2010), may be read online at http://health.groups.yahoo.com/group/AAHistoryLovers/message/6252.

_____. "Re: Is Bill responsible for this quote?" AAHistoryLovers message no. 4395. At https://groups.yahoo.com/neo/groups/aahistorylovers/conversations/messages/.

_____. *Shame & Guilt*. Second edition, revised and updated. Hindsfoot Foundation Series on Treatment and Recovery. Lincoln, Nebraska: iUniverse, 2007. May be read online at http://hindsfoot.org/eksg.html.

_____. Telephone conversations with Glenn F. Chesnut in March 2011 and April 2012.

_____ and Katherine Ketcham. *Experiencing Spirituality: Finding Meaning Through Storytelling*. New York: Jeremy P. Tarcher / Penguin, 2014.

_____ and Katherine Ketcham. *The Spirituality of Imperfection: Modern Wisdom from Classic Stories*. New York: Bantam Books, 1992.

Kurtz, Linda Farris, DPA. *Recovery Groups: A Guide to Creating, Leading, and Working with Groups for Addictions and Mental Health Conditions*. New York: Oxford University Press, 2015), p. 30.

_____. *Self-Help and Support Groups: A Handbook for Practitioners*, Sage Sourcebook for the Human Services. Vol. 34. Thousand Oaks, California: Sage Publications, 1997.

_____ and Adrienne Chambon, Ph.D. "Comparison of Self-Help Groups for Mental Health." *Health and Social Work* 12 (1987): 275-283.

Lambert, Alexander. "Care and Control of the Alcoholic." *Boston Medical and Surgical Journal* [now called the *New England Journal of Medicine*] 166 (April 25, 1912): 615-621.

_____. "The Obliteration of the Craving for Narcotics." *Journal of the American Medical Association* LIII, 13 (1909): 985-989.

Laporte, Jean. *La doctrine eucharistique chez Philon d'Alexandrie*. Paris: Éditions Beauchesne, 1972.

Lash, William (Barefoot Bill). "Tex B. (Sober 2/6/47)." Describing early A.A. in the Chicago area. AAHistoryLovers no. message 1881 (June 22, 2004), at https://groups.yahoo.com/neo/groups/aahistorylovers/conversations/messages/1881.

Lattin, Don. *Distilled Spirits: Getting High, Then Sober, with a Famous Writer, a Forgotten Philosopher, and a Hopeless Drunk*. Berkeley: University of California Press, 2012.

_____. *The Harvard Psychedelic Club: How Timothy Leary, Ram Dass, Huston Smith, and Andrew Weil Killed the Fifties and Ushered in a New Age for America*. New York: HarperCollins, 2010.

_____. Interview of him by Ron Roizen in *Points: The Blog of the Alcohol and Drugs History Society* (October 15, 2012) at http://pointsadhsblog.wordpress.com/2012/10/15/the-points-interview-don-lattin/.

_____. "What Bill W. told Carl Jung About his Awesome LSD Trip." Blog Post by Don Lattin, Oct. 16, 2012, see http://redroom.com/member/don-lattin/blog/what-bill-w-told-carl-jung-about-his-awesome-lsd-trip.

LeBerthon, Ted. "Why Jim Crow Won at Webster College." *Pittsburgh Courier*, 5 Feb. 1944, p. 13.

Leroy, Pierre, S.J., "Teilhard de Chardin: The Man." Pp. 13-42 in Pierre Teilhard de Chardin, *The Divine Milieu*. New York: Harper & Row, 1968; this Eng. trans. first pub. 1960, orig. pub. in French as *Le Milieu Divin* in 1957.

Lewis, C. S. *The Magician's Nephew*. London: Bodley Head, 1955.

_____. *The Screwtape Letters*. London: Geoffrey Bles, 1942.

Lewis, Todd and Kent Bicknell. "The Asian Soul of Transcendentalism." Available online at http://www.asian-studies.org/eaa/EAA-16-2-Lewis-Bicknell.pdf.

"List of A.A. Groups—as of Dec. 31, 1941." Available online at http://hinds foot.org/dec1941.pdf.

Lobdell, Jared. "Re: Emmet Fox's secretary." AAHistoryLovers message no. 7249 (March 19, 2011) at https://groups.yahoo.com/neo/groups/aahistorylovers/conversations/messages/7249.

_____. "Re: Can anyone tell me a little more history about Al S.," AAHistoryLovers message no. 6761 (Jul 29, 2010) at https://groups.yahoo.com/neo/groups/aahistorylovers/conversations/messages/6761.

Lonergan, Bernard J. F. *Insight: A Study of Human Understanding*. London: Longmans, Green & Co., 1957.

Lord, Daniel A. *Played by Ear: The Autobiography of Daniel A. Lord, S.J.* Chicago: Loyola University Press, 1956. May be read online at http://archive.org/details/playedbyear001277mbp.

Lord, Daniel Aloysius, S.J. Wikipedia article. http://en.wikipedia.org/wiki/Daniel_A._Lord.

Louÿs, Pierre. *The Songs of Bilitis*. Translated from the Greek. Trans. into English by Alvah C. Bessie. New York: Macy-Masius Publishers, privately printed for subscribers in 1926.

Low, Abraham A. *Lectures to Relatives of Former Patients*. Boston: Christopher Publishing House, 1967.

_____. *Mental Health Through Will-Training: A System of Self-Help in Psychotherapy as Practiced by Recovery, Inc.* Boston: Christopher Publishing House, 1950.

_____. *The Technique of Self-Help in Psychiatric Aftercare*. 3 vols. Chicago: Recovery, Inc., 1943.

"Loyola Academy." Wikipedia article at http://en.wikipedia.org/wiki/Loyola_Academy.

Loyola, St. Ignatius. *The Spiritual Exercises of St. Ignatius*. Trans. Anthony Mottola. Introd. Robert W. Gleason, S.J. New York: Doubleday Image Books, 1989; this Eng. trans. orig. pub. 1964.

_____. *The Spiritual Exercises of St. Ignatius*. Trans. from the autograph by Father Elder Mullan, S.J. New York: P.J. Kennedy & Sons, 1914. Available online at http://www.nwjesuits.org/JesuitSpirituality/SpiritualExercises.html or http://www.sacred-texts.com/chr/seil/index.htm.

Loyola, San Ignacio de. *Los Ejercicios Espirituales*. The Spanish text of Loyola's *Spiritual Exercises*. At http://www.librear.com/archivosebookstres/Loyola%20Ignacio%20de-Ejercicios%20Espirituales.pdf.

Lupton, Rev. Dilworth. "Mr. X and Alcoholics Anonymous." Sermon preached on November 26, 1939 at the First Unitarian Church, Euclid at East 82nd Street, Cleveland, Ohio. Can be read online at http://silkworth.net/aahistory/mr_x.html.

Mann, Marty. "The Pastor's Resources in Dealing with Alcoholics: Alcoholics Are Consumed with Guilt; They Do Not Need to Be Reminded of Their Sins." *Pastoral Psychology*, Vol. 2 (13), April 1951. Available online at https://groups.yahoo.com/neo/groups/aahistorylovers/conversations/messages/1283.

A Manual for Alcoholics Anonymous, often referred to as *The Akron Manual*. The original 1942 version can be read online at http://hindsfoot.org/akrman1.html and http://hindsfoot.org/akrman2.html. The printed version which is currently available for sale at Dr. Bob's house in Akron is a later revised edition with some material removed, including the reading list.

Martin, James, S.J. *My Life with the Saints*. Chicago: Loyola Press, 2006.

McBrien, Richard P., ed. "Cana Conference." *HarperCollins Encyclopedia of Catholicism*. San Francisco: HarperSanFrancisco, 1995. P. 214.

McGlin, Joseph T., S.J. *Backstage Missionary, Father Dan Lord, S.J.* New York: Pageant Press, 1958.

McGloin, Joseph T., S.J. *I'll Die Laughing!* Milwaukee: Bruce Publishing Company, 1955.

McQuade, James. Obituary of Fr. Edward Dowling, S.J. (1898-1960). *News-Letter, Missouri and Wisconsin Provinces*, May 1960, Vol. 20, No. 8. Available online at http://boards.ancestry.com-localities.northam.usa.states.missouri. counties.stlouis-4261-mb.ashx.

Mel B. Commentary on Emmet Fox's "Making Your Life Worthwhile." Available online at http://hindsfoot.org/fox1.html.

_____. "Emmet Fox's secretary and Al Steckman (correct spelling)." AAHistoryLovers message no. 4001 (January 5, 2007). Available online at https://groups.yahoo.com/neo/groups/aahistorylovers/conversations/ messages/4001.

_____. *My Search for Bill W.* Center City, Minnesota: Hazelden, 2000.

_____. *New Wine: The Spiritual Roots of The Twelve Step Miracle*. Center City, Minnesota: Hazelden, 1991.

_____. "Re: Conference Approved Literature." His gratitude for Emmet Fox's book on *The Sermon on the Mount*. AAHistoryLovers message no. 1861 (June 15, 2004), at https://groups.yahoo.com/neo/groups/aahistorylovers/ conversations/messages/1861.

Merrill, Kenneth G. "Drunks Are a Mess." In the A.A. prison group magazine *Bar-less* (1965; orig. published c. 1954). The article is written under the pseudonym Junius Senior. May be read online at http://hindsfoot.org/

nsbend2.html. Extended excerpts from the article are given in Chesnut, *The Factory Owner & the Convict*, pp. 18-24.

Meyer, F[rederick] B[rotherton]. *The Secret of Guidance*. New York: Fleming H. Revell, 1896. Available on the internet at http://www.ccel.org/m/meyer/guidance/guidance.htm.

Migne *Patrologia Graeca* — see Gregory of Nyssa.

Millard, Joseph. "Divorcées Anonymous." *Reader's Digest* 56 (May 1950): 15-18.

Miller, William R. and Janet C'de Baca. *Quantum Change: When Epiphanies and Sudden Insights Transform Ordinary Lives*. Afterword by Ernest Kurtz. New York: Guildford Press, 2001.

Mitchell K. *How It Worked: The Story of Clarence H. Snyder and the Early Days of Alcoholics Anonymous in Cleveland, Ohio*. Washingtonville, New York: AA Big Book Study Group, 1999. Some of the references in this present book are to the typescript for the revised 2nd ed. when it was under preparation in 2014.

"A Miracle at Christmas — a Man Re-born." A.A. *Grapevine*, Vol. 3, No. 7, December 1946.

Morgan, Oliver J. "'Chemical Comforting' and the Theology of John C. Ford, SJ: Classic Answers to a Contemporary Problem." *Journal of Ministry in Addiction & Recovery*, Vol. 6(1) 1999: 29-66.

Mullett, Michael A. *The Catholic Reformation*. Abingdon, Oxfordshire: Routledge, 1999.

Murray, Neville, M.D., and M/Sgt William Swegan, USAF. "To Tranquillize or Not to Tranquillize." *Quarterly Journal of Studies on Alcohol* 19, no. 3 (September 1958): 509-510. Excerpts reprinted in the 1958 yearbook of the *American Peoples Encyclopedia* (a popular set of volumes distributed by Sears Roebuck).

Newman, John Henry. Sermon 14. "Saving Knowledge." Pp. 151-161 in *Parochial and Plain Sermons*, Volume 2. London: Longmans, Green, and Co.,

1908. Available online at http://www.newmanreader.org/Works/parochial/volume2/index.html.

Olson, Nancy. *With a Lot of Help from Our Friends: The Politics of Alcoholism*. Ed. Glenn F. Chesnut. Hindsfoot Foundation Series on the History of Alcohol Treatment. New York: iUniverse / Writers Club Press, 2003.

Olson, Nancy *et al*. Brief biographies of the Big Book authors, from the AAHistoryLovers, see online at http://www.a-1associates.com/westbalto/HISTORY_PAGE/Authors.htm.

Otto, Rudolf. *The Idea of the Holy: An Inquiry into the Non-Rational Factor in the Idea of the Divine and Its Relation to the Rational*. 2nd ed. Trans. John W. Harvey. Oxford: Oxford University Press, 1950. Original German published 1917: *Das Heilige: Über das Irrationale in der Idee des göttlichen und sein Verhältnis zum Rationalen*.

Patrologia Graeca — see Gregory of Nyssa.

Packard, Vance. "New Cure for Sick Marriages." *American Magazine* 161 (May 1956): 30-31, 96-100.

Pass It On: The Story of Bill Wilson and How the A.A. Message Reached the World. New York: Alcoholics Anonymous World Services, 1984.

"Patty Crowley: founder of the Christian Family Movement dies." *Catholic New Times*, Dec. 18, 2005. Available online at http://www.highbeam.com/doc/1G1-140304355.html.

Peter John De Smet, S.J. (1801 - 1873): Life and Times of a Blackrobe in the West. See the section entitled "The Museum of the Western Jesuit Missions in Florissant," p. 307. Available online at http://users.skynet.be/pater.de.smet/pj-e/pagina307.htm.

Pearson, Bob. *A.A. World History 1985* (unpublished draft).

Pfau, Ralph. *The Golden Book of Sanity*. Indianapolis: SMT Guild, 1963.

Pfau, Ralph (Father John Doe) and Al Hirshberg. *Prodigal Shepherd*. Indianapolis: SMT Guild, orig. pub. 1958.

Pittman, Bill. *The Roots of Alcoholics Anonymous.* Center City, Minnesota: Hazelden, 1999; orig. pub. as *A.A.: The Way It Began* by Glen Abbey Books in 1988.

Plato, *Republic.* 2 vols. Trans. Paul Shorey. Loeb Classical Library. London: William Heinemann, 1935–7.

Poulain, Augustin, S.J. *The Graces of Interior Prayer: A Treatise on Mystical Theology.* Translated from the 6th edition by Leonora L. Yorke Smith. London: Kegan Paul, Trench, Trubner & Co., 1921.

Puhl, Louis J., S.J. *The Spiritual Exercises of St. Ignatius: Based on Studies in the Language of the Autograph.* Chicago: Loyola Press/Newman Press, 1951.

"Pressure Grows to Have Catholic College Doors Open to Negroes." *Pittsburgh Courier*, 19 Feb. 1944, p. 1.

Prowitt, A. "Divorcées Anonymous." *Good Housekeeping* 130 (Feb. 1950): 35.

Pulitzer, Joseph. "The Post-Dispatch Platform." The famous paragraph from his retirement speech on April 10, 1907, first published in the *St. Louis Post-Dispatch* for April 11, 1907. See the Wikipedia article on the *St. Louis Post-Dispatch*, available online at http://en.wikipedia.org/wiki/St._Louis_Post-Dispatch.

Ray, Mary Augustina. *American Opinion of Roman Catholicism in the Eighteenth Century.* New York: 1936.

"Religion: Conversion." *Time* magazine, 22 May 1939. Available online at http://www.time.com/time/magazine/article/0,9171,761385,00.html.

"Remembering Patty Crowley, Godmother of Call To Action." An article on the website of Call to Action: Catholics Working Together for Justice & Equality, at http://www.cta-usa.org/News200601/PattyCrowley.html.

Renee (Eastern Missouri District 51 Archivist). "From Golden Moments of Reflection: 1st A.A. meeting in Missouri at Gibson Hotel on Enright October 30, 1940." AAHistoryLovers message no. 5881. Available online at https://groups.yahoo.com/neo/groups/aahistorylovers/conversations/messages/5881.

Rodriguez, Juan. "Ralph Pfau instead of Big Book in early Spanish language AA." Message 5584 (February 23, 2009) in the AAHistoryLovers. Available online at https://groups.yahoo.com/neo/groups/aahistorylovers/conversations/messages/5584.

Roizen, Ron. Interview of Don Lattin in *Points: The Blog of the Alcohol and Drugs History Society* (October 15, 2012) at http://pointsadhsblog.wordpress.com/2012/10/15/the-points-interview-don-lattin/.

"St. Louis U. Lifts Color Bar: Accepts Five Negroes for Summer Session." *Pittsburgh Courier*, 6 May 1944, p. 1.

"St. Stanislaus Kostka: Novice Religious." In *The Jesuit Curia in Rome: The House of the Superior General*. Available online at http://www.sjweb.info/jesuits/saintShow.cfm?SaintID=42.

"St. Stanislaus Seminary, Florissant, Missouri." Waymarking.com. Available online at http://www.waymarking.com/waymarks/WM88V6_St_Stanislaus_Seminary_Florissant_Missouri.

Sartre, Jean-Paul. *La Nausée*. Paris: Gallimard, 1938.

Seeger, Pete. "Which Side Are You On?" On You Tube at https://www.youtube.com/watch?v=msEYGql0drc and at https://www.youtube.com/watch?v=5iAIM02kv0g.

Sharpe, William. *The Dual Image*. London: H. A. Copley, 1896.

Shoemaker, Samuel Moor, Jr. *Children of the Second Birth: Being a Narrative of Spiritual Miracles in a City Parish*. New York: Fleming H. Revell, 1927.

_____. *Extraordinary Living for Ordinary Men: Excerpts Selected from the Writings of Sam Shoemaker*. Grand Rapids, Michigan: Zondervan, 1965.

Silkworth, William D. "Reclamation of the Alcoholic." *Medical Record* (April 21, 1937). Available online at http://www.aa-nia-dist11.org/Documents/silk.pdf.

Sikorsky, Igor I., Jr. *AA's Godparents: Carl Jung, Emmet Fox, Jack Alexander*. Minneapolis: CompCare Publishers, 1990.

Snyder, Clarence. *Sponsorship Pamphlet*. Available online at http://www. barefootsworld.net/aasponsorship1944.html

Sodality of Our Lady. An account of its history at http://www.sodalityadw. org/History.html.

Speer, Robert E. *The Principles of Jesus*. New York: Fleming H. Revell, 1902. Available online at http://archive.org/details/principlesofjesu00spee.

Starr, Samuel M. "'Divorcées Anonymous' a Remarkable Success." *Virginia Law Weekly: Divorce and Family Relations*, 50-52.

Steckman, Al. *Bert D.: Hardhat, Inebriate, Scholar*. Memphis: Harbor House, 1976.

Swegan, William E. with Glenn F. Chesnut, Ph.D. *The Psychology of Alcoholism*. Hindsfoot Foundation Series on Alcoholics Anonymous History. Bloomington, Indiana: iUniverse, 2011; orig. pub. 2003 as Sgt. Bill S. with Glenn F. Chesnut, *On the Military Firing Line in the Alcoholism Treatment Program*.

Swegan, William E. See also Neville Murray, M.D.

Talbot, Matt. Wikipedia article at http://en.wikipedia.org/wiki/Matt_Talbot.

Teilhard de Chardin, Pierre. *The Divine Milieu*. New York: Harper & Row, 1968; this Eng. trans. first pub. 1960, orig. pub. in French as *Le Milieu Divin* in 1957.

_____. "Hominization" (1923). In the collection of his essays entitled *The Vision of the Past*. New York: Harper & Row, 1966.

"They Mend Broken Marriages." *American Magazine* 149 (June 1950): 107.

Thomsen, Robert. *Bill W: The absorbing and deeply moving life story of Bill Wilson, co-founder of Alcoholics Anonymous*. New York: Harper & Row, 1975.

Tiebout, Harry M. *The Collected Writings*. Center City, Minnesota: Hazelden, 1999.

_____. His talk at the Alcoholics Anonymous International Convention in St. Louis (1955). A transcript of the talk is given in pp. 245-251 of *Alcoholics Anonymous Comes of Age.*

Tom C., "Re: First black A.A. group was in Washington D.C. — or Chicago?" AAHistoryLovers Message 5754, June 3, 2009. Available online at https://groups.yahoo.com/neo/groups/AAHistoryLovers/conversations/messages/5754.

Travis, Trysh. *The Language of the Heart: A Cultural History of the Recovery Movement from Alcoholics Anonymous to Oprah Winfrey.* Chapel Hill, North Carolina: University of North Carolina Press, 2009.

Trevor, Fraser. Blog for May 1, 2013, entitled "One man who influenced Bill Wilson greatly was Gerald Heard. Tom Powers often said that Heard was one of Bill's sponsors." In *Dream Warrior Recovery*, at http://dreamwarriorrecovery.blogspot.com/2013/05/one-man-who-influenced-bill-wilson.html.

Twelve and Twelve = *Twelve Steps and Twelve Traditions.*

Twelve Steps and Twelve Traditions. New York: Alcoholics Anonymous World Services, 1952, 1953.

Wayman, Norbury L. *History of St. Louis Neighborhoods.* Baden-Riverview Churches. Available online at http://stlouis.missouri.org/neighborhoods/history/baden/churches2.htm.

Wilson, Bill — see Bill W.

Wing, Nell. *Grateful to Have Been There: My 42 Years with Bill and Lois, and the Evolution of Alcoholics Anonymous.* 1st ed. Park Ridge, Illinois: Parkside Publishing, 1993. 2nd ed., revised and expanded. Center City, Minnesota: Hazelden, 1998.

Wright, Henry B[urt]. *The Will of God and a Man's Lifework.* New York: The Young Men's Christian Association Press, 1909. Available online at http://archive.org/details/willofgodandman00wrig.

CPSIA information can be obtained
at www.ICGtesting.com
Printed in the USA
FFOW04n1425150815

9 781491 770856